Dec 2016

Barbara — Thank you
for your
interest +
support

Best
Mel
Scanlon

Communings
of the Spirit

Mordecai M. Kaplan, c. 1934.
(Courtesy Library of the Jewish Theological Seminary.)

Communings
of the Spirit

The Journals of
Mordecai M. Kaplan
Volume II 1934–1941

Edited by Mel Scult

Wayne State University Press
Detroit
Published in cooperation with the Reconstructionist Press

20 19 18 17 16   5 4 3 2 1

Library of Congress Cataloging Number: 2016947893

ISBN 978-0-8143-4161–2 (hardcover); ISBN 978-0-8143-4162-9 (ebook)

Permission to reprint material from Mordecai Kaplan's diary has been granted by the Jewish Theological Seminary of America, which owns volumes 1–25 of the diary. Volumes 26 and 27 are owned by Reconstructionist College. Permission has also been granted by the Kaplan family.

∞

Typeset by E. T. Lowe

Composed in Electra LH

To Allen Scult,
my brother, philosopher extraordinaire,
and my most significant intellectual other.

Contents

Preface

The originals of the first twenty-five volumes of Mordecai M. Kaplan's journal are at the Jewish Theological Seminary. The last two volumes are at the Reconstructionist Rabbinical College in Wyncote, Pennsylvania. I am grateful to Chancellor Arnold Eisen; Dr. David Kraemer, librarian of the Jewish Theological Seminary; and Rabbi Deborah Waxman, president of the Reconstructionist Rabbinical College and the Jewish Reconstructionist Communities, for allowing me to reproduce material from the volumes in their possession.

This published work exists only because of the generosity of Rabbi Kaplan and his family. First of all, I am indebted to Mordecai Kaplan himself, who allowed me a very long time ago to have my own copy of the journals.

My friends and colleagues have been extremely helpful, though they are not responsible for my errors. I want to thank my brother, Professor Allen Scult, with whom I have discussed many of the central issues connected with the journal and its meaning. Our conversations are unfailingly valuable. My colleagues Professor Robert Seltzer and Professor Emanuel Goldsmith continue to be supportive and helpful on many levels. The following colleagues and friends were consulted on specific issues: Ann Eisenstein, Rabbi Ira Eisenstein, Jethro Eisenstein, Judith Eisenstein, Miriam Eisenstein, Rabbi Ed Feld, Jonathan Helfand, Rabbi Richard Hirsh, Avraham Holtz, Seth Jerchower, Sara Regeur, Israel Schepansky, and Jerry Schwartzbart.

I am very much indebted to my fellow board members at the Kaplan Center for Jewish Peoplehood. Their encouragement and activities perpetuating Kaplan's legacy have been very important to me. I am particularly indebted to Dan Cedarbaum, the executive director of the Kaplan Center, for his energetic and creative activities on behalf of Mordecai Kaplan. I am extremely grateful to Jack and Kay Wolofsky of Montreal for their generous support of this volume.

Kathryn Wildfong, of Wayne State University Press, has been unfailingly supportive, and I am much in her debt. I very much want to thank my editor, Mimi Braverman, for her thoroughness and her expertise.

The material in this volume consists of approximately 75 percent of the journal for the period covered. Our principles of selection mirror Kaplan's major interests and focus. He lived in many worlds but is primarily known as an ideologue; thus a significant amount of space here is given to his thoughts on religion in general and Judaism in particular. Some mistakenly believe that Kaplan gave up God rather early in his life. The truth is that he thought about God and the belief in God all the time; that thinking is reflected here. I have given particular attention to issues and concepts that are not found in his published works.

Kaplan's journalizing changed over time. In the beginning (1913) the journal consisted almost completely of philosophical material—actually notes for his lectures and sermons. Kaplan functioned as a rabbi throughout his life, sometimes with a congregation and sometimes without. I have included some sermon outlines that deal with the Torah portion of the week or with holy days during the year. Kaplan's ideas also appear in casual conversations he had with different individuals, sometimes colleagues or sometimes unknown people who might come to him seeking advice or counsel. He did not enjoy the ministerial functions of the rabbinate, but from time to time he did perform a wedding or a funeral; some selections are included that describe his experiences on these occasions.

On the whole I have followed the journal itself in terms of the way it allots space. The titles in this volume are my own, but the title of the volume is Kaplan's.

A Few Matters of Style

The diary is not a finished product and was not prepared for publication. There are sentences that are awkward. In all cases the language of the original text has been retained except where there was a small obvious mistake in Kaplan's original (e.g., "of" for "at"). Punctuation has been changed in places to aid in understanding. There is no indication when a selection ends in the middle of a paragraph or at the end of a sentence. Three dots indicate when a selection ends in the middle of a sentence. A given selection under a certain date is not necessarily the first paragraph under that date. If a selection runs to more than one day the new date is indicated. A new title is given if a completely new subject for the same date is discussed. Each day contains many subjects.

Most people mentioned in the diary are described in detail in the glossary. If a person is mentioned only in passing or is a historical figure, his or her information is given in an accompanying note.

Square brackets are used for editorial comments, and parentheses are used for Kaplan's comments. When an obvious word is omitted in the manuscript it is supplied in brackets with no comment (e.g., "organized [life]"). Some Hebrew expressions are explained in the text in square brackets, some in the notes.

Kaplan usually wrote Hebrew words in Hebrew characters but not always. When a word is written in Hebrew characters the word *Heb.* appears. All Hebrew words are transliterated and translated. Although in the 1930s I imagine Kaplan pronounced Hebrew in the Ashkenazic mode, I have transliterated in the current Sephardic mode. Kaplan did not look up the references he cites, and so minor errors do creep in. These errors have been corrected. The transliteration is designed to be consistent and accurate. Kaplan often did not write out the complete Bible verse or prayer text he was citing; thus I have provided the portion of the verse or prayer that does not appear in Kaplan's Hebrew citation in the translation.

If Kaplan spelled the name of a person differently from the standard, the original spelling is kept in the text and the accepted spelling is given in a note. Archaic spellings, when not the name of a place or the name of person, are simply left as is, for example, *yeshiba* instead of *yeshiva*.

If there is a different spelling for the name of an East European town from the standard contemporary spelling, the original Kaplan spelling is kept with the present spelling in brackets afterward.

Kaplan frequently wrote over passages. When this is done, the text will include the revision without noting that this was done. If the write-over is a significant change, the addition appears in square brackets after the original text.

The original of the whole diary can be found online at www.Kaplan-center.org (follow the links: Our Reference Desk, then Kaplan Diaries, then JTS Digital Collection; then click on the box on the left labeled HTML). This digitized version of the diary is a result of the efforts of Dr. David Kraemer, the librarian of the Jewish Theological Seminary.

Introduction

Mordecai Kaplan was not only the founder of Reconstructionism and a leading Jewish thinker of twentieth-century America but also the most prodigious diarist on record. Kaplan's diary runs a full 27 volumes, from 1913 to the late 1970s, with some 8,000 pages and more than 2 million words. In terms of length, Kaplan's diary is longer than both Samuel Pepys's and Ralph Waldo Emerson's. The original notebooks of Kaplan's diary are housed in the rare book room of the Jewish Theological Seminary alongside Maimonides and Judah ha-Levi. Since 2001, selections from the years 1913 to 1934 have been available to the reading public. The complete diary is also available online.[1]

The present volume contains selections from 1934 to 1941. It begins with the aftermath of the publication of Kaplan's magnum opus, *Judaism as a Civilization*, and ends with the Japanese attack on Pearl Harbor and America's entry into World War II. To fully appreciate the diary selections in the present volume, we must be acquainted with the life of Mordecai Kaplan and with his philosophy.

Mordecai Menahem Kaplan (June 11, 1881–November 8, 1983) was born in Sventzian, Lithuania. He was the son of Rabbi Israel Kaplan, a prominent Talmudic scholar, and Anna Nehama Kaplan. At the age of 8 Kaplan emigrated to America with his family. They lived in New York City, and later Kaplan attended City College of New York (1900) and Columbia University. He received rabbinical ordination from the Jewish Theological Seminary (1902).

In 1909 Kaplan was invited by Solomon Schechter, the head of the Jewish Theological Seminary, to become principal of its newly created Teachers Institute. He enthusiastically accepted the position.

Kaplan remained at the Jewish Theological Seminary, the center of the Conservative movement, training rabbis and teachers, until he retired in 1963. As the first director of the Teachers Institute, he laid the foundations for Jewish education in America. Working closely with Samson Benderly, the director of the

---

1. The online link to the complete diary can be found at www.Kaplancenter.org (follow the links, starting at Our Reference Desk, then Kaplan Diaries, then JTS Digital Collection; click on the box labeled HTML to access the diaries). The earlier years of the diary have been published: M. M. Kaplan, *Communings of the Spirit: The Journals of Mordecai M. Kaplan*, vol. 1, *1913–1934*, ed. Mel Scult (Detroit: Wayne State University Press and the Reconstructionist Press, 2001).

Board of Jewish Education in New York City, he helped train all the educational leaders of the next generation.[2] Although Kaplan was critical of Benderly because of the latter's secularism, we might say that Benderly was his best friend. When the Teachers Institute was in what is now called the East Village, Benderly and Kaplan frequently met for lunch.[3]

Kaplan was a strong personality and a demanding teacher. For many years, including the period covered in this volume, he taught homiletics and Midrash (classical rabbinic homilies) to rabbinical students at the seminary in addition to the philosophies of Judaism. Critical of his colleagues who seemed to be concerned only with scholarly issues, Kaplan dealt with the central religious questions that troubled his students. His own graduate studies, in which he had concentrated on sociology, led him to formulate a religious ideology that emphasized the link between religion and experience. The primacy of experience remained a central concept for Kaplan in his analysis of religion and Judaism (diary entries for November 14, 1936, and July 9, 1940). Because experience changes, religion changes, and it is important, Kaplan believed, to find ways in which beliefs and rituals could function in the modern era as they did in the past. To do this, one might need to change a ritual, dropping it completely or substituting something new.

Readers may be interested in the whole controversy regarding Kaplan's *New Haggadah*, published in 1941 with its many changes (see the diary entry for March 24, 1941). Heavily influenced by the Utilitarians and by William James, Kaplan called himself a functionalist. He was ready to pursue the path most likely to make religion and particularly Judaism functional in the American setting.[4] Kaplan's *New Haggadah* was quite radical for its time. In the effort to modernize, Kaplan omitted the plagues (because they were miracles), inserted Moses as a prominent part of the Passover liturgy (he is not found in the traditional Haggadah), and omitted the chosenness formula completely (Kaplan rejected chosenness for ideological reasons).[5] Most important, Kaplan's *New Haggadah* shifted the emphasis of Passover from a celebration of God's power in redeeming the Israelites to a celebration of freedom. This emphasis was certainly much needed in 1941 and has come to dominate the contemporary understanding of the holiday.

---

2. See the fine work on Benderly by Jonathan B. Krasner, *The Benderly Boys and American Jewish Education* (Waltham, MA: Brandeis University Press, 2011).

3. For Kaplan during this early period, see the excellent work by Jeffrey S. Gurock and Jacob J. Schacter, *A Modern Heretic and a Traditional Community: Mordecai M. Kaplan, Orthodoxy, and American Judaism* (New York: Columbia University Press, 1997). For the biography of Kaplan, see Mel Scult, *Judaism Faces the Twentieth Century: A Biography of Mordecai M. Kaplan* (Detroit: Wayne State University Press, 1993).

4. For an early statement by Kaplan on functionalism, see Kaplan, *Communings of the Spirit*, 1: 62 (January 13, 1914).

5. For an extended discussion of chosenness and a complete analysis of Kaplan's ideology, see Mel Scult, *The Radical American Judaism of Mordecai M. Kaplan* (Bloomington: Indiana University Press, 2013).

Although the perfection of the individual might be the aim of religion and the meaning and goal of Judaism (see diary entry for May 17, 1939), Kaplan believed that this goal could be achieved only within the context of a community. He held that Jews must have more in common than their religion for Judaism to survive in the secular culture of the modern era. Throughout the ages Judaism, as the evolving religious civilization of the Jewish people, bound them together into a vital organic entity. A vigorous Jewish life in America could be brought into being, Kaplan maintained, only with the creation of new institutions appropriate to a democratic, technologically advanced society. Kaplan's most incisive statement on the relationship of the individual to community actually is found in a later entry in the diary. In the mid-1950s we find the following: "This, indeed, is the main paradox of the spiritual life: the way to achieve salvation is to bend all of one's efforts to render the people to which one looks for salvation capable of providing it" (August 18, 1956).[6] Kaplan envisioned the expanded synagogue as the vehicle for the survival of Jewish civilization. In 1917 the Jewish Center on West 86th Street in Manhattan, a magnificent building with many recreational facilities in addition to a synagogue, "the pool with a shul and a school" was dedicated with Kaplan serving as rabbi. It quickly became the prototype for many other synagogue centers in the United States and Canada.[7]

Kaplan's thinking became increasingly radical, leading to his departure from the Orthodox Jewish Center in 1922 with a large group of supporters to organize the Society for the Advancement of Judaism (SAJ), also in New York City. He attempted to establish his ideology, which he called Reconstructionism, as a school of thought within the Jewish community rather than as a separate denomination in order not to contribute to the fragmentation of American Jewry. Reconstructionism defined Judaism as an evolving religious civilization and stressed Judaism's quest for social justice as well as individual salvation or fulfillment as the primary values of Jewish life.

In 1934 Kaplan published his magnum opus, *Judaism as a Civilization*, which became the landmark for second-generation American Jewish leaders, who were desperately seeking a way to live both as Jews and as Americans.[8] He held that one could live in two civilizations (the Jewish and the American) without any sense of tension or contradiction because the two cultures were absolutely compatible. Kaplan's major thrust was to set the Jewish people, their past

---

6. Later in this introduction, I will explain more fully Kaplan's concept of salvation, which is central to his system.

7. On the Jewish Center, see Scult, *Judaism Faces the Twentieth Century*, 154–73. There is much information on the Jewish Center in Kaplan, *Communings of the Spirit*, vol. 1. See the index to that volume. See also the excellent work by David Kaufman, *Shul with a Pool: The Synagogue Center in American Jewish History* (Waltham, MA: Brandeis University Press, 1999).

8. See the most recent edition, Mordecai M. Kaplan, *Judaism as a Civilization: Toward a Reconstruction of Jewish Life* (Philadelphia: Jewish Publication Society, 2010).

experience, and their present welfare at the center of his conception of Judaism (see the diary entry for August 24, 1941).[9] The Torah (Hebrew scriptures), revelation, and God were all explained in terms relating to Jewish peoplehood. Because Kaplan did not see Judaism as a system of dogmas or a set of laws, he helped even the most skeptical of modern Jews to relate to Jewish civilization. At the same time, his students at the seminary wanted to know why Kaplan continued using the word *God* (see the diary entry for January 29, 1935) when he rejected the belief in a supernatural deity. It was the central repository of the spiritual quest of the Jewish people, Kaplan told his class.[10]

Kaplan also maintained that all Jewish laws were in reality customs of the Jewish community that had enduring value. He wanted Jews to observe as much as they were able to in terms of religious ritual rather than feeling that they were dealing with a set of laws which were either kept or broken. These guidelines for observance were spelled out in *A Guide to Jewish Ritual*, later published by the Reconstructionist movement.[11]

Kaplan's use of the term *civilization* fit into the modalities of American thought of the time and had the effect of countering an incipient anti-Semitism. In the 1920s and 1930s there was a rise in American nativism, culminating in restrictive immigration laws. This further motivated Kaplan to emphasize the multicultural nature of American civilization and to maintain that Judaism was also a civilization. It should also be noted that for Kaplan *civilization* was a more inclusive term than *culture* and included the latter.[12]

The assertion that Jews lived in two civilizations was enormously helpful for the Jews of the 1930s. To the children of immigrants and to those on the fringe of the Jewish community, Kaplan would say, "Yes, be American, but you can also be Jewish and have not one civilization but two." Judaism and Americanism share the same values, so there is no inherent contradiction.[13]

Although Kaplan was wedded to Jewish peoplehood on many levels, he was profoundly American. Early in his career he saw democracy in America

---

9. Kaplan outlined his basic philosophy many times. In the August 24, 1941, diary entry he lists the basic principles of Reconstructionism with an emphasis on the Jewish people and community. For a full discussion of Kaplan's concept of Judaism as a civilization, see Scult, *Radical American Judaism*, 5.

10. For a full discussion of Kaplan's concept of God, see Scult, *Radical American Judaism*, ch. 6 and 7.

11. See *A Guide to Jewish Ritual*, introduction by Ira Eisenstein (New York: Reconstructionist Press, 1962). It is not clear who actually wrote this pamphlet, although, of course, Kaplan would have had final approval. For an early formulation of the *Guide*, see Mordecai Kaplan, "Toward a Guide for Ritual Usage," *The Reconstructionist* 7 (November 14, 1941): 7–13. For a full discussion of Kaplan and ritual, see Scult, *Radical American Judaism*, 177–205.

12. For the most interesting account of Kaplan's use of the term *civilization*, see Noam Pianko, "Reconstructing Judaism, Reconstructing America: The Sources and Functions of Mordecai Kaplan's 'Civilization,'" *Jewish Social Studies* 12.2 (winter 2006): 39–55.

13. For a sermon on the American flag, which, however, Kaplan was quite dissatisfied with, see the diary entry in this volume for February 22, 1941.

as a threat, but in the end he came to understand its inevitability and that it could work to help save the Jewish people. He freely embraced the fundamentals of democratic culture, including the rule of law and the primacy of individual rights. His emphasis on individualism was the core idea of his notion of salvation. Kaplan was the quintessential modern person, and he understood that the process of modernity is a movement from "fate to choice" (diary entry for November 21, 1936). Jews must choose, Kaplan would say. In *Judaism as a Civilization* he dismissed the notion of the Jews as the chosen people but retained the concept of the Jews as the "choosing people." He continued to ponder this problem for many years (see the diary entry for May 31, 1940).

Judaism as a Civilization privileges heterogeneity. Kaplan's views of the nature of civilization and its pluralistic emphasis were confirmed by the writings of Horace Kallen, who vigorously opposed the notion of a one-dimensional American nationalism. Kallen rejected the melting pot ideology, where homogeneity was the goal; instead, he opted for the cultural pluralism model. He preferred the metaphor of an orchestra in which all members maintain their individual identities yet play together in harmony.

The question was whether both of these thinkers were also willing to accept cultural pluralism among the Jews. The answer was a definite yes. Kaplan completely rejected the idea that there was only one way to be Jewish. Indeed, he maintained that any way in which a person nurtured the "life-force" of the Jewish people was a valid contribution to Jewish survival (see the diary entry for September 4, 1934). He was pluralist to the core, believing that we must learn to live with a maximum amount of individuation, which translates into the idea that the more ways of being a Jew, the better. In favoring variety over uniformity and traditionalism, Kaplan would certainly approve of the astonishing range in the Judaisms of our time.

Kaplan's radicalism had been a problem at the Jewish Theological Seminary from the beginning of his tenure there. He was the first at the seminary to openly support biblical criticism. This textual methodology maintains that the Pentateuch was not written by Moses and was authored by many hands. Solomon Schechter, the great scholar and savant who was president of the seminary when Kaplan began to teach there, referred to biblical criticism as higher anti-Semitism.[14] Kaplan, on the other hand, emphasized that the significance of the Torah was not determined by its origin but by the function it performed in Jewish life. It had been central and could be again if it were reinterpreted so that it was functional for contemporary American Jews.

Kaplan never felt completely comfortable with his colleagues at the seminary. Neither his ideology nor his need for innovation appealed to them. He

---

14. On the relationship between Kaplan and Schechter, see the index to Scult, *Judaism Faces the Twentieth Century*; and Scult, *Radical American Judaism*, 10, 11, 53, 116, 119, 169. See also the index to Kaplan, *Communings of the Spirit*, vol. 1.

often considered leaving the seminary and in 1927 resigned to take a position at the more liberal Jewish Institute of Religion that Stephen Wise had organized a few years before. However, in the wake of persistent urging by his students and many seminary alumni, Kaplan returned to his position within a few months. By remaining at the Jewish Theological Seminary until his retirement in 1963, Kaplan in effect prevented Reconstructionism from becoming a denomination, because a separate party was impossible without the Reconstructionist movement establishing its own rabbinical seminary.

Kaplan writes often about the seminary. He tells us, for example, of the financial problems of the seminary that were part of the economic hardships of the Depression era (diary entry for February 5, 1935), of his discomfort during seminary faculty meetings (December 22, 1939), and of his disgust with his rabbinical school students (January 17, 1940). He writes in graphic detail of president Cyrus Adler's funeral (April 9, 1940) and of the advancing career of Rabbi Simon Greenberg (March 15, 1935), who was destined to become a key player in the Conservative movement of the 1940s and 1950s. The seminary faculty reacted strongly to Kaplan's *New Haggadah* (June 24, 1941), although Kaplan believed that some seminary professors had their own brand of heresy (October 22, 1941).

Kaplan's radicalism must also be understood against the background of the social and political problems of the 1930s. In the wake of the stock market crash of 1929 and the economic hardships that followed, the appeal of the Communist Party grew considerably. Kaplan, though he rejected Communism, because of its militant stand against religion, did find it appealing on many levels. Describing his ambivalence under the metaphor of having several selves, he declared, "I believe I shall be better off if I henceforth identify them [his several selves] as two separate entities, even to the extent of naming them as though they were two distinct persons. I shall call one Mordecai (the old Adam) and the other Menahem (the regenerated me). Mordecai is a liberal bourgeois. Menahem is an out and out Communist" (diary entry for July 25, 1934). Kaplan goes so far as to spell out what it is about Communism that attracts him and what it is that repels him. Kaplan found difficulties wherever he turned. During these years he taught at an institution called the Graduate School for Jewish Social Work. He reports the problems of dealing with students who were dedicated to the communist ideology (diary entry for April 2, 1935).

Kaplan was a lifelong Zionist and believed that Jewish civilization required the natural setting of its own land in order to flourish and grow.

Rabbi Isaac Jacob Reines, the founder of Mizrachi (a religious Zionist group), had been the rabbi in Sventzian, where Kaplan grew up, and was a close family friend.[15] Deeply influenced by the cultural Zionist Ahad Ha-Am, Kaplan later stated that this Zionist thinker revealed to him "the spiritual reality of the

---

15. Kaplan received *semichah* (traditional rabbinic ordination by laying on of hands) from Reines in 1909. See Gurock and Schacter, A *Modern Heretic*, 52.

Jewish people." At the same time, Kaplan found Ahad Ha-Am deficient in that his approach to Jewish life was "wanting in a basic appreciation of Religion." Kaplan had a rare brand of nationalism, which might be called nonstatist. Peoplehood was at the center of his philosophy but in a unique way. He had a mystical feeling toward the Jewish people but feared the excesses of nationalism.[16]

The uniqueness of the present volume consists partly in the fact that from 1937 to 1939 Kaplan was in Jerusalem teaching at the Hebrew University in the Department of Education. We are treated to a front-row seat during this period with such personalities as Martin Buber making many appearances.[17]

In one of the most fascinating entries, Kaplan chanced to meet Buber at the bus stop and they rode together up to Mt. Scopus and the Hebrew University. Of course, what would Buber and Kaplan riding on a bus talk about but their concepts of God.

> Yesterday morning at 10:30 a.m. a meeting of the Faculty Senate took place. As I waited for the bus on Talbieh Street, which would take me to the bus that goes to the University, Buber came up. This time I decided not to be the one who begins the conversation, as I have been on all the occasions I have met him. He has never asked me anything about myself, and I had to goad him into a conversation. The events of the preceding days have upset me so much that they left me no initiative to pull the tongue of anyone, even Buber. But after two or three minutes he began by saying that these days he is reading my book, *The Meaning of God in Modern Jewish Religion.*
>
> In the meanwhile the bus came, and from that moment on, throughout our ride on both buses, we conversed about the idea of God in my book. He expressed his objection to my approach and said that my god is not a god, because he is entirely immanent. The God of the simple Polish Jew is the God of Israel and the God of the universe. I tried to show him that I devote an entire chapter to the idea that God is a force outside ourselves.[18] He responded that this idea does not appear as central, but I think that he has not yet gotten to that chapter in my book.
>
> He promised me that he would write a review of my book in the form of a letter addressed to me. I cannot say that we thoroughly enjoyed the conversation, but the fact that, at least, Buber behaved

---

16. On Ahad Ha-Am, see Scult, *Radical American Judaism*, 2.

17. When Kaplan was in Jerusalem from 1937 to 1939, he wrote the diary in Hebrew. This portion of the diary has been translated by Rabbi Nahum Waldman, z"l.

18. Kaplan is referring here to Chapter 7 ("God as Felt Presence") in his book *The Meaning of God in Modern Jewish Religion* (New York: Behrman House, 1937; and Detroit: Wayne State University Press, 1994).

himself humanly, taking into consideration the interests of his colleague, pacified me somewhat. (Diary entry for July 9, 1938)

Of course Buber's notion of the "eternal thou" is hardly any closer to the simple shtetl Jew than Kaplan's notion, but that is a discussion for another time.

The immediacy of the situation in Jerusalem is conveyed in the following entry.

Apropos of the habit I cultivated of taking my daily constitutional on the roof instead of walking down King George Rd. through Ben Yehuda down to the Zion Cinema, which I used to do formerly, I said to Lena the other day, "There's nothing like having a roof under your feet." It was at her suggestion I made the change last August, when shootings and bombings in the heart of the new city became rather frequent. (Diary entry for March, 28, 1939)

Kaplan's personal life is inseparable from his life as a rabbi and ideologue. He is justly famous for introducing the bat mitzvah into American Jewish life in 1922, when his daughter Judith attained the age of 12 and a half.[19] He used to say that he had four reasons for introducing the bat mitzvah, meaning, of course, his four daughters. As a father, he had the same problems that all fathers have in trying to lead their children into the path they consider the right way. In Kaplan's case it involved their observance of Sabbath restrictions (see diary entry for August 19, 1934). It is interesting to note that the issue of more "bar" than "mitzvah," which sometimes characterizes our time, was also present for Kaplan. At times he had to attend "wild" bar mitzvah parties, which made him uncomfortable (see the diary entry for May 4, 1935).

Kaplan's own religious observance reflected his efforts to free himself from meaningless ritual at the same time that he could never completely reject his traditional past. He continuously had issues with writing on the Sabbath and feeling guilty about it (see diary entries for September 21, 1934, and April 18, 1936).

His ritual regimen was similar to that of many Conservative rabbis of the time. He did not ride on Shabbat when at home, but when away, he accepted a ride to the synagogue if it was unavoidable. His house was kosher (two sets of dishes, etc.), but when he was away on speaking tours, he often ate in the house of his hosts without questioning their adherence to kashrut. It was his custom to pray (daven) every morning, although this became more irregular as time went on. At times, we get a view of the rather rigid attitude toward religious ritual on the part of some Conservative Jews, as when a young rabbi lost a position because

---

19. For details of the bat mitzvah of Judith Kaplan, see Scult, *Judaism Faces the Twentieth Century*, 301–3, 415n31.

he took a bath on the Sabbath, a practice that was forbidden by a strict interpretation of rabbinic law.[20]

Rabbi Ira Eisenstein, Kaplan's son-in-law, reports a rather interesting episode regarding Kaplan's praying. In 1940 the Eisensteins (Ira, Judith, and the family) spent the summer with the Kaplans at the Jersey shore. Eisenstein told me that he observed Kaplan praying on a regular basis, donning tallis (prayer shawl) and tefillin (phylacteries) and using the traditional *siddur* (prayer book). But sometimes, Eisenstein said, "Kaplan would put on tallis and tefillin and read from John Dewey or Ahad Ha-Am." This might be called davening (praying) from Dewey.[21]

The diary also obviously contains material that is purely personal and reflects Kaplan's passing moods. Sometimes he is depressed and lonely (e.g., see diary entry for December 14, 1939). At times he is annoyed with everyday details (July 29, 1939) and thinks about the matter of failure, including his own (June 5, 1934). Throughout the period covered in this volume, Kaplan lived near Central Park and frequently walked around the reservoir, sometimes thinking about the distraction of a pebble in his shoe (see diary entry for June 20, 1934). Although Kaplan had a fine background and had no trouble reading Hebrew sources, classical or modern, he did have trouble with speaking Hebrew in public and notes it in the diary (see, for example, diary entry for October 3, 1939).

The period covered in this volume is also the time of the gathering storm arising from the advent of Hitler and Nazi Germany. Rather early on Kaplan felt the need for the democracies to arm themselves against Fascism and Nazism (see diary entry for November 18, 1938). Kaplan reacted strongly and provocatively to Hitler and Nazism as he attempted to understand how this brand of nationalism differed from the Jewish nationalism that he so fervently embraced. The great events of the time gain a moving immediacy. We experience with him the Nazi-Soviet nonaggression pact (diary entry for August 24, 1939). We feel his rage at the annexation of Czechoslovakia.

Another Hitlerian earth-quake. The Nazis have annexed Czecho-Slovakia. What next?

---

20. See diary entry for October 27, 1935, about Rabbi Parzen, who took a bath on Shabbat and lost out on a job. Parzen was apparently being interviewed for a position at a Conservative congregation. Herbert Parzen (1897–1985) was a rabbi ordained at the Jewish Theological Seminary, an author, and state director of the United Synagogue of America, as well as a chaplain in the New York City Department of Correction. He was also a Kaplan supporter.

21. The facts here were reported to me when I asked Eisenstein about Kaplan's praying habits. The expression "davening from Dewey" is my own. Ahad Ha-Am (Asher Ginsberg) is the well-known cultural Zionist. See glossary and Scult, *Radical American Judaism*, esp. ch. 3 ("Nationalism and Righteousness: Ahad Ha-Am and Matthew Arnold) and ch. 4 ("Universalism and Pragmatism: Felix Adler, William James, and John Dewey").

Last night I heard Chamberlain's speech over the radio which he delivered at Birmingham Town Hall. To me it seemed to say that we are on the brink of war. Had Nazi nightmares in my sleep. (Diary entry for October 1, 1938)

Kaplan also reacted strongly to the fascism he saw among the Jews themselves. For example, he had no patience for Zionists on the right. In 1939, with the horrendous events in Germany on the horizon and a conference in London that resulted in the White Paper and the subsequent restriction of immigration, student followers of Jabotinsky, leader of the ultranationalist party of the right, were demonstrating at the Hebrew University and disturbing classes in protest. Kaplan had no patience with them (see diary entry for February 1939).

Once the war starts, Kaplan feels the strong impulse to guide his congregants but also finds it difficult: "I have to preach and lecture on what to think and what to do in this crisis. Like a captain leading his band to a forlorn hope in battle, I must combine for myself and for others the experience of expecting the worst and hoping if not for the best, at least for some good. That is no easy matter" (diary entry for May 16, 1940).

The diary contains philosophical passages that continue to amaze. Almost everyone, including those who knew Kaplan well, think of him as a sociological thinker and a disciple of John Dewey and William James. But in the following passage and many like it, Kaplan comes close to a provocative metaphysical statement when he writes of mind as the fundamental reality of the universe. He sounds much more like the German idealists of the nineteenth century than the American Pragmatists.

The point which I then made was that mind, which is the very ground of reality and experience, is experienced as self on the hither end and as God on the end of one's self. This makes self and God correlative terms. The fact is that self has always been a correlative term. What the correlate was depended upon the cultural and social development of the individual. Usually the correlate was the most inclusive group. Its totem idol, flag, or other sancta were the gods which served as correlates. By this time, nothing less than the cosmos will satisfy the individual as being the seat of the correlate to the self. Hence his God is no longer tribal or national but cosmic.

I believe that the foregoing assumption that self and God are correlative terms might form the starting point of an interesting adventure in thought. (Diary entry for October 3, 1939)

Readers of this second volume of Kaplan diary selections are in for a treat, much pleasure, and a moving provocative read.

1

June 3, 1934–March 24, 1935

On the Flyleaf of Volume 7: Kaplan Quotes from Books He Is Reading[1]

"How can I be substantial if I fail to cast a shadow? I must have a dark side if I am to be whole."

> —C. G. Jung, *Modern Man in Search of a Soul*, 40. [Copied] May 14, [19]34

"Unless he is proficient, the man who claims to be modern is nothing but an unscrupulous gambler. He must be proficient in the highest degree, for unless he can atone by creative energy for his break with tradition, he is merely disloyal to the past."

> —*Ibid.*, 229. [Copied] May 15, [19]34

"Those who live experimentally must suffer great pangs and great terrors; others can live comfortably in comparison."

> —Henry N. Wieman, *The Wrestle of Religion with Truth*, 65. [Copied] June 2, [19]34

The Sabbath and Salvation

JUNE 3, 1934

I believe I have struck a capital idea in making the Sabbath symbolic of the striving after salvation. That coincides with the rabbinic interpretation of the Sabbath as a foretaste of the world-to-come. The next problem is to find a good

---

1. On the flyleaves of his diaries, Kaplan copied quotations from books he was reading. Those listed here are a selection.

working conception of salvation. I believe I have also solved that problem by making salvation synonymous with the synthesis of individualism and collectivism with the achievement of a maximum of cooperation plus a maximum of individual self-fulfillment. From that standpoint the holiness of life would mean the assumption that there are elements in the universe, which if properly reckoned with, are in rapport with the achievement of that synthesis. I was helped by Wieman's[2] definition of God. His definition would have proved much more fruitful if he had applied it, as I do, to holiness. To be sure, the concept of God is a precipitate of the quality of holiness, but as a substantive concept it obscured the denotation of quality.

On Accepting Failure

JUNE 5, 1934

It was only something I happened to read yesterday in Wieman's *The Wrestle of Religion with Truth* that made me go to the *siyyum hazman*[3] of the Friedlaender classes.[4] I refer especially to the chapter, "How Religion Cures Human Ills" and especially the sentence in it "To know how to accept failure is quite as important as to be equipped for mastery. For some undertakings in every man's life must certainly fail" (page 114, Wieman). The primary reason for my wanting to attend the *siyyum hazman* was undoubtedly the lack of anything specific to say. I know that it is very hard for me to speak when I am in that state of mind. Nevertheless, the sense of duty and my obligation to Chipkin[5] impelled me to disregard the possible failure I might incur. Undecided as to what I was to do, the passage from Wieman's book turned the scales and I went. The speech wasn't any too good, but it wasn't altogether bad either. But I am spared at least that terrible sense of maladjustment which overcomes me whenever I shrink from performing an unpleasant task.

Salvation and the Sabbath

TUESDAY, JUNE 12, 1934

Of the many things I want to work on, the interpretation of the Sabbath and Festivals seems at the present time to attract me most. The suggestion that the Sabbath should serve as a symbol of salvation as the aim of life simply fascinates me. But now comes the question, What shall we understand by salvation?

---

2. Kaplan is referring to Henry Nelson Wieman, whom Kaplan read throughout his life and was influenced by. Kaplan found that he shared much with Wieman. Emanuel Goldsmith has done much work on Kaplan and Henry Nelson Wieman; see, in particular, Emanuel Goldsmith, "Religious Naturalism in Defense of Democracy," in *Religious Experience and Ecological Responsibility*, ed. Donald A. Crosby and Charley Hardwick (New York: Peter Lang, 1996), 317–35.

3. *Siyyum hazman* is a traditional expression marking the end of a term.

4. Adult education classes at the Jewish Theological Seminary (JTS) named after seminary professor Israel Friedlaender.

5. Israel Chipkin was the director of the Friedlaender classes at the time.

The first idea that comes to mind is that the various answers given to that question constitute the history of man's spiritual development. That history has taught us that one of the most tragic errors has been the assumption that salvation must mean the same to all human beings who want to achieve it. Especially was that the case in the days of other-worldly religion. But even nowadays social reformers assume that there can be but one objectively true conception of salvation.

The lesson to be derived from the past is that a scheme of salvation which is imposed from above is bad, but not that we can afford to get along without some scheme of salvation, which is the result of cooperative study and thought. In fact, if the Sabbath is to serve as a symbol of salvation, it should be so not in the sense of holding up some fixed and final conception of salvation but rather as a reminder that we must keep on constantly thinking and planning cooperatively if we want to know what salvation means and how to achieve it. The Sabbath day should be chiefly dedicated to that kind of thinking and planning. That will make of the Sabbath Day a means to spiritual growth.

Milton Steinberg Has Ambitions of His Own

JUNE 14, 1934

I have been asked by Rabbi Samuel Cohen to prepare a series of special prayers similar to those I worked out for the Rosh Hashanah of last year. The request has been confirmed by a letter from [Louis J.] Moss, the president of the United Synagogue. In order to facilitate the task for myself, I invited Rabbi Milton Steinberg to collaborate on it with me.

Much as I like him, I must admit that he irritates me with his persistent refusal to cooperate with me. He is ambitious to achieve a scholarly reputation by getting his Ph.D. for an academic piece of work. Although he has allowed all kinds of interruptions to interfere with his work on his thesis, he uses his desire to get done with it as an excuse for refusing to collaborate with me every time I ask him. This is the third time he has turned me down.

An Unproductive Sabbath and Ambivalence Toward
Henry Rosenthal

SATURDAY NIGHT, JUNE 16, 1934

It is already ten o'clock at night. The whole day passed away without my having anything to show for it. At this morning's service there were about fifty people present. I couldn't allow them to leave without having them feel that they had learned something. Today's Sidrah being Korah[6] I gave them the rabbinic

---

6. Sidra is the Torah portion of the week read aloud in the synagogue. Korah tells the story of a famous rebellion against Moses. The portion runs from Numbers 16:1 to 18:32.

portrayal of Korah as a demagogue who tried to prove to the Israelites that Moses and Aaron exploited the people, especially the poor, using the divine sanction for their purpose.

For some reason or other, no matter how little I exert myself at a service, I feel tired when it's over. That together with the Sabbath meal makes it necessary for me to take a long nap after lunch. After that I managed to read a few pages of *Magic Mountain*.[7] At 4 [Henry] Rosenthal and his wife came. A little before 5 Ira and Ella Kaplan came and stayed till 7:45. Supper till about 8:30. Not having had any exercise the last few days, I thought it advisable to take a three-mile walk.[8] And so the whole day went.

Rosenthal came at my request. I suggested to him that he collaborate with me on the formulation of the prayers I have been asked by the United Synagogue to prepare. He too turned me down. He has been at work for some time on a novel, and he wants to use every minute of his free time during the coming weeks solely on that.

Strangely enough, I seem to have gotten to a point where I wanted him to refuse. Something within me hoped that he would not accede to my request, though I went on making it and advancing arguments why he ought to work with me on the prayers. It is probably the less worthy self in me wanting all the glory for itself that did not cherish the idea of his sharing credit with me. Perhaps—and I believe this is the more plausible reason—it was the fear that Rosenthal's name appended to the prayers might prejudice some of the Conservative or Orthodox diehards who have no particular liking for Rosenthal.

The Seminary Students and Faculty—A Sickly Bunch

TUESDAY, JUNE 19, 1934

At the Seminary Faculty meeting [Cyrus] Adler reported that out of the twenty-five Seminary students who had been recently given a medical examination, only three were reported as of normal health. All the others had either ear trouble or gastric disorders or chronic bronchitis; one was cardiac, and nearly all were flat-footed. It turned out that those who had been reported as doing poor work had something physically wrong with them.

How symbolic of the general decay in Jewish life—an old sickly and decrepit faculty of nine members appointed to train two dozen more or less diseased

---

7. *Magic Mountain* is a novel by Thomas Mann.

8. Kaplan was a regular walker. He walked frequently around the reservoir in Central Park and regularly from 100th Street down to 59th and back. He often took colleagues and students on the walk around the reservoir, including Judah Magnes, Louis Finkelstein, Max Kadushin, and Ira Eisenstein. They often discussed the *parsha* [Torah portion]. This information is from my interviews with Kaplan.

youngsters of very mediocre mental ability as spiritual leaders in an age of great turmoil and crisis!

Walking Around the Reservoir with a Pebble in My Shoe

WEDNESDAY, JUNE 20, 1934

As I walked on the cinder path around the reservoir this morning and one pebble after another got into my half shoes, at first scraping the foot and then working their way down under its arch, I thought of the petty irritations and annoyances that vex us and to which we manage to adjust ourselves after a while.

A Modern Reading of Psalm 27

JUNE 22, 1934

It has just occurred to me that a fitting theme for a prayer at the beginning of a New Year would be one based on the 27th Psalm, which is traditionally recited during the penitential season. To have that psalm yield a theme that might prove fruitful to the modern way of thinking, it is of course necessary to exploit its metaphorical implications. By this I mean finding equivalents in our present-day ethical thinking for the various elements that constitute the experience of the psalmist. Thus there figure in it (1) the enemies: these should serve as metaphor for the main causes of our fear and anxiety, viz., privation, sickness, failure, bereavement, temptation, disillusionment, and death; (2) God: He represents the sum of the forces, conditions, and relationships in the world that make for the enhancement of human life in the individual and in the group; (3) the sanctuary to which the psalmist looks for shelter; the equivalent of this is the inner act of thought and will whereby man divests himself of his self-centered ego and identifies himself in intention and activity with all those forces that spell God.

A New Prayer for Rosh Hashanah

JUNE 26, 1934

The ideal form for creative writing is poetry. But, unfortunately, I have no gift for rhyme or rhythm. The next best is poetic prose in the style of *Also Sprach Zarathustra*.[9] But how shall I acquire that style? It occurred to me while I was taking a walk today around the reservoir, that I might adopt the following procedure: (1) work out a regular sermon outline; (2) develop an antiphonal prayer on the basis of that outline; (3) convert that prayer into apostrophic form. Let me try it with the Yom Kippur Eve Prayer which I have recently formulated.

---

9. F. Nietzsche's aphoristic work. It is clear that Kaplan knew Nietzsche well. On the flyleaf of an early diary he put a quotation from Nietzsche: "I read only those who write with their blood."

1. In the conscience of mankind, God has revealed Himself to you; without such guidance you would be like lost and forsaken wanderers in a trackless desert.
2. Each Atonement Day He lovingly pleads with you to Cast away all your transgressions and make you a new heart and a new spirit; why will ye die, O House of Israel; pray that He grant you the wisdom to grasp the full import of His message and the ability to pattern your lives in accordance with its behests.
3. If you but knew Him aright, you would know His will; and knowing His will, you would not fail to recognize your transgressions.
4. Human beings have mistakenly sought to discern Him in the blind play of directionless forces and in the whirl of chance events; they have read His intent into the arbitrary doctrines of self-deluded guides.
5. Human beings groan under the weight of sin each time a flaw would mar the rites they performed to placate some god of their imagining; but sensed no wrong in depriving men of their due and despoiling the weak and the defenseless.
6. No qualms troubled them when grinding the faces of the poor, or when shedding human blood; no scruples mingled with their remorseless use of power or their pitiless torment of the innocent.
7. Be grateful that this criterion of sin no longer obtaineth; and that in its place a worthier standard has been vouchsafed to you.
8. For you know that against God you sin most grievously when you darken the lives of his children; and when by your selfishness you extinguish in them the light of faith and hope.
9. You sin against Him when you profane the person of a fellow being by using Him as a tool for the fulfillment of your desires.
10. You sin against Him when you allow envy of a neighbor's good fortune to breed in your hatred and spite and when in your pride you humiliate those of fewer possessions and lesser achievements.
11. You sin against Him when you besmirch a good name and gloat over the downfall of those you deem your rivals.
12. Pray to Him to help you root out your degrading habits and break the shackles of pernicious custom, to fashion your hearts anew and redirect your will in accordance with his purposes.
13. Else, you whom He called to proclaim His law of righteousness would forfeit both the right and the reason for being, and become an aimless and forlorn clan, the shattered ruin of a once glorious sanctuary of His spirit.
14. Let a new spirit of compassion move you to banish from your hearts evil purposes and cruel designs you harbor against one another; let a new spirit of lovingkindness unite you all in the endeavor to establish on earth God's kingdom of justice, freedom and peace.

Salvation — An Explanation

JULY 18, 1934

Salvation is that organization and adjustment of life which enables us to do the best we can and to bear the worst that befalls us.

"The best we can" means giving expression in integrated fashion to all phases and capacities of our personality in terms of the true, the good, and the beautiful.

The worst that befalls us includes both suffering and sin in the various degrees to which they afflict us. What are the requisites to our being able to do the best we can? Work, health, knowledge, leisure, and love . . .

Under the heading of love I include all those relationships — family, community, nation, etc. — which integrate the life of the individual with the life of others in an organic sense and not merely mechanical. These are the relationships which give the human being the feeling of adequacy, dignity, and self-respect.

The second half of the problem of salvation would deal with the task of finding what we must think, feel, and do to retain our equilibrium in sickness, bereavement, humiliation, poverty, and helplessness in the face of the wrong and cruelties of life.

In this analysis we must assume that reality is of such a nature as to help man achieve salvation, if he only knows how. This fact about reality constitutes its element of holiness. The hypostasis[10] of that element is expressed in the concept of God.

Salvation — Preaching vs. Practice

JULY 20, 1934

From the apparently little effect which all these exalted ideas about salvation seem to have upon me personally — considering how far I am from doing the best, etc., — I began to suspect the value of those ideas. But then I recalled two facts which reconciled me to the paradox of urging something upon others which has but little effect on myself. First, the fact clearly pointed out by Aristotle that a desirable state of character cannot be attained through knowledge merely. It calls for long and arduous habituation, and not having been habituated to live my ideas, I am condemned to keep on talking about them. Secondly, physicians who are cardiacs and consumptives are said to have an advantage over those who are well in having firsthand knowledge of the diseases they try to cure.

Being Ambivalent — This Time about Communism

JULY 25, 1934

It seems that the only way a man in my position can manage to exist is deliberately to split his personality and lead a sort of Jekyll and Hyde existence.

---

10. Hypostasis is an underlying reality, the substance or essence of something.

Otherwise I am likely to go insane or be a complete failure. All this fine talk about integrating one's personality is mere piffle. That doesn't mean to say I shall not wax enthusiastic about it, but I shall do it with that part of my personality which is bourgeois and parasitic. There will undoubtedly continue to operate a certain osmosis between the two personalities in me, but I must recognize the class struggle as existing between them no less than between the capitalists and the proletariats. I believe I shall be better off if I henceforth identify them as two separate entities, even to the extent of naming them as though they were two distinct persons. I shall call one Mordecai (the old Adam) and the other Menahem (the regenerated me). Mordecai is a liberal bourgeois. Menahem is an out and out Communist.

Life Goals

AUGUST 5, 1934

I think that the following formulation of the objectives of life-management is even better than that suggested by Lyman in the opening paragraph of his *Meaning of Religion*: To render life assuring (free from fear), interesting (free from boredom), and fulfilling (free from frustration).[11]

Getting the Children to Observe the Sabbath

SUNDAY, AUGUST 19, 1934

As soon as we were through with Sabbath dinner yesterday, Naomi asked, "Can we go to the beach with the car?" "You can do whatever you want," I said, "but it's not my idea of spending a Sabbath afternoon." Then the storm broke loose. For over two hours Judith, Hadassah, Naomi, and Selma, reinforced by Ira,[12] kept up a barrage of arguments under which, I must confess, I finally crumpled up. They demolished my defenses of the customary restrictions on the Sabbath and incidentally also those of *kashrut*.

After I rose from the table, I went to take Mrs. Epstein for a walk, and it was the same story all over again. Her children had all gone to the beach with their car, but not without having pleaded with her to come along with them. She too would not yield. Why? Habit.

Pluralism—Any Way You Nurture the Jewish Life Force Is OK

SEPTEMBER 4, 1934

Rabbi Fischer of Arverne—a man, by the way, whom I like very much because of his sincerity and devotion to his calling—contributed an important

---

11. The book Kaplan is quoting from is Eugene William Lyman's *Meaning and Truth of Religion* (New York: Charles Scribner's Sons, 1933).

12. Judith, Hadassah, Naomi, and Selma are Kaplan's daughters. Ira is Ira Eisenstein, who was married to Judith and was thus Kaplan's son-in-law. See glossary for individual notes.

idea with regard to what constitutes a true understanding of Jewish life. I had stressed the need of recognizing the organic relationship among the various phases, and having the synagogue function chiefly as a means of stressing this relationship. Fischer, however, raised the point that it would be asking the impossible of the average Jew to expect him to participate in all Jewish activities. The value of regarding Judaism as a civilization (this is my own addition) is in making it possible for the Jew to feel that he is contributing to Jewish life no matter what phase of it he fosters. To this I added the proviso that he realize the place of his contribution in the context of the totality of Jewish life.

A Tragedy at Sea—A Traditional Theological View

SUNDAY, SEPTEMBER 9, 1934

The sermon which I have worked out for tomorrow, the first day of Rosh Hashanah, is based on the idea that the comparison of life to a book should remind us that if we want life to have meaning for us, we must link up our lives with those forces which make for the unity of mankind and the development of personality.

When I read this morning about the disaster on the steamer *Morro Castle*, which caught fire off the New Jersey Coast, and that 250 people lost their lives, my train of thought about life being like a book received a severe jolt and was almost thrown off the track. In order to continue the run, I had to add the following thought: The disaster has as little to do with God (as I understand that term) as the fact that a passage in the copy of a book is blotted out through some accident. In the mind of the author, that passage lives. So if among the number who perished there were men and women who contributed to the meaning of life, they became part of the external context which lives in the mind of God, irrespective of what happened to their bodies.

Communist Thinking Oversimplifies

SEPTEMBER 13, 1934

The trouble with [Rebecca Pitts's] analysis of the situation,[13] it seems to me, is the same as with communist thinking in general, namely, the tendency to oversimplify the problem. With all my bitterness against the profit system, I cannot for the life of me come to think of the class struggle as a struggle between two diametrically opposed camps. There is also the psychological fact that people hold on to the old not because they believe that it is the best, but because they

---

13. Kaplan had been reading Rebecca Pitts's 1934 article "Jews Face Fascism" in *Opinion: A Journal of Jewish Life and Letters*. Pitts called for Jews to support the notion of "national in form and proletarian in content."

don't know that the new would be better. The fear of the untried is not something that exists in some and is altogether wanting in others, so that it might serve as a basis of distinguishing one class from another. Likewise the division into haves and have-nots is an unreal one. There is a third group which consists of those who don't have what they have because at the slightest turn of fortune they are apt to lose what they have. There are people who are absolutely poor, who believe in individual enterprise, and [there are the] well-to-do, who would readily part with their wealth for any system that would free them from the worries and responsibilities of their wealth. And what of the fact that there is hardly an individual who is homogeneous within himself? Most thinking people of the so-called middle class have the class struggle going on within their own souls.

A Loyalty Oath at the Seminary

MONDAY, SEPTEMBER 17, 1934

At the meeting of the Seminary Faculty last Friday printed slips stating "I swear (affirm) to uphold the Constitution of the United States and of the State of etc." were passed around for our signatures.[14] Prof. [Israel] Davidson expressed deep resentment at being asked to sign such a statement. The rest of us signed it without protest. Adler defended the legitimacy of the demand of the Legislature and pointed out that, as members of an institution, which is chartered by the State, it is our duty to abide by the ruling of the Legislature. I don't know whether Davidson finally signed or not.

Writing on the Sabbath and Feeling Guilty

FRIDAY, SEPTEMBER 21, 1934

I am writing this at 12:00 midnight and am thus violating the Sabbath ordinance against writing. Although I managed to emancipate myself from the habit of conforming to that ordinance a few years ago, yet the old habit has persisted and I have not used the pen on Sabbaths. In consistency with my permitting the playing of piano on the Sabbath, I ought frankly to permit writing, which satisfies the need for self-expression as much as playing an instrument does. But I suppose the feeling that writing is regarded as much more of an infraction of the Sabbath spirit prevents me from being consistent. Even now, as I began writing, Selma happened to walk into the study and, instead of continuing to write, I put away the pen and made believe I was only reading this journal. I am sure she noticed my embarrassment, but she acted as though she didn't.

---

14. The Red Scare of the 1920s led some states to require a loyalty oath from faculties of educational institutions.

A *Rather Chaotic Family Funeral*

Friday, October 5, 1934

The funeral was conducted in the semi-barbaric fashion of the ghetto. When I got to the house (1000 Simpson St.) at the time scheduled for the funeral, I learned that the body was still being prepared for the coffin. The small rooms were crowded with people, and my uncle's wife was sitting in the bedroom wailing and delivering a monologue in which she gave a detailed account of her husband's business relations and of numerous incidents that she recalled of his life. The women around her joined in the refrain of weeping. When the obsequies [funeral rites] were about to begin, the oldest son, Milton, asked me to conduct them. I suggested a procedure, but before I had a chance to start the services, bedlam let loose. A few women lay prostrate over the coffin and began screaming and shouting protests against death. The face of the deceased was uncovered and everybody began crowding to take a last look. But once they got near, they were rooted to the spot. Finding myself in this human whirlpool, I took the situation in hand, insisted upon drawing the black cloth over the exposed face of the deceased, and stopped the procession of morbid gazers. I was surprised at the readiness with which the mob yielded to my demand and at the quiet which reigned while I read the psalm and spoke. My brother-in-law Phineas,[15] at whose house Jonas was a frequent visitor, due to my mother staying there, delivered a brief eulogy. After that the coffin was taken downstairs, but instead of placing it in the hearse, it was carried through the street over a distance of about a thousand yards, in the course of which a busy thoroughfare had to be crossed on the way to the Hunts Point Talmud Center. I don't suppose such a thing is allowed by city ordinances, but in such crowded sections the people are left to themselves to do what they like. I understand that some of the neighbors advised strongly against putting the body on ice during the day before the funeral, claiming that it was more appropriate to have the body rest on the floor. A relative suggested that by placing bread and salt near the body, the same purpose would be served as putting it on ice.

First Meeting of the Reconstructionist *Editorial Board*

October 25, 1934

This morning I called the first meeting of the Editorial Board of the bi-weekly periodical I am planning to issue beginning January. It is to be published by the SAJ [Society for the Advancement of Judaism].[16] Present were Milton Steinberg, Benjamin Boxer,[17] Eugene Kohn, and Ira Eisenstein, besides me. Henry M. Rosenthal was invited but is afraid to join us because of the shakeup

---

15. Phineas Israeli married Kaplan's sister Sophie.
16. The SAJ was Kaplan's congregation, founded in 1922.
17. Kaplan probably means Ben Zion Bokser.

which had taken place in the YMHA [Young Men's Hebrew Association, similar to the YMCA], whose directors oppose any forward or liberal movement. Fischer of Arverne was invited but didn't show up. Robert Gordis had to be coaxed, but will probably cooperate.

My suggestion that it be called *The Reconstructionist* was accepted. The periodical should prove a wholesome and significant influence in Jewish life. Contact with those mentioned above was to be very exhilarating.

Difficulties of Speaking Hebrew in Public—and Sentimental Nationalist Slush from the TI Faculty

MONDAY, OCTOBER 29, 1934

Last night the formal opening of the TI [Teachers Institute] and Seminary College classes took place. This is another one of the ordeals I have to go through annually. My suffering on these occasions is due to my inability to speak Hebrew as fluently as I should be able to do, if I am to trust myself in the presence of all the Hebrew-speaking "bears" who constitute the TI faculty.[18] Having aroused the ire of some of them last year when I spoke in justification of the use of English, I was going to speak in Hebrew this time. I went so far as to formulate my thoughts in Hebrew and to conduct the sessions in Religion also in Hebrew so that I might twist my tongue into shape for a Hebrew speech. But when I rose to speak, I was dead tired and lost all confidence in myself and accordingly reverted to English. The students who followed me spoke in Hebrew very fluently and wittily much better than I did in English. Scharfstein gave the principal address. He delivered a regular harangue for more than a half-hour, in the course of which he made slurring references to rabbis who know Hebrew only from the book, and harped upon the importance of conversing in Hebrew. I was even more incensed at this attitude when later in the evening I read his article in the *Ha-Doar*,[19] in which there is a veiled allusion to my attempt to adjust Jewish life to American conditions. He is all for self-withdrawal into a Hebrew ghetto and preparing oneself to settle ultimately in Palestine. This is the philosophy of most of the members of the staff. That exempts them of any obligation to think through the problem of Jewish life as a permanent possibility in this country.

I can't help feeling that theirs is nothing more than a Jewish jingoism which does duty for serious consideration of the problem of Jewish life. Whereas I addressed the students on the need of their being intellectually and morally

---

18. When the Teachers Institute opened in 1909, the language of instruction was English, but the Talmud Torahs under the aegis of Samson Benderly did so well that in 1915 the language was switched to Hebrew. See Jonathan B. Krasner, *The Benderly Boys and American Jewish Education* (Waltham, MA: Brandeis University Press, 2011).

19. *Ha-Doar* was a Hebrew journal that appeared regularly in the United States from 1921 to 2002. It was published in New York City by the Histadrut.

honest with themselves as a condition to their being honest with others, and on the importance of their reinstating the honor system which has had to be abandoned, Scharfstein swept aside my remarks as if they were beside the point and sailed forth Fascist fashion into the sea of sentimental nationalistic slush. The entire experience sickened and depressed me, and it was by sheer force of will that I have managed to snap out of the mood which it got me into.

Organizing The Reconstructionist *Magazine*

NOVEMBER 5, 1934

On Thursday, October 25, Milton Steinberg, Ben Zion Boxer, Eugene Kohn, Ira [Eisenstein], and I met at my home to discuss the publication of a periodical. We decided to call it *The Reconstructionist* and to use the following motto: "Dedicated to the advancement of Judaism as a civilization, to the upbuilding of Palestine as a Jewish Homeland, and to the furtherance of universal freedom, justice, and peace." We also decided to organize ourselves into an editorial board which is to meet bi-weekly and to discuss the opinions to be expressed in the editorial columns.

Speaking in Troy, New York—Audience of the Subnormal Kind

NOVEMBER 15, 1934

Tuesday night I spoke at the Jewish Community Center in Troy. When I arrived at Albany at 7:09, I was met at the station by Rabbi Joel S. Geffen, who took me to his home, where I had dinner with him and his wife. During the six-mile trip from the station, Geffen managed to give a bird's eye view of the community and of the place of his congregation in it. The Jewish community numbers about 3,000 souls. His congregation consists of about 150 families. It is Conservative and has among its members the most influential Jews. Most of them are children of Lithuanian Jews who had rather worse than the average amount of Jewish knowledge possessed by our laymen. . . .

The audience I addressed was of the usual sub-normal kind. I had to speak in the most elementary terms possible to hold their attention, in which I succeeded.

The chairman, in introducing me, said that he had been told about my book that it was the greatest work of the kind since Spinoza's *Guide to the Perplexed*.[20]

Daughter Hadassah Gets a Marriage Proposal

FRIDAY, NOVEMBER 30, 1934

Last night Sidney Musher asked Hadassah to marry him. May God bless them. Lena and I are happy beyond words. I spent with my family (including Ira

---

20. Kaplan is demonstrating the chairman's subnormal understanding. Of course, *The Guide for the Perplexed* was written by Maimonides, not Spinoza.

and Judith and Sidney and Hadassah) an enjoyable and serene evening last night after a hearty Thanksgiving dinner. Sidney had not yet proposed, but everything pointed that way. During the night (about 2:30) Hadassah walked into our bedroom and told us the good news.

The Difficulties of Being a Rabbi

DECEMBER 25, 1934

A young daughter of Mrs. Harris (an SAJ member) is dangerously ill with the sleeping sickness. The mother had someone ask me to have prayers said for her child. What could I do but grant her request.

Speaking at a Federation Conference and Morris R. Cohen Answers

JANUARY 13, 1935

I was followed [in my talk at the meeting of the Council of Federations and Welfare Funds] by Prof. Morris R. Cohen.[21] He deprecated the organization of communal life on a permanent basis. His main objection against it was that it would destroy the freedom of Jews to do as they pleased and would bring back the ghetto as pictured by "Mendele Moher S'forim."[22]

There were questions from the floor, for the most part addressed to Cohen by those who agreed with me.[23] But the questions were put in such a way as to give him the better of the argument. It was only at the very end that a question was put to me in such a way as to enable me to show the sophistry of his position. He didn't like the idea of being refuted. He was white with anger when he said to me after the meeting broke up, "I am an assimilationist. I am sorry I wasted time in my youth on the study of Talmud. If I had used that time for the study of science or law, I would have been better off."

I understand that Harry Lurie, in summing up the discussion of last Sunday afternoon, said that I represented the neo-Orthodox traditional Jewish Catholic point of view, and that Cohen expressed the enlightened and liberal point of view.

A Wealthy Man Likes the Miracles in the Bible

TUESDAY, JANUARY 22, 1935

The following illustrates the topsy-turvy condition of Jewish life: Lewis L. Strauss, who is connected with Kuhn, Loeb, and Co., is a member of the Seminary

---

21. For more on Cohen and Kaplan, see Mel Scult, *Judaism Faces the Twentieth Century: A Biography of Mordecai M. Kaplan* (Detroit: Wayne State University Press, 1993).

22. Mendele Mokher Seforim (Shalom Jacob Abramowitsch) (1835–1917) was a well-known Hebrew writer.

23. Kaplan does not give the substance of his remarks here.

Board of Directors. He has a child whom he wants to teach the Bible stories. Not satisfied with any of the published books dealing with those stories, he undertook to write them out himself. He was afraid, however, that the English might not be of the best; so he asked the Seminary to send him a student who would revise the text which he had written out. The Seminary sent him Morris Adler, one of the members of this year's graduating class, and this is what Strauss said to Adler:

> I object to the usual way in which the Bible stories are told to children for two reasons; first, the tendency to talk down to the children; secondly, the miracles are either under-emphasized or denied altogether. I remember when I was a child of ten in my hometown in Virginia, the rabbi who taught me Bible told me that all the stories of miracles were mostly legends. When I heard that, I ran out of the room. The man who said that was none other than Morgenstern, the present head of the Hebrew Union College. After many years Morgenstern asked me to contribute to the College. But I thought here was a chance to have my sweet revenge on him, and I took advantage of the opportunity by refusing to contribute. Only recently when they were looking for someone to succeed Vogelstein as head of the Union of Hebrew Congregations, they asked me to accept the presidency. Again the desire to repay Morgenstern for daring to tell me that the miracle stories were legends asserted itself and I refused the offer.

This same Strauss was mentioned recently in one of John Spivak's articles in the *Masses*[24] as having financed some Fascist group which was at the same time engaged in spreading anti-Semitic propaganda.

Students Want to Know Why Kaplan Continues to Use the Word "God"

TUESDAY, JANUARY 29, 1935

How little the Seminary authorities have any idea of the religious unrest among the very men who are studying for the rabbinate! Could they imagine for a moment that in a class at the Seminary there could go on the kind of discussion that went on during the hour in Homiletics this afternoon. In discussing the outline I had given them on "Humanism Is Not Enough," I was bombarded with questions as to why I insist upon retaining the name of God in the ethical pattern of thought. The usual arguments about the misconceptions in the minds of those who hear it used were advanced with a great deal of clarity and force by the best men in the class.

---

24. A socialist publication of the time.

In answer to the argument that by using the term *God* I've only reinforced the anthropomorphic conception in people's minds, I made the point that what I am urging is not merely that the name God be retained, but that we center all our efforts upon educating the people to put new content into that name. That is at present our main function as religious teachers.

In answer to the argument that some of the most worthwhile people are alienated from Jewish life and ethical endeavor along Jewish lines because we insist upon using the name of God, I replied, first, they are alienated because we do not engage frankly in the task of putting new content into the term *God*, and secondly it is not the use of the term *God* that repels them but rather the whole nexus of legends which most of our people insist upon teaching as factual and historical.

In answer to the argument that it is impossible to retain our prayer book if we are to use the term *God* in the sense in which I suggested, I said that I hold no brief for the prayer book. Why not write new prayers in conformity with the modern conception of God? Why have a prayer book at all? Why not prayers which can be used at discretion and in accordance with actually felt needs?

Remembering the Beginning of the SAJ and Seeing the Larger Context of His Own Work

FEBRUARY 2, 1935

Today we of the SAJ [Society for the Advancement of Judaism] celebrated the 13th anniversary of the first service held under our auspices. In the morning I delivered a talk in which I addressed myself particularly to the eight of the twenty-one founders of the society, whom I had called out by name, and who after they had marched around the synagogue led by the cantor (Beimel substituted for [Moshe] Nathanson) carrying the Torah, seated themselves immediately in front of the pulpit. In my remarks I stated that the purpose of the anniversary was to keep alive the enthusiasm and sense of purpose which animated the group when it organized the SAJ. Like all creative movements, it had its origin in revolt and faith—revolt against a condition that had become unsatisfactory and faith in the possibilities that had been dormant. I then went on to describe the break with the Jewish Center and the physical and moral difficulties against which we had to contend during the first years of our existence. I gave them credit not only for dropping their investments in the Jewish Center[25] but also for following one, who at that time, stood practically alone in my ideas about Judaism. I spoke of the SAJ as the second attempt in American Jewish life to reckon with the requirements of the present-day environment. The first was the Reformist movement inaugurated by Isaac M. Wise.

---

25. On Kaplan and the Jewish Center, see the index to Scult, *Judaism Faces the Twentieth Century*.

During all these years that I have been advocating the conception of Judaism as a civilization, I have sought to find a method of implementing that conception. At first I thought that if the synagogue were transformed into a center that would house the leisure activities of our people, the problem of Jewish life in this country would be solved. Before long I realized that that was far from enough. Without an ideology reconstructed on lines of what is best in modern thought and social endeavor, I realized the mere physical transformation of the synagogue would not get us very far. It was this in particular that brought the SAJ into being. But now I am convinced that even the best of ideologies is not enough. The next step must be the reconstruction of the communal life of our people. Without a social environment to fortify Jewish thinking and Jewish living, all our endeavors were merely like trying to heat the street.

I closed with an appeal to the members that they rededicate themselves to the covenant by which we had bound ourselves in establishing the SAJ, a covenant that bore resemblance to the one our ancestors entered into at Sinai under the leadership of Moses. (This was said in allusion to today's Torah reading, which was *Mishpatim*.)[26]

A Talk with Cyrus Adler—Financial Problems at the Seminary

TUESDAY, FEBRUARY 5, 1935

This afternoon at 4:30 I went to see Dr. Cyrus Adler[27] in reference to the budget of the Teachers Institute and Seminary College for next year. The teaching load (to use the slang of the social workers) before 1931 was 148 hours. Now it amounts to 103 hours. The retirement was made possible by cutting out all post-graduate courses, arts and crafts, and doing away with the Freshman class in the Teachers Institute. Most of these courses have to be reinstated, if those who are to be graduated are to fulfill the usual requirements. Moreover, many of the graduates are asking for courses in advanced Hebrew and some want to proceed with graduate work. All this calls for a larger budget than the one we have been living on these last few years.

When I stated these facts to Adler, he gave the same reply that he had given me at least twice before in answer to similar demands on my part. (1) The income from the endowment has shrunk. Government bonds will not yield more than 2%, mortgages no more than 3% to 4%, etc. Dropsie College[28] is even worse off, because it has no popular support to draw from. The $19,000

---

26. This Torah portion is from the book of Exodus.

27. For material on Adler and Kaplan, see the index to Scult, *Judaism Faces the Twentieth Century*.

28. Dropsie College was a graduate institution established in Philadelphia and named after its principal benefactor, Moses Aaron Dropsie. The college granted degrees in Semitics from 1907 until 1986, when it was absorbed into the University of Pennsylvania.

interest the college was to have received this month has not been forthcoming due to litigation. All the universities except Columbia are in difficulties. Penn. U. has lost $1 million of its annual income. (2) The income from membership since July (for seven months) is over $3,000 more than last year ($12,000 in all). (3) Block (the accountant who has been the bane of my life the last eight or ten years) says the seminary will have a deficit of $20,000 this year. (4) I shouldn't complain. The Library that used to spend $10,000 a year spends about $250. (5) Three of the Seminary Faculty should by right be retired but the Seminary hasn't the means.

I also mentioned to him the possibility of my asking for sabbatical leave for a year. He said that I should put the request in writing, because he didn't want to grant me the leave without the consent of the Board of Trustees. In fact, he was taken to task by the Board for having permitted Prof. [Louis] Ginzberg to go to Palestine a year ago for the purpose of acting on the Committee to reorganize the Hebrew University. The Board felt that Ginzberg had been away a year and had been sick another half a year and it was not right to allow him to miss more of his work.

Not that the committee did any good, Adler went on to say. Although their report did not appear in the press, it is circulated by word of mouth, especially in Palestine where the least rumor is exaggerated. They found fault with Kligler and Magnes as not being up to the academic standard of the European universities. It seems that they did not think very much of American academic training. At one of the meetings he pointed out to the members of the committee that the American universities had the advantage over the European, for not only did they take over the best traditions of the European universities whence their first teachers came, but were less provincial than the European universities because they draw on more than the one tradition. It is just this kind of garrulity that has made him the "great man" he is.

First Printing of Judaism as a Civilization *Sold Out, But Kaplan Bought Half*

FEBRUARY 9, 1935

Much to my surprise, the first printing of my book was exhausted about a month ago. I understand that Macmillan had printed 1,500 copies, of which I received 650. The publication of the book cost me about $3,800, of which I have received back a little over $2,000. I ordered a second printing of the book yesterday. The understanding is that I am to buy 500 copies at $1.65. Macmillan will sell the other 500 at the regular price, and I expect to sell my copies at a reduced rate to those who will buy in quantities of five or more.

Leading a Dual Life — Maybe Zionism Isn't the Way

SATURDAY NIGHT, FEBRUARY 9, 1935

Tonight I worked out a plan whereby they [the rabbinical students] would make themselves responsible for a statement that would refute the indictment [communist attacks on Zionism] point by point.[29]

After they left, I proceeded to read [Samuel] Dinin's summary to the end. When I came to the charge against Zionism, I could not but see the justice of most of the contentions against the entire movement. I dread to think that I have deluded myself and others all these years, yet I shall not wince from drawing that conclusion if I shall find after further thought that I have been on the wrong track. I swear by everything that is sacred that I want to do what is right and to teach nothing but what I believe in with every fiber in my being. These are times when it seems impossible to commit oneself to any cause wholeheartedly without sinning against one's better nature that refuses to be narrow and dogmatic and that cannot accept the cruel judgment which communism passes upon the idealism (even if mistaken) of thousands of mankind's leaders.

Here I am the victim of conflict that is raging in my soul. If I could only find some way of engaging in work that would not require my committing myself to either horn of the dilemma. Only this afternoon I was making plans to go to Palestine. After the summary I have read tonight, I feel that I would only be aggravating the inner conflict if I were to implicate myself more deeply in the Palestine project. This business of leading a dual life is getting to be unbearable.

Communism Is Attractive and Kaplan Looks for a Synthesis Between Communism and Zionism

SUNDAY, FEBRUARY 10, 1935

Viewing my situation realistically, there is no possibility of my identifying myself with the communist movement. It would involve too much of a physical wrench, and even psychologically there are many things in communism which repel me: its materialistic dogmatism, its ruthlessness toward the middle class and white collar slaves, etc. But there is much in communism which I regard as indispensable to the welfare of a society. Some of it I openly avow and preach. The doctrines of classless society, of the abolition of profit, and the principle from each according to his abilities and to each according to his needs, I have preached from the pulpit and am embodying in my "The World as It Ought to Be."

My greatest difficulty is in squaring the communist analyses of anti-Semitism and Zionism with my pleas for communal organization and the

---

29. Kaplan planned to give the rabbinical students communist pamphlets that attacked Zionism. He wanted to prepare them to refute such attacks.

upbuilding of Palestine, or to put it more correctly, between the communist approach to the Jewish problem and mine. What I have been attempting all along
has been to effect a synthesis between the two. That has required my sublimat-
ing some of my communist beliefs. But that is something I cannot get others to
do. They prefer to take communism whole and unmodified and to forget about
Judaism altogether.

If the only way out of this impasse is just to live empirically and not
worry about the ultimate outcome, then I should try to confine myself to my work
at the Seminary and give up the idea of reconstructing Jewish life. But then the
problem arises as to what I am to teach if I am to evade the fundamental issues
of present-day Jewish life and thought. Perhaps I might succeed in effectuating
the sublimation of the above-mentioned doctrines best by casting them into the
form of "The World as It Ought to Be." In any event, just now I am in no mood
to make preparations for spending the year of the sabbatical leave in Palestine.

To Be Unethical or Neurotic

FEBRUARY 10, 1935

I know quite well that my vacillation, compromises, and opportunism
do little credit to my ethical reputation, but I prefer to be conscious of these
tendencies in myself to being ashamed of them and by repressing them develop all kinds of neuroses. I frankly prefer to be "psychologically associated"
and ethically unadjusted to being half-adjusted ethically and "psychologically
dissociated." If I were to pursue this subject casuistically, I might even prove that
it is more ethical to be half-adjusted ethically and psychologically whole than
to strain for complete ethical adjustment at the expense of my psychological
health. In short, Koheleth was right when he said *al tehi zadik harbey* [Heb.,
Don't be too righteous].

We All Need to Be Emotionally More Mature (Freud Is Right)

WEDNESDAY, FEBRUARY 20, 1935

Why do most people who know a good deal hold their knowledge the
way a glass holds water and not the way a stomach holds food? It may be because
the knowledge which they acquire retains the mind pattern of the one who im-
parted it to them. Instead of breaking up that knowledge so as to be assimilable
by their own type of thinking, they try to hold it in the form given to it by the
mind pattern of the one who transmitted it to them. That is why we are afflicted
with the presence in academic circles of so many learned ignoramuses, and why
knowledge in general is so little educative.

It was not before I hit upon an integrating idea arising out of the general
problem of human conduct I am concerned with that I found myself capable of

assimilating the contents of the book by [J. C.] Flugel [*The Psycho-Analytic Study of the Family*]. That integrating idea was the following one: One of the basic causes of maladjustment in human life is the fact that while intellectually most people outgrow entirely their infantile state, emotionally very few do so. Intellectually we may be grown-up men and women, but emotionally we are still infants. If we were not deceived by appearances, we would realize that when we see parents bringing up children, we are really witnessing big babies trying to bring up little babies. We shall not get very far with the best-laid schemes of social and economic reform unless we at the same time reckon fully with the prevailing infantilism of human nature. Beneath the austere presence of statesmen, bishops, financiers, and dictators rages infantile emotions made dangerous by the power and knowledge they possess. The problem of human life will remain insoluble so long as we remain ignorant of the conditions necessary to emotional maturation. This is where the Freudian approach to the subconscious can help us. Freud's discovery of the presence of unconscious motives and unresolved conflicts deals with the conditions responsible for the arrested development emotionally of most human beings. However much Freud, Jung, and Adler differ among themselves as to the nature of the unconscious motives, they are agreed that it is in the parent-child relationship where the problem of directing their development begins. From this point on one can see the connection between the ideas thus far worked out in the series and the main principles of psychoanalysis.

Possibly I am as much in need of being stimulated to outgrow infantilism as the people in my audience. It may therefore be that this course of lectures will have a good effect on me.

Ira Eisenstein's Thesis Topic Discussed at a Seminary Faculty Meeting

FEBRUARY 17, 1935

Some time ago Ira [Eisenstein] (after consulting me) sent an application to the Seminary for candidacy for the DHL [Doctor of Humane Letters] and as the subject of his thesis he suggested "Otherworldliness in the Jewish Ethical Literature." The application was read at the Faculty meeting this afternoon. It was no sooner read than [Louis] Ginzberg interposed that the subject was vague and Davidson chimed in that he didn't know what otherworldliness meant. It was apparent that both men identified the subject as one which constituted an indirect challenge to their denial of otherworldliness as characteristic of Judaism. I could not help saying that it was part of the very thesis to discuss the term *otherworldliness* and to define accurately the sense in which it was to be used. But, of course, they had their way and it was decided to ask Ira to specify the meaning of the term.

Should Jews Join the Communist Movement? A Surprising Answer

MARCH 10, 1935

Shall the Jews join the communist movement? It holds out the promise not only of making them the beneficiaries of the better world order but very definitely of eliminating anti-Semitism. To explain the answer which I am at present prepared to give and which I may have to change later because of new circumstances which I do not as yet foresee, I must state that I am speaking as one who is interested first and foremost in the survival of Judaism as a contributing factor in the world toward making it what it ought to be. Because of my keen desire to see it survive, I cannot conscientiously advise against joining the communist movement on the ground of anything that Judaism teaches, because I would thereby only add communism to the enemies and destructive forces that are already arrayed against it. If, on the other hand, I were to advise Jews to join communism, I would be augmenting the danger which goes with being made the scapegoat for the sins of the present social order.

The only way out of this predicament is for Jews to avoid regarding their Jewishness as being either a hindrance or an incentive to their joining the proletariat in the class struggle. They should refrain from taking sides in a collective capacity. They should approach the problem as individuals, and as human beings who find the present social regime unbearable.

It is in that capacity that I, for one, weigh the alternatives of communism and socialism and decide that I want to throw in my lot with the latter, although there is the possibility that the forces of reaction might become so menacing as to leave no other choice but communism. For the present my objections to communism are, first, its insistence upon becoming not only an economic system, but a new philosophy of life to be based on dogmatic materialism. Secondly, its tactics of declaring civil war instead of resorting to civil war as a last measure. Thirdly, its strategy of class war. Such strategy is totally unsuited in a country like ours which has so large a middle class, which, contrary to Marx's prediction, is not being forced into a fighting proletarianism but either into white-collar respectability or into resigned mendicalism. The chances of success in a civil war are so balanced that the greater part of the population would be wiped out before any decisive victory would be won and there is no telling whose the victory would be.

Some Jews Oppose Hebrew in the High Schools—Kaplan Holds Meeting to Support It

MARCH 15, 1935

Some time ago [Israel] Chipkin asked me to invite a few people at my home to meet Associate Superintendent Jacob Greenberg and Commissioner of

Education Louis Posner. In his efforts to have Hebrew introduced into the High Schools, he encounters a good deal of opposition from the Jews in the system, and when he finally succeeds in getting the educational authorities to yield, he discovers that the Yeshiva crowd headed by [Bernard] Revel tries to horn in on the situation in order to exploit it for their own glory. He therefore expressed to me his desire that the educational authorities should become acquainted with some of us who are engaged in Jewish educational work and should learn to turn to us for advice and cooperation instead of the Yeshiva crowd. I acted on his suggestion and called for the informal conference, which took place at my house last Wednesday. I had invited [Zevi] Scharfstein, [Samson] Benderly, Dinin, Profs. [Salo W.] Baron, [Shalom] Spiegel, and [Louis] Finkelstein, and Ira. Finkelstein had promised to come but didn't show up. Baron didn't even acknowledge the invitation, and Spiegel wrote he had an engagement to speak.

The two facts which emerged from the discussion were: (1) that if not for Chipkin, there would have been no Hebrew courses in any of the high schools; (2) that his success has been due to his persistent lobbying. Whether the movement for Hebrew is to make headway still depends upon personal whims and political wire pulling. Because Posner had nominated a certain Dr. Roberts for the superintendency of the high schools, he can hint to Dr. Roberts that he should not obstruct Chipkin's efforts.

Kaplan Resents Finkelstein Advancing Simon Greenberg

MARCH 15, 1935

Simon Greenberg is temperamentally opposed to my entire philosophy of Judaism and in sympathy with Finkelstein's simiosities[30] in thought and conduct. Finkelstein, seeing in him a kindred soul, has been grooming him for the Seminary faculty and got Adler to appoint him for the course in education in spite of the fact that Chipkin was the only logical man for the position. The students apparently see through F's schemes, which they deeply resent. But what they cannot endure is G's arrogant fashion of lecturing them for daring to hold views that differ from his.

Judaism Seems to Be an Autumn Thing and an Interesting Home Group Meets

SUNDAY, MARCH 17, 1935

The inroads made into Jewish life by the long summer vacation have within the last decade been supplemented by the newly acquired habit of the

---

30. Kaplan may have meant to refer to the word *simious* (i.e., *simian*); hence simiosities means ape- or monkey-like nature. This is obviously sarcasm on Kaplan's part.

more comfortably situated among our people to go to Florida or California during the winter season, and by the still more recent tendency to take a trip to Palestine during the spring season. Judaism in this country is thus coming to be an autumnal style of living.

Last night the "Community Group" met at M. J. Karpf's home. This was in deference to [David de Sola] Pool's objection the time before last to having the group meet all the time in my house, because, as he put it, "The whole thing might appear like a Kaplan affair." I conceded he was right, and so we came to meet in Karpf's home. Since Milton Steinberg had apparently dropped out, I felt I could invite Ira to join us, and I proposed his name to those who were present at the previous meeting. Accordingly, the following attended the meeting last night: Salo Baron, Benderly, Eisenstein, Glucksman, Karpf, Poole, Shalom Speigel, and myself.

I presented a statement envisaging an organic Jewish community both in its ultimate and its immediate form. My main point was that instead of the fiscal approach, we should develop the psychological approach, which I defined as being based on the need of generating in the individual Jew a desire for status in Jewry as a permanent historic group functioning actively as a whole in all of its parts.

The discussion which followed was quite constructive.

The Significance of Maimonides

MONDAY, MARCH 18, 1935

I have to speak the coming Wednesday at Plainfield, on Maimonides. The celebration of M's octocentenary is a welcome relief from the usual round of Jewish activities, which are confined to anti-Semitism and fund-raising. For once the Jews engage in something inherently interesting and cultural, and for these days when Jews should be wrestling with the problem of self-adjustment, there could be no more significant focus of attention than the personality and influence of Maimonides. We cannot learn from what he taught how to meet our own problems today, but we can learn a good deal about Judaism and the spiritual possibilities that inhere in it if we realize what it means for his teachings to have found a place in it. It is true that Maimonides effected a reconciliation between Jewish tradition and Aristotelian philosophy. But in the process of reconciling, he so changed the entire perspective of Jewish tradition that it lost its original character and became something different. If the intention of an act determines its character, certainly the intention of an entire system of life and thought gives character to that system. What M did was to ascribe to the social heritage of the Jews an intention derived from Greek civilization. He imposed upon Judaism a pattern of meanings previously unknown to it and foreign to its spirit until his day. How is it that Judaism was capable of assimilating his teachings and accepting him as the foremost teacher since the Judah ha-Nasi?[31] The answer is that, Judaism not being an interpretation of life but a segment of life, not being a religion but a civilization, must admit of various interpretations. If, however, Judaism is to be prevented from disintegrating as a result of diversity of interpretation, its constituent elements and its sancta must function as objects of vital interest. The reason M was able to change the perspective of Judaism without being excommunicated was that he participated in Jewish life and devoted himself to rendering its sancta capable of being observed. If he had not been the great Talmudist he was and had not written his *Yad Ha-Hazakah,*[32] his interpretation of Judaism would have been repudiated not merely by a zealous minority but by the entire Jewish people. To appreciate the force of the principle here posited, viz., that Judaism permits great latitude of interpretation, provided the interpretation is accompanied by an active interest in the activities and sancta of Judaism, it is necessary to know the pattern of the entire Maimonidean thought structure.

A Conversation about German Jews Immigrating to Palestine — Some Insist on Keeping the Ways of the Old Country

MARCH 23, 1935

This afternoon a German Jew by the name of Hirsch called. He left Germany about two years ago and established himself in Palestine. He is in this country on business and intends to sail for Palestine in a few weeks. I gathered from him a few interesting facts about the German Jews who had migrated to Palestine the last two years. Of the twenty-odd thousand who have come there, about 5,000 are in the colonies identified for the most part with the Haluz [pioneer] movement. About the same number represent the assimilated element who have come to Palestine much against their will and who would like to reproduce there the kind of life they led in Germany. The chief problem presented by the German element is how to get them to learn Hebrew. They wanted to have a German newspaper and a special group with the B'nai B'rith, but the Hebraic forces led by [Menahem] Ussishkin have put up a strong resistance. The fact that, while nothing but Hebrew is allowed on public occasions, other languages are in use in the homes, makes it very hard for these newcomers to acquire the language.

---

31. Judah ha-Nasi was a second-century rabbi who was the chief editor and redactor of legal work known as the *Mishnah.*

32. *Yad Ha-Hazakah* is another name for the *Mishnah Torah* of Maimonides, which is his code of Jewish law. It has fourteen divisions and covers every aspect of life. It was written in a simple Hebrew that would have been quite accessible to the average Jew, thus making study of the Talmud superfluous except for advanced scholars and rabbis.

The conversation turned upon the religious aspect of the life there. Hirsch remarked that the synagogues have absolutely no influence in shaping the mind of the Jews there. Rabbi Kook's[33] influence in that direction is also nil. I voiced the yearning to settle in Palestine in order to bring to bear upon the situation such ideas as I was in the habit of articulating. He was very much in sympathy with such a move on my part and even suggested that some of the Seminary graduates be encouraged to settle in Palestine for the purpose of supplying the missing religious note in its life. He has evidently been thinking about this problem, because he mentioned an idea that he had cherished, namely, the need of organizing a kind of Jewish religious order or brotherhood.

The Difficulties of Being an Editor—Rejection of a Review of Rav Za'ir's Book

MARCH 23, 1935

Yesterday afternoon I had to play a reverse role. I had received an angry letter in Hebrew from Dr. [Chaim] Tchernowitz. He wanted to know whether I was responsible for the letter he had received from Ira saying that the *Reconstructionist* could not publish any review of his recent book on the development of the Halakhah because very few of the subscribers to the *R* are familiar with Hebrew. The real reason for my asking Ira to write him that letter was that I could not see my way clear to giving a favorable review of the book, which seemed to me very superficial and of little scientific value. In order not to offend him by publishing an unfavorable review, I thought the best thing would be to avoid reviewing it altogether. Ira's letter stung him to the quick, and I had some job formulating a Hebrew letter that would pacify him. Since I very seldom write in Hebrew, I had to spend several hours reading the *Moznayim* [a Hebrew journal] to get myself into the proper mood. And then came the task of finding the proper formula that would be diplomatic without being untruthful. I think I managed in the end.

Musing on Whether to Continue the Journal—Realities of Shabbat at SAJ

MARCH 24, 1935

As I am concluding this, the seventh volume of the Journal, I am wondering whether I ought to start an eighth volume, and if I do, whether I ought to write it in English or in Hebrew. My reason for questioning the value of this Journal is that its scope is so limited and the story so monotonous, to say nothing

---

33. On Kaplan and Rabbi Abraham Isaac Kook, the first chief rabbi in Palestine under the British Mandate, see Jack Cohen, *Guides for an Age of Confusion: Studies in the Thinking of Avraham Y. Kook and Mordecai M. Kaplan* (New York: Fordham University Press, 1999).

of my inability to write in such a way as to enliven the account of the persons and incidents I refer to. The only possible value of this Journal is that it helps me locate in time some things I did in the past, which I would otherwise forget completely. If I hadn't entered the item concerning my visit to Plainfield in Jan. 1933, I wouldn't have known whether I was there a year ago or five years ago. I wonder what this inability to locate in time past actions or events is a sign of.

This lack of enthusiasm about beginning a new volume of the Journal is but a phase of the discouragement I experience about life in general and American Jewish life in particular. Although personally I have no reason to complain, the misery of the millions who are unemployed, the uncertainty of the future to which the youth look forward, and above all the impending clouds of war that threaten to destroy whole populations, take all the zest out of living. The fact that my own middle-years are soon to end and that I am beginning to feel the aches and pains that augur old age wouldn't worry me in the least if there were some sign that the insanity which has seized the nations is beginning to subside and the slightest indications anywhere evident that humanity will finally come to its senses and not commit hari-kari. And as for American Jewish life, I have come to a point where I feel as though I were choking for lack of air to breathe. It is almost a physical sensation with me and never so painful as on Sabbath mornings at the services of the SAJ when I sit on the platform and watch the few old timers going through the services mechanically. The Torah is taken out, the *Shamash Mentscher* [sexton] reads in his monotonous drone those outlandish portions about the Tabernacle and all kinds of lepers, the scroll is put back, a few people straggle in. I count the number present—hardly fifty people. It is soon *Musaph* [additional service]; a few young people slink in. By twelve o'clock they still keep on coming. The maximum is attained—125. Either Ira delivers the sermon or I do. There is no progression of ideas. We always have to begin from the beginning. After all these years Ira had to try to answer in today's sermon the question "What Is Religion?" Failing to get an adequate answer, the audience was left in complete confusion as though neither Ira nor I had ever said a word about religion all these years. The services are over. A few people come up and say *Gut Shabbos* [traditional Sabbath greeting]. A whole week passes—a void. The next Sabbath or festival comes. It finds everybody just where they were a week ago, a year ago, a decade ago, minus all the strength and hope of improvement that have kept on oozing out ever since I have been engaged in Jewish work.

2

April 2, 1935–August 12, 1936

On the Flyleaf of Volume 8: *Kaplan Quotes from Books He Is Reading*

"Most men live lives of quiet desperation."

> —Thoreau

"Many of my arrows left my bow only to seek my own breast.
And the flier was also the creeper;
For when my wings were spread in the sun their shadow upon the earth
    was a turtle.
And I the believer was also the doubter;
For often have I put my finger in my own wound that I
might have the greater belief in you and the
greater knowledge of you."

> —*The Prophet*, Kalil Gibran. Copied Sat. night, Jan. 4, 1936

"As a person" (John Middleton Murray) "I was quite extraordinarily underdeveloped and chaotic. Every man seen from within looks to himself indefinite. A cloud from within looks like a fog. A lake, if you are inside it, is just water." (Clearly enough Murray was sensitive and found life a painful experience.)

> —Arthur Colton in *Sat. Review*, July 18, 1936. Copied Wed.,
>   July 22, 1936

"In one of Bernard Shaw's plays, *Too True to Be Good*, at the end of the first act a player declares 'The play is now practically over, but the characters will continue to discuss it for two more acts.'"

> —Jerome Davis, *Capitalism and Its Culture*, p. 519

"I cannot help suspecting that our schools and universities must largely share the blame with those ancient perverters of the truth (prejudice and self-interest). And if they are to blame, it is because they make learning the first thing and thinking the second place, the tradition of knowledge before the training of the mind."

— James Ward, *Psychology Applied to Education*, 87. [Copied] June 20, 1938

"God offers to every mind its choice between repose and truth. Take which you please. You can never have both."

— Emerson. [Copied] June 25, 1938

Communism at the School for Jewish Social Work — What to Do

TUESDAY, APRIL 2, 1935

For a long time I was debating with myself whether to continue writing this journal in English or to attempt to write it in Hebrew. But when I thought of the very first matter I would have to record in it, there seemed to be something incongruous in trying to record it in Hebrew. I am therefore postponing the fulfillment of my ambition to make a practice of writing in Hebrew until I come to Palestine, where Hebrew will enter into the very fiber of what I shall have occasion to comment upon.

The matter I refer to is the tempest in the teapot, let loose by M. J. Karpf, the director of the Graduate School for Jewish Social Work.[1] Last Wednesday night he came to see me to tell me of the communist mimeographed sheet called "The Radical Therapist" issued by a group of students in the School, and of his resolve to send in his resignation to the Board of Trustees. He assumes that the rest of the faculty would do likewise because of the scurrilous attack on them and the Trustees. Being at heart only too glad to find an excuse for discontinuing the course I am giving at the Graduate School, because I find it futile to try to overcome the negative attitude toward things Jewish on the part of the majority of the students, I readily assented to his decision.

On Thursday, however, a change took place. The Faculty met at Prof. Salo Baron's home from 11 to 2 (I got there at 12:00) and decided to proceed slowly and to put it up to the students to find some way of dealing with those responsible for "The Radical Therapist." When the discussion veered to the fundamental

---

1. The Graduate School for Jewish Social Work was established in New York City in 1924 and lasted until 1950. Kaplan was active and taught there from time to time. The Communist Party, established in 1919, became quite active in the 1920s and 1930s because of the economic hardships of the time. Many Jews were attracted to the party and to Marxism in general. For Kaplan's opinion on Communism and Marx in particular, see Mordecai M. Kaplan, *Judaism in Transition* (New York: Covici Friede, 1936), ch. 3 ("The Communist Challenge").

problem of reconciling social work with the radical trends in present-day society, it became evident that the only way to do it was by giving a more intensively and affirmatively Jewish direction to the work at the school. I even went so far as to suggest that every student be expected to engage in some specifically Jewish project, like leading a Young Judea Club or other work of a similar character, in order to become more deeply interested in the possibilities of Jewish life.

Last Monday Karpf met the students and stated the grievance which the Faculty had against them and left it to them to make answer. The only outcome of the meeting with the students, which took place subsequently, was a repudiation of the attitude expressed in the "Radical Therapist." The Faculty met again later, this time to draw up some general principles to [regulate] the future students' activities and publications.

Aches and Pains and Whether to Spend a Sabbatical in Palestine

APRIL 3, 1935

Although I have managed to escape colds since the one I had during the first week in January, I have not been free from the muscular aches and pains which discourage me from undertaking tasks that call for the exertion of much physical energy. Especially the last two or three weeks I have been troubled, as I have been for a number of years around these months, with weariness in the legs and pains in the feet. Much as I would like to ignore my physical condition and to go on working and planning and acting cheerfully, I find I cannot do it.

I am still uncertain as to what would be the wisest thing for me to do next year, if my health will permit my doing anything at all. Should I spend the year in Palestine or utilize the leave of absence to make propaganda for the Jewish Community idea? From various quarters I get reports of growing interest in the idea. Now it needs somebody to fan that interest into a flaming desire for integrated organic communal life.

Lecturing in Wilkes Barre — Rabbi Louis Levitsky Is a Model

APRIL 14, 1935

From Rochester I went to Wilkes Barre [Kaplan was on a lecture tour]. There I found conditions which are the very antithesis of those in Rochester, and which prove affirmatively what the latter proved negatively, that the fate of Judaism in this country hangs upon the kind of spiritual leaders the seminaries send out. I could not say the seminaries produce, because they have a very small share in the actual training for the rabbinate. It is in the selection of the men for the rabbinate that the seminaries play the most important part. If a seminary like the one I am in were to know what it ought to do, it would have seen to it that a man like Levitsky with his remarkable executive and educational ability should somehow be enabled to put that ability to such use as to have the other men profit by it. A man like Levitsky should have been appointed by the Seminary as a sort of consultant and visiting rabbi to visit the rabbis in their various communities, and suggest improvements in the rabbis' method of functioning wherever needed.

What Levitsky did with his congregation, which he built up from the very bottom, is a marvel of accomplishment. His present membership is 250 families. The budget, including interest on a $100,000 mortgage, amounts to $34,000. Of that amount $11,500 goes for educational purposes, in comparison with $6,000 spent in 1929. He preaches twice a week to an attendance that shows not the least sign of dwindling, although he has been in the community these last 13 years. The educational work with the adults has been kept up with unwavering regularity. I have met some young women who five years ago did not know an alef from a bet, have learned to read and translate modern Hebrew poetry, and who are still going strong at the rate of five hours' homework per week.

The first thing Levitsky spoke to me about was the interest displayed by his people in my book, as a result of the two lectures he had delivered on it preparatory to my visit. With us in the car was a Mr. Weiss, who had come with him to meet me at the station. Levitsky later described to me this Mr. Weiss as a young man, about 35, who since the war had worked himself up from a borrowed $1,000, with which he opened a shoe store, to the ownership of 42 stores. Yet there was not a single lecture of Levitsky's that Weiss ever failed to attend. Nor was Weiss the only one who, though at first completely disinterested in Judaism, had under Levitsky's influence become an active participant in Jewish cultural work.

Levitsky was not content with my merely giving the lecture I had been scheduled to give. He had the Board of Trustees and their wives take supper together in my honor and had asked me in a letter that I be their guest and say a few words to them in recognition of the contribution over $500 they had made to the Seminary. I had accepted the invitation, and when we were through with supper, Levitsky and a certain Mr. Cohen (head of the educational committee) said some nice things about me and I reciprocated by saying some nice things about Levitsky and the congregation. This reception as well as the pleasure of seeing some evidences of what can be done to build up Jewish life, if there is the proper leadership, put me into a good mood for the address I had come to give. The additional circumstances that I had worked it over and improved its organization and that the audience seemed far more capable of following with interest the subject I was lecturing on, contributed to the success of the evening.

Kaplan Peddles His Book

April 14, 1935

This morning I spoke in Rabbi Jacob Katz's synagogue to a motley group of about 175 people. The reason I accepted his invitation was that he had promised to take 25 copies of my book. That was also the reason for my going to Cleveland. I hoped to succeed in the same way with Rabbi Magil of Buffalo. I expect to be in Buffalo next Saturday night to speak before the Regional Council of Federations. Magil wanted that I would occupy his pulpit the Friday night preceding. But apparently he has not been able to get his people to promise to buy the 25 copies. I charge them $3.33 a copy. It costs me $1.65. Having ordered 500, I shall have to pay Macmillan $825. That is for me a large sum of money, but I don't see how I would have refrained from ordering a second printing, since there is still some demand for the book.

More Books, More People

April 28, 1935

Friday morning I left for Buffalo. . . . The services began at 8:00. By 8:45, when I started speaking, there were about 700 people in the audience. I gave again the talk on "What to Live For as a Jew." The people seemed to have liked it, although I myself have been growing tired of it. It lacked the freshness it had for me when I gave it at Cleveland.

Writing on the Sabbath—A Different View

April 28, 1935

All day Friday on the train I was at work thinking about what I was to say (in the next speech) and to my regret found myself compelled to spend some hours on Saturday in putting down my thoughts in writing. I don't mind writing on the Sabbath. In fact, I sometimes feel that the prohibition of writing is an unnecessary restriction when it inhibits the expression of ideas that might otherwise be lost. But to write under pressure is, in my opinion, a definite violation of the Sabbath. I therefore hope I won't ever have to do that again.

Adler Fumes at Remarks by Norman Bentwich and Milton Steinberg on Palestine

Tuesday, April 30, 1935

I attended the second annual meeting of the Seminary Branch, which took place tonight at the Seminary. The two main speakers were Norman Bentwich and Milton Steinberg. Bentwich spoke on Judaism in Palestine. In the course of his address he mentioned the fact that the Jews in Palestine lived their Judaism as a civilization. Milton Steinberg made the point that the cultivation of Jewish higher learning was necessary as a means of counteracting the possible effect of anti-Semitism on the Jew. When Steinberg was through, Adler got up and voiced his disagreement with both speakers, but it was chiefly Steinberg who seemed to have irritated him in emphasizing the problem created by anti-Semitism. Adler spoke very excitedly, repeating for the thousandth time Schechter's bon mot about refusing to be a problem, and shouting that if Jews had led decent lives, there would be no problem. Then alluding to Bentwich's remarks, Adler said that the law will not go out from Zion but will have to go from the Diaspora to Zion (unless, I suppose, the Jews in Palestine will act differently from the way they do).

To utter such words as "problem," "ideology," "Jewish civilization" in the hearing of Adler is like waving a red flag in front of a bull.

Symptoms—Wild Bar Mitzvah Parties and All That

SATURDAY NIGHT, MAY 4, 1935

Among the symptoms of disintegration of Jewish life, in addition to those referred to in preceding entries, are the following:

1. Bar mitzvah celebrations are occasions for wild cocktail parties and ribald vaudeville acts. The upstart Jewish rich spend money on entertainers, among whom are semi-nude chorus girls who perform indecent dances in front of the table where the bar-mitzvah and his young friends are seated.
2. On Pesach and Shavuot Jewish hotels in seashore and mountain resorts do a big business by holding services. Freelance cantors and choirs conduct those services.
3. The provisional synagogue is an evil of old standing.

Petrified mediocrity—that's Cyrus.[2]

Kaplan Muses on and Expresses His Anger

MAY 6, 1935

Something must have been annoying me to have made me lose my head [Kaplan had lost his temper at an SAJ meeting and in a class at the Graduate School for Jewish Social Work]. Probably the suppression of my real feelings at the SAJ meeting last night, and the failure of the students today to display a genuine interest in the problem that was being discussed were the cause for my outbreak. If I could only discipline myself so that I would remember what Felix Adler[3] said about anger as in need of being resisted because of its tendency to upset the very purposes one cherishes most, I would not have to be wasting my energy in trying to live down many a thing I say in the heat of anger.

2. Kaplan probably has Cyrus Adler in mind.

3. Felix Adler was a philosophy professor at Columbia University with whom Kaplan studied. On Kaplan and Adler, see Mel Scult, *The Radical Judaism of Mordecai Kaplan* (Bloomington: Indiana University Press, 2013), ch. 4 ("Universalism and Pragmatism").

In one of the preceding volumes I find fault with the ancients for their having pictured God as very wrathful (*eyl za'am*) [Heb.]. I see now that they weren't altogether wrong. They projected into their conception of God what anyone who is sensitive to the stupidities and cruelties of human beings in their dealings with one another must feel. The more one learns of what is going on in the world, the higher must one's blood pressure become. When I read this morning about the iniquitous apportioning of land to the Bedouins who were unable to cultivate it, and withholding land from the Jewish legionnaires whom it was the duty of the British government to assist in their effort to settle in Palestine, I was wild with indignation at the injustice perpetuated on our people. That too may have contributed to the unhappy frame of mind during the session at the Graduate School. All in all, outside of the desire to contribute to the happiness of my own family, which is the only worthwhile purpose I still can do something to further, there is practically nothing I can live for wholeheartedly. I am one of the helpless victims of the infernal capitalistic system. May God's wrath descend upon it with the fury of a thousand hells and shock it into death with the voltage pent up in the storms of vindictive rage engendered in the hearts of the innocent and defenseless against their pitiless tormentors.

Rabbinical Assembly — Politics and Ideology

May 15, 1935

The thirty-fifth annual convention of the Rabbinical Assembly took place at Temple Beth El, Rockaway Park, May 13–15. That is where Robert Gordis functions as a rabbi. Having been chairman of the convention arrangements committee, he was instrumental in gaining the consent of the Executive Committee of the RA to hold the convention in his temple. The fact that it might be interpreted as exploiting the RA for his own prestige apparently did not even enter his mind, because he seems to be so Seminary-bent at the present time that anything which might contribute to his getting there is certain to appear to him as perfectly legitimate. Now that Finkelstein is fully grounded, he is in turn grooming his prospective underlings and they in turn are industriously rehearsing the parts they will have to play. Simon Greenberg[4] and Robert Gordis have been cast for their parts and everything is hunky-dory. Alexander Basel hovers about in the wings in the capacity of super flunky in the hope [of] being able to get Adler to bring into his Schiff Center (or more correctly All Saints Center) the Jewish "big shots" for the purpose of getting them to throw in some "maxima" into the coffers of his institution. He is then sure of saving up enough money to retire from the ministry and from the cemeteries, where he functions as a sort of

---

4. At this point, Simon Greenberg was the rabbi at the Philadelphia Congregation Har-Zion.

educated and high-class *maley* [Heb., "Oh Lord full of compassion," from the prayer for the dead] reciter for all and sundry.

To be in the good graces of Adler, one has to be identified as an anti-Kaplanite. Such an opportunity presented itself to him when Gordis was making up the part of the program in which my book was to be discussed. Basel offered to take up the cudgels for traditional Judaism. How he carried out his mission is part of the subsequent story.

I was unable to attend the sessions on Monday. But I came to the evening sessions described in the program as the "Public Academic Session." I had been hesitating whether to go or not but finally decided to go in order to carry out the promise I had made to Dr. [Louis] Ginzberg that I would ask the members of the Rabbinical Assembly to purchase sets of Judah Kaufman's edition of the *Moreh*.[5] I don't know why I allow myself to be inveigled into doing things I don't like. With Mrs. Kaufman pestering me and Ginzberg seconding her, I was unable to say no. But I regretted it later. This is what happened. I listened with a sense of resigned boredom to Adler's address on Schechter and to Abraham A. Neuman's talk on Freiman's edition of Maimonides' *Responsa*.[6] Then Margolis called on me to say a few words about Judah Kaufman's edition of the *Moreh Nevuchim*. The sight of an audience melting away after the long ordeal, and Margolis' turning to me as I went up the platform and making a sort of Eddie Cantor[7] face at me as he urged me say a *few* words, sent the blood to my head and I found it hard to make the simple announcement I had intended to make. When all was over, I took Margolis to task for his arrogance, and we let go at each other the pent-up feelings that we entertain for each other. I am glad to say that last night he and I made up, and that I had the good sense to take the initiative.

I attribute that extra dose of good sense to the fact that I had a successful day yesterday. In the morning Basel was the first to discuss my book as part of the program titled "Toward a Vital Program for American Judaism." The subheading was "Dr. Kaplan's Philosophy of Judaism." I had been after him all last week to let me have a copy of his paper. He promised me twice solemnly that he would let me have it, and in the end did not let me have it. The reason was that he had read only a few chapters of the book and glanced hurriedly at the rest of it. He thought that all he needed was to snipe at some of the main points and he would achieve his purpose. Many of the members of the Assembly were disgusted with the attitude he displayed toward his task and with the inanity of his remarks. He was followed by Max Arzt of Scranton, who had prepared a 35-page carefully worked

---

5. Maimonides' classic work *The Guide for the Perplexed* (*Moreh Nevuchim*).

6. *Responsa* contains rabbinic answers to legal questions. In general, responsa have been a traditional mode of legal dealings for many centuries. Someone asks a rabbinic authority a legal question, and the authority answers in writing, which then may become a legal precedent.

7. Eddie Cantor (1892–1964) was a singer and comedian.

out essay. When my turn came, I sailed into Basel for assuming that he didn't have to know the book before he criticized it. I countered his attack with body blows that sent him reeling. It was as merciless an onslaught as I ever wielded against a combatant. I could see that there were many in the audience who were delighted with the pummeling I administered to him. Arzt, on the other hand, I treated cordially and seriously. He had done me the kindness of sending me his paper in time for me to mull over it. That enabled me to discover what was basically wrong with his entire approach. I came to realize that he was attempting to bolster up the philosophy of Conservative Judaism by adopting the vocabulary of Judaism as a civilization. This preconceived purpose of his prevented him from realizing the implications of the very ideas in the book which he agreed with. I exposed his fallacies one after another and succeeded in making out a good case for my approach, at least as far as the majority of those present were concerned.

Fortunately I was sufficiently collected and self-possessed to maneuver my counter-attacks in such a way as to render the most telling. I knew enough not to continue with my discussion while the people were getting hungry. I asked for permission to postpone the conclusion of my remarks for the afternoon session, and when at that session I realized that I might not get a chance to conclude my argument if I permitted the reports which I had given the right of way to continue, I had the courage to ask for the floor which I had surrendered. It was granted to me and I finished my job. This put me into good spirits for the rest of the day.

The rest of the afternoon session was taken up with a pseudo-scholarly paper on "The Canons of Interpretation of Jewish Law" and the discussion of it by Ben Zion Bokser and Robert Gordis. Then came Louis M. Epstein's proposal concerning "The Adjustment of the Jewish Marriage Law to Present Day." At the last meeting of the Committee on Law, I urged that it be authorized to recommend the form of adjustment he had worked out as the one we all agreed to as the best under the circumstances. My belief is that it is advisable to get the Rabbinical Assembly into action in law pertaining to *dine ishut* [Heb., personal law]. This might in time lead to genuine adjustment of Jewish law to life. Of course I refer only to relationships *beyn adam le'havero* [Heb., between man and his fellow man]. In all matters *beyn adam le'makom* [Heb., between man and God] I would abrogate the category of law for the simple reason as I had occasion to explain in answering Arzt: that law is a category which is applicable only to cases where sanctions are enforced. Since that is no longer conceivable in all ritual matters, they cannot possibly be classified under the concept of law.

Should I Retire into My Shell or Migrate to Palestine

MONDAY, MAY 20, 1935

The accompanying picture was taken last Thursday when Lena and I went downtown to arrange for our passports to Palestine.

In my free moments my thoughts revert to the problem [of] what to do when I get to Palestine, whether to stay there only during the summer, to spend there the whole of the sabbatical year, or to plan to settle there permanently. If I were satisfied to let well enough alone and could manage to become absorbed in some literary or scholarly work that would not touch upon contemporary issues, I would be able to lead a far happier and more peaceful life than most people I know. But I am too restless, too ambitious, and too socially minded to retire into my shell. This is why I am continually agitated and in a state of inner turmoil.

Seminary Graduation—Cyrus Adler Attacks Kaplan

JUNE 11, 1935

On Sunday, June 2, the graduation exercises of the Seminary took place in the quadrangle. Because the TI completed twenty-five years of its existence a year ago June, I had been invited by Adler to give an address on the TI. Although I had experienced considerable difficulty in the writing of the address, it turned out to be rather good. But even this year the element of ordeal was not wanting, as far as I was concerned. Israel Levinthal's address was a cluster of homiletical sophistries based on falsification of rabbinic dicta and was meant to serve as an attack against me. Then came the climax, when Adler made the statement, which he said he did at the request of the Board of Trustees, to the effect that the Jews were a religious community long before the destruction of the Second Commonwealth, and that to say we are a race or a culture (meaning, of course, a civilization) is to place a weapon in the hands of our enemies.

On Monday, June 3, I addressed the Israel Friedlaender classes. This time my talk was a success. I made the point that the addresses at the Seminary graduation exercises indicated the diversity of opinion that existed in Seminary circles. But with it all there was the common denominator—the desire to see Jewish life lived to the maximum degree possible and the deprecation of minimum programs.

A Comment on Henri Bergson

AUGUST 13, 1935

I have read through on board Bergson's *Sources of Morality and Religion*.[8] I had had an idea of the book from Bergman's article on it in his *Hogei Ha-dor* [Heb., Contemporary Thinkers (Jerusalem, 1935)] which I had read in Jerusalem. While I was impressed when I read it, as one must be by Bergson's

---

8. Henri Bergson (1859–1941) was a French philosopher. The book mentioned here is *The Two Sources of Morality and Religion*, trans. Ashley Audra (New York: Henry Holt, 1935).

apt analogies and occasional poetic flashes, I am disappointed when I think of it as a whole. The main idea which I derive from the book is that the concept of humanity as the unit of ethical duty instead of the particular nation to which one belongs is not the outcome of the same biological process as that which has given rise to group morality, but is a new creative act of the vital impulse. Likewise the identification of God not with any of the national or church deities, but with the vital impulse itself is not in direct line of development from the various group religions (which are the outcome of the biological process) but a new creative act of the biological process. Incidentally, I find my distinction between personal and folk religion very similar to his distinction between mythological and mystical religion. But what troubles me about his analysis is that it lends itself to the inference that the creative acts of the vital impulse which give rise to higher religion and higher morality are not means of reinforcing the life current but, on the contrary, of weakening and defeating it. This is what Bergman seems to get out of the book. (The unfortunate analogy of contraception confirms the foregoing impression.) Bergson should have shown that these creative acts have become necessary for the sake of enabling the human species to exist. With the various groups having been brought into such close proximity with each other that each is affected by the fate of all, the morality of the closed groups is suicidal. Likewise, with the development of intelligence rendering the mythological religions untenable, there is no other resort for man if he wants to overcome the added contingencies which he envisages and fears than to achieve the higher type of religion. The creative act—whether of morality or of religion—is not confined to the prophets and the mystics but embraces the large number of human beings who apply their intelligence to the newly acquired knowledge of man and his environment.

Even more disconcerting than the way Bergson develops his main thesis are some of his applications. These remind me of his war pamphlet, in which he proved that the Germans represented matter and the Allies spirit. His evident desire to make out a case for Christianity leads him to regard it as the bearer of the idea of a universal morality—a fact which is contradicted by its having been used by Rome as a last resort in holding the empire together. Likewise, his sympathy with Catholicism leads him to find in the Catholic mystics the originators of the true universal religion. All this is utter nonsense. There is much more of the sense for humanity and for that cosmic unity and creativity which gives meaning to life in the social idealists of the last three centuries than in the self-intoxicated mystics, who, if they really got at the secret of godhood, were unable to communicate it in spite of their proliferate verbosity and their bizarre actions.

Philosophical Thoughts—Facts and Values

WEDNESDAY, AUGUST 14, 1935

The two discussions I had in Jerusalem with [Gershom] Scholem, [Samuel H.] Bergman, [Akiba Ernst] Simon, and the others have stimulated my thinking considerably. I wish I had a similar group of people in New York with whom I could discuss fundamental problems.

Those discussions started me thinking anew about the problem of values. By this time the following has crystallized itself in my mind:

The content of consciousness consists of (1) objects, (2) events, (3) relationships, and (4) values. (1) Objects are things mediated by one or more senses; (2) events are changes noted in those things; (3) relationships are connections among things and changes; and (4) values are relationships of things and changes to human life with its wants and needs.

The classification of values into the good, the true, and the beautiful formulated by the Greek philosophers has become traditional. Its inadequacy becomes apparent the moment we realize that the term *good* is not coordinate with the other two. Plato identified the Idea of God as the supreme idea, thereby making truth and beauty phases of it. I would therefore have "good" coextensive with value or meaning in all its aspects conceived affirmatively, as conducive to the fullness of human life.

The natural division into which those aspects fall is suggested by the three aspects of the mind's functioning, viz., will, feeling, and thought.

Since our interest in values is usually accompanied by the pragmatic purpose of having those of an affirmative character prevail, the aspect of will ought to be treated as the base or substance with those of feeling and thought as its modes.

Taking, then, the aspect of will as the base—which is equivalent to treating feeling and thought as aspects of conduct—we find it necessary to introduce into the analysis of that aspect the four different levels on which human conduct may be carried on. The difference in levels is a difference in the extent to which the element of intelligence, self-consciousness, or human individuality or personality is present.

First is the level of impulse, second the level of authority, third the level of morality, and fourth the level of ethics.

The four levels of conduct are crossed by three concentric horizons representing the three main frames of reference to which the conduct is related. They are (1) the body, (2) the group, (3) the cosmos.

The nature of the science, philosophy, and esthetics cultivated by human beings in the various stages of their development depends upon the level and the horizon within which such science and esthetics find expression.

Finishing Up the Next Book with a Chapter on Judaism and Marxism

SEPTEMBER 3, 1935

Since last Saturday night I have been working feverishly to finish the revision of *Judaism in Transition*,[9] which I expect to send to the publishers this week. I had given the manuscript to Eugene Kohn[10] and asked him to make the necessary revisions, but after spending eighteen hours on it, he brought it back practically without a single change in the text. Seeing that he was of no help in that respect, I buckled down to the task myself. In the essay on Judaism's attitude toward "the Disinherited" I had to do a good deal of tailoring and to sew together with it the greater part of what was originally to have appeared as a separate essay under the heading of "Marxism and the Jewish Religion."

A Visitor to the SAJ Objects to Rabbi Ira Eisenstein's Comments on Isaiah

SEPTEMBER 7, 1935

With all my effort to be tolerant toward the traditionalist and Orthodox Jews, I find it very hard to condone the injury they are inflicting upon Jewish life and thought. What they do to Jewish life was brought home to me by the description of Toronto Jewry given me by Rabbi Treiger and his wife, who called last Saturday. The large element controlled by the immigrant Polish rabbis are unamenable to communal organizations, mainly because those rabbis put all kinds of obstacles in the way of organizations. Though they are for the most part unable to render any kind of social service, they insist upon being supported by the community, and when the latter makes no provision for them, they deliberately wreck it.

An illustration of how Orthodoxy perverts the mentality of the Jews came to my attention this morning after the services at the SAJ. Ira spoke briefly on the prophetic reading. In the course of his remarks he referred to the fact that the reading was taken from the second part of Isaiah, which according to modern scholarship is regarded as not coming from the Isaiah of the first part of the book that bears his name. Among those that came up to greet us was a man who described himself as a former student of the Yeshivah. He was not a rabbi, he explained, but was in the coal business. That being his background, he felt he had a right to object to Ira's statements about the second Isaiah. Although it

---

9. This work by Kaplan was published in 1936. In addition to the manuscript on Marxism mentioned here, this rather neglected work contains a significant discussion of Maimonides.

10. Rabbi Eugene Kohn was a loyal Kaplan supporter and collaborator on many projects. Ira Eisenstein cast him as the third persona in a Jewish triumvirate: the father (Kaplan), the son-in-law (Ira Eisenstein), and the holy ghost writer (Kohn).

was the truth, it was *epikursos* [heresy] to present it. "Do you yourself believe it is the truth?" I asked. "Yes," he replied. "Still I maintain it is wrong to preach it." "But our people here are accustomed to being told the truth. They want to know the truth," I said. "How about the belief in God?" he questioned. Apparently he is quite in doubt as to the existence of God, but he protests vigorously against denying the Isaiahic authorship of the second part of Isaiah.

Dangers of Nationalism as Great as Dangers of Communism

SUNDAY, SEPTEMBER 8, 1935

[Earlier] I stated only one side of the dilemma in which we Jews find ourselves—the danger of being destroyed both as a people and to a large extent also individually, if we identify ourselves with Communism. The other horn of the dilemma is the impossibility of isolating ourselves from the rest of the world. I subscribe fully to the following by Hans Kohn (*New Republic*, July 31, 1935):

> In a world of political and economic nationalism, a nationalistic solution of the Jewish problem seems natural. But for the world in general there is no hope in political and economic nationalism. Both lead ultimately to more conflict and growing chaos. There are no easy solutions. The transitional age in which we live apparently does not allow a sheltered and peaceful life. The solution of the Jewish problem, as far as it is a political and social problem, seems to be bound up more than ever with the solution of the general problems of mankind.

I certainly could not state more clearly the case for the inevitability of Jewish intervention in the class struggle.

A Critic Comes with a Question about Unruly Jewish Students

WEDNESDAY, SEPTEMBER 11, 1935

About two weeks ago Dr. Moses Jung called. He is a brother of Leo Jung, my successor at the Jewish Center, representative of the Agudah[11] and a violent opponent of mine. When we meet in the street, I feel embarrassed, for as a colleague I ought to greet him, but as the object of frequent attacks on his part, I ought to ignore him. He probably feels the same way about me. I was therefore quite surprised to learn from Rabbi Gershon Levi, one of the recent Seminary graduates, who was at Jerusalem at the same time I was there, that Moses Jung, who teaches religion in the State University of Iowa, wanted to get my advice about some matter. I also learned that Moses Jung was married to a sister of

---

11. The Agudah refers to the ultra-Orthodox.

Gershon Levi's and was more human than his brother Leo. He happened to be in Palestine about the same time, but somehow was prevented from meeting me there. He therefore came to see me after I got back. What the Levis had told me about Moses Jung being a very agreeable person and nothing like his brother turned out to be true. I really enjoyed his company and was delighted to hear him talk sensibly about matters of common interest to us. I was very much disturbed by what he came to get my advice about. Among the Jewish students who come to his and other western universities from this part of the country, there is a large contingent—about 25%—who are not only intellectually below standard, but even more so morally. They make themselves extremely offensive on the campus and outside. The consequence is that prejudice against Jewish students in general is on the increase, and before we know it, they will find it hard to gain admission into the state universities. I advised him to write to the Jewish national bodies like the American Jewish Committee, the Jewish Congress, IOBB [International Order of B'nai B'rith], and Arbeiter Ring [Workmen's Circle] to organize a committee that would act as a sort of clearinghouse for information concerning students applying to any of the universities. The authorities of the universities could get the information it needs from the Committee. That would help to keep out the undesirable elements and make the desirable ones realize that there are some people in Jewish life with whose opinion they must learn to reckon. This might serve as an entering wedge into the present state of communal irresponsibility in American Jewry and enable our people to realize the need for having some kind of authoritative agency for the expression of Jewish public opinion.

Jewish Survival and the Great Ideologies of Our Time

THURSDAY, SEPTEMBER 12, 1935

Destiny seems to have brought us to a point where either we commit ourselves as a people to some world-saving cause, whether it be Communism or pacifism, and the resulting collision with the forces of greed and reaction perish in a code of fire and uproar, or we keep on compromising with those same forces only to die a lingering death and dwindle slowly into nothingness.

Difficulties of Speaking in Hebrew in Public

SUNDAY, SEPTEMBER 22, 1935

The day on which the opening exercises of the Teachers Institute takes place is one of the days each year I look forward to with a great deal of trepidation. This is the case because of the inner conflict that it starts. I don't know whether I should speak in Hebrew, which I would like to but can't do sufficiently well in, or in English, which, no matter how well I do in, is bound to strike a jarring note. As a rule—to which there have been but few exceptions—I start by preparing to speak in Hebrew, but when the decisive moment comes, I weaken and give the talk in English. The consequence is that I feel frustrated. Today, fortunately, I did not weaken and gave my talk in Hebrew. For this I feel quite grateful and happy.

Work on a New Prayer Book

OCTOBER 1, 1935

Milton Steinberg on various occasions asked me to organize and lead an editorial committee that would undertake the revision of the prayer-book.[12] In the past I failed to respond to his suggestion wholeheartedly. But when he made it again yesterday, I consented to act on his suggestion. The committee is to consist of Steinberg, Eugene Kohn, Ira, Boxer, Lang, and myself. We decided to prepare a *mahzor* for the High Holy Days. I've already worked out the *maariv* [evening] Rosh ha-Shanah.

A New Course, a New Book, and Worries about War

WEDNESDAY, OCTOBER 2, 1935

This has been a happy day for me as far as my personal affairs are concerned. I accepted the invitation of the local YMHA (92 St.) to give a course of six lectures on "The Reconstruction of Jewish Life." The remuneration of $300 will make it considerably easier for me to incur such incidental expenses as are necessary to expedite the publication of the literary material I have on hand.

Secondly, Miss Shiffen of the Macmillan Co. called up to tell me that there was a favorable report on the ms. I had submitted, and that they will proceed with the publication of it as soon as we come to terms.[13]

But it seems almost a shame to enjoy one's own good luck at a time when mankind is about to plunge once more into the abyss of war. The papers this evening carry the news that Italy has begun hostilities. God knows what lies ahead.

Capitalism and the Opening of the Hayden Planetarium

FRIDAY, OCTOBER 4, 1935

Last Wednesday night I attended the opening of the Hayden Planetarium adjoining the Museum of Natural History. The ceremonies were impressive, but one thing marred them for me and that was Hayden's opening statement

---

12. It is not absolutely clear what Kaplan is referring to here. The likelihood is that he started to work on the *mahzor* and then at some point changed over to the Sabbath prayer book. The Kaplan *mahzor* came out a few years after the Sabbath prayer book.

13. Kaplan may be referring to his *Judaism in Transition. Judaism as a Civilization* was published by Macmillan in 1934 with a subsidy from Kaplan. For the full story, see Mel Scult, *Judaism Faces the Twentieth Century: A Biography of Mordecai M. Kaplan* (Detroit: Wayne State University Press, 1993), 338–41.

about the necessity of turning men's minds to the wonders of creation and getting them to think of life in spiritual terms, especially "in these days when Bolshevism and Socialism" are turning men's thoughts to material things. So naive a confession only a simple-minded American capitalist could utter. Realizing the failure of the churches to provide effective opiate, the *plunderbund*[14] is intent upon capitalizing the visible heaven for that purpose. It is to be hoped that Communism will not use this fact as a reason for prohibiting the admiration of the heavens.

Buber Has What Kaplan Lacks—but Kaplan Has What Buber Lacks

OCTOBER 4, 1935

Yesterday I received a copy of Ludwig Lewisohn's *Rebirth—A Book of Modern Jewish Thought.*[15] I was surprised to find myself included among the twenty-five from whose writings Lewisohn chose selections for his anthology. The uncomplimentary remark he makes about my failure "to draw power from those primordial emotional and metaphysical forces which are . . . the necessary origins of human change and action" is undoubtedly inspired by his comparing me in his mind with Buber, whom he regards as "the most distinguished and influential of living Jewish thinkers." Buber, according to Lewisohn, possesses what I lack. I am entirely in agreement with Lewisohn. Buber is a poet and I am not. But on the other hand, I believe that Buber lacks what I possess: a sense for the realities of life.

Sukkot and the League of Nations

THURSDAY, OCTOBER 24, 1935

On the first day of Sukkot (Sat. Oct. 12)[16] I preached on "internationalism." Taking as my text the Rabbinic reason given for the seventy bullocks prescribed as the number to be offered during the Sukkot festival,[17] I dwelt upon the fact that the Jews were the first people in the world to think in terms of humanity. The unity of God is fundamentally an expression of the wish to see all mankind as one kingdom. The principle of human equality should be extended to nations. This is possible only when both stronger and weaker nations are subject to some supernational authority. To that end, it is necessary that nations form not only

---

14. An organization that exploits the public.

15. Ludwig Lewisohn (1882–1955) was born in Berlin and was a novelist and critic; he was on the faculty of Brandeis University.

16. The Jewish festival of Sukkot is known as the Feast of Booths. It occurs in the fall of the year and commemorates the time in the desert when the Israelites lived in booths. Kaplan interpreted Sukkot as an effort to return to a simpler life.

17. Rabbis assumed that the number of nations in the world was seventy, and so the number of bullocks connected to the holiday, being seventy, is a metaphor for the whole world. Deuteronomy 32:8 is conventionally interpreted as referring to the seventy nations.

a League of Nations but a Federation of Nations. This implies the surrender of national sovereignty pertaining to matters of an international character.

I was so carried away by the idea that I went out of my way to deplore the fact that our Jewish young people find it necessary to turn to Communism for a course worthy of their interest and devotion, when they could turn to the ideal of internationalism as a means of preventing war. At the same time, they would be pursuing an ideal which is in keeping with the moral and spiritual tend of Judaism.

For this digression I was taken to task by Ira, Judith, and Naomi. We argued at considerable length the question [of] whether it is possible to stop war by fighting state sovereignty without fighting the present economic system. At first I held my ground, but upon reflection I realized that I had made a mistake. The mistake would have plagued me had I not decided to disavow it in the address that I was to deliver on *Shemini Azeret* [the end of the festival of Sukkot]. I carried out my decision to the satisfaction I am sure not only of my own children but of quite a number of young people who had been in the audience on the first day of Sukkot.

Rabbi Parzen Takes a Bath on Shabbat and Loses a Position

Sunday, October 27, 1935

Rabbi Parzen,[18] one of the few graduates of the Seminary who has a conscience, displays a scholarly interest in things Jewish, and is a fairly good preacher, had to leave his position out West because his wife could not stand the climate there. For the last two or three years he has been trying to get a position in the East, but has had no luck. Recently he tried for the pulpit in Peekskill. Everything seemed to be in his favor, but as fortune would have it, he happened to have stayed with one of the members on the Sabbath he was out there. In the morning before going to synagogue he took a bath. This was discovered by the member and reported at the meeting at which Parzen was being considered for election as rabbi. The outcome was that he was not elected. When he asked what was wrong with taking a bath on Sabbath morning, "But you used soap," was the reply.[19]

Communism or Judaism? Even at the Teachers Institute

October 27, 1935

I have just come from the initial meeting of an honor group that has been organized at the Teachers Institute. After going through the mechanics of organization, the question arose what was to be done at the meetings of the group. It did not take very long for those present to arrive at the decision that the burning problem just now for them was Communism vs. Judaism. They can't make up

---

18. Herbert Parzen (1897–1985), ordained JTS, was an author, state director of the United Synagogue of America, and chaplain for the New York City Department of Correction.

19. Apparently, using soap violated one of the thirty-nine prohibitions of work on the Sabbath.

their mind with which to identify themselves, and they look to the discussions to be conducted by the group to aid them in deciding.

Talking with Finkelstein about Rabbi Akiba

THURSDAY, NOVEMBER 14, 1935

We had Louis Finkelstein and his wife for dinner on Thursday, Oct. 24. He had mentioned to me having done work on a biography of R. Akiba.[20] I took that as an evidence of his desire to break down the aloofness in which he had kept himself last year, and I took the first opportunity I had this year of inviting him for a personal chat. We had also Ira and Judith with us for dinner, and on the whole we spent a pleasant evening. The one interesting topic of discussion Finkelstein and I had was the problem of the synagogue vs. community. I succeeded, I believe, in breaking down some of the main arguments he advanced to prove that Jewish life in this country must organize itself around the synagogue. In compliance with the request I made of him, he sent me the manuscript of his work on R. Akiba a few days after his visit. I think he could do much better. He has tried to combine scholarship with literary form, or as Ira put it, to introduce something analogous to Schechter's studies, but very definitely failed. By attempting to derive R. Akiba from the formula of economic determinism which he has worked to death, he has destroyed whatever likelihood he had of portraying a real personality. The formula with which he has been working has been applied by a writer in German to Pharisaic Judaism (I recall distinctly having come across that interpretation of Pharisaism) and has been applied with a comparative degree of success by F. in his published article on Pharisaism. But he gets himself involved in a tangle when he tries to read that formula into all the opinions of the scholars at Yabneh.[21]

In addition, the work deals perhaps more with the men with whom R. Akiba came in contact than with R. Akiba himself. Moreover, the talmudic and midrashic material which forms the basis of the generalizations about Akiba and the others is of such trivial character that one wonders what all the ado is about. When I pointed out these things to F. Tuesday a week ago, he admitted that he himself realized these shortcomings but unfortunately there was not sufficient material on R. Akiba that was of intrinsic interest.

It seems that F. had been at work on this book for a long time, and had rewritten it several times in accordance with the suggestions of people to whom

---

20. Louis Finkelstein, *Akiba: Scholar, Saint, and Martyr* (New York: Atheneum, 1970). Rabbi Akiba was a late first-century rabbi who was a leading contributor to the *Mishnah* (the first part of the Talmud).

21. The *Yabneh* (or *Yavneh*) was the center of Jewish life after the destruction of the Second Temple. It was established by Rabbi Yochanan Ben Zaccai during the war with Rome. According to some scholars, it served as a prisoner of war camp for the Romans. If Rabbi Yochanan Ben Zaccai gave himself up before the war ended, he would have been sent there. See H. H. Ben-Sasson, ed., *A History of the Jewish People* (Cambridge, MA: Harvard University Press, 1976), 319–20.

he had submitted the manuscript. Having begun it as an article for the *Harvard Theological Review,* he enlarged it with the expectation of having it appear in book form, because, as he said to me, what you write in a magazine is as good as buried. But to put out a book involves paying the publisher. He hoped, apparently, that by popularizing it, he would get a publisher who would put it out without asking him to contribute toward the cost of the publication. Failing that, he circulated the ms. among some of the Seminary trustees, as I gather from the fact that he had shown it to Morrison, in the hope that they would help him defray the cost of publication. With all that annoying experience and suspense after having put in so much effort on the book, he was not in a very receptive mood to my suggestion that he rework the material of his book into a book on "The Vineyard," on the Academy of Yabneh, and show how the Jewish people was transformed from a state into a church.

Judaism in Transition—*Getting the Book Published*

Nᴏᴠᴇᴍʙᴇʀ 14, 1935

A most unexpected and to me most valuable outcome of F.'s visit was his offer to introduce me to Covici of Covici Friede publishers. He wrote to Covici as he promised, and I met Covici and had lunch with him on Monday, Nov. 4. For once I met a layman who was interested in knowing my conception of God and who was responsive to my presentation of basic ideas concerning Jews and Judaism. I really enjoyed every minute I was with him. I left with him my ms. of *Judaism in Transition.* Yesterday I spoke with him over the phone, and he agreed to publish the book at $2.50 on the understanding that I was to purchase 300 copies at 40% discount and 10% royalty on the sales. Macmillan had asked me to purchase 600 books at that price. The practical outcome of Finkelstein's visit is a saving to me of $450 and doing business with a Jewish firm and with publishers who take a personal interest in the negotiations. Even the casual suggestion that Covici made to me over the phone yesterday—that I should not refer to the book as a sequel to *Judaism as a Civilization* or as a collection of essays—is more than I got in all my dealings with Macmillan.

Fighting Assimilation—A Kaplan Responsum: Two Cases with Well-Known People

Nᴏᴠᴇᴍʙᴇʀ 14, 1935

I am about to finger the wounds of the Jew in me. Case No. 1. Last week Sidney Matz, the son of Israel Matz . . . , called me up to ask me the following *she-elah:*[22] In the Matz mausoleum they are about to put in a stained

---

22. *She'elah* is a Hebrew term that means "question" but is used in the Jewish tradition to designate an inquiry of a legal or halachic nature.

glass window. In view of the fact that his father is active in the cause of pacifism (something I had never known before), he wants to affix an appropriate motto to the window. "Would it be proper to have as a motto the words from the New Testament 'Peace on earth and good will to men'?" he asked. "His father," he added, "could see nothing wrong in having that motto on his mausoleum." I gave him to understand that such a motto would be in very bad taste, especially since there is the far more appropriate one in Isaiah: "Nation will not lift up sword against nation," etc. He thought at first that there were too many words in that verse, but after a while he withdrew the objection.

Case No. 2: One of Felix M. Warburg's sons who had been married to a Gentile, and after being divorced remarried a Jewess, got a Hebrew teacher for his children. In giving instructions to the teacher as to how he should handle the children, young Warburg told him he should be careful to break the news to his children about their being Jews gently.

Kaplan Lists All His Writing Projects

NOVEMBER 14, 1935

In taking stock of the literary projects I am working on I find that I am engaged in the following: (1) *The Meaning of God in Jewish Religion* (nearing completion); (2) *A New Approach to the Problem of Ethics*; (3) *Jewish Ethics*; (4) *Home Devotions and Prayers* (with Eugene Kohn); (5) *A Service for Sabbath Eve* (with Steinberg, Eugene Kohn, Ira, etc.).[23] As though that wasn't enough—O yes, I forgot a sixth undertaking, *The Ethical Conception of the State*, in collaboration with Ira. A seventh project has taken hold of me recently: a book on the fallacies people commit constantly in their reasoning, fallacies which are responsible for much of the distorted and vicious thinking about most of the problems which arise in our human relationships.

This last explains how it happened that I have failed to make entries into this journal since Oct. 27. I begrudge the time spent on writing up all these things. On the other hand, I don't feel happy if I allow experiences which to me

---

23. Item 1 on Kaplan's list was published: Mordecai M. Kaplan, *Meaning of God in Modern Jewish Religion* (New York: Behrman's Jewish House, 1937) (reprinted by Wayne State University Press, 1994). Item 2 in Kaplan's list is the well-known ethical work *Mesillat Yesharim: Path of the Upright* by Moses H. Luzzatto (Philadelphia: Jewish Publication Society, 1936), which Kaplan translated and edited. For more information on this book, see Scult, *Judaism Faces the Twentieth Century*, 108. Although Kaplan lists a work on Jewish ethics (item 3 in his list), he never published it. Item 4 also was never published, although I have seen prayers for home devotions in the Kaplan Archives at the Reconstructionist Rabbinical College. Kaplan's prayer book (item 5) appeared in 1945 and was the basis for his excommunication. On the prayer book and the excommunication, see Mel Scult, *The Radical American Judaism of Mordecai M. Kaplan* (Bloomington: Indiana University Press, 2013), 195–99. For more information on the excommunication, see also kaplancenter.org/excommunication-mordecai-kaplan-zachary-silver.

are so significant to go unrecorded and in a short while to be completely forgotten as though they never happened.

Changing the Torah Blessings

NOVEMBER 14, 1935

In a newspaper clipping I received this morning I note that Louis I. Newman has broadcasted the changes I have made in the benediction before the reading in the Torah, where instead of *mikal ha-amim* [Heb., "from all the people's" (Blessed be Thou, Lord our God, King of the universe who has chosen us from among all peoples [by giving us His Torah])],[24] I say *la-avodato* [Heb., "to your service" (Blessed be Thou, O Lord our God, King of the universe, who has brought us nigh to Thy service [and given us Thy Torah])]. The first time I recited the benediction in the changed form was on Yom Kippur, when I was called to *maftir yonah* [Heb., prophetic portion on Jonah]. Before reciting it, I explained to the congregation the reason for the change. I had spoken on that reason in the sermon last Shavuot.[25]

Birth of Kaplan Grandchildren and Thankfulness to the Forces That Make Life Worthwhile

TUESDAY, DECEMBER 3, 1935

This morning at 10:38 Hadassah gave birth to a son weighing 7 lbs 14 oz. Mother and child are doing wonderfully. The parturition was perfect. Brother Isador, G. bless him, is the attending physician. May God grant Judith as easy a parturition. She expects her baby sometime in April. God (the sum of those forces that render life worthwhile and significant) has been, to use the conventional parlance, mighty good to me and my family. I feel happy and grateful. Would to God that all human beings had occasion to be as happy and grateful as I am.

I was lecturing this morning at the Seminary. The passage in the Midrash I was interpreting was in *Gen R XXX*. It read *tinok ben yomo* [Heb., a newborn infant].[26] I made the point that such is the significance of potentiality in human life that everything is subordinated to it. Potentiality is the end to which all else is the means. As soon as I was through with the lecture, Lena phoned the good news. When I spoke to [Adolf Judah] Nadich at lunch, I told him that I had just become the grandfather of eight pounds of potentiality.[27]

---

24. Kaplan, in rejecting the concept of the chosen people, changed the language of the blessings where the expression for chosenness was used. Here, he is referring to the Torah blessing, but he mentions only part of what he took out and part of what he inserted. For the full language of his blessings as he formulated them in his prayer book, see the Torah service in Mordecai Kaplan and Eugene Kohn, eds., *Sabbath Prayer Book* (New York: Jewish Reconstructionist Foundation, 1945), 160.

25. Kaplan does not discuss the sermon he is referring to in the diary.

26. Kaplan may be referring to *Midrash Rabba* 30:8, which deals with Noah.

27. The baby announced here was Jeremy Musher, who became a noted physicist and died in 1974.

The Death of Morris Levine, JTS Faculty Member

SUNDAY, DECEMBER 22, 1935

When I was through with the lecture on Midrash, I went down to the office to tell Miss Gruner, who had informed me of Lena's telephone call, that she had been the bearer of good news. At that moment [Samuel] Dinin and [Abraham] Halkin came into the office and told me that Morris Levine was in the hospital and that he had asked that the members of the Faculty be apprised of his condition. At once the other half of the passage I had been interpreting came to my mind,[28] and the dread thought that it augured Levine's death disturbed the happiness which the birth of my first grandchild brought me. Of course, I soon dismissed that thought and almost became convinced that it was an idle fancy when, upon visiting Levine in the hospital on Friday, Dec. 6, Dr. Epstein, his friend and physician, told me that Levine, who had been operated on Wednesday, would be able to leave the hospital after two or three weeks. As a matter of fact, Levine's face resembled a death mask. I shuddered as I looked at his distended nostrils. The only sign of life were his eyes peering from under the poultice that lay on his head. His right hand was held in an elevated position. With his left hand, which was free, he motioned to me that I should come near to him. I did and held his hand in mine for a while and wished him a *hazak ve'amatz verefuah shlaymah* [Heb., be strong and of good courage, and a speedy recovery]. That was Friday. Sunday morning at 10:00 he died.

The funeral took place Monday, Dec. 9 at 1:30 at the auditorium of the old Seminary building. The ones who spoke were I, [Zevi] Scharfstein (in Hebrew), and Finkelstein. Eugene Kohn was to have read a psalm but just as he entered the room where the final arrangements for the funeral were being made, Finkelstein reminded himself that Kohn was a *koheyne* and ought not to participate in the ceremonies.[29]

A word about Levine. He came to this country in 1898 as a youth of 17 after having attended the yeshibot of Wolozhin and Eishishok.[30] His knowledge of Hebrew brought him into the circle of Hebraists who in the early years of this century constituted the *mefetzay sefat eyver* [Heb., spreading of the traditional tongue (Hebrew); a movement for the revival of the Hebrew language]. After having completed the course at CCNY in 1904, he entered the Seminary. On graduation in 1908, he was called to head the Hebrew Institute in Chicago. After two years or so he gave up that position and headed a Talmud Torah in Brooklyn. In 1912 I asked him to join the staff of the Teachers Institute. He rejoiced in the fact that at

---

28. It is unclear what passage Kaplan is referring to.

29. According to traditional practice, a *kohane*, or priest, may not enter a cemetery except for the funeral of a direct relative.

30. Volozhin and Eisheshok were well-known European yeshivas.

the Institute he could devote himself completely to teaching. That was his métier. He gave himself unsparingly to the students and to the preparation of the work to such an extent that he left himself no time to do any writing. Naturally of a rather austere and somewhat pedantic nature, the lingering illness of his wife, who died about seven years ago, and his own subsequent illness rendered him rather unapproachable and the last years extremely cranky and nervous. To express an opinion he disagreed with was to court his wrath. In all the years that I knew him, I never had occasion to spend an hour with him in the discussion of any of the ideas pertaining to Judaism. Time and again I felt as if I wanted to get closer to him and to learn about his Jewish outlook, but somehow I never succeeded. It was probably my fault as much as his. But what a sad commentary this is on our mode of life. Here were two men working side by side in the same institution for 22 years, both devoted to the same cause and yet completely insulated against each other, as it were, by a perfectly superfluous and stupid reserve which each of us kept up. O how little we know of the art of living together! and how much of life's value we thereby miss.

Kaplan Wants Gordis to Replace Morris Levine at JTS

DECEMBER 22, 1935

On Tuesday, Dec. 10, I asked Finkelstein to join me at lunch. I discussed with him the question as what should be done about the hours of instruction in Bible that Levine used to give. Since Levine had taught Bible both at the Seminary [the JTS rabbinical school] and at the [Teachers] Institute, I took for granted that anyone who would be appointed as Levine's successor at the Seminary would likewise teach Bible at both departments of the Seminary. I suggested that [Robert] Gordis, who had been specializing in the study of the Bible and who is a very able teacher, take over the work at both departments. Finkelstein, apparently seeing in the present situation an opportunity for saving some money for the Seminary, did not approve heartily of the idea of having Gordis take over the work in both departments. He made the counter-suggestion that the hours at the Institute be divided among the present instructors. I deprecated this move on the ground that it would impair the effectiveness of the Institute. We parted with the understanding that he would not come to Adler with any suggestion without first consulting me. The next day he called me up and urged me to accept his counter-suggestion. He repeated his argument that the sources of the Seminary were low. He would have Gordis take over the work at the Seminary, at a salary that would enable him to get an assistant for his rabbinical duties; but the [Teachers] Institute would have to get along without Gordis. I was very indignant at his attitude and insisted that if Gordis is to be engaged for the Seminary, he should also teach at the Institute. He promised faithfully that he would make no recommendations to Adler before we came to an agreement in the matter.

On Saturday two things happened which took the fight out of me. One was a sermon I delivered that day on the Jewish conception of peace and the other a letter from Dinin asking me to consult with the other members of the Institute Faculty before approaching Adler in reference to providing for the hours left vacant by Levine's death. In the sermon I made the point that peace was above everything and that in its interests we must go far in submitting to compromise. And Dinin's letter made it evident that he and the other members of the TI [Teachers Institute] Faculty would view my recommendation that Gordis take over those hours as an unfriendly act.

When I came to the Institute on Sunday, I learned that F. had gone to see Adler. I understood that he would forget his promise to me and make it impossible for my plan to be carried through. I called together the members of the TI Faculty and told them of my intention to write Gordis, explaining at the same time my reasons for doing so. Nevertheless, I stated that I would not proceed without their consent. The first one to speak up was [Paul] Chertoff, who maintained that the hours ought to be divided among the present instructors and that the difference between the cost of the instruction and the amount that Levine used to receive should be applied to the increase of the salaries of the other men.

When I saw F. on Wednesday at the meeting of the Seminary Faculty, I had to ask him what had been done about the question of the hours. Since the time he had spoken to me on the phone the week before, he had not said a word to me, but I made up my mind I won't let his crooked dealings annoy me, and I therefore approached him after the meeting to find out Adler's decision. I did not betray the least anger or resentment in talking to F. All he told me was that Adler said that he would not have any new men take over the hours at the Seminary. I suspect that F. himself must have made that suggestion to Adler, because from what I have heard, he doesn't like Gordis overmuch and is probably obstructing his appointment.

A Young Jacob Agus Criticizes Kaplan

WEDNESDAY, DECEMBER 25, 1935

Before the summer, *Opinion*[31] received an article from Rabbi Jacob B. Agushewitz[32] which dealt critically with the thesis of Judaism as a civilization. I

---

31. Kaplan is referring to *Opinion: A Journal of Jewish Life and Letters*, published in New York City from 1931 to 1956.

32. Jacob Agus (Agushewitz) was a U.S. rabbi and philosopher. After the events described here, Agus left Orthodoxy. He differed with Kaplan on a number of issues, but the two men admired each other. Agus wrote Kaplan in 1967 that it was because of Kaplan that Agus went to Harvard, where he studied with Harry Wolfson and William E. Hocking. Hocking had a major influence on Kaplan's life. On Kaplan and Hocking, see Mel Scult, "Kaplan and Personality," in *Reappraisals and New Studies of the Modern Jewish Experience: Essays in Honor of Robert M. Seltzer*, ed. Brian Smollett and Christian Wiese (Leiden: E. J. Brill, 2014), 162–80. On Agus, see Zach Mann, "The American Judaism of Jacob B. Agus," PhD diss., Jewish Theological Seminary, 2012.

was asked by *Opinion* whether I wanted to publish a reply. I was glad to do so, and the reply appeared together with his article. When I returned from Palestine, he [Agus] sent me directly a statement attacking my thesis from a somewhat different angle. I immediately wrote him back a reply. I have asked Eugene Kohn to expand that reply for publication purposes. Both Agushewitz's statement and this reply will appear in the forthcoming issue of the *Reconstructionist.*

Agushewitz is 24, a graduate of the Yeshibah, and he has a position at Norfolk, Va. Coming on a visit to his folks, he called on me this evening. Despite the Yeshibah environment in which he received his education, both Jewish and general, he is well read, thinks clearly, and writes with considerable verve. His views are anything but Orthodox—in fact, they border closely on Reformism. But in his teaching and preaching he is staunchly Orthodox. When I asked him point blank how he could reconcile that attitude with the ethical standard of honesty, he answered that he saw nothing wrong in it from the standpoint of higher expediency and quoted the well-known rabbinic dictate about Aaron having acted as peacemaker by inventing goodwill stories and God departing from the truth for the sake of domestic peace. He defended his work as being a means of bringing sweetness and light to the people he administered to. He also mentioned the case of Mona Vana.[33] The complete cynicism in all this sophistry left me almost speechless, and I blurted out some incoherencies about the duty of a man telling the whole truth and not being satisfied with merely refraining from flagrant lies—which he regarded as morally adequate. He admitted that he was the victim of inner conflict, but he accepted his situation, it appeared to me, with more than legitimate acquiescence. I am afraid the Gemara [talmudic] psychology is too much part of him for him to be able to be intellectually honest or to feel the exhilaration of intellectual freedom.

He mentioned the fact that some of his fellow alumni had taken him to task for engaging in a controversy with me. They maintained that in repudiating the fundamental principle of Orthodoxy—"supernatural revelation"—I read myself out of Judaism. They sure are a bunch of fakers, those Yeshibah boys.

Should We Keep Pidyon Ha-Ben?

Saturday night, January 4, 1936

Last Wednesday we celebrated the *Pidyon Ha-ben* [Heb., redemption of the firstborn from a priest (*kohane*)] of Jeremy Israel.[34] I haven't made up my mind whether *Pidyon Ha-ben* is a tradition that merits conservation. The main

---

33. Perhaps "Mona Vana" refers to any number of paintings depicting *Monna Vanna* (a vain woman). It could also refer to the play by Maurice Maeterlinck or Sergei Rachmaninoff's unfinished opera based on it.

34. Kaplan's first grandson.

point against it is that it recalls a barbaric practice. The points in favor are (1) the paucity of rites in Jewish life, and (2) the value of tracing our religious development to primitive beginnings.

A Family Argument at the Dinner Table

JANUARY 4, 1936

Last night's Sabbath meal with Ira and Judith at our table ended in a bitter altercation between me and the children. The exchange of sharp words began with Judith's snappiness toward Ira and Lena and was reinforced by Selma's saying to Lena, "You've got a hell of a nerve," and her being taken to task for that by Judith. Then I sailed into Selma by saying, "What else can you expect from a New College product?" This let loose upon me a storm of abuse from Judith, Selma, and Naomi.[35] By that time our nerves were taut. Just then, we started discussing the communist attitude toward Palestine. Naomi made some remark justifying the communist opposition to the Jewish settlement of Palestine on the ground that it crowds out the poor Arabs. This roused my indignation, and I waxed hot over the recent attempt on the part of some communists in Palestine urging the Arabs to make a pogrom on the Jews. Naomi replied that she didn't think that was right of the Communists. "I thank you," said I in bitter irony. Then pandemonium set in. Judith, Selma, and Naomi ran away shouting from the table. I remained seated. I rounded them up, and we said grace in a most unhappy frame of mind.

I took a long walk by myself and formulated my thoughts on what had happened. I came to the conclusion that all my efforts to build up Jewish life were absolutely futile. If with the home background such as my children have, they can even for a moment question the legitimacy of the Jewish hope to find a home in Palestine, then what can I expect of the thousands of young people who have never had a chance to learn of the high ethical and spiritual values latent in Judaism or to see some of its beautiful and highly significant aspects? I was convinced that my life was a failure, and I saw that the only reasonable thing for me to do is to give up all speaking and writing outside of what I have to do to earn my living. Just how I would manage to do that in a spirit of despair about the future of Jewish life I could not clearly make out. But at least I would be free from the strain of trying to do too many things at the same time, and resign myself to a life of passivity for the rest of my days. At that moment I felt like withdrawing *Judaism in Transition* from publication, and not going ahead with the Haggadah or with any other literary work on the subject matter.

When I came home, I told Lena, Ira, and the children (Judith, Naomi, and Selma) the conclusion I drew from Naomi's and Selma's negative attitude

---

35. Kaplan's daughters mentioned here are Judith Eisenstein, Selma Jaffee-Goldman, and Naomi Wenner.

toward Judaism. Then it was Judith's and Ira's turn to prove to me that I was wrong. Selma joined in and presently also Naomi. The discussion lasted till after 12:00, and when we separated, every trace of rancor was gone, due mainly to Ira's influence.

The foregoing experience exhausted me to such an extent that I was too tired to attend services this morning.

Handing in the New Haggadah

MONDAY, JANUARY 6, 1936

I handed in today the Haggadah[36] material to Charles Bloch of the Bloch Publishing Co. He promised to give me within a week an estimate of the cost of publication. In trying to explain to him the difference between the biblical verse and rabbinic interpretation, I learned that he couldn't even read the punctuated Hebrew. And this man is the head of a Jewish book concern that is more than eighty years old. He himself is in the early seventies.

Israel Levinthal happened to be in the store while I was negotiating with Bloch. I told Levinthal what I had come for and showed him the Haggadah material. He approved of it highly, but deplored the fact that I omitted the *makot* [Heb., plagues]. He pleaded that I reintroduce them if I want the Revised Haggadah to be used on a large scale. He even suggested that I do something with the *Shefokh hamatha* [Heb., "Pour out thy wrath upon the nations"].[37] Of course I couldn't seriously entertain any such proposals.

God as an Abstraction and God as a Particular Being

JANUARY 6, 1936

In discussing the conception of God recently both from the lecture platform and in the classroom, I have been stressing an aspect of it which I have never done before. I think I have a better insight now into one chief source of confusion between the religious and the philosophical conceptions of God. The conception "God" [in philosophy] is a generic term like "man." Whereas, however, in religion, "God" as a generic term is frequently used as the predicate of a [judgment] sentence, it is never the subject of a sentence. The Bible uses "man"

---

36. Kaplan's Haggadah was eventually published in 1941 for the Jewish Reconstructionist Foundation: Mordecai M. Kaplan, Eugene Kohn, and Ira Eisenstein, eds., *The New Haggadah for the Pesach Seder* (New York: Behrman's Jewish Book House, 1941). The Haggadah was revised in 1942 and 1978; the 1999 revised edition by Gila Gevirtz incorporated many changes.

37. This prayer from the Haggadah calls on God to punish those who have oppressed Israel. Although Kaplan strongly opposed the rising power of Nazi Germany, he thought that this prayer directed against Israel's enemies was inappropriate for the Passover seder. Removing it from the Haggadah may have been primary in the thinking of those who excommunicated him in 1945 for his prayer book. In terms of the Nazi threat, it is well to remember that this is 1936. On the excommunication, see Scult, *Radical American Judaism*, 7–27, 195–96.

in the generic sense as a subject, *Adam le-hevel damah* [Heb., "Man is like a breath, his days are a passing shadow," etc. (Psalms 144:4)], but never "God" in a generic sense. Even in the opening chapter of Genesis, where it would seem that "God" is used in the generic sense, the fact is that the term *Elohim* [Heb., Lord] refers to a specific being. The fact that God is made the subject not only of "created," but also of "saw" and "said," and especially in the sentence "Let us make man in our image," we have all the evidences of a specific being or entity and not of God in a generic sense [concept].

The philosophers, on the other hand, did make God in the generic sense of the term the subject of reflection. That reflection concerned itself with what they considered essential in the numerous gods that were worshiped by the pagan world. The philosophers themselves could conscientiously continue worshiping the various deities. They saw no conflict between that and their philosophic preoccupation with the generic concept "God."

The confusion began with those thinkers who like Euhemerus[38] or Philo[39] sought to identify the generic concept "God" with some particular god or gods of historical or natural religion. This process of identification had been made easier by the preparatory work of the Prophets, who had applied the process of elimination to the various deities they knew and had arrived at the conclusion that only YHWH was a god. It was one step from this conclusion to the conclusion that YHWH was God in the generic sense of the term.

I think that the incongruity of synthesizing the notion of a particular deity with the generic concept God was felt by the early Christian theologians. They thought they overcame it by arriving at the concept of the Trinity, God the father being God in the generic sense; God the son being a particular deity; and God the Holy Ghost being the equivalent of godhood or that quality which constitutes the differentia of a god. It is evident that while in thought each aspect is considered separately—the generic, the particular, and the attribute as such, are each hyposta[ses]—in actual being they are identical. I believe that something like the foregoing reasoning led to the formulation of the doctrine of the Trinity. I can see quite clearly why Christian theologians would be irritated with the Jewish philosophers, because once a philosopher accepts the reality of a specific entity as a god, he cannot remain a philosopher unless he at the same time acknowledges the concept God as a generic term and the attribute godhood as such, in other words, [he] becomes a trinitarian. The reason I could not believe in the Trinity is that I deny the existence of a specific or particular entity who all by himself incarnated or particularized godhood as such. To me, godhood is that aspect of reality which manifests itself in creativity and salvation. If I had

---

38. Euhemerus was a Sicilian philosopher who lived around 300 BCE. He held that the gods of mythology were but deified mortals.

39. Philo was a first-century Jewish philosopher of Alexandria.

been born a Christian, I could easily have reinterpreted the doctrine of Trinity in accordance with this perfectly rational interpretation of reality. All of which goes to show, as I have always contended, that the difference between Judaism and Christianity is not a theological one, but a difference of otherness.

As for Spinoza, I believe that of the three possible meanings of God, viz., the particular, the generic, and the substantive (= godhood), he made use of the last one only in his *Ethics* and made it identical with Substance or Nature.

Kaplan's Ideas the Same as a Traditional Medieval Work

TUESDAY, JANUARY 21, 1936

To my amazement, I discovered last week when I read with the seminar group the first chapter of Aramah's *Akedot Yizhak*[40] how much there is in common between my own approach to the God idea and that of Orthodox medieval theology. To me the term God is a hypostasis[41] of those aspects of reality that make for man's salvation, aspects such as creativity, unity, etc. Radically different as this idea may sound from Orthodox theology, it is essentially the same as that advanced by the latter, when it continually stresses the fact that God cannot be known as he is in himself, but only by means of the effects of his functioning in the world, or of those aspects of the world which may be regarded as manifestations of his existence. Aramah reads that thought into the Midrash from *Gen. R.* [*Genesis Rabbah*] which points out the difference between a human potentate and God. The potentate first identifies himself, then proceeds to announce his titles or achievements. But God first declares his works—the fact that he created the world—then makes himself known. It would be just as easy to read into this Midrash what I say about God being the hypostasis of creativity.

A Talk in Reading, Pennsylvania

JANUARY 21, 1936

Last Tuesday (Jan. 14) I spoke at Reading in Rabbi [Max] Routtenberg's synagogue. The lecture was given under the auspices of the Seminary Institute of Jewish Affairs. My subject was "Judaism as a Civilization." There were about 300 to 350 present. I gathered that this was the first time those people heard of that version of Judaism. They were very much aroused by the frank analysis of the Jewish situation and the novelty of my presentation to Judaism. They apparently had never heard about it from their rabbi.

---

40. *Akedat Yitzhak* is a popular sixteenth-century philosophical work by Isaac Ben Moses Arama. It contains many sermons that incorporate philosophical ideas. Kaplan frequently met with students for extra study.

41. Hypostasis is the substance or essential nature of anything.

The Status of Women Must Be Changed

JANUARY 21, 1936

Yesterday I delivered a talk on "The Status of the Jewish Woman" before a gathering of women at the Unterberg Memorial Bldg.[42] of the Seminary. The meeting was sponsored by the three groups—Hadassah, Council of Jewish Women, and Women's League of the United Synagogue—whose branches are conducting jointly the classes which are an extension of the work of the Friedlaender Classes.[43]

In my talk I ridiculed the opiate administered by the writers and speakers on the subject of the Jewish woman. They always make it a point to idealize the part she played in the past and evade the problems that arise out of the status of inferiority, which is the status of the woman in Jewish Law. I pointed out the urgent need on the part of the Jewish women to launch a movement for their religious, civic, and juridical equality. The audience was pleased with what I had to say, but gave no indication of carrying out my suggestion.

A Speech in Boston and a Discussion with Louis Epstein on Conservative Judaism

SATURDAY NIGHT, FEBRUARY 1, 1936

On Wednesday, January 22, I went to Boston to deliver the lecture on "The Evolution of the Jewish Religion" at the Brookline synagogue where Louis M. Epstein is the rabbi. I went there at the insistence of the Seminary Institute of Jewish Affairs. When I came, I found the Men's Club having dinner and having movies taken of them. I utilized the few minutes of conversation I could have with Epstein to orient myself with regard to him. He was among the first classes I taught at the Seminary. Being the son of an active Orthodox rabbi in Chicago, and having studied for a time in the Yeshiva, he has developed a vested interest in Talmudism, and having made it a practice to be Prof. [Louis] Ginzberg's neighbor every summer in Maine, he has become an aspirant to archaeological scholarship and a *Wissenschaft* snob.[44] When in the course of the conversation I asked him whether he gets the *Reconstructionist*,[45] he replied, "No, I see it once in a while, but I don't get it because I am not interested in theology." If at that moment I had not had to abide by the conventions of civilization, I would have punched his face. Instead I merely smiled sardonically and went on to the next subject, suggested by his telling me that he was giving a course of lectures Friday nights in his pulpit on the meaning of Conservative Judaism. I was curious to

---

42. The Unterberg Memorial Building is named for Israel Unterberg.
43. Adult education classes at JTS named after Israel Friedlander.
44. *Wissenschaft* refers to the science of Judaism or serious historical scholarship about Judaism.
45. The *Reconstructionist* was the magazine Kaplan began to publish in 1935. It was a primary outlet for his ideas and those of his followers.

know how he managed to keep his lectures theology proof, so I asked him to tell me briefly what he considered to be the difference between Orthodox and Conservative Judaism. His answer was that whereas Orthodoxy left no room for any choice between divergent opinions of rabbinic authorities, including even those to our own day, Conservative Judaism believed in the right to exercise such choice, except in those instances where the Talmud itself has laid down the principle that there is no choice. I can understand his answer, but from the standpoint of present-day problems in Jewish life, it is as relevant as Chinese Astrology.

A Speech in Baltimore

FEBRUARY 1, 1936

Last week I gave a series of three lectures at the YM & YWHA of Baltimore. The first night, Tues. Jan. 28, on "Judaism as a Civilization," the second (Jan. 29) on the "Evolution of the Jewish Religion," and the third night on "The Organization of American Jewish Life." The series was very successful. It was attended by an audience of about 250.

A Speech in Harrisburg and Some Community Problems

FEBRUARY 13, 1936

On Monday, February 3, I spoke at the Harrisburg Jewish Community Center on the question "Can a Modern Jew Be Religious?" [Jacob] Golub was responsible for getting me to speak there. I had an audience of about 250, and my talk was well received. After the lecture some of the communal leaders, including Rabbi Gelb, Mr. Brenner, and others, went together with me to the home of a Mr. Kaplan for the purpose of discussing the problem of communal organization.

The Welfare Board[46] is trying to consolidate the various institutions into a United Jewish Community. The main difficulty in the way of such consolidation is the existence of the congregations which cannot confine themselves to worship but must engage in social and cultural activities to justify their existence. They therefore duplicate and compete with the activities of the Center. This problem takes on a personal character when the rabbis, on the one hand, and the Executive Director, on the other, are unable to work out a modus vivendi between themselves. In this instance Gelb might have managed to come to an understanding with Golub, but at the last convention of the Rabbinical Assembly he presented a paper on the need of having the synagogue and center merge into a large communal unit. Louis Finkelstein, fearing that such a step might lessen the influence of the congregational group and ultimately weaken the position of

---

46. The Jewish Welfare Board was formed during World War I to aid Jewish soldiers. It was later expanded to support and coordinate activities of Jewish centers.

the Seminary, went hammer and tongs at Gelb. This had the effect of intimidating Gelb into taking an antagonistic attitude toward the Community Center and treating it as a rival to his synagogue. When I was at Harrisburg, I could see that Golub and Gelb were not getting along so well with each other.

A Speech in Bensonhurst

FEBRUARY 13, 1936

On Tuesday, Feb. 4, I gave the first of two lectures I had been scheduled to deliver at Bensonhurst. These lectures are part of a series arranged by the Welfare Board with the Jewish Community Center there. The series is designated "Judaism as a Civilization" and is being interspersed with artistic evenings. My two lectures are to be followed by four which Ira is scheduled to deliver.

I had an attendance of over 400. The questions came for the most part from defenders of Orthodoxy.

Fees for Speeches

FEBRUARY 13, 1936

The fee at Baltimore was $150 for the three lectures. At Harrisburg they took 25 copies of *Judaism as a Civilization* at $3.33 a copy as fee for the lecture. At Bensonhurst that was the fee for the 2 lectures. At Jamaica I got $50, of which Miss Grossel took $10.

Outlook for the Teachers Institute — Not Very Good

THURSDAY, APRIL 16, 1936

The last few days I have been having one of my occasional fits of mental dissipation and depression. The immediate cause of its onset is the obligation to write a 9,000-word article for the Historical Volume to be issued by the Seminary on the occasion of the fiftieth anniversary of its establishment.[47] The article has to deal with the work of the Teachers Institute. If I were permitted to tell the truth, I would have to blame the Seminary authorities, both directors and faculty, for the failure of the Institute to conquer the problem of Jewish education in this country. Jewish education is at present very much on the downgrade. The Teachers Institute may have slowed down somewhat the speed of the descent, but it certainly has not stopped the descent. The Seminary has missed its opportunity. It has permitted a whole generation to pass without laying the groundwork of Jewish life in this country. The chief blame rests upon Schechter and Adler,

---

47. Mordecai M. Kaplan, "The Teacher's Institute and Its Affiliated Departments," in Cyrus Adler, ed., *The Jewish Theological Seminary of America: Semi-Centennial Volume* (New York: Jewish Theological Seminary of America, 1939), 121–34.

whose imaginations never ranged beyond the little congregational school in a quiet small town community. Such a school constituted the objectives of all their ideas about Jewish education. Somehow, with all their talent for archaeology and history, or perhaps because of it, such men have no real understanding of the social forces at work in our own day. They are blind and deaf to the surging and whirling of the floods of change that are sweeping away the little that is left us Jews of our past. Thanks to leadership such as theirs, a man like Schiff donates $50,000 as a fund, the income of which was expected to half-suffice for the maintenance of a training school for Jewish religious teachers. Compared with what that kind of school ought to cost, that donation was a mere bagatelle. My heart sank within me when I opened the TI in Sept. 1909 with a handful of applicants, most of whom followed me from the Congregation Kehilath Jeshurun, where I had functioned as rabbi for five and a half years. So anxious was I to get away from Orthodoxy that I was glad to do anything for a living. But I knew from the first moment that my hopes and ambitions to work Jewish life on a scale commensurate with its needs would be hedged about by the unimaginative conceptions which the Seminary authorities entertained concerning Jewish education. When Benderly came along and the Kehillah gave promise of developing Jewish education on a community scale, I had to fight Schechter and Judge Greenbaum to permit me to cooperate with Benderly and to enlarge the scope of the TI. But with the collapse of that communal venture, due to Magnes' and Benderly's bungling, and during the last few years, as a result of the economic depression, the TI is today operating in a vacuum. The entire business of Jewish education is today financially and, what is worse, spiritually bankrupt. There is practically no demand for Jewish knowledge. The limited energy and resources that might be used for Jewish purposes are nowadays being drained off by the numerous drives to help our European brethren in Germany and Poland and to provide for them havens of refuge.

Conflicts about Writing on the Sabbath

SATURDAY NIGHT, APRIL 18, 1936

Last night I wanted badly to write in this journal some of the things I had on my mind, but I could not get myself to do it. Some years ago I managed to overcome my scruples against writing on Sabbath, but I have not been able to develop complete equanimity with regard to writing on the Sabbath as I have developed, say, with regard to turning on the lights. Basically, I believe the main cause of the inhibition against writing on Sabbath is not any inherent objection on the ground that writing is not in consonance with the Sabbath spirit. On the contrary, affording me as it does spiritual pleasure, I should feel perfectly at ease about it. I think, therefore, that I have been inhibited mainly by the consideration that even those who are in sympathy with my views are under the impression that I do not write on the Sabbath. I therefore do not want to do anything in the privacy of my room which I would not do freely in their presence. The Rabbinic principle *davar he-asur mi-shum marit ayin afilu be-hadrei hadarim asur* [Heb., something which is forbidden because of appearances is forbidden even in the most private place] is undoubtedly valid from an ethical standpoint.[48]

Article on the Teachers Institute Interrupts the Journal

APRIL 26, 1936 [ENTERED MAY 18, 1936]

More than the usual exertion of will power is required for me to resume this journal. The inward resistance, however, is overcome by the momentum of the long established habit to record experiences. That habit gives me no rest until I insert the main items of what has happened since the last recording. The principal reason for the interruption has been that I wanted to use every available moment to get through with the 9,000-word article on the Teachers Institute. That task lay like an incubus on my mind; otherwise I would hardly have gotten through with it within the time set for it. I was so anxious to free myself of it that I had it done almost a week ahead of time. The paper grew to about 11–12 thousand words, and has turned out to be quite readable. Thank God for that.

Law Committee and the Agunah Problem

WEDNESDAY, MAY 6, 1936 [ENTERED MAY 18, 1936]

I took part in the meeting of the Rabbinical Assembly Committee on Law. The meeting took place at Prof. [Louis] Ginzberg's home at 3:00. The subject of discussion was the *agunah*[49] problem. The suggested *takanah*[50] has raised a storm in Orthodox circles. For some reason, mainly negligence, the Committee had been acting on this matter without having consulted Ginzberg. He resented his being ignored in so vital a question, whereas in the question of wine for sacramental purposes—a question that arose during the Prohibition days when many Orthodox rabbis went into the bootlegging business—he had been induced to

---

48. For other instances of Kaplan writing on the Sabbath, see Mordecai M. Kaplan, *Communings of the Spirit: The Journals of Mordecai M. Kaplan*, vol. 1, *1913–1934*, ed. Mel Scult (Detroit: Wayne State University Press and the Reconstructionist Press, 2001), 170 and 452. The principle of not violating this prohibition in public seems to have been Kaplan's guiding principle most of the time.

49. An *agunah* is a married woman who is separated from her husband and cannot remarry either because she cannot obtain a divorce from him or it is not known whether he is alive. According to Jewish law, the man grants the woman the divorce; if the man disappears or refuses to give a divorce, the woman is still tied to him. Conservative rabbis tried to solve this problem in the 1930s. For some it is still a problem. See, for example, Irving Breitowitz, *Between Civil and Religious Law: The Plight of the Agunah in American Society* (Westport, CT: Greenwood Press, 1993).

50. A *takanah* is a directive enacted by halachic scholars that has the force of law. The matter of the *agunah* was ultimately resolved for Conservative Jews (in 1954) with the insertion of a clause into the *ketubah* (marriage certificate) enabling an *agunah* to force her recalcitrant husband to come to Jewish court or ultimately to a civil court for arbitration.

write a lengthy legal disquisition which was not heeded then and is forgotten now. The absence of Ginzberg's imprimatur exposed the Rabbinical Assembly to a wild attack from the Union of Orthodox Rabbis. Realizing their mistake, the Law Committee came to Ginzberg imploring his help. Louis Epstein of Boston is the head of the committee. [Michael] Higger, Boaz Cohen, Greenstone, and Drob are the other legal minds. Epstein had written a pamphlet defending the *takanah* which he had suggested. When in the course of the discussion that pamphlet was mentioned, Ginzberg remarked that he hadn't read it, although he thought highly of Epstein and read everything else Epstein had written. The reason was quite evident. He felt hurt he hadn't been consulted.

Although they decided to go on with the fight to introduce some *takanah* that might alleviate the *agunah* evil, I doubt whether much good will come out of their decision. I am convinced that so long as they will try to use the method of legal fiction or any other device in order to remain within the traditional law, they will get nowhere. I ventured to suggest the advisability of *takanah* in the sense of legislation, but, of course, no one in Ginzberg's presence would even dare approve of such a procedure.

A Good Word about Louis Ginzberg

MONDAY, MAY 11–THURSDAY, MAY 14, 1936 [ENTERED MAY 18, 1936]

I attended the sessions of the *kallah* [conference] led by Prof. Ginzberg. He gave little more than what he stated on his first set of notes covering the Mishnah of Kiddushim.[51] I am glad I managed to attend, first because I had carried out something I had made up my mind to do in spite of the press of other work. Secondly, because I feel that a man of Ginzberg's ability deserves all the recognition he could get and more. If I had been Enelow,[52] I would have gotten Mrs. Miller[53] to contribute the $20,000 for the publication of Ginzberg's commentaries on the Talmud rather than for Davidson's *Thesaurus*.[54]

Kaplan Attacked in the Press Because of His Book

ENTERED MAY 18, 1936

The April 29 issue of the *Christian Century*[55] carries a savage attack on the interpretation of *Judaism as a Civilization*. At the editorial meeting of the

---

51. This may be a reference to Louis Ginzberg's commentary on the Jerusalem Talmud.

52. Hyman Enelow (1876–1934) was a noted Reform rabbi, scholar, and author who apparently helped raise money for Israel Davidson's *Thesaurus*.

53. Linda Miller (1877–1936) was a patron of learning and literature in New Rochelle; she donated several rare manuscripts to the JTS.

54. Israel Davidson (1870–1939) catalogued the first line of more than 35,000 medieval Hebrew poems in his *Thesaurus of Medieval Hebrew Poetry*, published in four volumes from 1925 to 1933.

55. *Christian Century* was a liberal Christian periodical.

Reconstructionist we formulated a reply which Steinberg wrote up and which we revised at a subsequent meeting. It was sent to the *Christian Century*, but they answered that they want Morrison, who had written the editorial in which he assailed me, to reply. But since he is in England at present, it will be some time before our letter can be published.

In the meantime, some irresponsible scribblers in the Anglo-Jewish press are talking of the defense of Judaism, and the first thing they do is to throw me to the wolves. An anonymous scribbler in the Detroit *Jewish Chronicle* speaks of my book as a *curiosa Judaica* which nobody takes seriously. That surely hurts, but it doesn't make me in the least unhappy because I know it's not true.

"Jewish Reconstructionist Papers" — The Book

WEDNESDAY, JUNE 10, 1936

I handed in today to Louis Behrman,[56] the publisher, the material of *The Jewish Reconstructionist Papers*,[57] which I edited. The idea of publishing such a collection evolved from a suggestion made by Ben Zion Boxer [Bokser] at one of the meetings of the *Reconstructionist* Editorial Board about three months ago. His suggestion was that we publish a book of sermons to demonstrate the application of our point of view to preaching. But in the discussion it became apparent that very few people would be interested in reading a collection of sermons. The idea was then sprung, I don't remember by whom, whether by me or by someone else, that we collect the representative papers and editorials that have appeared in our magazine.

I believe the publication of these papers will give Reconstructionism a boost.

Good Things Happen at the Seminary

MONDAY, JUNE 22, 1936

Although official contacts with the Seminary authorities, especially faculty members, usually irritate me and make we want to get away from the Seminary building as far as possible, informal chats with them, which come about through casual meetings, make me feel as though I would want to stay around on the premises most of the time. I enjoy exceedingly the physical surroundings of the place. Academic atmosphere is veritable oxygen to me, provided it is

---

56. Behrman House also eventually published *The New Haggadah*.

57. Mordecai M. Kaplan, ed., *The Jewish Reconstructionist Papers* (New York: Behrman's Jewish Book House, 1936). A valuable collection.

accompanied by congenial exchange of ideas. The following matters came my way and were disposed of today:

1. I talked over with Dinin the question of allocating the $2,540 available from the late Levine's salary for TI and Seminary College budget. I needed this talk before meeting Adler, to whom I wanted to make a number of suggestions pertaining to the TI budget, yet it came about accidentally merely as a result of my having come into the building.

2. If I had not come then, I would have forgotten that when I was there last Friday, I had decided to tell the girls in the office not to allow my reports of the TI work and other records to lie around where anybody who went into the office could read them. I also reminded myself to ask Dinin to clean up the storage room of the TI.

3. When I came into the cafeteria, I sat down at Louis Finkelstein's table. He expressed the fear that the community, by displacing the existing organizations, would become totalitarian in character and come to be dominated by aggressive politicians. Using the parallel of the Federal government, he said that it would be as fatal for Jewish life to give up its existing organizations as it would have been for the American government to replace the individual state governments.

The fact is that I have been so much concerned with the federal idea, so to speak, in Jewish life, that I have paid little attention to the question of the autonomy of the constituent groups. To my way of thinking, the main problem today is to break down the resistance to integration of all Jewish activities. Finkelstein argues as if everybody accepted the principle of integration, and he already fears its consequences to a degree that leads him to oppose it altogether. Whether such opposition is motivated by a genuine fear, or is generated by a desire to antagonize, no one can tell, probably not even he himself.

In any event, the discussion with him has led me to call up Behrman's [suggestion] not to proceed with the setting up of my introduction to the *Reconstructionist Papers*, because I want to insert a paragraph or two to meet the objection he raised.

4. Another interesting encounter was the one I had with Dr. Abraham Halkin, who is a member of the TI staff. He had been invited by the Editorial Board of the *Reconstructionist* to become a member. Before accepting the invitation, he said, he wanted to learn from me more about the policies of the *Reconstructionist*. I asked him to come into my office, and we had a long discussion in Hebrew on what, to my great surprise, I learned was to him the part in my philosophy he found it difficult to accept, namely, the God

idea. Having long ago given up the traditional concept of God, he has not been able to achieve any other conception. His observances of religious customs and attendance at synagogue are basically part of his self-expression as a Jewish nationalist and are prompted by a vague sentimental attachment which he is unable and does not care to intellectualize. This started me arguing along the same lines I do in the class, especially with students of the Graduate School for Jewish Social Work. I wonder whether I shall succeed in getting Halkin ever to accept my approach to the problem of religion.

5. The interview with Adler, which was the main reason for my coming to the Seminary building, was formal and factual. He asked me to send him a record of my suggestion, since, as he said, one doesn't know what may happen to one (apparently that thought is in his mind), there should be no question as the decision arrived at.

6. On my way home I managed to attend to a matter of business. I met Covici[58] and explained to him why I had not given him the forthcoming *Reconstructionist Papers*. I also found out from him what should be done with the digest of *Judaism as a Civilization*, which Ira has practically completed.

Getting Away from the Anthropomorphic Conception of God

MONDAY, JULY 13, 1936

The main difficulty in effecting the transition from the anthropomorphic to a rational conception of God could be overcome, it seems to me, by the following approach: accustom yourself to the thought that the reality of God cannot be grasped by any effort at visualization. Without in any way inferring that godhood is a force in the same sense that electricity is a force, resort to the analogy of electricity. The reality of electricity is not experienced by any of the five senses. An electric shock is experienced by the muscle nerves. Likewise the reality of godhood is experienced not by any of the physical senses but by the mind in its emotional functioning. *When you are happy to the point of gratitude, or when you react to anything with a genuine feeling of holiness, you are actually experiencing God* in the same sense as a feeling of shock is evidence of your contact with electricity. The fallacy which has to be unlearned—an unlearning in which the analogy to electricity may be of help—is that any experience of God must, like the experience of our neighbor's presence, apprehend Him in his entirety. This is where anthropomorphism throws one off the track. Habituate yourself to the idea that it is no more possible to be aware of the whole of God in any single experience than it is to sense all of electricity in a single shock. The fallacy of identifying any one

---

58. Kaplan published *Judaism in Transition* (1936) with Covici Friede Publishers.

experience or even cluster of experiences as the revelation of Deity in His fullness gives rise to idolatry.

God as Presence

MONDAY, JULY 20, 1936

I am working at present on *The Meaning of God in Modern Jewish Religion*. I find that I have to rewrite some of the material almost entirely, but the effort is worthwhile. Just now I am rewriting the chapter on *Shemini Azeret*. The significance which I am now ascribing to it is that it stresses the importance of fostering worship or communion with God. This significance requires emphasis nowadays so that God be not merely held in the mind as an idea but felt as a presence.

Difficult to Be Hopeful in These Times

WEDNESDAY, AUGUST 12, 1936

I find it extremely difficult to set down in writing the dark thoughts that flit across my mind. When I read what is happening to the Jews in Palestine and in Europe, I feel as though I were in the midst of a cyclone or an earthquake. The phrase *omdim alenu lehalotenu* [Heb., "They stand ready to annihilate us" (from the prayer book)] keeps on thundering in my mind. All summer I have stayed in the city for the purpose of working on the edition of the *Jewish Reconstructionist Papers* and on my own book *The Meaning of God*, etc. All that work is predicated on there being some ground for the hope that a better time is coming, that the ideals of justice, freedom, and peace will some day be realized, that our own Jewish people will live on a footing of equality with the rest of the world. Instead, reaction and violence are becoming more strongly entrenched than ever, and the Jewish people is confronted with the menace of gradual extermination accompanied by mental and physical torture.

3

August 22, 1936–September 22, 1938

Despair over the Future of Judaism in America

SATURDAY NIGHT, AUGUST 22, 1936

I am still struggling with the question of whether I am not deceiving myself that there is hope for Judaism in this country. Should not the state of loneliness with regard to Jewish life and interests into which I am plunged at the very moment that I am engaged in teaching and lecturing have convinced me that this country, with respect to Judaism, is a desert and a wasteland? It swallows and destroys every remnant of our identity. Indeed, I think that ultimately factors of the era and of will power will themselves force me to draw the conclusion that, if I want to achieve any satisfaction in my life, I must dedicate what is left of my energies to our people in Eretz Yisrael. Only there lies any hope for our future. Is it not better for me to cast my lot with those who have life in their future rather than with those who are doomed to die? Were I still young, I would certainly move my residence to the Land of Israel, but now it is almost too late. I will therefore try to send the fruit of my thoughts to Eretz Yisrael. What brought me to this decision was the visit of Mr. Shimon Halkin, who came to see me ten days ago with regard to the deliberations about bringing him onto the faculty of the Teachers Institute.

Mr. Halkin suggested that I publish some articles in the press of Eretz Yisrael, especially *Davar*, as an introduction to my ideas.[1] Only then would it be worthwhile to translate my book on the concept of God (*The Meaning of God in Modern Jewish Religion*) into Hebrew. The resistance to tradition in Eretz Yisrael

---

1. Kaplan did publish a number of articles in the newspaper *Ha-Aretz*. See Emanuel S. Goldsmith, Mel Scult, and Robert Seltzer, eds., *The American Judaism of Mordecai M. Kaplan* (New York: New York University Press, 1990). For a full bibliography of Kaplan's publications, see pages 415–72 in Goldsmith. Although Gerson Cohen is given credit for the bibliography, it was actually compiled from cards given to him by Kaplan himself. This information comes from my 1972 interview with Kaplan.

is so intense that no one will pay attention to a book dedicated to the concept of God. There theophobia dominates.

Hebrew Will Redeem Kaplan Like English for Vanzetti

AUGUST 22, 1936

In the course of my work these days I chanced upon a volume of letters by Vanzetti,[2] who has been condemned to death in spite of his innocence of the crime for which he has been brought to trial. His knowledge of English was almost zero, but in the course of his confinement in jail, he learned to read and write in an incisive and beautiful style. Would that I too would succeed like him in my personal jail to learn the language (Hebrew) through which I can establish living bonds with my people and redeem my soul from despair.

Feeling Excommunicated

SUNDAY, AUGUST 24, 1936[3]

I will certainly be thought of as an ingrate—and perhaps, rightly so—that I compare myself with a man in prison. How dare I kick against the conditions in which I have been placed, conditions of freedom and security, in contrast to the tension and fear to which our people are subjected in Eretz Yisrael? Only a year ago did Dr. Louis Billig[4] make my acquaintance, a man about 38 years old, an expert in Arabic and a lecturer in Arabic studies at the [Hebrew] University. Miss Miriam Cohen, whom he was courting, introduced him to me. He was short, his face was black and pinched, and only the charm of a great scholar redeemed them from ugliness. . . . Yesterday the newspapers reported that he was killed in his home by unidentified killers while he was sitting and working on the scientific study of Islam. And here I sit in peace and quiet and yet I am bitter. The answer is that, as long as we live, it is hard to be content with less than what one's energies can attain. Limiting the fulfillment of our potential causes frustration and feelings of being hampered and hemmed in. It is not incarceration that makes the prison but excommunication. Weeks and months pass for me without any serious dialogue with anyone on Jewish or general matters, in which I have a certain competence; I feel as if I were excommunicated.

---

2. Nicola Sacco and Bartolomeo Vanzetti were Italian immigrants who were charged with the murder of a paymaster and guard on April 15, 1920. The murder trials, including appeals, lasted seven years (1920–1927), and both men were found guilty and sentenced to death. They were executed on August 8, 1927. There was much controversy over the measure of justice in this trial, and many thought that the fault of these two men was their radical, anarchistic views.

3. Kaplan has misdated this entry. Actually, August 23 was the Sunday.

4. Louis (Levi) Billig (1897–1936), an Arabist, was born in London. In 1926 he was appointed the first lecturer in Arabic language and literature at the Hebrew University. He was killed by Arab terrorists.

Problems with the Hebrew Language

TUESDAY, AUGUST 25, 1936

Ah, the Hebrew language. my right eye I would give if I only knew that through this sacrifice (writing the diary in Hebrew) I would gain command of it. It is so meager and poor and in need of limitless encouragement and support so that one will not become disgusted by its agonies. I was revolted when I read *Ha-Aretz*. There was a long argument over the question of whether it is correct to vocalize the plural of *lavi'* ("lion") as *leva'im* or *levi'im*. From time to time I want to find the exact translation of an ordinary English word, turning to the English-Hebrew dictionary in vain, and concluding that, in that dictionary, what has been broken down is greater than what is standing. I wanted to translate the expression "My muscles are stiff" and could not find a Hebrew word for "stiff." If someone would only gather all the words and phrases that do not yet have a precise Hebrew translation, he would then force the scholars and writers to deal with filling the void which prevents tens of thousands from using the Hebrew language.

Attacks on Jews—The Nature of the Problem

MONDAY, AUGUST 31, 1936

Two things which we raised and cultivated have turned into a weapon against us. We gave the nations our concept of God, and they have used that very same concept to prove that we have rebelled against our God and are deserving of destruction. We emphasized the importance of nationalism and raised it to the level of religion, but the result has been that the nations have learned to develop their feelings of nationalism in such an intensive manner that they can only look upon the nationalism of their neighbors with hostile eyes. We the Jews, are thought of as strangers in lands where we have lived 1,000 years or more and whose cultures have penetrated into our souls.

Bigotry of the Dead and the Living

FRIDAY, SEPTEMBER 4, 1936

Wednesday evening Samuel Inselbuch, the son of Rabbi [Elias] Inselbuch, who died recently in Palestine, visited me. He (the father) had been a rabbi in Brooklyn until a few years ago and was known as a courteous and quiet person who mixed well with people. The reason for the son's visit was to show me a copy of his father's will, in which he warns his children not to dare to recite Kaddish [memorial prayer] for his soul in a Reform or Conservative synagogue and that he will not forgive them if they disregard his wishes. This prevents his son's participation in Sabbath and holiday services in the Society for the Advancement of Judaism. When he showed me the copy of the will, it appeared as if he was asking my advice. Knowing that it would be useless to advise him to disregard his father's will, I counseled him to abide by it. Really, what is the right thing to do in these circumstances? To defy the written word of the dead or to yield?

I am horrified when I encounter the abbreviation of S"T (*sefardi tahor*), "a pure Sephardi," with which Sephardim, who are arrogant about their race, sign their names. How are we better than the Nazis? And much worse than this abomination is the attitude toward *kohanim* [priests].[5] Several times have I counseled individuals in our congregation to eliminate the recognition given to the priesthood when men are called to the Torah, but they did not honor my request. Thank God they have eliminated the ceremony of the priestly blessing.

On Writing and Publishing—Kaplan Joyously Reviews His Publication Meaning of God

WEDNESDAY, SEPTEMBER 9, 1936

Considering my private life, I can count myself blessed. Today I turned over to the printer the manuscript of my *Meaning of God in Modern Jewish Religion*,[6] upon which I have been working for six straight weeks to clear it from errors and from sections written in a difficult style. As I have already noted in this diary, there is nothing better in life than to complete a project which demands much work and effort, whether its value is great or small. From my childhood I have aspired to write books, partly for the sake of my ego and partly for their own sake. As soon as I gained certainty about the problem of religion, I did not rest, because of the desire that was stirred up in me to express the innovative ideas that had begun to be woven in my mind. At first I wrote many articles— this was between 1910 and 1915—on education and religion, which I read in annual conferences of the students of the Jewish Theological Seminary. Those articles remained in manuscript because in those years there was no newspaper interested in new opinions which required one's having a strong background for their clarification. Besides this, during those years I was working on the Torah's method of explanation as I had learned it in the Teachers Institute. Summer after summer I sat on the porch of the house we rented in Long Branch [New Jersey] from morning to evening, pondering how to find the key idea which joins the stories together in the book of Genesis. I remember how much I labored to integrate the story about Dinah into the narrative continuity of that part of

---

5. Reconstructionist congregations generally do not follow the practice of dividing Torah honors among priests (*kohanim*), Levites, and Israel. Kaplan believed that the ancient priesthood passed on through families was essentially racial and that it did not belong in the modern period.

6. The latest edition of this book, with a new introduction by me, is M. M. Kaplan, *The Meaning of God in Modern Jewish Religion* (Detroit: Wayne State University Press, 1994).

Genesis. However, after I had completed my commentary on Genesis,[7] I did not dare publish it, because I feared it would be accepted neither by the Orthodox, because it takes biblical criticism seriously, nor by scientists, because of the commentary's basic assumption that, despite the different sources upon which the Torah drew, the final editor fused the sections into a single unit through his nationalistic and religious aspirations and views.[8]

The first impetus to publish my thoughts came to me from Henry Hurwitz,[9] editor of *The Menorah Journal*. He encouraged me to write a series of five articles. There was a time when I wanted to combine these articles into a book, but with the passage of a few years I was no longer pleased with a significant part of their contents. In 1924 I published a small book—with two articles—in which I expressed the need to pave a new road to the solutions of the problem of Judaism. In the meantime, I was invited to give the course on Judaism at the Graduate School for Jewish Social Work. This course, too, served as a stimulus to the writing of various articles. If not for the stimulus which came from the establishment of the Rosenwald prize,[10] I would not have applied my energies to concentrate into the book the scattered material that I had. My success with my first book strengthened my desire to publish some more ideas on the problem of Judaism, on religion and ethics, and it also prepared me to work in a more systematic manner. And today, now that I have submitted my third book, apart from

7. Among Kaplan's papers at the Reconstructionist Rabbinical College there are many scattered references to the Torah. Kaplan apparently used cards, on which he wrote the outlines of his weekly sermons. Hundreds of these cards are found in the Kaplan papers. Someone could write a book using these cards as the source. Kaplan apparently shared his ideas and some of his manuscripts with Rabbi Gunther Plaut, who wrote an important Torah commentary. It may be that Plaut used Kaplan's interpretations without giving credit, but I cannot be sure. There are also a number of manuscripts in the Kaplan papers offering interpretations of the Torah.

8. For Kaplan's early views on biblical criticism, see M. M. Kaplan, "The Supremacy of Torah," in *Students' Annual, Jewish Theological Seminary of America* (New York: Jewish Theological Seminary, 1914), 180–92.

9. Henry Hurwitz, a friend and admirer of Kaplan, founded the *Menorah Journal* in 1915 and edited the journal for many years. Ideologically he was opposed to political Zionism and believed in reinterpreting Judaism in an American vein.

10. On the Rosenwald contest and the publication of *Judaism as a Civilization*, see Mel Scult, *Judaism Faces the Twentieth Century: A Biography of Mordecai M. Kaplan* (Detroit: Wayne State University Press, 1993), 338–41. The contest involving the prize mentioned here was financed by Julius Rosenwald, the president of Sears, Roebuck and Company. The essays were to deal with the way that Judaism could best adjust itself to modern life. Kaplan submitted his manuscript, which was later published as *Judaism as a Civilization*. The prize money was divided among the three top submissions, with Kaplan receiving $3,500, which he gave to Macmillan to underwrite the publication of his book. The submissions to the contest, which numbered about forty, are found among the papers of Samson Benderly, who was the executive director of the contest. Ira Eisenstein gave those papers to me, and I intend to give them to the American Jewish Historical Society. They constitute a valuable time capsule from the early 1930s of views of American Jewish ideologies.

the book *Essays on the Renewal of the Spirit of Judaism*,[11] which I edited with no help from anyone, I give thanks to God, who is the source of all human creative aspirations and the energy making possible their realization.

But my joy is mixed with bitterness over the tragedy which has overtaken one of the young men who was so dear to me because of his positive attitude to Judaism and his moral qualities, apart from his creative efforts in the Jewish Institute on 85th Street.[12] Two days ago Isaac Kaplan informed me that George Hyman is suffering from cancer and his days are numbered. This terrible news shocked me and put a cloud over my life.

Rabbi Abraham Isaac Kook's Failure

THURSDAY, SEPTEMBER 10, 1936

In *Ha-Aretz* of 3 Elul 5696, there is a series of articles about Rabbi Kook,[13] who passed away a year ago. From the thousands of words which the authors of the articles pile up in his praise, it turns out that he had outstanding talents and moral qualities which were wasted in his Orthodox and somewhat barbarian surroundings. Despite all the praises which his admirers sing in his honor, Kook brought up only clay in all his literary exertions. What depresses me is the phenomenon that in Eretz Yisrael, where there is a need for a new and healthy life to develop, they still continue to deceive themselves that the Talmud and its weapon-bearers can help them to solve their spiritual and social problems. Our tragedy is the yeshiva education, and as long as its influence is widespread, it will do us harm. Many of those educated in the yeshiva are dominant in lecturing and journalism, and they cover the nakedness of their folly and their ignorance of the principles of systematic logic with empty phrases with which they mislead their innocent readers.

---

11. The work referred to here is most probably Mordecai Kaplan, ed., *The Reconstructionist Papers* (New York: Behrman's Jewish Book House, 1936).

12. Kaplan is referring here to the Central Jewish Institute (CJI), established in 1917 and directed by Albert Schoolman. The institute had a variety of classes and clubs and at its peak boasted 3,500 members. Camp Cejwin (the name incorporates the initials of the institute), in Port Jervis, was founded by the CJI. Schoolman was a friend, a reconstructionist, and a strong supporter of Kaplan. For more information on the CJI and Kaplan's involvement with it, see Scult, *Judaism Faces the Twentieth Century*, 199–202, 400n42.

13. Rabbi Abraham Isaac Kook was the first Ashkenazic chief rabbi of Palestine. His views were mystical but pluralistic. On the affinities between Kaplan and Kook, see Jack Cohen, *Guides for an Age of Confusion: Studies in the Thinking of Avraham Y. Kook and Mordecai M. Kaplan* (New York: Fordham University Press, 1999). This work was originally written in Hebrew, with the title *Morim le-zman navokh*, and was translated by Cohen himself. See also Yehudah Mirsky, *Rav Kook: Mystic in a Time of Revolution* (New Haven, CT: Yale University Press, 2014). For a more detailed work, see Benjamin Ish-Shalom, *Rav Avraham Itzhak HaCohen Kook: Between Rationalism and Mysticism* (Albany: State University of New York Press, 1993).

Asking the Right Questions — Prof. Hugo Bergman's Review

SATURDAY NIGHT, SEPTEMBER 12, 1936

This morning, when I opened the *Judisches Rundschau*[14] of September 11, I was surprised to find a review of my book *Judaism in Transition* [New York, 1936] by Dr. Hugo Bergman, Rector of the Hebrew University in Jerusalem. Understandably, he disagrees with my views on Judaism because I negate the reality of the category of things that are considered to exist outside of nature. His system is that of Buber and Rosenzweig, author of *The Star (of Redemption)* and he cannot make peace with humanism. By his very opposition, however, he assigns great value to my book.

FRIDAY, OCTOBER 23, 1936[15]

A few weeks ago I was surprised to see in the newspaper *Judisches Rundschau* a critique of my book *Judaism in Transition* by Hugo Bergmann. Yesterday my surprise was even greater when I received from him a copy of a critical article in Hebrew, which had appeared in *Ha-Aretz* on the 23rd of September. In general, the Hebrew article repeats the content of the one in German, but the last sentence conveys a much warmer evaluation of my book, despite Bergmann's opposition to my views. This is what he says: "Kaplan dared ask of Judaism questions which we are accustomed to pass over in silence, and he tried to answer them according to his viewpoint without prejudice, without fear, and with relentless consistency. In this he has rendered religious Judaism a great service. His books are of the category of those whose errors are more important than the truths one finds in many books by others." I never anticipated such praise from one who is a follower of Buber.

Comments on Genesis

SATURDAY NIGHT, SEPTEMBER 12, 1936

These days I am busy preparing my sermons for Rosh Hashanah. It is my intention to make my listeners aware of the unique character of the human being, which is his awareness of the concept of "time." This awareness reaches its height when it is able to distinguish between that which is fleeting and that which is permanent. [Such awareness] gives birth to the human striving to recognize what is permanent and to identify with it. There are two qualities involved in differentiating what is permanent from what is not: one is self-assertion and

---

14. *Judisches Rundschau* was a weekly journal of the German Zionist Organization. It was founded as the *Israelitische Rundschau* in 1896 and was published in Berlin. The name was changed in 1902, and the journal appeared as the *Jüdische Rundschau* until 1938, when it was discontinued.

15. Although this diary entry does not follow the previous one chronologically, I have inserted it here because it is relevant to the earlier entry.

the other is self-fulfillment. The story in the Torah which symbolizes these two qualities is the story of the Garden of Eden. The Tree of Knowledge of good and evil symbolizes self-assertion. The Tree of Life symbolizes self-fulfillment. All the calamities that one brings upon oneself come from the quality of self-assertion. This is what drives a person to increase their efforts to gather treasures and to achieve domination. It is through power over others that these people hope to attain that essential something that can escape from the ravages of time. The function of classical faith is to convince the person that the success of the self-assertive is only imaginary, for [that success] will evaporate, leaving behind it frustrated aspirations. The self-assertive person is evil because he trusts in his own power to gather wealth and to bend to his will those he can exploit. The main idea in the Bible is that the wicked person will perish, while the righteous, who strives for self-fulfillment, will remain in the world. When experience denies or contradicts the claims of classical faith, the latter finds ways of escaping from the confusion. With the help of the imagination, faith creates another world [i.e., the world to come], wherein is preserved the difference between what is transitory and what is permanent. . . .

When we survey what is happening in our time, we see that iniquity is stamped upon all the grand and powerful worlds which man has created through the force of his self-assertion. The emotionalism and insecurity which prevail in our time are clear proof of the assumption of classical religion that it is impossible for humans to achieve their desire, permanence, so long as they seek it through self-assertion.

What is the quality of self-fulfillment? It is the quality based upon the recognition that only through communication with others in relationships of love and devotion can one recognize that which is permanent and identify with it.

Self-Doubt about Hebrew

Tuesday, September 15, 1938

At times I am so wearied and agitated over my difficulties in expressing my thoughts in Hebrew that I am almost ready to consign the whole matter to Hell (Azazel). Though my ability in linguistics is average, I am still not inferior to most of those who we desire will acquire proficiency in the Hebrew language, and if I, who all my life have been absorbed in study and reading in Hebrew itself and whose interests have a relationship to Hebrew, have to cope with spiritual torture and stumbling over barriers on all sides, and finally, when I do begin to walk, my feet are chained, what will the others do? . . . For example, I wanted to express in Hebrew a simple sentence, "The Loyalists gained adherents for their cause," and I could not. When I looked in my English-Hebrew dictionary, I became even more aggravated over the lack of authentic equivalents for the expression of a simple sentence like this.

Jesus Appears in a Dream

MONDAY, SEPTEMBER 21, 1936

How vast is the difference between our reaction to dreams and that of our forebears. Last night, for example, I saw in my dream Jesus of Nazareth. He appeared to me when it seemed that I was in trouble and in need of help. If I had any inclination to mysticism, like Buber[16] and Rosenzweig,[17] and, all the more so, if I were influenced by Hasidic fantasies, I would certainly interpret this dream in a serious manner, expressing sympathy for Christianity. However, I am so far removed from this nonsense, and mystery in religion is so alien to me, that this dream made no impression on me, and had I not wanted to use it as a subject for an exercise in writing Hebrew, I would have forgotten it immediately.

Kaplan Compares Himself to I. J. Singer

THURSDAY, SEPTEMBER 24, 1936

These days I am occupied from time to time with proofreading the galleys of my book [*The Meaning of God in Modern Jewish Religion*], soon to appear. At times I feel great pride in the contents and the style. In addition, I am working on the sermons I am to deliver. In the meantime the recently published new book by I. J. Singer,[18] *The Brothers Ashkenazy,* came to hand. I read a few chapters and skimmed through other parts. I was astounded at the breadth of the canvas which the author unrolls before us, at the accuracy of his personal knowledge and at his microscope-like penetration into the souls of his characters. In the face of a talent like that of I. J. Singer, of what value is my ability to challenge prejudices in religion or politics? Nonetheless, I will continue my work knowing, as I have written in this diary, that happiness does not depend specifically upon actions of great value but rather in the carrying-out of a project which has entered my thoughts, whether it has a great or a small value.

Daring to Lecture in Hebrew

WEDNESDAY, SEPTEMBER 9, 1936

Before every opening session of the Teachers Institute, I struggle with the question, In what language to address the students, English or Hebrew? I

---

16. Martin Buber was a German Jewish philosopher who embraced a version of Zionism that stressed a cultural center in Palestine. He dealt in many of his works with the mystical world of Hasidism and with the centrality of the interpersonal.

17. Franz Rosenzweig was a German Jewish philosopher and educator who worked with Martin Buber on a German translation of the Bible. After Rosenzweig's death in 1929, Buber continued alone.

18. Isaac Joshua Singer (1893–1944) was the older brother of Isaac Bashevis Singer and a significant novelist in his own right. He immigrated to the United States in 1933. *The Brothers Ashkenazi* was published in 1936.

certainly would prefer to speak in Hebrew, but when I know or fear that I will stumble in my speech, I use English. The result is that a feeling of inferiority, which disturbs my thought processes, overwhelms me for a time. However, this year I am more involved with Hebrew than has been my earlier custom, and if I did not lecture in Hebrew because of the aforementioned fear, I would despair completely of ever knowing how to speak and teach in Hebrew. Moreover, I aspire to conduct my courses in Hebrew, and so I must succeed this time in my experiment. Thank God I spoke fluently and did not stammer at all. I cannot prepare a speech and memorize it, so I must rely upon the possibility that the correct phrases will come when I need them, and that is what happened.

After me, Rabbi [Paul] Chertoff spoke. He recently returned from Eretz Yisrael and the subject of his speech was the current situation there. He spoke in a rich and variegated style, which captured the attention of his listeners. It seems that he felt his superiority over me in Hebrew, for immediately after his speech he whispered in my ear that he prefers hearing me lecture in English, for he feels the absence of my incisive and polished English style when I lecture in Hebrew.

Concept of God Same as Concept of Government

Sunday, October 11, 1936

How did the belief that the Torah was given at Mount Sinai and that it was revealed from heaven come about? First of all, we must leave our thought world and try to penetrate the thought world of our forebears. There was a time when it was impossible to conceive of the existence of any nation without it having a god who was its father and patron, just as it is impossible for us to conceive of any nation without a government which unites it and makes it into a unit. Indeed, the concept "God" played the same role then as the concept "government" does in our time. This being so, the bond between the nation and its god existed from the time it became a nation. And because the Children of Israel believed that they had become a people before they entered the Land of Israel, they drew the conclusion that the bond existed in the wilderness where they wandered about before entering the land. Because the concept "God" filled the same function in the past as does the concept "government" for us, the result is that the basic bond between God and the nation is expressed through the statutes and laws by which it is governed. Therefore they had to attribute to God all the laws by which they lived.

In other words, where there is no information about the past based upon facts and experience, reason and imagination attempt to describe it, and that is what happened to our ancestors when they sought to shed light on the darkness of their past. This aspiration in itself has great value and does honor to our forebears. But those who are stubborn in their faith, [such] that it is impossible to conceive of the past in any way other than the imaginings of our ancestors, block the path of our people's spiritual development.

Meetings with New Teachers

SUNDAY, OCTOBER 18, 1936

Yesterday Dr. H. L. Ginsberg, who is a candidate for the teaching of Bible in the Seminary, visited me. He is one of two candidates for Bible instruction, the other being Dr. [Robert] Gordis. I was very happy when I became aware that he is very modern, not only in his views, but it seems that he will also be so in his teaching. I greatly enjoyed his straightforwardness with respect to modernism, in contrast to the twisting of Gordis.

Judaism as a Civilization—An Answer to the Demand for Aliyah

SUNDAY, OCTOBER 25, 1936

Yesterday I received from Dr. Abraham Schwadron of Jerusalem a copy of his article "The Decline of Ahad Ha-Amism," which appeared in *Moznayim* [a Hebrew periodical] of February 1933. I do not know Dr. Schwadron. It seems he was moved by the critical review of Dr. Bergmann [Samuel Hugo Bergman], which I have mentioned above on this page [i.e., the entry for October 23, 1936], to send me his article in which he condemns the approach of the Zionists who make peace with the eternity of the Diaspora. The article shook me up considerably, precisely because in my own thought I have arrived at the conclusion that it is impossible for Judaism to survive in the American environment, but despite the consistency of this conclusion, it is impossible for me to make it the basis of Jewish life here. Therefore I have been compelled to yield to the demands of life and to find a compromise by the call to consider Judaism as a civilization. I justify this compromise on the basis of the pedagogical need for the American Jew to consider the Jewish community as a national and not a religious unit. This is the primary condition. It is also important to cultivate in him the proper attitude to the problem of the Jews. In his present condition he is under the influence of the erroneous assumption in which he has been schooled for two thousand years, that he belongs to a holy congregation. He cannot deal with this otherwise than by accepting this assumption and considering himself a member of a unique faith, or by denying it and cutting himself off from Jewish life. Therefore, it is no less than absurd to force upon him the conclusion that he must emigrate to Eretz Yisrael if he wants to be a Jew. He prefers not to be completely liberated from the Jewish problem. From this point of view my compromise and its rationale are no more than a philosophy of rationalization. Indeed, for me personally this compromise must appear only as rationalization, because in general I see the degeneration of Judaism in this country as assuming awesome proportions, and I should have fled to Eretz Yisrael. Why did I spend all my time here?

Philosophy of Education

SUNDAY, NOVEMBER 1, 1936

The push I needed yesterday was based on the first chapter of the book of Kilpatrick[19] on "Sources for the Philosophy of Education." The main idea of the chapter is that education cannot do without a basic philosophy and that the philosophy establishes the nature of the education. I was not satisfied with this simple idea, but I delved into the question, What is a Jewish philosophy? My answer is that a philosophy which serves as a basis for life and education is made up of three elements: (1) an orientation toward the world in general and specifically to the fate of man. Such an orientation receives support from the narratives of the Torah on creation, sin, death, the chosenness of the people of Israel, etc. The chain of ideas which I have found in the beginning of the book of Genesis and which I mentioned in my sermon on *Shabbat Bereshit* [Genesis][20] are the unity of the creation, the unity of the human race, and the possibility of conquering death. Indeed, thanks to the development of human life, we need additional means of guidance. The navigators of a sailboat could be satisfied by knowing how to guide their vessels by the stars in heaven, but the aviator needs different instruments which will guide him in his journey through the air. It is not enough for him to know the order of the stars. Similarly in modern life, which, compared to the lives of our ancestors, is like the airplane compared to the sail boat, we need at least (2) guidance and training through a synthesis of two kinds of requirements or demands to which man must be subject and which by their nature contradict one another, such as the tendencies to community and to isolation, nationalism and cosmopolitanism, the physical and the spiritual, Judaism and assimilationism, etc., and (3) a ranking of all things in terms of their importance or value in having the potential to help us reach our goal in life, as defined by the first two principles.

Problem of Science as a Solution to Our Problems

SATURDAY NIGHT, NOVEMBER 7, 1936

The traditional point of view helped man find his direction and feel at home in the world. The traditional program provided man with certainty as to the nature of happiness and his appointed place. Even if he did not live according to that program, he still believed that through divine grace he would succeed in obtaining the happiness ordained for him.

---

19. Kaplan is referring to William Heard Kilpatrick's *Sourcebook in the Philosophy of Education* (1926). Kilpatrick (1871–1965) was a writer on education. His other books include *Foundations of Method* (1925–1926) and *Group Education for a Democracy* (1940).

20. On each Sabbath a portion of the Five Books of Moses is read in the synagogue, and the Sabbath here takes its name from the first portion in the book of Genesis. Judith Kaplan, in her diary, comments on the sermon that her father gave on *Bereshit*. The entry was written when she was a teenager and was quite sophisticated, given her age. Her diary is in the possession of Anne Eisenstein.

The traditional world outlook became obsolete for well-known reasons. Can man live without a world outlook? Does he not need a position which will help him find his way? Does he not need a program which will help him reach his destination?

The answer is that man deceived himself by believing that he would arrive at a new world outlook based on the assumption that he would reach his goal in this world if he developed science. He hoped that, through theoretical science, he would reach a position with regard to existence which will have greater authority than the traditional outlook, and that, through applied science, he will attain new powers which will enable him to find his happiness in this world. But what are the facts? Theoretical science is now in such a tangled state that the experts themselves are confused about the very foundations of their knowledge. And applied science, from which we anticipated such great things, it too has disappointed us. What great things [did we anticipate]? (1) The increase of wealth through technological inventions, (2) providing peace and rest to the masses of humanity, so that they can reach a higher level of living, and (3) the providing of information which will help attain social, political, economic, or educational goals.

The disappointment in all three hopes is well known.

For these reasons there are many who think of science as a false messiah. In my opinion, science is not a false messiah. Science itself needs a true messiah. A true messiah means a modern world view which essentially identifies with the traditional one but which adapts its position in accordance with the basic assumptions of science. This means that its foundation is the unity of the universe, the unity of the human species, and man's yearning for eternity. And for its program of perfecting the soul (salvation), it must have a modern world outlook differentiated in actuality from the traditional view, in that, instead of the helplessness which was the foundation of faith in the past, the manifold powers which practical science affords will serve [his needs]. In the light of this, how great is the folly of those who hold the opinion that religion must not interfere in social problems but must limit itself to *spiritual* matters!

The Meaning of Religious Experience

SATURDAY NIGHT, NOVEMBER 14, 1936

The subject of my talk today (Shabbat) was "What Is the Meaning of Reality in Our Concept of God?" This is the Hebrew version of the question in English: What is the meaning of religious experience? A literal translation says nothing to anyone who is not familiar with the English terminology. For example, how distant is the expression *nissayon dati* from the precise meaning of "religious experience"! I prefer, therefore, to translate the subject of the talk freely.

Primitive man had a sense of reality in his awareness of God because he identified objects or certain living creatures as gods. When man developed, he ceased identifying common objects as gods and attributed to the divinity only the matters of his intellect or imagination. If it is really correct to attribute to divinity such a revelation is doubtful, even though a scholar like William James assumed that it was proper to do so. But many people who believe in the reality of God need to fortify this faith by the feeling of reality which flows not from the senses or the imagination but from intellectual conclusions. There are two types of conclusions upon which most people base their faith in God. One includes reactions of fear (from the point of view of feeling) to decrees which may not be questioned (from the point of view of will and lack of knowledge, from the point of view of the intellect). Those whose tendency is to react to the phenomena of life in these ways mostly do not connect their religion with their interpersonal relations and are therefore bound to be corrupt in their moral qualities. To the second group of conclusions belong reactions to the phenomena of life which identify divinity with all that inspires confidence ("The Lord is for me, I have no fear"), with the best moral qualities ("Just as He is merciful, so be you merciful") and with the power of reason ("He who teaches man knowledge").

Kaplan Thinks of Dedicating His Book to JTS

MONDAY, NOVEMBER 16, 1936

This evening there was a social gathering of the students of the Teachers Institute with [Cyrus] Adler and the faculty. There was no formal program and even the few words Adler customarily delivers at these meetings were not spoken. After we entered the dining room to partake of sandwiches and drinks, I said to Adler that I had a suggestion to make to him. We sat at the table alone, and I asked him if he would be comfortable were I to dedicate my forthcoming book on the concept of God [*The Meaning of Modern Jewish Religion*] to the Jewish Theological Seminary in honor of its 50th anniversary. He could not give me an immediate answer because I revealed to him that I was concerned that the book, because of its ideas, would stir up attacks on the institution.

A Sermon on the World in the Making

SATURDAY NIGHT, NOVEMBER 21, 1936

My sermon this morning was very successful. Its subject was "The World in the Making." I set optimism and pessimism opposite each other as I proved that the first basis is the confidence that the situation of man is gradually improving, and that the second basis is the view of Koheleth [Ecclesiastes] that there is nothing new under the sun. The Jewish tradition is the first expression; the Greek tradition, the second expression. Jewish tradition tells of the creation of the universe with the condition that man will complete it by adding the extra measure of his own that he is obligated to give. With the power of choice that has been given to him, he could either add to the world or destroy it, and he has chosen to destroy it. Therefore God has found it necessary to repair the world which man has destroyed and to encourage the individuals who have walked in his way to make up the loss which has been caused by other people. However, in the end man will not succeed in repairing the world, and it becomes the obligation of God to restore to it the completeness which he impressed upon it at the beginning of creation. That is the new earth and the new heavens which will comprise the world to come. In the meantime, the mystics tried to fathom the depths of the universe and to perfect it to a certain degree without waiting for the end. The summation of all the theories and struggles which flow from the spirit of Judaism is that the world is not a definite, fixed entity and can be changed either for better or for worse.

Opposite this is the development of ideas whose source is Greek tradition. It has emphasized the rule of fate, an emphasis better recognized than all the developments that have flowed from it. In philosophy the belief in fate clothed itself in the form of the belief in the connection of cause and effect. After this, Greek culture emphasized the function of nature, a function that cannot be changed. During the centuries which followed, there grew the belief in astrology. At the dawn of the modern period began the reign of science. In the 18th century Newton gave the concept of cosmos the shape of a machine, all of whose parts, which represent the laws of nature, are fixed. In our time, this view has found expression in all aspects of life, in art, in economics, etc., etc.

In my opinion, only by a synthesis of the two extremes can we deal properly with existence. Such a synthetic view is meliorism. In order to understand it, we must know the events in the realm of science in the past generation. These teach us that the scientific illusion that the universe is eternally fixed is progressively weakening. The system of Bergson[21] is more correct with regard to the laws of nature. They are the very factors which are undermining the assumption that there is nothing new under the sun. For my part, I add the fact that in the multiplicity of changes and combinations lie possibilities which negate the fixity of the world and introduce numberless innovations. We see this particularly in chemistry, with the great power of the catalyst. I compare to the physical catalyst the grasp and understanding of man, through which he is liberated from the forces which control him, not, of course, that he nullifies their function, but that he uses their functions to reach his own destination.

The conclusion is that the future is not fixed. The world is in a state of "If." This is meliorism, if man prepares to extract the good from all that happens. He must repair the world, for if he does not, he will destroy it.

---

21. Henri Bergson was a well-known philosopher of the interwar years. His book *Creative Evolution* had a strong influence on Kaplan.

The Invitation from Hebrew University

TUESDAY, DECEMBER 29, 1936

Today I received a response from Dr. Dushkin. It seems that the committee for the appointment of a professor of education is ready to submit my name, but on the condition that I agree to teach the course for at least two years and not one, as I had proposed to Dr. Dushkin in my earlier letter.

THURSDAY, DECEMBER 31, 1936

Yesterday I told Dr. Adler about the letter I had received from Dr. Dushkin, in order to ascertain if the Trustees of the Seminary will permit me to be on leave from my position for two years. At first he minimized the value of the position at the Hebrew University and also tried to prove that the promise of [Judah L.] Magnes is not so reliable because his colleagues on the faculty are trying to wrest away from him his control of the University. When I told him (Adler) that not only Magnes but the entire committee for the appointment of a Professor of the Principles of Education are unanimous with regard to me, he tried by other arguments to diminish the position in my eyes. Finally, however, he admitted that, with all the changes in the political situation which are due to come, the University is the only institution which has a secure future.

The Limitations of the Talmudic Rabbis

THURSDAY, DECEMBER 31, 1936

In the afternoon I listened to lectures held before the Bible Society. Professor [Erwin R.] Goodenough[22] proved that, despite the objections of the *Tannaim* and *Amoraim* [early Talmudic rabbis] to art and sculpture, there are to be found in synagogues and on tombs [in that period] survivals of art and sculpture. From this he drew the conclusion that the sages lived their lives separated from the masses. If his conclusion is correct, then the Talmud does not reflect at all the lives of the masses in those generations. The lecturer based himself on the contents of the Talmudic passage *Avodah Zarah* [Talmudic tractate dealing generally with idolatry], ch. 3. The reason for my being present at the meeting of the Bible Society was the participation of Dr. [Louis] Ginzberg in the lectures. He lectured on the influence of Greek culture upon the sages of the Talmud. According to his remarks, the talmudic sages were innocent of any Greek influence. Both papers support my assumption that the talmudic sages were in general limited in reason and imagination.

---

22. Erwin Ramsdell Goodenough (1893–1965) was born in Brooklyn, New York, and was a scholar of Jewish philosophy and art of the Hellenistic period. He is the author of *Jewish Symbols in the Greco-Roman Period* (1953–1958).

Education and Philosophy

SATURDAY NIGHT, JANUARY 16, 1937

This year a change was introduced into the curriculum of Columbia University, which sheds light on the problem of education. In recent years the University has demanded that all students in the freshman and sophomore years take the course which offers a general survey of the state of world civilization. Now they have added another requirement: a course in the human culture of the world (anthropology). It seems that [educators] have begun to feel that the students are boors in their knowledge of the literary culture of the ancients and the moderns and prefer scientific studies, apart from their practical value.

From this it is clear that one must divide the subject matter into two parts: (1) cultural studies and (2) scientific studies. The second category is further divided into (1) natural science and (2) the science of human life. Prior to the modern period education dealt only with the student of culture. At the beginning of the modern period educators began to pay attention also to scientific studies. Now attention is being paid to the study of human life. In the meantime, the interest in culture has receded, primarily because its contents reflect the living conditions and the state of knowledge of ancient times.

SUNDAY, JANUARY 17, 1937

I believe that the main function of philosophy at this time is to emphasize the two-sidedness or polarity of everything in existence and existence itself. With regard to the latter, this concept is distinguished from the one which expressed itself in dualism, or [the belief in] two gods. According to the dualistic system, the relationship of the two sides or poles is one of opposition. However, according to the polarity system, the two sides or poles complement one another. It seems to me that my concept is similar to the dialectical system of Hegel. The system of polarity must of necessity serve as an important solution for many problems in education. Examples of polarity: "Great is study, for it leads to deed" (*TB Kiddushin* 40b) [Talmudic tractate] and "If I am not for myself, who is for me; when I am for myself, what am I?" ["Ethics of the Fathers" [*Pirkei Avot*], 1:14).

How Can Reconstructionism Be Brought into the Community?

THURSDAY, JANUARY 21, 1937

On Tuesday evening I was in Chicago, where I lectured before a large audience in the synagogue Kehilat Anshe Emet where Rabbi Solomon Goldman is the spiritual leader. The topic of my lecture was "Reconstructionism." I spoke for an hour and a half, and there was no time to answer questions from the audience. After the lecture there gathered in [Rabbi] Goldman's home Dr. [Leo] Honor, Judge Fisher, and their wives, and we argued primarily over the importance of the Hebrew language from the point of view of establishing it in the lives of Jews here (in America).

On Tuesday morning, [Rabbi] Goldman, [Rabbi] Felix Levy (the Chairman of the Conference of Reform Rabbis), and Dr. Honor gathered, and we dealt with the question of how to realize the program of Reconstructionism.[23] We agreed that it is not worthwhile to set up a [new] organization for this idea alone but to propagate it within the framework of existing organizations. For this goal it is best to begin with institutions which are Zionistic (in the American understanding) in their scope and are religious in their function. That is, the two rabbinic organizations, the Conservatives and the Reform, and the two associations of religious communities. Instead of coming to these congregations with a complete program, we should spell out for them the flaws and faults in the behavior of communities and also in the situation of the rabbinate, whether from the point of view of [the inadequacy of] preparation or its actions and influence, and we must demonstrate to them that the primary reason for the depressed state of Jewish religious life here lies in the network of community organizations which are really nothing more than clubs made up of the bourgeois class and [thus] are an obstacle to the development of communities broad in scope and activity.

Evaluations of Rabbi Abraham Isaac Kook

THURSDAY, JANUARY 21, 1937

These days I have been reading the small book *Mishnat Ha-Rav* (The Teachings of the Teacher). With regard to Rav Kook, of blessed memory, too, I have changed my opinion positively because I found in the book fresh and original thoughts, even though they are not really new in the world of ideas. Only at the end of the book, where there is a pronounced similarity of ideas to those of Judah Halevy, both with regard to the sacrifices and the people of Israel, I could not endure the reversion to views which perhaps had their place a thousand years ago but which in the twentieth century cannot be defended.

Kook Sounds Like Kaplan to Kaplan

SUNDAY, JANUARY 24, 1937

The subject of my sermon today was the system of Rabbi Abraham Isaac Kook, of blessed memory. I based my sermon on the contents of his small book, *Mishnat Ha-Rav*. I emphasized that, though the main discussion of his book is divinity, he never defines it in itself but notes the human tendency to yearn for God. What he does is to identify as a yearning for God the desire for and

---

23. Kaplan uses here his own Hebrew coinage *mechadshanut* (renewal).

aspiration to completeness or to actualize the possibilities which are unique to the human species as against the rest of creation. Such an approach to the problem of faith in God is humanistic, not religious or psychological. I also laid emphasis upon Rav Kook's attitude to the matter of disbelief, for which he finds "a legitimate right to survive temporarily." In general there is much in his system on divinity which so resembles what I have written in my book on God (*The Meaning of God in Modern Jewish Civilization*) [*The Meaning of God in Modern Jewish Religion* was the final title] that it was easy for me to penetrate into the depths of his thoughts in this matter.

The Advantage of Yiddish

THURSDAY, MARCH 11, 1937

Last night I spoke to the Women's Division of the Society for the Advancement of Judaism. Some men were also present. I suggested that they learn Yiddish. All attempts to learn Hebrew end in naught because of the difficulties bound up with the Hebrew language. As against this, if they would be learning Yiddish, they would experience success in their studies and would be bound to their people with meaningful bonds. As of now, all spiritual ties are progressively growing weaker.

Tension in the Seminary

WEDNESDAY, MARCH 24, 1937

After the meeting of the faculty of the Seminary, I showed Adler the letter of invitation which I received from Schocken[24] (an invitation to be a visiting member of the faculty of the Hebrew University), and I asked him to advise me what to answer. His response was that the meeting of the Board of Trustees will take place on the 7th of April, and even though he will recommend that they give me a leave of absence, he does not have the authority to grant this permission by himself. I knew this from the start, but I wanted to see his reaction to my receiving the letter of invitation. This is the third time that I have spoken to him on the subject of my going up to Eretz Yisrael [Kaplan used the term *aliyah*], and each time he repeated the same things about the situation there, which he painted almost entirely in black. However, the atmosphere of the Seminary oppresses me so much—specifically, the lack of friendship from my colleagues and the attitude of contempt that they take toward my ideas and books, depriving me of so much of my peace of mind—that the dangers which lurk in Eretz Yisrael do not frighten me.

---

24. Zalman Schocken, the rector at Hebrew University at the time. See the fine biography by Anthony David, *The Patron: A Life of Salman Schocken, 1877–1959* (New York: Henry Holt, 2003).

Louis Ginzberg, Louis Finkelstein, and Robert Gordis

SUNDAY, MAY 30, 1937

On the 20th of May (Thursday) Gordis visited me. The purpose of the visit, it seems, was to follow up on the idea of Finkelstein to seek out the friendship of the Seminary faculty. Gordis himself mentioned this idea in his remarks. Finkelstein had suggested this to him so that Ginzberg would not be an obstacle to him. Three years ago an article by Gordis appeared in the *Jewish Quarterly Review*. Ginzberg criticized the article, particularly its attitude to tradition. Gordis responded. Though he (Gordis) certainly did not insult him in any way, Ginzberg would not forgive him for attempting to respond, according to Finkelstein. Gordis should have kept silent and accepted Ginzberg's rebuke in love.

I used this opportunity to chastise him (Gordis) for his custom of identifying my approach to Judaism with Conservative Judaism. But he is an unmatched sophist and you cannot grasp him in your hand. Alas that such a talent like him nullifies, through his quality of misrepresentation, the good that he could continue to do for Judaism in America.

Individual and Collective Despair: A Binational Plan for Palestine

SATURDAY NIGHT, AUGUST 7, 1937

Though I can single out one or two accomplishments during the last weeks — such as the completion of reading the two translations of my book [*The Meaning of God in Modern Jewish Religion*], the Hebrew and the Yiddish — my heart within me is broken by the world's pain in general and the pain of my wretched people specifically. A few weeks ago I was called upon to eulogize a young woman, 26 years old, and tomorrow, again, I must eulogize a young woman who died from wounds received when the flame she used to light the gas burst forth upon her. Tragedies such as these crush my spirit and wreck the world of faith which I am trying to construct for myself and others. And as for the proposal of the Royal Commission for the partition of Palestine, what shall I say and what shall I speak?[25] The entire matter emphasizes in a painful way our position in the world: on the outside the hatred of the Gentiles brings bereavement, and alienation of hearts causes it from within. Who knows what our end will be?

I am very fearful of the attempt to establish an independent Jewish state. If I had any influence, I would recommend that the Jews propose to the Arabs

---

25. The proposal Kaplan refers to is the Peel Commission Report (July 1937). The Royal Commission recommended partition because the Mandate had become unworkable as a consequence of the hostilities between Jews and Arabs. Jewish leadership accepted the plan in principle, but Arab leadership rejected it.

that they participate equally in the government and that the population [of Jews] be permanently adjusted to the number of Arabs in the country.

Departure for Palestine — Last Minute Thoughts

THURSDAY, SEPTEMBER 9, 1937

I am now sitting on the deck of the ship *Excalibur*, which I boarded with my wife and my daughter Naomi on Tuesday of last week. All summer I worked almost without stop on the preparation of courses that I must give at the [Hebrew] University: the course on the history of education and the one on the fundamentals of education. The only disturbances, aside from the disturbing ones which I mentioned in the list above, were the dismantling of the apartment so that it could be repaired and repainted for the next tenant and the packing of my books for transfer to Palestine or to my office in the Seminary.

Two events took place, which are worthy of mention: one, a discussion I had with Finkelstein in the week before I left New York. Though the purpose of the conversation was official—that is, that he could obtain my agreement to his filling my place in the administration of the Teachers Institute—we spoke, one to the other, with complete openness, in a manner which had become unusual for us for a long time. He admitted to me that Judaism in America cannot survive if it does not adapt itself to the needs of modern life and that the time has come that something be done for its survival. But what? He stopped at this point and did not add one new item over what he had suggested to me several times in our conversations in past years. Now that I am trying to summarize the outcomes of our conversation, it seems to me that at least the wall of frost that had stood between us during the last two years has melted and the relationship between us is on the level of *status quo ante*. I am happy that we parted from one another with feelings of friendship. The second event was the party my friends, the Society for the Advancement of Judaism, held in my honor on Tuesday, August 24, in the hall of the Savoy Plaza. The initiator of the party was Mr. Albert Rosenblatt. At first I was opposed to it, but finally I made peace with it, and after it was over, I was very pleased that I had parted from my friends with a suitable ceremony and did not sneak away from them in secret.

On the Ship — Talking of the Chief Rabbi Herzog

MONDAY, SEPTEMBER 27, 1937

After the ship left Marseilles, a Mr. Beck introduced himself to me. He was a banker in Brooklyn, the President of Public Bank. He settled in Palestine six or five years ago and lives in Haifa. In one of our conversations he told me about Chief Rabbi [Isaac] Herzog. He told me that at the time the Royal Commission was busy hearing testimony about the situation, Rabbi Herzog committed a great folly. This was in connection with the testimony of the Mufti,[26] who was so extreme in his objection to Jewish settlement that the Chairman of the Committee, Lord Peel, became so disgusted with him that he could not conceal his contempt. One of the claims of the Mufti was that the Jews are plotting to capture the holy places sacred to the Moslems. The absurdity of his claim did much to alienate him from the members of the Commission. What did Rabbi Herzog do? A day or two after the Mufti testified before the Commission, he (Herzog) lectured before his associates, and among the things that he stressed was the hope that not too much time will pass and we will again be able to worship the God of Israel through the offering of sacrifices as in the past. These words appeared in the Anglo-Jewish *Post* and a short while afterward they appeared in an Arabic newspaper in which the writer demanded that Herzog clarify his remarks. Not only did his folly consist of bringing up the matter of sacrifices at such a dangerous time as this, but he added folly to his folly by not making use of this opportunity to save himself from his error but instead by answering in such a manner as to give an opening to our enemies, when he said that those present at his lecture knew what he was referring to. This is the political wisdom and expertise of the person who stands at the head of the Hebrew community. I learned also from a man other than Beck . . . whom I met in the Telsh Hotel in Haifa, that Herzog is of limited stature in his entire grasp of his role and opportunities as Chief Rabbi.

From the fall of 1937 to the summer of 1939 Kaplan was in Jerusalem teaching at the Hebrew University. During this period he wrote in his diary (Volume 8) in Hebrew. The Hebrew portions of the diary have been translated and edited by Rabbi Nahum Waldman, z"l, who passed away in 2004. The Hebrew portions are not a translation of the whole diary but are only selections. The notes for this section were written by Rabbi Waldman.

Moral Problems in Palestine

WEDNESDAY, OCTOBER 6, 1937

In the meantime some details relating to my positions have become known to me. Most of my work, it seems, will not consist of preparing lectures

---

26. The mufti at the time was Haj Amin al-Husseini (1893–1974), a militant Arab nationalist who was appointed mufti (religious leader) in 1921 by the High Commissioner Sir Herbert Samuel. Husseini inspired the anti-Jewish riots of 1920, 1929, and 1936. In 1937 he was exiled by the British to Damascus, and in 1940 he moved to Iraq, where he collaborated with the Nazis in the carrying out of a pro-German coup.

but in building a network of relationships around the Department of Education which will be effective in improving the situation of education in general. And there is no aspect of education in Palestine which demands greater improvement than the moral one, which is in a very bad state. A few weeks before I arrived, a scandal took place. Right before the final examinations all the test papers of the graduating classes of the high schools were stolen, and the robbery was not a mere robbery — it was organized like the American rackets, with cars and pistols and gangsters. Everything according to the rules. There were students who paid ten pounds for examination papers. When the "scandal" became known, there were public meetings and court sessions, and it was ordained that no graduate of this class would receive a diploma. This frightening story was told to me by Prof. [Hugo] Bergman and repeated by [Alexander] Dushkin. Even though these details give a dim picture of what happened, there is still enough in them to demonstrate how the members of our people have degenerated in their moral qualities. Our land cannot be built with human material such as this.

Kaplan Gives His Inaugural Speech at the Hebrew University

Sunday, October 24, 1937

On Wednesday of last week (October 20), the University [program] was opened in a festive ceremony in the reading room of the library. Speeches were given by [Judah] Magnes, [Zalman] Schocken, and [Samuel Hugo] Bergman. All who were connected with the faculty sat on the stage in a semi-circular arrangement (literally, the Talmudic "a round half-threshing floor"). I sat on the extreme right, and next to me sat [Samuel] Klein,[27] and next to him, [Joseph] Klausner. One half of the audience was made up of men and women interested in the University, and the students made up the other half. Magnes, as is his custom, preached for recognition of the fact that what is being created here is not merely a Hebrew culture but a Semitic one. I was amazed at his bravery. Based on the program, there were many who feared that a demonstration against him would take place, but, thank God, everything was peaceful. My lecture on the development of the educational process lasted a full hour. Because of the abundance of material in it, I was forced to read it at a fast pace. This made comprehension difficult for the listeners, but the lecture made a good impression and was received with cheerful faces.[28] After the ceremony we gathered in the social

---

27. Samuel Klein (1886–1940) was a historian and geographer of Eretz Yisrael.

28. Kaplan's inaugural lecture was published by the Hebrew University. It was given in Hebrew, and the published version has both a Hebrew and an English title. The English title is *The Evolution of the Educative Process* (Jerusalem: Hebrew University Press, 1937).

hall of the University to celebrate Magnes's sixtieth birthday. Schocken spoke again, this time to inform the public that a section of the University campus has been dedicated to "Judah." Bergman also spoke and presented Magnes with a collection of articles written by members of the Faculty of Liberal Arts and the Faculty of Science. Magnes responded to their greetings. Everything proceeded with feelings of exaltation.

Reaction to a Terrorist Murder

TUESDAY, NOVEMBER 9, 1937

A few minutes ago I was informed of the murder of five young men [by Arab terrorists]. Mrs. Dushkin, who had been a patient in Hadassah Hospital in the morning when their bodies were brought in, was the one who brought me this shocking piece of news. She told me that the murderers were not satisfied to kill them with shots but also mutilated their bodies. Magnes came to the funeral and remarked to Mrs. Dushkin that our leaders will exploit this event too, to stir up our feelings of patriotism and fortify the developing anti-compromise position. On the other hand, Dr. [Hayyim] Yassky, director of the hospital, remarked to her, how does Magnes dare to show his face at this kind of funeral?

More on Terrorism

SUNDAY, NOVEMBER 14, 1937

Today was another day or horror. While I was showering in the morning at 6:30, I heard three shots and immediately bitter outcries and the call "Police." When I came out for my post-breakfast walk, I saw a group of workers on the new house belonging to the Jew who, like me, lives on Talbieyeh Street talking together. I asked them what happened, and they told me that two Arabs were shot in the Rehaviah neighborhood; one died and the other is badly wounded. When, in the course of my walk, I reached bus line no. 9, I learned that in the Bet Yisrael neighborhood on the way to the University there was a clash between Jews and Arabs and four Arabs were shot. I was to lecture that day at the University, but my neighbor, Mrs. Feigenbaum, said that the entire city was in uproar and she advised me to stay home, and she herself called the University to tell them that I was not coming. The excuse she used was that Lena was sick and that I could not leave her.

SUNDAY, DECEMBER 5, 1937

Actually, Lena was sick all of last week with something which could have turned into an emergency. Her nose and face swelled up because of some toxin that spread under her skin, she had pains in her mouth, and her temperature was continuously unstable.

The Influence of Eliezer Ben-Yehuda

WEDNESDAY, DECEMBER 8, 1937

Today I heard a lecture delivered by [Joseph] Klausner at the faculty club of the University on Eliezer Ben-Yehudah.[29] I was disturbed by the memorializing of the day of his death [which occurred] fifteen years ago. I confess that I do not understand the genius of Eliezer Ben-Yehuda any more than I understand the musical genius of Beethoven. How was it possible for Ben-Yehuda to have hoped that our people would return to this land and revive its culture and language when not one of the leaders of the national revival . . . believed in this possibility? How is it possible for a human being to be so devoted to an ideal which everyone thinks to be impossible? There is no doubt that it was not just his stubbornness which had the power to revive the Hebrew language, and he certainly did not rely upon a miracle from heaven to create the conditions necessary for revival. On the basis of what signs in his time did he conclude that the Jews would have to return to the land, and on the basis of what political teaching did he believe the gates of the land would be opened for them? It is hard to deny the influence of personality forces upon human history when we consider personalities such as Ben-Yehuda.

The Need for a Think Tank of Ethics

TUESDAY, MARCH 8, 1938

The book *Beyond Conscience* by T. V. Smith has made a shocking impression on me. I have not finished it, but in the part I have read, especially the chapter "The Idealistic Implementation," it seems to me that it is directed against the thrust of my thinking in *The Meaning of God* and especially against my assumptions in the chapter "God as the Power That Makes for Righteousness." Alas that in matters of morality and human relations [the conditions for] scholars and researchers [to] work together on these problems upon which the future of humanity depends do not exist as they do in the natural sciences. If only it could be possible for me to organize a small group of people who are concerned with these problems and who would be able to devote a number of hours a week to researching them. The first step: to prepare a bibliography of books that really have something to contribute to the clarification of the questions. The second: to work up a program for reading these books and the writing of abstracts and critiques. The third: to lay the foundation for a consistent and comprehensive method [to create] a philosophy of life and an ethical path.

---

29. Eliezer Ben-Yehuda (1858–1922) was a writer, journalist, lexicographer, and advocate of the revival of spoken Hebrew. He demonstrated his commitment by his strict rule to speak only Hebrew to his family, by his word-creation efforts in the *Academy of the Hebrew Language*, and in his compilation of the monumental *Dictionary of the Hebrew Language*.

The Crises of the Day

WEDNESDAY, DECEMBER 8, 1937

Out of a fascinating discussion which we had in our house last night . . . , I came to the conclusion that (a) in order not to despair and to find value in life, a person must either create values or help others live and (b) neither the creation of values nor the will to be helpful is enough to improve human life at all if the values created or that which is beneficial is not measured against the criterion of the well-being of the group, such as the greatest benefit for the greatest number of people.

The background of the aforementioned discussion is the darkening of the world through the victory of Hitler in his joining of Austria to Germany, with none of the governments [of the West] making a peep or a chirp, and the defeat of all the hopes which people placed in Russia, which is now executing the great revolutionaries who made Russian revival possible. Besides this, in China and Spain people are being killed by the hundreds and thousands by airplanes which drop death bombs upon cities and their inhabitants who are taking part in the war. Treaties and covenants are not worth the paper they are written on. The whole world seems ready to explode within moments.

Judah Magnes on Moral Cowardice

WEDNESDAY, MARCH 23, 1938

Today Lena and I visited Magnes and his wife. In his conversation he described well the inner situation in Eretz Yisrael. The discussion meandered over to the question of why one does not see any signs of reaction to the horrors which are developing in Europe and China and especially with respect to the Jews. In his response he demonstrated to what extent people are afraid to express their feelings out of the fear that such expression is bound to bring calamity to the Jews here and in all places. He cited some examples: He was opposed to the transfer [of population], but he could not protest against it because through it, it became possible for thousands of Jews to strike roots here. In Haifa there was an exhibit on behalf of Republican Spain, and when they wanted to move it to Tel Aviv, the government forbade it because it included a caricature of Mussolini. Here in Jerusalem, too, it is forbidden to display this exhibit. A few days ago Prof. [Frederick] Bodenheimer came to him holding in his hand a telegram he had received from a professor in Spain, who asked that he make contact with influential people who will protest against the barbarism committed by Franco in Barcelona. Magnes was willing to send a telegram of support to Barcelona, but Bodenheimer remarked that there is danger in this: if Barcelona falls into Franco's hands, this telegram in the name of the Hebrew University will be discovered and another pretext will be found for pouring out wrath upon the Jews. On the basis of facts such as these, Magnes reached the conclusion that, in contrast with the opportunity in a city like New York to join with people who are interested in the human and ethical side of current life and to demonstrate against violence and barbarism, we here are deprived of the freedom to express our protest against the evil that is being done in the world. We lack ethical freedom, and the reason is that we are placed in a situation of threat on all sides; on the one side, the government (which imprisoned a number of guiltless Revisionists in Akko, and only because it had imprisoned a number of Arabs); on another side the [political] parties; and yet on another, the rabbinate. Still, he [Magnes] found it necessary to demonstrate that the situation with regard to parties, for which he lays the blame on the European environment in that they do not know how to value properly the value of the minority, has improved. And to my question, "What is the reason for the improvement of the situation in this aspect?" he responded, "Because each party has learned from experience to be one of the pursued, and, especially, what is happening in Europe has served as an instructive example of what the results of party strife are."

A Frustrating First Meeting with Martin Buber

TUESDAY, APRIL 12, 1938

Yesterday I visited Martin Buber. He was appointed Professor of Philosophy of Society at the same time that I was appointed to teach education. For a time he was the candidate for the teaching of education, but it seems there was opposition to him on the part of [Israel Jacob] Kligler and Dushkin and also on the part of Shubow[30] and others because of the mystical line in his approach to Judaism. Still, it was impossible that they not find a place for him in the University, as he is one of the greats of our generation, even if it is not so easy to fit him into the framework of our familiar values.

I must admit that I was somewhat disappointed with my meeting with him yesterday, which was the first. In our conversation it fell upon me to be the stimulus, while he was simply reacting to my questions and comments. The discussion moved to the idea he expressed in the book that was translated into English as *I and Thou*.[31] It seemed to me that what he is striving to express—be it in a deep manner—with regard to the relationship of one human to another is the same idea which Whitehead expresses in his book *Science and the Modern Mind*, when he says, "The concrete enduring entities are organisms, so that the plan of the whole influences the very characters of the various subordinate organisms which enter into it." But all of this is theoretical: he has in effect never documented the possibilities between the *I* and the *Thou* with respect to our own

---

30. I have been unable to determine who Shubow is.

31. The earliest edition of Buber's work in English is Martin Buber, *I and Thou*, trans. Ronald Gregor Smith (Edinburgh: T. and T. Clark, 1937).

discussion. He did not ask me one question with regard to my views, my goals, my work. The attainment of practical results is, it seems, a simple matter that only cheap pragmatists like me demand. The matters of mystery do not need such pragmatism.

Circumcision—A Primitive Rite

SATURDAY NIGHT, APRIL 30, 1938

Last Thursday I was present at a *brit-milah* [circumcision] which took place at the Hadassah Hospital. The father of the baby, Elkus, is a graduate of the university and one of my students here. The invitation was for 8:30 a.m. When I arrived with Dushkin, I already found Prof. [Joseph] Klausner and his wife. We waited for over an hour until the *mohel* [the person who performs the circumcision] arrived. In the meantime two or three circumcisions took place in the small house by the gate. It seems these were Sephardic families, and when the ceremony was finished, we heard a kind of long whistling to signify the end of the ceremony.

In the room where the infant was to be circumcised there was a holy ark, a Chair of Elijah, and a long bench. The people who crowded into the room were mainly people with long beards, dressed in dirty clothing, and among them circulated some who were asking for alms. A boy of thirteen, with long *pe'ot* [earlocks], wearing a long coat which reached down to below his knees, whose eyes were infected by disease, was also one of those circulating. Finally, when the ceremony began, it was announced that Klausner would be the *kfater* [godfather]. I was given the honor of being *sandek* [the one who holds the baby during the circumcision]. The child was placed in my lap, and around me stood all these people, whom, from a sanitary point of view, it seems to me, the director-ship of the hospital should never permit. But all this is nothing against the primi-tivism of cutting the foreskin. All the participants in the ceremony were wrapped in filthy *tallitot* [prayer shawls], and the *mohel*, after he cut the foreskin, put the organ in his mouth and sucked the blood. I do not understand how they permit such a barbarian ritual which suits the wild tribes of Central Africa.

The Implications of "Nevertheless"

FRIDAY, MAY 13, 1938

Because of the debate of the students in the course on the principles of education, I have come to the decision to write about Judaism from the point of view of "nevertheless."

Therefore it will be good to begin the first chapter with the Talmud's suggestion concerning a non-Jew who comes to convert. We demonstrate to him that it is very hard to be a Jew, but if he says, "Nevertheless," we convert him.

After that it would be appropriate to quote from what Bertrand Russell said in his article on the free worship of truth and with regard to an attitude to the world, which parallels what is demanded of the convert. When we analyze this attitude, we see that, just as a person must create an artificial environment in order to survive, so we must create an artificial world of thought. The artificial environment is not totally in opposition to the natural environment. It is a unique juncture of factors and forces, the same forces and factors that make up a part of nature; if not for this, the juncture could not exist. The hut that the primitive builds and the fire that he is warmed by and on which he roasts his meat constitute an artificial environment that he needs to protect himself from the forces which rule outside of it, but nevertheless they are the same elements bound to the same forces. Thus man must organize a thought world which is in part derived from reality and is in part in opposition to it. Correspondingly, the Jewish people must create its own world of action and thought, which in part is derived from the best in the human environment and which in part deliberately defends itself against it. Through anti-Semitism the nations show themselves ready to destroy us, but if we want to survive, we must do what man does when he considers the wild forces threatening to destroy him. He does not allow those wild forces to breathe despair into him or to make him turn his eyes away from the forces which are able to help him. Thus in our relations with the nations we must reveal as much as possible the human inclinations and the seeds of righteousness, uprightness, truth, and beauty, and on these foundations to build our world. Even if a wave comes and sweeps us away, nevertheless, as long as we live, let us live in such a manner as to not be ashamed of ourselves.

Kaplan on His Own Observance

SATURDAY, MAY 21, 1938

I am beginning not to feel my absence from synagogue just as I have ceased feeling the absence of putting on tefillin,[32] and this is because no ritual has been developed that applies to the current situation. Is it a wonder that most of those whose horizons have been expanded see no reason for ritual? They see only one possibility: either the traditional ritual or nothing.

How can I refrain from this writing on Sabbath? In the morning hours my spirit is like an overflowing fountain and my ideas flow in abundance. If I don't write them down, they are lost. Even if from a general point of view they have no value, from the point of view of my own personality, they are all that I have, they are the essence of me, and if I allow them to be forgotten, I lose a part of my personality. . . . (By the way, it is possible to draw the conclusion that a

---

32. Tefillin, also called phylacteries, are a set of small leather boxes worn by observant Jews during weekday morning prayers. They contain verses from the Scriptures.

change in environment causes the forgetting of ideas. Therefore we swiftly forget what we dreamt in our sleep.)

The Thoughts of Jessie Sampter

MONDAY, JUNE 6, 1938

On Friday we traveled to the convalescent home at Givat Brenner, and we spent the Sabbath and Shavuot, which came yesterday. There resides Ms. Jessie Sampter, who counts me as one of the influences upon her. In her childhood, until her seventh year, she was educated in a non-Jewish spirit and did not even know that she was Jewish. Afterward, she came under the influence of the Ethical Culture Society, founded by Felix Adler.[33] For reasons unknown to me, she came in contact with Ms. [Henrietta] Szold and became a Zionist. In the years 1914–1915 she studied privately with me. At that time she became interested in my writings. Clearly, her being in Eretz Yisrael has changed her perspective on the problems of the survival of Judaism in the Diaspora, but she began to feel that she is moving away from ideas. But now that I have come to Eretz Yisrael and am trying to adapt to the conditions here the main points of my approach in the past, she is putting her hopes on me that I will be able to stimulate the youth to a positive attitude toward tradition from a scientific point of view. My discussions with her interested me greatly. I marveled at her Hebrew poems and especially over her thoughts, expressed in fragments over various matters. She gave me The Discussions of Krishnamurti,[34] which I read with great pleasure. Even though I do not agree with all his thoughts, he directed my mind to the practical side, which I tend to overlook.

I recited the Kiddush for the Sabbath and the festival before the evening meals. I had in mind to say in the Festival Kiddush "Who has sent us prophets of truth and bestowed upon us lofty aspirations" in place of "who has chosen us, etc.," but after reading The Discussions of Krishnamurti, I became convinced that it is not right to glory in ideals. I phrased the beginning of the blessing thus: "who redeems us from slavery and makes us rejoice in His salvation."

The Ultra-Religious vs. the Scholars

SATURDAY NIGHT, JUNE 11, 1938

The degree to which we can look forward to a Kulturkampf [cultural war] was demonstrated by a small incident that took place in the Jeshurun Synagogue.

33. On Kaplan and the Ethical Culture Society and Felix Adler, see Scult, Judaism Faces the Twentieth Century, 79–81; and Mel Scult, The Radical American Judaism of Mordecai M. Kaplan (Bloomington: Indiana University Press, 2013), 66–87. Felix Adler was a major influence on Kaplan when Kaplan was a graduate student at Columbia. Adler's universalism was deeply appealing to Kaplan as well as to Henrietta Szold and Jessy Sampter.

34. Jiddu Krishnamurti (1895–1986) was a well-known speaker and writer on spiritual and philosophical subjects.

On the Sabbath before Shavuot, Prof. Joseph Klausner lectured on the Scroll of Ruth. Immediately upon his expressing his opinion about the time in which it was written and stating that he does not accept the opinion of the Gemara [Talmud] in *Baba Batra* (14a, that the Prophet Samuel wrote Ruth), there was a stir among a number of Yeshivah *bahurim* [young Orthodox men] who had come to hear the lecture, and one of them rose, ascended the platform, and began rebuking Klausner for the heresy in his lecture. There were also some rabbis present, among them Rabbi Berman (who is in charge of Mizrachi education and is considered a sort of rabbi for the Jeshurun congregation), who joined the protesters and demonstrated against Klausner by leaving the synagogue. A few days later a letter was received from Chief Rabbi Herzog, chastising the congregants for allowing such lectures. I was told that Levanon, the chairman of the congregation, tried to effect a compromise between Klausner and his opponents by saying that the heresy in Klausner's remarks on Ruth is not so serious, although he is opposed to it, and he argued with Klausner. Klausner continued his lecture to the end.

Kaplan and Buber Talk about God

SATURDAY NIGHT, JULY 9, 1938

Yesterday morning at 10:30 a.m. a meeting of the Faculty Senate took place. As I waited for the bus on Talbieh Street, which would take me to the bus that goes to the University, Buber came up. This time I decided not to be the one who begins the conversation, as I have been on all the occasions I have met him. He has never asked me anything about myself, and I had to goad him into a conversation. The events of the preceding days have upset me so much that they left me no initiative to pull the tongue of anyone, even Buber. But after two or three minutes he began by saying that these days he is reading my book, *The Meaning of God in Modern Jewish Religion.* In the meanwhile the bus came, and from that moment on, throughout our ride on both buses, we conversed about the idea of God in my book. He expressed his objection to my approach and said that my god is not a god, because he is entirely immanent. The God of the simple Polish Jew is the God of Israel and the God of the universe. I tried to show him that I devote an entire chapter to the idea that God is a force outside ourselves. He responded that this idea does not appear as central, but I think that he has not yet gotten to that chapter in my book.

He promised me that he would write a review of my book in the form of a letter addressed to me. I cannot say that we thoroughly enjoyed the conversation, but the fact that, at least, Buber behaved himself humanly, taking into consideration the interests of his colleague, pacified me somewhat.[35]

---

35. Compare this experience with Kaplan's first meeting with Buber in the entry for April 12, 1938.

The Daily News Is Painful

MONDAY, JULY 18, 1938

How awful is the situation in the world, in Eretz Yisrael, in my heart! All my waking moments I am in the shadow of a nightmare. All day I await with eagerness my sleeping hours, although at times they too are disturbed by dreams of terror. At the sound of "The Voice of Jerusalem" over the radio, my heart trembles, and still I cannot refrain from listening. My hands tremble after reading *Davar* and *Ha-Aretz*, but I do not have the strength to restrain myself and not read.

Treachery and Increased Violence

SATURDAY NIGHT, SEPTEMBER 3, 1938

It is very hard for me to live peacefully in this emotional environment. Two events have shaken me to the depths of my being: first, the treacherous act of the leaders of the Jewish community in Iraq, who sent a telegram to the League of Nations in which they attack Zionism and intervene on behalf of their Arab "brothers" whose rights are endangered . . . : "The Jews of Iraq deplore Zionist politics and support their brothers, the Arabs of Palestine, and urge you [the League of Nations] to treat them with justice and to restore peace and tranquility to the Arab Middle East." . . .

The second matter that worries me is the spread of the custom among the Arabs in the last two weeks to wear the *kaffiyeh* and the *aqal*, the Bedouin headdress, in place of the *tarbush*. I believe that this fashion parallels the black shirt of the Fascists or the brown one of the Nazis.

A Yiddish Poem of Hope

FRIDAY, SEPTEMBER 9, 1938

In one of the essays that the students in my course handed in to me, a small poem by Y. L. Peretz[36] is quoted. I mention it here because it hits the mark of the ideas in my book *The Values of Judaism and Their Renewal*:[37]

> Let the world be waste!
> And we,
> We Sabbath-holy,
> We Festival-ready,
> We extra-soul-graced Jews
> Will march over its ruins!

---

36. Yitskhok Leybush Perets (1852–1915), a writer, editor, social critic, and modernist, was one of the masters of modern Yiddish literature. He later turned to Hasidic themes and folk materials.

37. Kaplan's book *The Meaning of God in Modern Jewish Religion* was translated into Hebrew with another title. The title here is a translation of that Hebrew title.

To Go Home or to Stay?

THURSDAY, SEPTEMBER 22, 1938

After I formulated my letter of resignation, I showed it to Dr. Kligler last Friday. In his opinion my resignation at this time is bound to make an unpleasant impression. Only in the event of war, in his opinion, am I permitted to return to America.

Following Kligler's advice, I had an appointment on Sunday with [Solomon] Ginsberg,[38] Administrator of the University. These are days of no (University) administration, and no one in the city is stepping in. I showed him the letter that I intended to send Magnes. First, he told me that, from a practical point of view, the address on the letter is not correct. Since Magnes has been stripped of all administrative authority, with respect to my letter he also has none. Second, he expressed his surprise, because my first decision had been not to remain here after the two years. Third, my resignation would harm the University's Department of Education. I did not attempt to argue with him because I saw that he was right. I must therefore make peace with the necessity of keeping my word. England and France can annul the treaties they established to define Czechoslovakia against attacks from Germany, and I, an individual, must keep my word. That is the way of human beings!

The portion of the diary written in Hebrew stops here.

---

38. Solomon Ginsberg, an associate of Dr. Judah Magnes, the president of the Hebrew University, became the administrator of the university when Magnes was relieved of his administrative authority and "elevated" to the office of president in 1935.

4

November 12, 1938–February 19, 1939

A Typical Jerusalem Night—War and Peace

SATURDAY NIGHT, NOVEMBER 12, 1938

Golden sunset, music, Plato interpreted by his most eminent virtuoso, Jowett, and I sitting solitary in a flat in Jerusalem, having just brought up emergency water which I pumped downstairs from a reserve supply, because the water pipes which were smashed somewhere near Ras el-Ain about a week ago are still unrepaired, I am wondering what sort of a world this is, which can harbor such violent contrasts of good and evil. All this makes my life like that of an extinct volcano, idyllic peace without and seething chaos within. Exactly at 11:00 tonight there was a break in the calm which has prevailed in these parts for some time, and shooting—single shots followed by machine gun firing, like that which marked the weird nights when the Old City was invaded by the bandits—has started again. An end to the idyllic peace!

Kaplan's Shyness

THURSDAY, NOVEMBER 17, 1938

The water supply was resumed last night after an interruption of fully five days.

While the meeting of the Senate yesterday was proceeding, we heard a shot that seemed to come somewhere near the building we were in (Mathematics Institute). The secretary, Dr. Ben-David, then informed us that this was part of the student target practice, which then kept up for some time.

I am at my worst and unhappiest at faculty meetings, apparently because I find it hard to form opinions worth expressing concerning the matters usually discussed at such meetings. I felt that way in all the years I took part in the meetings of the Seminary faculty, and I feel the same way here. The added difficulty of speaking freely in Hebrew is a contributory cause as well.

111

Going Home and Buber on Religion

NOVEMBER 17, 1938

Some time ago I said to Prof. [Samuel] Hugo Bergman that I wanted to see him and talk to him about myself. Yesterday when we met at the University, he suggested that he better come to see me because in his house he is disturbed by telephones. I made the appointment for this afternoon at 4:30. When he came, I told him of my decision to go back to America at the end of this year. He of course had heard about it, and he expressed his regret. I then made the suggestion which I had made also to Dr. Senator some weeks ago at the same time that I told him of my decision, namely, that I be invited to give a series of lectures once every two years during the summer semester, which usually lasts ten weeks after Pesach [Passover]. He as well as Senator thought well of the suggestion.

Bergman then made a remark which took me by surprise. He said that when some weeks ago word got round that I intended to return to America, Buber said to him that it was his (Bergman's) fault that he (Bergman) made no special effort to persuade me to stay.

I then got to talking with Bergman about Buber. I have always been wanting to know what Buber's ideas were about religion and the specific questions of belief, so I thought here was a good opportunity, since Bergman was or is one of his disciples. And this is what I learned: that Buber's outlook has undergone a radical change. Before the war Buber was a pantheistic mystic, but he has since evolved into a dualistic theist. He now holds practically the traditional view of the divine personality as an entity external to the world. I then went on to ask whether Buber believes in the historicity of the miracles recorded in the Bible and in supernatural revelation as external events, and Bergman replied in the affirmative. In answer to my question "How about Jean d'Arc and others like her who claimed they heard voices?" again Bergman said that, according to Buber, in those cases too supernatural events actually took place. Without that, Bergman said, Buber does not believe in the necessity of practical observances.

I can now understand what moved Buber to take strong exception to my ideas about God, which he had read in *The Meaning of God . . .* , as he told me in a casual conversation we had on a bus on the way to the University in the beginning of the summer.[1]

We Must Be Armed Against Fascism

FRIDAY, NOVEMBER 18, 1938

Typical of the atmosphere here these days is the sight of a number of students who came to my house wearing *ghaffir*[2] uniforms and carrying rifles

---

1. The conversation Kaplan is referring to here is recorded in the diary entry for July 9, 1938.
2. Jewish settlement police.

when they had to appear before the committee—Dushkin, Brill, and myself—to be interviewed for admission to the Pedagogy Department of the University. I noted that when those who had had some military training were called into the room where we were sitting from the backroom where they had been asked to wait, they clicked their heels in military fashion.

I think this military training is a wonderful thing for our Jewish youth. If we are to survive in this cruel world, we must have lots of fighting courage. I am referring to those few places in the world where we still have a fighting chance. For the same reason, I believe that it is the duty of democratic countries to arm to the teeth in defense against Fascism and Nazism. Otherwise they are bound to be swamped. So long as the antidemocratic forces were ill-defined, there really was no excuse for democracy to arm. Military preparations could then be employed for one purpose, viz., conquest and imperialism. But when there is no mistake about the aggressive polity of three such powers as Germany, Italy, and Japan and about their intention to act in concert to dominate the world and suppress every vestige of democracy, it is nothing less than criminal negligence to leave democracy defenseless and exposed to their ravages. In fact, they don't even have to go to the trouble of going to war; all they need is to rattle their sabers and the democratic peoples are frightened out of their wits and are ready not only to yield whatever is demanded of them, but even to surrender their democratic institutions and freedom of expression in order to conciliate those who have practically become their masters.

Kaplan and Buber Discuss the Bible

NOVEMBER 19, 1938

This morning I called on Buber. Somehow I couldn't warm up to him in all the time that he has been here since last Pesach. I had expected him to return the visit I paid him at the hotel when he arrived here recently, but he did not show up. Yesterday I received from the University a copy of an article by him on *shmuel ha-navi* [Heb., Samuel the Prophet], which I have read with a great deal of avidity. For once I learned something worthwhile from Buber. Having practically made up my mind some time ago that I wouldn't stand on ceremonies but call on him again, in order to establish closer relations with him, I was impelled by the favorable impression his article made on me to carry out my resolution. So, taking along a copy of my *Erchei ha-yahadut* [Heb., *Meaning of God* . . .],[3] I went to see him.

The subject matter of his article constituted the basis of the first part of our conversation. (I can't help remarking again, as I did after my first visit with him, that with a man of such parts and with so many books to his credit, I should

---

3. Kaplan's book *The Meaning of God in Modern Jewish Religion* in its Hebrew version.

have to be the one to make conversation. To this day I recall that whenever I would go to visit Schechter, I would never have to worry what I should talk about with him because I was always sure he would provide the stimulus. That was the reason, I suppose, his company was so enjoyable.) In that article Buber makes the point that when Samuel saw that the hereditary priesthood with the Ark failed the Israelites during the crisis brought on by the victories of the Philistines, he tried to reestablish the early charismatic type of prophecy as the directive and administrative factor in the life of the people. When I called to his attention the fact that the verse in Psalms 99:6 *Moshe ve-aharon* . . . [Heb., "Moses and Aaron among his priests, and Samuel among them that call upon his name; they called upon the LORD, and he answered them"] didn't exactly jibe with that reconstruction of Samuel's role, he offered the usual explanation: "The reference to Samuel was added later." He found the other argument I offered somewhat harder to parry, namely, the fact that the prophets never meddled with the law. His reply was that the prophets regarded Moses as their forerunner, as having revealed the law once and for all. As for the association of *Torah* with the *kohane* [priest], he remarked that *Torah* meant interpretation, not legislation. In any event, he felt he should look into the question further.

I then took another tack. "What can be done," I asked, "to develop in the schools here the type of approach to the Bible that is represented by such interpretive studies of both the history and the inner meaning of the text?" This question seemed to rouse him. He thought at first that it was necessary to interest a group of people here in an effort to introduce a new spirit into the teaching of the Bible. "To my way of thinking," I said, "it might be more advisable to attack first the problem of working out the necessary content. Once we possessed such content, it should not be difficult to interest some group in the practical effort of introducing that content into the schools." I furthermore pointed out to him that since I was going back to America, where the same problem exists, it would be highly important for the two of us to get to work on the problem of content, because in that way we might establish a cross-current of influence between Jewry here and Jewry in America. The idea appealed to him very much, so that before I left him, we decided to formulate a plan for such a cooperative undertaking and to meet again in about two weeks from today to discuss it.

"Civilization" Better than "Nation"

TUESDAY, NOVEMBER 22, 1938

The full implication of the concept of Judaism as a civilization is now beginning to dawn on me, as I have become aware more than ever that the term "nation," as applied to the Jews in the past, has very little of what is connoted by that term nowadays, whereas it does have most of the elements of what is connoted by the term "a culture" or "a civilization" (which includes the element of social unity and structure). If we were to regard the Jews as a nation, in the sense in which that term is used nowadays, we would have to consider its habitat as exclusively Palestine, and all the rest of Jewry who no longer accept the Torah as supernatural or authoritative in a legal sense would be left without any status. Thus there is much more involved in identifying Judaism as a civilization. Mere nomenclature. The question whether there exists any social concept that fits the case of the Jews is really a question of whether the Jews who no longer accept the Torah in the traditional sense have anything but the common fate of persecution to serve as a common denominator. A common fate of persecution only without any common cause to render the persecution significant is bound to have a degrading effect.

Jessie Sampter's Death

NOVEMBER 27, 1938

The news of Jessie Sampter's death came as a shock to me. The very fact of her having been able to hold out so long in spite of her frailty seemed to give promise of her being able to live on indefinitely, as it were. She is one of the few people who not only succeeded in overcoming her tremendous physical handicap but in actually achieving a rich and contentful life. She lived out fully and wholeheartedly what she believed in, and by her life demonstrated the validity of her faith, which is what can be said of so few. But thank God that there are some at least of whom it can be said.

Lena went with Miss [Henrietta] Szold and Julia Dushkin to attend the funeral of Jessie Sampter at G'vat Brenner. Lena marveled at Miss Szold's vigor in first delivering a eulogy in Hebrew at the grave and then addressing the group of 62 youngsters, recent German immigrants, in German, on Miss Sampter. Later Miss Szold said with a feeling of bitterness that the Hebrew language has made her dumb. She deplored the fact that she could not use Hebrew with that same ease that she felt in the use of German nor express all that she wanted to say. It seems, then, that I am not the only one whom the Hebrew has rendered tongue-tied, in spite of all the years put into reading and studying it.

Buber-Kaplan Collaboration Falls Through

TUESDAY, NOVEMBER 29, 1938

The Buber-Kaplan combination is off. It was silly of me to entertain the thought even for a moment that the two of us could work together. We are worlds apart in our temperaments and ways of thinking. But I am so starved for cooperation that I followed even what I knew in my heart was a will-o'-the-wisp. The last time I saw him, we arranged to meet last Saturday, but I didn't want to be kept in suspense unnecessarily; so I took along the first part of my commentary on Genesis, and the collection of my comments on *Midrash Rabba*, to illustrate to him what type of work we might collaborate on. I no sooner began to talk to him than I saw that he was trying to get out of any joint undertaking as gracefully as possible. So that's that.

Buber Doesn't Relate Well

THURSDAY, DECEMBER 1, 1938

The more I see of Buber and of his actions, the less I am impressed. He is not what you call a big man. He lacks a sense of humor and displays little interest in you when you talk to him. He is interested mainly in Buber. I have heard much about his having exerted a great deal of influence on the Jewish youth of the Central European countries. Yet I have not met a single person, and I say this advisedly, who waxed enthusiastic about him. In fact, to the contrary, every one who has spoken to me about him ran him down to an extent that I would feel uncomfortable hearing an outstanding Jewish personality so disparaged.

With all my desire to be charitable, I cannot but find such a program as he has drawn up for his courses at the University on the philosophy of society, which he identifies with sociology, quite charlatanish. The idea of a man treating under distinct headings the sociology of religion, the sociology of custom and ethics, the sociology of art and literature, the sociology of science and technology, and the sociology of education, and omitting all consideration of economics, law, and politics, as if these matters had nothing to do with society. This constitutes his program for a three-year course in sociology, and this is what the Senate passed yesterday as one of the courses that is to be recognized as a minor, where with all the theoretic material that enters into the pedagogic training, it has pleased the Senate to refuse last year to recognize pedagogy as one of the minors that a student might choose for his degree, after they voted two years ago to afford it such recognition.

A Home Meeting to Discuss Various Issues

DECEMBER 4, 1938

Last night I took part in a type of meeting which I have become accustomed to in America. It was called by Joseph Bentwich at his home for the purpose of seeing what can be done to reconstruct our Jewish religious life. . . .

After the introductory talk by Bentwich, each one of us had his say. B. [Bentwich] was for starting a Jewish Protestant movement, H. [?], and [Akiba Ernst] Simon dwelt upon the ugliness and absurdities which mark Jewish practice as regulated by the rabbinate in this country, such as the marriage and burial rites, the administration of inheritance laws, etc., the fiction of selling the fields to the Arabs in order to get around the law of *shemitah*.[4] This last was carried out by the authorities of the Keren Kayemet[5] at the behest of the rabbinate. Roth,[6] as is usual with him, belittled the effort as a whole and saw its value only insofar as it afforded an opportunity for theological "discussions," and in seeing what can be done with the question of religion in the schools. The one who contributed most to the discussion was Dushkin. He emphasized (1) that it was not a question of formulating abstract truths but of meeting concrete wants, (2) that the main problem was with the parents and adults generally, and (3) that the way to begin was by instituting the practice of devoting every Sabbath morning to the consideration of the entire problem, such consideration to be itself treated as Torah and a form of religious exercise.

The World Is Closing In on the Jewish People

WEDNESDAY, DECEMBER 7, 1938

Every time I read a newspaper or a piece of contemporary writing, my whole frame is shaken by the mental torture of the awareness that the whole world is closing in on us Jews. The world has become like a den of wild beasts ready to spring on us and tear us to shreds.

In today's *Palestine Post* there is a quotation from a letter sent to the London *Times* by a group of Christian missionaries who have lived and worked here. With a heartlessness and cold-blooded disregard of our legitimate claims to Palestine and of our tragic situation in Europe, these sanctimonious gentlemen proceed to intercede on behalf of the "oppressed" Arabs and to recommend amnesty for the leaders of the rebels. The fact that the rebels have compelled the majority of Arab notables to flee the country is turned into a specious argument for treating with those rebels before they lay down arms. It takes a certain kind of Englishman, who comes to these parts to earn his livelihood and who combines in himself the worst elements present in the English makeup—snobbery and stupidity—to concoct such proposals.

Only an hour before this bit of unpleasantry came to my attention, I got a shock when, in the course of paging through a delightfully humorous little book, *With Malice Toward Some*, I came across an incidental reference to the existence of a considerable Nazi group in Sweden and the statement that in the next year Sweden will fight on the side of Germany.

---

4. The *shemitah* is the sabbatical year in which the land is to lie fallow and debts are eliminated. See Exodus 23:10.

5. Keren Kayemet l'Yisrael is the Hebrew name of the Jewish National Fund, which was established in 1901 to buy and develop land in Israel.

6. Leon Roth (1896–1963) was a professor of Jewish philosophy at the Hebrew University.

But what are these pinpricks to the mental agonies one experiences when one's thoughts revert to the harrowing news from Germany and Austria and to the systematic efforts of Italy and Germany to provoke war?

Education Must Give a Cosmic Orientation

THURSDAY, DECEMBER 8, 1938

The first of the three requirements which Jewish studies must meet in order to qualify for centrality in the school curriculum is the ability to help the educand [student] achieve a cosmic orientation. No education fulfils its function if it fails to enable the child to orient himself cosmically. The need for cosmic orientation is to the human being just as natural as are the needs for health and sustenance. With his extraordinary capacity of memory, imagination, and reason, man actually lives in an environment that infinitely exceeds in space and time the one he exists in physically. The range of his sensitivity exposes him to suffering from all manner of calculable to incalculable evils. He is therefore all too easily upset, and all too readily feels himself lost in the windy vastness of his thought world and is accordingly in need of a compass, as it were, to help him regain and retain his bearings. Comparing life as he finds it with life as he would like it to be, he has sufficient reason to become discouraged. But if he is to go on living without being weighted down by a sense of frustration and despair, he must have some reservoir of faith to draw upon. To that end, his education must be so directed that when fears and disappointments begin coming, he is well prepared to meet them. Say what one will about the traditional education, it was just this need that it seemed to fulfill more so than any other. To be sure, it was much easier to meet this need in the past, because man's cosmos was comparatively smaller and simpler than the one which he mentally inhabits now, and he was far less critical than he is now of the consolations offered him.

Nevertheless in spite of the difficulty involved, education must not shirk its task of helping the student orient himself. In fact, just that should be the main function of the central studies. But the question is, How can Jewish studies, the contents of which arose at a time when the thought world or universe of discourse was radically different from what it is now, help the Jewish child orient himself in the new thought world or universe of discourse? It is important that we do not delude ourselves as to the extent to which these two universes differ from each other. In addition to all the changes effected by the sciences like astronomy, physics, biology, and psychology, which have transformed the very meaning of our physical environment, there is the complete change of center from the other world to this world as the stage of man's self-realization, with all that such change implies in our moral and religious life. The only way in which Jewish studies can contribute to the cosmic orientation of the student is by evolving a method of interpretation that will take all these facts into account and by making that interpretation as much an integral part of Jewish knowledge as the interpretation given to the biblical tradition constituted an integral part of Jewish knowledge during the Rabbinic period.

The second requirement is that of inculcating a sense of nationhood which is free from the objectionable elements which marked it in the past and which mark it in the present. It is evident that the principal purpose of giving the central position to Jewish [people] can only [be done through] the inculcation of a Jewish national consciousness. This raises the question, What kind of national consciousness? What is to be the conception of the Jewish nation vis-à-vis the other nations? The answer implied in all of traditional lore is unmistakably that the Jews constitute an altogether unique kind of nation in no way to be compared with the other nations. This is the case because it was assumed that we stood in closer relationship to God than any other nation, as attested by our exclusive possession of God's law for man. Implied in national consciousness is a sense of national destiny. Here again the question arises, How is this destiny to be conceived? And again the reply of tradition is plainly to the effect that Israel is destined to be the supreme people in the world. Neither teaching of tradition is compatible with a modern orientation. It is possible to soften the harshness of national egoism implied in the traditional conception of national destiny by the process of interpretation which would set that attitude against the ancient background and which would draw inferences that point rather to a sense of national responsibility than to that of national variety. But the fact remains that, outside a very limited number of passages in the prophetic writings, the preeminence of Israel's destiny, as conceived generally in traditional Jewish lore and above all in rabbinic writings, is of such character that no amount of reinterpretation can render it compatible with ethical nationalism as we now understand it.

This fact leads me to conclude that when it comes to the matter of Jewish nationalism, traditional Jewish subject matter cannot by itself occupy a central position in the curriculum unless it is to be supplemented by material taken from modern social sciences, which would set forth the history of nationalism, the moral and spiritual factors which render nationhood indispensable, and the moral and spiritual dangers to which it is subject and against which we Jews must especially be on our guard. There can be no question that we Jews have contributed the constellation of ideas which has helped nationalism to develop wherever the economic and political circumstances favored it. The modern nations learned what nationhood is by imaging themselves for a long time as in direct line with the Israel of the Scriptures. By being instrumental in fostering nationhood in the rest of the world, we may have rendered mankind a service; but for the present, the aspect of disservice outstrips that of service. It is in the name of nationhood that certain nations now carry on like beasts of the jungle, and we Jews are their most hard beset victims. This fact imposes upon us the logical responsibility of making a close study of nationhood with a view to drawing the danger line in order to indicate just where and when nationhood ceases to be a good and becomes a menace. This calls for new subject matter on the entire problem of nationhood. Without the new subject matter, it is not possible to see the traditional subject matter in the proper light, from the standpoint of its teachings concerning nationhood and national destiny.

The third requirement is that of inculcating acquiescence in a code of law which is based on the ethical conception of personality. A common national consciousness and a sense of common destiny are empty phrases unless they include acquiescence in a national code of law of some kind, which is recognized as authoritative and which is actually operative. This means that there is no use trying to inculcate a national consciousness so long as nationhood has nothing of its appurtenances of statehood. The essence of statehood is a functioning code of law. There was accordingly more real nationhood in the pre-emancipation era than there is in Palestine today. Language, literature, and even a common past are not sufficient to evoke that sense of identity with one's people, which is implied in the term "nationhood." They are indispensable, but not sufficient. A civil code of law goes much further than they do, and therefore is even more indispensable than they are.

But, it will be said, this lies outside the field of the educator. That is true if he conceives his calling so narrowly as not to think of it in terms of conditions which affect it and excludes from his consideration social problems, though they have a direct bearing on the work of the school. If, however, he is socially minded, he considers it his duty to take an active part in removing social evils which prevent him from properly fulfilling his function as educator. If, accordingly, he is convinced that the character development and the inner and outer integration of the child necessitate his being given a sense of nationhood, he cannot but assume the responsibility for giving effect to that necessity by seeing to it that the main condition to nationhood be fulfilled. That main condition is undoubtedly the indispensable element of statehood, as expressed in an authoritative law code. No Jewish teacher can at present regard himself as doing his duty with respect to the inculcation of Jewish nationhood unless he agitates for the codification of Jewish civil law. Since in this whole argument we assume that we are dealing with teachers and educators who are intent upon adjusting the child to modern life, the civil law for which they must agitate should not be other than that based on the ethical conception of personality and on the conception of justice in which human happiness rather than precedent is the criterion.

German Atrocities and German Music—A Question

DECEMBER 9, 1938

The hair-raising atrocities which are being perpetuated these days on the German Jews render life for the thinking Jew a horrible nightmare. That human beings should be capable of thinking up such diabolic schemes of subjecting their fellow beings to such unspeakable tortures is sufficient to rob life of all meaning. The most tragic outcome of all this is, to me, symbolized by the fact that music has had its spiritual valiancy belied. If a people so musically gifted as are the Germans can act so fiendishly, then music must be one of Satan's inventions to beguile man into believing himself a god and into behaving as no swine at its worst could behave.

Kaplan's Future Plans for Teaching at Hebrew University

SATURDAY, DECEMBER 10, 1938

Thursday night I called on Dr. [David Werner] Senator at his invitation. He wanted to know whether I had definitely made up my mind to return to the States and whether I still abide by the suggestion I had made to him several weeks ago that I would be willing to come to the University every other year for the summer semester, which begins after Pesach, to deliver a course of lectures (about 40 to 50 hours) on the principles of education, if the matter could be arranged between the University and the Seminary. I replied in the affirmative to both questions.

The Medieval Thinker Albo, His Concept of God, and Holiness

DECEMBER 11, 1938

The attempt to get behind an ancient text, or complex of ideas, in order to arrive at an understanding of what universal human wants were trying to make themselves articulate is to engage in the type of creative interpretation which enables us to discover the elements common to the authors of that text, or idea complex, and to us. It is thus that we achieve a sense of desirable continuity with the past. One of the ways to carry out this project successfully is to bring into the scope of material to be interpreted other material which is closely related to it. This rule can assist us in trying to formulate the desiderata implied in the traditional belief that Judaism is a supernaturally revealed civilization.

The cognate material that we should take into account for this purpose is none other than the three fundamental principles which Albo[7] regarded as the sine qua non of Judaism as a supernaturally revealed civilization, namely, the existence of God, the revealed character of Torah, and reward and punishment. By applying to these three principles the method of creative interpretation, we are likely to discover not only what desiderata they represent, but why such

---

7. Joseph Albo (c. 1380–1444) was a Jewish philosopher and rabbi who lived in Spain during the fifteenth century. He is known chiefly as the author of *Sefer ha-Ikkarim* (Book of Principles), a classic work on the fundamentals of Judaism.

desiderata are a prerequisite to a civilization, if it is to help the society which lives by it to achieve self-fulfillment or salvation.

The first of these root principles is the belief in the existence of God. What are the significant facts in Albo's discussion of this principle? First, Albo does not ask us to believe in the existence of God, as Judah Ha-Levi does, on the basis of an assumedly historical event, but on the basis of highly abstract reasoning. This ill comports with the very opening statement of his book, in which he takes for granted that "it is not possible by the human intellect alone to arrive at a proper knowledge of the true and the good. There must therefore be something higher than the human intellect by means of which the good can be defined and the true comprehended in a manner leaving no doubt at all." Yet he admits that reason is capable of adducing the existence of God. The rest follows naturally. Reason, which is thus cavalierly dismissed at the front door, is invited back through the window and made to feel quite at home (cf. [*Sefer ha-Ikkarim*] I, 2, p. 49). Second, Albo is very emphatic in denying that it is possible for man to know God or to apprehend His essence. "The term *existence* when applied to God denotes nothing else but his quiddity.[8] But his quiddity is absolutely unknown, as Maimonides says . . . the side of God's existence which is possible of comprehension is the consideration that all existing things are due to his influence and that he is their cause and maker" (II, 1, p. 5). Like the previous fact, this one too is a great concession to reason which, as far as the belief in God is concerned, goes no further than identity within actual experience of those aspects which constitute God's functioning in the world.

Both of these facts are entirely alien to the conception of God either in Scripture or in rabbinic [texts]. They are taken over almost bodily from the philosophy of Aristotle. Yet that does not militate against their being incorporated into Jewish teaching. The reason is that, from the standpoint of a living civilization, what counts is the way ideas function and not their verbal formulation. That is especially true of the God idea in its relation to a civilization. Its function is not to acquaint us with the metaphysical essence of reality, but to impel us to utilize that civilization in such a manner as to help us behold the manifestation of the divine in the world. What constitutes such a manifestation? Aristotle said power and perfection, and all his followers repeated his answer. Modern thinkers equally entitled to a hearing have furnished us with a more plausible answer, namely, worthwhileness and holiness. These appeal to the modern mind as those aspects of experience which give meaning to human life and redeem its existence from the chaos of meaninglessness. What more than this did, practically speaking, all those who affirmed the existence of God really have to say that can stand the test of experience? But it is sufficient. On the other hand, for life to be

---

8. Quiddity, a medieval philosophical term, is the nature of a thing, its "whatness," that which makes it what it is.

regarded as worthwhile and holy, it must necessarily be such as to enable man to attain salvation. Thus the God idea as part of a civilization implies that it is the function of that civilization to enable those who live by it to achieve salvation.

Here, then, we have the first principle that is to be applied to Judaism as a civilization. Its teachings must be such as to bear out the assumption of life's holiness and worthwhileness, and its practices and institutions much be such as to make for the salvation of the Jew. If some still hold to the traditional belief of a God who can be influenced by petition to grant man's wishes—that is, if they find that only this conception of life renders life holy and worthwhile for them—they certainly have a right to their views. If, on the other hand, there is a growing number of those who are learning to find life holy and worthwhile on other terms, they should be permitted to live in accordance with their idea of God. But a civilization which does not contribute to the experiencing of life's holiness and worthwhileness, both on the part of those within and those without that civilization, is definitely a barbarism. In ancient times that distinction was expressed by speaking of the civilization which fulfils that requirement as supernaturally revealed, and of the others, as human. But the basic truth that the ancients sought to express about what constitutes the primary criterion of a civilization is that to which mankind will have to subscribe if it is to be saved from barbarism, namely, that it must be conducive to the belief in God as well as be based upon such belief. That belief to the modern-minded man means that life is holy and worthwhile.

In the light of the foregoing, the conventional distinction between secular and holy, religious and nonreligious, falls away. Everything in the life of the individual and of society can be treated as having no meaning beyond itself, or perhaps only in relation to some thing immediately next to it, or it may be treated as opening up new worlds of meaning and render life more abundant and exhilarating. In the former case, experience is permitted to remain drab, meaningless, profane. In the latter instance, life proclaims the glory of God. Worship is from this standpoint the stimulation of the mind and heart by means of assembly, song, and the spoken word to guide efforts in the direction of whatever makes for life being holy and worthwhile to the greatest number possible.

Reconstructing Reward and Punishment

Monday, December 12, 1938

A second root principle, which Albo names as basic to the acceptance of the Jewish civilization as supernatural or divine, is the belief in reward and punishment. Before attempting to get at the underlying desideratum that is implied in this belief, it is necessary to study it in its traditional setting. In that setting the belief in reward and punishment is integral to two fundamental assumptions, one about the world and the other about man, which in their literal form have, as a matter of course, become untenable. The one concerning the world is that the physical world in which we live is a deteriorated form of the one God originally created and that at some future time God will reconstruct it and eliminate all the evils of nature, suffering, and cruelty. That is the world to come, wherein the righteous and those whose sins have been duly expiated will dwell forever. The assumption concerning man is that he is essentially immortal and therefore not to be classed with other living beings. Consequently, this world where he spends but a limited number of years, and these mostly in sin and frustration, cannot possibly be his real home. The center of his existence can be only in the world to come.

Again, it is necessary to be reminded that the foregoing two assumptions did not constitute part of a particular phase of human life called religion, in contrast to other phases called science, art, practical affairs, etc. Those assumptions were inherent in the whole of premodern civilization. Every phase of that civilization, to the extent that it was thought out consistently, was permeated by those assumptions; the latter were basic not to religion as we understand it, but to each of the three great civilizations of those days: the Jewish, the Christian, and the Moslem. The belief in reward and punishment merely expressed the logical basis of those assumptions and to a large extent also their historical origin. Not being the result of experience but rather a method of interpreting experience, that belief undoubtedly voiced a deeply felt human postulate, namely, that cognizance be taken of the difference between goodness and evil, justice and wrongdoing. How could life have meaning if it made no difference how we behaved and if no one took cognizance of our behavior? In ancient times, when men were not given to close observation, the belief in reward and punishment encountered no difficulties. But when men reflected more, the evidences to the contrary became overwhelming. . . .

What we need now is to separate out of the foregoing thought complex the postulate that cognizance must be taken of the difference between goodness and evil, and weave it into the modern universe of discourse. This means treating that postulate in relation to a normative civilization as Albo and the other theologians treated the belief in reward and punishment in relation to a divine civilization. If we want Judaism to function as a normative civilization, we must see to it that it functions in such a way as to enable the difference between goodness and evil, justice and wrongdoing, to be taken cognizance of in the fullest measure.

It is not difficult to state what that principle implies in terms of civilization. It implies the existence of ethical standards in all human relationships, standards that are not honored in the breach but in the observance. There is nothing more destructive of the meaning of life and of all its higher values than the dualism which prevails ordinarily, when, on the one hand, we profess the primacy of the virtues and, on the other hand, confer genuine honor and prestige on those who attain success in violation of the fundamental laws of justice. A state of society in which he who possesses might succeed in gaining not only more might but also the applause of their fellows, while he who has a conscience has to pay for it dearly in deprivation and failure—such a state of society is not a civilization but a barbarism. With the center of gravity of human life definitely shifted to this world, the only possibility of that life realizing to the full the good latent in it, is a civilization in which there is the law of reward and punishment; that is, one in which the whole weight of that civilization—its education, its public opinion, and its ethical standards—bears down upon the wrongdoer, however powerful, and uplifts and encourages the righteous, however humble.

Kaplan on Torah

WEDNESDAY, DECEMBER 14, 1938

And finally the root principle of supernaturally revealed Torah. There are two elements to this principle: Torah and supernatural revelation, both of which have to be transposed into the key of modern thinking. Torah is essentially the organon of national life. Its ideology defines the place of the nation in the life of mankind and helps to orient the nation cosmically. Its laws and institutions are intended to regulate the relationships of the individuals and groups among themselves and of each toward the people as a whole. The belief in the supernatural revelation of the Torah should be equated with the function of enabling man to achieve salvation. Stated in modern terms, that belief means that Jewish civilization [*dat*] should help the Jew achieve perfection, *shelymut ha-enoshi* [Heb., human perfection], and realize his highest potentialities or attain salvation. The organon of his national life, namely, the ideology and laws of the Jewish people, must be deliberately calculated to achieve that end. This principle provides us with the norm which must govern the development of Jewish national ideology and of Jewish law, namely, the purpose of furthering the human perfection or the personal salvation of the individual Jew. When, therefore, a number of Jews find any element in the traditional or prevailing ideology or codes of laws that fails to further that purpose, and all the more if it hampers that purpose, they are duty-bound to see to it that such element be removed. Whenever that kind of situation exists, we should act in keeping with the traditional rendering of the scripture *et la-asot la-donai hafer toratecha* [Heb., "To do for God it is time to disregard the Torah"] and regard modification of Torah the only means to its preservation.

Even if the entire weight of tradition were to resist modification of the Torah, as it apparently seems to do, it would be necessary to proceed with such modification, since the weight of experience counterbalances that of tradition, and that experience points to the irresistible fact that intransigence must lead to moral disaster. But the truth is that part of the weight of tradition is in line with yielding to change when necessary. There is, of course, the incontestable fact that what constituted Torah both in terms of ideology and law for one age was very much different from what constituted Torah in another age. To insist, as the traditionalists do, that the Torah has been absolutely the same since the days of Moses, is to beg the question and to ask those who are familiar with modern ethical studies to subscribe to assumptions that violate the fundamental laws of thought. The same applies to Talmudic ideology and law. The main difficulty with such changes, however, is that they came about on the whole quite unawares, with those who effected them generally being convinced that they were merely reinstating preexisting teaching or practice. This is why it pays to reckon with Albo's argument pertaining to the question of modification of the Torah in [Albo's *Sefer ha-*] *Ikkarim*, III, 13–14.

Before examining that argument, it is necessary to bear in mind that both rabbinic and medieval Jewish theologians had particular reason to be sensitive to the suggestion of the Torah as subject to modification. They were confronted by the challenge of Christianity and Mohammedanism, which by no means ignored the Mosaic Torah, but on the contrary regarded it as supernaturally revealed. Why, then, did not Christians and Mohammedans accept it as binding on them? Because they maintained that it had been superseded by subsequent revelation. The Jews, to justify their adherence to the Torah, had to protest this claim with all their vigor. It was not the Torah's modifiability as such that the Rabbis and Jewish philosophers resisted, but the Torah's supersession by Christianity and Mohammedanism. With the grounds for such apprehension no longer in existence, they certainly would not have felt as strongly against the revision of Jewish ideology and law. And surely there can be no grounds, since the very demand for change arises from convictions that would relegate Christianity and Mohammedanism to the domain of the outlived, even for their own peoples.

And now for Albo's argument. Raising the question ([*Sefer ha-Ikkarim*], III, 13) "whether it is possible that a given divine law of a given people should change in time, or whether it cannot change but must be eternal," he replies that it cannot change for reasons based upon a consideration of the giver, or the recipient, and of the law itself. To the consideration of the giver, God, he devotes one short paragraph. His point is that since it is inconceivable that God should change His will, it is inconceivable that He should change one law for another. To the consideration of the law itself, he devotes also only one short paragraph. The point there is that since "the purpose of the divine Torah is to teach men intellectual conceptions and true opinions, there can be no reason for its changing at any time. For true opinions can never change." Here we are on shaky ground. In the first place, Albo narrows down the broad conception of human perfection as the purpose of the Torah to the one of teaching men intellectual conceptions. Second, he too begs the question when he says "true opinions can never change." It all depends what the opinions are about. True mathematical opinions may not change, although even that may be questioned, but certainly opinions about the nature of things, human relations, etc.—that is to say, what may have been true at a certain stage of knowledge and mental development—may not be true at another stage.

But it is to the consideration of the recipient that he devotes most space, and it is there that he practically gives the argument away and actually arrives at the opposite of what he sets out to prove. He sets out to prove that since the nation which received the law is the same, there is no reason why the law should change in the course of time, especially as there is no analogy between a nation and an individual in the matter of changing with time. But as he develops the argument, he proceeds to prove the very opposite, namely, that change may occur on the part of the recipient. In fact, he utilizes the traditional beliefs stated in the Torah itself to the effect that what had been forbidden to Adam was later permitted to Noah, and that when Israel came, the law was changed again, to prove that "divine commandments change with the times." But, of course, what he means is that God Himself can change His laws, not men. For our purpose, however, the issue is not affected by the limitation which he sets up, since that limitation belongs to the traditional approach. Though, in effect, he certainly would not concede man's right to abrogate any law in the Torah, his attitude is entirely different from that of Maimonides, who makes the immutability of the Torah one of the thirteen cardinal doctrines. According to Albo, the reason the Torah is still in force is that Moses, through whom it was revealed, has so far been the greatest of all prophets, not because of the precept in the Torah "Thou shall not add thereto, not diminish from it," on which Maimonides bases his doctrine.

In all this there is no intention to make the deliberate attempt to reconstruct Jewish tradition square with the traditional attitude toward change. The point made in the foregoing is that even in the armor of traditional teaching, with all its effort to be consistent and unyielding, there are pregnable places. Change is the law of life, and no living Judaism could possibly evade that law. But in recent years the process of changes has accelerated to a degree which necessitates deliberate reckoning with it, no matter what phase of human life we happen to deal with. After all, our object is not to justify the repudiation of the traditional Torah for some radically new revelation. On the contrary, our interest is to maintain as far as possible a sense of continuity with the past, but not at the expense of maladjustment in the present. The principle of "Which if man do, he may live by them" is to be our main guide.

Kaplan the Poet

Friday, December 16, 1938

When I woke up early this morning, long before it was time to get out of bed, the following lines kept on repeating in my mind and didn't let me fall asleep again until I got up and jotted them down:

Who am I?
I am I.
What am I?
Dust that breathes,
Breath that sings
Song that dies,
But in dying, Lives in You.

Lecturing on the History of Education

MONDAY, DECEMBER 26, 1938

I resumed today my lectures on the History of Ed. after the week's interruption on account of Hanukkah vacation. Recalling that I was not satisfied with the way I lectured two weeks ago, because I had worked on other matters in the morning, I decided to use this morning for going over in my mind carefully what I was going to lecture on today. As a result, I am sure the lecture proved far more interesting to the students.

But as so often happens here, something always turns up before long to mar one's contentment. On the way home I noticed that there was again one of those ominous crowds in front of the Hadassah Hospital. The chauffeur informed me that a Jewish young man was killed two hours ago in the neighborhood by an assassin who fired 4 bullets at him.

Teaching Bible to Your Children

JANUARY 7, 1939

My Hadassah[9] asked me in one of her letters when she should begin teaching Jeremy [Kaplan's grandson] Bible stories. In my answer to her I merely said that she better put off telling him those stories as long as possible, so as not to take away his zest for the Bible when he gets to study it at school. But what really should be said about the Bible is that the time to begin teaching it is when you can teach it as consisting of three layers of ideas: one, the primitive layer, which expressed the thoughts and interests of those who first wrote or spoke them, mainly the latter; second, the layer which consists of the meanings which the first layer assumed for the compilers; and third, the layer which consists of what the Rabbis read into the text. Incidentally, writing up such a three-layer text of Bible interpretation is a project that holds tremendous fascination for me. I wish I had the time and the energy to undertake it.

---

9. Hadassah Kaplan Musher, Kaplan's second eldest daughter.

Sabbath Discussion with Hebrew University Colleagues

JANUARY 11, 1939

There were only six present this morning at the Sabbath discussion which took place at Dushkin's house. Besides Dushkin and myself, there were Rieger, [Joseph] Bentwich, Ben-Zeev, and [Akiba Ernst] Simon. Dushkin tried to sum up the substance of my remarks from the two previous sessions, but I had to remind him of my main point, which was that before we can discuss the reconstruction of Judaism, we must be clear in our minds as to what we understand by Judaism and the relation of religion to the other aspects of Judaism. In my remarks I tried to point out that even in *medieval Judaism*, where the philosophic writers speak of *dat* (usually but wrongly translated as "religion"), the modern conception of religion is unknown, and what they had in mind was "a civilization." To them, Judaism was not a religion but a supernaturally revealed civilization.

Bentwich reiterated the objections to my approach that he had stated to me before the summer when I almost gave up trying to discuss my views with him. His main contention was that religion was a distinct and separable element in civilization, intended to set forth the absolute truth about God as the Unknowable who exercises directive influence on our lives. Our problem therefore consists in formulating this truth and fostering it to the best of our ability. Fortunately this time I thought of an excellent analogy that brought the fallacy in his thinking into bold relief. That analogy was suggested to me by something he himself mentioned in an article he wrote. There he quotes Madame de Stael[10] as saying that "mathematics cannot cultivate the logic needed in practical life, because a mathematical idea is either all false or all true, whereas in life truth and falsehood exist in a combined state." Bentwich himself is especially interested in mathematics. This enabled me to point out that his thinking about religion was vitiated by his mathematical approach, which required that the ideas in it be wholly true or wholly false, whereas to my thinking, religion no more exists apart from life than the mathematical aspect of reality can exist apart from reality. Plato, discovering the significance of abstract thinking and the value of abstract ideas, came to regard them as the essence of reality and all physical embodiments as detractions from reality. This hypostasis or reification of abstract ideas has given rise to what I designated as "civilized idolatry" in contrast with the "primitive idolatry" of ancient mankind in general. This "civilized idolatry" was later incorporated into Christianity and helped to create the Christian dualism between this-worldliness and other-worldliness. This dualism is a source of moral danger, which we Jews should seek to avert.

---

10. Madame de Stael (1766–1817) was a writer and intellectual who actively participated in the political and intellectual life of her time.

[Akiba] E. Simon tried to indicate that he held a middle ground between Bentwich and me. He quoted Husserl approvingly in favor of an absolute external truth. But what struck me as peculiar was his conception of the Torah, which he said was also that of Rosenzweig and Buber, namely, that the Torah as we have it was not as Maimonides taught, literally dictated by God to Moses, but that at Sinai there began the process of translating into words the supernaturally revealed will to Moses and subsequent seers.

On the whole, I came away from the session quite upset by two things: first, that even the handful of people who have joined it do not take it seriously enough to make a special effort to come and to begin on time, and second, that with such a stubborn insistence on supernaturalism or superrationalism as the essential element of religion, as manifested by Bentwich and Simon, we shall never be able to arrive at a working basis of any kind.

Ultimate Purpose of Education

Friday, January 13, 1939

The major problem in education is how to tame power. In ancient times education was used in the interests of power. With the appearance of the great thinkers, sages, and reformers, the notion arose that education should be used as a means of taming power. But with the rise of the State as a veritable god, many thinkers have become its priests and are foremost in proclaiming power as the worthiest end of human life.

Lecturing in Tel Aviv

Tuesday, January 17, 1939

Last Friday afternoon Lena and I went to Tel Aviv. We stopped at the San Remo Hotel during our weekend stay. The weather was mellow, and we did quite a bit of tramping through the town. I, for one, could not help admiring what our people have accomplished in so short a time, considering the lack of all experience in town building and self-government.

We visited with the Davidowitzes, the Bachs, and Joshua Neuman and his family, with whom we had supper on Sunday night. Emanuel Neuman's family was also there. Sunday morning we spent two hours at the art museum. In the evening of that day I gave my talk for which I had come to Tel Aviv. The talk was given under the auspices of the Tel Aviv "Friends of the University."

There were about 175 people present. But I knew no one in the audience and they didn't know me, and there was no discussion after I was through with the talk. The person who was supposed to introduce me didn't come on time, so I simply proceeded with the lecture without the formality of an introduction. I can't say that it was a thrilling experience, but I am glad I did my duty.

New Projects after Returning Home

JANUARY 17, 1939

Now that my thoughts are beginning to turn homeward, various undertakings come to mind, things I should like to work on when I get back. Here are some of them: (1) A revised edition of *Judaism as a Civilization* that would bring it up to date. (2) A systematic presentation of those ethical teachings of the Rabbis that are still valid. This requires going through the Talmudim and Midrashim [ancient commentaries on Scriptures], the halachic [legal] as well as the aggadic [nonlegal] sections. This has to be a cooperative affair. (3) In teaching the course in religion at the TI, I should like to make use of E. Kaufman's 3 vols. of *Golah venechar* [Heb., In Diaspora and Foreign Lands]. (4) In Homiletics I should like the students to read Allport's *Personality*.

Going Home Versus Staying in Jerusalem

JANUARY 22, 1939

Last night I met the committee consisting of [Zalman] Schocken, Ussishkin, and the rector Prof. [Abraham H.] Fraenkl that was appointed to ask me to withdraw my letter of resignation. We met at Schocken's house. Ussishkin delivered a long speech at me. He wanted me to tell him why it was that the University has not been successful in retaining those who come from America. The late Max Margolis, Louis Ginzberg, and Israel Davidson could have been identified with the University. But each of them preferred to go back to America after having taught here for some time. He quoted what he had said to Edmond Rothschild, when the latter was nearing his eighties: "If instead of giving your millions to Palestine, you would come to settle here, you would be doing much more for Palestine than you are doing now." Likewise, he said that I would be helping Zionism far more by working here than by working for it in America. Apart from the value he attached to my work here, he considered it important for the University to attract men who did not come here because they found it difficult to function elsewhere. So far, the majority of those on the staff have come here not as a matter of choice.

What could I say? I tried to rationalize my going back by pointing out that under the difficulties which the Pedagogy Department labored at present, I felt I could make more of a contribution to Jewish life in America than here. This Ussishkin rebutted by saying that whatever work I did here, even under difficulties, ultimately meant more for Jewish life in America than anything I did there.

Prof. Fraenkl repeated in different words the hope that I would withdraw my letter of resignation. I don't think he was very deeply concerned whether I went or stayed. Schocken, on the other hand, was really anxious that I should change my mind about going.

Where family spirit is strong, community spirit is weak. If I hadn't felt responsible for sending $60 monthly to my folks, and Lena and I hadn't been so attached to our children and kinfolk, we might have made a go of it here. Even then the problem of personal security would have to be taken into account. In case the Arabs kick up, or there is war, or England plays the Jews dirty—and it is very likely that all three things are liable to happen—what then?

On Love and Good Will

JANUARY 22, 1939

Probably at no time in human history has there been such a challenge to faith or to the feeling that there is some meaning to human life as there is today. The effect of the Lisbon disaster[11] in the 18th century on thinking men and women was slight compared to that of the present inhumanity of man to his fellows, such as practices in countries like Germany, Italy, and Japan and to some extent also in Russia. As I see it now, it is futile to try to restore that faith by means of Aristotelian teleological cosmology, or Aquinas' synthesis or revelation and Aristotelian or Hegelian dialectic. Kant was right after all in looking to man himself and not to the universe outside him for the basis of faith. But he was wrong in believing that such faith is an act of intellectual willing. It seems to be that unless we can identify some basis for faith within accessible experience of the average person, life is bound to lose all worth and meaning. The fact is that before a person can have faith in human life as a whole, he must first have faith in himself. We put the cart before the horse if we want to find reason for faith in mankind before we have cultivated any genuine ground for faith in ourselves. The problem of faith can be met only if we go about it the other way around. If upon looking into our own souls, we become aware of something in us which, if universalized, would render life as a whole worthwhile, then we cannot be mistaken. The only thing of which that can be true is love and goodwill. If we can discover in ourselves evidences of love and goodwill, we are bound not only to have faith in ourselves but in humankind as a whole. The reason for this should not be hard to understand. We cannot help concluding that there must be many others in whom there is this quality of love and goodwill. Once we become aware of that fact, we have a veritable sheet anchor for faith. If that quality is more or less inherent in human nature, it will ultimately assert itself. That a long time will pass before that will happen does not alter the fact of its presence and slow but sure predominance. That fact should be sufficient to render life significant and worthwhile. However, this conclusion can be arrived at only if we ourselves

---

11. The Lisbon earthquake occurred in November 1755 and was one of the deadliest in history, killing more than 10,000 people and destroying the city of Lisbon. The earthquake was widely discussed among Enlightenment philosophers in connection with theodicy, or the problem of evil.

possess sufficient love and goodwill to have faith in ourselves. This is not a matter of abstract belief but of practical demonstration. The more love and goodwill we practice, the more natural it is for us to feel that other human beings are likewise endowed with those qualities which, were circumstances favorable, would find outward expression. This experience is bound to restore any flagging faith in the worthwhileness of human life. The solution of the problem of faith lies therefore in the domain of deeds of love and goodwill.

A Conversation with Schocken

THURSDAY, JANUARY 26, 1939

Yesterday afternoon I went to see Schocken, as we had arranged, and he showed me the text of the letter he intended to send to Adler in reference to the possibility of my coming once every two years for the summer semester.

In the course of the conversation about the status of Jews in America, compared with the status of the Jews in Germany, he said that he had been reading considerably about the attitude of the German Jews toward German culture and politics, and he found that beginning with Borne,[12] Jews who were prominent in letters and politics always said and did things to irritate the natives. Borne's criticism of Goethe was the subject of some critic in the [18]60s who made it the occasion for anti-Semitic attacks on Jews. Lassalle's[13] sensational opposition to Bismarck did the Jews no good. The Jews in England, said Schocken, are making the same mistake, and he mentioned Sachar, Brodetsky, and Laski,[14] who are identified with the Laborites, as pursuing the same tactics. For one who professes to have come out for Zionism when it was highly unfashionable in Germany, this policy, which would have the Jew refrain from voicing his honest opinion about the life and thought of the country in which he lives, seems rather incongruous. But after all, he is a rich man, and economic interests outweigh his Zionist sympathies.

Terror Incidents in Jerusalem

SUNDAY, JANUARY 29, 1939

There has been no letup in the terrorist campaign of violence. The last few weeks not a single day has passed without shootings, woundings, and killings in and about Jerusalem. Last Tuesday at 2:15 in the afternoon a Jewish taxi driver was shot in front of Magnes' home. I've heard that the University staff have urged him to move out of the section near Herod's Gate [wall of the old city], where he

---

12. Ludwig Borne (1786–1837) was a German Jewish political writer and satirist.

13. Ferdinand Lassalle (1825–1864) was a German Jewish jurist, socialist, and political activist.

14. Harold Laski (1893–1950) was an English political theorist, economist, author, and lecturer who served as chairman of the Labour Party.

has been living these few years, and that he informed them that he had decided to do so of his own accord. A strange man, this Magnes, with an unusual dose of saintliness and courage in an environment so abounding in courage that it takes his courage for granted and so lacking in saintliness that it has nothing but contempt for his saintliness.

Last night a bomb was thrown on Ben-Yehudah Street near the Orion Theater. Six Jews and one British soldier were wounded.

Music Lessons

JANUARY 28, 1939

Since Thursday, Jan. 19, I have begun to take lessons twice a week in learning to read music at sight. My teacher is Mrs. Berlin, who had been recommended by our neighbor Mrs. Feigenbaum, whose children take music lessons from her.

The Diaspora Is Permanent

JANUARY 28, 1939

And now for the talk I have to give on the radio.

The story of David at Ziklag[15] is illustrative of the attitude which is often taken by those at the front toward those who for some reason are compelled to remain behind. Thus those placed by choice or by circumstances in Palestine, the front line of Israel's struggle for existence, refuse to share with those who remain behind what they achieve in terms of Jewish values, self-confidence, and hope of a Jewish future. They are all too apt to look upon the Jews of the Diaspora as laggards who have no share in the God of Israel. This is what one might infer from (1) the attitude of blame or contempt toward those who accept their fate as destined to remain in the Diaspora, (2) the sweeping assumption that Judaism in the Diaspora must disappear, and (3) the complete absence in the educational content of the schools to indicate any intent in or responsibility for Jewish life outside Palestine.

The Desire for Immortality and Group Consciousness

MONDAY, JANUARY 29, 1939

It seems to me that the yearning for individual immortality is an individualization of the feeling of oneness with the herd to which one belongs. It is an

---

15. In 1 Samuel 30:21–26, David asserts that the spoils must be shared, even with those who did not go into battle.

attempt to compensate for the loss of that self-identification with the group which enables the individual to transcend himself or the limitations of his bodily existence, the limitations both in space and in time. The process of individualization naturally begins with the leaders. They are therefore the ones to feel first the loss of that instinctive self-identification which is common to the rest of the human herd or group. Accordingly, they are the first who are singled out for immortality. As the solidarity of the human group begins to break up and individualization progresses, there are more and more candidates for immortality. It is then that religion takes the form of otherworldliness.

In course of time, however, the untenability of individual immortality becomes too apparent. As a result, the attempt is made to restore by artificial means the sense of identity with the group which had disintegrated with the process of individualization. It is then that we witness a new eruption of nationalism. With Judaism and Christianity losing their force as otherworldly religions, as means of assuring immortality to the individual, their adherents find it necessary to resort to national patriotism to satisfy the need for self-transcendence in time and space. And so we find Ahad Ha-am fifty years ago urging the Jews to achieve a passion for nationhood and in our day the exaltation of national patriotism to spiritual hegemony.

Though it is difficult to draw the line between the conscious and unconscious in the various manifestations of life, it is possible to mark off distinct stages in the development of consciousness. Thus in the human race as a whole and in the individual human being as such, we cannot help discussing a different stage of consciousness evolving when the primitive races achieve civilization or when the child enters on his fourth or fifth year, when conscious memory begins to operate. From the standpoint of stages in consciousness there can be no question that with the advent of Greek science and philosophy, mankind entered upon a new stage of consciousness. What is not generally recognized, however, is that the last two or three centuries represent a further stage of consciousness than that of Greek science and philosophy. With the rise of the historical, psychological, and social sciences, man learns to view the achievements of the stage of consciousness represented by Greek science and philosophy in the light of the various factors that operated at the time that consciousness evolved. Likewise, all ideas are no longer viewed as absolute and independent but in relation to their setting. No longer are they viewed as static but as dynamic and as functions of continually changing and developing situations. In other words, we have really reached the stage of consciousness which is as much more complex than the one of Greek science and philosophy as the relativity view of the physical universe is more complex than the Newtonian view.

Kaplan Unhappy with His Class and Terror in Jerusalem

TUESDAY, JANUARY 31, 1939

I was not altogether pleased with the way my lecture came off yesterday at the University. I don't think I succeeded in interesting the students sufficiently, because I read too much from the notes instead of driving home the main points by speaking extemporaneously as I have learned of late. I was therefore especially anxious that today's three-hour session in the "Principles" should come off better. But as luck would have it, the subject of the paper for today, "Some Obstacles in the Way of Progressive Education," was one on which I had not yet developed any especially compelling idea, and the paper itself was very poor. I finally did come upon some integrating idea, but I wasn't sure I would be able to do much with it. Nevertheless, the session turned out to be one of the most successful during the entire time I have been teaching here.

But now comes the interesting thing. Almost invariably, every time I leave the University satisfied with myself for having done a good job, I come upon something that is frightfully upsetting. It is usually in the form of news which the taxi driver conveys to me about someone having been wounded or killed a short while before. When the taxi passes either the Hadassah Hospital or the Bekur Cholim Hospital or King George Road, we encounter a crowd, and the taxi driver stops for further information about what has happened. Last week, for example, I learned in that way about the taxi driver who was killed in front of Magnes' home. Now today there was a variation on that kind of upsetting experience. This time, as is usual on Tuesdays, I had Prof. [David] Yellin and Klein in the car with me. We no sooner neared the New Hadassah Hospital grounds than I saw a large bonfire in front of the new building, and our car veered suddenly into the hospital roadway on the right, and as it did so, I heard a shot. There I saw several ghaffirs[16] with their guns and some workmen. The faces of the two ghaffirs and of one of the workmen were covered with blood. When I asked what happened, they seemed dazed and didn't know what struck them. In the meantime, I saw one of the ghaffirs run with his gun into the field on the other side of the high road and kneel ready to shoot. Not hearing any further shots, I told the taxi-man to drive on to the city. His theory is, which I think is correct, that the shots came from remains of explosives that came in contact with the bonfire. But for the time being, the temporary mood of satisfaction was cut short.

Terror in Jerusalem

WEDNESDAY, FEBRUARY 1, 1939

While I was at the faculty meeting this afternoon, I happened to see a copy of the *Davar* [a Hebrew newspaper]. From there I learned that at 10 this

---

16. Ghaffirs were Jews who served in the British Mandatory police force.

morning a Jew had been killed in Talbiah [a neighborhood in Jerusalem] about 500 feet from where I live. He was selling coffee to Jewish customers he had in these parts and was set upon by a couple of Arabs, who shot him dead on the spot. Alex Dushkin afterward told me that Julia [Dushkin's wife] was holding a meeting in her house when she heard the shots. As they went out to see what happened, they saw the Arabs running. A few steps from the house they found the victim breathing his last.

Disturbances in Class at Hebrew University from the Revisionists

WEDNESDAY, FEBRUARY 8, 1939

As I was going to the lecture room yesterday, I met Dr. Ben David, the Secretary of the University Senate, and he told me that I should be prepared for disturbance of the lecture, because the Revisionists[17] ordered a strike in protest against the opening of the London conference on the Palestine question, which had taken place yesterday. Fortunately there was no such disturbance in my class. I learned, however, that Alex Dushkin had some tussle with a few who tried to stop his lecture. If I were ever tempted to discover any traits in our people that pointed to moral superiority over other peoples, the presence of such savages among us as the Revisionists would put all such thoughts out of my mind. To me they are as depressing a sample of humanity as the followers of Hitler and the Mufti.

Changing Sabbath Laws—The Proper Process

FEBRUARY 11, 1939

A procedure to be avoided in arriving at a working conception of Sabbath observance for our day is that of allowing the new life needs to determine what reforms are to be introduced and then juggling the traditional law until we find a basis in it for those reforms. We only delude ourselves when we think we conserve the traditional law that way, and we at the same time evade the need of formulating a rational principle for such changes as we advocate. The proper prerequisite, therefore, is to recognize the inherent character of the traditional laws and the agency entrusted with its enforcement and to determine in the light of the fundamental reinterpretation given above of Judaism as a whole what character Sabbath laws must assume for our day and what agency or agencies must be entrusted with their enforcement or general observance.

---

17. The Revisionist movement was a strong statist movement founded by Vladimir (Ze'ev) Jabotinsky. Its London conference resulted in the White Paper of 1939, which restricted Jewish immigration to Palestine.

The first step in the advocacy of any reform measures is a clear apprehension of the fact that the sanction for the traditional Sabbath laws was their supernatural origin. It was that sanction which was regarded as making the Sabbath holy and its observance a means to the sanctification of life in the individual and in society.

Nationalism, Chauvinism, and Tradition

FEBRUARY 18, 1939

Thus far I have treated the subject of nationhood merely from the descriptive point of view. I have tried to define its essence as an existential fact. I shall now take up the normative or ethical aspect of nationhood. That is the aspect implied in nationalism which is a philosophy or tendency that stresses the need of fostering nationality and national consciousness. The normative aspect becomes an object of consideration when there arises the need for making a choice between alternatives in which nationality is involved. We must therefore know which choice is in question before we can state our attitude toward nationalism. There are three possible choices, viz.: (1) A choice between nationalism, which recognizes a priority of obligation to the members of one's nationality, and cosmopolitanism, which recognizes no such priority, would have one treat all human beings as equally entitled to whatever consideration duty or love impels.

(2) A second choice is between nationalism, which insists on one's nation being sovereign and autocratic and recognizing no higher law than its own will and needs, and internationalism, which, admitting a high degree of autonomy to each nation, advocates the submission of each nation to a sovereignty higher than its own and representative of a group of nations but preferably of all nations. (3) A third choice is between nationalism, which insists upon a member of a nation remaining loyal to the nation into which he was born despite all odds, and the moral right to surrender such membership and become a member of another nation.

In order to determine the moral issue involved in making any of the foregoing choices, we have to fall back upon what we have found to be the essence of nationality and the content of national consciousness.

The first moral choice is, in terms of what we have found to be the nature of national consciousness, a question of whether the we-feeling which human beings naturally entertain with reference to those with whom they have in common the elements of nationhood—namely, language, history, laws, and folkways—should be regarded not only as normal but as normative and involve a greater intimacy and sense of responsibility on their part than is involved in the case of those with whom we do not possess any of these elements in common, or is this differentiation or partiality morally wrong or undesirable? The answer which naturally suggests itself is that ethics has generally approved the preferential treatment of the member of one's own family. Ancient man always saw the nation merely as an extension of the family bond. Historically this may well be questioned. But from an ethical point of view it should be regarded as an advantage that man naturally regards the bonds which are the product of mental and spiritual factors on the same plane of intensity as physiological factors. As a matter of fact, the issue of nationalism vs. cosmopolitanism flared up only among a few rationalist thinkers in the 18th and 19th centuries but never really attained any serious proportions. It is generally taken for granted nowadays that, other things being equal, a person owes the members of his nation more interest, cooperation, and love than those who are of a different nation.

SUNDAY, FEBRUARY 19, 1939

With human nature being what it is, cosmopolitanism lends itself readily rather as an excuse for not doing one's active duty by one's own nation than as a stimulus to active participation in the welfare of other nations. The nationalism which deprecates cosmopolitanism has proved itself morally justified.

A more serious question at the present time is presented by the second type of nationalism, which sees a danger to a nation not only in cosmopolitanism but in internationalism. According to this type of nationalism, a nation should seek to be self-sufficient economically and morally. Any tendencies or movements within the nation which transcend the boundaries of national life are a menace and should be suppressed. This applies in the first place to economic affairs as a whole and to economic reforms in particular. A nation should realize that it is regarded as a competitor and potential enemy by all other nations, and it must therefore do all in its power to render itself secure against them. Any measure that renders it dependent on other nations or implies cooperation with individuals of other nations not sanctioned by the state is bound to prove a source of weakness. Hence even moral and religious movements, to say nothing of economic movements or pacifist activities, that aim at general human and international welfare are, in light of this type of nationalism, entirely unwelcome. But it would go further and insist upon each one regarding his nation as not only unique but as superior to all other nations, as fulfilling more adequately the meaning of humanity than any other nation. One's nation must be regarded as divinely chosen, as enjoying a greater share of the divine spirit than any other. Its language must be regarded as the most beautiful, its laws as the most sacred, its history as the one most divinely guided, its morals as the most just, and its folkways as the most humanizing. "My nation can do no wrong" must be the motto for each citizen. Whatever adventures it enters upon to extend its dominion or to improve its will on others are a manifestation of its superior energy and will be a means of bringing other peoples within the circle of its bliss. It is not hard to recognize in all this the type of nationalism preached by Chauvinists and now emphatically avowed by Germany, Italy, and Japan.

Merely to state what this type of nationalism means is to make evident its immoral character to those who take for granted that a doctrine which implies that any one group of human beings is alone entitled to the distinction of humanity, whereas all other groups represent lower types of humanity, cannot be considered moral. What, then, shall we make of our own tradition, which apparently conforms to this type of nationalism, in that it would have the Jew regard his people as divinely chosen, its Torah or civilization the most perfect, and only those who become proselyted and accept its authority as eligible for the life of bliss in the hereafter? To be sure, there are stray passages in rabbinic literature which sound a universal note, and it is possible to offset R. Judah ha-Levi's[18] conception of Israel as being as much superior to the rest of mankind as the latter is to the animal world, with Maimonides' contention that all human beings are eligible to eternal life. But the main burden of Jewish tradition is undoubtedly inclined to be strongly nationalistic, in the sense of this second type of nationalism.

If we mean to be consistent in our condemnation of this kind of nationalism, the only possible reply to the charge that such is the nationalism taught by Jewish tradition is: In the first place, for the very reason that we would have every national tradition subject to the laws of universal reason and morality, we find it necessary to reject as obsolete the kind of nationalism taught by our tradition. Second, in justice to tradition, we must realize the circumstances which led to its teaching that kind of nationalistic doctrine. Both of these considerations point to the conception of Jewish tradition not as something fixed and eternal but as subject to modification in response to growth in the knowledge of reality and the wisdom of life. With the world constituted as it was in the past, with all nations regarding one another as moral enemies engaged in a deadly struggle for existence, with each knowing very little of the inner life of the other, this kind of nationalism seemed to have been the only kind that gave a nation a chance to survive. Neither Plato nor Aristotle, despite their extraordinary moral insight and intellectual grasp, achieved the idea of universalism. The very idea of an evolving Jewish tradition is but part of the moral general idea of which our moral conceptions also keep on evolving. What is deemed immoral now may have been perfectly moral in the past.

But in the specific case of the nationalistic doctrine taught by Jewish tradition, there are very definite extenuating circumstances which must be taken into account. The struggle for existence waged by the Jewish people since the destruction of the Second Temple called for a far greater measure of inner reinforcement than that waged by other nations. Only an extraordinary faith in its own worth and destiny could arm it against a cruelly hostile world bent upon destroying it. And the only way our ancestors could keep such faith alive was by promulgating that conception of Israel which we find in rabbinic literature and

---

18. Judah ha-Levi (c. 1075–1141) was a *philosopher*.

which we border so closely on the nationalism we deem objectionable. To realize to what extent this kind of nationalistic teaching was a defense nationalism called forth by the predicament in which Jews found themselves after they lost their state, we need only compare the attitude of the Prophets, when prophecy was in its prime. How little that attitude chimes in with rabbinic teaching is evident from the way the rabbis condemn it.

The main task which confronts Jewish leadership today is to define anew the meaning of nationality (or nationhood) and national conscience, in terms that will not only render tenable but will invest with purpose and dignity the status of the Jews who must indefinitely remain scattered among the various nations of the world. They must point the way to a conception of Jewish nationhood that would make it compatible with unquestioned loyalty to whatever non-Jewish nation they cast their lot with. This task involves a spiritual insight into the potentialities for good that inhere in nationhood and the practical wisdom to translate those potentialities into a way of life not only for Jews but also for the rest of the world. It would be nothing less than poetic justice if the Jewish people, which more than any other has supplied the inner forces that have made of nationhood a potent influence in shaping history, an influence unfortunately at present most viciously abused, should also contribute toward the elimination from nationhood its dross of collective selfishness and sacred egoism and render it essentially a means of social creativity and individual betterment.

5

February 20, 1939–October 8, 1939

On the Flyleaf of Volume 9: Kaplan Quotes from Books He Is Reading

"Now it happens curiously enough with philosophical meditations, that precisely that which one has thought out and investigated for oneself is afterward of benefit to others; not that, however, which was originally intended for others."

> —Schopenhauer, Preface to his works. Copied Nov. 7, [19]39

"It would be a difficult task to reconcile the picture I have of myself with the one which other people make of me. Who is right? And who is the real individual? When we go further and take into account the fact that man is also what neither he himself nor other people know of him—an unknown something which yet can be proved to exist—the problem of identity becomes more difficult still."

> —Carl Gustav Jung, *Psychology and Religion*, p. 100. Copied Jan. 9, [19]40

"Ducunt fata volentem, nolentem trahunt." [Seneca, c. 30 CE]
God is not reflected in nature; He is refracted.[1]

> —[Copied] July 23, 1940

---

1. The translation of the Latin quote from Seneca, according to LatinR.com, is "The Fates lead the willing and drag the unwilling." The relationship between the two statements here is not clear to me.

Fascism at Home and Abroad

MONDAY, FEBRUARY 20, 1939

Individually, I am as well as one has a right to expect to be, but as a Jew, I am experiencing mental tortures of hell. On the one hand, I read of the insanely sadistic attacks of the anti-Semites, and on the other hand, I learn of the fanaticism and stupidity of some of our own people. A reprint from an article by Joshua Starr in *Jewish Social Studies* (I, 1, 1939) on "Italy's Anti-Semites" brought home to me the fact that rattlesnakes are angels compared to creatures like Pregisi, Interlandi, Farinacci,[2] and the rest of that whole damned crew. The papers presented by students for the seminar tomorrow, in which they deal with the subject of religion, make me sick at the thought of what addled brains we have among our teachers and rabbis. Nor was I much edified by the stories Prof. [Harry] Torczyner told me this afternoon about the stone-throwing campaign, led by Rabbis Amiel and Uziel[3] in Tel Aviv, aimed at automobiles driven by Jews on the Sabbath, and their success in having an educational group cancel their invitation to him to lecture on the Bible because of his scientific approach to its study. If at least I myself command a facile pen and a power of eloquence to combat human stupidity, I might have been able to fight off the spiritual depression under which I labor. But when I realize my shortcomings, when I see, for example, how dull and heavy-footed is the argument on nationalism in the preceding pages, especially in the beginning, I am just too discouraged to hope for better things.

Democracy and Education

FEBRUARY 21, 1939

It is strange that, after having translated the greater part of Dewey-Horne's *The Democratic Philosophy of Education*[4] and having taught it last year, its real significance is first dawning on me. I think Dewey's book would have had a far greater vogue if he had brought out that significance more clearly. The thesis of the book—that education should aim at the growth of the educand [student] and at the democratization of society—would have stood out more sharply if Dewey had developed the antithesis which his book seeks to negate. That antithesis is the traditional conception of education for the man as the inculcation of obedience to society and its traditions, and for the few as a training in leadership or domination.

---

2. Roberto Farinacci (1892–1945) was a leading Italian Fascist politician and an important member of the National Fascist Party.

3. Apparently, local ultra-Orthodox rabbis.

4. H. H. Horne, *The Democratic Philosophy of Education: A Companion to Dewey's Democracy and Education.* Horne (1874–1946) was a spokesman for philosophical idealism in education and advocated a spiritual and religious approach to education.

A summary of the history of education from this point of view would have livened up the book. After that he could have pointed out that most of the modern versions of education are essentially the traditional conception in modern garb, especially the idealistic versions. Certainly Herbert's version of education merely supplies the traditional conception with a powerful instrument—his methodology.

Reaction to the White Paper of 1939

MONDAY, FEBRUARY 27, 1939

Days of dread are again on us.[5] The British Government, to win the support of the Arab world in the coming greater World War, is repudiating the Balfour Declaration.[6] God knows what's in store for us here and abroad.

More Arab Terror

TUESDAY, FEBRUARY 28, 1939

Again everybody is under great tension. The dastardly Arabs found it necessary to celebrate their victory by killing three Jews in Haifa and committing other acts of violence. And the Jews retaliated in wholesale fashion after months of self-restraint, during which time not a day passed without some Jews being murdered. A bomb was exploded in Haifa, killing 27 Arabs and wounding 34.

Different Conceptions of Nationalism

WEDNESDAY, MARCH 8, 1939

There are four different conceptions of nationhood: (1) the racial, (2) the theological, (3) the political, and (4) the cultural. The Jews, in defining their nationhood vis-à-vis Christendom, which claims to have become heir of "Israel," uphold it on racial-theological grounds. In the past Judah ha-Levi[7] [held the racial-theological view] in his contention against both Christendom and Islam; in modern times Steinheim,[8] Rosenzweig, [and] Buber [hold this view]. Believing as I do that it is more important to reckon with the modern political conception

---

5. This diary entry was written in response to the White Paper of 1939, which was a British policy statement that abandoned the policy of partition, established one government in Palestine of Jews and Arabs in proportion to their numbers in 1939, and established a quota for Jewish immigration of 75,000 for the years 1940–1944.

6. The Balfour Declaration (November 1917) was a letter from Arthur Balfour, England's foreign secretary, to Baron Rothschild, leader of the Jewish community, expressing British support for a Jewish homeland in Palestine. The declaration led the League of Nations to establish the British Mandate in Palestine.

7. Judah ha-Levi (1076–1141) was a medieval Jewish philosopher and poet best known for his explanation and defense of Judaism in *The Kuzari.*

8. Solomon Ludwig (Levi) Steinheim (1789–1866) was a German physician and poet.

of nationhood, I think it is more to the point to counter that conception with the cultural one. This is what I mean to imply by designating Judaism as a civilization.

The racial conception of nationhood which has been revived by the Nazis is based on the assumption that blood kinship is the supreme factor of human life; the theological attaches supreme importance to the God-consciousness, the political to power, and the cultural to civilization.

In reality, all the four above-named factors play a significant role in the making of nationhood. The problem is, Which factors should be treated merely as existential and which as normative? Here again is where we differ along the lines indicated before. Here again is where the cultural approach shows to advantage. It alone, of all the four, points to what may be regarded as the normative conception of nationhood. The other three make for international bitterness and war. They are unamenable to reason. On the other hand, it is the cultural approach alone that is translatable into the analogy of the orchestra of nations and that is compatible with the supremacy of reason.

The theological approach treats the history of the world as the history of God and of human salvation.

The chief point in the application of the conception of Jewish nationalism to education should be the following: In education it is unwholesome to inculcate in the children the notion that the Jews belong to a unique category of human beings or that the Jewish nation possesses racial or ideological characteristics that justify its being regarded as divinely chosen. This is especially dangerous to children of a minority group. When in the past the Jews said that they were a chosen people, they affirmed what the overwhelming majority of other peoples claimed concerning themselves. In other words, they used a generally accepted category and applied it to their own status. The principle illustrated in the interpretation that the Jews give to their nationhood is that they tend to utilize whatever prevailing category they regard as valid to identify their own status. It was in this spirit that Josephus tried to represent the Jews as a philosophic sect, and in modern times Jewish thinkers adopt whatever social or philosophical category they happen to regard as true or authoritative.

A Meeting to Respond to Gandhi's Article on Zionism

MARCH 8, 1939

I came a little while ago from the meeting at Magnes' [house]. Buber and Magnes read the statements they have worked out in answer to Gandhi's recent statement about the Jews in Germany and Palestine.[9] Buber's statement was worked

---

9. In November 1938, Mohandas K. Gandhi published a short essay, "Zionism and Anti-Semitism," which included an unprecedented critique of Zionism, Judaism, and the Jews in Germany, who were then suffering from the evils of Nazism. In February 1939 Martin Buber sent a letter to Gandhi that profoundly criticized his essay.

out very carefully and effectively. Magnes', on the other hand, was very weak and shamefully apologetic. Among those present were Benjamin, Bergman, Sholem, Baer, Koebner, Gutterman, Miss Szold, Schlesinger, and quite a few others.

Thursday, March 9, 1939

The session at Magnes' home last night had a depressing effect on me. In the first place, that a man of Gandhi's reputation and influence should have permitted himself to advise Jews in their present tragic plight to immolate themselves—this is what his message amounted to—and to charge them at the same time with being usurpers in that they try to recover their homeland, without as much as an attempt to hear the Jewish side of the case, helped to weaken my faith in human goodness, the only faith left me these days. It is all too apparent that he allowed himself to be influenced by the politicians in his entourage who are interested, as are the British, in courting Mohammedan goodwill. Second, the allusions to Jewish suffering, past and present, in both Buber's and Magnes' statements, and the sad pass to which we have come to— that we have to be continually fingering our wounds and exposing our miserable lot—have no purpose whatever. The mischief Gandhi's article set on foot is potent, far-reaching, and enduring. What chance have any replies to it to make any impression? And finally, the self-degradation to which we submit for fear of hurting the feelings of one who so shamefully wrongs us as to condemn us without even giving us a hearing. I was especially disgusted by the tone and contents of Magnes' letter. It was most unmanfully apologetic and most childishly put together.

Traditional Judaism

Monday, March 13, 1939

Traditional Judaism consisted of the following elements: (1) self-government, which was made possible through the existence of civil law, of men trained in it and of a system of courts, and above all through the political set-up of ancient society which necessitated the corporate status of Jews; (2) a world outlook and an ethical attitude based on supernaturalism and otherworldliness and on hopes for this world of a messianic and millennial character; and (3) an elaborate system of ritual observances and prohibitions which were regarded as a prerequisite to the enjoyment of divine favor.

Modern Judaism is broken up into various trends which stress only one or the other of the foregoing elements. National Judaism stresses the first, Reformist Judaism the second, and neo-Orthodox Judaism the third.

Hitler Annexes Czechoslovakia — You Are There

MARCH 16, 1939

Another Hitlerian earthquake. The Nazis have annexed Czechoslovakia. What next? People here are storing food. For once the Bible seems to have a message that is to the point. It is this: *hoi shoded ve-atah lo-shadud . . .* [Heb., "Oh you ravager who are not ravaged, you betrayer who have not been betrayed! When you have done ravaging, you shall be ravaged; When you have finished betraying, you shall be betrayed" (Isaiah 33:1)].

SATURDAY NIGHT, MARCH 18, 1939

Last night I heard Chamberlain's speech over the radio which he delivered at Birmingham Town Hall. To me it seemed to say that we are on the brink of war. Had Nazi nightmares in my sleep.

Reason, Peace, and World Unity Must Curb Nationalism

MARCH 20, 1939

I believe I have come upon a promising solution to the problem of pluralism by discovering that the crux of it is to be found not in the question of the state vs. all other corporations, with the church as one of them, but rather in that of the church vs. all other corporations, with the state being one of them. In other words, it is the growing spirit of democracy that is mainly responsible for the state-church controversy, because it is democracy that gives a naturalistic and ethical significance to the invisible forces which govern society. Hitherto the upholders of democracy have maintained that only when the invisible forces are conceived in supernatural fashion is there reason for their being represented by a special agency of government, a church, but that with the identification of these forces as human and ethical, there is no need for their having such an agency. This assumption constitutes the main weakness of democracy as it has thus far been realized. Fascism, especially the Nazist phase of it, has taken advantage of this weakness and has placed the agency representing the invisible forces, national patriotism, and imperialism with the nation as the deity, in control of the state of all the corporations which represent the material interests and fighting strength of the people. The only salvation of democracy lies in realizing that no people can exist without an organized agency in control of its spiritual forces. What it must do, therefore, is to identify those spiritual forces as the antithesis of Fascist jingoism, namely, as reason, peace, world unity, etc., and have those who can speak in their name constitute a governing agency to act as a check and a guide to the governing agency representing the state. The former agency would be a modern rational and ethical equivalent of the church.

WEDNESDAY, MARCH 22, 1939

The essence of democracy should not be identified either with parliamentarism, which happens to be one of the methods of implementing it, or with individual freedom and consent of the governed, which are prerequisites to it. The types of parliamentarism that have been tried have failed. This is no reason why other types should not be tried. But democracy as such is a social order which is based on the assumption that justice can be willed and that, through willing it, it becomes the decisive influence in the conflict of human interests. I would define justice practically in the terms used by Plato, namely, as that governing principle in human relationships whereby one's duties correspond to one's abilities and one's rights correspond with what one needs to be able to fulfill one's duties. It is necessary to realize that in recognizing this principle as a determining factor or force in human life, we merely articulate in our own fashion, which is in keeping with our rational world outlook, the principle implied in all religious and ethical systems, viz., that the career of mankind is not determined by the interests which answer to the blind impulses but by forces which the best way man has been able to identify has been by calling them invisible. There is an ancestry to the principle of justice as defined above. That ancestry is to be found in the gods, spirits, and ancestors who from of old have been the objects of worship.

Education and Nationalism

MARCH 22, 1939

At the initiative of Buber, Bergmann, and Fraenkl, a symposium on educational aims is being organized for Thursday and Friday, May 25–26. They were going to make a big splurge and invite all the educational organizations to take part, which of course would have meant inviting all kinds of political complications. Fortunately they called in Alex Dushkin and me at the initial stage of their planning, and we succeeded in holding down the affair to modest proportions. In the program which has finally been agreed upon I shall have to give the opening lecture. Its subject is to be "The Meaning of Nationalism and Its Place in Education."

All education, insofar as it aims to integrate the individual into the group, seeks to generate in the child a we-feeling in reference to his people. This we-feeling should not be identified as due to common ancestry or to unique racial characteristics. Such identification breeds jingoism. It should rather be identified as due to common objects, places, persons, etc., which serve as sources of value and which give meaning and direction to one's life — in other words, with the sancta of a people. It is not the fact of common descent that generates attachment between two persons but the *consciousness* of some common person or persons as constituting an objective of love that is responsible for such attachment.

The sharing of sancta, of values, is the real source of we-feeling. Hence all that speculation about unique qualities or ideals is pure nonsense.

Expecting a War Any Time and Difficulties in Concentrating

FRIDAY, MARCH 24, 1939

These days I have again been listening frequently to the radio to learn about the latest development of the international crisis. Typical of the present state of mind is this experience of mine last night: I was writing up the lecture on "The Democratic Ideology," which I am scheduled to give under the auspices of the Friends of the University here on April 12. Anxious as I was to know the latest news, I was afraid to turn on the radio for fear that I might hear bad news and would not be able to go on with the writing of the lecture, which I was about to complete. It required some exercise of will to allow the minutes when the news was being transmitted to keep myself down to work. At six o'clock this morning I made a dive for the *Palestine Post* [now the *Jerusalem Post*], which is left early in the morning in the door handle, to see whether war hasn't been declared yet.

Fascism vs. Democratic Nationalism—Again

SATURDAY, MARCH 25, 1939

I no sooner got through with my lecture on "The Democratic Ideology" than I began working on the lecture which I am scheduled to give at the educational symposium which is being arranged by the University. My subject is "The Meaning of Nationalism and Its Place in Education." So far the following is to be the thought I develop:

It is generally admitted that the aim of education from the standpoint of the social group which conducts it is to integrate the child into the society into which he was born. That society is not an amorphous mass. It has an inner unity, organization, and life of its own and sufficient traits to mark it off from other units of a similar character. In the past that unit might have been a clan, tribe, city-state, or nation. In civilized society as it is constituted today, it is a nation. The purpose of integrating the child into the nation is to inculcate in him a we-feeling or we-attitude toward all members of the nation, past, present, and future. At once, we come upon an important distinction between the elements upon which education has hitherto been based, and to a large extent still bases its efforts, to inculcate the we-attitude from those upon which democratic education hopes to base its efforts. Traditionally, education assumed four factors as constituting nationhood, namely, (1) blood kinship, (2) land, (3) culture, and (4) self-government. The methods which it has used to inculcate a we-attitude with regard to these factors have been (1) training in habits of obedience and (2) exalting the value of each of these factors as being of supreme worth to the self-fulfillment of the individual. An additional tract of traditional education was its assumption of a supernatural sanction for the four factors. Fascism is an attempt to revive the traditional conception of nationality and the traditional method of education. It is the culmination of modern nationalistic trends which have been crystallizing since the last quarter of the 18th century, when supernatural sanctions lost their effectiveness. Among those nationalistic trends have been our own, which have emphasized the same factors and have resorted to the same type of educational appeal.

In contrast to both the traditional and the Fascist conception of nationality and education of national we-feeling is the democratic. In the first place, it eliminates blood kinship as the basis of nationality. The fiction of common ancestry was created in the past to account for collective life and cooperation, because the ancients reasoned by analogy from the family. Objectively, it is not the kinship itself that generates the we-feeling even in the family, but the cooperation to which it leads. Nowadays that fiction is deliberately invoked in the face of the most irrefutable facts in order to foster national solidarity. There remains for democracy, therefore, the three other factors, viz., land, culture, and self-government. In contrast with the traditional and the Fascist nationalist approach, democracy would inculcate the we-feeling with regard to them not by representing them as intrinsically of supreme worth, but as of supreme worth only to those born into the nation, as a means of their self-fulfillment. The land can be such as affording security, the culture as affording self-expression, and the institutions of self-government as affording means of self-control. To the extent that these factors fall short of being such, it devolves upon the members of the nation to make them such. Hence the ideal, if implicit, obedience is out of place in democracy, since it would preclude the improvement in those factors, which is necessary to render them fully effective as a means of salvation to the members of the nation.

At this point it is necessary to illustrate the traditional Jewish teaching with regard to the Land of Israel, Jewish culture, viz., the Hebrew language, the national literature, folkways, etc., and the system of morals and jurisprudence, and to point out what the evaluation of them would be from the democratic standpoint.

Lamenting Events in Czechoslovakia

MONDAY, MARCH 27, 1939

What a wealth of implications in the following I heard over the radio a few days ago. In Paris the Czech Embassy is draped in black. Inside there is a large book into which passersby are asked to inscribe their names to a protest against Germany's rape of Czechoslovakia. The inscription on the door reads, in the words of *Eyha: Lo alekhem koll ovrei derekh* . . . [Heb., "May it never befall you All who pass along the road—Look out and see; Is there any agony like mine, Which was dealt out to me When the lord afflicted me On His day of wrath?" (Lamentations 1:12)].

Random Thoughts on Plato and Aristotle

TUESDAY, MARCH 28, 1939

Plato and Aristotle seem to have defined for all time the two poles between which all thinking must move, namely, idealism and pragmatism, Plato having stressed idealism and Aristotle pragmatism. In politics these two points of thought are represented, respectively, by the Fascist trend and the democratic trend.

Adler Froze to the Occasion

MARCH 28, 1939

I received a letter from Cyrus Adler yesterday in reply to Schocken's letter of Jan. 25. Every one of his official letters reminds me of the phrase "He froze to the occasion." Of course he turned down Schocken's suggestion that I should come to the University for the summer semester once in two years. Devoid as he is of imagination, how could he sense the value of a personal contact between the Seminary and the Hebrew University?

Fear of Terror Alters Kaplan's Morning Walk

MARCH 28, 1939

Apropos of the habit I cultivated of taking my daily constitutional on the roof instead of walking down King George Rd. through Ben Yehuda down to the Zion Cinema, which I used to do formerly, I said to Lena the other day, "There's nothing like having a roof under your feet." It was at her suggestion I made the change last August, when shootings and bombings in the heart of the New City became rather frequent.

Fascism and Democracy Contrasted

THURSDAY, MARCH 30, 1939

In contrast to traditionalism and Fascism, on the one side, is the approach of democracy on the other. In the first place it [democracy] repudiates common ancestry as the basis of nationhood. Second, it dispenses with the assumption of the absolute and supreme worth of the principal factors in the life of the nation. Third, it would not sacrifice individuality to inner national unity. And fourth, it would not place the nation above international law.

A Random Thought on High School Civics

MARCH 30, 1939

It seems to me that it ought to be possible to work up the Supreme Court decisions into educational content for high-school instruction in civics.

Source of British Hostility Toward the Jews

SUNDAY, APRIL 9, 1939

At the Dushkins', with whom we visited last Friday night, the question came up why it is that many English officials who come here with the best of intentions to understand the Zionist movement and to help it along become alienated from it after a while and throw in their sympathies with the Arabs. Judge Khassan of Haifa, Dushkin's brother-in-law, who is a native Palestinian, explained that the change in the attitude of these Englishmen is due to the differences between the treatment they receive at the hands of the Arabs from that at the hands of the Jews. The former are deferent and hospitable. The latter are disputatious and keep aloof. During the Turkish regime, Jews were wont to act very deferentially toward the Turkish officials, to invite them to their homes, and to send them gifts. With the advent of the English regime, the Arabs act toward the English officials the way the Jews did formerly toward the Turkish officials.

One thing is certain: that if Jews had possessed social cleverness, they could have made friends of both the Arabs and the English. Instead, those who began coming here after the Balfour Declaration regarded the Arabs with contempt and the English as aliens, from whom they wanted to receive no favors so as to be under no obligations to them. Of course, it is the unfortunate sense of inferiority which has been beaten into us by the rest of the world that is responsible for our social awkwardness. But there that awkwardness has cost us dearly, and our leaders should have had sense enough to insist upon our overcoming it.

Individual and Collective Suffering and Thoughts on the Problem of Evil

APRIL 9, 1939

After all I have read—and there is really not very much to read—about the question of good and evil and after all I have pondered on it—and that I have done a good deal—I am as helpless as a babe in coping with the present state of the world. The chief Italian gangster who has been undone by his German understudy is apparently trying to recover his championship. Hence the rape of Albania. The plight of tens of thousands of human beings who have been put to flight from their homes by these two demons, and who are crowded into boats that wander about the seas trying to find a haven for the refugees, cries in vain to heaven no less than to men. . . .

Last night, I went over to the Dushkins' to meet Miss Henrietta Szold and her two sisters, who had come to fetch her back to America. She is 78 and her heart is fast breaking up. With the utmost reluctance she is letting go of one task after another. She is about to make a trip through the country in connection with her work for the Youth Aliyah. It is to be her last trip. This combination of large-scale human cruelty, meaningless suffering, and death due to sheer chance in the lives of so many human beings, and at best the fading out of a well-spent heroic life in a blaze of keen self-awareness—all this is too much for my reeling brain.

Let me try to reason all this out for the ten-thousandth time, though I am sure to land in the same blind alley. If there is no God, there surely is no point to all this cruelty and suffering, and the sooner life—human life—becomes extinct, the better. If there is a God and He permits all this to go on, then human beings ought to commit suicide to prove their moral superiority to Him. It is impossible, however, that these two alternatives should exhaust reality, for the following reason: The very protest at the apparent meaninglessness of life cannot be part of that meaninglessness; it must stand outside it. Moreover, that protest proceeds from moral assumptions in the light of which it condemns God for permitting all this evil to go on. Why not rather conclude that God—if He exists—must be inclusive of our highest moral assumptions and cannot be such as to be identified with the God of either of the above alternatives. In other words, we cannot help concluding that life has meaning—except that we must readjust our idea of existence as meaningful—and that there is a God—except that we must give up our notion of him as almighty in plan and execution. This is the furthest I ever get.

The "Stupidity" of Synagogue Services

MONDAY, APRIL 10, 1939

I have just come from the Jeshurun synagogue.[10] The services were well attended, probably due to the Yizkor [memorial prayer for the dead recited on certain holidays] part. I think our national stupidity never stands out so sharply as at our religious services. Such an indiscriminate collection of prayers and readings, such infinite repetition, such complete disregard of vital realities and needs at a time when people are ready to give expression to their deepest feelings are entirely unforgivable. Take, for example, the Yizkor part. If we do think it important to remember the departed in the course of public services, we ought to have some prayers or readings that would articulate that importance. Instead, all that our great sages and poets could formulate for us is that vulgar promise to pay a couple of shillings—a sort of bribe to the Almighty, he shouldn't be so hard on our poor

---

10. Yeshurun Synagogue was founded in 1923 with the support of the chief rabbi, Abraham Isaac Kook. The present building dates from the 1930s and still stands. It was a spiritual and religious center of the Orthodox community during the Mandate period.

relatives. After the congregation stands on its feet for a long time, not knowing what to do after it has recited that promise, the cantor breaks out with a great lament, which after a while turns out to be a memorial prayer for somebody's great-grandfather or some such individual. In the meantime, the entire congregation stands on their feet swaying to the sad tune. When the cantor is through, he starts all over again with a slight variant of the same tune. When he comes to mention the person for whom the prayer is intended, it turns out to be the entire host of victims of the terrorist campaign in the country. The congregation keeps on swaying with not the slightest indication that the tragic actualities of life invaded the services for a fleeting moment. This is followed by the cantor giving the signal for the congregation to mill through that horrible concoction of verses beginning with the phrase "Father of mercies." Could anything appear more bizarre . . . ?

Passover in Jewish Settlements

APRIL 10, 1939

My Naomi spent last Thursday at Mishmar Haemek and Friday and Saturday at Eyn Hashophate.[11] She tells me that they eat leavened bread there during Passover, although they also have matzot and celebrated Seder night. It is only the third year since they've started having seder at Mishmar. There is no question that Jewish life is bound to evolve here its appropriate religious expression. But what I marvel at is the success with which both the pietists and the radicals—or is it only the radicals?—are managing to sidestep a *Kulturkampf* [culture war].

A Letter from Solomon Goldman

APRIL 13, 1939

Yesterday I received a letter from Solomon Goldman dated March 21. Among other things he says that he regrets that I am not remaining in Palestine. There is an unreality about our efforts here that makes all of our work futile. In some of the letters I received from Ira Eisenstein last year, he sounded the same note. If that is the way the sincere rabbi feels, why should the average layman be expected to be interested in Judaism?

Pressure from the SAJ to Return to America

APRIL 13, 1939

In reply to my letter of Feb. 24 to A. T. Thomson, then chairman of the SAJ Board, in which I asked him to present my request to the Board to appoint me Emeritus, I received a letter from him dated March 29 in which he says that he did not present my request to the Board. "The first and foremost prerequisite

11. Mishmar Haemek and Eyn Hashophate were two kibbutzim (collective settlements).

to get our people interested from a financial standpoint was my assurance to them that at the expiration of your leave of absence *you would come back and assume your post with us as in the past.*"

Roosevelt Calls for a World Disarmament Conference but Fears War

SATURDAY NIGHT, APRIL 15, 1939

Just heard over the radio about Roosevelt's cable to Hitler and Mussolini urging them to promise they won't attack any of the thirty nations he enumerated and pleading for a world disarmament conference. I feel like uttering the benediction *Barukh she-asani ezrah amerikani* [Heb., Blessed (is the one) who hast made me an American citizen].[12]

Being Bound in German and Other Cultures

SATURDAY, APRIL 22, 1939

At Lena's suggestion, a local bookbinder has been working on an extra-fine binding for my copies of *Judaism as a Civilization* and my two other books. The other day his wife brought me the bound copies, and I refused to accept them because he stamped my name on top of the back and the title of the book at the bottom. His wife said that he has been accustomed to do it that way right along. It then occurred to me that the Germans probably have all their books bound that way—the author's name first and then the name of the book. I took a look at the books in my library and sure enough every German book is bound that way, while on every English book the author's name is second. I believe that a national difference of this kind has psychological significance and confirms the general impression that egotism is a German characteristic. It is interesting, incidentally, that the Hebrew books follow the German practice; this should be of sociological significance, indicating the predominance of German influence on Jewish life.

God and Peace Are Indivisible

SATURDAY NIGHT, MAY 6, 1939

I learned last night that Litvinoff,[13] who has recently had to resign his post as Foreign Secretary of Russia, was the one who coined the phrase "Peace is

---

12. Obviously a benediction made up by Kaplan. Kaplan's Americanism is also illustrated by the publication of a book of songs and prayers to be used for American holidays: *The Faith of America: Prayers, Readings, and Songs for the Celebration of American Holidays*, comp. Mordecai M. Kaplan, J. Paul Williams, and Eugene Kohn (New York: H. Schumann, 1951). These prayers are an example of what has come to be known as civil religion.

13. Maxim Litvinoff (1876–1951) was a Russian revolutionary and diplomat. He was from a prominent Jewish family.

indivisible," which implies that peace cannot be secured unless those countries which really want peace cooperate with that end in view. It occurred to me this morning that the conception of God as one and indivisible might likewise be interpreted as in physics that ideals like freedom, justice, peace, and love, which in their totality are symbolized by the God conception, cannot be achieved if applied only partially. Lincoln's statement, for example, that America cannot be a nation half-free and half-slave carries out the same idea. Monotheism, therefore, in addition to voicing the aspiration for a united mankind, also reflects the will to have all mankind benefit alike by ethical ideals identified with the God concept.

Optimism in Reaction to the White Paper of 1939

WEDNESDAY, MAY 17, 1939

Tonight the substance of the White Paper will be broadcast. Its contents are sufficiently known by this time. The Yishuv[14] is like a seething cauldron. A general strike and demonstrations have been called for tomorrow. God knows what the outcome will be. I simply find it impossible to grasp the implications of this perfidious act of England by which she hands us over to the mercies of the savage Arab hordes, after we have sunk in the conversion of this God-forsaken wilderness into a habitable land some of our most precious possessions—human lives and age-long hopes. I can visualize the consummation of this piece of cruelty as little as I can visualize death. So long as one lives, one cannot help but hope. Ultimately I think the prophet who said *Utzu etzah ve-tufar* . . . [Heb., "Hatch a plot, it shall be foiled; Agree on an action—it shall not succeed. For God is with us" (Isaiah 8:10)] will be vindicated.

The Sacredness of Individuality

MAY 17, 1939

I still believe that, before all else, we Jews ought to answer ourselves the question, To what end? What are we Jews for? Without some kind of a satisfying answer, our condition ceases to be even tragic and becomes completely meaningless. There can be no evil greater than meaningless suffering. I say that we must redeem this suffering of its meaninglessness, and I don't think it is so difficult. The existence of mankind as a whole, bound up as it is with every conceivable evil, would appear nothing less than a cosmic error, if we were not to attach significance to consciousness, spirit, mind, reason—a significance that all the infinite universe of dead matter cannot destroy. If man thus dares to affirm his right to existence in the face of a vast universe that woke him to life only

---

14. The Yishuv is the Hebrew term referring to Jewish settlements in prestate Israel.

to crush him with its infinite ponderousness, why should not the Jew have the courage to defy the savage element of mankind that seeks to annihilate him? It is man's function to assert the right of the mind to exist. So it is the Jew's function to assert the right of human individuality, which is the most important expression of the mind. The minority status to which Jews seem to be condemned is the opportunity which the Jews must exploit to affirm the right of the human being to be something else besides being a creature of the herd, to be himself. This human dignity, which it has fallen upon the Jew to defend, is what the Jew should live for as a Jew.

White Paper—An Invitation to Violence

MAY 27, 1939

I attach very little significance to the demonstrations that were held here during the last weekend. They belong unfortunately to the class of necessary evils. If they had not been held, it would have appeared as if we were too weak or too cowardly even to object. As a matter of fact, the very statement of the White Paper is an invitation to violence. Does it not say that its provisions will go into effect if the two peoples will show that they can live together in peace? The logical conclusion is that if they don't want those provisions to go into effect, they should shed each other's blood. England is in this respect true to form: Divide and rule.

But as far as we are concerned, all this business of trying to negotiate with England or with America to get them to support us in our efforts is futile. To this type of negotiation the teaching of the prophets who deprecated political alliances and intrigues with the imperial nations applies even today. The antithesis of the policy of political negotiation is planned cooperation with the natives. By "planned" I mean not the setting up of ideal aims which are at present unrealizable. The vast difference in standards of living rules out immediate large-scale cooperation in employing Arab labor and buying indiscriminately from them. But it does not rule out gradual cooperation by introducing such measures as [Chaim] Kalvarisky has been advocating for years, viz., organization of groups comprising in the farm areas, Jews and Arabs for purposes like the following: credit loans, publication of agricultural information, engaging physicians, opening schools where Hebrew would be taught to Arabic children. The trouble with the [Hebrew word illegible in the original] is that it is run by the Histadrut[15] and is more like a Zionist propaganda paper to Arabic-speaking Jews than a paper that represents the Jewish side of the case from the standpoint of Arab interests. (I learned incidentally that Brandeis contributed $10,000 toward it.) I owe most of the foregoing ideas about Jewish-Arab relations to talks I have had with Manyeh

---

15. The Histadrut was an organization of workers in the Land of Israel.

Shohet of the old Ha-Shomer[16] of the Second Aliyah [second wave of immigration] and Kalvarisky [formerly of the Department of Arab Affairs of the Jewish Agency], who reorganized Baron Rothschild's colonies with a view to eliminating the element of dependence to which the colonists had become used. Kalvarisky is undoubtedly right in what he said to me this afternoon: "This blow (the White Paper) has come to us because of our failure to treat with the Arabs."

More Terror

MONDAY, MAY 29, 1939

It is 11:20 at night. Lena had just fallen asleep when the bell rings excitedly, and Mrs. Feigenbaum, our neighbor, having just come back from town, informs us that two Jews were shot dead in Bezalel St. in the alley behind one of the large cooperative apartments on King George Road, and that a bomb exploded in the Rex Wirre House, killing a number of Jews and Arabs. We had heard the explosion when it occurred about 8:20, but we naturally explained it away as caused by automobile exhaust pipes.

A Nightmare

TUESDAY, MAY 30, 1939

I had a nightmare during the night. I dreamt that three Arabs tried to trip me and were preparing to shoot me.

Kaplan Gives Lecture on Humor

MAY 30, 1939

For the first time in my life I delivered a full-length lecture today on Humor as part of the course in "Principles of Education," and it wasn't bad at that. One of the students had read a paper on "Humor and Its Place in Education." There wasn't much to what he said. My talk was based on the assumption that the most predominant form of humor consists in the destruction of somebody's hierarchy of values. The ancients allowed humor only at the expense of individuals whose hierarchy of values was antisocial or based on deception of self or of others. Nowadays we should use humor to undermine the hierarchy of values of vested interests and established traditions which stand in the way of general happiness and progress. For that reason I suggested that the entire discussion of the place of humor in education falls under the category of "Intelligence."

---

16. "Ha-Shomer" is short for Ha-Shomer Ha-Tzair (The Youth Guard). Ha-Shomer was a Socialist Zionist secular youth movement founded in Austria in 1913. It is also the name of the group's political party in the Yishuv and after the founding of the State of Israel. The organization continued in Israel and in the United States as a significant Zionist group.

Conservative Judaism — Nostalgia for Tradition

MAY 30, 1939

Could anything describe more neatly the difference between the traditional conception of salvation and the conception implied in Conservative Judaism than the following two phrases taken from Edman's[17] *The Contemporary and His Soul*: "The safest refuge from time is eternity" (p. 79); "the safest refuge from the present is the past" (p. 105). Nothing hits off so smartly the attitude of historical Judaism as the title of Ch. V in that book, "Nostalgia for Tradition."

Idealist Nationalism vs. Realist Nationalism

JUNE 9, 1939

As a result of my work on the "Modern Trends in Judaism," I have discovered that the Jewish people, in its struggle for existence, has resorted for survival to values which are not only the product of the Zeitgeist, but generally to those which are appealed to by its enemies to justify their hostility. The most recent illustration of that practice is the resort to the values of nationalism. . . . I have been reading and thinking intensively for the better part of the last week on Nationalist Judaism. I found a great deal that is stimulating to the mind but depressing to the spirit in Ezekiel Kaufmann's *Golah ve-nekehar*.[18] But I can't understand why he devotes considerable space to Smolenskin and mentions Herzl only in passing. Herzl's name isn't even in the index.

I believe that the classification which I have at last hit upon — Idealist Nationalism and Realist Nationalism — ought to bring some order into the mass of facts and ideologies pertaining to Jewish nationalism. I define Idealist Nationalism as that theory which bases the need for activating Jewish nationhood on spiritual and ethical values, assumed as inhering in nationhood, and Realist Nationhood as the theory which bases the need for activating Jewish nationhood upon the status of alienage, which is bound to adhere to the Jews because they are not rooted in the land in which they dwell, and upon the consequent inevitability of chronic anti-Semitism.

Mistaking Terror for Something Else

JUNE 9, 1939

Last night at 9:45, as I was sitting and working, I heard a series of loud explosions. Lena and I went out on the back veranda to see what happened.

---

17. Irwin Edman (1896–1954) was a philosopher and author identified with Columbia University, where he taught for many years. He was a supporter of John Dewey. Kaplan valued his work.

18. Ezekiel Kaufman, *Golah ve-nekehar* [In Strange and Foreign Lands]: *A Sociology of Jewish History* (Tel Aviv: Dvir, 1929–1932). The book was a favorite of Kaplan's. Kaufman's view of biblical religion dominated the Jewish Theological Seminary at midcentury.

There was nothing to be seen except continuous flashes from a searchlight coming from the northwesterly direction and the glimmer of what looked like a conflagration somewhere in the center of the town. The electric lights in the house flickered for a moment. This morning I learned that the electric workers were bombed and that a third of the city was plunged into darkness.

The interesting thing is the way Lena and I tried to make nothing of the explosion. She said it was thunder. This was suggested to her by Naomi's letter, which said that a few days ago it thundered and lightninged in Beirut. And I said the explosions were due to fireworks in honor of the King's birthday, which was yesterday.

From the Back Flyleaf of Volume 8: Kaplan Quotes from Books He Is Reading

"It is no more possible to argue with the Nazi state of mind than with the germ of some foul disease. It must be considered as a Thing, no more capable of reason and decency than dirt. Civilized human beings find it offensive even as a topic of discussion, but must discuss it because it is there, swollen and horrible to sight, smell and intelligence, right outside the window of the homes of the human race and beginning to spread disease."

> —Westbrook Pegler in *World*, Wed., Nov. 16, 1938. Copied in Jerusalem on Dec. 19, 1938

"I ask myself why I keep this journal. . . . I say to myself that hereafter in these pages it will be as if memory had fashioned itself into a friend who has heard my confidences and can respond with sympathy. It is an attempt also to fix the fluid insulatantiality of the spirit."

> —Paul Elmer More, *Pages from an Oxford Diary VIII*. Copied in Jerusalem, Jan. 3, 1939

[And then Kaplan added his own thought]

"When I am on speaking terms with myself, I record in the Journal." (February 19, 1939, Jerusalem)

Volume 9 of the diary begins here.

Kaplan Ends His Stay in Jerusalem

TUESDAY, JUNE 13, 1939

This afternoon I brought to a close my two years' work at the University. I think that, on the whole, I have reason to be satisfied with the results for myself of the study I have made of the history and principles of education and with the results for a number of students who took the work seriously. It is really too much to expect that very many of them should take the pedagogy courses seriously, first, because they receive no academic credit for them, and second, they are overburdened with studies besides having to do outside work to pay their way through the university.

I took leave this afternoon of Yizhak Epstein. He is one of those who laid the foundation of Hebrew education here, and a high-minded personality. The frightful misconduct of our people here at the present time, which like that of our zealots and gangsters, *biryonim* [Heb., Talmudic term for cruel extremists before the destruction] of old, is destroying our chances of survival, is weighing heavily on his mind. He is old and his strength is failing. He wept when I said goodbye to him. It was all I could do to restrain myself from weeping.

It was he who told me that five Arabs were killed this morning at Haifa by a bomb.

Training Rabbis at the Hebrew University?

JUNE 14, 1939

When we were through with this matter [the Department of Education], Schocken wanted to know my opinion of the plan which is being sponsored by Profs. Asaf, Klein, and Albeck with the cooperation of Chief Rabbi [Isaac] Herzog and his entourage to establish a rabbinic department in the University. The understanding, of course, is that it is to train men for the Orthodox rabbinate. Profs. [Julius] Guttman[19] and Scholem are strenuously opposed to such a move. They are afraid it would hamper their freedom. Ussishkin and Schocken are likewise opposed. In my opinion, which I voiced to Schocken, it would be a mistake for the University to ignore the rabbinic training altogether, but it would also be a mistake for the University to confine itself to one type of rabbinic training. The much wiser policy would be to have the various religious trends, or at least the Reformist and the Conservative as well as the Orthodox, represented in the rabbinic department. To that end, as well as for the general good of Jewish life, it would be advisable that the University should become the center of the network of the rabbinic training schools in the Diaspora and make arrangements whereby students would be able to take courses both at the University and either

---

19. Julius (Yizhak) Guttman (1880–1950) was a philosopher and historian of Jewish philosophy.

finish or begin their studies at one or the other of the rabbinical seminaries in Golut. If our people had vision, what tremendous possibilities for the unity and development of Jewish life could be realized through such a plan!

The Buddhist Notion of the Self

SUNDAY, JUNE 25, 1939

Whether it is because I am extremely impressionable or because what I read happens to coincide with my own thinking, the fact is that, chancing upon an account of Southern Buddhism, I was thrilled by its doctrine of the self as an illusion. This doesn't mean to say that I am ready to accept that doctrine. After all, I have wrestled with it in its more modern guise of behaviorism. But purely from the standpoint of adjusting oneself to human existence, with its infinite suffering, frustration, and cruelty, I can't help thinking at times that the negation of the self, which might make one at all times look forward to death itself as redemption, is more helpful than the affirmation of the self. For even if we happen to enjoy health and happiness, we must be quite callous not to have that enjoyment marred by the awareness of the multitudes whose bodies are tortured by pain or whose minds are wrung by fear.

On Board Ship Reading Herzl

FRIDAY, JUNE 30, 1939 (ON BOARD *Champollion*)

We got to Haifa on Tuesday and stopped at Hotel Zion. On Wednesday at 6:00 we boarded the *Champollion*.

I have been reading Herzl's and Nordau's Zionist addresses. I must say that I do not find them particularly edifying. Having to create a popular movement, they were probably forced to vulgarize their appeal and reduce Zionism to the simplest terms of flight from Jew hatred. If they had kept to those terms, one could find no fault with their elementary approach to the Jewish problem. But they do once in a while take up complex issues like assimilation and "mission." Those issues cannot be discussed in offhand fashion, and yet they are dealt with summarily in those addresses. Herzl's argument against assimilation seems to me to be forced. The fact is that if the Jews are let alone, they are absorbed by the general population. Witness how entire communities like those that existed three or four centuries ago in Italy have not left a trace behind them. Granted even that anti-Semitism is inevitable, one expects some social analysis of the causes of anti-Semitism, if one is to regard Zionism as the only solution. I was jarred by the one statement of Herzl's to the effect that if the nations won't help the Jews find a land of their own, the latter will breed revolutions.

Ezekiel Kaufman Is Very Valuable and Should Be Studied More

JULY 3, 1939

There can be no question that Ezekiel Kaufman[20] is the most scholarly and prolific thinker we have today. I do not understand why he is not better known. The reason probably is that his writings are all in Hebrew. Ahad Ha-Am has had better luck because of his brilliant style and his direct attack of the Hovevei Zion movement in his day. Perhaps the very fact that Kaufman is so prolific and not given to the fragmentary type of thinking which characterizes our spiritual guides is against him. No one has time to read through a book like *Golah ve' Neychar* [Heb., In Alien and Foreign Lands], much less to study it. But why isn't study of it required in the rabbinical training schools? Because the problems it discusses are too vital and too challenging.

Reconstructing the Notion of Hillul Ha-Shem

WEDNESDAY, JULY 5, 1939 (ON BOARD THE *Normandie*)

When we got off at Marseilles, we went to the ticket agency to arrange for the rest of the trip. An interpreter, who was a Jew, helped the passengers to make themselves understood to the officials of the agency. Among the several languages he used was also Hebrew. We learned later that he had lived several years in Jerusalem. Being anxious to get as many customers as possible for his hotel, which is right opposite the office, he gets the officials to give the Jewish passengers wrong information about the trains going to Paris, so that instead of leaving at once for Paris, they are led to believe that they must stay over in Marseilles till the evening, when they have to take a night train. In the meantime they are induced by the Jewish interpreter to take meals and stay over for a day at his place.

Against conduct like the foregoing, the fear of *hillul hashem* [Heb., profanation or desecration of God's name] formerly acted as a powerful deterrent. The question we ought to consider is, What should be done with the concept of *hillul hashem* [Heb.] if we want to have an equally deterrent effect in our day? It is the one concept about which there can be no doubt that it synthesized the idea of God with the idea of Israel in such a way as to give pragmatic reality to the former and high ethical significance to the latter. This synthesis disproves the contention of E. Kaufman that Smolenskin, Ahad Ha-Am, and the other nationalist thinkers are wrong in using nationalism as a means of revitalizing the religious values, since in the past the reverse was the case: the religious values were used to reinforce the nationhood of the Jewish people. The truth is that the two ideas—the religious and the national—were always mutually supplementary and each was incomplete without the other.

---

20. Yehezkel Kaufmann (1889–1963) was a biblical scholar, sociological thinker, and essayist.

It is evident that the motive of *kiddush ha-shem, hillul ha-shem* [Heb., sanctification of God's name, profanation of God's name] is to function nowadays [such that] the Jews must be so identified with his people that he would realize that any wrong that he does reflects on the entire people. This realization must be not merely intellectual but deeply emotional. Such identification presupposes the existence of a tangible collective Jewish life, national and communal. Thus we find that in our desire to keep alive the motive, we are actually striving for the regeneration of Jewish national life. We then cannot help being concerned about the quality of that national life. We want it to be of an ethically high level. This brings us back to the inevitable conclusion that if we want any ideal in Judaism to function, we must make the revitalization of the Jewish people and the raising of its standard of life the two chief objects of our concern. By aiming at them, we are bound to make Judaism a living force in the life of the Jew.

Kinship with Hermann Cohen but not with F. Rosenzweig

SATURDAY, JULY 8, 1939

From Bergman's account in his *Hogey ha-Dor* [Heb., Contemporary Thinkers] of Hermann Cohen's philosophy,[21] I am inclined to believe that there is much in common between that philosophy and Dewey's. From the little I read of Cohen's *Die Religion der Vernunft* [Religion of Reason out of the Sources of Judaism (1919)], I find that his method of interpretation of traditional Jewish concepts is very much like the one I follow in my *The Meaning of God*. I was especially struck by his interpretation of the God concept, which is almost identical with the one I give in my book, namely, as the "guarantee that what ought to be will be." Entirely identical with my reinterpretation of the traditional belief in creation as creativity is his interpretation of that belief. My approach, however, differs from his in that I recognize the fact that I am re-interpreting—consciously revaluating tradition—whereas he assumes he is merely making explicit what tradition actually meant to say. This is why he has to indulge in homiletic license, which I abhor.

But while I can endure Cohen's fanciful renditions of traditional texts, I am revolted by [Franz] Rozensweig's absurd metaphorical interpretations. The one he gives of the Magen David [Star of David] and of the Cross is nonsense. Rozensweig, personally, was undoubtedly a highly sensitive soul. Spiritually he seems to have been an incarnation of what Jesus is reputed to have been. But intellectually he is merely an adolescent who loves to play with abstract concepts as though they were little blue-winged cherubs.

---

21. Hugo Bergman, *Hogey ha-Dor* [Contemporary Thinkers] (Jerusalem: Hebrew University Magnes Press, 1935). The discussion of Cohen's philosophy is on pages 70–83. Hermann Cohen (1842–1918) is widely considered the most important Jewish philosopher of the late nineteenth and early twentieth centuries. Kaplan valued him highly. See Kaplan's book on Cohen: Mordecai M. Kaplan, *The Purpose and Meaning of Jewish Existence* (Philadelphia: Jewish Publication Society, 1964).

Arriving Home with Mixed Feelings

SATURDAY NIGHT, JULY 22, 1939

I cannot say that I do not feel hurt at the way the Seminary ignores me. The only two people connected with the Seminary from whom I received a word of greeting are Scharfstein and Romanoff (the curator of the museum with whom I seldom come in contact). Chipkin met me at the boat, and Chertoff came to see me. Finkelstein was in town the day after I arrived. He should have had the decency to call me up or drop a line welcoming me, but so far not a word. Suspecting his attitude toward me is part of what looks like a studied plan to cut me, I am exceedingly annoyed. I know that it is foolish of me to mind the hostility of my colleagues, but I can't rid myself of a sense of discomfort bordering on fear when I realize how much more difficult it will be for me to put up with Finkelstein as president than with Adler, or with a Board of Trustees including men like Strauss, Hendricks, Edgar Nathan, Drob, Israel Goldstein, [and] Krasne than with the late Judge Greenbaum or Judge Lehman. Sometimes I imagine I shall be deprived even of the security of tenure (without which I could not have accomplished anything) as a result of the way these people who are now in control of the Seminary feel toward me. If I only could pull myself together and go on with my work without caring a fig about what they think of me at the Seminary. But for that my work itself would have to be much more exhilarating than it is.

I am sick and tired of the Jewish problem, which is what I am working on at present. I happened to reread yesterday the concluding chapter of *Judaism as a Civilization*. If what I say there has had no effect, I don't see how anything that I can ever say will move our people to do anything about Judaism. Feeling as hopeless as I do about the future of Judaism in this country, it is veritable torture for me to restate the case for Reconstructionism.

Discussing the Concept of Freedom with Ira

JULY 22, 1939

In discussing with Ira yesterday and this morning the subject of freedom, which he is working on for the doctorate, I got to the point where I realized that it was a mistake to attempt to make any affirmations about freedom as such because, abstracted from specific situations, it was empty of all content and was entirely meaningless. Freedom is a quality of human acts and relationships, the desirability of which can be determined only when considered as part of some particular act or relationship. There is no such thing as freedom to do something. The trouble with a concept like freedom is that in its abstract form it has honorific implications which render it fit material for propaganda. But when it comes to regulating our affairs, the abstract principle of freedom is totally useless. I believe, for example, that the propaganda of the Nazis should be suppressed in a democracy, because they advocate violence. It is nonsense to maintain that the freedom of speech must include the freedom to advocate violence any more than it includes the freedom to yell "fire" in a crowded theater as a practical joke.

Annoying Everyday Details, Like the Rest of Us

SATURDAY, JULY 29, 1939

It doesn't take much to upset me. The other night about 12, as I looked through the material I was to correct the day following, I discovered that there was a page missing. It meant having to bridge the gap, which is not a pleasant thing to do when one is in a hurry. So for about an hour I was in a panicky state of mind, and it took me a long time to fall asleep after that. Fortunately next morning, with a little effort, I made good the damage and my normalcy was resumed.

Just now I am again annoyed because I forgot to take out the watch from the trousers which I have to be pressed. The watch is a cheap one but much more handy than the gold one I have. The loss of it is enough to upset my equilibrium for a while. Thank goodness it's all straightened out. At the suggestion of the colored maid, I called up the cleaner's and sure enough the watch was there.

Teaching Civics and Teaching Torah

JULY 29, 1939

Although I have only a brief reference in the previous volume of this Journal to the possibility of including statutes and court decisions in the teaching of civics,[22] I have been really anxiously looking forward to getting to work on that idea. The preparation of the Chicago lectures has necessitated my keeping that matter in abeyance. But suddenly, as out of a clear sky, the opportunity to bring the suggestion to the attention of the public has presented itself, and I have to look into it while in the very midst of the work on the lectures. I refer to the address which I have undertaken to give at the "Congress for Education in Democracy." What better means of inculcating democracy than by means of the specific statutes and decisions which illustrate and apply its meaning? This is an infinitely superior way of developing democratic habits and attitudes than through the use of glittering generalities and inspirational slogans. The relation of this suggestion to what I have to say about Judaism's contribution to education for democracy is quite clear. The traditional practice of the study of Torah, in which every Jew is expected to engage, plus the fact that the great part of that study was devoted to civil and marriage law, constitutes an educational precedent which might well be adopted in the high schools as part of their training in civics.

---

22. See diary entry for March 30, 1939.

Kaplan's Nonstatist Zionism and Dual Loyalty—1939 Version

AUGUST 3, 1939

The fact that I would have to discuss with Garrison the matter of double loyalty led me to formulate once again my position with regard to our status as Jews. The following is probably more to the point than anything I have had to say thus far: The dispersion of the Jews must be accepted as a permanent condition. This being the case, the Jews cannot hope ever again to become a nation with a central state to unite them. Their status must henceforth be that of a nationality with a common religious civilization as their band of unity. A civilization is a manifold of social institutions, language, literature, ethics, art, and religion. While the Jewish civilization has to be religious, there must be as much room for individuality in outlook, taste, and self-expression as in the other elements of the civilization. In this set-up, Palestine—even if it succeeds in becoming or harboring an independent Jewish state—will not function as a central state for Jews in the Diaspora. It will be only the cultural and religious center of Judaism—their secondary civilization. This should put an end to all charges of double allegiance against those who subscribe to Judaism as a civilization.

Facts as the Key to Action—The Pragmatic Kaplan

AUGUST 5, 1939

All those things [in the Museum of Science and Industry in Chicago] hold me spellbound when I learn about them, and I could probably go on enjoying them indefinitely if I had the time. But they also produce in me a strange sense of frustration. I find it as difficult to hold knowledge which I can't translate into action as to hold liquor. I get drunk on half a wine glass of liquor and the knowledge of many facts at a time gets me dizzy. This is probably why newly observed facts take on easily a symbolic meaning for me. This symbolization is the nearest I ever come to action.

A Visit from N. N. Glatzer

AUGUST 7, 1939

At 11:30 I had a visitor by the name of Dr. N. N. Glatzer (1353 East 56 St., Chicago) who had attended the three lectures I have given here thus far. He said he wanted to come to thank me for them and that he was very much interested in them because he had read what I had written. He is apparently in his thirties. He taught Bible and History at Biram's for four years and came to this country about a year ago. He teaches here in Rabbi Mishkin's Hebrew High School. He prefers his work here because it leaves him time for the pursuit of his own studies. He must be a well-informed man, because he succeeded Buber in the teaching of the history of the Jewish religion in the University of

Frankfurt-am-Main. Although at one time a follower of Buber's, he hinted his discontent with what he described as a certain narrowness in his approach. The opening subject of our conversation was the Jewish-Arab relations in Palestine. He wanted to know to what extent were the youth being imbued with the importance of establishing harmonious relations with the Arabs.

Democracy, Mobocracy (Fascism), and Judaism

AUGUST 10, 1939

Though I have the general idea of what I want to say at the Congress on Ed. for Democ., I do not find the working out of it so easy. Let me try to work it out here.

After mentioning the two factors which have contributed to the rise of mobocracy, viz., (a) the stupendous machinery of communication which unites millions into a seething sea of human emotion and (b) the failure of democracy to make good its promise of bringing special privilege under control, I want to point out the principal devices which mobocracy uses as a means of fortifying itself. They are (1) xenophobia, (2) chauvinism, and (3) ignorance of law.

1. The rulers in a mobocracy know that they can gain control of the masses by instilling in them hates and fears of some common enemy who has to be augmented to gigantic proportions if he is comparatively insignificant and harmless, and who has to be invented if he is non-existent. For their purposes mankind must be treated as broken up into classes or nations or tribes that are engaged in a mutual life and death struggle. The purpose of propaganda is to fan the flames of hate.
2. Chauvinism is the method used by these rulers to arouse a megalomania in their own people or class. This is the other function of propaganda.
3. These rulers find it advantageous to keep their followers in ignorance of whatever invokes the exercise of reason and is based on a conscious regard for justice. Since authority is the only basis of social order in a mobocratic regime, the less the individual knows of how the law to which he must submit has come into being, the better.

Now what can religion do to counteract these devices? While I can speak only for the Jewish religion, I cannot but feel that it is subject to the same danger as all other religions, viz., that of lending itself to evil as well as good uses. The apothegm of Satan quoting the Bible is all too true. A well-known theologian (Thomas Aquinas, whose name I suppose I should not mention in this connection in the presence of Catholics) based the principle that the king was not responsible to the people on the verse in Psalm 51 which reads "to thee alone have I sinned," and in 1749 (?) the English petitioned the king to withdraw the bill from Parliament which proposed granting Jews civil rights on the biblical ground that God himself denounced the Jews, etc.

It would be far from the truth to say that Judaism has throughout its history, the first 1,000 years of which are reflected in the Bible, taught the gospel of democracy as we understand it, whether in opposition to special privilege or to mobocracy. Judaism is an evolving religious civilization, and one must expect to find in its early stages much that has become unacceptable. To teach Judaism as an eternally fixed system of truth is to prevent it from being a force for democracy. On the other hand, taught from the evolutionary standpoint as a pattern of life, the beauty and meaning of whose design unfold gradually to meet the developing needs of life in general, Judaism has a tremendous role to play as a factor for democracy. Thus it is in the light of this need for democracy that we can discern in Judaism three important tendencies with which to counter the devices of mobocracy.

(1) To counter xenophobia, it is necessary to stress the significance in the Jewish tradition of the teaching concerning the unity of mankind and the divinity that is in all men. This is the main pragmatic implication of its monotheism. (2) To counter chauvinism, it is necessary to appreciate the role played by the true prophets. (3) To counter ignorance of whatever is conducive to reason and justice, it is important to revive the educational practice of Torah as the study of the civil law as a means to social justice. Since the Jewish civil law is defunct, I venture to submit to religious schools the suggestion that selection should be made from the vast towers of legal decision of the higher courts and state and federal legislation, which may be regarded as the authorized tradition or interpretation of the Constitution, which is the principal safeguard of democracy.

Kaplan Meets with Conservative Rabbis at Camp Tabor

AUGUST 20, 1939

Friday I left for Camp Tabor near Como Lake [in Pennsylvania], which is owned by Rabbi Jacob Grossman. He has been asking me to visit his camp for the last 12–15 years. The reason I went this time was that I wanted to meet the rabbis who usually spend their vacation there. If I really want Reconstructionism to make headway, I must make friends among the rabbis and break down their antagonism. Like all social ideals, Reconstructionism has a political aspect to it, which should not be ignored.

Although there were but few rabbis there, I am not sorry I went because among the few some are key men. I refer to Israel Levinthal, Simon Greenberg, and Max Arzt. Besides them there were the following: [Max] Kadushin, who is a loyal disciple; Louis Epstein, one of the arch opponents; [Paul] Chertoff, a personal friend but unsympathetic to Reconstructionism; Lipis of Camden; Louis Grossman of Mt. Vernon, an adherent; [Reuben] Kaufman [at Temple Emanuel] from Paterson, a fanatical opponent; Boaz Cohen, the bibliographer; and Alex Birnstine, quite an ardent disciple.

Ritual Must not Be Law

August 20, 1939

On Saturday afternoon nearly the entire group of rabbis called on me and engaged me in discussion. Epstein started the discussion by asking me to answer the following question: Since it is a fact that Jewish life throughout the past was conserved by the law, why is it that the non-religious elements in Palestine omit the reinstatement of the law from their national activities? I mentioned the fact that with the present need of eliminating all possible occasions for dissension, the Jews are wary of raising the issue of reforming the law as handed down from the past. I added, however, that if such an issue were raised, it could only concern itself with the civil and marriage laws and not with ritual observances. These cannot constitute matter for law to those who are modern minded. Observances there will be, and there is a definite tendency to create new ritual forms, but they cannot come under the category of the law.

Synagogue vs. Community—and Kaplan's Pluralism

Monday, August 21, 1939

Yesterday at Camp Tabor I had a long discussion with Simon Greenberg on the problem of the community. He has been one of the most strenuous opponents to my idea of making not the synagogue group but the community consisting of all groups, religious and non-religious, the principal unit of Jewish life. The main reason, of course, for my unwillingness to have the synagogue the main unit of Jewish life is that it identifies Judaism with religion only in the narrowest sense of the term. If the synagogue could do what the Catholic Church does, and identify salvation with self-fulfillment in the hereafter, it would be holding out the most powerful motive for cooperation—eternal life. But, since it can no longer do that, the center of gravity in Jewish life must necessarily be wherever the real interests of the Jews happen to find maximum expression. But those interests must not only be Jewish; they must be directed toward a Jewish future. Here we come upon the most difficult element in the problem of Jewish life in the Diaspora. The synagogue as such is practically devoid of any active Jewish interests, but it represents very definitely the general desire for Jewish survival and survival on a high level. The Jewish interests which are furnished by the various communal activities do not on the whole concern themselves with the Jewish future. This applies to the Zionist movement almost as much as to JDC[23] and other philanthropic movements. Even though the Zionist movement contemplates a future for the Jewish people, that future is limited to those who will live in Palestine. It is not interested in providing a Jewish future for those in the Diaspora.

The question therefore arises, Which should constitute the locus operandi for Jewish life: the synagogue, which upholds the idea of a Jewish future but does next to nothing to implement that idea, or the community activities, in which the most immediate interests of Jews as Jews find expression but where those interests do not reckon with a Jewish future? It is impossible to expect all Jews to join the synagogue as it is now constituted, or to crowd all their activities within its scope. On the other hand, it is just as difficult to expect that out of the temporal or temporary communal activities, there evolves a consciousness of their significance for a Jewish future.

Nazi Soviet Nonaggression Pact—Its Meaning

THURSDAY, AUGUST 24, 1939

At this very moment Germany's armies may be marching into Poland (8:00 a.m. New York time). If that is the case, Russia's non-aggression pact with Germany will prove to have been the match that set off the explosion. Throughout the years she has been pretending to be the great factor for peace. No doubt with her queer dialectics she will prove that war is peace and peace is war, but the fact remains that all people who had faith in the possibility of a better world as a result of Russia's experiment have had the faith completely shattered. When one bears in mind that those terrible blood purges of hers were carried through on the pretext that those who were executed had been conspiring with Germany, the Stalin Regime appears to have been playing a devilish farce. For those who reposed their entire trust in communism, there is nothing left to believe in or hope for. Of course, if they had realized the implications of Marxian communism or the so-called scientific socialism with its historic materialism, they should have left all faith and hope behind. Marxian communism regards faith and hope as useless baggage. But who thinks a thing through to its implications?

It seems to me that in most of the writing which deals with the present world chaos, there is not enough stress laid upon the new phenomenon in human society: the formation of great human amalgams through the rapid

---

23. The American Joint Distribution Committee, which is frequently referred to as the Joint. The committee is a Jewish relief organization. It is headquartered in New York and is active in seventy countries worldwide.

means of intercommunication. These human amalgams will take a long time to become human and amenable to reason. In the meantime they function like Frankensteins or golems.[24] Nationalism, Fascism, Communism represent effective amalgams that crush all individuality. From a theological viewpoint, they are the penalty for the greedy selfish individualism of the capitalist regime. But they differ from supposed penalties like earthquakes and plagues in that they contain the correctives to a degree of the evils they result from. Viewed in this light, what is happening now will appear not as world turned into chaos, but as chaos pregnant with a world yet to be, the creation of human amalgams that shall have the divine within them.

The Great Conflagration — The War Begins

MONDAY, SEPTEMBER 4, CEJWIN CAMPS [PORT JERVIS, NEW YORK]

On Friday Sept. 1, the supreme madman of the world started the great conflagration. God knows what the outcome will be. The mind simply refuses to contemplate the dread possibilities.

Yesterday England and France declared war on Germany. After their long record of criminal selfishness and stupidity which converted the German nation into a maddened herd, I was afraid that they might have become so corrupt as to permit this horrible creation of theirs to have its way. So dreadful has life become that one has to find relief in two such empires — or shall I say vampires — declaring war on a rattlesnake like Hitler.

The Value of Milton Steinberg — Reconstructionist Institute at Camp Cejwin

SEPTEMBER 5, 1939

Yesterday morning Milton Steinberg spoke on the problem of communal organization. He is a masterful speaker. His fluency, diction, and wealth of vocabulary are astounding. He certainly is an asset to the movement and could make it more powerful than Reformism, if he were to give himself to it heart and soul. The trouble is that he doesn't. He hasn't been maddened into doing it. Prashker (one of the Benderly group about 25 years ago, who long ago left Jewish education, went into Law and now teaches law at St. John's College) quoted Boaz Cohen, whom he had seen the week before at Wildwood, as saying that the only one of the graduates whose adherence to Reconstructionism he regrets is Milton Steinberg.

---

24. A golem is a clay figure brought to life by magical means. It has its origins in Jewish folklore of the seventeenth century.

Kaplan vs. Finkelstein—This Time on Salary

SEPTEMBER 7, 1939

At 12:00 Finkelstein came to my office. I had made the appointment with him yesterday. The entire conversation was conducted in a spirit of quasi-amity. Not even the sensitive point of the policy of the Teachers Institute— whether it is to be one of expansion or retrenchment—did anything to increase my blood pressure. I managed to maintain a suave temper all the way through until he answered in the affirmative my question about the raise of salary which the other members of the Faculty got and which had been denied me. Chertoff happened to have mentioned that fact incidentally when he came to see me about two months ago, and it rankled in my mind since then. When I protested the injustice of the procedure, Finkelstein's face assumed its characteristic satanic expression, with his lips curling into a cynical smile that is enough to drive one to commit violence. And when I added, "I don't think I have done the Seminary any harm," implying that I deserved better treatment at its hands than to be thus discriminated against, his silence eloquently said, "You certainly have harmed the Seminary." I choked down, however, my rising resentment and said I would write directly to Adler asking him to rectify the mistake, if mistake it was. He tried to dissuade me from writing to Adler by telling me that Adler was too sick to read any letters. He suggested that I discuss the matter with the treasurer, Oppenheimer. I did not accept his suggestion.

In the course of the conversation he intimated that he had suggested [Saul] Lieberman of Jerusalem for the work that Hyamson had been doing in addition to taking over the Talmud courses formerly given by the late Davidson. He referred to Lieberman as a Talmudic scholar second only to Ginzberg.[25] [Hillel] Bavli is to take over the courses in medieval Hebrew literature. He has an eye on Milton Steinberg. Just what he expects Steinberg to teach I couldn't tell. He expressed his philosophy of the organization of the Faculty as being that of having it divided, as it were, into two groups—the scholars and the men of influence.

Something tells me that I am in for a great deal of humiliation and mental distress at the Seminary, such as I have never experienced with Schechter and Adler.

Incidentally, I understand now why Lieberman was so effusive in his praise of Finkelstein when I last saw him in Jerusalem.

---

25. Besides the information on Louis Ginzberg in the glossary, see Mel Scult, *Judaism Faces the Twentieth Century: A Biography of Mordecai M. Kaplan* (Detroit: Wayne State University Press, 1993), 209–13.

Kaplan Distracted by a Finkelstein Letter and Delivers His Sermon Poorly

SEPTEMBER 15, 1939

A contributing factor to what I regard as the unsatisfactory delivery of my sermon yesterday was the letter from Finkelstein that came with the morning's mail and which I read before going to services. It said that the letter I had addressed to Dr. Adler in reference to my salary had been sent to him by Mrs. Adler with the request that he attend to the matter. The idea that Finkelstein should wield such authority illustrated to me quite emphatically the moral chaos that exists in the world. I might have found it easy to talk about overcoming the chaos by means of the divine spirit in us, so long as that chaos did not hit me personally. But immediately after I felt its impact, the blow was too staggering for me to be able to retain my composure. The result was that the sermon did not become sufficiently part of me, for the words to come trippingly from my lips. I had to hunt for the right word most of the time, and the effort left me mentally and spiritually exhausted.

In the afternoon, Lena, who had read Finkelstein's letter, sensed what was wrong with me and drew out from me how I felt about it. She helped me greatly with the wholesome attitude she took to it and which she communicated to me.

Kaplan Humiliated at a Seminary Faculty Meeting

SEPTEMBER 22, 1939

Yesterday afternoon I attended the meeting of the Seminary faculty. This time I came into open clash with Finkelstein and suffered as humiliating a defeat as did Poland at the hands of Hitler. This happened in the discussion of suggested changes in the curriculum. After Hyamson's suggestions and those made by Finkelstein and the men in charge of the Bible teaching, I asked Louis Ginzberg, who acted as chairman in place of Adler, why I had not been requested to send in suggestions. Instead I was handed a copy of suggestions drawn up by the four men who had given the courses in Homiletics during my absence—Levinthal, Goldstein, Greenberg, and Steinberg. In their report they took occasion to make the sweeping statement that "the students do not learn to preach at the Seminary." The reply was that the request was not sent to me because the idea of discussing the curriculum was taken up only last May and the office waited till I was back to inform me of that request. (Then why did the office have to wait till yesterday? I didn't put this question because I saw that the odds were against me.)

But the worst blow came when I touched upon Finkelstein's suggestion which centered upon the need of having a course at the Seminary which would present a systematic Jewish Theology. He suggested Milton Steinberg as the man that ought to give the course. I felt that I ought to mention the fact that the main part of my work in Homiletics necessarily consisted of the presentation of a systematic Jewish theology as the basis of what the men were to preach. The answer came at once from Louis Ginzberg that my work dealt with theology only in incidental fashion. It was therefore necessary to have someone give it for its own sake. This of course was supported by Finkelstein. Then the old babbler Hyamson repeated his long disquisition on Homiletics in which he—in his pastoral fashion—condemned the very idea of a theology having anything to do with Homiletics. The proper function of Jewish homiletics is to give the men the traditional sources—Midrash, Talmud, medieval sermons—but not a philosophy of Judaism. That each man must arrive at for himself.

After the faculty meeting broke up, I followed Finkelstein to his office to argue the point further. I only got deeper into the bog by indicating that my main interest was not in the Homiletical technique but in the underlying philosophy of religion. He had the advantage over me in being able to contend that such a suggestion was not within his scope to deal with. He would not declare himself on that question before consulting Adler. No amount of my practically begging him to express his opinion as a friend elicited a reply from him. He finally rose as a sign that he had to leave. I went away a broken man.

There was no use arguing that my book *The Meaning of God in Modern* etc. plus the chapters on religion in the other two books was as good a systematic theology as anything in Niebuhr and Lyman, whom he held up as exemplars of what he had in mind. He would have pooh-poohed the idea. It is so easy to make nothing of anything one wants to disparage. If I were inclined to accept the Seminary's attitude to belittle my work, I would regain my self-confidence from a letter like the one I received this morning from Dr. N. Glatzer, who is a scholar and a seeker after the truth.

At times the mental torment to which the Seminary subjects me makes me extremely depressed to the point of giving rise to insane wishes. But then I remind myself of what I have to say from the pulpit and apply it to myself. I spoke of Creation vs. Chaos only a few days ago. This situation at the Seminary is itself part of the universal chaos of greed for power and of unreason. I should indeed welcome the opportunity of experiencing firsthand the sinister reality of this chaos, its hampering and its sabotaging of reason and good will. Why should I expect to lead a sheltered life when there is so much suffering in the world due to man's cruelty to man? In fact, in those moments when I forgot my experiences at the Seminary, I was ashamed of my security. So now I ought to be grateful for having this hateful object to contend with and to rob me of my peace of mind.

Sermons Are So Ephemeral

THURSDAY, SEPTEMBER 28, 1939

Begrudging the time spent on sermonizing, I came to the services with a bare outline of the idea I was to expound this morning. As a matter of fact I had occasion to repeat the substance of the sermon to three different people, and I managed to make my point clear to them. But when I got to the pulpit, I was seized with what is ordinarily termed stage fright. Actually it was not that. It was a fit of inarticulateness. There was, of course, the uncongenial atmosphere of the audience, heterogeneous to the extreme, lacking as far as I could see all the elements of cohesiveness and insulated from me by many rows of empty seats. But I do not blame the audience for my failure. If I had worked on my idea sufficiently, I might have developed enough heat to fuse the heterogeneity into something of common-mindedness and to break down the insulation. To achieve this result, I would have to spend at least three full days on a sermon. I cannot get myself to waste so much of my time and energy when I consider how ephemeral is the effort of the best of sermons.

Kaplan's Brother-in-Law in a Freak Accident

TUESDAY, OCTOBER 3, 1939

This morning my brother-in-law Edward Rubin died as a result of an accident. A few days ago, as he was calling for his morning newspaper through the dumbwaiter shaft, the dumbwaiter went down on his head and threw him down to the bottom of the shaft. He had had a bad heart and was unable to overcome the effect of his internal injuries.

He was a peculiar type of man. He came as a poor youth to this country and ended by being the head of a great concern. He had a remarkable head for business. He owed his success in it as much to a strong sense of business honesty as to his shrewd insight. But in his personal relations he was on the whole quite a crank. His inner life was tense and stormy. Yet he somehow elicited from his children a loyalty—not love—which had nothing to do with their dependence upon him.

Still Having Trouble Speaking Hebrew in Public

OCTOBER 3, 1939

I began teaching at the Teachers Institute on Sunday, Sept. 17. I did not find teaching in Hebrew the strain it was before I went to Palestine. Nevertheless when it came to delivering the opening talk last Sunday (Oct. 1) at the Students' Assembly, I found myself to a large extent under the same handicap as in previous years. My poor memory stands in the way of my being fluent as a public speaker. I lack all powers of concrete illustration and I have to grope for my words even in English. These difficulties are augmented a hundred-fold when translated into Hebrew.

Self and God — A Fundamental Theological Statement

OCTOBER 3, 1939

In spite of the many years I have been teaching at the [Teachers] Institute the subject "Jewish Religion," I have not succeeded in working out the subject matter to my own satisfaction. This year I am trying out something new. With the third-year students I am reading the section on Judaism in Vol. II of G. F. Moore's *History of Religions*. This is to be followed by Kaufmann's *Toldot ha-emunah hayisraelit* [Heb., A History of the Religion of Israel].[26] With the fourth-year class I am trying out something new. I am taking the fundamental religious concepts in the order in which they occur in the Bible and translating them into terms of experience which a modern-minded person can identify.

The first two lessons were devoted to the description of the range of experience of a modern-minded person. That range has been widened as a result of the following principle discovered by ancient philosophy: (1) that the senses are no guide to reality [and] (2) that the relationships which fall under the various categories of thought are real in the sense that they make a difference in the essence and operation of things and persons. In addition, there are the following principles discovered by modern philosophy: (1) that because of our inability to think and discourse about relationship realities, we fall into the tendency to hypostatize them and into all kinds of errors as a result of such hypostasis; (2) that of the various relationships those which belong to the category of values are no less real than those that belong to the category of space, time, cause, etc.; (3) that the very ground of all reality, mind is the least capable of being named or described. Whatever we can know about it is not its noumenal but phenomenal aspect. Yet we experience its reality with an immediacy which cannot belong to any of its objects. On the other hand, this experience is non-communicable, whereas that of its objects is communicable.

The point which I then made was that mind, which is the very ground of reality and experience, is experienced as self on the hither end and as God on the end of one's self. This makes self and God correlative terms. The fact is that self has always been a correlative term. What the correlate was depended upon the cultural and social development of the individual. Usually the correlate was the most inclusive group. Its totem idol, flag, or other sancta were the gods which served as correlates. By this time, nothing less than the cosmos will satisfy

---

26. Yehezkel Kaufmann, *The Religion of Israel: From Its Beginnings to the Babylonian Exile*, trans. Moshe Greenberg (Chicago: University of Chicago Press, 1960).

the individual as being the seat of the correlate to the self. Hence his God is no longer tribal or national but cosmic.

I believe that the foregoing assumption that self and God are correlative terms might form the starting point of an interesting adventure in thought.

Steinberg, Finkelstein, and the Seminary

OCTOBER 3, 1939

Chancing to meet Milton Steinberg at the SAJ today, I opened up to him about my tilt with Finkelstein at the last meeting of the Seminary faculty. I find it a pleasure to talk with Steinberg because he is transparently honest. I don't have to suspect any mental reservations in whatever he tells me. As a result of the conversation I had with him this afternoon, I became clear in my own mind as to what he ought to do in order not to be used by Finkelstein as a pawn to checkmate the Reconstructionist movement. If he would accept the invitation to conduct the Seminar in systematic theology as Finkelstein proposed at the Faculty meeting, he would necessarily compromise whatever work in theology and philosophy of Judaism I give as part of the course in Homiletics. It would come to be regarded as contraband which I smuggle in under the name of Homiletics. I therefore suggested to him that if he is offered the post in theology, he should insist upon coordinating his work with the work in my department as well as with that of Finkelstein. He agreed heartily with any suggestion and promised to show me and have me pass on the letter he would write in answer to an invitation from the Seminary.

True Religion — Reconstructing the Concept

OCTOBER 8, 1939

Yesterday it was my turn to preach at the SAJ synagogue. The sermon I gave was the most successful of those I have delivered this year. It was based on the Haftarah Isaiah 42–43. The following is in substance what I said:

The "mission idea" developed by Reformism is not found in the Torah, nor even in the early Prophets. That fact does not indicate what's wrong with it. Before pointing out what's wrong with it, we must understand the meaning of true religion for the dissemination of which God is supposed to have designated Israel.

True Religion Makes Men Free

The criterion of what constitutes true religion is given in Is. 42 as being that which makes men free. We have there the forerunner of the famous New Testament statement (in John) about the truth making men free. In biblical days the antithesis of true religion was image worship. The question to be answered today is, What is the false religion from which true religion should emancipate us?

In the domain of the intellect there is the thralldom of the idolatry of nature. True religion is based on the primacy of the spirit. In self-awareness man has the means of mastering nature instead of being its bondman.

In the domain of the emotions there is thraldom of the idolatry of limited loyalties, in particular, chauvinistic nationalism. The antithesis is the God of unlimited loyalty, of loyalty to loyalty (as Royce puts it).

In the domain of the practical there is the thraldom of the idolatry of power. Salvation is with the God of righteousness. The difference between might being right and right being might is that illustrated by Hitler's present proposal to hold an international conference now that he has crushed Poland, whereas he had refused to join such a conference before he was in a position to dictate terms.

And now for the question of the mission. It is absurd to maintain that only the Jews are capable of appreciating the difference between true and false religion. The fact is that while a few exceptional poets and teachers understood that difference and dedicated themselves to the promulgation of true religion, the bulk of the Jews were not sufficiently appreciative of the difference between them to be regarded as its missionaries. The anonymous prophet himself says that more were so deaf and blind as those who should have been most keen in their sight and hearing. But the element of truth in the mission idea is that whereas other nations can manage to survive disaster because they have adequate means of survival, the Jews depend more than any other people upon commitment to the cause of true religion. Instead, however, of making the adoption and demonstration of true religion as a function of the Jew in the dispersion, it were best to treat [it] as the function of the resurgent Israel both in Palestine and in the Diaspora.

6

October 9, 1939–March 14, 1940

God and Emergence of Our Sense of Self

MONDAY, OCTOBER 9, 1939

I believe that I have the right clue to a method of experiencing the reality of God in the idea that the belief in gods has its origin in the adjectival aspect of important, significant, indispensable by which certain objects, places, people, etc. are identified. They become the sancta of the tribe. The question is, What are the steps whereby man can come to have a truly objective conception of God?

God and Personality

The first step is that of personification, which is itself a process that goes through various stages. When man begins to personify the objects which he regards as indispensable and therefore as holy (or endowed with mana-power that one must handle with care, etc.), he is still extrovert. The child personifies the doll before it is conscious of itself as a person. When the human being matures racially and culturally, he becomes aware of his own personality. The biblical statement of man's having been created in the image of God is historically more correct than the reverse, which is the usually accepted idea of the process in which the God-self relationship evolves. The fact is that man at first and for a long time regards the gods as more real and important than his own being. He is very little aware of the latter. The individual self is the latest stage in human development. Does it not seem then that *pari passu* [on equal footing] with the crystallization of the conception of God there takes place the crystallization of the self? So long as human beings believe in gods, which are merely the personification of the quality of indispensability, the self is identified with the body of the individual or is regarded as its ethereal double. With the rise of monotheism there necessarily arises a new conception of the self. The implications of the belief in the one God, the creator of the world, who governs it in righteousness, evolve [into] the conception of a self that regards itself as responsible for its conduct, etc. What happens when one's scientific approach to reality eliminates all need for assuming the existence of God? The tendency is to infer that the self too is nothing but an illusion and that there is nothing more to man than the physical and chemical forces that operate in him. Consciousness is a superfluous assumption, according to the behaviorists. Such a conclusion is a reductio ad absurdum of the scientific approach to reality, which sees in it nothing but blind forces operating at random. The experience of self, which is too real and immediate to be denied, should lead us to revise or at least to supplement the mechanistic conception of the universe.

The upshot of the foregoing reasoning is that God is that aspect of reality which gives rise to the fact and experience of personality in each of us.

Books for the Philosophy of Religion Class

FRIDAY, OCTOBER 13, 1939

Last night 13 students of the 3rd- and 4th-year classes at the Seminary met at my office for the first session of the Seminar. The work will consist of discussion of reading assignments in recent works on the philosophy of religion. The first book to be taken up is Knudson's *Philosophy of Personalism*.[1] This is to be followed by Garnett's *Reality and Value*.[2]

Water and Life in Hebrew

SUNDAY, OCTOBER 15, 1939

Is there any significance to the fact that the Hebrews gave the plural form to the nouns for water and for life?

Difficulties of Socializing with Louis Ginzberg

MONDAY, OCTOBER 16, 1939

Saturday night Prof. and Mrs. Ginzberg visited with us. They had attempted to call on us the second Rosh Hashanah night, but we were then with Judith and Ira.

I must say that I don't feel altogether at ease whenever I meet him socially. Being bookmen, we should occasionally touch upon problems dealt with in books. Being instructors of young men who are being trained for the rabbinate, we ought sometimes discuss the prospects of Jewish life. Working in the same

---

1. Albert C. Knudson, *The Philosophy of Personalism: A Study in the Metaphysics of Religion* (New York: Abingdon Press, 1927). For an analysis of personalism in Mordecai Kaplan's thought, see Mel Scult, "Kaplan and Personality," in *Reappraisals and New Studies of the Modern Jewish Experience: Essays in Honor of Robert Seltzer*, ed. Brian Smollett and Christian Wiese (Leiden: Brill, 2014), 162–80.

2. A. Campbell Garnett, *Reality and Value: An Introduction to Metaphysics and an Essay on the Theory of Value* (London: Allen & Unwin, 1937).

institution, we ought naturally to have something to say to each other about the way the institution is conducted. Yet all of these subjects are mentally ruled out by us as taboo, because we do not have a common language in which we could discuss them. So different are the universes of discourse in which the two of us live. Hence, when we get together once in a while, I have to make conversation, as in the case of Buber. I don't understand why I should be the one to assume the task of preventing the conversation from coming to a halt. But somehow these people are so satisfied with themselves that they don't see any reason for keeping me entertained or informed. And so I make use of the Talmudic method of association of ideas of passing on from one subject to another that is cognate to it. And when I am through, I feel as though a burden is off my mind.

Under circumstances such as the foregoing, the conversation is as flat and insipid as a cold cup of overboiled coffee. Not a scintillating idea is elicited from me or escapes my interlocutor. The highest point reached in the conversation may be illustrated by the following two remarks of Ginzberg's. One was in reference to Ussishkin, who, when he came to this country, said to Ginzberg referring to the fact that when Ginzberg had been in Jerusalem in 1928–29, he had never visited Ussishkin. To this Ginzberg quoted himself as replying, *ani yahid be-dor* [Heb., "Am I the only one in this generation?"]. The second remark was the one concerning his son Eli. Someone had asked Ginzberg whether he read his son's recent book. Ginzberg replied: Has Eli[3] read my books?

Uniqueness of Jewish Life in the Yishuv

OCTOBER 17, 1939

Today I started teaching at the Seminary. Instead of being able to devote the greater part of yesterday to preparing the lessons I was to give today, on Midrash and Homiletics, I had a number of appointments with people who came for advice and assistance, and I had to think of what to do today for the students of the Seminary who had invited me to a luncheon which they were to give in my honor today after the class. I spent three hours without finding a central idea. After a while as I was brushing my teeth, the sought-for idea popped up. It was the following: The difference between Jewish life in Palestine [in the Yishuv, i.e., the prestate Jewish community in Palestine] and that in America is that the former is characterized by physical security and spiritual insecurity. Among the factors for spiritual security I stressed the University. There for the first time the Jewish people and not merely individual Jews were destined to make contributions to general civilization, in that whatever discoveries or creative achievements Jews would be responsible for would be the outcome of collective Jewish support and encouragement.

───────────

3. Eli Ginzberg (1911–2002) was an economist, author, and advisor to President Eisenhower.

Graduate School for Jewish Social Work—How It Ended

WEDNESDAY, OCTOBER 18, 1939

I lunched today with Maurice J. Karpf and his wife. Karpf told me the story of the Graduate School for Jewish Social Work,[4] which he heads and which has been in financial difficulties since 1937. Then the two funds—the New York Foundation and one other the name of which I don't remember—gave notice that they would discontinue their annual contribution of $25,000 and $15,000, respectively, toward the support of the school. The budget had amounted to $75,000. Felix Warburg contributed $10,000 annually. When the question arose that year whether a new class should be admitted, Warburg promised he would secure an additional $10,000 to make it possible for the new class to conclude its studies. To carry out his pledge, he wrote during the summer of 1937, while he was in Europe, to his son Edward, who had come into possession of money which, according to Karpf, he didn't know what to do with, that he should give $10,000 to the school. The son was very much annoyed that his father dictated to him, but he paid in the money anyhow. When in October of that year Warburg died, it became evident that unless some new resources were found, the school would have to discontinue. In June 1938 a number of Federation executives of different cities and their trustees met to consider what to do with the school. It looked as if the Federations would save the school when Frank Sulzberger, head of the Chicago Federation, made a vehement attack on the school as being a sheer waste. When in April 1938 a report was brought in by a committee of those who met in January, the prospect for the continuance of the school was diminished, although the report endorsed the school and recommended that the work be reorganized in view of the limited resources. In the meantime, the Federations began to feel the added strain due to the overseas emergency relief which drained their income and were not inclined to contribute toward the maintenance of the school. Finally, in the spring of this year the directors of the school decided to liquidate it.

Kaplan Has More Influence than He Thought

OCTOBER 21, 1939

I have had a great deal of praise heaped on me this week on two occasions: at the reception given to me by the students on Tuesday and at the SAJ *seudah*[5] this afternoon. In addition, I found myself sprawling big in the *Proceedings*

---

4. The Graduate School for Jewish Social Work was established in New York City in 1924 and closed in 1940. It was an experiment to combine issues of general welfare with a particularist Jewish perspective. Kaplan noted the student body's strong interest in communist ideology. Kaplan taught at the Graduate School from time to time. Among Kaplan's papers are student writings that contain case studies of Jews who needed help.

5. Kaplan is referring to *seudah shelishit*, the third Sabbath meal eaten between late Shabbat services. It is a mitzvah to eat three meals on the Sabbath.

of the Rabbinical Assembly Conventions 1933–1938. I am beginning to realize that people think much more of me than I do of myself. I find the awareness of this discrepancy quite uncomfortable.

Israel Davidson—A Candid Portrait and Some Gossip

OCTOBER 31, 1939

Today . . . Boaz Cohen sat at the same table with me at lunch in the Seminary cafeteria. We naturally got to talking about the memorial exercises for Israel Davidson [who had died in June]. This led him to say many things about Davidson which did not do the latter's memory any credit. According to Cohen, Davidson was a supersensitive man who suffered from a sense of inferiority. Once he took a dislike to anyone, there was no way of breaking down his antipathy. Boaz Cohen mentioned the incident of his having worked out a bibliography of Davidson's writings and coming to present it to him on his 60th anniversary. Cohen did this at Marx's and Finkelstein's suggestion, in order to break down the ill-will which Davidson had borne against him for no good reason. The greeting which Cohen got was, "I am not dead yet."

According to Cohen, it was this sense of inferiority that drove Davidson to work on incessantly so as to make up in quantity what he lacked in quality. His *bête noire* was [Louis] Ginzberg. He always imagined that the students treated him as inferior to Ginzberg. Although he received more public recognition than did Ginzberg, he was always unhappy and he let out on those students whom he could afford to victimize.

What a difference between the public and the private character of celebrated people!

Torah and Natural Law

OCTOBER 31, 1939

In the absence of a concept of natural law to express the orderliness which obtains in the physical world, the concept of Torah or divinely revealed law functioned for the Sages as a means of accounting for that orderliness. In modern thinking the reverse is true. With natural law as an assumed fact and with revealed law subject to doubt, religionists extend the idea of natural law into the spiritual world and the Orthodox treat the Torah as an embodiment of that extension. If the latter were to write Midrash-Aggadah [traditional rabbinical commentaries], they would say God looked at the laws which are the foundation of the world and wrote His Torah for Israel in keeping with them.

An Outline of the Nature and Function of Religion

OCTOBER 31, 1939

I think I have finally gotten the outline of the lecture I am scheduled to give next week at Providence and which I expect to repeat the week following at Philadelphia. Here it is:

The Jewish Religion of Tomorrow

Introd. The Jewish religion is not coextensive with Judaism. The latter includes the entire context of Jewish life, its culture, organization, and institutions. The Jewish religion refers specifically to that element in Judaism which has to do with the idea of God.

Jewish religion will have a tomorrow only if Jewish civilization will have a tomorrow, if there will be a center of Jewish life in Palestine and a communal Jewish life in America.

On the other hand, Jewish civilization will have a tomorrow provided it will have not merely religion but true religion. The conviction which Jews had that their religion was truer than those of the other peoples kept Judaism and the Jewish people alive.

In ancient times it was not difficult to distinguish between true and false religion. Polytheism, worship of subhuman beings and of inanimate symbols, exalted rites over morals. For our day we need a criterion to help us distinguish the one from the other [i.e., true religion from false religion]. Such a criterion is offered us by the prophet: to open men's eyes to the truth which should set them free.

To apply that criterion to religion, it is necessary to deal separately with each of its three aspects: (1) the mystic, (2) the metaphysical, and (3) the ethical.

The function of the mystic aspect of religion is to help us adjust to the destructive forces which are beyond control and retain the willingness to lie under the most difficult circumstances. That aspect can be dealt with in a manner that is enslaving—viz., theurgy and magic—or in a manner that is liberating—viz., union with the ground principle of being. Such adjustment takes the form of resignation, trust in God, faith.

The function of the metaphysical aspect of religion is to orient us to the universe by helping us get at the nature of reality. The false orientation is the fatalistic of ancient times (including other-worldliness) or the materialistic-mechanistic of our day. The true one is that which leaves room for freedom, initiative, and human responsibility.

The function of the ethical aspect is to help us bring under control our insatiable desires. The false method is that of some limited type of loyalty, the true one of loyalty to the greatest good of the greatest number, irrespective of race, color, or creed.

Doctoral Examination of Henry Rosenthal

NOVEMBER 2, 1939

I've just come from the [doctoral] examination of Henry M. Rosenthal [at Columbia University], which took place this afternoon at Room 311 of the Low Memorial Building. Besides Fries and Schneider, under whom Rosenthal studied, the examining committee consisted of Prof. Lyman[6] of the Union Theological, Prof. Parkhurst (anthropologist), Prof. [Irwin] Edman, Prof. Murphy (psychologist), [and] Drs. Randall and Guttman.

The hypothesis, as worked out by Rosenthal, did not stand up well under examination. The reason I was swept off my feet on my first reading of it was that it coincided with my conception of the relation of religion to culture, and for the moment I imagined that everybody would see the point. But as I read the dissertation a second time more carefully, I felt as all the other members of the committee felt: that it assumed altogether too much and that Rosenthal didn't trouble himself to clarify some of the most disputed points.

I think that if Rosenthal had not made it a practice to avoid stereotypes by using abstract terms in unwarranted fashion, but instead had tried to be concrete and simple, he would have gotten much further both in his thinking and his writing. There is a striking freshness to his point of view and at times an epigrammatic succinctness—as when he said today, "We have stopped talking about God and we talk about religion"—but there is hauteur about him which at times leads him to affect a certain obscurity in his style. In his hypothesis, for example, he got himself all entangled by his use of the term "emotional system," which to this moment I still fail to understand.

The committee voted to ask him to revise his thesis and to reckon with the questions raised in the course of the examination.

A Family Discussion at Lunch

SUNDAY, NOVEMBER 5, 1939

At lunch today Lena happened to refer to the various levels of conduct, viz., impulse, habit, and intelligence. (According to this classification, authority belongs to the level of social habits.) Thereupon Naomi popped up with the question, Is there anything to warrant placing sex taboos in the category of intelligence? To which I replied: There can be no family life without sex taboos. This led me to make the following point: As man becomes sophisticated, he becomes unaware of the relation of means to such ends as he originally achieved instinctively in the same way as sub-human beings. When the end to be achieved is

---

6. Kaplan read Eugene William Lyman with interest, especially *The Meaning and Truth of Religion* (1933).

remote, there arises the conflict between the urge of the impulse and the remote purpose. Thus the mediation of knowledge, concerning the relation of means pursued authoritatively to ends felt intuitively, is the main cause of sin. This fact is basically the meaning of the story of the Fall. The knowledge of good and evil, especially in matters of sex, is the same as man's yielding to temptation.

Mysticism and My False Teeth

SUNDAY, NOVEMBER 12, 1939

Yesterday I preached at the SAJ services on "Mysticism—True and False." I gave the first part of the lecture I had given at Providence. I found it necessary to work it over in my mind again before I preached it, otherwise I am quite sure I would not have succeeded with it as I did. Anyone who wants to do good work must exercise considerable persistence and concentration. But I certainly require a great deal of both, if I want to speak or write effectively. My effort with a sermon is very similar to that with the bridge in my mouth. Whenever I have to put back the bridge, I have to shut out all thoughts and to concentrate on the groove in my left molar. Otherwise I can't get the bridge into place. As soon as I get my mind focused on the groove, the bridge clicks. That is exactly what happens to the sermon if, before delivering it, I focus my mind on it. Isaac Eisenstein (Ira's father), as if he knew of this analogy which had occurred to me before I gave the sermon last Sabbath, said to me after the services, "This time it clicked."

Faculty Salaries at the Seminary—Some Difficult Problems

NOVEMBER 12, 1939

Friday afternoon [Hillel] Bavli and [Paul] Chertoff—members of the Teachers Institute faculty—came to see me. They told me that they and the other teachers had received each a $200 raise. Of this raise they were notified in an impersonal note by the accountant Block. This meager raise, coming after five years of a much reduced salary and after Finkelstein had led them to believe that he would endeavor to satisfy the teachers by rendering their salaries adequate, only deepened their resentment against him. The money used for these beggarly raises comes from what [Abraham] Halkin had renounced by giving up ten hours of instruction. The classes had to be reorganized, and each instructor has to teach many more pupils than in previous years. It is no wonder that the instructors feel that they are being wronged.

But what could I do to help them? I had to tell them that due to Finkelstein's intriguing, or to the complete reliance which Adler and the Trustees put in him, my prerogative to have a deciding vote in the budget and in the allotment of salaries has been completely nullified. I am a dean in name only.

Reality Both Good and Evil

MONDAY, NOVEMBER 13, 1939

Have I come upon the truth, or am I deluded in believing that [God or][7] Reality is polar? It is both body and mind and couldn't be one without the other. It is both good and evil. *Borey hoshekh oseh shalom u'borey rah* [Heb., "He creates darkness, makes peace, and creates evil" (Isaiah 45:7)]. He therefore is ever at war with himself. He prays to himself. Since we exist in Reality or are part of it, we too consist of good and evil and [are] ever at strife with ourselves. (God prays with us when we pray to Him. God prays to God.)

TUESDAY, NOVEMBER 14, 1939

God should not be equated with Reality any more than consciousness with man. God is the positive pole of Reality. The positive, in its striving against the negative, hypostatizes itself, abstracts, and becomes conscious of itself, in the case of man. Likewise the cosmic positive becomes aware of itself in its struggle against the negative. In man his cosmic positive finds expression in the awareness of God or gods.

Truth and Illusion and Reading Otto Rank

NOVEMBER 18, 1939

Rank—Illusion as Essential to Survival

Reading Rank's *Truth and Reality*[8] has started me thinking on a new tack. It has dampened my enthusiasm for Reason as the panacea for all our ills. What he says about the destructive tendency of self-consciousness when carried to the limit is quite convincing. Likewise is his contention that illusion is indispensable to survival. At least this is what I gather from his book. What he says seems to be borne out by ordinary experience. For one thing, art, for example, is inconceivable without the element of illusion. But we don't have to go so far. How odd and unnatural life would become if we were seriously to act on the truth that colors are not in objects. The blue of the sky, the horizon of the earth, the entire complex of experiences which are what they are as a result of illusion would disappear if we were to insist on objective truth, and we would be far from being the better for it. What Kant designates as the dicta of practical reason, or what are commonly spoken of as "values" would naturally fall within the category of "illusion." This, of course, would apply also to the God-idea as it is meant to function in religion and not necessarily in metaphysics.

---

7. Words in brackets were crossed out by Kaplan.

8. Otto Rank, *Truth and Reality* (New York: Norton, 1978). Otto Rank (1884–1939) was an Austrian psychoanalyst and one of Freud's closest colleagues.

Polarity in Rational Interests

This brings up, perhaps, the most serious problem of human thought and conduct. There can be no doubt that the truth is to a large extent indispensable to life, and certainly to life at its best and highest. On the other hand, from the foregoing it is quite evident that illusion is no less indispensable to life. It is apparent that we come here again upon the principle of polarity as a characteristic of life. But the question is, Where shall we draw the line between the areas where truth should function and those which belong to illusion? The mere admission of illusion as necessary to life opens the door wide to all kinds of superstition and humbug. How is one ever to know what to do and what to believe?

True Conception of God

NOVEMBER 18, 1939

Intellectual Conception of God

Let me try to state the difference between the true and the false conception of God, from the standpoint of the intellectual apprehension of that conception. Intellectually we should expect the conception of God to deal with the following: (a) the nature of ultimate reality in relation to known reality—is it altogether the same as the latter, is it radically different from the latter, or is it neither? (b) the relation of that ultimate reality to the existence of evil; and (c) its relation to the freedom of the human will.

a. Fate and mechanism identify the ultimate reality or God with what is. The dualistic religions regard the ultimate as the absolute antithesis of what is. Hence the otherworldliness. Either view leads to false religions. True religion identifies God with the process of growth or creativity.
b. From the fatalistic or mechanistic viewpoint there is no good or evil. From the dualistic viewpoint evil is an illusion. From the creationist standpoint evil is a phase of ultimate reality to be overcome without which there would be no meaning to life or creativity.
c. From the fatalistic or mechanistic viewpoint, there can be no freedom of the will. From the dualistic viewpoint it is a supernatural gift wherewith man is endowed at creation, and which as a rule he forfeits in the course of his earthly life. From the creationist standpoint, freedom is a progressive achievement of the human being, which is the functioning of God in man.

Should a Jew Talk to Arabs?

SUNDAY, NOVEMBER 19, 1939

Last night at the Dushkins' I learned that a Zionist had approached him with the request that he write a letter to the *Reconstructionist* pointing out that I was wrong in what I had said in my article on Palestine Jewry concerning Zionist responsibility for the failure to urge the reformulation of Jewish civil law and about the prevalence of a chauvinist spirit in the schools. Dushkin hadn't read the articles, but he replied that he could well imagine what I had to say about the former matter and that he was in accord with my view about it. As for the matter of chauvinism, he also agreed with me. To prove the point, he told this Zionist the following story: In 1938 members of the vigilance committee of the Bet Hakerem community [in Jerusalem] asked him to dismiss Anna Machlowitz from the Bet Hakerem community where she was teaching English because she was reported to have conversed with Arabs in the street and to have invited Arabs to her home. On investigating what had happened, he learned that as she was one day waiting for the autobus, she overheard two young Arabs speaking a beautiful Hebrew. She was so intrigued that she got talking with them to find out where they had learned Hebrew, and she invited them to come to her home. The vigilance committee did not make the slightest effort to find out the facts but proceeded to charge her with being a spy and with trying to get Arabs to move into the neighborhood. A Jew, they claimed, should not be seen talking with Arabs.

Kaplan's Radicalism with Respect to Mitzvot

NOVEMBER 23, 1939

Monday night I had dinner with Dr. and Mrs. [Maurice] Karpf and Dr. [Julian] Morgenstern of the Hebrew Union College. . . . We had dinner at Trotzky's because they knew I would not eat anything but kosher. After dinner Karpf drove us in his car to his home on Central Park West and 108th (?) St. In the course of the conversation Morgenstern asked me whether my stay in Palestine had any effect on my views. All I had a chance to say was that it has led me to shift my interest from nationalism to religion. Mrs. Karpf then came out with the silly remark that in spite of any radical thinking, I was still Orthodox in practice. This led me to give a lengthy explanation of my position. To prove how unorthodox I was from the standpoint of practice, I mentioned my eagerness to see the Sabbath moved to Sunday by means of a legal fiction like moving the clock 24 hours.

Simon Greenberg

NOVEMBER 23, 1939

Last night I lectured at Har Zion synagogue [in Philadelphia], headed by Rabbi Simon Greenberg. He is a peculiar type of individual. I have not been able to make him out. He is one of those who have not seen eye to eye with me. He is either by nature or upbringing too conservative-minded to find my radicalism acceptable. But being sincere himself, he respects my sincerity, and being appreciative, he is grateful for whatever he learned from me. He is especially jealous for the centrality of the synagogue in Jewish life, and he feels that the effect of my conception of Judaism is to negate that centrality. In this he happens to be only half-right.

Ever since he has been cultivated by Finkelstein and brought by him into the Seminary Faculty, he has naturally become even more alienated from me. Although I do not regard him of much significance from the standpoint of creative thinking, he possesses enough personality and administrative ability to cut an important figure in the rabbinate. For that reason he would be a strong asset in the Reconstructionist cause. For this reason I accepted his invitation to address his Men's Club Forum.

In the course of the conversation I had with him last night, he expressed certain opinions about Jewish law which made me even more eager to win him for Reconstructionism. He said that he would favor an altogether different procedure in the solution of the *agunah*[9] problem from the one that Epstein was working on. His solution would include the insistence upon the Jewish court as the authoritative body to grant a divorce, but it would extend that prerogative to the point where it could grant a divorce to the woman as well as to the man. I felt on the whole that he had grown less Conservative than I had known him to be in the past. But I am afraid that he would hesitate before he would take any step that might antagonize Finkelstein.

A Moment of Depression — Loneliness

FRIDAY, DECEMBER 14, 1939

It is only two weeks and one day since I last wrote in this Journal, and already I find it so difficult to resume writing in it that I have a good mind to discontinue the Journal altogether. I am weary and disheartened. I do not see anything that gives any evidence of revival of Jewish life in America. I have no spiritual companionship of any kind. This last fact especially is eating me up. I am by nature so dependent upon stimulation and cooperation that I feel lost without them. And unfortunately the older I get, the more lonely I feel.

---

9. An *agunah* is a woman whose husband will not give her a divorce. According to Jewish law, the man gives the woman the divorce, and if the man disappears or refuses to give a divorce, the woman is still tied to him. Conservative rabbis tried to solve this problem in the 1930s, and Rabbi Louis Epstein was in the forefront of these efforts.

Seminary Faculty Meeting—A Plan Embarrassed

FRIDAY, DECEMBER 22, 1939

I look forward with considerable annoyance to the meetings of the Seminary Faculty. They all rub me the wrong way. Perhaps it is I who move the wrong way, thereby setting up electrical friction. I therefore solemnly resolve every time I have to attend one of those meetings to exercise all the self-control I can possibly summon. If my nerves don't give way, which is seldom the case, I feel that day like Little Jack Horner.

Everything went along smoothly at the Faculty meeting last Wednesday morning. I actually took part in the discussion and had no occasion to make any extravagant statement. When the item of the agenda came up in which the Faculty looked to me to make a report on the Homiletics suggestions that Finkelstein had handed to me at one of the previous meetings, I acted as if there was nothing to those suggestions and referred merely to the one suggestion with regard to the interval between the time the student read his sermon in class and the Sabbath on which he delivered it in the synagogue. All I said was that I had accepted that suggestion.

Finky [Louis Finkelstein], however, thought here was an opportunity to score against me. After one of the sermons delivered recently, a young lady approached him and asked him why it was necessary for the student-preacher to deliver a tirade against Chamberlain in connection with the present war. I calmly replied that I had asked the student to omit that part of the sermon and even had occasion to cross it out from the written sermon which he handed in later. Why it was necessary for Finky to try to embarrass me, by putting me on the defensive, he and the devil know.

Seminary Politics—Max Arzt

DECEMBER 22, 1939

Rabbi Arzt, formerly of Scranton, has been added to the Seminary staff in the double capacity of membership campaign organizer and lecturer on practical theology. He is not a bad sort of a chap; he has a good sense of humor and he knows a thing or two. He generally admitted to having learned something from me, but always made it a point, like Greenberg, to emphasize the fact that he disagreed with me on important fundamentals. This qualified him for Finky's retinue, and Finky has made sure that Arzt will be immune to the Reconstructionist virus by drawing him into his ambit and adopting him as a satellite. Finky is pursuing the same strategy with regard to Milton Steinberg, and probably by the beginning of next year Steinberg too will be revolving around Finky.

This Rabbi Arzt has been on my neck [that] I should have a seminary membership drive in the SAJ. I sent out about 55 to 60 letters to SAJ people asking them to come to my house to discuss what was to be done in reference to the

Seminary and the *Reconstructionist*. Nine promised to come and four actually showed up.

On Unions and Businessmen and Speaking Out and Being Disgusted

DECEMBER 22, 1939

Today I had lunch with Joe Levy and his son-in-law Finn at Longchamps on 5 Ave. and 12 St. In addition to repeating his complaint concerning the apathy of the older members and the poor attendance at our services, in comparison with that of the Jewish Center, he found fault with the *Reconstructionist*. After trying to get him to state specifically what he so resented in the *Reconstructionist*, he stated that the attacks on [Frank] Hague, the mayor of Jersey City, in the *Reconstructionist* of last year were out of place and unwarranted. Hague was, according to him, perfectly justified in keeping out the CIO from Jersey City. This meddling in controversial issues of our economic character is bound to do us Jews harm. An organ like the *Reconstructionist* should confine itself to discussion of matters of strictly Jewish concern. In the pulpit and in the *Reconstructionist* righteousness in general may be urged, but no stand should be taken on specific issues. This latter sentiment he kept on repeating again and again.

He said that union leaders had presented him with an ultimatum that he must give them $20,000 in American currency, if he did not want to have a strike on his hands in a few weeks from today when the contract with the workers would expire. If this is true and the union leaders are really racketeers who are selling out the union, then I cannot blame him for being bitter against the unions and resenting any attempt to take up cudgels on their behalf. Withal that I don't think that he has any right to dictate to me what to preach and what not to preach. There is no question that, under the guise of friendship, he wants to muzzle me, as did Joseph H. Cohen, Abe Rothstein, [and] Ike Phillips in the Center.[10]

All in all, I wish I could either grow cynical and reconcile myself to a career of lying and flattering and toadying for the sake of what the world calls success, and hate the whole damn brood of men and women who destroy my soul, or have the courage to pay with suffering and death for the privilege of being true to my innermost convictions.

Is it possible that all the world and myself included are intrinsically so morally corrupt, so selfish, so cruel, as to belie the reality of all genuine goodness and kindness, in other words, the reality of God? I confess that I feel very much depressed and hopeless about human life in general.

---

10. The three men were members of the Jewish Center. For more on Kaplan and the Jewish Center, see Mel Scult, *Judaism Faces the Twentieth Century: A Biography of Mordecai M. Kaplan* (Detroit: Wayne State University Press, 1993), 154–78.

And why should I find fault with the world in general? In my own little family I see from time to time the outbreak of the most violent hatreds. Judith, Hadassah, and Selma[11] with their husbands were with Lena, Naomi, and me at dinner this evening, which happened to be Lena's 55th birthday anniversary. After dinner we sat in the living room and were enjoying ourselves over a silly little book that was put out by a daughter of one of the members of the SAJ. At about 11:30 Judith happened to drop some remark about Lena's having had to take care of Selma,[12] when Selma flared up in a temper as though a thousand furies had taken possession of her, and screamed and cursed as though she were stung by a serpent.

In view of all these experiences, I must admit that I find it hard indeed to keep on affirming that there is any worthwhileness to life. I find life to be a veritable hell, despite the fact that materially I am infinitely better off than probably nine-tenths of the people in the world. What, then, must it be for the nine-tenths?

The Communist Party and Gone with the Wind

DECEMBER 23, 1939

Yesterday's *Times* carried an item about the motion picture reviewer of the *Daily Worker* [newspaper of the Communist Party] who had lost his job the day before because he refused "to mold his criticism of *Gone with the Wind* to fit snugly on the Communist party line." I quote this to convince myself that it makes no difference where and with whom one works; there is no such thing as independence of mind or interest in truth for its own sake. We are slaves of those who hold us in their power because we are slaves of the will-to-safety.

Impotence in the Face of Evil

DECEMBER 24, 1939

It is no wonder . . . that when the human being finds himself helpless in the face of overwhelming evil that he would prefer death to life. The evil by which one is overwhelmed is not only outside oneself but is also within one's self. Allowing oneself to be overwhelmed is experiencing defeat and the impotence of one's self. To be thus impotent is a living death. This is why complete death is then preferable.

More on the Family Argument — and Its Significance

MONDAY, DECEMBER 25, 1939

As much as I was shaken by Selma's actions last Friday night at my house, so much was I heartened by Judith's coming with her Miriam[13] to my

---

11. Kaplan's daughters.

12. This would seem to be some childhood issue. Selma was 24 at the time.

13. Miriam Rachel Eisenstein (1938–) is the daughter of Ira and Judith Eisenstein. She was a lawyer for the Civil Rights Division of the Justice Department and retired in 1999.

house yesterday and acting toward Selma as friendly as though nothing had ever happened between them. When I see human beings acting rationally and kindly, I am thrilled to the point of believing in God again. To me, a simple act of forgiveness is a source of genuine religious experience. I don't have to resort to any such extravagant experience as that recorded in James' *Varieties*[14] to come in immediate contact with that aspect of reality which is to one God. But the fact that such normal experience is to me significant of God is entirely the result of reflective thinking and of the rational process. James is all wrong when he assumes that there is no element of the conceptual in all those identifications of certain experiences as divine, which he records in his book.

Apropos of the intellectual function of religion, what more important task can there be for religion than to build up that entire conceptual structure of thought whereby we can learn to think about reality from the religious point of view in an ordered, consistent fashion analogous to that which we employ in our scientific approach? The fact that religion is not possible without some basic experience is certainly no reason for concluding that we can dispense with reflection and orderly thought to interpret that experience. Certainly science is meaningless without sense experience, yet who would maintain that all we need is sense experience?

Finding Literature on Socialism Valuable

WEDNESDAY, DECEMBER 27, 1939

I wish someone would write on Socialism as developed by Eduard Bernstein,[15] Ferdinand Lassalle,[16] and Hermann Cohen and point out their ethical approach to it in contrast with the so-called "scientific" but actually power approach of Karl Marx.

Besht Operates a Placement Office

DECEMBER 27, 1939

A realignment of the rabbis which would make possible for those in sympathy with Reconstructionism to constitute a homogeneous and effective group is not possible so long as the present rabbinical organizations control the placement of their members. The only likelihood of a Reconstructionist organization coming into being is when provision is made for the placement of men

---

14. William James, *Varieties of Religious Experience*, which has been published in many editions. For a valuable study, see Charles Taylor, *Varieties of Religion Today: William James Revisited* (Cambridge, MA: Harvard University Press, 2002).

15. Eduard Bernstein (1850–1932) was a well-known theoretician of evolutionary socialism.

16. Ferdinand Lassalle (1825–1864) was a German jurist, philosopher, and socialist political activist. Lassalle is best remembered as an initiator of international-style socialism in Germany.

in positions where they can earn a livelihood. When Jacob Joseph Cohen, who was rabbi of a community in Podolia, became a disciple of the Besht [Baal Shem Tov], he was compelled by the Mithnagdim there to resign. The Besht saw to it that Cohen obtained a position in Rashkov, where he served for four years (1748–52). When Cohen had to leave this position too, the Besht secured for him another post in Niemirov. Idealism even when supplemented by belief in miracle-working cannot dispense with economic considerations.

Salvation, Not God, Is Chief Concern of Religion — Criticism of James Otto

DECEMBER 27, 1939

I've read through the greater part of *Theories of Religious Experience* by J. M. Moore.[17] He gives an excellent analysis of James Otto's and Bergson's conceptions of religious experience. There is very little left of their theories after Moore has done with them. It seems to me that the very way in which they state their problem is all wrong. The very notion of trying to discuss experience of any kind apart from the object experienced seems ludicrous to me.

If we want to avoid treating the idea of God as the essence of religion, because as an idea it limits religion to the cognitive type of experience, we should do well to treat salvation or self-fulfillment as the essential object or objective of religious experience. Such an object is necessarily comprehensive and inclusive of every phase of psychological reaction. The comprehensiveness of salvation gives a different significance to the various elements which constitute religious experience from what they have by themselves. Take the notion of fear. Otto struggles hard to distinguish between ordinary fear and religious fear and comes to the conclusion that the latter is numinous fear. What this numinous object is he tries to explain. But as Moore rightly implies, were it not for the particular cultural background which Otto assumes, it would not occur to him to characterize the numinous object as an object of religion. It seems much simpler to account for the unique character of religious fear by the fact that it is not so much fear of the object as fear for the forfeiture of salvation or its equivalent. Fear of a ghost is not religious fear, but fear that the ghost is an omen of loss of salvation is undoubtedly religious fear.

If the function of religion is to help the human being achieve salvation — and religion would then be the complex of attitudes, beliefs, and behavior dominated by the purpose of salvation — it is important to control its emotional, intellectual, and social functions so that it will help the individual achieve salvation. What our religion is to be, therefore, depends upon our notion of salvation, which is determined not by religion but by the social and cultural development. Nevertheless

---

17. John Morrison Moore, *Theories of Religious Experience with Special Reference to James, Otto, and Bergson* (New York: Round Table Press, 1938).

it is part of the intellectual function of religion to formulate a conception of salvation that shall be so integrally related to actual needs as defined by the current social and cultural conditions as to give meaning and direction to the whole of a person's life. The main trouble with the historical religions has been that the conception of salvation which has come down from them is out of keeping with the rest of human life. Though they have not insisted that their traditional conception of salvation be taken seriously, they have not had the courage or wisdom to formulate a modern workable idea of salvation.

By this time the threefold function of religion seems quite clear to me. The intellectual function is to formulate the meaning of salvation, the emotional to indicate the proper method of overcoming fear, and the social is to arrive at a proper synthesis of individual self-realization and social cooperation.

Shifting Ritual to the Home

DECEMBER 30, 1939

Part of the general problem of Jewish life is the question of religious services, which are coming to be less and less regarded as worthwhile. Once the theurgic [magical] conception of public worship is given up, no matter how beautiful or interesting it be made, it ceases to play an important part in a person's life. If religious services are to be judged by esthetic standards, they necessarily enter into competition with the manifold offerings in art, music, [and] entertainment, and even when successful in this competition, they cannot be counted on to become a regular spiritual diet. The tendency to be fed up is one to which religious services are likely to give rise as any form of entertainment, even to the best.

Perhaps the time has come when we must think of shifting the center of gravity of worship from the public gathering to the home. If the family were to become the main unit in religious services, or the home the principal place for divine communion, the practice of worship might be given a new lease on life. In general, it seems to be that if we want Jewish life to survive within the present political and economic framework, it will be necessary to decentralize it in certain of its aspects as well as to centralize it in others.

The New Haggadah — Not Good Enough

SUNDAY, DECEMBER 31, 1939

One of the ways of shifting the center of gravity of Jewish religion from the synagogue to the home would be to issue a book or books of home devotions. Eugene Kohn and I have done some work in that direction. We worked out a revised Haggadah,[18] which I put into Behrman's[19] hands a few weeks ago. But Dina

---

18. The Haggadah is the liturgy for Passover. The title of Kaplan's version is *The New Haggadah*.
19. Behrman House was the publisher of Kaplan's *New Haggadah*.

Behrman discovered that it was not up to the standard of what was expected of us. The revised Haggadah, to make an impression, would have to be poetic and much richer in content. I put in the greater part of a week's work on it again, and Eugene Kohn wrote a couple of poems for it. But again Dina Behrman pointed out that while it was a great improvement on the original text I handed in, it was still far from perfect. I must confess that I respect her judgment in this matter, even though it means a year's delay in the publication of the Haggadah.

Salvation — The Will to Life Abundant

DECEMBER 31, 1939

I have a feeling that in making the will to salvation instead of the God-idea the essential element in religion, I am effecting a Copernican revolution analogous to that which Kant did in his theory of knowledge when it occurred to him to treat time, space, and the logical categories as forms of the mind instead of as derived from sensation. After he formulated his theory with regard to our knowledge of the world, he proceeded to apply the same method of discovering in the mind itself the forms by which it knows reality to the field of morality. There again he arrived at the imperative moral category which, according to him, constitutes the form that the mind imposes on human relationships. Religion did not receive any special place in Kant's conception of the original nature of the mind. It was to him simply the moral law viewed as divine. It seems to be that this defect in his theory would be made good if instead of the moral imperative being regarded as a form of the mind, we were to regard as the basic form of the mind which operates in all matters of a practical character, the will-to-salvation. The will-to-salvation is the will-to-live as it functions in the human mind. From a psychological standpoint, to be sure, the will-to-live expresses itself in the will to particular activities. But that should not prevent us from regarding all these specific expressions as manifestations of one underlying form, of which only man, by dint of his power to think abstractly, can identify. In the human being the will-to-a-desired-end, by becoming an object of consciousness, renders the ends themselves subject to comparison. Thus arises not merely will-to-a-desired-end but will-to-most-desirable-ends. This fact, when generalized, means that the human being, as a result of his power of self-awareness or awareness of the ends he strives for, possesses not only a will-to-live but a will-to-maximum-life, or life abundant. This is the will to salvation.

Prayers Should Speak of God in the Third Person

MONDAY, JANUARY 1, 1940

Once in a while I get into a kind of praying mood. It is usually the result of my coming across some well-formulated modern prayers. It is never the result of my reading the book of Psalms. The Psalmist's enemies are not my enemies, and he shouts so loud about his troubles that I can't make out what they are. I don't know much about Francis d'Assisi's prayers, but I have a hunch from the little that I do know about them that they would fit my needs much more than do the prayers of the Psalmist. But there is one point in which I would differ in the formulation of prayer from both [the Psalmist and St. Francis] and from most people who have written prayers. I would speak of God in the third and not in the second person. Buber to the contrary, notwithstanding. I regard the style of *Yitgadal ve-yitkadsh shemay rabbah* [Heb., "May God's name be magnified and sanctified"][20] as much more fitting for my conception of God than that of *Baruch atah adonai . . .* [Heb., "Blessed art Thou, o Lord our God"].[21]

Should Rabbis Speak Out on "Non-Jewish" Social Issues?

WEDNESDAY, JANUARY 3, 1940

I somehow could never accept Karl Marx's version of what he calls the class struggle. All I could see was that there are people who have power and those who lack it, but the former exploit the latter and are on the lookout for any signs of rebellion on the part of the exploited. But once in a while I cannot help being impressed with the reality of the class struggle. Ira and I have a difficult time with the few leading members of the SAJ because they sense that we are not in sympathy with the status quo. They sabotage the *Reconstructionist* because once in a while it comes out with an editorial attacking some flagrant evil of the present social order. The following are instances of what we have to put up with: Jacob Levy at a meeting of the SAJ[22] Board last year expressed his resentment at the editorial in the *Reconstructionist* which had made a plea for justice to Mooney.[23]

Harry Liebovitz, the most reasonable of our reactionary group, was finally convinced by me, in the course of the conversation at my house last Monday, that Jacob Levy was wrong, when I mentioned the fact that even the *Atlantic Monthly* had an article by Frankfurter vindicating Mooney. All the facts which pointed to the tissue of lies had no effect apparently on Liebovitz. But my statement about the *Atlantic Monthly* (I'm not sure whether it wasn't *Harpers* that had the Frankfurter article) silenced all his doubts and convinced him that the *Reconstructionist* was justified in coming out last year with a plea for justice to Mooney.

Bernard Semel said to Leibovitz, "Have you ever read the *Reconstructionist* platform? It is anti-capitalistic." As if there could be nothing more criminal. This is the basis of all his fault-finding with the SAJ.

---

20. First words of the Kaddish prayer.

21. First words of blessings. Key phrase in many prayers.

22. Jacob Levy was a key member of Kaplan's congregation, the Society for the Advancement of Judaism.

23. Kaplan is probably referring to Thomas Mooney (1882–1942), an American political activist and labor leader who was convicted of a bombing in 1916. Many believed that Mooney was wrongly convicted; he was freed in 1939.

Joseph Levy stated to me at one of the luncheons I had with him a couple of weeks ago that the *Reconstructionist* had no right to attack Mayor Hague of Jersey City for keeping out the CIO from his city, nor to condemn the action of the Jewish Center there which compelled Plotkin to resign because of his having attacked Mayor Hague. Joseph Levy said that the *Reconstructionist* should confine itself to matters of direct Jewish interest only, and that in our preaching and writing we should avoid dealing with specific evils, but try to uphold the general principles of ethics.

The Ethical Is Objective

JANUARY 3, 1940

If the source of our knowledge of God is the will to salvation, the crucial factor in human life is our conception of salvation.

The Place of Reason in Human Life

This conception is determined by the general status of our cultural development. But if there is to be any meaning to cultural development, if there is to be any standard by which we can distinguish between lower and higher values, we must assume an objective norm of truth and value. The assumption of such a norm and its imperative character are part of the functioning of reason. No matter how much reason is eclipsed by the drivers of instinct and impulse, its presence somehow does not fail to assert itself. It is the only hope of mankind, and to that extent it becomes an integral part of our idea of salvation. The violation of it in ourselves brings with it self-contempt. The highest conception of God, or of the power that makes for salvation, is achieved when we consciously accept reason as the true law of our being, which gives us no rest unless it finds fulfillment in us. From that standpoint, I think that the Stoics and Spinoza achieved the highest conception of God.

Why People Embrace Supernaturalism

JANUARY 3, 1940

Why Some People Demand Supernatural Sanctions

What place in the foregoing analysis shall be assigned to the kind of religion which takes shelter in authority because of its distrust of reason? Does not the fact that many who have been familiar with the functioning of reason have fled from it and its works, indicate that we are unwarranted in placing our reliance upon it and in making it the sole true revelation of God? The answer is that those who distrust reason really do not repudiate reason but the various human impulses and interests that assume the guise of reason. Unfortunately, pure reason is seldom given a chance to operate in our thinking. When people fall back upon the religion of authority, it is because they deem authority as speaking with the voice of reason. Of authority they feel sure that it is not colored by their personal likes and dislikes. They have little knowledge of the way authoritative teachings arise. Especially if they regard such teaching as supernaturally revealed are they prone to consider it free from all contamination of the subjective and the arbitrary. It is no wonder, therefore, that for want of a reliable criterion of the functioning of pure reason, men have for so long hoped to find the only expression of true divine reason in some supernaturally revealed teaching.

Thinking about Psalm 94

JANUARY 4, 1940

What I said above about the Psalmist's prayers[24] does not apply to his ideas and sentiments. I find the latter for the most part both stirring and exalting. I just happened to glance at the 94th Psalm. It is too bad that he makes use of the term *nekama* [Heb., vengeance (Psalm 94:1, "God of retribution, Lord, God of retribution appear")]. Very few know that he uses that term in the sense of "justice" and takes for granted that he really means "vengeance" in the old barbaric sense. But otherwise it is a great psalm. I was especially touched by the feeling he voices of finding himself alone in his struggle against evil doers: *mi yakum li em me'reyim* [Heb., "Who will take my part against evil men? (Who will stand up for me against wrongdoers?)" (Psalm 94:16)]. It takes, however, the "American Translation" to bring out the full value of the text.

When I read the verse *ha-notea ozen ha-lo yishma* [Heb., "Shall He who implants the ear not hear (He who forms the eye not see)" (Psalm 94:9)], I was tempted to conclude that it represented the only sample of teleological thinking in the Bible. In fact, Knudson quotes this verse in the course of his argument about teleology.[25] But when I examined the context, I noted that it had nothing to do with proving the existence of God, but rather with the fact that God cared and that it sought to contravene the statement of the wicked, who say *lo yireh yah ve'lo yavin* [Heb., "The Lord does not see it, the God of Jacob does not pay heed" (Psalm 94:7)].

The Morning Walk

FRIDAY, JANUARY 5, 1940

I love these half-hour walks in the morning with their yield of fruitful ideas. I have just come back with the following: The theory that the will to

---

24. See the diary entry for January 1, 1940.

25. Kaplan is probably referring to Knudson's *Philosophy of Personalism*, the book Kaplan used with a student group. See the diary entry for October 13, 1939. Albert C. Knudson, *The Philosophy of Personalism: A Study in the Metaphysics of Religion* (New York: Abingdon Press, 1927). On Kaplan and personalism and especially on the significance of Knudson, see Scult, "Kaplan and Personality."

salvation is the source of our belief in God throws a new light on the concepts of freedom of the will and immortality. Freedom of the will, from the viewpoint of that theory, is the freedom man has in choosing what he shall consider salvation or life abundant. Even if environmental influences play a great part in determining one's conception of salvation, there is always some flaw in the armor of those influences. Moreover, if we view the problem of freedom not as an individual one but as one in which society as a whole is involved, there can be no question that the opportunity to choose the higher, the more socialized and spiritual type of salvation is always present.

Venting One's Spleen in Prayer

SATURDAY NIGHT, JANUARY 6, 1940

I don't suppose preachers often resort to prayer as I did today when I used it to vent my spleen against Joseph Levy,[26] the Little Napoleon of the SAJ. In this respect my use of prayer probably comes nearest to that of the Psalmist. But if ever anyone will read this, he will at least know what I objected to in my "enemy," whereas the Psalmist never took the trouble to tell us specifically what kind of people his enemies were. The following is what I said in part before the Ark after the scroll of the Torah was put back:

> Give us understanding and we shall live. Give us understanding of what we ought to be and what we ought to do. Make us realize how often we either thoughtlessly or deliberately flout what we know to be the right. Let us not deceive our conscience or imagine we can deceive Thee by using our human weakness as an excuse for our vanity and our greed. Keep us from using Thy name in vain. Put fear into our hearts against the desecration of any sacred cause that is dedicated to Thy service as a shield for our selfish purposes. Grant that the faith we profess with our lips may shame away our mean intents and so purify our hearts of all dross of selfishness that we may serve Thee in sincerity and truth.

Joseph Levy was in the audience. I used a special device to catch his attention. Having heard him once quoting with approval the verse "Give me understanding and I shall live," which I would use in the reading before the Scroll was taken out, I inserted that verse in the prayer in the hope that it would compel his attention to the rest of what I had to say.

---

26. Joseph Levy, one of the founders of the SAJ, was frequently at odds with Kaplan over many issues, but he was a strong supporter of the SAJ nonetheless.

The Meaning of Reconstructionism

FRIDAY JANUARY 12, 1940

The problem which confronts the Jew today is, How should he carry on this struggle for individual existence in the face of anti-Semitism? He can carry on that struggle in one of two ways. One way is to spend himself in combating anti-Semitism in order that he might become entirely assimilated and cease to be a Jew. If anti-Semitism would abate, he could identify himself so completely with the totalitarian tendencies of the modern nations as to throw in his lot completely with its power-politics. Or he can join his individual struggle for existence with that of his fellow Jews, and transform the common predicament into the collective struggle of the Jewish people for survival. In the very effort at collective survival it is inevitable for him to evolve ideas and ideals which are a very [large] part of a democratic nationalism. The struggle for Jewish survival is a struggle for an order of society in which right and not might is to govern the relations of the state to the citizen and of the state to other states. Thus, by choosing the alternative of Jewish survival, the Jews vow allegiance to a conception of salvation which spells universal justice and peace.

In order, however, that the Jews shall choose the second course and that, in making this choice, he should feel that he is moving in the direction of its objective, it is necessary to formulate a plan of Jewish living in which there is an intelligible connection between the purpose of Jewish survival on a high level of existence, creative survival, or salvation, and the means to it. It is at this point again—the point of counteracting the consequences of the shattering impact of the tremendous upheaval—that Reconstructionism asserts its realism. This realism involves dealing with Jewish life organically. No one type of effort which concentrates upon one aspect of the Jewish problem as if it were the whole of it can remedy matters. This does not mean that everyone must try to do everything to strengthen the synagogue, be an active Zionist, do anti-defamation work, take part in educational endeavor, try to help in the relief campaigns. There is need for division of labor, and for more Jews to take part in all these activities. But it does mean correlating all Jewish endeavor and bringing them within the framework of the dominant purpose of Jewish survival.

Ezekiel as the Patron Saint of Reconstructionism[27]

SUNDAY, JANUARY 14, 1940

If Jewish life were inclined to take unto itself patron saints, I would choose the prophet Ezekiel as the patron saint of Reconstructionism. Both the circumstances of his age and the message of his prophecy correspond accurately to those which are part of Reconstructionism. Then as now, Jews in the Babylon diaspora

---

27. Although Kaplan rarely gave titles for his diary entries, this title is from Kaplan.

saw no future for their people, and then as now the most pertinent message is "Wherefore shall ye die, O house of Israel?" Ezekiel even went so far as to lay down the principles of reconstruction which we should do well to follow in our own day: reconstruction in ideology as illustrated by his emphasis on individual responsibility and reconstruction in organizational aspect of Jewish life as illustrated by his utopia for the returned captivity portrayed in the closing chapters of his book.

Disgust with the Rabbinical School Class

JANUARY 17, 1940

On the contrary, the more I see what those in a position of leadership in Jewish life are doing, and how unqualified those whom the Seminary is training for leadership are to understand the magnitude of their task and responsibility, the more despondent I grow. When I asked the class in the Seminary yesterday to read the Midrash, there wasn't even one out of about 40 men who was prepared. I was beside myself with exasperation at the complete apathy of the entire student body. And when I upbraided them, all that they could say was that they had 15 different subjects and could not find the time to prepare. I know that this is all humbug. If the men really cared, they could find time. They waste plenty of it. The real reason is that they don't care. All that they are interested in is to pass in subjects like Talmud, History, and Bible, where it is a question of knowing a number of dry, unrelated facts which have nothing to do with the dangers and problems that confront us today and which call for no deep personal concern or wholehearted interest in the Jewish struggle for existence. How little fundamental knowledge they get in those sources, how little they actually understand even those subjects which they are compelled to cram, comes out again and again in the sessions with me. I had to spend nearly a whole hour yesterday to impress upon them the fact that it is impossible to understand important sections of Bible and Rabbinics without having an idea of the mental concept of the universe with which the ancients operated. One imagines that long before they entered the Seminary, they would learn the world picture implied in the account of creation, the story of the Flood. And yet even those who are about to be graduated are completely ignorant of such basic facts.

Listening to Reinhold Niebuhr

JANUARY 17, 1940

I attended the first luncheon lecture of this "Interfaith" business. It was given by Niebuhr[28] of the Union Theological. It dealt with prophetic religion.

28. On Reinhold Niebuhr, see the glossary and especially Daniel F. Rice, *Reinhold Niebuhr and John Dewey: An American Odyssey* (Albany: State University of New York Press, 1993). Kaplan's approach is more generally identified with Dewey than with Niebuhr.

He spoke fluently and impressively, but what he said was basically unsound. He is a Barthian.[29] Nothing plays so conveniently into the hands of obscurantists and hypocrites as Barthianism. Hence its danger to present-day Judaism, whose only hope is the healing light of human reason and disinterested integrity.

Meeting Jacob Agus

JANUARY 17, 1940

Rabbi Jacob B. Agus (formerly Agushewitz) is a graduate of the N. Y. Yeshibah but a sympathizer of Reconstructionism. His rabbinical position, however, does not permit him to come out openly with his views. Not long ago he got his doctorate at Harvard. His thesis dealt with Buber and Hermann Cohen. When he came to see me about a month ago and told me these facts about himself, I asked him to let me read his thesis. I got it last week and read it through. I found it to be a very clear and organized statement of the two philosophies of religion. He thinks clearly and writes well and is genuinely interested in the problem of religion.

The Realities of Synagogue Life

FEBRUARY 4, 1940

Yesterday I preached my monthly sermon at the SAJ services. Yesterday was typical of those days when I go through mentally the most grueling experience. This is what takes place: On Friday I feel I have an important message to convey. My topic is "Religion and the State." It all seems so clear. I want to point out the superficiality of the "Back to Religion" slogan one hears these days and to indicate the kind of religion we need, if we want to find a way out of our present crisis. It should be a religion which emphasizes not merely cult and belief but mainly justice. And justice must mean not only redress of wrongs and harmonization of conflicting interests but also equal distribution of power. Hitherto the State, which represents the organization of power, has been based on concentration of power in the hands of the few. If we are to have an ethical state, the religion to which we should turn should counter the tendencies of power to gravitate into the hands of the few. All power states — theocracies, stratiocracies,[30] plutocracies, bureaucracies, and the proposed technocracy — resort to religion for sanction. But their religions, instead of combating the concentration of power, actually help to maintain it.

Satisfied that I have an idea that is worth preaching, I walk down to the synagogue Sabbath morning. I get there about 10:00, and I discover about two

---

29. Barthian refers to Karl Barth (1886–1968), a prominent twentieth-century Swiss theologian who is identified with neo-Orthodoxy.

30. A stratiocracy is a form of government headed by the military.

dozen strangers seated together way in the front, while the rest of the synagogue is practically empty. I know at once that there is a bar mitzvah, and I am annoyed that I hadn't been told about this before. [Moshe] Nathanson [the cantor] drones the service mechanically. I sit down in my chair on the platform. By the time the reading in the Torah is begun, a few SAJ worshipers who are not members straggle in. Lubetkin, the SAJ member of the Board who acts as usher (a service he has rendered faithfully since the founding of the SAJ), divides the *Aliyot*.[31] I see him ask about four or five people of the bar mitzvah party to accept an *Aliya*, but they refuse because they can't recite the benedictions. Very few of those who do come up are able to recite those benedictions. Lubetkin informs me that all these people are recently arrived refugees. The reading of the Torah is gone through mechanically. Some more people have in the meantime come in. The important SAJ members are conspicuously absent. They are away in Florida. The few who are present—I begin to think—will be no more sympathetically disposed to my sermon than those who are away. When I get up to speak, I find myself confronted by new people who don't understand English. I have to keep my eye on the three or four people whom I wish to interest and my eye on the typewritten notes which contain additions by hand—hard to make out. I lose sight both of my listeners and of the notes. The sentences come out in lumbering fashion. I find it hard at times to get the right word. I feel my voice getting strident, and that I am out of touch with my audience with which I am struggling hard to establish connections. And so I labor for about 55 minutes. I am all in a sweat. Just that day Nathanson takes it into his head to lengthen out the service; we get through much later than usual—about 12:45.

All in all a Sabbath at the SAJ is to me generally a heartbreaking experience. The exceptions are rare.

WEDNESDAY, FEBRUARY 7, 1940

Perhaps I underestimated the favorable reaction of the audience to my sermon. The accompanying correspondence from E. W. Fiss and S. E. Osserman would seem to indicate that they were impressed by what I had to say. So what?

Father Coughlin and the Jews—A Trivial Incident

FEBRUARY 7, 1940

A trivial incident—but significant of the spread of anti-Semitism—is the following: I was walking yesterday morning to the Seminary. On Broadway between 121 and 122 St. a group of small boys between the ages of 8 and 10 were on their way to the Catholic school, which is located on 121 St. near Broadway.

---

31. The blessings recited during the Torah service (reading of the Torah), often by congregation members who ascend to the pulpit to recite them.

As they noticed me, one of them walked over toward me, and viciously called out "Hello, Comrade!" This shows how far Coughlin's[32] anti-Semitic propaganda is poisoning the minds of the Catholic masses against the Jews.

I believe that the anti-Jewish campaign of the Catholics may be accounted for on the ground that it is intended to divert the minds of the non-Catholics from the Catholics who are charged with un-Americanism because of their recognizing the authority of the Pope as supreme. Since the best defense is attack, and since it would not do to attack the Protestants, the Coughlinites proceed to attack the Jews, thereby hoping to vindicate their own Americanism.

The Grapes of Wrath — *The Movie*

FEBRUARY 7, 1940

Last night I went to see the movie *Grapes of Wrath*, based on the novel of that name by Steinbeck. I seldom get full esthetic satisfaction from the best of movies, and this one was no exception. But as a social sermon it had a tremendous effect on me in that it called my attention to one of the flagrant injustices of American democracy. I regret that I hadn't seen it before I delivered my sermon last Sabbath. It would have helped me drive home the point I was trying to make about the failure of religion hitherto to function as an ethical force. I was very much affected by the part played by the preacher who had discovered the irrelevance of his preaching. It struck home.

Theological Self-Doubt and the Value of Jesus

FEBRUARY 7, 1940

How can I be otherwise than disoriented when, on the one hand, I am struggling to formulate a conception of religion based on the thesis that religion is essentially the search for salvation and not for God, and, on the other hand, I am weighed down by a terrible sense of futility from the standpoint of alleviating the misery which human beings inflict on one another. The very blessings of my sheltered life weigh heavily on my mind when I think of the millions to whom the world is an inferno where their bodies and minds are tortured daily by friends in human guise. How can I sit calmly in my study and formulate ideas about self-fulfillment, life abundant, life satisfactory, salvation, when people are driven off their lands on which they had lived for generations, and that they had cultivated with the sweat of their brow?[33]

---

32. Charles Edward Coughlin (1891–1979), known as Father Coughlin, was a Catholic priest popular on the radio in the 1930s. His broadcasts had a strong anti-Semitic content.

33. Kaplan is thinking here of the movie *The Grapes of Wrath*, which he had just seen and which made a deep impression on him. See the diary entry for February 7, 1940.

Then again, if I were to do nothing but yield to passive grief over the fate of the suffering millions of human beings, neither my lot nor theirs would be in the least improved. I can take an oath [that] Jesus never had the slightest notion of the depths of misery into which human beings are sunk, and that it never occurred to him that he might bring them redemption by giving his life for their sake. That story as a historical fact is the height of absurdity. As a myth, however, not of theological sin but as representing the wish-thought of anyone who is sensitive to the man-inflicted human agony in which the great part of mankind spend their lives from the cradle to the grave, it is incomparable. Who with any human feeling would not pray to be crucified a thousand times, if such crucifixion would be an end to persecution and exploitation?

Secular Religion (Kaplan) vs. Prophetic Religion (Finkelstein or Niebuhr)

FEBRUARY 10, 1940

Finkelstein is trying to convince everybody that I, the Teachers Institute, and the *Reconstructionist* are trying to foster secular religion, whereas he and the Seminary are fighting for the genuine kind of religion which is "prophetic religion." I believe that when he realized that I emphasized religion in all that I write and taught and he could no longer charge me with outright secularism, he resorted to the new strategy of drawing a distinction between secular and prophetic religion. As a matter of fact, this time he happens to be right as regards the distinction, but I don't think that he himself really believes in what he implies when he speaks of prophetic religion. He wishes to give the impression that he regards religion as of transcendent origin and as supernatural. At the same time, that term suggests to most people the ethical emphasis. For his purpose he could not make use of a happier term. It brings him into line theologically with Kaufmann Kohler and with Paul Barth. Reinhold Niebuhr uses that term. Finkelstein may have gotten it from him. In any event, as a weapon of attack, it is as dangerous as a sharp rapier and can be used by a Jesuitical theologian with tremendous effect against a rationalist humanist theology, such as I seek to develop. It enables a Finkelstein to hunt with the hounds and run with the hares, to be at home among the Reformists and among the Orthodox. Reconstructionism plays into his hands by presenting a shining mark of attack, which furnishes him a raison d'être for his "prophetic religion." This "prophetic religion" is entirely compatible with the denial of the Orthodox doctrine of the supernatural revelation at Sinai, and yet it has a supernaturalism of its own, so that one who holds to it can play fast and loose with his religious beliefs and utilize it as a cover for whatever move he wants to make to acquire more power. There is wherein its jesuitry lies.

It seems to me that the principal implications of Judaism as a civilization could best be explained by stressing the primacy of environment. Judaism as a civilization is Judaism as environment.

Some Prominent Guests Talk about Zionism in Kaplan's Living Room

FEBRUARY 10, 1940

Last night we had Salmon [Zalman] Schocken, Dr. [David Werner] Senator, and Dr. and Mrs. Klieger for dinner. After dinner, Dr. Senator led a discussion on the [following] questions: What is necessary to make of Palestine the cultural center that Ahad Ha-Am hoped it would become? And what should the University do to help Palestine become such a center? His idea is that Jewry in the Diaspora, including America, should not wait till anti-Semitism forces it to engage in menial labor and to accept a lower standard of living, but that of its own accord, impelled possibly by some religious drive like that of the Hindus who are fighting British domination, it should redirect its economic life and break away from its present occupancy of the white-collar professions. The example of the *haluzim* [pioneers] in Palestine should be followed by Jewry everywhere. He did not state what he had in mind about the University. But Klieger argued that the University ought to abandon the scholastic standards which were in vogue in Germany until recently and devote itself to the specific social, economic, and political problems with which Palestine Jewry is wrestling. Assuming that they would be dealt with in an ethical spirit, the solutions arrived at would constitute a contribution to civilization.

Fifth Anniversary Celebration of The Reconstructionist

WEDNESDAY, FEBRUARY 14, 1940

The celebration last Sunday of the fifth anniversary of the *Reconstructionist* came off far more successfully than I had expected. It took place at Pierre's on Fifth Ave at 61 St. There were about 200 at the dinner. Most of the guests were from the SAJ. A large number of Seminary students came in for the speeches. Milton Steinberg acted as toastmaster. The entire Editorial Board with the exception of Mortimer Cohen were seated on the dais. The only entertainment was provided by Madame Gorby, who sang Hebrew and Jewish songs. Steinberg with his usual matchless fluency set the proper tone to the celebration. I liked very much his accentuation of the ideological rather than the personal side of the movement. My address on "The Meaning of Reconstructionism" took an hour and ten minutes. I managed to hold the attention of the audience, in spite of the fact that except for the first five minutes the entire address was read. I made a special effort, however, to approximate the style of address that is given extemporaneously. After I got through, Steinberg announced the formation of the Reconstructionist Foundation and he called upon Guzik, a lawyer and a member of the SAJ, and Botein, a lawyer and member of the Park Ave. Synagogue, both of whom are members of the Board of the Foundation, to say a few words. They both spoke well and to the point. Finally Ira was called upon and in a brilliant little speech appealed for memberships and contributions to the Foundation. I understand that about 60 became $5.00 members and that $1,100 came in in contributions. Harry Liebovitz contributed $500.00. Everybody went away highly elated and inspired.

Some Reactions to Student Sermons, Including Moshe Davis's

WEDNESDAY, FEBRUARY 21, 1940

Why is it that people don't realize that the fundamental question with which human beings will have to grapple is not the abstract one of whether there is a God or there isn't but rather whether life is worth living. The fact is that with the increase of knowledge and sensitivity on the one hand and with the persistence and augmentation of stupidity on the other, life is getting to be more and more unbearable.

I am led to make the foregoing observation as a result of a tussle I had a little while ago with a seminary student, Moshe Davis.[34] His sermon on "The Function of Art in Jewish Life" turned out to be a keen disappointment. Though quite talented artistically and dramatically, he does not shine in the formulation and systematization of ideas. The consequence is that even after trying to make something out of the sermon he gave last week in class, he feels that he has not had much of a share in the development of its main thought. This led him to find fault with the way I teach the Homiletics, referring particularly to what I did in class yesterday with a sermon that was presented by another student, Greenberg, and by two others who gave outlines, [Israel] Kazis and Jacobson. I found so little in what they said that I had to reformulate the idea which they tried to state, and to develop it on altogether different lines from those they followed. This procedure of mine seems to have displeased the three concerned. To me, all this information came as a shock, because I had been rather pleased with myself for having done what I did with the threadbare proposition about all things not being good or evil in themselves but being one or the other according to the uses to which they are put. The text was the one about the jewels of the Israelites in the wilderness having been used both for the golden calf and for the tabernacle. What I made out of the

---

34. Moshe Davis, the registrar of the Teachers Institute in the early 1940s and the founder of the Institute for Contemporary Jewry at the Hebrew University, was a strong supporter of Kaplan. He helped to reconcile Kaplan and Finkelstein, an accomplishment he was proud of and mentioned every time I met him in Jerusalem.

text was that we misdirect our efforts toward improving human life if we condemn the instruments which men employ as their evil purposes. But what are evil purposes? The concept of idolatry supplies the answer. For idolatry is essentially either abandoning oneself to some dominant impulse or playing the God.

What the men want is to be praised. They are terribly thin-skinned and envious of one another. It is probably ridiculous of me to expect them to be otherwise. But then, what is this whole damn business about ethics, religion, and spirituality? We expect those who go in for athletics not to be flabby. Why shouldn't we expect of those who train to be moral athletes, supposedly, to show that they possess a little more moral fibre than the average. Is that asking too much? At least, if they don't possess any moral fibre, why aren't they ashamed of their lack but parade it as though it were something to be proud of?

Two Plays and Gone with the Wind

FEBRUARY 24, 1940

I saw last week *Juno and the Peacock*.[35] I found it to be excellent character portrayal and splendid acting. The ever quoted remark of Aristotle in his *Poetics* about the purgative effect of tragedy somehow strikes me as unreal every time I see tragedy on the stage. That this Irish household went smash is shown in this play to be due to Paycock's constitutional laziness. What's there so grand about that? For all I know such laziness may be due to some glandular defect or some other congenital cause. So how does that help me? Can I feel more hopeful or more heroic as a result of this meaningless suffering?

This week I saw one play and one movie. The play was Maxwell Anderson's *Key Largo*[36] with Paul Muni as King. For some no good reason the critics did not take to it and it is going off the boards the coming Monday. To me it was a great play from every point of view. It tore open the basic problem of all human life. Is there any meaning to it? And it left one wondering, as a great play should, since the arguments on both sides are equally balanced. Here, if anywhere, Aristotle's remark does apply. For plumbing the depths of reality, it is in my humble opinion, worth ten Hamlets. *Hamlet* the play abounds in quotable gems of poetry that have become imbedded in the English language, but as "holding up a mirror to nature," it strikes me as quite irrelevant.

---

35. *Juno and the Peacock* is a play by Sean O'Casey (1880–1964), the first playwright to write about Dublin slums. The play deals with difficulties of life in the slums of Dublin during the Irish Civil War of 1922–1923.

36. Maxwell Anderson (1888–1959) was an American playwright. *Key Largo* was written in blank verse. On stage, Paul Muni played a veteran of the Spanish Civil War who deserted under fire and redeems himself in death, defending the family of a true war hero. The noteworthy movie of the same title (released in 1948) starred Humphrey Bogart and Lauren Bacall and was directed by John Huston. The play was modified by Huston.

The movie which I saw was *Gone with the Wind*, based on Margaret Mitchell's novel of that name. It is a grand spectacle, but the love story strikes me as sheer carpentry, an artisan-like putting together of a lot of commonplaces about a woman running after a man whom she in her inner-inner-innermost heart doesn't love and forever running away from and repelling the man whom she in her inner-inner-innermost heart does love. That kind of imaginary character naturally affords opportunity for endless episodes for fat novels and movies that last for hours on end.

Last night Selma, Saul,[37] and Hadassah were with us for dinner, and Selma, Hadassah, and Lena set me straight (although I still have my doubts about their interpretation) concerning the real nature of Scarlett O'Hara's love for Ashley. We got into such a heated discussion that we called up Judith and Ira to give us their version, and they sided with the women folk.

Later Albert and Bertha Schoolman and [Israel] Chipkin[38] came over. After the children left, I had a very warm and interesting discussion with them on the question of the status of the Jews among the peoples of the world. It seems that only we professional Jews are drawn into the discussion of basic Jewish questions. It is just a significant little fact like this one that raises "thick banks of gloom" around me.

On Keeping a Journal

WEDNESDAY, FEBRUARY 28, 1940

Like the much quoted character in one of Molière's plays who suddenly discovered he had been talking prose all his life without being aware of it, I've discovered that I've been living up to the advice that every one ought to have some hobby without being aware of it. My hobby is keeping a journal. I herewith declare all my hitherto avowed reasons in previous volumes for keeping a journal null and void. This only goes to show that one knows one's own mind as little as one knows anything else in the world. The truth in my case probably is that I am trying to rationalize my inability to indulge in some real hobby like sculpting, stamp collecting, photography, etc. So I try to palm off my journal as a hobby. If my life depended on giving an accurate accounting for what it is that impels me to go on with this journal, I couldn't do it.

The fact that we know so little about the self is an added reason for treating it, if not as an illusion, at least as an exceedingly exaggerated entity. This is why I feel so fully the force of the truth that life is not in us but that we are in life. We probably have as much to do with what we think as with the beating of our hearts. A truer description of what happens when we think would probably

---

37. Saul Jaffe was Selma's first husband.
38. Both Schoolman and Chipkin were strong Kaplan supporters.

be to say "it thinks in us," the "us" being merely a conventional term which "it" or "life" has achieved to facilitate its own processes.

Kaplan vs. Steinberg: God of All Reality vs. God of Salvation

February 28, 1940

Milton Steinberg, who is on the hunt for certitude, keeps on insisting that the God of religion must be identical with the whole of reality or being. He therefore objects to my assumption that the God of religion is only that aspect of reality which makes for human salvation. I believe this is a very fundamental issue that ought to be thoroughly canvassed. It seems to me that one of the main reasons religion has been ambivalent in its functioning, instead of being solely a force for good, is just this very tendency to make God co-extensive with all of reality, including evil. This has led to the defense of evil and to the toleration of it instead of to unequivocal effort to eliminate it from human life. Take a simple illustration. As identical with all of being, God was bound to be regarded as the cause of sickness as well as of health. Hence it was necessary to explain sickness as punishment for sin, as discipline, trial, etc. The book of Job with its failure to explain evil whether as suffering or as sin is testimony to the inconsequential complications we become involved in when we insist on making God responsible for all that is, instead of viewing him as the power that makes for all that ought to be.

What is there outside God? Chance, accident, chaos, and in man's world all kind of human blundering. No one is responsible for them. That is just the point which is missed by the dualistic religions, any more than anyone is responsible for darkness. This does not imply that chance, chaos, etc. are nonentities and unreal. They certainly are real, but the fact that no one is responsible for them is the very reason for their existence and hope of the possibility of their elimination as soon as the power that is responsible—God—succeeds in invading them and bringing into them his order and his will.

In any event, in the foregoing we have a real fundamental issue in the philosophy of religion, whereas the question of belief in God vs. belief in the God-idea is an unreal one and can only be a matter for future logomachies.[39]

Jewish Survival and Student Sermons

Friday, March 1, 1940

This morning I had a stormy conference with three seminary students who came to discuss the sermon which they had to prepare for class. The main sermon has to be written by J., a fourth-year man, and the outlines by C. and

---

39. A logomachy is an argument about words.

D.J.[40] had chosen as his topic, What Jews must do to survive as a people despite persecution. Before he proceeded very far with the explanation of his topic, which I got him to formulate only after much cross-questioning, I realized that he was skiing over his subject and taking big leaps over difficult places instead of flowing through it. I finally succeeded in having him ask this question: What is that fullness of Jewish life which would enable Jews to survive? and in having him itemize the answer as follows: (1) a definite system of belief about God, Torah, Israel; (2) a sense of unity experienced through living a communal life; (3) the practice of *mitzvot* and study of Torah; (4) Jewish cultural values. Before, however, I brought him to that point, he tried to be evasive and was resentful of my effort to pin him down to an accurate formulation. He thought he would get away with a lot of hot air about educating the children and attending services. It hadn't occurred to him that he was tackling the basic problem of Jewish life and that he must reckon with hard realities and perhaps insufferable difficulties. When I pointed out to him that it was impossible to expect Jews to find Jewish life desirable, unless we had community, he answered that the average Jew would regard the establishment of community so difficult that he would despair of Judaism, if that were made the condition.

At one point of the discussion he was so sullen that he lost track of the connection of the ideas, and I was about to break off the conference. He apologized and I continued with the development of the thought. After he himself realized that one ought to know what to believe in as a Jew, if one is to defy persecution, he admitted that he himself did not know what a Jew must believe in. As far as he himself is concerned, the traditional theology is out of question. But so far he hasn't found anything to replace it.

This was said by a young man about to be graduated, in the presence of two other students. He is a good-looking chap, makes a good impression, oratorical like Israel Goldstein, married, and an occupant of a pulpit for the last year or two. Everything points to his becoming perfectly sleek and self-satisfied, and here I come along with my upsetting talk about problems and realities. He even has the degree "doctor," which he got from the Brooklyn law school for a trifling little paper on a legal subject. In the heat of my tirade against the rabbis who by their refusal to reckon with the realities are permitting the devastation of Jewish life to be consummated, I opened the Bible and pointed to the verse in Isaiah 56:10: *tzofu v'rim kulam lo yada'u kulam kelavim ilmim* . . . [Heb., "The watchmen are blind, all of them, / They perceive nothing. / They are like dumb dogs / That cannot bark; / They lie sprawling, / They love to drowse"].

The men were shocked out of their torpor by those sledgehammer words of the prophet. It seems that J. finally saw that I was not altogether wrong in

---

40. Because Kaplan is critical here, I have used the initials of the individuals involved. The full names are in the original diary.

demanding of him a radically different approach to the subject he was to preach from the one which he had taken at first. I pointed out to him that it would not be taken amiss if he were to postpone dealing with that subject until he has learned more about Judaism. If, on the other hand, he insisted on treating it now, it would be necessary for him to admit that the question of belief is too complex for discussion in that sermon. When he realized what I was driving at, he said, "But we have never been taught to see problems. Where in our general education are we made to feel that there are problems for the solution of which we are responsible? The people certainly don't want to be made aware of problems."

Could anything be more revealing of the inner rottenness of Jewish life than the experience I had yesterday with K. and today with J.?

A Conversation with Shalom Spiegel

SATURDAY, MARCH 9, 1940

A week ago today Shalom Spiegel[41] called. I like him personally as much as I ever did, but I wish I knew how to break down the barrier that divides him spiritually from me and that prevents him from joining the Reconstructionist group. Is it a barrier of belief or of temperament? The fact is that I cannot get to the bottom of what he believes about God, prayer, the Jewish people. Is he a mystic or isn't he?

He quoted Steinschneider[42] as having said that the function of *Judische Wissenschaft*[43] was to provide Judaism with a decent funeral. It looks as though the Jewish scholars, with their complete avoidance of anything that has to do with the burning problems of the present, are verifying the truth of Steinschneider's observation.

Spiegel also mentioned the fact that I was the only one with whom he ever got a chance to discuss the present status of Jewish life. Often, as he goes to see Prof. [Louis] Ginzberg, he never ventures to broach such questions to him because the mere mention of them would cause Prof. Ginzberg to tremble with excitement. Apparently these scholars are afraid to face the realities of the present and prefer to forget them by escaping into the past. I see in this a most ominous portent for the future of our people.

---

41. Shalom Spiegel, a scholar of Hebrew literature, often lectured eloquently at the SAJ. He was much admired by Kaplan.

42. Moritz Steinschneider (1816–1907) was an Austrian bibliographer and orientalist. He is a key research interest of Ismar Schorsch.

43. *Judische Wissenschaft* means "Jewish science." The *Judische Wissenschaft* was a nineteenth-century movement among German Jews to apply Western modes of thought and research to the Jewish tradition in order to help make classical sources more respectable. *Judische Wissenschaft* is a key concept of Conservative ideology.

A Word on the Kabbalah

MARCH 9, 1940

At the present time I am trying to formulate the place of Kabbalah and Hassidism in traditional Judaism. I find it difficult to do so in terms of ideology, because except for the emanation theory (the exact significance of which it is questionable whether the Kabbalists really grasped), there is hardly anything in Jewish mysticism that is not read out of the rabbinic tradition. There are ideological divergences from rabbinic theology in Kabbalah and Hassidic writings. But I find that both divergences and agreements are quite immaterial when we want to determine the place of [Kabbalah] and [Hassidism] in traditional Judaism. The important fact about them is that they succeeded in giving a new vitality to the Bible and rabbinic writings by reinterpreting them in terms of those new theosophic and theurgic interests which appealed to the Jews of medieval and pre-modern times.

A Practice School for TI Students

WEDNESDAY, MARCH 13, 1940

On Monday (March 11) [Israel] Chipkin, [Samuel] Dinin, and I met at Dushkin's office with [Alexander] Dushkin to discuss plans for the practice school which the Jewish Education Committee is likely to subsidize for the Teachers Institute. I regard this as the most auspicious development in the history of the Teachers Institute. Throughout all the years that the Institute has been in existence, it has not received the least recognition or encouragement from the Seminary Board of Directors. Its function and personnel are entirely alien to them. If it weren't for [Cyrus] Adler's sanction of its budgetary requirements, it would have been liquidated long ago. But even Adler, [who] as he grew older and under Finkelstein's influence crystallized in his own mind the stereotype that I was the incarnation of a secularized Judaism, became more alienated from the work of the Teachers Institute. This new development, I hope, will redeem the Teachers Institute from the danger of ineffectiveness to which Finkelstein has been trying to reduce it.

Personally I have all the reason in the world to be grateful for this finding myself working with Dushkin and Chipkin (Chipkin is now vice-director [of the Jewish Education Committee] to Dushkin) in this project, because we understand one another and are interested in helping one another in furthering the aims to which the three of us are heartily devoted. I consider myself fortunate in having both of them as my friends.

Jewish Philosophy and Jewish Mysticism

MARCH 13, 1940

Of late I have resumed work on the series of lectures I delivered last summer at the University of Chicago. My problem at present is how to interweave in the description of Traditional Judaism the philosophic and the mystic trends. . . .

In the first place, is it necessary to find a category which might cover both philosophy and mysticism in relation to the two constituent elements of Judaism? As a rule, they are treated as parallel developments in Judaism. I believe this is based on a mistaken notion of their relative importance in traditional Judaism. It is as though one were to consider the movie industry on a part from the standpoint of recreational significance, with a few little theatres in which highly artistic productions are experimented with. In reality, mysticism was entirely integral to traditional Judaism. It was bone of its bone and flesh of its flesh, even though some of the breath of life was derived from non-Jewish sources. On the other hand, the philosophic writings were culled forth by the challenge of Greek philosophy, especially Aristotelian—a challenge which troubled only the intellectually elite. In meeting that challenge, Judaism necessarily recognized the validity of the rival method of salvation—reason—and at the same time placed itself in the position of being on the defensive. This could not contribute to the popularity of philosophy, which thus remained esoteric despite its appeal to reason, while mystic love, which is generally regarded as esoteric, achieved great popularity.

. . . If mysticism is the acceptance of an idea or a practice on the evidence of intuition or of faith, where there is the alternative of experiment or reason, then surely the entire traditional ideology may be characterized as mysticism. Kabbalah and Hassidism merely elaborated further on those evidences of both intuition and of faith which constitute the content of rabbinic teaching.

THURSDAY, MARCH 14, 1940

The prestige which the mystic trend enjoyed in traditional Judaism was further enhanced by the pragmatic interests it sought to serve. They were threefold: (1) the redemption of the soul from the taint of mortality and the assurance to it of immortality by being united with or absorbed by God; (2) the attainment of desired objectives in this life through the wielding of such theurgic means as prayers, incantations, etc.; and (3) the achievement of national redemption by resorting to such theurgic means—prayer, fasting, flagellations, etc.—as would hasten the coming of the Messiah. These three purposes were not pursued simultaneously. Historically, one of these purposes was dominant for a time, while the other two were kept in the background and in some cases entirely ignored, though never excluded. Beginning with the close of the Talmud down to Abulafia,[44] the first was the dominant purpose. Abulafia initiated attention to the second purpose, and the Safed[45] school emphasized the third purpose. The Hasidic movement was in the main an elaboration of the means to the achievements of the second purpose. Thus, in addition to utilizing the national sancta for the attainment of its purposes, Jewish mysticism in course of time came to stress purposes which dealt with both the individual and the nation, and which at the same time reckoned with the yearning for well-being now and immortality in the hereafter.

All mysticism is essentially mythologizing. What differentiates it from primitive myth-making and gives it a speculative character analogous to that of philosophy is its tendency to introduce the element of inner consistency and coherence in whatever series of mythical notions it operates with.

---

44. Abraham ben Samuel Abulafia (1240–1291) was born in Spain and founded the school of prophetic Kabbalah. Abulafia's Kabbalah inspired a series of writings that can be described as part of his prophetic Kabbalah, namely, as striving to attain extreme forms of mystical experiences.

45. Safed is a city in northern Israel that since the sixteenth century has been a center of Kabbalah; it is very much worth visiting.

Kaplan at the Jersey shore, c. 1931.
(Courtesy Hadassah K. Musher.)

Seminary graduating class and faculty, 1918.
(Courtesy Library of the Jewish Theological Seminary.)

Reading room at the Seminary.
(Courtesy Library of the Jewish Theological Seminary.)

The Jewish Center, West 86th Street, New York City,
as it looked on its twentieth anniversary, 1937.
(Courtesy Rabbi J. J. Schachter, The Jewish Center.)

Alexander Marx (1878–1953), colleague of Kaplan's at JTS. (Courtesy Jewish Theological Seminary.)

Louis Ginzberg (1873–1953), colleague of Kaplan's at the JTS and his primary adversary in the 1920s and 1930s. (Courtesy Library of the Jewish Theological Seminary.)

Teachers Institute faculty meeting, early 1940s.
(Courtesy Library of the Jewish Theological Seminary.)

Kaplan and Dr. Louis Finkelstein, c. late 1930s.
(Courtesy Library of the Jewish Theological Seminary.)

Rabbi Kaplan, Lena Kaplan, Judith Kaplan Eisenstein,
and Ira Eisenstein, 1930s.
(Courtesy Judith Kaplan Eisenstein.)

*Lena Kaplan and Kaplan's mother,
late 1930s.
(Courtesy Reconstructionist
Rabbinical College.)*

*Judith Kaplan.
(Courtesy Judith Kaplan Eisenstein.)*

Kaplan family in the early 1930s. From left: Naomi Kaplan, Lena Kaplan, Ira Eisenstein, Judith Kaplan, Mordecai Kaplan, Selma Kaplan, and Hadassah Kaplan. (Courtesy Reconstructionist Rabbinical College.)

Sixtieth birthday celebration for Kaplan at the Hotel Commodore, New York City, May 1942. (Courtesy Reconstructionist Rabbinical College.)

Rabbi Mordecai Kaplan and Lena Kaplan, early 1940s. (Courtesy Judith Kaplan Eisenstein.)

7

March 16, 1940–July 10, 1940

Intrigues—Milton Steinberg and **As a Driven Leaf**

SATURDAY NIGHT, MARCH 16, 1940

It is too bad that I find it necessary to interrupt the serene contemplation of such ethereal subjects as mysticism, Gnosticism, etc. with a tale of woe about some of the ugly realities with which I have to contend. I have been quite unhappy for the longest time about the lackadaisical attitude of the members of the Editorial Board of the *Reconstructionist*. Outside of Ira [Eisenstein], who puts his whole heart and soul into the magazine, and Eugene Kohn, to whom it has become the sole prospect of earning anything, the other members of the Board take a sort of Platonic interest in Reconstructionism. Henry Rosenthal has joined the Board only recently. He at least has attended every meeting regularly and has carried out whatever task was assigned to him. I cannot say the same of the rest of the Board.

But my complaint against those men is not so much that they fail to participate in the responsibility for the work on the magazine or for getting the funds necessary to carry out the Reconstructionist program. A much more serious consideration is the fact that they don't measure up morally or spiritually to the standard that one has a right to apply to people who undertake to inaugurate a movement like Reconstructionism. The following will illustrate what I mean. One of the main objectives of our editorial policy is to combat the intimidation and suppression of freedom of speech and press by such bodies as the Anti-Defamation League and the American Jewish Committee.[1] Just this afternoon, I waxed indignant over what Isidore Hoffman,[2] Chairman of the Committee on

---

1. The American Jewish Committee and the Anti-Defamation League are Jewish organizations that fight anti-Semitism.

2. Isidore Hoffman (1898–1981) was active in peace organizations and the Synagogue Council of America. He was friendly with Solomon Schechter and lived with the Schechters while attending the rabbinical school at JTS.

Social Justice of the Rabbinical Assembly,[3] whom I met at Ira's, had told Ira—namely, that the American Jewish Committee sent Rabbi Abels to the Rabbinical Assembly with the "ukase" [order] that the latter body issue a protest against Bertrand Russell's[4] appointment on the City College Faculty in support of Bishop Manning's and other churchmen's protests. After I got through denouncing the American Jewish Committee, Ira unfolded to me this tale about Milton Steinberg, one of the main pillars of our Board:

The Hadassah[5] organization, which had felt beholden to [Milton] Steinberg[6] for the services which he had rendered it, wanted to make sure that the review of his novel *As a Driven Leaf*,[7] which was to appear in its *News Letter*, would be acceptable to him. Those who edit that publication took special pains to find a reviewer of journalistic reputation. They thought of Maurice Samuel and asked Steinberg whether he approved of their selection. He was pleased with that selection, and Samuel wrote what to me or any objectively minded person seems like a most glowing review of the book. He expressed, however, the opinion that the chief character of the book, Elisha ben Abuya, emerges from the story as a contemptible intellectual prig, or something like that. For venturing to express and publish his opinion about Elisha, Maurice Samuel and the National Board of Hadassah have called down on themselves the furious wrath of Milton and his wife Edith, especially the latter, who has let loose a storm of scandal and blackmail. At her insistence, Bobbs-Merrill, the publisher of Steinberg's novel, sent their man to the editors of the Hadassah *News Letter* to tell them that his publishing house had intended to put in a big "ad" for the book, but withdrew it as a consequence of Samuel's review. The members of the Hadassah National Board are very much disturbed over the incident, because they dread losing his cooperation.

As the matter stands, it is the same kind of disgusting intrigue as goes on in the world about us, where honesty and freedom are being squelched by those

---

3. The Rabbinical Assembly is the official organizational arm of the Conservative movement, including Conservative Rabbis.

4. Bertrand Russell (1872–1970) is a well-known British philosopher. In 1940 his appointment to the City College of New York was revoked before his arrival as a result of public protests and a legal judgment in which Russell was found to be morally unfit to teach at the college.

5. Hadassah is a women's Zionist organization founded in 1912 by Henrietta Szold (1860–1945). It is devoted primarily to medical work in Israel. Ms. Szold and Kaplan knew each other well. Henrietta Szold is an intellect of the first rank.

6. Milton Steinberg (1903–1950) was a rabbi, author, and Zionist instructor at City College of New York and the JTS. He was a disciple and a favorite of Kaplan's, but was critical of him in his later years. He was philosophically sophisticated, and his works are worth reading. His papers can be found at the Jewish History Center in New York City. His book *Basic Judaism* is a fine introduction to Jewish belief.

7. *As a Driven Leaf* is a novel by Milton Steinberg about the heretical rabbi Elisha Ben Abuyah. The novel is still in print and is still popular.

who have power. What right have we Reconstructionists to take others to task for a wrong of which one of our foremost colleagues is as clearly guilty as they are? Apart from the fact that the review is effusive in its laudations of the book and should delight the most vain and praise-hungry, the criticism of the chief character of the book should itself have been accepted as the highest praise by Steinberg, since such a portrayal speaks for the artistic objectivity of the author. But suppose Samuel had honestly believed the book itself to have been no good and had had the courage to say so. Would it have been right for the Hadassah to suppress his review after having asked him to write one? And would it have been honorable for Steinberg—a rabbi, a preacher of justice, and interpreter of the word of God—to engage in what amounts to blackmail?

And now the question which I put to myself is, How can I go on with the magazine, when I lack not only the active participation of the members of the Editorial Board—with the exception of those I mentioned above—but also the encouragement to fight for Reconstructionism, which can come only from being associated with men who have a high sense of honor and of the right? I wish I knew how to extricate myself from the predicament without being guilty of moral cowardice. If I break with Steinberg, I will bring on myself untold complications which will destroy my usefulness—whatever that is in the way of teaching and writing. And if I let the matter go, I feel I am condoning wrongdoing when I should be castigating it.

Thoughts on Hadassah and How Well Run It Is

MONDAY, MARCH 18, 1940

As Jewish organizations in this country go, I believe I am not mistaken in regarding the Hadassah as the one organization that makes for affirmative Jewish life, in the sense that it not only maintains professional Jewish workers who have a vested interest in Jewish survival but that it succeeds in winning among the laity believers in Jewish survival. For that reason I treat with respect the request that came to me from the members of the National Board of the Hadassah to expound to them my conception of Jewish nationhood. I am to meet them Wednesday night. This means diving once again into the subject I dealt with in the preceding volume of this journal. But then I was in Palestine, and now I am in New York. This makes all the difference in the world, because then I could afford to take the will-to-Jewish survival for granted, whereas now that will itself is in question.

A Program for Zionism

MARCH 18, 1940

The two main propositions I wish to set forth are: (1) In all policies pertaining to Palestine we should have a long-range view of what we want in order to know how to evaluate what we get; and (2) our approach to the upbuilding of Palestine must be integral to an interest in the survival of Jewish life in the Diaspora.

Before the impact of Western civilization on the life of the Jewish people, two important factors gave definite direction to that life: (1) a definitive ideal concerning Palestine, Messianism, with all that it implies, and (2) a definitive status of the Jews as a corporate group—a theocratic nation in exile constituting everywhere an alien body.

Western civilization, in granting civic rights to Jews, has rendered both factors inoperative. But its ambivalent and vacillating attitude toward the Jews has thus far interfered with their evolving two other factors in place of the two traditional ones which have become inoperative. We cannot afford to proceed with the upbuilding of Palestine without a definite idea of our ultimate objective. We must envisage at least its main political aspects.

1. We must definitely disavow the notion of getting all Jews into Palestine.
2. The question of boundaries is of secondary importance as compared with the main political significance of Palestine, namely, that of serving as a home for all Jews whom the nations do not want to harbor in their own lands.
3. The Jews in Palestine must be permitted to constitute the majority population in Palestine.
4. They must possess sufficient political independence to exercise cultural and religious autonomy.
5. Beyond that they should be willing to have Palestine become part of a large political body, such as Arab Federation, British Dominion, or League of Nations, so as not to have to maintain any military organization of their own, or to conduct any foreign policy of their own.
6. The relation of Palestine Jewry to the rest of world Jewry must be non-political but purely cultural and religious. All forms of cooperation between Palestine and Diaspora Jewry must be on a voluntary basis.

With the foregoing as an ultimate program, anything that Jews are compelled to accept which falls below that program should be accepted under protest as a temporary compromise, whether it be a matter of boundaries, immigration, land sales, etc.

Cooperation with Arabs in Palestine is extremely important but should be confined to the field of economic, social, and cultural endeavors. No political negotiations can be entered into except on the basis of the Mandate.

Interpretation to the Arab world of the Jews' claim on Palestine, and of their ultimate objective is no less important than to the Western nations.

Nationality, the Most Appropriate Category for the Jews

MARCH 9, 1940

The two types of permanent status possessed at the present time by human groups are those of church and nation.

1. The church status is based upon conformity to a particular conception and program of salvation. This cannot apply to the Jews because of the wide diversity in the conceptions of salvation.
2. The status of nation is applied to a group that is governed by a central state which can exercise coercive power over *all* the members of that group. The Jews have not been a nation (they have *had* a nation) in that sense ever since the destruction of the first commonwealth (Jews have lived in Diaspora since then).
3. The status of nationality is applicable to a group which, though lacking a central state, possesses a civilization that is the product of its life and which is governed by a common code of ethics and law. This was actually the status of the Jews before the end of the eighteenth century and must continue to be such if they are to function as a group.

[A primary] prerequisite to Jewish survival is a clear understanding of the relation of our status as a nationality to our historic role as a religious group. This involves a conception of religion that can enable us to view it as a natural phenomenon of group life, hence as evolving in complexity and diversity simultaneously with the complexity and diversity of the group to which the particular religion belongs.

A religion viewed naturally is the self-awareness of a group, as it expresses itself in the assumption, on the part of each member in that group, that the group is an indispensable means to his salvation.

This implies a keenly felt need for self-identification with the group life. Such identification takes place when the individual enables the sancta of the group to function in his consciousness as a means of eliciting the best that is in him.

Hence, from the standpoint of Jewish survival, it is essential that for the individual Jew the sancta of the Jewish people have such vital significance as to elicit the best in him.

So viewed, Jewish nationhood fulfills a religious function and is entitled to the rights accorded to religious groups known as churches, viz., to engage in cooperative effort on a communal scale. This solves the problem of correlating our status as members of the Jewish nationality with our status as American citizens.

WEDNESDAY, MARCH 20, 1940

[Another] prerequisite to Jewish survival is to develop Jewish content and activity. The real problem of Jewish survival is what to do with it as an end in itself. We are so busy trying to explain *why* live as Jews that we neglect the question of *how* to live as Jews. If Jewish life would provide an outlet for creative thought, activity, and self-expression, there would be no need of explaining why live as Jews. This calls for the elaboration of a three-fold program.

1. The fostering of constructive thought dealing with the social, the economic, the political, and the religious problems of Jewish life in Palestine and in the Diaspora.
2. The organization of communal life on such a basis as to call for participation of every man, woman, and child in some Jewish activity.
3. The encouragement of esthetic creativity in all the arts with a view to giving esthetic articulation the entire range of emotions from those evoked by the most ridiculous aspects of Jewish life to those evoked by the most sublime experiences in Jewish religion.

Messiness at the SAJ—A Contentious Divorce

FRIDAY, MARCH 22, 1940

I often wonder what bearing all these abstract and highbrow discussions have on the humdrum life of human beings. The following items which I shall record deal with the mutual conflicts of people which arise out of their being thorns in each other's side. The conflicts will apparently go on like the weather, regardless of all attempts of moralists, social reformers, and revolutionists to change the world.

About ten days ago Mrs. Irving F. came to see me. She is an only daughter of the M.'s who were members of the SAJ. I officiated at her wedding about seven years ago. She has now a child of five. Her husband is a son of the F.'s; his mother is the president of the organization which supports the institution for the blind known as the "Lighthouse." The F.'s have lost their money and the young Mrs. F. (apparently at the instigation of her parents) divorced her husband. He has refused to consent to the divorce which she got at Reno. She cannot therefore be married in this state, but she can get married in Conn[ecticut]. She is now considering getting married, and to please her parents, she came to ask me to persuade her former husband to grant her a Jewish divorce. I suspect that her parents probably thought that getting a Jewish divorce would enable her to get married in this state, because I can hardly imagine that they would care sufficiently for Jewish law to wish to comply with it to that extent.

I felt I had to do my duty and to use my influence with her former husband's parents to see to it that she obtain a Jewish divorce. Expecting resistance on their part, I came to the SAJ Board meeting Wednesday a week ago and suggested the appointment of a committee of Jewish law and custom to deal with situations of the kind described above. But fearing that the matter would be unduly delayed, if left to a committee, I arranged to have the mother of Irving, Mrs. F., come to see me. She came last Saturday with her husband. When I told them what I wanted them to do, Mr. F. simply wouldn't hear of it. He felt that the M.'s had wronged them too deeply and he didn't see how Irving could consent to grant a Jewish divorce after having refused a secular divorce. The mother thought that I had called them for the purpose of suggesting a reconciliation. Both of them spoke well of the young woman and put the blame entirely on her parents. After much urging, I got them to promise to deliver the message, which they did. During the week Irving called up and definitely refused my request.

Prayer Will Not Survive Unless It Has a Rational Value

SUNDAY, MARCH 24, 1940

I am very doubtful whether it will ever be possible to render public worship as intrinsically indispensable to people as it was in the past when it had a theurgic[8] significance. It is more likely to be dispensed with altogether, unless someone invents for it a therapeutic value that is compatible with reason. Among us Jews attendance at public worship on the part of those to whom it has no theurgic significance is dwindling so rapidly that I doubt whether many more new synagogues will be built in neighborhoods with a permanent Jewish population.

If there were still any vitality in us Jews, we would be evolving esthetic values to take the place of the theurgic values which are becoming defunct.

The Contribution of Greek Thought

MARCH 24, 1940

The unique contribution of Greek philosophy to the evolution of the human mind is no doubt its calling attention to the need of subjecting the process of knowing as such to close scrutiny. Without a dependable theory of knowledge, all speculation about being is merely mythology. Actually, very little progress can be said to have been made in epistemology. Superficial philosophers like Durant deride epistemology as being useless logomachy.[9] At the present time, I am reading with the men of the seminar, which meets every other week on Thursday nights, Garnett's *Reality and Value*. I find the discussion there of epistemological problems very helpful in my general thinking, and vice versa.

---

8. *Theurgic* is Kaplan's word for "magical." Kaplan has in mind here that one can influence events through prayer.

9. Battle of words.

Cyrus Adler Dies and Kaplan Remembers His Early Life

MONDAY, APRIL 8, 1940

Cyrus Adler died last night. The funeral will take place tomorrow from his late home in Philadelphia. I recall his having said some years ago at a banquet in his honor that he had written in his will that no eulogies be pronounced at his funeral.

I cannot talk very kindly about him because he never liked me. My very first contact with him was one of conflict. That was in 1902. The Seminary was then in the process of re-organization. Adler was then head of the committee which, having come into possession of new funds contributed by [Jacob] Schiff, [Louis] Marshall, the Strausses, [Ludwig] Lewisohn, etc., was about to take over the old Seminary.[10] When the old Seminary had become bankrupt, they decided to reorganize it and to invite [Solomon] Schechter to head it. In order to start out with enough students to justify engaging a new faculty in addition to Schechter, and to be able to graduate a class after two years instead of four, the outgoing class of 1902, to which I belonged, and which had stayed in the Seminary about eight years, was told that it was expected to stay two years at the new Seminary, after which it would be graduated. There were about five or six of us who had counted on getting our rabbinical degree in 1902. We had been led to believe that by the late Joshua Jaffe, who was our instructor in Talmud, by Bernard Drachman, who taught us Bible, Jewish philosophy, history, etc., and by the then existent Board of Trustees, among whom were Simon Reeder, Percival Menken, and Max Cohen. The late Pereira Mendes was acting president (I believe). The entire affair was a ramshackle condition, and we students were anxious to go out into the world. Nevertheless, we would have been perfectly happy to continue studying another two years. But we were told that we were to be put together with the new students and to be taught the same subject matter at the same time with them. No account was to be taken of our having spent eight or more years at the old Seminary. Knowing, as I did, who some of the new students were to be and how completely ignorant of Jewish knowledge they were, I for one resented being put into the same class with beginners. Charles I. Hoffman, who was then a man of 35 with a wife and five children, who had been a Philadelphia lawyer, and who had made up his mind to go into the ministry, was to be one of the new students. He had engaged me to read with him the *Mekhilta*,[11] and I realized how little Hebrew he knew. I thought it would be ridiculous for me to be put into a

---

10. On the founding of the new seminary and the figures mentioned in this paragraph, see Mel Scult, "Schechter's Seminary," in *Tradition Renewed: A History of the Jewish Theological Seminary of America*, ed. Jack Wertheimer (New York: Jewish Theological Seminary, 1997), 1:43–103.

11. *Mekhilta* is a rabbinic midrash. An English translation can be found in Jacob Z. Lauterbach, ed. and trans., *Mekhilta de Rabbi Ishmael*, 2 vols. (Philadelphia: Jewish Publication Society, 1949).

beginner's class. None of us had any idea of the cycle system which Schechter was planning to introduce.

I was at that time president of the student society known as the Morais-Blumenthal Society,[12] and we formulated a letter in which we asked that those of us who were about to be graduated should have our previous work taken into account and not be made to sit together with beginners. For daring to make such a request, Adler came specially from Philadelphia to give us a bawling out, telling us that it was impudent on our part to send such petitions. Abramowitz, Kauvar, and Israeli were graduated in June of that year (1902) and they got out-of-town positions. I did not get any position so I attended courses during 1902–1903. In the fall of 1903 I was given charge of the school at Kehilath Jeshurun and had to preach once a month. From that time on (1903–1904) I became somewhat irregular in my attendance at the new Seminary, and made no attempt to be graduated again. Elias Solomon was the only one of our group who complied with the new arrangement and received his rabbinical degree from the new Seminary in 1904.

At one time during my ministry in Kehilath Jeshurun (East 85 St.),[13] I was so unhappy with my work that I wanted to quit. Before doing so, I went to see Adler in Philadelphia. I don't remember now what made me go to him for advice. I wanted to go into selling life insurance, and I probably expected him to give me the necessary recommendation. (Incidentally that was not the only thing I wanted to escape to from the rabbinate. At one time I wanted to take up farming and join an agricultural school.) When I told him what I had in mind to do, he pooh-poohed the idea and told me that when I felt depressed, the best thing to do was to take a long walk and the blues would disappear. He said that was the way he would overcome his own jimjams.

It seems that in 1909, when Schechter offered me the principalship of the Teachers Institute and he apprised Adler of that fact, Adler was not altogether happy about Schechter's selecting me for the Institute post. As a matter of fact, I owed that post to a chance remark that Miss Szold let drop about my religious school at the 85 St. congregation. Somehow she had learned that I had built up a successful school and she mentioned that fact to Schechter. One day in June 1909 I was holding forth to the Alumni of the Seminary on the need for a Copernican revolution in our thinking about Judaism (see introd. to *Judaism as a Civilization*) and Schechter was present and joined in the applause when I got through. The same morning he invited me to his office and offered me the

---

12. Sabato Morais (1823–1897) was a Sephardic rabbi, and Joseph Blumenthal was a member of the board of the old seminary.

13. Kaplan was given the title of Minister at Kehilath Jeshurun and served there from 1903 until 1909. In 1905 Moshe Zevulun Margolis joined the administration of the synagogue. In 1909 Kaplan became principal of the newly formed Teachers Institute. Kehilath Jeshurun is at present an Orthodox congregation that operates the famous Ramaz School named after Margolis. Needless to say, they would rather forget that Kaplan was rabbi there.

position. Apparently he then wrote to Adler, and he must have gotten in reply a letter questioning my fitness for the position. This is the inference I draw from Schechter's reference to me in Bentwich's biography of Schechter.[14]

In the course of my stay at the Seminary, there was a time when they thought of grooming me for the presidency, first Schechter and then Adler. But I made myself impossible when I began to publish my views. During one of the years that Schechter was away from the Seminary, when he took a trip to South Africa to visit his older daughter [Ruth],[15] who was then married to a certain [Morris] Alexander, I started a seminar with a group of the more advanced students. I believe it was in 1911–12. At the Seminar I began developing my new outlook on Judaism. The freedom from the rabbinic yoke was exhilarating (and Schechter's absence was also helpful), and I gave free rein to my eagerness to find some solid intellectual basis for Judaism. When Schechter came back and heard about the seminar, he was quite put out and he said to me, "Listen here, I am here (at the Seminary) to teach theology. You can teach your theology at the Teachers Institute." At some time later I had occasion to show him the interpretation of Genesis, which I had worked out and which I then expected to publish some time. I made no secret of my departure from the traditional view of the Torah. He returned the manuscript to me with a few dissenting comments. Not long after that, he tried to interest me in working on the text of *Shir ha-Shirim* [Heb., Song of Songs][16] in the hope that I would have something to my credit in text scholarship and at the same time be diverted from my theological speculations. My first article in the *Menorah*[17] got Schechter wild with anger because I dared to question his view about dogmas in Judaism. He said he would answer me in the *Menorah*. But he died before he had a chance to do so.

Adler too entertained for a while the idea of grooming me, I believe, but time and again I made myself impossible. Every additional article of mine that

---

14. Norman Bentwich, *Solomon Schechter: A Biography* (Philadelphia: Jewish Publication Society, 1938). Bentwich knew Schechter when Bentwich was a boy. The Bentwich Papers at the Central Zionist Archives in Jerusalem contain an enormous amount of information on Solomon Schechter, much of which is not included in the biography. There are many Schechter letters in the archives that Bentwich did not use. In the text, fitness probably refers to Kaplan's relative lack of experience. He had held one position at this point.

15. For a biography of Ruth Schechter, see Baruch Hirson, *The Capetown Intellectuals: Ruth Schechter and Her Circle, 1907–1954* (London: Merlin Press, 2001). When she lived in the Union of South Africa, Ruth Schechter became involved with Olive Schriner, a well-known early feminist. She also knew Mohandas K. Gandhi, who stayed at her house the night before he left for India. During Solomon Schechter's visit to South Africa, he spoke at many congregations in and around Capetown. For information on this visit, see the Morris Alexander Papers in the archives at the University of Capetown.

16. The reference here is to the Midrash on the Song of Songs. Kaplan had brought back from Europe in 1909 a manuscript of *Shir ha-Shirim Rabbah*. For the full story, see Mel Scult, *Judaism Faces the Twentieth Century: A Biography of Mordecai M. Kaplan* (Detroit: Wayne State University Press, 1993), 108 and 388n25.

17. See M. M. Kaplan, "What Judaism Is Not," *Menorah Journal* 1.4 (1915): 208–16.

appeared in the *Menorah* helped to alienate him from me. This was especially the case with the one in which I refer to the stories in Genesis as half-mythological. He took me violently to task for daring to use such an expression about the Bible. Another occasion when he delivered a broadside against me was in January 1922, just as I had broken with the Jewish Center and was about to launch the Society for the Advancement of Judaism. The occasion was a paper I read on "The Place of the Synagogue in Jewish Life" in the auditorium of the old Seminary building on 123 St. at an annual convention of the United Synagogue. In that paper I gave expression to my newly acquired ideas on the relation of the synagogue to the rest of Jewish life. In a talk which Adler gave in the afternoon of that day, he berated me in no uncertain language. The only one who ventured to come to my defense was Eugene Kohn. All this happened while I was outside the auditorium.

The last straw must have been my resignation [in 1927] from the Seminary with a view of accepting Wise's invitation to join the Jewish Institute of Religion.[18] It was about that time that Finkelstein was drawn into Adler's orbit, and since then his star has been rising. Nothing would make me happier than to see Finkelstein succeed in putting the Seminary on the map. All I pray for is that he should learn to be honest, to say what he means and mean what he says.

Cyrus Adler's Funeral

TUESDAY, APRIL 9, 1940

As one of the four "senior" members of the Seminary Faculty, I was asked to attend the funeral of Cyrus Adler, which was to be strictly private from his home in Philadelphia. I arranged with Prof. [Louis] Ginzberg to meet with him at the Penn. Station this morning, and he, [Alexander] Marx, and I sat together and talked about all sorts of things on the way to Phila. When we got to the house, I found it to be very old-fashioned and drably furnished. There must have been about 100 people distributed in four rooms, two on the lower level and two on the upper. A. A. Neuman, rabbi of the Mikve Israel Synagogue[19] and the member of the Dropsie Faculty[20] whom Adler groomed for the presidency of Dropsie, officiated. He read a few Psalms in Hebrew and English and delivered

---

18. For the saga of Kaplan and Wise, see Scult, *Judaism Faces the Twentieth Century*, 268–69. My biography of Kaplan contains a detailed account of all the events Kaplan refers to here. When researching the biography, I found a letter from Wise to Judge Mack, written after the whole saga between Kaplan and the Jewish Institute of Religion was over, in which Wise writes, "We may have overestimated Kaplan." When I published my first article on Kaplan and Wise in 1975, I left out the reference to this letter. Kaplan was then still alive.

19. Mikveh Israel is a Sephardic synagogue in Philadelphia, Pennsylvania. It was founded in 1740.

20. The Dropsie College of Hebrew and Cognate Learning was a secular graduate institution concentrating on Semitics. It was founded in 1907 with money from the legacy of Moses Dropsie (1821–1905). It granted more than 200 doctorates before it closed in 1986. The college merged with the University of Pennsylvania in 1993.

a prayer in which Adler's nine lives [?] were mentioned. The car in the funeral cortege in which Ginzberg, Marx, and I sat [was also carrying] the Solis Cohens. After the funeral we were treated to lunch at a club to which Cohen and his friends belong, and at 3:00 we took the train back to New York.

On the way back we talked again about all kinds of things. Never in all the time that we were together did any one of us mention Finkelstein's[21] name.

Reconciling with Milton Steinberg

APRIL 11, 1940

The second occasion for satisfaction was my conference with Milton Steinberg. I had been provoked against him lately, first, because of what I had heard concerning his attitude toward Maurice Samuel's criticism of his book, and, secondly, because of his failure to appear at important meetings both of the *Reconstructionist* editorial board and of the Rec. Foundation and to bring any of his congregation into line for the Recon. I had finally decided that nothing would be gained by sulking or bearing a grudge against him, and that the sensible thing to do was to awaken in him a sense of responsibility for the progress of Recon. I asked him to come to see me, and when I did so, I intended to take him to task for his negligence and lack of cooperation. But upon thinking the matter over, I realized that that was not the way to get his cooperation. Instead of rebuking him for what he had not done, I asked him what he thought all of us ought to do to speed up the R. movement. He replied that what we need is to dramatize the movement, and he suggested that we spend two weeks going from town to town in evangelical fashion and bring the message of Reconstructionism to the Jewish masses. A campaign such as that, adequately publicized, would focus attention upon our movement. He promised he would be willing to take part in that campaign. I was so thrilled by his interest and enthusiasm that I promised to contribute $300 toward conducting it. For once, it was necessary to impress upon our people with the fact that the R. group was in deep earnest about its ideals. We decided that such a campaign ought to be launched some time in November.

Reconstructionist Summer Conference

APRIL 11, 1940

The other matter I discussed with him [Milton Steinberg] was the summer institute. I had prepared in my mind a tentative program, and by the time I was through discussing it with him, the program assumed quite definite

---

21. Louis Finkelstein succeeded Cyrus Adler as president of the JTS. He and Kaplan had many conflicts, and Kaplan reported at one point that he suffered from Finkitis. They were eventually reconciled, due in part to the efforts of Moshe Davis. Kaplan recorded the efforts of Davis in his diary during the 1940s.

shape. We agreed that what was needed to make R. understandable was not merely a set of general principles but a kind of *Shulhan Arukh*[22] that would provide the Jew with a regimen of conduct and reflection for all sorts of situations and occasions. With that end in view, we should conduct the summer institute over a period of two weeks at Grossman's camp. The discussions should deal with the following topics and be led by the following men: (1) a Reconstructionist credo—Kaplan; (2) a regimen for individual and domestic use—[Milton] Steinberg; (3) communal organization, including function of synagogue—[Eugene] Kohn; (4) Jewish cultural activities—[Ira] Eisenstein; (5) Jewish education—[Samuel] Dinin; (6) Jewish group relations, including problem of anti-Semitics; (7) Palestine.[23]

The discussion of each topic should last two successive mornings, one morning to be devoted to orientation, the other to implementation. An interesting suggestion that developed from our discussion was that in the contemplated code, we should have three levels of attainment: a minimum, a normal, and a super-normal.

Tyranny—Anti-Semitism and Psalm 94

WEDNESDAY, APRIL 24, 1940

Yesterday I spoke on "The Last Tyranny." I worked very hard in preparing the sermon because of the intrinsic difficulty of the problem which I tackled. That problem is, What shall we Jews do when we realize the true nature of anti-Semitism as the concomitant of the tyranny of the masses? In contrast with the first three estates, or the classes, which had an interest in saving us from the onslaught of the masses at the same time that they invited the masses against us, the latter have nothing but hatred for us, a hatred implanted by the Christian myth and fostered by the Church. The fact that Germany, in her propaganda by which she expects to disrupt the various governments of the world in order to facilitate her penetration into their countries, makes use of Jew hatred to denounce as Jewish any and all forces that stand in her way, renders our predicament more tragic than it has ever been. The frightening fact about this new tyranny of the masses who are coming into power is that they possess all the stigmata of the organized mob, which knows neither reason nor pity. I believe that the emergence of this new psychological phenomenon—the collective or mass mind endowed with power—is more than the economic factor for the understanding of what is happening in the world today.

I had to fall back on the belief in God as the only solution. In the words of the psalmist, *berov sarafai bekirbi, tanhumecha yesha-ashu nafshi* [Heb., "When I am filled with cares, your assurance soothes my soul" (Psalm 94:19)].

---

22. The *Shulhan Arukh* is a sixteenth-century code of Jewish law widely accepted among Orthodox Jews.

23. All the invitees to the conference mentioned here were primary Kaplan supporters.

That entire Psalm 94 records an experience strictly parallel to our own in the face of the menace of anti-Semitism. It is the outcry of one who seemingly was just as puzzled and perturbed as I am. He calls on God to appear and render to the arrogant the punishment they deserve. His solution resolves itself to the affirmation that God will punish the evil-doers who crush His people. I mentioned that in my sermon and added that I did not regard his entire argument convincing. It seems to me that a more feasible solution is that implied in the rabbinic conception of God Himself as in need of redemption, *shelkha ve-shelanu ha-yesh geulah* [Heb., "Yours and ours is there redemption?"].[24] I pointed out that the will-to-live that is in us compels us to conclude that this mass tyranny cannot represent the last word in human development, because it is bound, first, to convert mankind into breeds of termite-like colonies engaged in eternal warfare with one another, and then to destroy the human race entirely, because the human termites are armed with every conceivable instrument of destruction. Such an outcome is a sort of reductio ad absurdum which the human mind cannot contemplate. Hence the truth of the words of Micah: *ki-eyshev be-hoshekh* [Heb., "Though I sit in darkness the Lord is my light" (Micah 7:8)].

Keeping Spirits Up

WEDNESDAY, MAY 1, 1940

On Monday, the 7th day of Pesach, I preached on "How to Keep Up Our Morale." I made a special effort again to get a firm hold on the sermon so that I would deliver it effectively. Although such efforts exhaust me, they at least save me from the blues which I experienced every time I gave a poor sermon. Of the twelve sermons I gave this year, only two were below par.

The second seder was held at the SAJ house and was participated in by about 110 people. We tried out the Revised Haggadah and it proved to be satisfactory.

This evening, as I was eating supper, a messenger brought a letter signed by Sol Stroock, member of the Seminary Board of Trustees, apprising me of Finkelstein's election to the presidency of the Seminary.

The International Crisis — Gloom

THURSDAY, MAY 16, 1940

The entire time since the preparation of the Pesach sermon I have been in very low spirits. It was then borne in on me as a result of my analysis of the world situation that we Jews are practically doomed, and that thought haunts me every waking moment. The recent victories of the Nazis in Norway, Holland, and Belgium and the dark outlook of the Allies, together with the likelihood of our getting into the war, almost make it impossible for any gleam of hope to break through the dark cloud of despair which hangs over my mind. The worst of it

---

24. The origin of the reference here is not clear.

is that my work, instead of distracting me from all these dark forebodings, continually keeps me aware of them. I have to preach and lecture on what to think and what to do in this crisis. Like a captain leading his band to a forlorn hope in battle, I must combine for myself and for others the experience of expecting the worst and hoping if not for the best, at least for some good. That is no easy matter.

Ideas for an Innovative Haggadah

MAY 16, 1940

Azriel Eisenberg, a graduate of the Teachers Institute who has been active for many years in the field of education, is at the head of the Jewish Educational Bureau in Cincinnati. He worked out a modern Haggadah on the basis of a new kind of *Mah Nishtanah*.[25] The Four Questions are pertinent and vital in present-day Jewish life. For answers to them, he used material from the *Reconstructionist*. I was especially delighted to see that he used the letter which Eugene Kohn, Ira, and I had worked out together in reply to a letter by a woman in Pennsylvania who wanted to know why we insist on remaining Jews.

It occurred to me as soon as I saw this modern Haggadah that it would be an excellent idea to publish it together with the more ambitious and more traditional one we worked out. To those who observe a second seder, or for those for whom our revised Haggadah is still too traditional, this modern Haggadah ought to appeal very strongly. I hope this suggestion will meet with the approval of the rest of the Editorial Board. I had no difficulty in convincing Ira and Eugene.

Max Kadushin and Kaplan—Politics of the Inner Circle

MAY 17, 1940

If I am not mistaken, Kadushin's[26] coming to me at this time is not just for the purpose, as he said, to work on the *Mekhilta*.[27] I think it is part of a little scheme Finky has up his sleeve, namely, to appoint him lecturer in Systematic Theology. It seems that Finky has dropped the idea of having Steinberg as lecturer. He senses that Kadushin has broken away from the type of thinking which I have

---

25. The Four Questions are part of the traditional seder and are usually asked by the youngest child present. The Four Questions are the organizing principle for the seder text. See Rabbi Joy Levitt and Rabbi Michael Strassfeld, eds., *A Night of Questions: A Passover Haggadah* (Wyncote, PA: Reconstructionist Press, 1999). Levitt and Strassfeld's Haggadah is the current Reconstructionist Haggadah.

26. For more on Max Kadushin, see Scult, *Judaism Faces the Twentieth Century*, esp. 332–33. When I interviewed Max Kadushin for my biography, he stated that he thought Kaplan exaggerated the importance of the chosen people concept in rabbinic literature. Kaplan thought that Kadushin left New York to get away from him and that it was due to Kadushin's wife that Kadushin was alienated from Kaplan. I have no way of knowing whether or not Kaplan's feeling had any basis. Kadushin was close to Kaplan and taught for him at the Jewish Center.

27. Max Kadushin, *A Conceptual Approach to the Mekhilta* (New York: Jewish Theological Seminary, 1969).

been urging as essential to the reconstruction of Jewish life, and has become an apologist for tradition. The organismic thinking which has become an obsession with Kadushin has the semblance of striking an original note in Jewish theology, and does actually warrant—if true—a certain intellectual chauvinism very much akin to that developed by the Nazis. In a time such as this, chauvinism is what the average person wants in answer to the chauvinism of which he is the victim. I can sense how Solomon Goldman and Simon Greenberg have found in Kadushin's organismic thinking just what they need to reenforce them in their chauvinist obscurantism. They in all probability have led Finky to consider Kadushin as the proper man for the lectureship in Systematic Theology, even to the extent of forgiving him his close association with me in former years. I have a suspicion that Kaddy's self-elimination from the *Reconstructionist* Editorial Board and repeated refusals to write articles for the magazine are due to his desire to free himself from his earlier association with me as a disciple, so that it would not count against him with the Seminary authorities, first Adler, then Finkelstein. If this change has actually taken place in his attitude toward my philosophy of Jewish life—and I believe it has—I do not in the least blame him for wanting to dissociate himself from me, or for having the ambition to teach his own kind of Jewish theology. If he will only remain open and above board with me and do nothing to sabotage what I am trying to do, my friendship for him will be as warm as ever.

The Threatening International Situation

MAY 21, 1940

In spite of preoccupation with our own immediate affairs, we cannot possibly forget what is going on in Europe these days. The mind is simply paralyzed with dread of the outcome of the rout which the Allies are suffering at the hands of the Nazis, who it appears have already reached the Channel and will probably occupy Paris in a few days. What is going to happen to us Jews, to Palestine, to all our hopes and dreams? Will America really stay out of the war, and will Germany reduce France and England to the status of Czechoslovakia? Will she succeed in destroying forever the promise of a rational, free, and just world which was implied in the French Revolution and the establishment of the United States of America? Despite the worst that may befall, we have to plan and work as though life had meaning and a future.

At a National Convention in Pittsburgh—Jewish Education

FRIDAY, MAY 24, 1940

It is some time now since I have taken part in annual conventions. I rather enjoy being together with a lot of people who are actively concerned in problems of Jewish life, although to very many of them I suspect that concern is essentially of a job-holding character.

I got to Pittsburgh Wednesday morning and put up at Hotel Wm. Penn, where the 1940 conventions of the three organizations were taking place: the National Conference of Jewish Social Welfare, National Association of Jewish Center Workers, and National Council for Jewish Education. Ira Eisenstein and Henry Rosenthal were with me most of the time during my stay in Pittsburgh.

Wednesday afternoon I took in two sessions. One was on "How the Center Develops and Encourages American Jewish Art and Expression"; the other was on "Research and Reports" (in Jewish education). At the first of these sessions I was especially interested in the remarks of a Dr. Gall, a church organist who has organized for the Pittsburgh YMHA a choral group which devotes considerable attention to Jewish music. About 40% of the group are Gentiles. His main point was that the Jews themselves are not interested. "Their apathy to Jewish music," he said, "is unbelievable." At the other session I heard Jacob Golub read a paper on the lines of research that ought to be conducted in Jewish education. Although what he said was true, I felt that at the present time we cannot afford to divert the energies of those who are engaged in Jewish education for the more immediately urgent tasks of creating in the parents a desire to send their children to a Jewish school and developing content of instruction in the Jewish school.

In the evening (Wednesday) I gave my talk on "The Implications of the World Situation for Jewish Cultural Life in America" before a large gathering at the ballroom under the auspices of the three organizations. The prepared address would have taken 1 hr & 50 minutes. Fortunately I had sense enough to omit parts of it and to get it down to 1 hour. It was listened to very attentively and seemed to express what most people felt was a timely message. Subsequently, however, I learned, as I shall have occasion to record, that there was another reaction to it. The discussants were A. M. Dushkin, S. C. Kohs, and Louis Kraft.

Yesterday morning I read my paper on "The Teaching of Religion in the Jewish School" before the National Council for Jewish Education. The paper was well received. The discussants were Rabbi [Barnett] Brickner of Cleveland and Dr. Louis L. Kaplan of Baltimore. Others who took part in the discussion were Hurwich of Boston, [Emanuel] Gamoran, and Rabbi Mishkin of Chicago. Hurwich and Mishkin tried to present the case of Orthodoxy. [Louis] Kaplan, who seems to be intelligent, suffers from some kind of lag in his thinking.

In the afternoon I listened to Dushkin's paper on his approach to his task with the Jewish Education Committee here. The discussion indicated to me that the principle of diversity in unity is accepted, if at all, as a matter of expediency, but that the acceptance of it as a norm of Jewish civilization is scarcely even considered.

Last night the National Council for Jewish Education were the guests of Charles Rosenblum, President of the Pittsburgh Federation, at the dinner given to them in the Cardinal Room of the hotel. He himself was toastmaster, and the speakers were Dr. Louis Kaplan (Chairman of the NCJE), Rabbi [Solomon]

Freehof, and Mark Eisner. Kaplan, in the first part of his remarks, pointed out that this was just the time to demonstrate our faith in God as the power that makes for salvation. But then he assailed the spirit of self-criticism in which we indulge. He deplored its psychological effect. I took his remarks to pertain to my talk of Wednesday night. If that was the case, I am sorry to find that a man of his ability should lend aid and comfort to our own demagogic forces which hamper the process of self-correction in Jewish life. This is what I had reference to when I said above that possibly there were many who were displeased by my denunciation of the escapists. But Freehof was the limit. He too tried to find fault with the attempt to get at the meaning of the God conception and then launched into a whiny diatribe against the schools for not teaching the Bible. From the way he spoke, one might infer that he would have his people read nothing but the Bible. He actually deplored the reading of many books, but the fact is that he makes the reviewing of all the latest books the chief attraction of his preaching activity. Seldom if ever does he lecture on any of the books of the Bible. The impression his talk gave was that of reflex action. He stands up, closes his eyes, tunes in on his nasal whine, and the sentences just form themselves mechanically. He is a typical false prophet.

Kaplan's Classes at the Teachers Institute

SUNDAY, MAY 26, 1940

Today was my closing session at the Teachers Institute. The course known as Religion 5–6, given to third-year students, was based on the chapter on Judaism in Moore's *History of Religion*, Vol. II,[28] and the course Religion 7–8, given to fourth-year students, consisted during the first term of the discussion of the three functions of religion—intellectual, emotional, and voluntaristic—and during the second term of the conception of God as the power that makes for salvation. I used during the second term the Hebrew translation of *The Meaning of God*.

The students of Religion 5–6 were few in number and of poor caliber, with the exception of two or three. Those of [Religion] 7–8 were many (about 32) and constituted a wide-awake group. The courses were conducted for the most part in Hebrew. I resorted to English at times at the request of the students when it would have been hard for them to express themselves in Hebrew.

Apparently the students of Religion 7–8 enjoyed the course. When I was through, they handed in a petition [that] I should teach them also next year.

Analysis of the Current Situation

THURSDAY, MAY 30, 1940

With what is going on in the world these days, it is extremely difficult to think coherently or to plan hopefully. Whatever I do is done under the drive of

---

28. George Foot Moore, A *History of Religions*, 2 vols. (New York: Scribner's Sons, 1919).

sheer necessity or mechanized routine. Yet now if ever is the testing time of the faith in the Power that makes for salvation. But this does not mean necessarily adhering to the easy-going optimistic conceptions of the values involved in that faith, conceptions which have been knocked into a cocked hat by current events. One fundamental oversight in the pre-war (the present one) optimism has been the failure to see in Nazism a world revolution directed against the hypocritical capitalist democracy. Unfortunately we Jews have been maneuvered into the position of having to defend this kind of democracy, because the moment we begin drawing distinctions between genuine and counterfeit democracy, we are accused of being communists. But the fact is that, viewed objectively from the standpoint of the masses of mankind, existing democracy has meant little more than freedom to starve. Mankind has grown sick of having to live even more precariously, because of the stupidity of its leaders in dealing with the overproduction due to technological improvement and with the selfishness of the plutocrats. Anything that gives the least promise of overcoming the fear of starvation and homelessness is seized upon like a straw by a drowning man. Totalitarianism is such a straw. For all anyone knows, it may prove a raft. If by force of the most unhappy combination of circumstances, we Jews have come to be in a position where, for purposes of mass propaganda, we supply the necessary concept of the "Devil" with which to belabor and damn plutocratic democracy, the fault is as much our own as that of our enemies. I am beginning to agree with E. Kaufmann and others among our Hebrew writers who maintain that the cardinal sin of our people is having permitted ourselves to remain in a state of alienage for so long a time. We should either have become absorbed or have found some land for ourselves. No matter how much the population of the various countries which are invaded by the Nazis suffer for a time, neither they nor their children can ever know the life-long mental agony of the average Jew.

On the Chosen People

MAY 31, 1940

The group of Seminary graduates that Jacob Grossman had haphazardly got together met with me again last Wednesday. Although the meeting of little over two weeks ago was to have been the final one this year, those in the group expressed a desire to meet at least once or twice more before the summer. On the other hand, I myself rather enjoyed the discussions, and I was really glad that they wanted to get together again. Present were: J. J. Newman, Schwartz, Miller, [Herbert] Parzen, I. Hoffman, Jacob and Louis Grossman, Goldberg (of 93 St. synagogue), and Radin.

The discussion turned on the question of the re-evaluation of the concept "chosen people." I called attention to my statement in *Judaism in Transition*, p. 124. Jacob Grossman then asked why it was not possible for the change I had made in the liturgy by substituting (p. 147) *asher kervanu le'avodato* [Heb., "Who has brought us near to his service"] for *asher bahar banu* [Heb., "Who hast chosen us"].[29] But Newman interposed with the usual argument that the people who came to synagogue needed to be emotionalized into Judaism and not merely to have the *siddur* [prayer book] changed. I agreed with him on his major premise but disagreed with him in his implied minor premise that the way to emotionalize them was not to tamper with traditional views or practices. Using the idea of chosen people as an illustration, I suggested some realistic facts and possibilities for which that idea might serve as a genuine index. None can gainsay the historical fact that our people achieved a collective self-awareness which found expression in ethical monotheism. If we are not a chosen people, our ancestors were. Our own claim to distinction can be only a conditional one. The condition is that we survive as a people. If we shall succeed in that, we shall give the greatest collective demonstration of the power of the spirit. If we can manage to retain a sense of unity, mutual responsibility, and common destiny, despite persecution, which is directed chiefly at our alienage and has nothing to do with traditional religion, despite our lack of a central authority or state and our dependence on voluntarism, despite the insistence of so-called liberals upon our giving up our individuality, and despite our differences in world outlook, then we are indeed a unique people in being able to transcend the limitations of human nature. Such survival implies that we are discovering new spiritual values in our very persistence, that we are capable of transforming heteronomous into autonomous sanctions, that we have the strength of will to say "nay" to well-meaning but mistaken friends, that we are capable of performing the great moral feat of discovering what men have in common amid the many factors that divide them. Any people that can attain such spiritual heights deserves to be called "chosen." Even if only a faithful remnant is capable of such achievement, it is entitled to this high designation.

Another aspect to the notion of "chosen people" is that suggested by the statement in Amos III 2.[30] The traditional view, which conforms with that statement, is that our alienage, with its attendant miseries, is the penalty for our sins. In the revaluation of the concept of "chosen people," we must find a substitute for the traditional connection between that concept and the fact of our wretchedness. We might find such a substitute if we analyzed the position into which we have been maneuvered by our relation to democracy. We are the beneficiaries

---

29. The liturgical phrase for the chosen people concept was changed by Kaplan in the late 1920s from the traditional to a new formula which he drew from the *Musaf* service for the pilgrimage festivals. It is used in the 1945 Reconstructionist prayer book and in all subsequent prayer books of the Reconstructionist movement. For a film on Kaplan and chosenness, see Joshua Gippin's *Not the Chosen*. Gippin interviewed Arthur Green, Deborah Waxman, Nancy Fuchs-Kreimer, Jacob Staub, and me for his film.

30. Amos 3:2 says, "You alone have I singled out of all the families of the earth—that is why I will call you to account for all your iniquities." This is a key verse dealing with chosenness.

of democracy. We should not, however, have become so enamored of the rights it conferred upon us as to have forgotten the duties which it should have been the task of democracy to inculcate in all who wish to live by it. We should have taken our "mission" seriously and not permitted ourselves to be guilty of the same selfishness and hypocrisy as the rest of the world in the application of democratic principles to politics and economics. Had we taken our religion seriously, we would not have condoned the adoption by our own ambitious Jews of the prevalent methods of heartless exploitation and ruthless competition. The very fact that our enemies have evolved the Jewish bogey as responsible for the sins of democracy indicates that, whether we want it or not, our very existence is bound up with that of democracy, more so than that of any other people. We might therefore paraphrase the statement of Amos to read: Only you of all families of the earth have I caused to be dependent upon the establishment of freedom, justice, and peace; therefore it is your fate to bear the brunt of the suffering in wake of the violation of these laws of Mine which you call democracy.

Finkelstein Trying to Divest the JTS of the TI

WEDNESDAY, JUNE 5, 1940

After the meeting of the Seminary Faculty this morning Finky[31] took me aside, and while we were both standing, he made a proposition concerning the Teachers Institute which left me stunned. Referring to the fact that [Zevi] Scharfstein and [Hillel] Bavli had come to see him with regard to the teachers' salaries, he said that it might be a good plan for the Jewish Education Committee to take over the TI. This interview to which he referred was reported at a recent meeting of the TI Faculty. Scharfstein then stated that F. had told them that the Seminary was running on a deficit and that there was no likelihood of anything being done about the salaries of the TI instructors. It is quite evident that F. is out to knife the TI.

. . . The fear and tension under which everyone labors in view of the Nazi threat to overwhelm the Allies and to challenge this country are enough to stifle all thought that has no bearing on the immediate danger.

I have this Finkephobia to overcome. Physically I have been under the weather for the last ten days due to sciatica in my hips. All in all I find myself at present bereft of that very hope and courage which it is my function to instill in others. Yet if men like Churchill and Reynaud can manage to carry on in the face of such national defeats and disasters as are their daily portion, no one worth his salt has a right to give in to such petty troubles and worries as the Seminary has been subjecting me for the last few years, and even to the very real dangers that hang over Jewish life.

---

31. Louis Finkelstein, president of the Seminary at the time.

Seminary Graduation — Alexander Marx Naps

JUNE 8, 1940

The baccalaureate sermon was given by [Morris] Schussheim. It was a very mediocre effort. He was very nervous. I don't blame him. It is very difficult to say anything encouraging nowadays in which one can believe whole-heartedly. The audience consisted for the most part of students and Faculty. (The Faculty are seated on the platform.) As soon as Schussheim began to speak, Prof. Marx went to sleep and did not wake up until the sermon was over. Marx does that invariably, and no one has ever taken him to task for it. It seems to be one of his vanities to boast of his inability to write a sermon or to listen to one without going off into deep sleep.

At the Seminary Synagogue — Which Torah Blessing to Use

TUESDAY, JUNE 11, 1940

Death, the further off it seems, the better it is braved. This is why, other things being equal, health and courage go together.

When I came to the Seminary synagogue last Sabbath, I knew that I would be given some honor connected with the reading of the Torah. The question arose in my mind what I should do in case I am called up. If I were to use the new version of the Torah benediction (*asher kervanu le'avodato*) [Heb., "who hast brought us near to his service"][32] instead of *asher bahar banu* [Heb., "who has chosen us"], I would offend the congregation. On the other hand, if I reverted to the traditional benediction, I would appear guilty of inconsistency. I had to make up my mind beforehand, so I decided to use the traditional form. But fortunately I was saved from compromising myself by being called up for the ceremony of raising the scroll. Whether it was a matter of chance, or whether Prof. [Louis] Ginzberg who apportions the honors wanted to forestall embarrassment on anybody's part, I cannot tell. But I am surely grateful for the *mitzvah* of *hagbah*.[33]

Failing to Deliver a Sermon Well

SATURDAY NIGHT, JUNE 22, 1940, DEAL, NEW JERSEY

Yesterday we moved into the cottage we rented for the summer. It is located in Deal, on the corner of Norwood and Philip Aves. Ira, Judith, and [their daughter] Miriam are with us.

---

32. In rejecting the chosen people concept, Kaplan substituted words in the service that did not refer to the chosen people.

33. This honor of lifting the Torah does not require any blessing so Kaplan had no problem. It is also a lesser honor than being called up to the Torah and saying a blessing.

On Wednesday, the first day of Shavuot (June 12), I experienced one of my occasional reverses. The sermon was a flop. I tried to give the very same talk that had proved eminently successful the Monday night before. But something must have upset me. Perhaps it was the poor attendance due to the fact that many of the members were in other synagogues where their friends were having their children confirmed. Perhaps [it was] the unexpected presence of Henry Rosenthal, whose hypocritical attitude has a disturbing effect on me. All I know is that the words I needed eluded me and the words that came to my tongue were the wrong ones. When I am under nervous tension, I suffer a kind of attenuated aphasia which shows itself in my forgetting names and in my failing to get the right word for the thought I want to express. The present condition of the world is naturally the main cause of my nervous tension. But at times I manage to overcome it, especially when I find myself in genial surroundings. This is hardly the case at services at the SAJ. The unaesthetic surroundings, the lack of proper musical rendition of the prayers or the Torah readings, the small numbers—all these things combine to depress me. And the result was the failure to put my sermon across.

The effect of such failure is to aggravate my nervous tension and to put me into a very black mood. It takes me some time to overcome that effect, depending on how soon I have the opportunity to redeem myself in my own estimation. I cannot say that up till now I have really redeemed myself, despite my having had one opportunity since then where I might have done so, if I had succeeded with it better than I did. That will be made clear in the sequel.

Meeting a Rabbinical Student Group at Home for a Special Summer Seminar

JUNE 22, 1940

Fortunately in my own case the task of having to meet a group of Seminary men who had asked me to conduct with them a seminar and discussion group has enabled me to overcome the depressive feeling. The following were in the group: Gershon Chertoff, [Abraham] Winokur, Tenenbaum, Gerstein, [Meir] Engel, [Benjamin] Kreitman, Barish, [Lawrence] Charney, [Moshe] Davis, [and] [Herman] Kieval. The first session was attended also by Sidney Greenberg. I took up with them Moore's *Origin and Growth of Religion*, of which I covered the first 4 chapters. I spent one half of each session on that book and one hour on the discussion of the paper on "The Function of the Rabbi in American Jewish Life," which I expect to present at the convention of the Rabbinical Assembly in Detroit next week. I met with the group 4 times in the course of the week, June 17–21, omitting Wednesday. Both the men and I enjoyed the sessions and found them fruitful.

Robert Gordis and Seminary Politics

SUNDAY, JUNE 23, 1940

Monday afternoon (June 17) Dr. Gordis came to see me.[34] I don't think I have recorded anything about him in this Journal thus far, but he is one of the dramatic personae of the Seminary Comedy (Comedia Divina). He is in my opinion the most brilliant graduate of the Seminary, not excepting even Milton Steinberg. He has preeminent ability both as a scholar and as a speaker and some excellent traits as a person. If it were not for a streak of pilpulism[35] that yellows both his thinking and acting, he would be almost a flawless kind of person. It is his capacity to think straight that I venture to say has led him to accept and even partly avow the Reconstructionist approach. But it is that pilpulistic streak which has led him to identify it with Conservatism and on occasion to disavow Reconstructionism.

The object of his visit was to tell me about his being offered a Chicago pulpit and to get my advice as to whether he should accept it. The pulpit is occupied at present by a "freelance," a certain Daskell who has been with his congregation for the last 20 years. The congregation is aware that its growth is impeded by Daskell. They want to retire him on a pension and to get a better man in his place. They are anxious to get Gordis, whom they are offering $8,000.00.

Gordis described his situation at the Seminary as one that is uncertain, due to Finkelstein's desire to economize and to his tendency to prevaricate. Among the most recent antics of F. is that of acting as apologist for Christianity in general and the Catholic Church in particular vis-à-vis the Jews. On one occasion he broke out in anger against Gordis for some imaginary offense to [William F.] Albright, who had done Gordis an ill turn, and he accused Gordis of failing to turn his other cheek. When F. was about to invite a Catholic missionary to the Jews to participate in the interfaith series of lectures, Gordis warned him not to do so. Instead of thanking Gordis for apprising him of the kind of person that Catholic priest was, he turned on him resentfully and excoriated him for suspecting innocent people.

When I asked Gordis how his wife felt about his making the change, he told me she preferred to remain in New York, mainly because she has all her relatives here. I then saw no point in advising him to make the change.

---

34. Robert Gordis was a leading Conservative rabbi. Kaplan expected Gordis's support in conflicts with the Seminary faculty but didn't get it. Gordis was an exceptional speaker, and his style was loud and fast, earning him the description Machine-Gun Gordis. For more on Gordis and Kaplan, see Scult, *Judaism Faces the Twentieth Century*, 226, 234. For the Seminary faculty generally, see Scult, *Judaism Faces the Twentieth Century*, 203–40. On Gordis and the Kaplan Haggadah, see Mel Scult, *The Radical American Judaism of Mordecai M. Kaplan* (Bloomington: Indiana University Press, 2013), 311.

35. Irrelevant Talmudic scholastic argumentation.

(I forgot to state in the preceding that at present he holds two positions: one as rabbi of a Long Island congregation, to which he gives most of his time and which pays him, I should judge, about $6,000. And the other is as lecturer in Bible which gives him $1,000.) There are two other men in the Seminary who teach Bible, H. L. Ginsberg[36] and [Alexander] Sperber. Ginsberg, who gives all his time to the Seminary, stands the best chance of attaining the professorship in Bible, which had always been Gordis' ultimate ambition. The one who is chiefly responsible for Ginsberg's accession to the Seminary is Albright, according to whom Ginsberg is the most promising Jewish biblical scholar. From what Gordis says, Albright, while trying to smooth Ginsberg's path, does everything to obstruct Gordis' chances. Albright went so far as to prevent three articles of Gordis' from appearing in the *Journal of Biblical Studies*. The fact that they were accepted immediately and without any reservations by three other reputable magazines shows that it was not because they were not good enough that they had been turned down.

Congregation Shaarey Zedek in Detroit, and the Rabbinical Assembly's Annual Meeting

JUNE 29, 1940

That same night I left for Detroit together with Ira to attend the convention of the Rabbinical Assembly. We got there Tuesday noon and drove directly to the Synagogue Shaarey Zedek, where all the sessions of the convention took place. That synagogue had been rebuilt quite recently, I believe about six years ago, and contains magnificent accommodations for worship, school, and social activities. The congregation Shaarey Zedek has been in existence over 70 years and includes among its members a considerable number of well-to-do Jews who come from intensely Jewish homes and had been brought up to place a high value on Jewish knowledge. This accounts for their being neo-Orthodox and for the hold which Rabbi Hirschman has on them. He is a man of about my age who came to this country after I did, after having gotten something of a Yeshivah training. He has been with the congregation for over thirty years. At present it has a membership of nearly 700 families with a Sunday school attendance of about 1,100. Of that number only between 50 and 75 attend the weekday Hebrew school. The younger people had been clamoring for years that Hirschman should get an assistant, because they were out of sympathy with his intransigence in the matter of Jewish belief and practice, and wanted to be served by a man who was more modern minded. This, however, was not the avowed reason for their demanding that the congregation get an assistant rabbi. Hirschman, on the

---

36. To me, Ginsberg was noted for his readiness to make changes in biblical texts based on ancient Near Eastern languages. He was my teacher and seemed to reconstruct the text as he taught.

other hand, has been inveterately opposed to having an assistant imposed on him. Finally he had to yield, and Morris Adler, one of the more recent Seminary graduates and a very able young man, is now assistant. Although Adler has been there only one year, the two rabbis are already at loggerheads. When I asked Hirschman how Adler was working out, he said to me that a congregation has no right to be so big as to require more than one rabbi.

The Rabbinical Assembly—Issues and Interactions

JUNE 29, 1940

Tuesday afternoon, papers were presented by Morris Adler, Armand Cohen, and David Goldstein on the rabbi and the community. Armand Cohen discussed his particular phase of the subject—the Center and the Synagogue—in the spirit of Reconstructionism. Simon Greenberg could not let such outspoken approval of Reconstructionism go unchallenged. He took exception to Cohen's suggestion that the community ought to take under its wing both the synagogue and the center. In the course of his remarks he made the statement that the only way rabbis can get money of Jewish activities is by influencing rich Jews to give. To illustrate his point, he mentioned the fact that the new hospital which was being erected in Philadelphia will in all likelihood make provision for kashrut, because the president of the hospital was a member of his congregation. I used this very example afterward to illustrate what I meant by the statement that the rabbi was functioning in a void, since he had to resort to "shtadlanut"[37] to achieve his Jewish objectives and had not a democratic base to build on.

In the evening a public meeting took place in the main auditorium of the synagogue and was addressed by Israel M. Goldman of Providence and Finkelstein. Goldman gave a well worked out, though lengthy address, on the Seminary. Finkelstein was supposed to speak on [Cyrus] Adler.[38] What he told about Adler was quite interesting, though it gave a highly idealized picture of the man. But then he digressed into an analysis of the present world situation, the danger in which civilization found itself, and what the Seminary proposed to do in order to save civilization. In the meantime, it hasn't enough funds to keep even the museum open. In the course of his ranting, he let drop a remark from which I gather on what pretext he bases his opposition to the group of educators like Dushkin, Chipkin,[39] etc. to whom Goldman had referred as the products of the Teachers Institute. That remark was that it is not enough to evolve the methodology of Jewish education. The Seminary will undertake to produce content. From that

---

37. *Stadlanut* is a historical term referring to Jews who attempted to gain money and power by lobbying or serving powerful non-Jews.

38. Cyrus Adler, president of the Seminary, who had just passed away.

39. Kaplan's supporters in education.

point he expiated on such important work as the inter-faith courses and the proposed council of 80 scientists, philosophers who will meet on Sept. 9. The truth is that in his eagerness to get financial support for the Seminary, F. is resorting to all kinds of sensational and spectacular methods that may appeal to certain rich Jews who have no interest in furthering Jewish life as such. But by [using] methods such as these, he is catering to and reenforcing the lowest standards of Jewish life and neglecting the intrinsic values which it ought to be the business of the Seminary to foster. It is interesting though saddening to see how he tries, by working himself up into a frenzy, to get himself to believe in this kind of sensationalism as not only justifiable but as indispensable to the salvation of the Seminary.

Wednesday morning and part of the afternoon were devoted to the discussion of the rabbi's function in the congregation. The particular aspects dealt with were preaching, arranging the order of worship, and influencing the home, from the standpoint of modern life and thought. Ira read an excellent paper on "Preaching Modern Religion." Eli A. Bohnen, one of the discussants of the paper, frankly said that he was troubled by the fact that he had no definite conception of God, though he was in quest of such a conception. The frankness was to be refreshing but the fact was discouraging. Morris Silverman read a good paper on "Vitalizing Public Worship," but the one by Eugene Kohn on that subject was much better. Henry Fisher, the second discussant, challenged the value of improved techniques when the very reality of God as an entity was being questioned. While admitting that he was not asking us to recover the belief in an anthropomorphic deity, of the kind that his mother, who prays devoutly, believes in, he said he was at a loss to advise in order that we might worship in the same spirit as did our ancestors. William P. Greenfield read a paper on the home. He likewise was challenged for not going to the root of the matter and failing to realize that the Jewish home is merely sharing the general disintegration of the home. All in all I was pleased both by the specific nature of the suggestions as to what may be done to improve the activities of the rabbi and by the repeated challenge to them on the ground that they failed to reckon with the more fundamental causes of what was wrong with those activities.

In the evening I listened to Herman Hailperin's M. D. Levine Memorial Lecture[40] in Hebrew on "Intellectual Relations Between Christian and Jew in Europe with Special Reference to Rashi and Nicolas de Lyra."[41] Though what

---

40. The lecture series is named after Morris Levine (1881–1935), a popular and much respected JTS faculty member. Levine was primarily responsible for bringing Hebrew to the Teachers Institute. When the Teachers Institute was established, the language of instruction was English. This changed in 1915 primarily as a result of the efforts of Samson Benderly in New York education.

41. Rashi refers to Rabbi Shlomo Yitzhaki (1040–1105), the most important commentator on Bible and Talmud. Nicholas of Lyra (c. 1270–October 1349), a Franciscan teacher, was among the most influential practitioners of biblical exegesis in the Middle Ages. He was a doctor at the Sorbonne by 1309 and ten years later was appointed the head of all Franciscans in France.

he said was rather commonplace, it was expressed in a clear style and articulate diction. When I recall what a poor opinion I had of him and of his intellectual attainments when he started on his career in the rabbinate, I am gratefully happy for the sake of Jewish life to note such vast improvement in some of the men entrusted with conserving it.

Boaz Cohen's report of the Committee on Jewish Law did not create a good impression on those present. (There were fewer members of the Assembly and more strangers than at the day sessions.) The main spirit of the report may be summed up by the *morte non possumus* [roughly, "because we are mortal, we cannot"].

Thursday morning came my turn. This was the best attended session of the entire convention, except, of course, the public one of Tuesday night. For once I delivered an important address with perfect ease despite the presence of unfriendly critics, disarming the latter and making new friends for the cause of Reconstructionism. The fact that I spoke extemporaneously, illustrat[ing] the most important points by references to what had come up in the discussion of the two preceding days and in general integrat[ing] the various papers into an organic unity, enabled me to hold the interest of the hearers for an hour and a half and to convey to them the basic principle of Reconstructionism. If I had come with a prepared address, I would probably not have had the courage to make explicit references to Reconstructionism. But I noted throughout the discussions of the preceding days that the speakers found themselves compelled to use the term "reconstruction" again and again. Each time the word was mentioned, there was a rustle of comment. I then realized as I had never before what an excellent term I happened to have chosen for our movement. From the advertiser's standpoint, nothing is so valuable as having the name of the product he is trying to sell creep frequently into discourse. Not being bound to a manuscript, I capitalized on what I had heard in the course of the discussions of the various papers that had been presented. I made use especially of Greenberg's remark that we Jews lack the power of taxation to prove my point about the rabbinate's functioning in a void, and of Lang's insistence upon dealing with the individual Jew to get him to want to be a Jew, to indicate that this was exactly what Reconstructionism stood for. Reconstructionism, I pointed out, differs from the existing movements in Jewish life in urging that the problems of readjustment which the rabbi has to solve as social engineer, educator, and theologian be dealt with not by the rabbis alone but by them cooperatively with the laity. Only by getting the laity to understand those problems and accept responsibility for their solution will Jewish life succeed in finding a place for itself in the modern world.

Greenberg again rose to speak, this time, however, not to take issue with what I had said but to say that he had found himself in greater agreement with me than ever before and to explain what he himself described as his "unfortunate" statement about working through the rich. Finkelstein naturally had to register that he differed with me theologically in reference to my definition of God not as entity but as process and socially in that he would rather stress the reconstruction of the world in which we live rather than the reconstruction of Jewish life. He did, however, approve wholeheartedly my suggestion that the Seminary give its students a basic three years' training in the subject matter of the Jewish heritage, and a two years' special professional training either in synagogue activities, social welfare, Zionist work, etc. so as to have men with a rabbinic background qualified to go into various phases of administrative work in the Jewish community.

There were about twelve of us on the train that left for New York that evening. Among them were [Louis] Finkelstein, Israel M. Goldman, Louis Levitsky, Boxer [Ben Zion Bokser], [Morris?] Adler, [Alexander] Burnstein, Harry Halpern, and others. We interchanged funny stories, "davened" Maariv[42] in one of the compartments, and listened later to the voting of the Republican Convention that was being held in Philadelphia. The only serious matter we touched on that evening was the organization of the adult classes to be conducted under the auspices of the Seminary. Goldman had been appointed by Finkelstein to organize the work.

In the morning Finkelstein and I chatted about what he had said with regard to reconstructing the world. I tried to explain to him that it was impossible to think of reconstructing Jewish life without at the same time reconstructing to some extent the general environment in which we lived. It seems to me that he is too much obsessed with his practical objectives to think clearly on any subject, especially one which calls for a thorough grounding in the fundamentals of sociology and philosophy. Later, while talking about the reluctance of our graduates to go to remote places where their services are highly needed, he mentioned what President Roosevelt had said to him about settling refugee Jews in the different South American countries. The governments there feared that Jews might isolate themselves and try to build up an "imperium in unperio." Roosevelt was therefore pleased to hear from Finkelstein that he had suggested to the JDC[43] to send rabbis to these new Jewish communities to help them adjust themselves to the new conditions under which they had to live and to become integrated into the general population. "What I fear," said Finkelstein to me, "is Jewish isolationism." Does he really believe that I am an isolationist, or does he merely want to believe that about me in order to feel justified in combating whatever influence I might have over the graduates? It seems that he and Cyrus Adler must have talked with each other into believing that about me. It is quite apparent that he has, out of gratitude to Adler for having made him president of the Seminary, allowed Adler's spirit and way of thinking to take full possession of him. This is how he has grown into the part of the typical pious assimilationist.

---

42. *Daven* means to pray. Maariv is the daily evening prayer.

43. Joint Distribution Committee. Founded in 1914 to aid needy Jews in Europe and Palestine, it now aids needy Jews around the world.

As for my own part in the convention, I am glad to record that I have managed to carry it through with complete satisfaction to myself from every point of view. It has given me greater confidence in myself and in the graduates of the Seminary and has added to my sense of security in the Seminary vis-à-vis Finkelstein.

Lecturing at the Jewish Institute of Religion Meeting—Kaplan's Concept of God

SUNDAY, JUNE 30, 1940

This morning I went to New York to deliver the lecture on "The Religious vs. the Philosophic Approach to the Belief in God" before the Summer Institute of the Jewish Institute of Religion.[44] All I did was to use part of the address I had given at Pittsburgh before the National Council for Jewish Education on May 23. I was surprised to find quite a large group of people taking part in the seminar. Most of the participants work quite hard during the academic year, and one would imagine that on a fine June morning like today's they would relax. But apparently most professionals are eager and ambitious to advance in their callings. It is good to see that those engaged in Jewish work also take their calling quite seriously.

I had in the audience Prof. and Mrs. [Ismar] Elbogen and Prof. [Shalom] Spiegel. They complimented me on my address. I gave only the part that dealt with the conception of God. That took me about an hour and a quarter. The questions were too few for me to judge how the audience reacted. The reason for the limited number of questions was that there was another lecture immediately following mine.

In going over the material I lectured on this morning, I had occasion to bring out a new and very important point. I drew a distinction between the belief in God on the one hand and the conception of God or the God idea on the other. The former I described as the articulation of the will to life abundant and as analogous to the forms which Kant ascribed to the mind; the latter I described as the particular idea of the Power that makes for salvation, which is determined by the level of cultural and social development and is analogous to the content of thought.

---

44. The Jewish Institute of Religion was founded by Stephen Wise. It was a Reform rabbinical school that later merged with Hebrew Union College. Wise wanted Kaplan on the faculty and perhaps as president in 1920, a complicated but important part of Reform Judaism's history. For the story of Kaplan's interactions with the school, see Scult, *Judaism Faces the Twentieth Century*, 268–75.

Worries about the Future of the Teachers Institute and Finkelstein's Strategies

JULY 8, 1940

Three times each year I send in a report to the President of the Seminary on the work of the Teachers Institute and Israel Friedlaender classes.[45] The latter report this year was the first one addressed to F. [Finkelstein]. In acknowledging the receipt, he added a number of questions about the Friedlaender classes which he wanted Chipkin to answer. The questions were many in number, calling for all sorts of statistics about the students, their attendance, marks, examinations, and also about the IF [Friedlaender] Faculty, the number of meetings held, etc. I referred these questions to Chipkin, but I could see at once that F. was out for some mischief. Sure enough, I was right in my guess. The other day I received word from Chipkin that he had had a long interview with F. and that he wanted to tell me about it. Today I waited to see Chipkin to get from him the account of the interview.

In brief, this is what F. said to him. "Did Kaplan tell you of my suggestion about the TI that the Jewish Education Committee[46] ought to take it over? K. turned it down. But how about the IF classes? I can use my influence with the other members of the JEC [Jewish Education Committee] to get them to take it over." (The very words he had used with me about the TI.)

"But," interposed Ch., "apart from the fact that the JEC could not take over the classes without violating the principle of treating all groups alike?"

"I can't see any difference between the TI, the Yeshiva Teachers Institute, and the Herzliah.[47] I received my training in all three kinds," answered F.

"But should not the fact that the IF Classes have been part of the Seminary for 20 years, and that they are a means of memorializing Friedlaender's sacrifice for Judaism be taken into account? After all there is a great deal of sentiment involved in all this," Ch. said.

"That shouldn't stand in the way," F. replied. "As for sentiment, Friedlaender didn't die for the Seminary. He died for the JDC."[48] What I suppose

---

45. Adult education classes at JTS named after Israel Friedlander.

46. The Jewish Education Committee supervised and coordinated Jewish education. The Board of Jewish Education (New York City) started in 1910 as the Bureau of Education. At this time Samson Benderly was the director. In 1917 the organization was renamed the Bureau of Jewish Education. In 1940 the Jewish Education Committee, founded in 1917, absorbed the Bureau of Jewish Education. During the same year, the Jewish Education Committee also absorbed the Jewish Education Association, founded in 1921. In 1970 the Jewish Education Committee changed its name to the Board of Jewish Education. (Information from the records at the American Jewish Historical Society.)

47. These were institutes in New York City for training teachers of Hebrew.

48. It was the American Joint Distribution Committee that sent Friedlaender on his fatal fact-finding mission to the Ukraine after World War I.

he meant was that the community and not the Seminary ought to memorialize Friedlaender's name. But whatever he meant, only a heartless brute could talk like that.

Apparently he is having a hard time meeting the Seminary budget. Either he or someone among the Seminary trustees is responsible for the contemplated investigation into the way the Seminary is conducted. The suggestion was made that Teachers College be asked to appoint the investigating committee. That was how the Graduate School for Jewish Social Work began to be sabotaged. But F. said that he would try to carry through the investigation himself. If what he did would not prove satisfactory, he would ask Teachers College to undertake it. At least that is the story he told Ch. in explanation for his asking Ch. to give him all those statistics about the Friedlaender classes.

I am very much afraid that the comparative peace of mind which I enjoyed in the Seminary hitherto belongs to an era that is past. This man F. is a trouble maker.

Kaplan Outlines His Theology, Which He Calls Soterics

JULY 9, 1940

Of late I have made considerable headway in my thinking on religion. The following thoughts on the subject should prove fruitful:

Toward a Science of Soterics[49]

Whatever truth there may be to Kant's distinction between the form and the content of thought, epistemologically, there is in it an important psychological truth. Psychologically all conation [impulse or striving] necessarily implies movement in a specific direction of which the mind (the totality of will, thought, and emotion) becomes aware, usually as a result of some obstacle which obstructs the movement. Awareness is a kind of converted "movement-in-a-specific direction," analogous to heat which results from collision of two objects. The converted "movement-in-a-specific direction" of the will or conation may be regarded as the *form* which the cognition assumes. As a result of the functioning of the imagination (which may be considered as the constellation of cognitive acts), that form is progressively filled with *content*.

The foregoing distinction, viewed psychologically, between the form and content of thought should prove helpful in understanding the nature and

---

49. Soterics is the name that Kaplan gave to his ideology. It comes from the Greek word *soter*, meaning "to save," and is meant to emphasize the centrality of salvation in his system. In the early 1940s Kaplan hoped to work out a whole system, which he would call Soterics. This system is much more theological and philosophical than what is now called Reconstructionism. In the 1950s Kaplan proposed that the Hebrew word *sheleymut* (wholeness or completeness) be used instead of *salvation*.

development of religion. In keeping with that distinction, we should distinguish in religion the *belief* in God from the *idea* or *conception* of God. The belief in God is cognitive *form;* the conception of God is cognitive *content.* As *form*, the belief in God is the constant factor in all the manifestations of religion. As *content*, the conception of God is the variable factor in religion, which varies with the level of social and intellectual development.

The belief in God is the cognitive *form* of the movement of the human will in the direction of deliverance or salvation. God as the object of religious *belief* is therefore the Power that makes for salvation.

The conception of God is the particular thought *content* which is put into the three elements of the belief in God: (1) the Power, (2) that makes for (3) salvation. At once we come upon an important fact about the conception or idea of God, viz., that it is not merely a conception of a Power, without at the same time being a conception of (3) salvation and of what (2) makes for it. The attempt to formulate a conception of God independently of our conception of the other two terms is like trying to define a person's character apart from any situations in which that person had a chance to display it.

The psychological order in which the three elements of the belief in God take on content is first "salvation," then "makes-for," and finally "God."

Salvation in its elementary aim of deliverance from some evil becomes an object of awareness as soon as some desire is obstructed, and the imagination, becoming active, envisages the thwarted objective. All thwarted desire is a form of evil. It is in the nature of pain to focus the entire mentality of the living being upon the actual or putative cause of the pain. When we have a festering hangnail, we find it difficult to keep our minds upon our most important affairs, for at that time our entire being is centered upon the hangnail and the wish to be relieved of the pain it causes. This centering of his entire being upon some focal point results in the case of man (whose memory retains strong impressions of these frequent states of obsession) in awareness of selfhood. Likewise, the desire for relief, becoming associated with the whole of one's being or self, becomes for the time being synonymous with self-fulfillment, to which everything is for the moment subordinated. We then have as the first step in the psychological process of the breaking up of the experience of the will to deliverance or salvation, the emergence simultaneously of the self as the subject of that deliverance or salvation.

The next psychological step is the awareness of conditions as "making for" that deliverance. In our eagerness to be relieved of what is troubling us, we "attack" whatever causes us the pain. How we "attack" it depends evidently upon what we identify as the conditions upon which our salvation depends.

But as little as we find it possible to attend to the source of the evil without bringing our whole self to bear on it, without becoming aware of self, so little do we find it possible to attend to the conditions which are regarded as capable of removing the evil without becoming aware of a power behind them, a power in whom or in which the conditions that make for deliverance or salvation receive their unity. Thus, by the same token that the awareness of the want of salvation leads to the emergence of selfhood, the awareness of the existence of conditions that make for the attainment of salvation leads to the emergence of godhood. The Power that makes for salvation is thus the necessary complement to the self, which is the subject of salvation. This accounts for the recognition, in time, of the possession by man and God of a nature inherently common to both. Thus the emergence of the belief in a Power or powers constitutes the third psychological step in the breaking up of the experience of the will to salvation.

The history of religion is the history of the various types of content prejudiced into each of the three elements of the belief in God, viz., (1) salvation, (2) make-for, and (3) Power.

At this point there should be anthropological material arranged in the order of the social and intellectual progress to illustrate the development in the *conceptions* of salvation, of what makes for it, and of the Power behind what makes for it.

In Jewish religion salvation is conceived as deliverance from self, by the practice of Yoga. The third element is left unfilled. Thus proving that the most determining element of the three in religious belief is the element of salvation.

Until modern times in the Western world salvation was regarded as immortality of the soul and bliss in the hereafter, the conditions that make for it as residing in the tradition of some supernaturally revealed law or person, and the Power who is the author of that revelation as a quasi-human being.

Nowadays there is confusion as to how to conceive salvation. The most plausible conception of it is that of contributing toward the establishment of a world in which there would obtain a synthesis of the maximum of individuality with the maximum of cooperation. The conditions making for it should be conceived as a progressive knowledge of human life and its natural environment and the utilization of that knowledge to achieve the salvation of individual and society. God should be conceived as a cosmic process analogous to human selfhood. As process, God's nature is one, but polar in character, harboring the evil which it is forever seeking to overcome and destroy. (Incidentally, this is what Kabbalah also taught. This is the first time that I find myself subscribing to the traditional conception of God as the author of both good and evil. Hitherto I conceived of God as identified with the good only.)

WEDNESDAY, JULY 10, 1940

To arrive at a working conception of God for our day, we should first arrive at a clear understanding of what is to constitute for us salvation. How shall we go about formulating a satisfactory conception of salvation? Two factors enter into the formulation: one is what we want, the other is what is possible. In ancient times, when people had no notion of natural law and regarded all existence as caused by personal and purposive will, anything that was wanted was considered possible. Thus, since the human being wanted to live forever and since he had no conception of death as inherent in the nature of things, he conceived of salvation as consisting of immortality. This world seldom if ever proved satisfactory. The mere fact that man wanted another and better world for his abode was considered sufficient reason for its ultimate realization. From these premises it followed naturally that man's true destiny lay beyond this world of space and time in some eternal realm that was unmarred by sin and suffering.

Nowadays, however, the notion of fixed laws in the physical and mental aspects of reality have become so integral a part of our thinking that we have learned to resign ourselves to this world of space and time as the only one in which the human being will have to achieve salvation, if he can achieve it all. It is much more difficult to formulate a conception of this-worldly salvation than it ever could be to formulate one of other-worldly salvation. The reason is evident. Besides having to be specific, where the other-worldly conception could afford to be vague, a conception of this-worldly salvation that would satisfy all and sundry is very hard to arrive at. In fact, it must be so formulated as to allow considerable latitude for a variety of tastes. Tentatively the following conception seems plausible:

Salvation for the modern-minded individual would be the conviction that human society will ultimately be redeemed from at least the major evils which have their origin in human nature as well as to a large extent from those which are the concomitant of physical nature, and the feeling that our life has made some contribution, however modest, to such a consummation. What are the major evils which are remediable, and what the goods which would result from their elimination? These are by no means easy questions to answer. We must remember that the elimination of one evil might lead to another. Let us say that human beings have finally eliminated war and have achieved a method of settling international disputes analogous to that used in settling disputes between individuals. There is plenty of injustice rampant in the world despite the fact that individuals resort to litigation instead of to dueling. What guarantee is there that for every evil that is eliminated, another might not come in its place?

Besides, the elimination of evil by itself is not sufficient to constitute salvation. For life to be truly worthwhile, it must yield some positive satisfactions. What shall they be? Tentatively I might suggest the following: maximum of self-expression plus maximum of cooperation in the various social relationships through which we function. Maximum self-expression presupposes health, both physical and mental, which accompanies the satisfaction of the needs for food, shelter, and sex experience. It also presupposes adequate opportunity for work and play, the adequateness depending upon the native capacities of the person. Maximum cooperation implies the development of satisfactory relations based on love, mutual respect, etc. in all dealings with other persons from the most intimate to the most distant.

Assuming that the foregoing is a feasible kind of salvation, we must not only have a general faith in its ultimate achievement but we must also correlate it with the actualities of the world we live in. We must identify the possibilities which inhere in human society and which have in them the making of the salvation we strive for.

There was a time when it was believed that if man would master the difficulties presented by the physical environment, if he could produce enough for his physical wants in the way of food and shelter, the basic reason for his being forever at war with his neighbor would be removed. But we now realize that the vast progress man has achieved technologically has rendered his life less secure and happy. This very technological progress has made man his own most dangerous enemy. Human nature, despite all the teaching and moralizing, has not become one whit better and kindlier. If anything, it has become more cruel and calculating in its viciousness. The deliberate use of propaganda and deceit on as large and unashamed a scale as it is resorted to nowadays could hardly have been contemplated in the past.

But if we believe in the existence of a Power that makes for salvation, we assume that there is meaning and direction to the course of human events, that human nature, despite its being dominated by forces that seem to have little to do with salvation, is made to bring man nearer to the fulfillment of the better and worthier possibilities that are in him. This is the belief which finds expression in the statement that Judaism has taught man to behold God in history. That is to say, the Jews discerned in the tangle of human affairs a movement in the direction of salvation conceived in ethical and not merely naturalistic terms. But in ascribing to human affairs such meaning or direction, they always insisted that it was injected in those affairs by a superhuman Power and not derived from the human agents themselves. Humanism, which became particularly articulate during the last century, refused to countenance this notion that whatever meaning human life and history possessed, they owed it to a source other than human. Comte and Hegel tried to prove that rationality was inherent in human history. Progress came to be regarded as inevitable. The last three decades have opened our eyes to the primeval chaos in which human life is still involved, and the apparent hopelessness of man's ever achieving genuine salvation by dint of his own natural powers and abilities. No wonder that we have with us thinkers like Barth, Berdyaev,[50] and their disciples who maintain that the divine element in human affairs, which compels them to make for man's salvation, does not derive from

---

50. Nikolai Berdyaev (1874–1948) was a Russian religious and political philosopher. His ideology might be described as Christian existentialism.

them but is superior posed as them. In other words, God is not within society but transcends it.

According to this new transcendentalism, the meaning which human affairs assumes by being regarded as constituting history instead of as a medley, is that which the will to live ascribes to human affairs as an act of faith and not as a logical inference from those affairs themselves. As a matter of fact, logical deduction would be inclined to interpret human affairs as meaningless by very reason of their being [treated as having] to have meaning.[51] For one of the most discouraging facts about human life is that it is weighted down by history, by habits and traditions and prejudices which derive their sanction from the mere circumstance that they have a long history. How much more readily human life would adjust itself to changing circumstances if it were not bound by the shackles of history and tradition! If despite that tendency we can still believe that history has meaning, that human affairs are making for man's salvation, it is because our will-to-live is such as to necessitate the existence of a Power that transcends human affairs and that superimposes his will upon them, thereby compelling them to make for the salvation of man.

(I never would have believed that I would find myself accepting the Barthian conception of God. Not so long ago, when I read one of his books, I was literally repelled by his presentation. Yet as I try to think the problem through, I find myself compelled to subscribe to the conception of God as essentially transcendent.)

---

51. "Treated as having" was typed in the original diary and then crossed out in pencil and replaced with "to have meaning."

8

July 12, 1940–August 30, 1940

Salvation and Being Delivered from Evil

Friday, July 12, 1940

Despite what I said in the last item about the inadequacy of the negative aspect of salvation, salvation as deliverance from evil, further reflection leads me to believe that inherently in the very notion of being saved or delivered, the predominant element is not attaining some good but escaping some evil. God, therefore, or the Power that makes for salvation, is the Power that helps man overcome evil. The conception of God is therefore determined by what man conceives as preeminently evil. We would have a better understanding of the history of religion if we made a careful study of what human beings in the different stages of their development considered as the cardinal evil or evils. Not only would we thus gain an itemized list of the different things human beings have regarded as evil, but we would realize that the human imagination plays an important role not only in conjuring up unwarranted fears of what are actually evils but also in representing as evil things that are really not evil. We shall also discover that many evils are considered so good as to constitute salvation.

. . . Neither in early Jewish religion nor in the other religions of mankind—outside the mystery religions which treated death as the cardinal evil but not sin—were sin and death regarded as cardinal evils. They did not constitute the main objectives of a god's redeeming function. In early Jewish religion the cardinal evils were enemies, famine, [and] pestilence (cf. the choice put before David after he counted the Israelites). Enemies meant exile or death by the sword. Famine and pestilence meant the torment of physical pain. God as savior or deliverer warded off all three. Where did the Christians get the notion that sin and death were cardinal evils? I have a hunch that they got it from Hindu philosophy through the medium of the Pythagoreans and the neo-Platonists.

What Moderns Regard as Evil—Economic Slavery and War

JULY 12, 1940

What to the modern man are the cardinal evils? Insecurity, disease. It would not be altogether correct to speak of poverty as a cardinal evil. When poverty, as in the case of monasticism, does not involve insecurity, it is indeed welcomed as a good. But insecurity, which has increased as a result of the fluctuations in the economic life of mankind, is certainly dreaded by the majority of human beings. As for disease, there is nothing new in regarding it as evil, but the increased knowledge of medicine has made the fear of disease an obsession with most people. An evil which may be termed "emergent," in that it is gradually coming to be recognized as such, by no means without resistance on the part of many who either accept it as neutral or even as good, is slavery. In the crude sense of buying and selling human beings as though they were chattels, slavery is considered formally as an evil. But in its disguised forms, such as unquestioning submission to authority, whether of those who speak in their own name or in the name of some tradition, or being dependent upon the arbitrary will of others for one's economic or social well-being, slavery is far from being considered a cardinal evil. In fact, the breakdown of democracy has led many to regard such submission to authority a veritable good. Catholicism definitely goes so far as to make blind submission to authority a high merit and prerequisite to salvation.

Another such emergent evil is war. The fact that democracy is inclined to treat war as an evil has placed the so-called democratic nations at a disadvantage in the world today, which sees the rising star of Germany and Italy because they have inculcated in their people the notion that war is not only not an evil but a good and a means to salvation. It was by means of a similar attitude toward war that Mohammed conquered the greater part of the civilized world in his day. In my book *The Meaning of God in Modern Jewish Religion*, where I have much to say about God as the Power that makes for freedom, I have nothing to say about His being the Power that makes for freedom from war. It would be entirely untrue to the spirit of the Jewish tradition to say that it regarded war as a cardinal evil. The same applies to Christianity. The emergency of war as a cardinal evil is the product of the modern realization that mankind is one and dependent upon the abolition of international war. The inference which Nietzsche drew from Darwin's thesis of the universal struggle for existence is wrong because the thesis itself has been shown by Kropotkin to be in large part wrong.

The point at which the metaphysical aspects of the Power that makes for salvation cannot be evaded is the circumstance that it takes the evils of insecurity, disease, slavery, and war to impel man to produce the conditions that make for their elimination. It takes evil to produce good. Thus from the side of evil, no evil is absolute, since up to a certain point it is a factor for good. On the other hand, every good is quiescent until aroused to action by evil. Hence good from its own standpoint cannot be absolute, since it requires evil to call it into action. Thus good and evil are polar to each other and constitute part of the same underlying entity—God.

This conclusion is a second significant change in my religious thinking. Whereas hitherto I was wont to identify God only with the good and to treat evil as outside God, in the sense that darkness is outside light and its negative, I am now inclined to view God as harboring evil, which is as much a part of Him as the good, but as eternally engaged in overcoming it. In fact, even the analogy of light and darkness as either two distinct entities or as an entity and its negative is misconceived. Properly conceived light and darkness are part of the same process and meaningless apart from each other. What is meaningless apart from anything else cannot have complete existence. Metaphysically speaking, one of the truest and most important definitions of God is that found in Is. 45: "I form the light and create darkness: I make peace and create evil."

Making Processes into Things

JULY 13, 1940

One of the main obstacles to salvation inheres in the inability of the human mind to conceive relationships and processes without hypostatizing[1] them as entities. This is the main source of all the misleading notions about the ego, the soul, and God. It does not seem far-fetched to regard the prohibition of idolatry as an intuitive antagonism to hypostatization of religious concepts. In any event, no religion that is intent upon truth can afford to omit from its reckoning the natural tendency to hypostatization. The best way to combat it is by reviving the prohibition of idolatry, a prohibition which figures so prominently in Judaism and early Christianity as almost to seem the main prerequisite to salvation.

Idolatry not only conforms to the hypostatizing tendency of them. It also brings easily into play the emotional and conative [striving] aspects of the mind. By personifying the gods or God, man can easily fall into emotional reactions similar to those which are aroused in him by his fellow beings. All anti-intellectualist trends in religion have an advantage over those which are based on the attempt to think clearly in being able to play on the emotions. But they are to be suspected of encouraging idolatrous tendencies.

In the light of the principle that it is as much a function of true religion to combat idolatry as to teach the correct conception of God (the conception arrived at as a result of dispassionate search for the truth, a search uninfluenced by authority), the two errors in traditional religion which have to be thus combated are anthropomorphism (including anthropopathetism) and theosophy (in

---

1. To hypostasize is to treat something abstract as a concrete reality. Kaplan has invented the wonderful verb "to thingify" to describe this process.

Judaism it is Kabbalah). The relation of anthropomorphism to the idolatrous tendency to hypostatize is evident. Theosophy is here understood as the system of thought and practice based on the assumption that the cosmos is operated in all its details by final or purposive cause and that it is possible for man to control both environmental and personal forces, entities, etc. by means of the category of final causes as embodied in the names of Deity, angels, demons, etc. in total ignorance or disregard of efficient causes (usually referred to by the term "nature").

The Self and Salvation

Sunday, July 14, 1940

The relation of the soul-self (personality in ethical and spiritual sense) to the ego-self (personality in the novice and salesmanship sense) or for that matter the relation of God to the individual may be conceived as analogous to that of the gravitational force of the earth to the weight of the stone. The commonsense assumption that weight inhered in the stone has given way to the scientific assumption that it is the pull of earth upon the stone that gives it the particular weight which it possesses. Likewise we shall in time consider it perfectly natural to view the soul-self or personality of the human being as residing in him by virtue of the spiritual gravitation of society or of the cosmos, and therefore as surviving the dissolution of the body.

The analogy must not be carried further. Physical gravitation acts with an inevitability that is absent in spiritual gravitation. It is due to that very lack of inevitability that spiritual gravitation is spiritual, for the essential mark of spirit is freedom. For that reason, both the soul-self and God do not by themselves determine the kind of personality the individual shall be. There is, as in physical gravitation, the factor of the receptivity of the individual, which is partly determined by his physical constitution and partly by his ego-self. But neither the ego-self nor the soul-self is a fixed or invariable process. Hence the element of unpredictability in the behavior of the human being.

. . . Throughout all that has been said thus far, we recognize consciously what has been acted upon unconsciously by most of the religious philosophers and theologians, namely, that the only source of our knowledge of God can be what we believe about our own abiding self, or soul-self, and not as they for the most part imagined: supernatural, revelation, or the traditional record of it.

Anthropocentrism Is Inescapable

Monday, July 15, 1940

The most difficult problem, it seems to me, we have to cope with is, What relation is there between the anthropocentric universe of discourse to which the conception of God as the Power that makes for salvation belongs and the scientific universe of discourse in which not only man but even the solar system cuts a relatively small figure? Before Copernicus there was no such problem, because there was only the anthropocentric universe of discourse. Even the Aristotelian conception to which Maimonides[2] subscribed and which negated the notion that the world was created for man left an important role for man in that it affirmed a relationship between God and man. But there is something so incongruous in associating the astronomical universe with man's destiny and salvation that it almost seems absurd to speak in one breath of the Power that holds these universes together as the same Power that makes for man's salvation.

Yet it is a fact that both mathematically, chemically, and physically, the same principles are at work in the remotest ends of space as on the earth. It is also a fact that the human mind has managed to fathom this vast universe and to discover these principles. It thus appears that the anthropocentrism which was thrown out through the front door of science comes back through the window of idealistic philosophy or epistemology. Perhaps we must resign ourselves to the fact that we are confronted with a mystery which the human mind will never be able to penetrate but which should not in any way make us doubt the reality to which it points, namely, that anthropocentrism is somehow inescapable. Objectively speaking, does it not seem as incongruous that so minute a creature as the human being should comprehend the astronomical universe and the laws that govern it as that the Power which holds the universe together should take cognizance of the human being, of his destiny and salvation?

Magic and Soterics[3]

THURSDAY, JULY 18, 1940

(I am still in the woods. I am having a hard time trying to disentangle the two strands in the history of religion which have been so interwoven that they are seldom recognized as two. One is the strand of religious practices and beliefs which should properly be designated as magic. The whole complex of activities centered about local divinities, saints, angels, and the whole host of extra-human or super-human beings identified with trees, springs, relics, amulets constitute one distinct strand. They are regarded as necessary to the attainment of specific objectives, like cures, fertility of the soil, fecundity of animals

---

2. Maimonides (Rabbi Moshe Ben Maimon, Rambam) (1135–1204) was a preeminent Jewish philosopher, rationalist, and rabbinic authority of the Middle Ages. He wrote the *Mishneh Torah* (Code of Jewish Law) and *The Guide for the Perplexed*.

3. In this diary entry Kaplan contrasts soterics to magic, which is a way man has attempted to meet his needs. Obviously what constitutes salvation differs from one era to the next and from one religion to the next.

or human beings, conquest of enemies, etc. They have in common the negative trait of not having reference to any kind of totality, whether of the person, or of the group or of society as a whole. They are intended to make for life, health, well-being, power, or whatever is at the moment regarded as desirable. They have the positive train in common of being based on the ignorance of cause and effect relationship in the operation of either the physical or mental world. Instead, they are based on the assumption of personal wills and final purpose as the agencies with which it is necessary to reckon in satisfying one's disparate wants or needs. It might help us to class all such activities under the heading of magical strand of religion.

In contrast with this strand, there has been in the history of religion another and more significant strand which we might designate as soterical. The characteristic of activities and ideals which belong to this latter strand is that they concern the totalities of personality, society, the world. They represent a high degree of self-consciousness or an awareness of selfhood in the conservation and enhancement of which men are deeply concerned. It is then that the moral and social aspects of religion emerge and with it the yearning for deliverance (salvation) from evils which beset one's whole being, whether it be one's soul, one's people, one's world of ideals with which one has come to identify oneself. The Power that makes for salvation or the maximum life, which is the fulfillment of the whole of one's self, is God, not the putative being or beings to which magic ascribes the changes which are desired for the attainment of specific objectives.

In the various religions of mankind, magic and soterics have been so entangled in each other that we must expect to meet with great difficulty when we try to get people to realize that, despite the superficial resemblance between the two, they (i.e., magic and soterics) represent qualitatively different trends of the will to live. Magic is simply an expression of the different wants of human nature which act disparately without regard to any totalities as such. In magic not even the will to live as a whole becomes aware of itself. On the other hand, in soterics, not only does the will to live as a whole come into play, but the very nature of the life to be striven after becomes an object of awareness. The factor of values and preference and the conscious straining after the maximum attainable of what is regarded as desirable is now prominent.

Selfhood and God

Sunday, July 21, 1940

Once we refuse to accept the traditional accounts of divine revelations, the only possibility of experiencing the reality of godhood is in discovering some phase of one's inner life which points to something that corresponds most nearly with what human beings have sought to express in the concept "God." The experience of selfhood should constitute the gateway through which we ought to be able to enter into the presence of God. But selfhood is not ready-made, waiting for us to enter. It does not even yield to command or wishful thinking. A command like *pitchu li shaaray tsedek* [Heb., "Open for me the gates of righteousness" (Psalms 118:19)], even taken allegorically, is not enough; we first have to build the *shaaray tsedek* [Heb., "gates of righteousness"]. It may be that the very crux of experiencing the divine is identifying what shall constitute for us selfhood and willing that it be. The very notion of choosing among several selves implies some standard as principle of selection. Both process and principle of selection are conditions making for the attainment of the particular self which is selected or for its salvation. The god of that person would either be the standard or be regarded as revealing himself through that standard, usually the latter. It is easy for us to admit the godhood of an ethical standard like the one we name "conscience" or "sense of honor." But what shall we think of selfhood which is centered on the attainment of power over others, like wealth or fame? What godhood are we to associate with the standard which the ambitious man applies to himself?

The answer is that for the ambitious man, godhood is undoubtedly manifest in whatever helps him attain the object of his ambition. In other words, there is no one absolute concept of godhood apart from what we regard as salvation of the fulfillment of selfhood. This answer, while logically correct, is from the religious standpoint unsatisfying. What the ethically religious man wants to be sure of is that the particular salvation which shall prevail shall be not of the kind that the ambitious man considers such, but the kind which the good man regards as such. Is there anything in nature or in history to fortify the good man in this wish of his?

More on Selfhood and God

JULY 21, 1940

The striving for salvation lies in the area of not mere consciousness but of self-awareness. What was said above about its being dependent upon an awareness of self and society and cosmos is proof of its being unthinkable on any other plane than self-awareness. When therefore we speak of God as the Power that makes for salvation, we mean that if we want to have an idea of the reality and nature of God, we must study the process of self-awareness as it functions in our will to salvation. For purposes of practical religion, it should be quite sufficient to identify God as that particular Power. Metaphysically we might want to know what the relation of that Power is to the Absolute, the Power that "keeps the stars in their courses." We would then have to enter into a detailed study of the relation of knowledge (self-consciousness) to consciousness and to life. Is it not apparent that this is by no means a problem which the human mind can readily, if ever, solve? To make religion therefore dependent upon our knowledge of the Absolute is to halt the wheels of life's machinery.

Life's Worthwhileness—A Fundamental Category

JULY 23, 1940

The foregoing makes it apparent that not the mere animal delights in living; the mere zest which comes with physical health or with the sense of triumph in a contest for power is what we should have in mind when we speak of life's worthwhileness. It does bespeak quite definitely a sense of triumph, but not in a contest for power or gain or fame, but over the forces of evil and suffering in oneself and in the world at large. They themselves may perhaps continue as of yore, but it is their inability to destroy the will-to-live that is here spoken of as triumph.

Only after having articulated this conception of salvation, I can understand the following in Nicolas Berdyaev's *Freedom and the Spirit*[4] (p. 39):

None of the attempts which have been made to base the certainty of a future life on the substantiality of the soul are at all convincing, nor can they bring us any real proof of it. They have their origin in the naturalist outlook upon the mysteries of the spiritual life, and life itself eludes this mode of thought. Human personality is immortal not because the human soul possesses substantiality, nor because the idea of personality necessarily involves the assumption that it is immortal, but because the idea of personality necessarily involves the assumption that it is immortal, but because there is a spiritual experience of eternal life, because that spiritual life is divine-human. . . . It is proved and demonstrated by the manifestation of immortality itself in the spiritual life. Immortality is indeed a spiritual and religious category, and not a category of rationalist metaphysics. . . . The immortality of man is not a prolongation into infinity of his metaphysical nature; it is a rebirth into the higher life. . . . It is eternal life which has conquered death. Immortality, that is, eternal life, is the revelation of the Kingdom of God and not merely another name for the metaphysical nature of being.

If the spiritual life is, as here assumed, the will-to-live, self-aware and intent upon the maximum of life, immortality is the affirmation of that will, despite

---

4. Nicolas Berdyaev, *Freedom and the Spirit* (London: Geoffrey Bles, 1935; reprinted San Rafael, CA: Semantron Press, 2008).

the dissolution of the particular body which happens to be the vessel in which the will-to-live functioned for a time.

On the Cosmos and Spirit

JULY 23, 1940

What is the relation of the spirit to the cosmos? To speak of the cosmos as utterly indifferent to the spirit makes no sense. If we bear in mind that the cosmos does not mean just a blind meaningless something that exists yonder, [then the] cosmos means a universe in which the human mind has learned to discern relationships, order, beauty, power, and, above all, the unity of vast uniformities. The sub-human, or even the primitive human, has no intimations of such a cosmos. The cosmos is the creation not of any particular human mind but of mind or spirit as it functions transcendentally. When we speak of the mind's or spirit's functioning in man, we naturally refer to man's will to live the life abundant. It is that will which was not satisfied with the immediate impressions it gathered in the course of its trying to live, and which aspired to more life through the medium of profounder and more extensive understanding of the environment both in space and time that has revealed to man the cosmos which is his habitat. Mind, as such, that can free itself from subjective notions, assumes a kinship between itself and its creations, and abhors begetting a universe that not only den[ies] it but belie[s] it, and declare[s] it vanity and illusion. Since there is indeed such inherent kinship, then mind or spirit has good reason to feel itself at home in the cosmos, even though, as it functions in man, it has not yet reached the degree of reasoned articulation to be able to detail the arguments to warrant that feeling.

Atheism is not only atheism; it is also acosmism and apsychism [i.e., atheism negates order and negates the spirit].

The Will to Live as a Religious Category

JULY 23, 1940

In all that has been said here about salvation being the objective of the will to live the life abundant, there is no intention to identify that will as a psychological category. The will to live is not viewed in this entire discussion externally but entirely from within, as the basic dynamic factor in all our thinking, feeling, and acting, and as that with which we think, feel, and act rather than as their object. As such, the will to live is a distinctly religious category, as a category for helping us to identify the soul-self, God, and salvation. An analogous error with regarding to reason will illustrate the distinction between viewing the will to live as a psychological and viewing it as a religious category. Reason has been taken off its pedestal on which it was placed by philosophers and scientists and reduced to a psychological function. Morris R. Cohen[5] has a good deal to say in refutation of this tendency to psychologism. Once we treat reason merely as a psychologic function, we are left without any standard by which to determine the rightness or wrongness of anything and we land in mental anarchy. Instead, I prefer to view reason as an inherent trait of the will to live the life abundant and as having for its objective the attainment of truth. From that standpoint, reason too is a religious category. By the same token, conscience should be viewed as a religious category, and likewise the esthetic judgment. (There ought to be a category for the appreciation and creation of beauty analogous to reason and conscience for truth and goodness, respectively.)

Reason — One Part of the Will to Live

Wednesday, July 24, 1940

One of the important implications of the soteric approach to the belief in God is that reason cannot by itself prove the existence of God, much less help us to experience the reality of God. Salvation involves the whole of the will to live, and only through experiencing that will in its totality from within can we know what godhood means. Reason is the expression of only one aspect of the will to live and is inherently not qualified to articulate that will in its entirety. Reason is bound to the law of identity, or at least it was considered so bound until Hegel came along and released it. It has become evident that it is impossible to exhaust the reality of any process if we adhere to the law of identity, because all process is becoming, and becoming is a synthesis of being and non-being.

Spirit and Cosmos

July 24, 1940

The Spirit reveals itself in the cosmos as nature, in society as the Kingdom of God, in the individual as salvation. The individual combines in himself the attributes of society and the cosmos. His body displays the attributes of the

---

5. Morris Raphael Cohen (July 25, 1880–January 28, 1947) was an American philosopher and legal scholar who united pragmatism with logical positivism. He was a childhood friend of Kaplan. Cohen taught at City College for many years and was known for his tough Socratic teaching method, which many students found difficult. Milton Steinberg was among Cohen's students and was rescued from his difficulties by Kaplan. Cohen received an Ethical Culture scholarship as a young man and went to Harvard to study philosophy. Kaplan was also offered such a scholarship from the Ethical Culture Society but rejected it on ideological grounds. On Cohen, see the fine book by his daughter: Leonora Cohen Rosenfeld, *Portrait of a Philosopher: Morris R. Cohen in Life and Letters* (New York: Harcourt, Brace & World, 1948). On Kaplan and the Ethical Culture Society, see Mel Scult, *The Radical American Judaism of Mordecai M. Kaplan* (Bloomington: Indiana University Press, 2013), 66–87.

cosmos, his mind the attributes of society (memory and imagination) which attain the level of reason and conscience. Spirit or God is the will to live. Nature is the myth which man fashions concerning his physical environment. That environment includes his body and extends to the furthest star. Into it he projects an order which is the creation of his reason (a phase of his will to live). History is to society what nature is to the cosmos. It too is a projection of order, which is the creation of man's will to live. But in this projection not only reason but also conscience is involved. Salvation is the achieved goal which the will to live the life abundant projects into the future. God is the Power that makes for the attainment of that goal, but He reveals Himself in the actual striving toward that goal. "Reveal himself" is here synonymous with "is," but it expresses the additional fact that God's being is in the individual human being only to an infinitesimally small extent or degree.

Key to Theology Is Faith in the Self

JULY 24, 1940

Logically prior to believing in God as the Power that makes for salvation is to believe in man as capable of salvation. In ordinary parlance, this means having faith in man, believing that he possesses potentially—at least, what we usually term a higher nature than the beast. This does not necessarily mean that the human being viewed either physically or psychologically needs to be regarded as harboring that something which should give us reason to expect better things of him. We may even despair, if we view man merely as a creature of nature, of his ever evincing any proof that he is generically different from other creatures. But if we can discern in man evidences of a higher order of being, despite their being overlaid with corruption and cruelty, then we can believe in God. But how can we ever discern any such evidences other than by discovering them in our own person. "There can be revealed to us only that which is revealed in us," says Berdyaev (*Freedom and the Spirit*, p. 93). The first step, accordingly, in achieving faith in God is to learn to have faith in oneself.

This faith in oneself is not merely faith in one's ability to do things. The latter is necessary as a part of mental health, and is as important as bodily health. The faith in oneself which is not only a prerequisite of faith in God, but is in a sense faith in God, implies being able to identify in oneself a principle of life which is not a derivative from one's natural capacities, but which belongs to a different order of existence. In the yearning for salvation, for life's worthwhileness, for truth, goodness, and beauty for their own sake, for freedom, justice, and peace in society, man experiences something supra-human or supra-natural. One who experiences that yearning in himself cannot be so vain or unreasonable as to believe that he is alone in the possession of such yearning. The most difficult step in achieving faith in God is thus the first one of achieving faith in oneself. The rest follows easily.

God and Evil

JULY 24, 1940

Where in this conception of God is the place of evil? It is not in necessity but in the creativity of God. Evil is not (as I formerly believed) mere chance or negation, but something very real. It would not be evil if it were mere negation of being. All evil may be reduced either to the destruction or lowering of life. It is the antithesis of life, and in man, of salvation. The first is physical; the latter is moral evil. The cruelty which pervades the whole of animal creation and which is referred to in the description of nature as "red in tooth and claw" is evil in as ontological a sense as is the good of any act of kindness, and it is folly to try to explain it away as mere chance and outside of God. It will not do to follow the example of Job's friends to absolve God of the responsibility for the evil in the world. In the Book of Job, they are rightly condemned for saying the wrong things about God, despite their zeal to formulate a theodicy. What we have to assume with reference to God in order that we may accept His godhood is not that He is without evil, but that He is struggling to free Himself of the evil in His being. The evolutionary process whereby life rises to self-knowledge and to the evaluation of evil is an expression of this divine struggle to overcome the evil it has generated.

But how did God come to harbor evil? The answer to that lies in the fact of God's being creator. All creation is freedom, and freedom implies possibilities of evil as well as of good. Having exercised that freedom as Creator, God has created not only good but also evil, not only the motherly love but the beastly hate. In man God as the Power that makes for salvation is God the Creator of good. But God is also in man the power that hinders his growth and lessens the abundance of his life. Man is thus the arena of God's creative power with the freedom that its exercise implies. In man's efforts to achieve salvation it is also God who seeks to exercise his creative power for good and achieves, as it were, His own salvation.

Primary Importance of Creativity and Unity

JULY 28, 1940

The sense of centrality as the creative activity of the mind gives man his world; it brings unity out of the chaos of his inner and outer life. As he goes on living, his world is continually being upset, and he is always reconstructing it. Whatever helps to restore the unity, man is deeply grateful for. It enables him to pursue his efforts at self-realization. Is it not to be expected that he would ascribe the restoration of the unity to the same Power that makes for salvation not ourselves—however he conceives that Power—which had originally bestowed on him the very ability to create his world? In other words, whatever restores the unity of one's world or confirms one in the feeling of that unity adds meaning to one's life. It renders life worthwhile and significant in that it reinforces the drive to salvation. It is a revelation of that original Power which has bestowed upon man the sense of his own centrality and unity of his cosmos. *Every creative act of man adds to the meaning of life and is a revelation of the Divine.* This is as true a conclusion in soterics as any theorem in geometry, and for the art of life infinitely more essential.

Soterics and the Will to Live

MONDAY, JULY 28, 1940

There is no danger that soterics might lose itself in the dark jungle of occultism and theosophy. As its name implies, it is rooted in the will to live the life abundant. For soterics, spirit is that will, which we experience with an immediacy and intimacy that amounts to identification with self. By exploring it and trusting ourselves to it, we become aware of freedom and creativity and other aspects of reality which can only be known when reality is viewed from within.

Goodness, Truth, and Beauty, but Especially Beauty

JULY 28, 1940

What are we to consider as making for salvation depends upon how we conceive truth, goodness, and beauty, which are the constituents of what make life worthwhile. In this regard there is a definite departure from the pre-modern way of life. Truth was regarded as fixed, static, and timeless and in its own nature completely actualized. As against this view, the modern man has come to regard truth as unfolding, becoming, revealing, and actualizing hitherto unrealized potentialities. Goodness was regarded as obedience to eternal and unchangeable law. It now is viewed as the creative fulfillment of freedom. Without freedom there can be no goodness. Except among the ancient Greeks, the spiritual meaning of beauty was unknown to the ancients. It is now recognized as indispensable to the attainment of the spiritual life. Dostoyevsky is quoted as having said that beauty will save the world. Of course that is an exaggeration. Its value, however, is in counteracting the disregard of form. Truth and goodness pertain to the substance of life. It is to the latter mainly that the ancients gave all their attention, leaving form to take care of itself. The Greeks made the remarkable discovery that substance and form are so integrally related that both must receive attention if we want life to achieve its full measure of perfection. Hence the spiritual significance of beauty, that is, its indispensability to salvation.

Kaplan's Reading Confirms His Ideas

JULY 31, 1940

Richard Cabot's *What Men Live By*[6] is an attempt to formulate a system of soterics, though he does not realize fully the implications of his own effort. The four things men live by, according to him, are work, play, love, and worship. *God and the Common Life* by Robert Calhoun[7] comes nearer to what soterics ought to be in that he senses the significance of work or vocation as life-fulfillment for the understanding of what God means in human life. But his book suffers from two defects. One, the identification (which he is not fully aware of) of salvation with vocation, is based on too narrow a conception of salvation. The other is the failure to derive the conception of God from the concept [of] salvation as such. All he does is to draw an analogy between the conception of God, which he thinks is metaphysical, and the essential aspects of vocation. Salvation as life abundant is realized by the human being through vocation, progeny, and the utilization of excess function in play, art, and worship.

How Ritual Fits into Kaplan's System

AUGUST 1, 1940

As for the conditions and laws which traditional religion upholds as the requirements that have to be met if salvation [i.e., fulfillment] is to be achieved, many of them will undoubtedly be found to be the same which actual experience has proved to be essential. This applies especially to the ethical precepts and laws. The Ten Commandments and the laws which prescribe the love of God and of our neighbor have been more than vindicated by the catastrophes which have come upon the human race because they were violated. But the problem is with ritual observances. The answer to that should not be difficult. If those observances have acquired meanings which experience has demonstrated as having intrinsic value, in that they can contribute to salvation, they should not only be retained, but also interpreted in such a way as to bring that value to the fore of consciousness. The Sabbaths and festivals suggest themselves as the principal illustrations of ritual observance that should be thus dealt with.

---

6. Richard Cabot (1868–1939) was a physician and medical educator whose interests included social work, religion and medicine, and medical ethics. From 1902 until 1934 he taught at Harvard University, where his courses were in the fields of clinical medicine, philosophy, and social ethics. He practiced at Massachusetts General Hospital from 1898 until 1921.

7. The Rev. Robert L. Calhoun (1897–1983) was the Sterling Professor of Historical Theology at Yale University and a leading figure in Protestant scholarship and ecumenism.

The Nature of Mysticism

Sunday, August 4, 1940

Reflective mysticism, as distinguished from [the] theurgic [magic], is a state of mind in which one experiences not only a sense of self-fulfillment but the feeling that such self-fulfillment is en rapport with a larger reality than one's self. It becomes religious mysticism when that larger reality is identified as God or the Power that has made possible this self-fulfillment.

The Nature of Ethics

August 4, 1940

Ethics, on the other hand, seeks to establish the basis for ethical action on some autonomous principle, like happiness, intuition, utility, or categorical imperative. The autonomy is in antithesis to the heteronomy of the ethical precepts taught by authoritative religion. Historically, the purpose of ethical science has been to build up a system of ethical conduct that would be based on human experience or reason and would not have to depend on the authority of supernatural revelation or organized religion. The need for such systems of autonomous ethics is felt whenever the supernatural revelation is called into question. The danger of social anarchy or of remaining without a dependable standard of human behavior, it is believed, might be prevented by means of an autonomous system of ethics. In France instruction in autonomous ethics was part of the educational system. It is probably possible to develop a series of rules for human behavior in various situations and relationships as it is possible to work out traffic rules. So long as there are authorities and sanctions to back them up, they are likely to be obeyed. They would be autonomous in the sense that they are not imposed by a supernatural agency or anyone speaking in the name of such agency. They would be as autonomous as any legislation of a self-governing society would be. But that would practically assimilate ethics to legislation. It would cease to be autonomous in the sense of expressing the innermost self of the individual and of representing his own free conviction.

Why indeed may not ethics be merely a traffic code upon which the members of society agree to act in order to avoid collisions and to make sure that each one gets to his destination, so to speak, with a minimum of inconvenience? As a matter of fact, we might have gotten much further with working out the actual necessary rules of the road—or of the way of life—if we had been more concerned with practical outcomes in terms of peace and social security and less with questions of rationale and sanction and abstract problems about values, etc. But the truth is that even ordinary traffic codes, in the literal sense of the term, to say nothing of constructive social legislation, presuppose the existence of an ethical code, in the same way as mathematics both simple and complex presupposes an inherent logic of mathematics. It is ethics, as the basis of all social efforts which find expression in actual codes of morals and laws, that is the subject matter of the science of ethics. The autonomy which that science seeks to establish is not merely the kind that belongs to social legislation, but that is at the very basis of individual behavior. In other words, in the science of ethics, we seek to identify that in the individual mind which enables him of his own accord to subordinate his impulses and desire to a more inclusive will.

Throughout the past the human being conceived that will as the will of God or gods who transcended him in power and in ethical qualities. Nothing would have seemed more absurd than to claim for oneself the motivation to ethical conduct. The ancients may have gone too far in their ascribing that motivation to an extraneous agency. But it is questionable whether the moderns have been able to work out a consistent theory of ethical conduct on the basis of entirely individual motivation. The reason probably is that in attempting to work out a theory of ethics on such a basis, they were as guilty in their way as the religious philosophers were in theirs. The religious philosophers have made the mistake of treating the idea of God apart from its context, which includes the idea of man. Likewise the ethicists have erred in treating the idea of man apart from its context, which included the idea of God.

Both of these mistakes point to the need of formulating the science of soterics in which both the idea of God and the idea of man would be dealt with in relation to their context. It would be a synthesis of religious philosophy and ethics, because the will to live the life abundant is the meeting point of human personality and the Power that makes for its salvation.

Explaining Mysticism Without Explaining It Away

AUGUST 4, 1940

It is only soterics that explains mysticism without explaining it away. By directing our attention to our own will to live, with all its human complications, it brings us face to face with the Ultimate. We stand in its presence but we cannot penetrate it. But the mere awareness of it gives us new energy and zest for living. The testimony with regard to reflective mysticism on the part of such thinkers as Bertrand Russell and Leuba,[8] whose attitude toward traditional religion and its God-Providence concept is entirely negative, deserves serious consideration. According to Bertrand Russell, mysticism is "the inspirer of whatever is best in man" (*Mysticism and Logic*, p. 4), and according to Leuba, "Whoever wants to know the deepest that is in man, the hidden forces that drive him onward, should become a student of mysticism. And if knowing man is not knowing God, it is nevertheless only when in possession of an adequate knowledge of man that

---

8. James Henry Leuba (1847–1946) was an American psychologist best known for his work on the psychology of religion. He argued for a naturalist understanding of religion.

metaphysics may expect to fashion an acceptable conception of the Ultimate" (*The Psych. of Rel. Mysticism*, p. 318). (Both quotations are from E. W. Lyman's chapt. "On Rel. & Mysticism" in his *The Meaning and Truth of Religion*.)

The adequate knowledge of man to which Leuba refers would necessarily be that knowledge of man which, in addition to knowing all the chemical, biological, and psychological acts about him, would also know him as a totality both individually and collectively enacting history, striving to make the most of life and the center of the cosmos, the creator and upholder of which he has always conceived as the Power making for his salvation.

History and the Belief in God

AUGUST 5, 1940

The demand for metaphysical validation of the belief in God stems from Greek philosophy. The Jews have taught the world to demand a historical validation. It is thus that they have come to give the world not a philosophy of nature but a philosophy of history. To prove the existence of God, the Jews pointed to their own history. They cast their traditions and annals into a coherent account not of any abstract ideas or trends but of God's way with man. They set that account into the framework of a cosmogony and ethnology. The growing danger of invasion, exile, and destruction and the actual impact of national calamities crystallized that philosophy of history. But in crystallizing it, they also rendered it highly particularistic and Israelocentric. During the latter part of the second commonwealth period, Judaism was on the point of becoming universalized. All who wanted to join the Jewish people were welcomed, and national expansion took the form of proselytism. But that did not alter the Jewish philosophy of history. It still remained particularistic in that it centered about the Jewish people.

By the same token, Christianity, which took over the Jewish philosophy of history, did not, in spite of appearance, transform the particularistic character of that history. The Church regarded itself as the true Israel, and applied to itself all the prophesies which gave meaning to Jewish history. The Church regarded itself as the chosen people for the sake of which the world had been created. The fact that it was ready to admit all who wanted to enter it, and even engaged in proselytizing efforts, does not in the least modify the particularism of its philosophy of history. The Jews for at least two centuries before Christianity (especially in Alexandria) and even during the early centuries of Christianity were just as anxious to have the rest of the world accept their religion.

The notion of a universal history of philosophy that would validate the belief in God was first broached in modern times and actually attempted by Hegel. But unfortunately the attempt miscarried because it ended up in being just as particularistic as was the traditional philosophy of history. While Hegel did include in his construction of history a number of nations and cultures, he ignored far too many and finally led up to two conclusions which vitiated his entire attempt. One is the acceptance of the status quo as the consummation of history, and the Prussian state as the highest embodiment of Reason or God. What Hegel thus achieved was to formulate a new particularistic philosophy of history concerning Prussia in place of the traditional one, which centered about Israel or the Church.

There have since appeared other philosophies of history, notably those of Marx, H. S. Chamberlain (*Foundations of the Nineteenth Century*),[9] J. B. Bury (*The Idea of Progress*),[10] and Spengler (*The Decline of the West*).[11] But they were not intended to validate the belief in God. On the contrary, some, like Marx's and Spengler's, even meant to refute the belief in God. It is quite certain that no one with a sense of reality will again attempt to formulate a philosophy of history in which any one people or group of peoples will be able to figure as incarnating the meaning of God or carrying forward any of the purposes associated with godhood. The only possibility of having recourse to history as a means of illustrating the functioning of the Power that makes for salvation is to treat mankind as a whole from the standpoint of progress in general (along the lines of *Morals in Evolution* by L. T. Hobhouse)[12] and from the standpoint of the ultimate realization of the unity of humankind.

A Philosophy of History

AUGUST 5, 1940

We have to learn to read history as an account of the progress of the recognition of the worth of human personality in the individual and of the unity of mankind as indispensable to the salvation both individual and collective. Such a history would have to include the account of the obstacles encountered and the occasional defeats and setbacks experienced. The career of mankind can be nothing other than the career of the individuals and groups composing it. Such a history would not merely validate the belief in God; it would actually set it forth in concrete terms.

---

9. Houston Stuart Chamberlain (1855–1927) was a British-born German author of books on political philosophy and natural science, and Richard Wagner. His racist works became popular with Hitler in Nazi Germany.

10. John Bagnell Bury (1861–June 1927) was an Irish historian and classical scholar who also wrote on the philosophy of history.

11. Oswald Spengler (1880–May 1936) was a German historian and philosopher. He is best known for his book *The Decline of the West*, published in 1918. *Decline* included a new theory of the life span of civilizations.

12. Leonard T. Hobhouse (1864–1929) was a British liberal theorist and sociologist who helped to establish sociology as a field of inquiry.

The Value of Introspection

AUGUST 7, 1940

As to the value of introspection as a means of revealing inner experience that may be regarded as reality and not as illusion, Prof. Judd makes the following statement (quoted by E. W. Lyman in *The Meaning and Truth of Religion*, p. 352):[13]

> In the sphere of feelings, where we experience likes and dislikes, in the world of dreams, and in the play of fancy, we find that introspection is the only method which we can employ to reveal the inner happenings of the individual life. . . . Introspection gives us an indispensable body of data which are necessary for the complete study and understanding of human life. . . . In every normal human being there is an inner world of ideas and of recognitions of values, for which inner world there is no counterpart in the world studied by the physicists or in life below the human level.

Selfhood or the inner psychical unity, which is the object of this introspection, is described by [French philosopher Henri] Bergson as follows:

> Besides the body which is confined to the present moment in time, and limited to the place it occupies in space, which behaves automatically and reacts mechanically to external influences, we apprehend something which is more extended than the body in space, and which endures through time, something which requires from, or imposes on, the body movements no longer automatic and foreseen, but unforeseeable and free. This thing which overflows the body on all sides, and which creates acts by new-creating itself, is the "I," "soul," "mind." [This is a reality] whose main purpose appears to be a ceaseless bringing of something new into the world. (quoted by Lyman, *ibid*. [*The Meaning and Truth of Religion*], 360)

Inges says (*Idealism and Mysticism*, p. 26), "By 'revelation' I understand with Emerson the announcements of the soul, its manifestations of its own nature."[14]

---

13. E. W. Lyman (1872–1948) was a professor of the philosophy of religion at the Union Theological Seminary in New York. He wrote several books on theology, two of which are *Theology and Human Problems* and *Experience of God in Modern Life*.

14. The reference here is to Emerson's essay "The Oversoul." Emerson continues, "These [revelations] are always attended by the emotions of the sublime . . . in these communications, the power to see is not separated from the will to do, but the insight proceeds from obedience, and the obedience proceeds from a joyful perception." This is amazingly similar to the biblical statement *na-aseh ve-nishma* ("we shall do and we shall listen [understand]"). I believe that Emerson had a significant influence on Kaplan. For their relationship, see Mel Scult, *The Radical American Judaism of Mordecai M. Kaplan* (Bloomington: Indiana University Press, 2013), ch. 3 ("Self Reliance: Kaplan and Emerson").

Lyman's statement (p. 360), "Unless there is an inner unity and coherence in the self it would be impossible to discover any coherence or system of laws in the outer world," confirms what was said above about the dependence of our interpretation of the cosmos upon our interpretation of the self.

Will to Live and Freedom Are Basic, Socially and Metaphysically

AUGUST 7, 1940

Likewise any metaphysical theory which would interfere with our will to live or even with our will to maximum life may a priori be condemned as false. This applies to metaphysical theories that negate the reality of consciousness, the ego, or soul or that deny any meaning to human history.

The outstanding metaphysical theory which interferes with the will to salvation is absolute determinism. That theory is the antithesis of the metaphysical reality of time and negates all creativity. This is in the main Spinozism. It not only rules out free will and moral responsibility but the very notion of more than one predetermined series of possibilities in the way of life appointed to the individual or collective self. All history is an illusion, for reality exists from the standpoint of the absolute, according to this theory, at one point of time, *sub specie aeternitatis* [under the aspect of eternity]. Hence the very striving for more life, and certainly for salvation, is merely living out in oneself that which has been predetermined and could not be otherwise. The experience of striving, of moving from a state of non-being to being, is one of those illusions which are the concomitants of our finite nature.

Wonderful Optimism

AUGUST 7, 1940

. . . The only meaning to history is to be found in the increase of creativity which men exert in the ordering of their lives, as individuals and as groups. Such increase is measured by the extent to which human beings can emancipate themselves from the blind drive of their biological tendencies and social heredities and can master them instead of being mastered by them. Anyone who on the whole can see human history as having followed that trend hitherto to some extent at least and can have faith that this measure of creativity will be augmented in the future can subscribe to the following by Charles A. Beard[15] (quoted by Lyman, *ibid.* [*The Meaning and Truth of Religion*], 454):

---

15. Charles A. Beard (1874–1948) was, with Fredrick Jackson Turner, one of the most influential American historians of the first half of the twentieth century. He published hundreds of monographs, textbooks, and interpretive studies in both history and political science.

For myself I may say that as I look over the grand drama of history, I find (or seem to find) amid the apparent chaos and tragedy, evidence of law and plan and immense achievement of the human spirit in spite of disasters. I am convinced that the world is not a mere bog in which men and women trample themselves in the mire and die. Something magnificent is taking place here and amid the cruelties and tragedies, and the supreme challenge to intelligence is that of making the noblest and best in our curious heritage prevail.

Even God Grows

August 7, 1940

For what else does the entire panorama as unfolded in the Bible convey, if not the fact that not even the divine fiat succeeded but that God himself has had to resort to the process of growth for the accomplishment of his purpose? God created a world by fiat, only to find the world recalcitrant, and that he had to resort to the method of educating a people to obey His laws. That is the method of growth.

Ultimate Significance of the Will to Live — Man as Life-Hungry

August 7, 1940

All this is transformed, if we recognize that the fundamental fact around which everything we think, do, or feel must revolve is the will to live, and that man by virtue of his ability to objectify that will, raises it to the will to live the maximum possible. Man is the most life-hungry *of all creatures and never knows when he has enough life*. It is not quantity alone that counts with him but also quality. He doesn't just go *through* life as do other living beings, but he also goes around it and smells it and paws it and plays with it and is both frightened and elated by it, as though it were a skein and he were a kitten. Out of this multifarious handling of it arise the various moral and esthetic values. Good is that which makes for more and better life, beautiful is that which gets the most of life out of or sees the most in any actual living moment. Suppose we strike a snag and find that there is not enough of either quantity or quality of life to satisfy our voracious appetite for it; suppose, in plain words, we find that men are cruel and unjust and hypocritical. Should we say, "I must make sure that the existential world supports the values by which I express what I think of certain conduct and of certain phases of reality from the standpoint of their increasing or diminishing the measure and richness of life"? It seems to me that such a demand is nonsensical. Will the leer on the face of a fawning hypocrite cease to be ugly even if I can't prove logically the existence of a God who detests hypocrites? Will the betrayal of a friend, will lying and cheating and breaking the plighted word be less damnable, if I am not sufficiently keen minded to understand the principle of metaphysical unpredictability which allows for freedom of the will and of panpsychism which introduces godhood into the grain of sand?

Suffering Must Become Love

AUGUST 7, 1940

But interpretation of evil . . . must be genuine. It is not genuine if it tries to prove that evil is an illusion or a necessary means to good. It is genuine when it tends to point out that evil is an integral part of the mystery of life, beyond the power of man to account for. The best thing to do is to fight against it, if we can, for in such a fight we are doing God's work, or God is working through us. Here is where *can* is *ought*. And if we cannot fight against evil, we should accept it, not in a spirit of blind resignation but make it part of life. When one is resigned to evil, nothing happens to it. When, however, it is made part of life, treated as that chaos which is the very occasion for creating it, it is somehow metamorphosed. This is actually the testimony of those who can reckon with evil in that spirit, as may be seen from the following by Katherine Mansfield,[16] a gifted author who died in 1922 at the age of 34, after a long struggle with disease:

> I should like this to be accepted as my confession. There is no limit to human suffering. When one thinks: "Now I have touched the bottom of the sea—now I can go no deeper," one does go deeper. . . . I do not want to die without leaving a record of my belief that suffering can be overcome. For I do believe it. What must one do? . . . Do not resist. Take it. Be overwhelmed. Accept it fully. Make it *part* of life. Everything in life that we really accept undergoes a change. So suffering must become Love. This is the mystery. This is what I must do. I must pass from personal love to greater love. (from her *Journal*, quoted by Lyman, *ibid.* [*The Meaning and Truth of Religion*], p. 412)

Note the statement "Be overwhelmed." This indicates at once between her kind of acceptance and the acceptance in a spirit of resignation. She advises not stoic hardness but a religious love, a kind of self-identification with God in

---

16. Katherine Mansfield Beauchamp Murray (1888–1923) was a prominent modernist writer of short fiction who was born and brought up in New Zealand. She settled in London and was friends with Virginia Woolf and D. H. Lawrence.

17. Gordon Allport (November 11, 1897–October 9, 1967) was an American psychologist. Allport was one of the first psychologists to focus on the study of personality and is often referred to as one of the founding figures of personality psychology. The book Kaplan mentions here is *Personality: A Psychological Interpretation* (1937).

His struggle against chaos. This is borne out by what she says later: "Suffering must become Love."

Eleanor Roosevelt—A Spiritual Genius

AUGUST 7, 1940

One does not even have to resort to the lives of spiritual geniuses. The lives of men and women who by self-discipline have made more of their lives than what their heredity and environment might have led one to predict are equally heartening and equally convincing as evidence of the Power that makes for salvation. In concluding her *This Is My Story*, Eleanor Roosevelt[17] says, "From the time of my marriage, the life I lived seemed more closely allied with the life that all of us know today [1937]. It was colorful, active and interesting. The lessons learned were those of adaptability and adjustment and finally of self-reliance and the developing into an individual which every human being must eventually do." Those lessons, which she learned from experiences that were at times far from happy, are lessons in the art of life. Adaptability, self-reliance, and individuality—what are they if not indices of greater quantity and quality of life attained? No salvation is conceivable without them, and they might in themselves constitute highly important elements in the good life, the life worthwhile or salvation.

Life Needs Life

AUGUST 8, 1940

Like all specific hungers, there must be something in the existential world to satisfy it. So it is reasonable to assume that man's insatiable hunger must have something in the existential world corresponding to it. The only reality that can satisfy an insatiable hunger for life is infinite life. This is exactly what we mean by God. However unfeeling and cold and disdainful the existential world and human society may be of all that we value, if there is in us sufficient elan vital, sufficient, nisus [striving], urge, or drive, we shall continue believing in God.

Definition of Personality and Its Centrality

AUGUST 8, 1940

Also the concept "personality" takes on concrete meaning, when viewed in relation to the human will to live or the will to salvation.[18] The term "personality"

---

17. Eleanor Roosevelt (1884–1962), the wife of Franklin Delano Roosevelt, was important in her own right as an American politician, diplomat, and human rights activist.

18. See Mel Scult, "Kaplan and Personality," in *Reappraisals and New Studies of the Modern Jewish Experience: Essays in Honor of Robert M. Seltzer*, ed. Brian M. Smollett and Christian Wiese (Leiden: Brill, 2014), 162–80; also available online at www.Kaplancenter.org and academia.edu.

has been defined in dozens of ways. Allport,[19] in his book of that name, enumerates about fifty. The particular sense in which the term is discussed here is the (p. 233?) honorifically [word not clear in the original diary] moral and spiritual one, that sense in which it is made synonymous with soul and treated as sacred. That is the sense too in which its attainment is deemed the acme of human achievement and that which gives worth to society and its institutions. In reality, it is the inner psychological product of successful striving for the life abundant or salvation. It is the consummation of the human differentia. Whereas "values" represent the significance of specific experiences from the standpoint of their relation to the will to salvation, "personality" stresses the significance of that will itself. To the extent that the human being has such will, he has the capacity to be a "person," and to the extent that he has strived for salvation, he has personality. In that sense, personality is the image of God and the destiny of man (see p. 242).

Destroy or Transform Evil

AUGUST 8, 1940

Intellectually the will to live is no less, if not more, of a mystery than the evil which that will seeks to overcome. Hence the primary and normal reaction to evil should not be to try to account for it, least of all to try to explain it away, but to destroy or transform it. Only secondarily should we theorize about it, when it is so potent that it defies our power to destroy or transform it, which means that it threatens to destroy or transform us. Then there is this value to interpreting it: Interpretation either makes it possible for us to go on with our efforts to destroy or transform the evil, or it neutralizes the power of evil to destroy us. In the latter case we transcend the evil which we cannot transform.

The Self—An Unanalyzable Unity

AUGUST 10, 1940

The soteric approach to religion is based on the assumption that the central interest in religion is not the conception of God but what constitutes salvation and the way to attain it. On that assumption all that the various religions hitherto have been chiefly trying to articulate is the meaning of salvation. On the further assumption that what the various religions have been trying to articulate has come from introspective contemplation and not from any supernatural revelation, they should have been able to offer better guidance with regard to salvation than they have done. They all agree that the answer to the problem of salvation turns upon

---

19. Gordon Allport (November 11, 1897–October 9, 1967) was an American psychologist. Allport was one of the first psychologists to focus on the study of personality and is often referred to as one of the founding figures of personality psychology. The book Kaplan mentions here is *Personality: A Psychological Interpretation* (1937).

a fundamental dualism: an evil to be averted and a good to be attained. But what the dualism is has been defined in various ways, none of which has been altogether helpful, if at all. Here are some of the pairs of evil and good as the various religions and philosophies of religion have stated them: matter vs. spirit, body vs. soul, death vs. immortality, natural vs. supernatural, finite vs. infinite, this world vs. the next world. If they do not help us to achieve salvation, it must be because they represent untrue dichotomies of reality. Are we then to conclude that we cannot rely on introspective contemplation of our inner life?

There is one important consideration which prevents us from accepting this conclusion. It is this: Whatever the introspective contemplation engaged in, it was vitiated from the very start by the fact that the self which was contemplated was not permitted to remain in its "analyzable unity," but was broken up at once into abstract concepts, like body and soul, matter and spirit, temporal and eternal, natural and supernatural, finite and infinite. As an "unanalyzable unity," the outstanding fact about the self which should have been noted at once is that it is nothing if not a synthesis of each of the two pairs of concepts. That would at once have pointed to the true nature of salvation as consisting in fulfilling the double character of the soul, and taking care not to break up that synthesis by emphasizing one side at the expense of the other. It is only thus that introspection would have resulted in what E. W. Lyman pleads for ([*The Meaning and Truth of Religion*], p. 422), namely, the realization that the only true dualism is the ethical dualism "between right and wrong, loyalty to truth and acceptance of untruth, love and its opposites of cruelty, callousness, greed, and hate."

More on Unity

SUNDAY, AUGUST 11, 1940

A very important corollary which derives from the emphasis upon the "unanalyzable unity" of the self as the source of our ethical and religious institutions has a bearing on the relation of God to natural evil and on the question of God's finitude. The self in its unity embraces both its actualities and possibilities. Ontologically, neither is conceivable without the other. But the process of ratiocination breaks up this unity into a duality. The desirable possibilities of the self are separated out more and more from the actualities of the self and are hypostatized into the ideal self. The realization of it is considered salvation. The Power that makes for salvation thus conceived is likewise separated out of the actual world, and He in turn becomes the hypostatization of all the possible perfections to the nth degree. He is infinite power, omnipotent and omniscient; He is infinite goodness, perfect.

Then the question arises, If He is infinite in power and goodness, why does He suffer so much natural evil to exist? To this day there has not come a genuinely satisfying explanation. All the theodocies are stilted and artificial. They only accentuate the incongruity of a world in which there is so much suffering and mutual slaughter of living things with the conception of all powerful God, who would have to possess a mere modicum of goodness to eliminate all that unnecessary evil. The main purpose of religion is to get us to love God and to worship Him. How can we possibly find it in our hearts to love and worship a God who, having the power to eliminate so much useless agony, does not do so? The further we get away from traditional religion, which paid very little attention to the claims of rationality and simply bid us suppress them, the less likely will it be possible for love and worship of God to figure in our lives, if we shall insist that only an omnipotent God is God, and that He is the author of the evil in the world as well as the good. This in the main is why we are religiously disoriented nowadays.

Reading an Anglican Divine

MONDAY, AUGUST 12, 1940

The following from W. R. Inge[20] in *Personal Idealism and Mysticism* (p. 2) confirms the central thesis of my approach:

> Our religion must based upon our own experience, and it ought to be so. Although God's thoughts are not as our thoughts, nor His ways as our ways, we are made in His image, and no higher category than our own rational and spiritual life is open to us in which we could place Him. . . . But what are "we"? Man is a microcosm, with affinities to every grade of God's creation. He is a little lower than the angels, and a little higher than the brutes. . . . Everyone of us in his short span of life, recapitulates and hurries through the whole gamut of creation. In the nine months before we see the light we pass through stages of evolution which in the race were spread over tens of millions of years. And in our upward progress may there not be some dim anticipation of another long period of growth, which the slow mills of God are grinding out without haste and without rest?

Embracing the Thoughts of Henry Nelson Wieman

AUGUST 12, 1940

It seems to me that Henry Nelson Wieman[21] has done more clear and constructive thinking on the subject of religion than any of the writers whose

---

20. William Ralph Inge (1860–1954) was an Anglican priest and prolific author who believed in the value of individual inspiration in understanding mysticism and religion.

21. Henry Nelson Wieman (1884–1975) was an American philosopher and theologian. See, for example, Emanuel Goldsmith, "Religious Naturalism in Defense of Democracy," in *Religious Experience and Ecological Responsibility*, ed. Donald A. Crosby and Charley Hardwick (New York: Peter Lang, 1996), 317–35.

works on the subject of religion or the idea of God I have read. His approach to the problem is straightforward and realistic and is not vitiated by hypostasis like those in which most writers on the subject of religion involve themselves. He doesn't make religion the subject of statements and affirmations. When he speaks of God, one knows exactly what he means by that term. The definition in which that meaning is set forth is a gem for clarity and is at once framed in an argument for the reality of God, which in simplicity and truth excels all the classic argument of theology. Here it is: "Whatever else the word God may mean, it is a term used to designate that Something upon which human life is most dependent for its security, welfare and increasing abundance. That there is such a Something cannot be doubted. The mere fact that human life happens, and continues to happen, proves that this Something, however unknown, does certainly exist" (*Religious Experience and Scientific Method*, p. 9).

From the foregoing it is evident how near Wieman comes to defining God as the Power that makes for salvation, for what else are security, welfare, and increasing abundance (of human life)? In the first chapter of that book he makes three points. First, he insists that our knowledge of God comes to us in the same way as all other knowledge, by way of a datum of experience (uninterpreted) which is then interpreted, and not as a direct and immediate intuition unlike all other knowledge. Secondly, he makes a distinction between knowledge by acquaintance and knowledge by description (which he uses somewhat differently from the sense in which they are employed by William James) and emphasizes the fact that our knowledge of God is knowledge by acquaintance. By that he negates a theory like that of Hermann Cohen (whom he does not mention), who regards God and the God idea as synonymous, because God, to Cohen, is the logical ground of reason, a logical entity and not an object of experience. God is to Wieman very definitely "an object that enters into our immediate awareness" and not merely known "through the logical consistency of propositions." He is not "purely a system of concepts." Thirdly, he samples religious experience. One is a quotation from Rufus Jones which tells of a man who experienced God just after the physician had told him that he was the victim of a disease that would make him deaf and blind and impair his memory. The other is from Geo. A. Coe which describes the experiences of survivors of the *Titanic* disaster and which records William James' reaction to the San Francisco earthquake. Then he adds instances taken from normal life.

Unity Is the Goal

Wednesday, August 14, 1940

The general function of soterics may be described as that of reintegrating the totalities of life and experience which the mind with its analytic tendency has broken up. The main instance of that function is of course that of reintegrating religion and ethics into the organic unity which they possess in life.

Goal of Salvation Is Growth

SUNDAY, AUGUST 18, 1940

How much clarity the soteric approach can bring into religious thinking becomes evident in the case of a religious philosophy like that of Wieman's. Thus in their *Normative Psychology of Religion*[22] God is defined more specifically than in *Religious Experience vs. Scientific Method*: "God is the *growth* of meaning and value in the world. This growth consists of increase in those connections between activities which make the activities mutually sustaining, mutually enhancing and mutually meaningful." If instead of identifying growth with God, they would identify it with salvation, they would find the concept of growth itself more fruitful without losing its connection with God. It is much truer to fact to say that to experience salvation means to experience growth in the meaning of one's life, that is, increase in the connections between the activities which enter within the horizon of one's personality, thereby enlarging that horizon. Insofar as God is the Power that makes for salvation or the increase of those connections, we have an immediate experience of His reality when we become aware of that increase. But that is not the same as identifying God with the growth of meaning.

A Moment of Depression — The Function of the Journal

FRIDAY, AUGUST 30, 1940

After having kept out for a long time from this Journal all entries of a personal nature, I find it difficult to resume recording them. As a matter of fact, the ideas on religion which fill the last 82 pages are as much part of my personal experience as what I do for and with others. That is perhaps one of the reasons I enter those ideas in this Journal instead of writing them up in a separate book. These ideas constitute the bulk of events in my very uneventful life. I imagine that without them there would hardly be any occasion for keeping a Journal. Being by nature, probably, an extrovert and yearning for activity and finding myself confined — or doomed — to a life of dull passivity, I try to make much ado about ideas, knowing full well that unless translated into action, they turn sour. I hoped that Reconstructionism would afford me an outlet for action, that it would cause a number of people to gravitate toward me with whom I could begin to bring some order out of the chaos of Jewish life. But unfortunately even the few who constitute the editorial board of the magazine have to be continually prodded into attending to the few duties which their association with the magazine calls for. Of course Ira [Eisenstein] and Eugene Kohn are exceptions. But I wish that even they were more zealously active than they are.

---

22. The work Kaplan is referring to here is Henry Nelson Wieman and Regina Westcott-Wieman, *The Normative Psychology of Religion* (New York: Crowell, 1935).

As usual, the summer months, with their cessation of all constructive Jewish activity, have a very disheartening effect upon me. During a period of almost four months Jewish life is in a state of absolute coma. The strain and excitement of the High Holidays are probably the only way in which it is possible for that coma to be shaken off. But to me they feel highly unnatural, like the last flickers of a dying flame, the gasps for breath of one who is on his deathbed.

The Funeral of Alice Seligsberg

AUGUST 30, 1940

The tragic senselessness of Jewish disintegration was brought home to me the last couple days through the death of Alice Seligsberg.[23] I learned to know her through Miss [Jessie] Sampter, who brought her to a group which I organized in the Teachers Institute in the winter of 1916. (I have elsewhere a record of the discussions which took place at those meetings.) She had come from a background of completely assimilated German Jews who constituted the main supporting group of the Ethical Culture movement. Under the influence, probably of Miss [Henrietta] Szold and Miss Sampter, and impelled by her own search after some kind of religious support and certainty, she alone of her entire family and entourage became a Zionist and eager to express her religious yearnings in a Jewish way. From time to time I would meet her, though very rarely, and discuss the fundamental problems of Jewish life. Her heart ached for the same reasons that mine does. If she had lived and had been strong, she would have made an excellent worker for Reconstructionism.

Last Tuesday night her brother Walter called me up and asked me to officiate. I went into the city the next morning to talk over the details of the funeral. He then told me that about five or six weeks ago she had spoken to him about her approaching end and had asked him to have me or Ira officiate at the funeral. I had him tell me about her life. He mentioned the fact that though the members of her family had not the least sympathy with her Zionist or religious interests, they respected her wishes and made it possible for her to observe the dietary laws and to keep the Sabbath. To the last Friday night of her life she had the Sabbath candles on her table.

It was then that I learned how she came to be interested in child welfare work. Her brother is or was a trustee of the Hebrew Sheltering Guardian. This institution was established by a group of German Jews who were not accepted by an older group of Jews who ran the Hebrew Orphan Asylum. There was such

---

23. For Kaplan's diary entry on an interesting conversation with Alice Seligsberg about his belief in God, see M. M. Kaplan, *Communings of the Spirit: The Journals of Mordecai M. Kaplan*, vol. 1, *1913–1934*, ed. Mel Scult (Detroit: Wayne State University Press and the Reconstructionist Press, 2001), 220–21.

bitter rivalry between those two institutions that they would frequently resort to litigation in their efforts to get children into their respective institutions. Miss Seligsberg's mother was the first one to do away with the prevalent custom of having all the orphans dressed alike, their heads shaved, and go through ceremonial routines when the directors came around. Only recently has the rivalry between those two institutions ceased.

Now here are all the directors of these and similar Jewish institutions. Most of them have become thoroughly habbitized [word not clear in original diary]. But there are among them some very fine people with high ethical standards. I imagine that is true especially of some of the old families like the Seligsbergs, who helped [Felix] Adler[24] organize his Ethical Culture movement. There could never be any direct and straightforward understanding about the policy to be pursued by those institutions, from the standpoint of Judaism, because the main supporters were out and out assimilationists, while the parents of the children and the general community would have resented turning the Jewish children into *goyim*. Hence the ambiguous Jewishness of the Reformist type. The Sunday School, the Confirmation, and a few other cold formalities conducted by people who themselves had no interest in them.

The East European Jews, especially in Russia, either become outright *goyim* or are on the way toward working out some genuine Jewish adjustment to the modern world. The German Jews developed a peculiar kind of ambiguous position, which is neither completely Jewish nor completely goyish. One has only to take a look, at the cemetery of the Ethical Culture Society, which I saw for the first time yesterday, to realize what a failure these Jews who wanted to become thoroughly dejudaized, made of their efforts at assimilation. It seems to me as much of a ghetto as there ever was one. The Ethical Culture School is usually spoken of by Gentiles as a Jewish School, not in a derogatory spirit, but for purely descriptive purposes.

Of course, if we want to be fair, we should ascribe this difference between the way the German Jews dealt with the question of assimilation and the way the East European Jews dealt with it to the difference between the attitude of the East European governments toward the Jews and that of the Western governments. The former remained unequivocally medieval; the latter posed as liberal and actually were ambiguous in their tolerance of the Jews. This ambiguous attitude of the Western governments is responsible for the failure of Jews in Western lands to be either thoroughgoing Jews or thoroughgoing *goyim*.

Having to officiate at a funeral of this kind was a new and difficult experience for me. If it were not for her wishes, her brother Walter would have

---

24. Felix Adler was one of Kaplan's teachers. Although he inspired Kaplan, ultimately Kaplan could not accept Adler's philosophy, which was a rejection of Judaism. See Scult, *Radical American Judaism*, ch. 4 ("Universalism and Pragmatism").

asked Dr. Elliot, the present leader of the Ethical Culture Society, to officiate. I knew that most of the people present would be these marrano Jews. The rest I knew would be her Zionist and Hadassah friends and associates. I struggled several hours to find an idea that would offend neither group and appeal to both.

Freedom and Creativity

AUGUST 30, 1940

The nineteenth-century theologians were wont to identify the spirit with freedom. It would be much more correct to identify the spirit with creativity and to understand by creativity the synthesis of freedom and necessity.

The concept of creativity as thus defined has important bearings on ethics, education, and religion. In religion it helps us hold in our mind the paradoxical fact about reality (not as it is in the abstract but) as it is related to man's salvation, namely, that God as the Power that makes for salvation represents the synthesis of necessity and freedom.

9

September 21, 1940–April 25, 1941

A Limited God

SEPTEMBER 21, 1940

A 4th-year student of the Jewish Institute of Religion came to see me yesterday to learn more about Reconstructionism, which he wants to write on in his graduation thesis. Although he had read what I have written, I found that he had messed up entirely on my conception of nationalism. He thought that mine was of the usual autarchic kind. I had to read to him from *Judaism as a Civilization* to convince him that I deprecated such a thing as absolute national sovereignty.

He questioned me on my conception of God and asked me pointedly whether I subscribed to the notion of a finite God. My answer was definitely in the affirmative. He then told me that Prof. Slonimsky[1] at the JIR held and taught the same view.

On Reading and Writing

SEPTEMBER 21, 1940

If I had been in my youth as eager to write as I have come to be in recent years, I would have published by this time a whole library of books. A day in which I do not write down some new thought seems to me wasted. Even reading what is worthwhile does not seem to satisfy me. I have read and enjoyed the last few days about 100 pages of Mann's *Joseph in Egypt*,[2] Wieman's *Issues of Life*, and the greater part of Annusias [?] *Makhshava ve-emet* [Heb., Thought and Truth, vol. 2]. But I have written nothing and that makes me restless. All I have

---

1. Henry Slonimsky (1884–1970), PhD, taught philosophy at the Hebrew Union College and at the Jewish Institute of Religion.

2. Kaplan means *Joseph and His Brothers*, a four-part novel by Thomas Mann retelling the Genesis stories of Joseph.

done was to rewrite on Thursday night the prayer based on the first Psalm, and to write one this morning based on today's reading in the Torah, *Ki-Tavoh* [Deuteronomy 26:1–29:8]. I read the latter at the services, and Ira and Lena said they liked it, but nobody else. (That I can honestly say doesn't bother me in the least.)

Experimentation and Ritual—Kaplan's Commitment to the Sabbath

SUNDAY, SEPTEMBER 22, 1940

I was very much impressed by a passage in Jefferson's tribute to Washington, which I happened to come across recently. "He has often declared to me," says Jefferson, "that he considered our new Constitution as an experiment in the practicability of republican government, and with what dose of liberty man can be trusted for his own good; that he was determined the experiment should have a fair trial, and would lose the last drop of blood in support of it." This reminded me of what I had heard Edwin E. Aubrey[3] of the University of Chicago say at the Conference on Science, Philosophy, and Religion. He described the experimental attitude as a "combination of commitment to a hypothesis for purposes of investigation and tentativeness in the acceptance of the results yielded." And he asked the question, "Can one commit himself whole-heartedly to that which at the same time regards as a tentative judgment?" The case of Washington proves that one can if one wants to, in fact must, if what one wants is true democracy. Unless human beings can cultivate that combination of flexibility and firmness, no worthwhile purpose in society can ever be achieved. This is true not only of democracy but also of Judaism.

Take the problem of Sabbath observance. I have been advocating a policy of reasonable adjustment to modern needs in the way the Sabbath is to be observed, but I am certainly opposed to treating it like an ordinary weekday. Yet most of my own colleagues find it difficult to draw the line between leaving it to the individual to determine what constitutes Sabbath observance and giving up the Sabbath altogether. I find that if I were to refrain from writing down some of the things that come to my mind, I would come to look upon the Sabbath as an obstacle to my self-realization. But that does not mean that I would spend the Sabbath afternoon packing books into boxes to have them ready for the moving van which is not due before ten days. This does not mean that I would do away with the beautiful ceremony of Havdalah. And yet Ira and Judith do go to the length which I believe is bound to destroy the Sabbath entirely. Why?

---

3. Edwin E. Aubrey (1896–1956) had a PhD in philosophy. He was a professor of Christian theology and ethics at the University of Chicago from 1933 to 1944 and later the dean of Crozer Theological Seminary.

Seminary Doings—Saul Lieberman Comes to JTS

Monday, September 23, 1940

This morning I met about a dozen rabbis—all of them Seminary graduates—to discuss with them sermons for the High Holidays.

This afternoon I attended a meeting of the Seminar faculty, which was devoted to the admission of new students. When Finkelstein passed out the schedule for the coming year, I noticed that Prof. Lieberman[4] was scheduled to teach Talmud. This is the Lieberman I met in Jerusalem. He has a reputation of being a great Talmudist. It would have been the gentlemanly thing for Finkelstein at least to apprise us of the appointment of Lieberman to the faculty. [Louis] Ginzberg and [Alexander] Marx were probably the only ones who were consulted. I suppose F. would consider his casual mention to me about a year ago that it would be worthwhile getting Lieberman on the faculty as having discharged his duty of consulting me. It so happened that at the Matz Foundation[5] meeting which took place at my home when I came from the Seminary, Dr. Schwartz asked me whether it was true that Lieberman was appointed on the faculty of the Seminary. Fortunately I was able to appear as though I knew all about the appointment. But if he had asked me the question earlier in the day, I would have felt embarrassed and humiliated.

When I left the meeting, Ginzberg and Marx followed me into the elevator. I expressed to them my resentment at what I indicated was an unfriendly thing to do. I don't know whether I should have said to them what I did or I should have just swallowed the insult. In any event I really and truly do not recall a single meeting with the Seminary people when I do not go away from them with my nerves frazzled.

Sacrificing for One's Ideals

September 25, 1940

When justice, freedom, and the dignity of human personality are at stake, we should expose our bodies to torture and death for their sake in the confidence that the sacrifice is not in vain. "A life sacrificed at the right moment is a life well spent," says L. Mumford in *Faith for Living* (p. 81),[6] "while a life too carefully hoarded, too

---

4. Saul Lieberman (1898–1983) was a rabbi and Talmud scholar who taught for many years at the Jewish Theological Seminary. For an informative work on Lieberman, see Marc Shapiro, *Saul Lieberman and the Orthodox* (Scranton, PA: University of Scranton Press, 2006). On the Finkelstein era when Lieberman was so central to JTS administration, see Michael B. Greenbaum, *Louis Finkelstein and the Conservative Movement: Conflict and Growth* (Binghamton, NY: Global, 2001). See also Neil Gillman, *Conservative Judaism: The New Century* (West Orange, NJ: Behrman House, 1993).

5. The Israel Matz Foundation supported Jewish writers. The organization is named for Israel Matz (1869–1950), who founded the Ex-Lax company.

6. Lewis Mumford (1895–1990) was an American historian, sociologist, philosopher of technology, and influential literary critic.

ignominiously preserved, is a life utterly wasted." "Life at its highest and intensest has nothing to do with the mere maintenance of the physical body" (*ibid.*, p. 140).

Reality and Expectations

SEPTEMBER 25, 1940

The illusion under which religionists and ethicists have labored is that while there may be technical differences in the formulation of what men regard as worth living for, they are at bottom agreed as to the meaning of life and the kind of life they consider as most worthwhile. Religionists have generally assumed that all human beings would concede that kindness is better than cruelty, truth better than falsehood, beauty better than ugliness. Ethicists merely wrangled as to what validates the superiority of one over the other, whether it was utility, intuition, or divine revelation. It must therefore come as a shock to realize that the very opposite is the case. The emergence of the Nazi barbarism has demonstrated that the human being can as easily set up a world of values which are the very reverse of those which were hitherto believed to be universally accepted as axiomatic.

Courses Kaplan Teaches

SEPTEMBER 25, 1940

It is so long since I have recorded the courses I have been giving [in the Rabbinical School] at the Seminary that I am not sure of the accuracy of the first three or four of the following items (cont. from Vol. VII, p. 148) [of the original diary].

1933–34	Midrash text (p. 274)	Judaism as a Civilization, part II
1934–35	"	Principles of Ethical Criticism (Soterics)
1935–36	"	The Meaning of God, etc. (mimeographed sheets)
1936–37	"	Judaism as a Civilization, Part I
1939–40	"	Modern Trends in Judaism, Part I
1940–41	"	Judaism as a Civilization, Part II
1941–42	"	Soterics
1942–43	"	[G. F.] Moore's *Judaism*
1943–44	"	Philosophies of Religion [Judaism][7]

---

7. It was important to Kaplan that this course be called "Philosophies of Judaism" in the plural, indicating that there was not just one philosophy. Up until this point Kaplan had taught homiletics and primarily Midrash.

Hindu Philosophy—Kaplan Gets the Point

OCTOBER 2, 1940

I can very well imagine the ancient Hindu thinkers going through almost the same process of introspection which I described above and which led me to a sense of identity between the self and God. For how else could they have come to regard Brahman, the self-existent creative principle of the world, as identical with Atman, the true self or inner being of man?

The assumption of knowledge is the very essence of man, and that its attainment means salvation comes probably as a result of man's fresh discovery of his ability to think and to arrive at a recognition of identities. The very ability to achieve so daring a formula as *tat toum asi* (That art Thou) must have so thrilled the discoverer of it that he felt himself at that moment not man but God. As God he was emancipated from the fears and anxieties under which he had always labored, chiefly that of the eternal wheel or endless round of transmigrations that doomed him to suffer for past existence and prepared him for future suffering. By means of such knowledge as that of identity between Brahman and Atman, the eternal wheel would at least be broken in two. This conclusion was probably based upon the experience of the momentary thrill generalized into a timeless principle.

Right at that point we have the beginning of the dualism between body and mind, which in Greek thought became the basis of the conception of salvation for the Western world. What this knowledge does, according to the Upanishads, is to emancipate man from all his desire. The Hindu regarded all the evils from which man suffers as having their root in desire, and desire is of course the life of the body. This is why the life of the body was to him not really life but its negation. True life was only in the mind, in knowledge, which as such had nothing to do with the body.

Kaplan Undermined by Finkelstein

OCTOBER 13, 1940

Finky has lots of secretaries, and he keeps on sending me letters, nearly all of which begin with the stereotype "I deeply appreciate" and end with "warm regards." But every now and then I get a note from him which is like the rattle of a poisonous snake warning that he is going to strike. I received such a note last Thursday saying I should come to see him to talk over some matters pertaining to the Seminary and Teachers Institute. Although he apologized for annoying me at this time, when he knew I was so busy, and implied that the appointment could wait till next week or so, I was too agitated and wanted to have it over with.

The first matter was about the Friedlaender classes.[8] He claimed that the expenditure of $4,500 per annum for 100 students (both of which figures I

---

8. Adult education classes at the JTS named after Israel Friedlander.

suspect to be false) was not warranted in view of the very elementary character of the work done. I myself have for the longest time been skeptical of the value of those classes, at least not to the extent of battling for them against opposition which had been growing during the last ten years, due I suspect, to Finky's persistent effort to undermine [Israel] Chipkin's influence. When, therefore, he said he would suggest that a committee be appointed to look into the work of the Friedlaender classes, I could not honestly oppose such a suggestion, although I took care to state that I was not sure that the Friedlaender classes deserved to be eliminated.

When he was through with that matter, he proceeded to introduce the next one, which he described as a "very delicate one." I knew at once that he was going to suggest something vicious. Like the snakes that cover their victims with slime before they begin to devour them, Finky emits a slimy froth of irrelevant sophistries before he comes out with what he is after. This time his preface began with a remark which he quoted Dr. [Leo] Honor as having made to him about two years ago at a banquet given by the Teachers Institute alumni in Dr. Honor's honor. The remark was that only the older classes were represented. This, according to Finky, meant that in the early years I was in contact with the students, whereas in the later years I have permitted [Samuel] Dinin, as he put it, to get between me and the students. He gave himself as an example of having prevented [Cyrus] Adler to get close to the students. Moreover, Dinin was doing altogether too much work. He ought to give up the work as registrar. The upshot of all this is that I should take over the job as registrar—which, of course, would mean a saving of about $1,000 to $1,500. I asked him how his consideration for Dinin, who he thought had been doing too much work, squared with his willingness to pile more work on me. Out of that he tried to wriggle by pretending that the last thing he wanted to do was to pile work on me. The secretary would attend to the details. Then he proceeded with a song and dance about what it means to have an efficient secretary. And so leaped from one sophistry to another like a nimble monkey leaping from one tree to another.

Fortunately I was able to control myself and to display no sign of resentment. I told him firmly that I am doing ten hours of actual teaching a week and cannot think of taking up more administrative duties. But I doubt whether I am through with him. It seems that I am destined to have him on my neck all the time. He even expressed the wish to take part in faculty meetings of the Teachers Institute.

Salvation and Suffering and Martyrdom

OCTOBER 23, 1940

We are bound to miss the full significance of the striving for salvation if we identify it merely with the maximum attainable goods. Maximum life is not necessarily limited to the attainment of outward goods. If we succeed in hold-ing on to life in the face of suffering, without surrendering to despair, we also manage to achieve life abundant. Even if that suffering becomes unbearable and we perish, we can actually attain maximum life by making of our death a redemptive agency in the life of the race. This is the truth in the doctrine of vi-carious atonement and of salvation through martyrdom. In order, however, that our death be the attainment of salvation, our life must be dedicated to the love of mankind. It must be a life depicted in Isaiah as that of the suffering servant, which it can be if it is lived in a spirit of saintliness, or as visioned by Shelley in his *Prometheus Unbound*, which it can be if it is lived in devotion to truth and enlightenment.

In a world in which life is fairly tolerable, salvation is naturally measur-able in terms of positive goods which we succeed in securing, goods on the level of organic needs, of acquired habits, and of creative urge. But a world in which life is as intolerable as it is today, salvation must consist in the strength and cour-age, which qualify one for martyrdom.

Humanism Is Not Enough

OCTOBER 24, 1940

The "Humanist Manifesto" of 1933 declares in its fifth article "that the nature of the universe depicted by modern science makes unacceptable any su-pernatural or cosmic guarantees of human values" (*The New Humanist*, 6:2).[9] There is as much sense to that statement as there would be to one which would affirm that the nature of the human being as depicted by modern science makes unacceptable the assumption of an ego or of personality or even for that mat-ter the assumption of consciousness. Strictly speaking from a narrowly scientific standpoint, Watson is right and behaviorism can adequately account for every-thing that we ascribe to consciousness without positing consciousness. Even il-lusion, from the behavioristic standpoint, is . . . what? illusion? That cannot be, for that would imply the objective existence of consciousness. The truth is that modern science makes unacceptable the very notion of values. So why bother about their supernatural or cosmic guarantees?

The trouble with this confused thinking of the Humanists is that they are still fighting windmills. It is about time that they realized that the issue is no longer the supernaturalistic or theurgic [magical] conception of reality vs. the naturalistic or scientific conception of reality. The problem which should engage us is, now that we have come to accept the scientific approach as valid and indispensable

---

9. "The Humanist Manifesto of 1933" can be viewed online at americanhumanist.org/ Humanism/Humanist_Manifesto_I. The manifesto was crafted by John Dewey and other humanist leaders. Kaplan supported it but was critical, as we see here.

within the sphere of reality, which has nothing to do with values, and now that we recognize that values have their origin in man's will to attain maximum life, how shall we recapture the sense of life's unity in our effort to achieve salvation? For the present both the ego as center of reference, and God as the frame of reference have meaning only in the realm of values. Must we resign ourselves to the conclusion that they are either irrelevant or untrue in the realm of science? It may well be that we shall have to resign ourselves, but not without awareness of the fact that science is only a provision method for obtaining a specific type of results, but not for telling us the actual story of reality?

If, then, we have to maintain the objectivity of human values apart from science, we have to trust the inevitable implications and inferences of such objectivity. One of these implications is cosmos. Cosmos is a meaningless term apart from a central organizing principle or center of reference. Certainly the very notion of value implies a center of reference, and a center of reference, which gives to Being the pattern of a cosmos, creates or implies a frame of reference. Self and God, as they function in a scheme of values, do not guarantee those values. That would be like saying the center and circumference "guarantee" the existence of the circle (in the geometric sense). The old way of speaking "Self" and "God" were supernatural entities. But as we now understand them, they are realities of a different order from those natural phenomena that science (in the strict sense of the term) deals with.

The upshot of it all is that the Humanist movement is of little help in solving the problem of values, in discovering what it is that we should identify as salvation or maximum life.

A Comment on Genesis

SATURDAY, OCTOBER 26, 1940

The story in Genesis which is intended to account for the existence of sin, suffering, and death in human life, describes Adam and Eve as having eaten of the fruit of the knowledge of good and evil and therefore having become, according to the serpent's temptation, like unto gods. The fact that the fruit should have made them like unto gods throws light on what we are to understand by the knowledge of good and evil. That knowledge of good and evil can be no other than the sense of power which often turns man's head and causes him to think himself a god.

Why the sense of power should have this effect becomes clear when we recall how easily one may effect the transition from the will to salvation to the Power that makes for salvation in the course of inner contemplation. It is as though the center of reference were to absorb into itself the frame or circumference of reference. When the ego is drunk with power of whatever kind, it is all too likely to think itself God, because there is nothing but humility to draw the boundary between the self and not-self in the region of the soul.

A Metaphor—How the Mind Ensnares Us

SUNDAY, OCTOBER 27, 1940

We would understand more easily the self-entanglement of the human mind in respect to its concern in the attainment of salvation, if we were to imagine the following situation: Let us assume that we make the discovery that what actually happens when we medicate ourselves to fight off some ailment and manage to recover, is that we have permitted nature to effect the cure. Now suppose instead of concentrating on the study of ailment, observing the conditions that bring it about, the changes that take place in the human organism when the ailment attacks it, and the conditions that favor the cure of the ailment, we concentrate on the general idea of nature and begin to speculate whether there is such a thing as nature, whether it is finite or infinite, interested in human beings and their welfare or not. We would then introduce into the problem of physical health the same kind of theological machinery whereby we have unnecessarily complicated the problem of spiritual health. We would then waste our energy in spinning out all kinds of arguments about Nature, cosmological, teleological, and ontological. Some would be saying that Nature is merely an idea with no power, and others would say it is power without any purpose. There would also arise various physidicies, on lines analogous to the theodocies, to prove that Nature has a beneficent purpose in inflicting ailments, and that they are necessary to give it occasion to exercise its curative powers. Let us further imagine that after all that cobweb spinning, we come to our senses and proceed with the scientific study of the ailment in question and its cure, continuing at the same time to realize that the natural forces or processes whose working we are intent upon observing are not created by us ad hoc, but are ever present, ready to help the patient, provided we know what to do that would expose him fully to their operation. Nature would not lose its sense of reality for us. We would merely become aware that the personification of it is only a shorthand way, or if you will, a poetic way of expressing our awareness of the process that makes for physical health.

Let us now translate this hypothetical situation from the problem of physical health to that of maximum life (or mental and moral health). There, too, whatever we do to overcome the ills that afflict us have value only insofar as they permit the forces and processes that make for maximum life or health to function unhindered. Those forces or processes are nature plus, just as maximum life or health is physical life or health plus. We call nature plus, God. But the trouble has been that instead of concentrating on the scientific study of conditions which obtain when human beings are frustrated or damned (or just plainly damned) and the conditions which come into being when the hindrances to the operation of the spiritual forces or of the process or Power that makes for maximum life are removed, philosophers, theologians, and ethicists have been busy discussing the various proofs for the reality of that process of Power.

It is from this aberration of the human mind that soterics might wean us away by centering our interest on the problem of salvation without dismissing the awareness of the Power, not ourselves, that makes for salvation as unimportant. But it will exploit that awareness in altogether different fashion from the way it has hitherto been exploited by the theologians and philosophers or even psychologists. The theologians and philosophers have accepted its reification of the process that makes for salvation, if not uncritically, at least as presenting the main problems to be studied from the standpoint of our interest in human salvation. Psychologists, especially Freudians, have treated this awareness as illusion. Soterics will study that awareness as an integral part of the very process that makes for salvation. In other words, it regards self-consciousness in general as part of the life-making process. Hence our awareness of the process that makes for maximum life is itself a factor for maximum life. It should therefore be cultivated.

Opening Up the Minds of Those Who Teach Teachers

MONDAY, OCTOBER 28, 1940

On Saturday night, Oct. 19, I had the members of the Faculty over to my house. This is the first of a series of social [or] semi-social gatherings of that Faculty which I expect to hold this year to become more intimately acquainted with them and to get them, if possible, to view the problems of Jewish life and education more intelligently. They are for the most part so shut in within their own little world that they really have no conception of the disintegration which is going on in Jewish life. They are therefore uncompromising in their demands of parents and teachers that the children be given an eight to ten hour a week education in Jewish subject matter. If that subject matter were intrinsically worthwhile, and made a difference in the life of the child after he grows up, such a demand would not be unreasonable. But with the present obsolete and irrelevant character of most of that subject matter, people simply will not listen. Somehow my colleagues have an absolutely closed mind to the realization of the actual character of the conventional Jewish subject matter. If as a result of more frequent discussions with them, I would succeed in prying their minds open enough to see the truth, I shall have accomplished what to me is as yet an unbelievable miracle.

The Primacy of Process and Growth

OCTOBER 29, 1940

From an existential viewpoint, the eternal never was on sea or land. *It is an infinite becoming and not an actual being.* That is why we should conceive of God as process and not as entity, for God is a term to designate all those phases of the new direction that life takes on in man which are indicative of life's infinite possibilities of growth.

On the Flyleaf to Volume 10: Kaplan and Thoreau

"Action from principle, the perception and performance of right, changes things and relations; it is essentially revolutionary and does not consist (*sic*) wholly with anything which was. It not only divides states and churches, it divides families; ay, it divides the *individual*, separating the diabolical in him from the divine."

—Thoreau. [Copied October 1940]

On Roosevelt's Reelection

NOVEMBER 6, 1940

If the church were wise, it would reconstruct its traditional attitude and adopt an attitude similar to that of the state. This means that it would have to give up the principles of supernaturalism and authoritarianism and adopt the principles of secularism and democracy. Should there arise then a conflict between the institutionalized conscience of the church and that of the state, there would have to be worked out a modus vivendi between them. From the standpoint of social progress, nothing could be more desirable than the development of a real spiritual check on the arbitrary power of the state.

WEDNESDAY, NOVEMBER 6, 1940

The adjoining entry was written at 2:30 when I could not sleep on account of joyous excitement over the reelection of Roosevelt. For Americans and for the Jews I thank God.

Soterics Defined

FRIDAY, NOVEMBER 8, 1940

The following is a tentative description of the scope of soterics:

When the will to live attains in the human being that point of development at which it becomes the will to make the most out of life (the will to life abundant or to salvation), it precipitates the belief in self; society (clan or nation) and the self, [and] society and God come to represent both the origin and the goal of the urge to salvation.[10] They are the common movers, the final cause of everything in the human being that contributes to his salvation. They are thus the source of soteric values which validate the pragmatic.

. . . So far, no more illuminating principle as to what is to constitute for us salvation has been articulated than that stated in Plato's writings and further

---

10. The original sentence in the diary is not clear at this point, and so I have reconstructed the best possible reading.

sharpened by Aristotle. It is the principle of "health" or wholeness, which they qualified by the principle of justice or harmony. The way to make the most out of life is to avail oneself of all the elements that go into the making of life, with due regard to such harmony among the elements as would enable *all* of them to be accorded the maximum measure of consideration possible under the given circumstances. To that end, it is highly important that every person know himself sufficiently to be able to live by that principle. It is at least as necessary to have some kind of frame of reference by which we might orient ourselves with regard to the elements that go into the making of human life, as it is to have an elementary knowledge of geography and of the astronomical conception of the universe. The former is infinitely far more important for the regulation of our conduct and inner life than the latter. Such a frame of reference, though it would be the barest outline of the elements that enter into the making of our inner life, could be made as integral a part of the average person's education as a knowledge of human anatomy. It is by no means any less essential. With increased knowledge, that soteric frame of reference could be filled in with details which would make it more specific and helpful.

Life and the Will to Power

NOVEMBER 12, 1940

All life is inherently the functioning of individuals' wills, and every will is a will to power so as to possess the means to life. The will to salvation is the will to achieve power to a maximum degree. By itself there is nothing in power that is good or bad. The fact that the means to life exist to a limited degree and that there are many claimants to those means gives rise to conflict of wills. The important thing to bear in mind is that the values of purpose in which the individual will seeks to realize itself are themselves based upon the relationship of conflict and coordination, between the individual will and other wills. It is in the very process of choosing that the will to salvation becomes conscious of the trinitarian element, self-society-cosmos (God). Consciousness of that trinitarian element is consciousness of its functioning as conscience.

The real problem therefore is this: How far can the consciousness of the trinitarian element, self-society-cosmos, detach itself from the process of choosing or of calculating which the will to salvation engages in, so as to judge with maximum impartiality the true nature of the choice? Ideally, it might attain sufficient detachment to be more than a rubber stamp to what the will, acting through the values of purpose, decides upon as the course to be taken. But as a rule, it merely echoes the decisions arrived at on the basis of the values of purpose. The prestige which conscience enjoys is the prestige of an ideal attainment and not of an actually achieved ability. The point to be made, therefore, is that there is nothing sacrosanct to conscience as such but to the ideal of detachment. This applies likewise to the two elements of the trinity: society and cosmos (God). Enough crimes have been committed in the name of society (nation, class, humanity) and cosmos (God) to have minimized their prestige. Nothing is gained by the effort to show them up to be humbugs. The fact is not that they are humbugs, but [that] we are, and the reason we are is that we refuse them that detachment from our own desires, interests, and ideals (values of purpose) which presumably we grant them. But if we were really to grant them adequate detachment, we would have morals, politics, and religion that could be depended upon to render true judgments on the choices of the will to salvation.

When do we presumably grant the self, society, and cosmos the detachment that should qualify them to pass true judgment? Every time we ascribe to them objective reality that is independent of our transient desires, interests, and ideals and regard them as surviving our individual will to live, the self as soul, society as some immortal group with a destiny of its own, the cosmos as God—the three elements of the trinity that emerges from the process of choosing among the values of purpose—are appealed to as the judges of the true meaning of life.

What is it that we want most? According to T. V. Smith, it is "a genuinely free self in a genuinely voluntary society."

On Freudian Categories

NOVEMBER 16, 1940

There seem also to be the following correspondences: between the values of the id and those of beauty; between the values of the superego and those of goodness; and between the values of the ego (intelligence) and those of truth.

Lecturing in Detroit

THURSDAY, NOVEMBER 21, 1940

It is some time since I went on lecture tours. Any change in my routine comes hard to me. It was therefore not easy for me to resume giving out-of-town lectures, which I did this week. The original engagement was for Detroit, where I had been scheduled to speak on "The Jewish Religion of Tomorrow." Last week I received an invitation from Rabbi Jehudah Cohen, the director of the Hillel Foundation at Ann Arbor, to speak under the auspices of the Foundation. I turned the matter over to Miss Weisman, and she arranged that I speak there the Tuesday of this week on the afternoon before I was to speak at Detroit.

I was not satisfied with my experience at Ann Arbor. There I found a group of young people—members of Avukah[11]—who seemed interested in

---

11. Avukah was a little-known student Zionist organization. It was founded as a Jewish social group at Harvard University in 1925 and eventually grew to several thousand members on campuses throughout the United States and Canada. Albert Einstein was a key figure for the group.

Judaism. But they were a mere handful, hardly half a dozen. The rest of the audience, which consisted of about 75 people, were a very heterogeneous group. I found it difficult to get into complete rapport with the audience while I spoke, and I had no chance to do so in any discussion after the lecture because the people had to rush off to supper.

Jehudah Cohen, who has been in charge of the Hillel Foundation on the campus of the Michigan University this last year, is a graduate of the JIR [Jewish Institute of Religion]. For several years he directed the work at the Jewish Center at Los Angeles. He was in Detroit when I got into Ann Arbor, but I learned to know him after the lecture. He spoke to me the entire time he drove me back to Detroit for the lecture I had been scheduled to give there. He strikes me as a very nice chap and as one who is deeply imbued with the philosophy of Reconstructionism. All the four sermons which he delivered on the High Holidays were devoted to the interpretation of Reconstructionism. From what he tells me, there is considerable Reconstructionist sentiment throughout the country. I have known that all along, but the question is, What can be done to crystallize that sentiment?

In Detroit my lecture was very successful. I had an attendance of about 300. It was a very representative and quite intellectual audience. Some of the important Yiddishists who are very active in Detroit were there, and they brought the noted Yiddish poet Lavik with them. I was in good form during the lecture and during the discussion which followed it.

I felt so good after that lecture that I accepted Rabbi Cohen's invitation to address in Hebrew a group of Hebraists known as the Kevuzah. Originally I had turned down that invitation, but under the influence of my exhilaration I withdrew my refusal. Strange to say, the talk I gave on Wednesday morning, which dealt with the question of isolation vs. assimilation, was worked up with very little effort and turned out to be successful from every standpoint. I have almost gotten over by this time the stage-fright feeling under which I had always labored when speaking in Hebrew to an adult audience.

After the Hebrew lecture I was given a luncheon at the Center by its executive Herman Jacobs and a number of other graduates of the Graduate School for Jewish Social Work. In my talk to them I urged them to constitute themselves into a Reconstructionist group for the purpose of mutual encouragement in the affirmative attitude toward Jewish life and of instituting the kind of religious services that would appeal to them. At present they are not identified with any religious group and are looked upon as secularists. Their influence on Jewish life beyond what they do professionally is at present almost nil. As a Reconstructionist group, they could exert a very wholesome influence. Among those present were Mrs. Sobolof (née Mazorfsky) (her husband is head of Federation); Boxerman, who is head of the Jewish council; Fleischman, who is on the staff in the Center; Harold Silver, director of Jewish social services; Goldie Goldstein, case worker;

Mr. & Mrs. Luchs (he is in charge of refugee settlement work); and Franck, a member of the Center staff.

Twenty-Fifth Anniversary of Solomon Schechter's Death

THURSDAY, DECEMBER 12, 1940

Last night the Seminary observed the 25th anniversary of Schechter's death.[12] The exercises were described as a convocation with Faculties and Trustees (of whom there were only four, including Mrs. Warburg).[13] The others were Sol[omon] Stroock, Hendricks, and Nathan, the last two nincompoops of Spanish Portuguese ancestry, all togged out in academic rags and boards with tassels. Finky spoke extemporaneously and well. But there was enough in what he said to indicate his tendency to falsify facts. I refer especially to the explanation he gave for Schechter's being as he put it "unhappy and lonely." According to F., the one and only reason Schechter was unhappy and lonely was that Judaism was being secularized. F. mentioned specifically the secularization of Jewish education. How false that explanation is one can realize on reading Bentwich's biography of Schechter.[14] Bentwich does not quote Schechter's letter to [Louis] Marshall in full. If he did, there would be quite a scandal.

The same gang that made Schechter's life miserable later formed the American Jewish Committee, which at present has a throttle hold on American Jewish life. I have sufficient circumstantial evidence that it is trying to knife me and to sabotage Reconstructionism. The releases which have been sent out to a number of Anglo-Jewish periodicals under the masthead of "The Reconstructionist Viewpoint" are being turned down. This, I am told, is the work of stooges of the American Jewish Committee, who see to it that nothing the Committee objects to is published in those periodicals.

The Federation leaders belong to the same tribe of Jewish fifth columnists. I [stirred] a hornet's nest with the editorial in the *Reconstructionist* titled

---

12. Solomon Schechter (1850–1915) was a rabbinic scholar and president of the Jewish Theological Seminary. See Mel Scult, "Schechter's Seminary," in *Tradition Renewed: A History of the Jewish Theological Seminary of America*, ed. Jack Wertheimer (New York: Jewish Theological Seminary, 1997), 1:43–103.

13. Frieda Schiff Warburg (1876–1958), the wife of Felix Warburg, was a philanthropist and community leader in New York City. She was on the board of the JTS, the YMHA, the Visiting Nurses, and Hadassah. I seem to remember, but I am not certain, that she donated the money for the gates at the entrance to 3080 Broadway. The gates, which looked like the gates of a prison, were recently replaced by glass. For a photo of the original gates, see Mel Scult, *Judaism Faces the Twentieth Century: A Biography of Mordecai M. Kaplan* (Detroit: Wayne State University Press, 1993), 204.

14. Norman Bentwich, *Solomon Schechter: A Biography* (Philadelphia: Jewish Publication Society, 1948). Bentwich's book is the standard biography of Schechter. For details on Schechter's personality, see also Mel Scult, "Solomon Schechter: Missing Person," in *Solomon Schechter in America: A Centennial Tribute* (New York: Jewish Theological Seminary, 2002), 63–75.

"A Bad Plea for a Good Cause," in which I (I gave the substance of the editorial to E[ugene] Kohn, which he then wrote out and I corrected) took [Joseph M.] Proskauer [to task] for sending out a two-page letter appealing for Federation, in which there was no reference to Federation's being a Jewish institution, or that those to be helped were Jews. Only one to whom the term "Jewish" is synonymous with whatever he wants to escape from and forget could have allowed such a letter to go out over his name.

Among the first repercussions to that article was a telephone call to [Israel] Chipkin from [Joseph] Willen. Willen is a highly paid (he is said to earn from $30,000 to $40,000 per year) Federation worker whose specialty is plying the richest Jews for funds. He ordered Chipkin, who is listed among the editors of the *Reconstructionist*, to write a letter repudiating the editorial. I say "ordered" because the same Willen is Roseman's right-hand man in the Jewish Education Committee. It was Willen who had Roseman appointed to the chairmanship of that committee because Burke, the executor of the Friedsam[15] estate, relied entirely on Willen as to the disposition of the million dollars left by Friedsam for some Jewish charity. Chipkin, being an employee of the Jewish Education Committee, can therefore be ordered around by Willen. At first Chipkin consented to follow orders, but on second thought he realized apparently at [Alexander] Dushkin's suggestion, that he would stultify himself if he were to write such a letter to the *Reconstructionist*.

Another illustration of how systematically these fifth columnists are trying to sabotage all affirmative Jewish efforts is what the JEC [Jewish Education Committee] is doing with a pictorial they are getting out for the Jewish schools. It is called *The World Over*. Recently there appeared in it a biography of Brandeis. I was told that the fact that he was a Zionist is not even mentioned.

Finkelstein is one of those who talk in superlative terms about things concerning which (or people concerning whom) they have no positive convictions.

Kaplan's Value System

SATURDAY NIGHT, DECEMBER 14, 1940

The distinction between pragmatic and soteric values makes it possible to distinguish between the prayer of the unenlightened and the prayer of the enlightened. The prayer of the unenlightened aims to obtain values of the pragmatic order; the prayer of the enlightened aims to achieve the values of the soteric order—the integrity of self, the inherent worth of humanity, the godhood of the cosmos.

---

15. Michael Friedsam (1858–1931) was the president of the department store B. Altman & Co., a civic leader, and a philanthropist in New York City.

The foregoing distinction might also explain the difference between the lower and higher type of morality as expounded by [Henri] Bergson in his *Morality and Religion*.[16]

TUESDAY, DECEMBER 24, 1940 (ALL THE PRECEDING ENTRIES SHOULD BE CORRECTED IN KEEPING WITH THIS ONE.)[17]

It looks as though I shall have to rename the different categories of values. Those I have been calling "pragmatic values" and purposive values I shall henceforth designate as content values, in that they constitute the content of living. The urges of instinct, habit, and intelligence are the very material of human life. Next come the "formal values": truth, goodness, and beauty. They constitute the forms which the various contents of life must assume if they are to render life satisfactory or worthwhile. What being worthwhile means is indicated by the final values, viz., self, society, and God. Other and less technical terms than self, society, and God as final values are the following: "a taste for life," "a reverence for life," "the sense of wonder at life," and "a proper and reasonable attitude toward life" (terms employed by Lin Yutang).

The formal values are the criteria to which the functional values are to measure up if they are to yield the final values. Thus in the statement "Whatever else science may do, it certainly does not destroy, but rather increases our sense of wonder at and reverence for life," we have expressed the idea that the knowledge of the truth increases our awareness of life's wonder or meaning.

THURSDAY, DECEMBER 26, 1940

The values to which self, humanity, and God give rise are, respectively, reason, democracy, and faith.

Reconstructionism — A School of Thought

FRIDAY, DECEMBER 27, 1940

I was away on a lecture tour the greater part of last week. I left Monday afternoon for Chicago, to get there in time for a Reconstructionist conference which Dr. Honor had arranged the week before. . . . The greater part of the discussion was devoted to the question of the relation of the Reconstructionist movement to the existing parties in Jewish life. To avoid the danger of becoming an additional party parallel to those which are already in existence, I urged that Reconstructionism be presented as the expression of a school of thought which has a contribution to make to the existing parties. I pleaded with the men that

---

16. Kaplan is referring to Bergson's *Two Sources of Morality and Religion*, which appeared in 1932. Kaplan also read and used Bergson's *Creative Evolution* (1907).

17. The parenthetical remark is in the original diary in the margin of the entry. Kaplan apparently wanted to remind himself that his final thoughts were in this entry.

they select from their congregations small groups of men and women whom they should train to think along Reconstructionist lines and live their lives in keeping with the Reconstructionist philosophy. This group should be definitely informed that what they are being given is Reconstructionism. The name is important. They can then act as ferment in their respective Jewish organizations to influence those organizations to conduct their activities in an affirmative Jewish spirit.

In the evening I spoke at Arnoff's synagogue. My subject was "A Pattern for Modern Jewish Living." I managed to hold the attention of the people, and the written questions surprised me by their number and by the intelligence they showed.

Next morning I left for Minneapolis. I was scheduled to speak at Rabbi Albert Gordon's synagogue on "The Jewish Religion for Tomorrow." There was too much wooden pulpit between me and the audience to permit me to get into close touch with them, and I was haunted by the feeling that I was not in rapport with the people. The questions were fewer in number than those I had got at Chicago, but that enabled me at least to speak in more concrete terms and to arouse a good bit of interest on the part of the audience.

Rabbi and Mrs. Gordon had not only invited me together with a number of people to dinner before the address, but they also had us at their house after the address. Dr. Barron, who is a member of the faculty at the University of Minnesota, was there with his wife, a Mr. Brin and his wife,[18] and a few others. I first met Dr. Barron when I spoke about 25 years ago before the Menorah Group at the University of Minnesota, which was led by Louis I. Newman, who has since become one of the leading rabbis in this city. In the discussion which took place at Rabbi Gordon's home, Dr. Barron gave as his conception of God the well-known Deistic one based upon the assumption of an initial cause or creator. My reply to that was that what I was mainly interested in was that we associate with the term God some identifiable and significant experience. If he as a scientist finds the notion of first cause significant, he meets that requirement. For most people, however, some more intimate experience is necessary as content of the term God. I found such experience in the will to salvation.

I stopped at Hotel Nicollet.

On Thursday I met a group of people from Al Gordon's congregation and two or three from Rabbi Aronson's at a luncheon, for the purpose of telling them about the Seminary, which is preparing the ground there for a membership campaign.

In the evening I had supper at Rabbi Aronson's. I like him personally but he is too much of a Talmudist to be free from sophistry. According to him,

---

18. Ruth Brin (1921–2009) was a poet, liturgical pioneer, and author. It is difficult to find a prayer book of any of the major denominations that does not contain her poetry. Her most important book is *Harvest: Collected Poems and Prayers* (Duluth, MN: Holy Cow! Press, 1999).

Reconstructionism is nothing but Conservative Judaism. He goes even further in that respect than Robert Gordis.

On Friday afternoon I met with the Hebrew teachers of Minneapolis and St. Paul and gave them, at Dr. Gordon's (the physician who is the principal of the Minneapolis [Talmud Torah]) invitation, a talk on the idea of God. The talk, which lasted about an hour and 10 minutes, and the discussion which followed were in Hebrew. I was perfectly at ease and thoroughly enjoyed the experience.

Rabbi Herman Cohen of St. Paul sent his son to take me to St. Paul for the Sabbath. I put up at Hotel Commodore there. In the evening I spoke at Rabbi Cohen's synagogue. The attendance was about 400 and I was in good form. My subject was "A Pattern for Modern Jewish Living." After the lecture a large part of the congregation gathered in the assembly room downstairs and I was subjected to a series of questions. I played with the audience and managed to get in considerable information concerning the Reconstructionist movement.

On Saturday afternoon I addressed a large gathering of the Hadassah women from St. Paul and Minneapolis at the St. Paul Jewish Community Center. The gathering took place in celebration of Henrietta Szold's 80th anniversary [of her birth]. After giving some personal recollections concerning her, I used the editorial on Miss Szold in this week's issue of the *Reconstructionist*. I had dictated the thought of that editorial to Ira and he wrote it out in full.

Both Rabbis Aronson and Cohen did an interesting thing with the high schools of their cities where a considerable number of Jewish children attend. They succeeded in getting the principals of those schools to arrange for a celebration of Hanukkah alongside the Christmas festival.

I left St. Paul Saturday night and got to New York last Monday morning just in time to take my class at the Seminary at 9:00. At 12:40 I went to take part in the second Faculty-student luncheon, which was in honor of Dr. [Moses] Hyamson, who had been retired from the Faculty. He started speaking at 1:40, and I left at 2:30 and he was still going strong.

Salvation — A Brief Explanation

SATURDAY NIGHT, JANUARY 4, 1941

I am still groping after some pattern into which all my ideas concerning salvation might arrange themselves. Accordingly, many of the preceding entries on that subject are bound to turn out incorrect, especially those which have to do with the main question: What shall constitute for us salvation?

To the extent that there is unity in the life of individuals and societies, that unity is both the cause and the effect of men's striving to make the most out of their lives, to achieve the greatest plentitude of which life is capable, or in brief, salvation. Until modern times the historical religions have sought to articulate the nature of salvation and the means to it. The modern man finds the traditional conceptions of salvation untenable, because they assume that man is unable to achieve it, under natural conditions of either the physical world or of human life. The modern man assumes that it ought to be possible to achieve salvation with the materials of the environment and of human nature as they are. So far, however, there has not emerged any tenable scheme of mundane salvation. It should be the purpose of soterics to formulate such a scheme.

A scheme of mundane salvation would therefore be one which would set forth a definite goal for human striving. That goal would be one to which we could give ourselves wholeheartedly. Insofar as we have faith in it and live by that faith, we make the most of our lives and do not live in vain. This means that we attain salvation to the extent possible to us under the circumstances and abilities which are ours. This would constitute for each of us intelligent living. What more should we expect from life?

Requirements for Salvation

JANUARY 9, 1941

It is impossible to achieve salvation so long as society is conceived as so constituted that violence must ultimately be resorted to as a means of settling the clashing demands of classes and nations.

It is impossible to achieve salvation so long as the self is conceived as so constituted that no amount of conditioning can render it capable of unselfishness.

It is impossible to achieve salvation so long as the cosmos is conceived as so constituted that life and mind are only temporary accidents in a senseless and chance concurrence of protons.

Youngstown, Ohio, and Rochester, New York

JANUARY 17, 1941

This week I lectured at Youngstown, Ohio, and Rochester. I gave my lecture at Youngstown under the auspices of the Jewish Communal Center. When I got to Youngstown on Tuesday at 11:40, I was met at the train by Berlatsky, who is in charge of Center programs. Whenever the Center has an out-of-town speaker, it has to make use of the auditorium of either the Reform Synagogue (Rodeph Sholom, of which Philio is the rabbi) or of the Conservative synagogue (Anshe Emet, of which Nathan Kollin is the rabbi). There is a third synagogue, an Orthodox one, which strangely enough is also known as a temple.

Berlatsky went with me to the Ohio Hotel, where I put up for the one day. I had him give me a general idea of the size and nature of the Jewish population in Youngstown. He told me there were about 7,500 Jews, of whom about 2,500 were affiliated with the synagogue. The number of children that were receiving a Jewish education was very limited. Only the Conservative congregation had a weekday school for about 150 children. Its president, Mr. Nadler, was insistent upon having the congregations take over whatever educational work was to be done in the community. He regarded any attempt on the part of the community to provide religious education to Jewish children as depriving his congregation of the chance to make members. According to him, the only bait a congregation could hold out was the religious school. This competitive attitude on the part of the congregations toward any communal endeavors of a cultural or religious nature is quite inbred in most of the key people in Youngstown Jewry.

When it was time for lunch, Berlatsky took me to a Jewish restaurant. Originally that restaurant was known as Commercial Club [and it] was a Jewish club. When the Depression came, it was taken over by an individual who runs it for profit. At Christmas time it is decorated with holly and a Christmas tree, but never is there a sign of the Hanukkah festival when that comes around.

After lunch I was asked to present at a conference of a committee of some of the key people of the community who were discussing what to do with the situation presented by the new law to have religion taught in the school. They asked me for my opinion, and I told them that the dog in the manger policy we Jews were pursuing was not doing us any good. The effect on the Jewish children who will have to take the regular school studies while their Gentile friends will be getting religious instruction in another part of the school will be demoralizing. It is therefore important that the Jewish community representing all elements should make provision for the Jewish children. Those present told me that any communal effort for that purpose would be strongly opposed by Rabbi Philo, who, it seems, is still repeating in polparrot[19] fashion the doctrine on which the Reformists placed all their hopes, viz., the separation of state and church. He had even told the members of his confirmation class they should refuse to take any Jewish religious instruction in case it is given in the public school.

At the conference and during the rest of my stay I renewed my acquaintance with Greenberg, whom I had met years ago in Kansas City and who was working in Youngstown in the capacity of executive director of the local federation. He seems to be a very sensible and quite capable fellow. He has been following the *Reconstructionist* and is in sympathy with its purpose. I urged him to collaborate with Nathan Kollin in getting Reconstructionism known among the more influential people.

As for Nathan Kollin, he is a nice chap and has a nice young wife and baby. He has served the community for the last six years but would like to change for some pulpit in a university town. He is quite a student but not much of a thinker and somewhat naive.

---

19. To repeat like a parrot.

Despite the small attendance, I managed to speak quite well on the subject of "American Jewry of Tomorrow." I had recast what I gave at the previous lectures.

From Youngstown I went to Rochester, where I had been scheduled to lecture on Wednesday night. At the Rochester station I was met by Judah Pilch,[20] who is in charge of the Jewish Young Men's Association, and a Mr. Goldstein, the president of the association. A little later they were joined by Rabbi Fisher. I had supper with Pilch, Fisher, Harris, [and] Israel Schoenberg.

The communal situation in Rochester is somewhat unique. Out of a Jewish population of about 22,000, more than half are affiliated with the synagogue in one way or another. Solomon Goldman told Pilch, when the latter left Chicago to go to Rochester, that he was going to a city of "frumakes" [traditional Jews]. The reason for their unique Conservative tendency of that town is that in about 1865 a group of intensely pious Jews laid the foundation of communal life there. Even their grandchildren today are strictly observant, although their knowledge of Judaism is limited to *siddur* "davening."

I gave the same talk as at Youngstown and proffered to Pilch and Fisher the same kind of advice about cooperating as I had offered to Greenberg and Kollin.

A Rabbinical Student Uncomfortable Talking about God

JANUARY 18, 1941

One of the men to be graduated this year from the Seminary is K. Yesterday he came to see me about the sermon he has to prepare for class. The text which he chose happened to be one that, if properly interpreted, called for a discussion of some phase of the idea of God. When I told him that, he said he had been trying to avoid dealing with the idea of God. In reply to my question why he was averse to preaching on the idea of God, he said he knew very little about it. I could not even get him to realize the abnormality of such a state of affairs.

Chaim Tchernowitz

JANUARY 18, 1941

Here's another lost soul. Chaim Tchernowitz.[21] Last Sunday there was a big celebration in honor of his 70th birthday. I hadn't been too anxious to attend it because of my inability to be at ease at that kind of an affair, especially as I would have to deliver an address or make a speech. Fortunately I had a good cause for staying away, because the SAJ had the second of this year's informal gatherings

---

20. Judah Pilch (1902–1986) was a well-known Jewish educator and author. He was the director of the American Association for Jewish Education.

21. Tchernowitz was a colleague of Kaplan, and his daughter married Henry Rosenthal, a professor of philosophy and a strong Kaplan supporter.

that same evening. I sent in a letter, however, to Dr. Bernstein, the chairman of the dinner committee, in which I said some nice things about Tchernowitz.

Why really have I not gotten together with him? Basically because we really could not work together. He lacks the modern sociological approach to the realities of Jewish life, future. It is too bad that that is the case, because he possesses both the personality and the pen[22] to get across anything intrinsically worthwhile.

Dislike of Officiating at Weddings and Funerals

January 24, 1941

Anyhow, officiating at weddings, which I do so rarely, perhaps because I do it so rarely, is next to officiating at funerals, the bane of my existence.

Lecturing at Barnett Brickner's Synagogue in Cleveland

Monday, February 3, 1941

Last week I went to Cleveland to give three lectures at the Euclid Ave. Temple where Barnett R. Brickner is the rabbi. One lecture I gave on Tuesday morning before the Institute on Judaism for Christian ministers, and the other two I gave on Tuesday evening and Wednesday evening before a lay group consisting of members of the congregation. All the three lectures were given at the small chapel which holds comfortably about two hundred people. The chapel was filled each time I spoke there. The subject of my first lecture was "Traditional Judaism and Its Reinterpretation." The subject of my second lecture was "A Pattern for Modern Jewish Living" and of my third lecture "The Jewish Religion of Tomorrow." I spoke each time between one hour and an hour and a quarter. After the first lecture there were oral questions, and after the other two, written questions. For once I feel I did a good job. I personally liked my first talk best. I spoke with considerable ease and fluency both in the lecture and in the answers to the questions. There were two questions which I had been sure would be put to me and I planned beforehand what to say in answer to them. They were "What do you think of Einstein's statement made at the recent conference on Science, Philosophy, and Religion?" and "If the Christians would give up the dogmas associated with Christ, would the Jews accept him as a prophet or eminently inspired man?"

---

22. Tchernowitz published many works in Hebrew, the most interesting of which is *Masechet Zichronotai*, a book containing brief portraits of all the major Hebrew writers living in Odessa in the first decade of the twentieth century. These short portraits are wonderfully incisive and elegantly written. It so happened that all the greats were in Odessa at the same time, for example, Mendele Moykher-Sforim (Sholem Yankev Abramovitsh), Hayim Nahman Bialik, and Ahad Ha-Am. They knew each other and met frequently, especially on the Sabbath.

On Wednesday Brickner had a few of his Temple people meet me at luncheon at a downtown hotel. At my suggestion he utilized that occasion to tell them about the existence of Reconstructionism and to mention the fact that he owed his approach to the various problems he dealt with and the spirit of the improvements he had introduced into the Temple activities almost entirely to Reconstructionism, and he made a plea for interest in it. I followed him with an explanation of our purpose to function as a school of thought in Jewish life with a view to giving it direction and program. The twenty-five people present seemed to respond quite warmly to the presentation.

I was the guest of the Brickners during my stay in Cleveland. I spoke with him and his wife Rivka for hours on end about the status of the inner life of our people. The following are some of the facts I learned about his congregation. Before he came to Cleveland 15 years ago, his congregation was headed by [Louis] Wolsey. The congregation of which [Abba Hillel] Silver is the rabbi had been headed, before Silver's coming, by Gries. When Silver replaced Gries, there was an exodus from Euclid Ave. Temple (now Brickner's) to Silver's Temple. When Wolsey left and was followed by Brickner, there was a return to Euclid Ave. Temple on the part of those who had left it. There are now 1,400 families affiliated with that Temple, which, incidentally, is in its 94th year. Many of these families were formerly members of the Jewish Center of which Sol. Goldman was rabbi when he was in Cleveland. (From this one can see how little stability there is to the congregation and how superficial is its influence upon the life of its members.) The Temple is without a mortgage and has an annual budget of $76,000. The dues range from $60 per family to $200. When I felicitated Brickner on the fact that his congregation was free from the burden of a mortgage, he replied that a mortgage is a good thing for a congregation. It gives the members something specific to work for.

From my discussions with him I gathered that the two important problems which deserve intensive study are: (1) Can the congregation become the coordinating agency in Jewish life, and can it go into neighborhoods which lack synagogue facilities and organize the people into congregations? And (2) In view of the waning interest in worship as the principal function of congregational affiliation, is it feasible to have its place taken on Friday night and Sunday mornings by other forms of collective activity, such as Oneg Shabbat and various educational projects carried out in a spirit of religion?

Reasons for Kaplan's Unhappiness

THURSDAY, FEBRUARY 27, 1941

If it weren't for the fact that discontinuing this journal, or the failure to record what I have done these last two weeks, would aggravate my present state of mental malaise, I wouldn't waste time writing up these things. Although my physical condition is good, and my financial condition secure, I am far from happy. The reasons for my feeling that way are three: (1) the menace of evil *madu'ah derech re'shaim tsalechah* [Heb., "Why does the way of evil people succeed?" (a Talmudic saying)], (2) the inherent desire of most Jews to escape from Jewish life, and (3) my own shortcomings — intellectual and spiritual.

Reconstructionist Work

SUNDAY, FEBRUARY 9, 1941

The staff of the Jewish Education Committee gave their chiefs, Dushkin and Chipkin,[23] a testimonial dinner on the occasion of their having concluded thirty years in the service of Jewish education. With the dark prospect for Jewish life as a whole and Jewish education in particular, I found it very hard to put together a few thoughts that would be appropriate for the occasion. I spent several hours preparing for the ten-minute talk I had been asked to give. But at least I had no reason for feeling depressed afterward, as is generally the case these days after I am through speaking, either because the talk is labored or the effect of it is nil.

MONDAY, FEBRUARY 10, 1941

The Reconstructionist Foundation Board met to act on my suggestion that Mrs. Jacob Grossman be appointed executive secretary. Something had to be done to get things moving.

SUNDAY, FEBRUARY 16, 1941

I addressed the Hillel Group of Rutgers College. I spoke to about 100 undergraduates. Rabbi Keller, a graduate of the JIR, has charge of the Hillel work. The address was part of a forum which he conducts at his Temple. I spoke glibly, but the entire atmosphere was depressing.

TUESDAY, FEBRUARY 18, 1941

Mrs. [Irma Levy] Lindheim is a voice crying in the wilderness. She would like to reconstruct the economic foundation of American Jewish life by introducing the Haluz movement into this country. She believes that if Jewish youth can be directed in the organization of agricultural collectives, animated by the ideal of conserving and developing Jewish life, there would be a veritable Jewish renaissance in America. She came to urge me to call a conference of Jewish youth and other organizations for the purpose of discussing the plan and taking steps to put it into effect. I promised to do what I can.

---

23. Both Alexander Dushkin and Israel Chipkin were strong Kaplan supporters.

Louis Ginzberg on Jewish Law

WEDNESDAY, FEBRUARY 19, 1941

Boaz Cohen, chairman of the Law Committee of the Rabbinical Assembly, arranged a special conference on Jewish law.[24] It began with a luncheon and concluded with a dinner and addresses following the dinner. At the luncheon there were about 70 graduates, and by the time Prof. [Louis] Ginzberg[25] gave his address, there were about 100. Apparently the men were really eager to get some constructive message pertaining to making Jewish law compatible with life. Both Boaz Cohen and Louis Epstein, who spoke during the first part of the conference, indicated by what they had to say that they were not altogether impervious to the realities of contemporary life. But Ginzberg was simply impossible. For over one and a half hours he dilated upon two points of ancient interpretation of the law. The substance of what he said could have been given in 15 minutes, or at the utmost ½ hour. The subject was announced as "Interpretation vs. Abrogation." That suggested that he would deal with the problem of Jewish law as it affects us today. Instead of which what he said was simply a rehash of two or three of the lectures he gives in class, interspersed with sarcastic remarks about everybody who presumes to express an opinion based on less knowledge of Jewish law than he himself had, and with deliberately concocted mannerisms to impress the heavens with his own greatness. Following the example of some of the Talmudic sages, who would begin with his first words "I'll tell you a story," there is a ha-ha and he pulls out one of his old chestnuts. Then he tells the men how glad he is to have them back in class. Then there is a series of statements, in themselves not uninteresting, but given with an air of being Copernican in their revolutionary character, when all they amount to is commonplace sociological truths. After he has spoken for an hour and has had four sips of water, which has been handed to him by Boaz Cohen, he pulls out a piece of paper and makes the remark, "I forgot to look at my notes." The men laugh and that pleases his vanity. He fumbles with the piece of paper and puts it back into his inside pocket, and the men laugh again. What's funny about all this is that I saw him go through exactly these same motions about four years ago when he gave a similar kind of lecture to the graduates.

Having thought that Ginzberg would really speak to the subject for which he had been announced, I was under the impression that he would attach the position I maintained with regard to ritual observance—that such observance does not come properly within the category of law—I prepared a statement in which I dealt with the relation of law to sanctions. Instead of entering into a discussion of ritual observances as such, I tried to prove that so long as

---

24. Boaz Cohen was the professor of Jewish law at JTS.
25. Louis Ginzberg was the senior professor of Talmud at JTS.

there was no Jewish society that could apply sanctions, it was meaningless to speak of Jewish law.

After dinner Drs. Tchernowitz and Greenstone[26] spoke. The attendance was very poor, and what both of these men had to say bore chiefly on [Louis] Epstein's suggested solution of the *agunah*[27] problem. Tchernowitz was by far the more sensible of the two. Greenstone was a model of timidity.

Kaplan Gives a Poor Sermon and the American Flag in Synagogue

SATURDAY, FEBRUARY 22, 1941

It was my turn to speak at the SAJ services. My subject was "What the Law Is For." I tried to say too much at one time, and the result was a poor sermon with the usual aftermath of self-disgust. It is already Thursday and, despite considerable activity since, I haven't altogether gotten over the demoralizing effect on me of that sermon.

At the end of the services we dedicated the American and the Zionist flags, which had been presented to the synagogue by the Judsons. (Even on an occasion like this and with no excuse for staying away, since it was Washington's birthday, Mr. Judson didn't come to services.) I am not so sure that in my earlier years I would have altogether approved of the idea of having flags in the synagogue, but I am getting tired of making an issue of such trifles when we are so beset by dangers that threaten the entire structure of life and civilization.

Admiration for Rabbi Isaac Klein, An Expert on Jewish Law

MONDAY, FEBRUARY 25, 1941

I spoke that night at Worcester [Massachusetts] before Israel Chodosh's congregation. I was pleasantly surprised at the large attendance he had managed to secure for me, and I was in quite good spirits. The result was that the audience, I, and everybody concerned were happy. Rabbi Isaac Klein[28] of Springfield (a seminary graduate and quite a Talmudist) met me on the train as it pulled into Springfield and offered to drive me in his car to Worcester. I accepted the

---

26. Julius Greenstone (1873–1955), a longtime friend of Kaplan's, was a religious educator and administrator and the principal of Gratz College. For more on Greenstone, see Scult, *Judaism Faces the Twentieth Century*, 183–84.

27. Agunah is the Hebrew legal term meaning "chained" and refers to a woman who is chained to her marriage because her husband has disappeared or refuses to give her a divorce (*get*). The agunah problem was a complex halachic problem to which Epstein suggested a solution in the early 1930s.

28. Isaac Klein was well known for his *Guide to Jewish Religious Practice*, which was the standard guide for Conservative Jews. That book has since been superseded by *The Observant Life: The Wisdom of Conservative Judaism for Contemporary Jews*, ed. Martin S. Cohen (New York: Rabbinical Assembly, 2012).

invitation, and on the way we had a very interesting conversation. I asked him frankly how, with his strict Orthodoxy, he could display such an interest in my unorthodox approach to Judaism. He replied that his Orthodoxy extended only to his conduct but not to his thinking.

Kaplan Feels Attacked

FEBRUARY 25, 1941

What is Finky up to again? The students at the Seminary on the History of Religion tell me that Prof. Paul Weiss,[29] who teaches religion at Bryn Mawr, has been giving a series of lectures as part of Finkelstein's seminar,[30] and that Weiss has taken occasion to attack my approach to Jewish religion as being pragmatic. Finkelstein was going to have Mortimer Adler[31] lecture this term, but somehow Adler couldn't make it. It looks as though Finky is now bringing in these men to combat my influence in the same way as Charles Hoffman fought to get Finky to teach theology to counteract the heresies I was [spreading] among the students.

Kaplan Misunderstood — Again

MARCH 9, 1941

According to [Joseph] Willen, I am regarded by those whom I charge with assimilationism as an extreme Jewish nationalist and as favoring ghettoism. In fact, they consider me quite un-American. Of course I pooh-poohed this notion they have of me and explained to him my conception of Jewish nationhood and of the place of Palestine from a political standpoint. When he heard what I had to say, he replied that if I were to get together with those I denounce, say, with a man like [Joseph] Proskauer, both sides would realize that they have much more in common than they suspect. He was especially pleased by my statement that I am willing to cooperate with assimilationists, provided they come out openly with their views on what is best for Jews to do. According to him, there has taken place a change of heart on the part of many of the assimilationists. They now realize that the door to assimilationism is shut. He thought that I, on the other hand, had retreated from my former position of intransigent nationalism. This, of course, is not true. I never was an intransigent nationalist.

Shortly after Willen saw me, he called me up to ask whether I could have him and Proskauer lunch with me on Saturday, March 15. I told him "gladly."

---

29. Paul Weiss (1901–2002) was a prominent philosopher mainly known for his metaphysical writings.

30. Finkelstein established the Institute for Religious and Social Studies in order to bring outstanding scholars of all faiths to the Seminary. The Institute published the papers from the many conferences it sponsored. These volumes are extremely valuable and are underused by students and scholars.

31. Mortimer J. Adler (1902–2001) was an American educator, philosopher, and popular author.

In Praise of Ira Eisenstein

SATURDAY NIGHT, MARCH 15, 1941

The dinner given to Ira in honor of the 10th anniversary of his ministry in the SAJ was a gala affair. Ira as usual was in excellent form. Finkelstein was quite good. In the course of his remarks he stressed the fact that the Seminary is unique in that it permits diversity in interpretation of Judaism. This, of course, is not true. The Jewish Institute of Religion was founded specifically on the principle of freedom of teaching and has lived up to that principle, whereas I have often encountered opposition and at times even hostility. But he knew it would please the audience to hear him make such a statement, so he said what he did regardless of what he may have to say elsewhere.

My talk, despite the considerable thought I had given to it, did not prove successful. It may be that I am too conscious of how much is expected of me. That, together with the fact that my memory fails me when it comes to getting the right word just when I need it undoubtedly contributes to the labored character of my remarks. Perhaps back of both factors is my chronic unhappiness about the world in general and Jews and Judaism in particular.

Yet how thankful I ought to be to God! What would I have done without Ira? Either the SAJ or I would have gone to pieces.

Speaking in Newark

TUESDAY, MARCH 18, 1941

Monday, March 10, I lectured in Newark. This was the first of a series of two lectures given as part of a symposium in memory of Aaron Robison,[32] who was executive director of the Newark YM & YWHA. The attendance consisted of about 200 people, among whom were many of the Jewish lay leaders of Newark and some rabbis. In my talk I followed the new tack of urging that Jewish life be reconstructed with a view to rendering it an asset instead of a liability to the Jew. I did fairly well, although when I saw a transcript of the address, I was shocked by the choppiness of the English in it. I was not at all satisfied with the manner in which the question period was conducted by Rosenthal, who acted as chairman.

Tuesday, March 11, I presented the case of Reconstructionism to a group of about 20 people at Harold Garfunkel's home. I believe that the talk I gave there was the most smooth-spoken I have given in a long time. It was also satisfactory from the standpoint of its effect on those present. The amount raised was not much—about $300 annually for a period of four years.

Sunday, March 16, I took part in the program of the opening of the Hebrew Week, which took place at the 23 St. building of CCNY [City College of

---

32. Aaron Robison (1893–1936) was a rabbi and community worker.

New York]. I had worked quite hard on the address I was to deliver, but I am not sorry I did so because it worked out quite well and it gave me occasion to get a whack at the isolationist Hebraists, whom I detest only second to the assimilationists. I believe the address will appear in the forthcoming issue of the *Hadoar*.[33]

A *Visit from a Representative from New America (Modestly Socialist)*

MARCH 18, 1940

Wednesday, March 12, Mr. Wright, representing a movement for democracy known as "New America," which has been active for five or six years, came to see me. I gather from the literature he had sent me that it is a movement to foster a modest socialism. It advocates nationalization of banks and natural resources. The literature I received consisted of a quarterly, a biweekly, and a monthly. I learned from Mr. Wright, who seems to be a field secretary, that the quarterly and monthly, both of whom are mimeographed, had a circulation, respectively, of 800 and 300. I asked him how large a fund he was trying to get and how much was promised toward it. He told me that he tried to raise $20,000 per annum toward which $11,000 was pledged. It struck me as odd—and I told him so—that we of the Reconstructionist group were out to raise $10,000 per annum and toward that amount a little over $5,000 was pledged and that we too have been on the scene for the last five or six years. Yet I cannot understand that with so basic an appeal and with the whole country to draw on, "New America" should be only about twice as widespread as the *Reconstructionist*.

An *Attack by Finkelstein*

MARCH 21, 1941

Today I had again one of those periodic shocks which upset me frightfully. I refer to Finky's taking me over the carpet for interfering with his Seminary campaign by addressing home meetings on behalf of the Reconstructionist Foundation and having Mrs. Grossman contact Seminary graduates for the purpose of holding Reconstructionist meetings. Incidentally, he indicated that the Teachers Institute is nothing but a liability incurring a deficit of $31,000 annually. He learned about those home meetings from a statement which Ira had inserted into the "Realities and Values" [column] in the *Reconstructionist*.

Of course, if I were sure that by resigning from the Seminary, I would be more effective in achieving what I am after—the reconstruction of Jewish life and thought—I would not hesitate for a moment and I would send in my resignation.

---

33. *Hadoar* was a Hebrew periodical published in New York City under the auspices of the Histadrut.

Resignation from the JTS and Merger of the JIR and the HUC

SATURDAY, MARCH 22, 1941

I was so wrought up yesterday by Finky's onslaught that on my way from the Seminary all kinds of plans were forming themselves in my mind whereby I could escape from his claws. The first thing I did when I got home was to call up Stephen Wise to arrange for an interview with him. Perhaps, I thought, he might help me out. I knew that the JIR[34] was about to be merged with the Hebrew Union College. Perhaps that very fact might open up some opportunity that would emancipate me from the Seminary. Wise said he could see me today in his office at 4:15.

In the meantime, after talking over with Lena and with some of the children the pros and cons of resignation from the Seminary, I decided not to broach to Wise any of the difficulties I was encountering. Instead, I was to show him the *New Haggadah,* an unbound copy of which I had just gotten, and to ask him about the merger of the JIR with the Hebrew Union College.

When I met him, he surmised that I came to learn about the merger. I spent a few minutes with him—he is always in such a damn hurry—showing him the new features of the *New Haggadah.* I managed to pin his attention down to what I was saying, but I saw that he was impatient and wanted to talk about the merger. And this is what he told me: About two years ago James Heller of Cincinnati suggested that the two institutions get together. He (Wise) could not and still does not understand why they should have been so eager for the amalgamation, except as he put it, they had this passion for uniting institutions and activities which had intrinsically little in common. He calls it "unionists." Union he says is not unity. When I interpolated that it was the passion for monopoly of control, he assented. (It seems peculiar that he should not have recognized it for what it is.)

The conditions are that he should take over the administration of the new institution and [Julian] Morgenstern would be co-President. Some of the faculty of the JIR would be retired, among them [Chaim] Tchernowitz. He thinks that with only three years for him to serve, since he would be seventy at the end of that time, both he and Morgenstern would be retired to make way for a young man.

The one condition on which he insists and which he thinks might stand in the way of the amalgamation is that the present JIR become a New York branch of the new institution. The rabbinical course would consist of five years,

---

34. The Jewish Institute of Religion (JIR) was the Reform seminary in New York City established by Stephen Wise in the early 1920s. In 1927 Kaplan resigned from the JTS to join the JIR, but after a few months he returned to the JTS. If he had stayed, the Reconstructionist movement might have been founded in 1927. For more on Wise and Kaplan, see Scult, *Judaism Faces the Twentieth Century,* 268–79.

two of which would have to be spent by every student in the branch here while the other three in Cincinnati.

The reason for his insistence [is that] it is absurd that Cincinnati, with its 20,000 Jews, should retain the same position today as in 1880, when it had about 15% of the Jewish population in the United States, and that [New York] City, with the area within a radius of 50 miles which harbors more than two million Jews, should leave the rabbinical field entirely to the Seminary. The Seminary was to him the president.[35] With Finkelstein as its president, it represented "stoogism for assimilationism," because, as he put it, Finkelstein was the "theological stooge of the assimilationists."

To prove his point, he mentioned one incident in connection with the Pan-American Jewish Congress to be convoked in Montevideo next July. When the American Jewish Committee learned of the plans to have the Congress meet in Montevideo, Finky was sent to interview Berle,[36] the undersecretary in the State Department, and to impress upon him the need of preventing the Congress from meeting there or anywhere else. The argument F. used was that the Congress was a political body, in contrast with the American Jewish Committee, which was spiritual in character. Berle called a meeting to which Wise had been invited to discuss the advisability but actually to point out the inadvisability of having the Congress meet. Wise did not attend, but went to see Berle by himself. He then told him that both Secretary Hull[37] and Welles[38] had been informed of the contemplated meeting of the Jewish Congress and that they had both given their full approval.

Seminary Dance in Kaplan's Honor

Monday, March 24, 1941

Last night the Seminary students held their formal dance, which they had dedicated to me. This is the first time they did any such thing. Despite my scolding them from time to time for their lackadaisical attitude toward the burning problems of Jewish life, I seem to be rather popular with them because they get from me what they need most for their calling—a point of view.

It was a very pleasant affair. Finky had to extend to me the greetings of the Faculty. I give him credit for the fact that he didn't say anything about me personally but used the occasion to point out the unity underlying the diversity of views represented by the different members of the Faculty.

---

35. I am not sure what Kaplan means by this sentence.

36. Adolf A. Berle Jr. (1895–1971) was a lawyer, educator, author, U.S. diplomat, and member of Franklin D. Roosevelt's "brain trust."

37. Cordell Hull (1871–1955) was an American politician from Tennessee. He was the Secretary of State from 1933 to 1944 and played a key role in establishing the United Nations.

38. Benjamin Sumner Welles (1892–1961) was an American government official and diplomat in the Foreign Service. He served as Under-Secretary of State from 1937 to 1943.

I had worked quite hard at the talk I was to give, and I was rewarded by the fact that it was successful. In addition to "kibbitzing," I developed the following idea: On the principle that good and evil are what we make of things (an idea implied in *kol mah d'asar lekha rakhmana shara lecha kevutah* [Heb., "Whatever the Merciful one forbade us, He permitted something correspondent"],[39] the dance may be a dance of death, as that of the golden calf, or a dance of life, as that of God and the righteous in the world to come.

New Haggadah *off the Press—Critical Reactions*

MARCH 24, 1941

The *New Haggadah* is off the press.[40] I have been showing the unbound copies which I received from Behrman [the publishing house] to Stephen Wise and to the Teachers Institute and Seminary students.

Wise didn't seem to know enough about the traditional Haggadah to appreciate the innovations in the new one. Neither did for that matter most of the students. But while most of them were very favorably impressed, some reacted very violently against it. In the Institute, when I showed it to the small class that takes Religion 7–8, Ben-Zion (a son of Rabbi Benjamin, a man of rather unsavory reputation) was almost livid with rage at finding the *Makkot* [the ten plagues] and the imprecation (*shefokh hamatkha al ha-goyim* [Heb., "Pour out thy wrath on the nations that do not know you" (Jeremiah 10:25)][41] excluded. He characterized the *New Haggadah* as meant for an inter-faith conference to show the goyim [non-Jews] what a fine people we are. Such an attitude at this time he said was *avdut be-tokh herut* [Heb., "slavery in the midst of freedom"].[42] This morning, when I showed it to the Seminary students, Abraham Goldberg, a member of this year's graduating class, was scandalized by the omission of part of the Hallel.[43]

---

39. This statement is from BT *Chulin* 109b. There the discussion deals with matters that are prohibited but similar to matters that are permitted; for example, the consumption of blood is prohibited, but we do have permission to consume liver. My thanks to David Kraemer for the source of this statement. Although the statement implies a certain leniency, I think Kaplan goes too far beyond the apparent meaning of the statement.

40. Mordecai M. Kaplan, Eugene Kohn, and Ira Eisenstein, eds., *The New Haggadah for the Pesah Seder* (New York: Behrman's Jewish Book House, 1941). For documents on *The New Haggadah* and the controversy over it, see Jack Wertheimer, "The Great Do-Nothings: The Inconclusive Battle over the *New Haggadah*," *Conservative Judaism* 45.4 (1993): 20–38.

41. This statement is part of the traditional Passover seder and is said after the meal, when the door is opened for Elijah. Many have had problems with the violent nature of the verse. It may be that Kaplan's complete omission of the verse played a major part in his excommunication in 1945. For more about Kaplan's excommunication and *The New Haggadah*, see Mel Scult, *The Radical American Judaism of Mordecai Kaplan* (Bloomington: Indiana University Press, 2013), esp. ch. 1.

42. This phrase is an allusion to the Ahad Ha-Am essay by the same name. On Ahad Ha-Am and Matthew Arnold, see Scult, *Radical American Judaism*, ch. 3.

43. Hallel is a group of Psalms (Psalms 113–118) that are part of the Passover seder and also part of the synagogue service for festivals.

He contended that with the Talmud devoting so much space to the discussion of the question of the Hallel, such ruthless slashing as we did showed a brutal disregard for the sanctity of tradition.

APRIL 10, 1941

The entire edition of the *New Haggadah*, which consisted of 3,000 copies, was sold out within ten days after it came off the press. Last Sunday there appeared a vicious attack on it by Gedaliah Bublick[44] in the *Jewish Morning Journal*.

Personally I am satisfied that this gave me an opportunity to bring out into the open the issue of the "Chosen People." It will be even harder to give up than the doctrine of revelation, although the latter is one of the three cardinal principles of traditional Judaism.

Worries about the Future of the Teachers Institute

SUNDAY NIGHT, APRIL 13, 1941

Again I received a letter from F. [Finkelstein]. Every time I receive any mail which I recognize as coming from the Seminary, I get the jitters. For a few weeks I had lost the sense of insecurity which F. had aroused in me when he put to me the question whether he ought not to suggest to the Board of Directors of the Seminary that the TI be turned over to the Jewish Education Committee. But it was awakened again by his recent machinations. The enclosed letter from him, dated April 10, is as full of contradictions as his own miserable character, and yet he has the gumption to make a bid for more and more power. However diabolical a creature Hitler is, his love of Germany is undoubtedly his supreme passion. As for F., I cannot trace in him the least evidence of genuine love for his people or of devotion to its future.

Preaching on Freedom

APRIL 13, 1941

Yesterday I preached on "The Freedom Indispensable to Democracy." I developed the thought that inner freedom consisted of an unreconciled heart, a challenging mind, and a will that is both dauntless and cooperative.

Kaplan Considers Leaving the Seminary

APRIL 16, 1941

We [Lena, Ira, Judith, and members of the family] discussed the possibility of my sending in my resignation to the Seminary right after Pesach

---

44. Gedaliah Bublick (1875–1948) was a Yiddish journalist and Orthodox Zionist. He also served on the Executive Committee of the World Zionist Organization.

[Passover].[45] The reason to be given should be that I cannot work with F., who is employing all kinds of tactics to force me out of the Seminary. Knowing full well that it would not be feasible to resort to any pretext which might impugn the ideal of academic freedom so dear to the heart of the late Dr. Adler, he resorts to the chronic deficit of the Seminary as an excuse for threatening to liquidate the Teachers Institute. If the threat were at least frank and forthright, one might know how to deal with it, but unfortunately his fondness for equivocation gets the better of him so that one does not know where one stands with him. His pretext is that it is his purpose to produce a sense of insecurity in the staff of the Institute, so that they might share with him his anxiety about the future of the Seminary. I cannot conceive that to be a genuine reason. To me it means only one thing: getting rid of Kaplan. If that is the way he feels about me, I prefer letting him have his wish to being badgered, intimidated, and humiliated by him after having served the Seminary for 32 years with all "my heart, my soul, and my might."[46]

I have always known Lena to be in complete accord with what I wanted to do, except in the case of my negotiations with Wise in 1923. But I have never seen her so determined in her urging me to resign from the Seminary, even though it means living on our limited savings.

Kaplan's Lectures for the Past Year

APRIL 17, 1941

This year I lectured at the following places: Ann Arbor ($75), Detroit ($100), Chicago ($75), Twin Cities ($200), Youngstown and Rochester ($175), Cleveland ($225), Worcester ($100), Troy ($75), New Brunswick ($75), Germantown ($100), Newark ($150), Flushing ($75). The total in fees amounted to $1,425, of which 10% was deducted by the Jewish Welfare Board.

Last year I turned in virtually all that I had earned from lectures to the *Reconstructionist*. It amounted, I believe, to a little over $400. This year I am contributing $200.

In figuring what I would have to live on in case I severed my connections with the Seminary, the need of having to depend on lecture invitations of the kind I have had this year does not strike me as very attractive. Whatever spiritual independence I might then enjoy would be frittered away in talking for talking's sake. The psychological effect on me of saying much and doing little is morally devastating.

---

45. Kaplan considered leaving the Seminary many times (e.g., in 1923 and 1925). In 1927 he actually resigned for a few months to go to the Jewish Institute of Religion. On Kaplan's unhappiness at the Seminary and the 1927 incident, see Scult, *Judaism Faces the Twentieth Century*, 268–79.

46. An allusion to the Shema.

More on the New Haggadah

APRIL 21, 1941

I learned yesterday from Ira [Eisenstein] that Zemach, a Seminary student of the graduating class, had given him an earful about the uproar caused in the various classes by discussion concerning the *New Haggadah*. Prof. [Louis] Ginzberg was especially bitter in denouncing it. It did not receive a good word from anyone.

Being used to and expecting such reaction, I was not at all surprised at what Ira told me. So that when I went to class this morning, I had forgotten all about the fuss. At the end of the first hour, however, Moses [Moshe] Davis approached me and told me that various members of the faculty had occasion to attack the *New Haggadah* and that I owed it to myself as well as to the students to devote part of the session today to answering the objections that had been raised.

I proceeded during the second hour with the reorganization of the sermon that had been delivered by Barish during the first hour. Finding that I still had 15 minutes left without anything further to say about the sermon, I proceeded to answer my critics. I began by saying that if my critics are of the opinion that the traditional Haggadah is adequate, then there is no use of discussing the subject. If, on the other hand, they too feel that the Haggadah is not adequate, why have they not done anything to make it adequate? Such indifference on their part to a condition that is in need of being remedied is unworthy of people with a sense of responsibility for the spiritual welfare of others.

In the course of the discussion which followed I had occasion to answer the following arguments:

1. *The New Haggadah* is bound to have a destructive effect by reason of its being issued by one who has influence in Jewish life. My reply was that there are plenty among the critics who have at least as great an influence. Why do they not formulate their views in the open? I am ready to meet their challenge point for point.
2. The making of Haggadahs ad libitum [freely] will introduce anarchy into Jewish life. In reply I said: Would that sufficient interest were aroused in the attempt to render the Seder vital and significant with the possible result that there would be a flood of Haggadahs. This is infinitely preferable to the present state of growing apathy to the Seder due to the meaninglessness of the traditional Haggadah.
3. Jewish unity is bound to suffer. Answer: If freedom means anything, it calls for diversity in unity. There would be greater and deeper unity in Jewish life if every Jew could observe Seder with a Haggadah entirely his own, than if only 25% of the Jews do with the old Haggadah while the rest disregard the Seder entirely.

4. The repudiation of the traditional doctrine of Israel's election is a greater departure from normative Judaism than even the Reformist omission of Zion from their Haggadah. In answer, I developed some of the ideas which I am at present trying to formulate concerning the doctrine of Israel's election.

5. The recital of the Haggadah is intended to create a mood and not to be taken too literally. This of course brings us back to the question whether it is successful in creating in the many the mood that it creates in the few who come to the Seder with long-formed habits of Jewish living. In my opinion that is certainly not the case. Furthermore, I question the value of a mood that is vaguely sentimental and that cannot be translated into meaningful terms for the life we have to live today.

Jewish Education and the Ethical Life

APRIL 24, 1941

An unusual opportunity for utilizing Jewish study as a means of raising the ethical level of life is presented by the current social issues which hinge upon the rights and wrongs of property, of the state vs. the individual, of individual and collective uses of power, of peace and war. The general ethical principles and the golden rules in which our ethical tradition is rich offer no specific guidance by reason of their abstract character lack and the force of public opinion necessary to activate them. What we need is the cultivation of an ethical sensitivity to the issues involved in the various conflicts of interests and something of that passion for righteousness, which is the eternal glory of prophetic religion. To experience passion, we must do more than merely study and analyze the prophetic writings; we must study and analyze the social situations, the poverty, the disease, the slums, the unemployment, and the main other social evils and note the extent to which they are due to selfishness, vanity, greed, and stupidity as well as to sheer inertia. It would not at all be amiss, after having acquainted the Jewish layman with some of the typical instances of talmudic lore, with a view to illustrating how Jewish ethical values were translated into law, to include the exposition of the Constitution of the United States and of outstanding legal decisions in the effort to utilize Jewish study as a means of sensitizing the Jews to ethical values.

Biblical Criticism and Jewish Education

FRIDAY, APRIL 25, 1941

Under this heading should come the entire problem of what to do with the biblical criticism. Certain it is that ignoring it cannot but lead to an attitude of negativity to religion as a whole. As bad, if not worse, is to recognize it and to deal with it in the artificially apologetic manner of Hertz's[47] commentary on the Torah. The bon mot of Schechter's,[48] to the effect that higher criticism was only higher anti-Semitism, was timely when he said it and even then had limited application. But when repeated ad nauseam as a reason for not dealing with the far-reaching implications of higher criticism for the understanding of the formative period of Jewish religion, it serves merely as an excuse for evading a frank discussion of the traditional doctrine that the Torah was supernaturally revealed. If we want our people to make the Torah an integral part of their consciousness, we must be outspoken as to whether we regard it as a monolithic text of supernatural origin or as a document of composite authorship. If I am not mistaken, the overwhelming majority who sponsor and take the courses in adult Jewish study cannot be gotten to subscribe to the traditional doctrine concerning the Torah. If that is the case, then we must do two things in teaching Torah, one from the standpoint of Jewish literacy and the other from the standpoint of Jewish experience. From the standpoint of Jewish literacy, we should give in popular form the history of the scientific study of the Bible, its present status, and some of the most important conclusions thus far arrived at by the principal schools of biblical research. In this connection it would be quite in place to indicate the contributions to biblical research made by Jewish scholars, whose theories about the Bible are certainly free of any Christian or anti-Semitic bias. From the standpoint of Jewish experience, we shall have to indicate how such a scientific approach is compatible with the evaluation of the Torah as indispensable to Jewish life, and how such indispensability does not preclude our treating some of its teachings and practices as obsolete. Above all, it will be necessary to treat the conception of God in the Torah as by no means the final form in which it must be accepted for all times, but rather as an incentive to such formulation as would guide us Jews individually and collectively in the living of the good life.

To sum up: If we want that Adult Jewish Study shall avoid the Charybdis of boredom and the Scylla of short-lived faddism, it must be made relevant to the problem of overcoming centrifugal tendencies in Jewish life, those which threaten Jewish solidarity, the Jewish ethics, and the Jewish religion. It must neither pontificate or speak with the kind of authority which treats all alternative views as either non-existent or as unworthy for consideration, nor must it speak with the aloofness of encyclopedic scholarship which cares not

---

47. Kaplan knew Joseph Hertz well and thought him pretentious because he once greeted Kaplan and Chaim Weizmann in his formal attire. Hertz was the first graduate of the Seminary, receiving ordination in 1893. Hertz's Torah commentary, *The Pentateuch and Haftorahs with Hebrew Text, English Translation, and Commentary* (popularly known as the Hertz Chumash), has been used widely since the 1930s.

48. Solomon Schechter was president of the JTS from 1902 to 1915. See also Mel Scult, "Schechter's Seminary," in *Tradition Renewed: A History of the Jewish Theological Seminary of America*, ed. Jack Wertheimer (New York: Jewish Theological Seminary, 1997), 1:43–103.

a hoot whether you take or leave what it has to offer. Jewish adult study must concern itself with Jewish literacy as a means to Jewish experience, with having ever increasing numbers of the Jewish laity identify themselves completely with the problem of Jewish survival and revival, for only then will that problem receive a satisfactory solution.

10

April 29, 1941–October 16, 1941

On the Chosen People

TUESDAY, APRIL 29, 1941

For once I have acted out a dream of mine. The elimination from the Kiddush in the Haggadah of the reference to our being a chosen people has called down upon me the vociferous protestations of the great do-nothings who command positions of spiritual influence in Jewish life but who, having a vested interest in the status quo, confine their activity to protesting against any move to blow off the sacred dust that has collected on the ancient stereotypes. I anticipated the storm which has broken loose and which may develop into a hurricane. But I had to dislodge from the Jewish mentality an idea which was bound to be most obstructive in any growth, reconstruction, and progress in Jewish life. The very act of affirming with all the solemn pretense of prayer an idea which is not taken seriously and which in fact is flouted and ridiculed is the greatest offense against elemental decency. That Jews could be so insensitive as to permit themselves such flummery would be evidence either of senility or degeneracy. I could not continue to work for the Jewish cause if it was to be inextricably tied up with such unfeeling disregard for the sanctity of prayer. Thank God I have had the courage to go through with the excision of such a cancerous growth from the Jewish consciousness.

WEDNESDAY, APRIL 30, 1941

Although I find that I have to make considerable changes in any address or article which I write out in this journal, I shall attempt to write out the talk I expect to give at the annual meeting of the Reconstructionist Foundation, because this journal has the effect on me of an interlocutor who draws out from me what I would otherwise have no occasion to say. My subject this time is to be "The Doctrine of the Chosen People."

The most challenging innovation in the *New Haggadah* and one which may come to have far-reaching significance for the future development of Jewish belief was the omission of hardly a dozen words from the traditional text. Those words state that God "has chosen us from among all peoples and has exalted us above all tongues"; they include also the allusion to God's having made the distinction between Israel and the nations as he does between light and darkness, between the seventh day and the six work days. This innovation was not made lightheartedly or without full realizations on the part of the editors that they were abandoning a doctrine which Jews in pre-modern times regarded as no less self-evident than the existence of God. While it is true that in the official creeds of an Albo or a Maimonides the doctrine that Israel is God's chosen people does not even figure, there is no disputing the fact that by implication and inference it is present in those creeds. It was to be expected, therefore, that the omission of the statement affirming this doctrine would raise a storm of protest and criticism, even in quarters where one is wont to meet considerable latitudinarianism.

That the teaching concerning Israel's election should be called into question, not by secularists but by those who stress religion as the soul of the Jewish civilization, and that they should indicate their refusal to subscribe to that teaching by deliberately omitting it from the liturgy which they otherwise accept, has so staggered critics that they have not been able to look into the possible reasons for so radical a step. The only motive they could think of as having actuated the editors was the wish to appease our enemies, who point to this doctrine of Israel as the chosen people as an evidence of the contempt which the Jews harbor for the rest of the world. One such critic naively asks how the editors could possibly hope to succeed in appeasing our enemies on that score, as long as there are enough copies left of the old Haggadah.

It should therefore be stated forthwith that no such considerations move the editors. The notion of appeasing hostile critics of Judaism was furthest from their minds. The assumption that Judaism is responsible for having given rise to the idea of race superiority, which is today creating havoc in the world, is only another of those absurd accusations which it is hopeless to attempt to refute, because they stem more from prejudice than from a careful weighing of facts.

To anyone free from prejudice it should be apparent that the doctrine of Israel's election belongs to an entirely different universe of discourse from that of the modern theory of race superiority. The former is religious teaching; the latter is political policy. At its narrowest, no religion would refuse admission to anyone who recognized its truth and accepts its obligations. Even though Judah Halevi came suspiciously near to ascribing to the Jews a definite superiority based on racial descent, and emphasized the denial of absolute equality to a proselyte, the very act of soliciting the Chazar King and his people to adopt Judaism implied in the entire argument of the *Kuzari*[1] indicates that we cannot take his theory of Jewish racial superiority too seriously.

As for making the Jews responsible for the Germanic adoption of the theory of race superiority, the actual source whence that theory was taken over by the Germans is well known. About 75 years ago the French writer Count Gobineau[2] wrote *Essay on the Inequality of the Human Races*, in which he tried to prove that the Nordic race was gifted with such extraordinary qualities of thought and action that it was entitled to be the master race of the world. Wagner, who translated into poetry and music the new theme of German superiority, was an intense hater of everything Jewish and could scarcely have been influenced by anything coming from that source. The Germanic notion of race superiority belongs rather to the class of ideas found in the childhood stage of mankind everywhere, when peoples naturally tended to be ethno-centric, when the correlative of inner solidarity of any group was always hostility to the out-group. All nature peoples, from the most primitive to the most highly civilized, regard themselves as the only genuine species of human beings. The answer which the Caribs give to the question whence they came is, "We alone are the people." Lapps and Esquimaux think of themselves alone in belonging to the category man. The Greeks and Romans regarded themselves as inherently qualified to be freemen, while the rest of the world were barbarians and only fit to be slaves. In their case we already have a definite anticipation of a political interpretation of race superiority. These examples suffice to prove that nothing could be more ridiculous than to hold the Jews responsible for a trait which is so inherent as to be universal.

THURSDAY, MAY 1, 1941

It is entirely from the standpoint of religion and for the purpose of having our religion as sanction only for what we sincerely believe to be ethically acceptable that we should appraise the doctrine of Israel's election. I conceive religion not merely as a matter of conforming to an established regimen of ritual practice. I therefore do not view the question of Israel's election as a question of whether or how we should recite a certain formula. It is a question of whether we can get ourselves with our present outlook on life to believe the fact which the formula states or to pray for the desideratum which the formula implies. Before we so proceed any further with the discussion of the matter, we must make sure that we get the full force of the distinction between viewing the question as one of ritual or as one of experience. The trouble with most of our discussions of

---

1. The *Kuzari* is a medieval polemic by Judah ha-Levi (1075–1141), Spanish-Jewish poet and philosopher, in which the king of the Khazars supposedly interviews leaders of Judaism, Christianity, and Islam to see which is the best religion.

2. Joseph Arthur Comte de Gobineau (1816–1882) was a French aristocrat and novelist who became famous for developing the theory of the Aryan master race.

religious problems is that they turn upon the propriety or impropriety of reciting certain formulas or performing certain acts. They seldom, if ever, probe to
fundamental problems of our fundamental experience. The first step, therefore,
[which] we must take in orienting ourselves to the problem of Israel's election is
to realize that our main concern is not whether in the light of the fact that the
Jewish people has throughout the ages regarded itself as divinely chosen; we have
or have not the right to tamper with that belief. Our main concern should be
whether there is any sense in which we actually believe that, as we are now constituted, we can conscientiously affirm that we stand in any closer relationship
to God than any other people. What we have to decide is not whether we should
or should not quote what our ancestors believed about themselves. When we
worship, our religion must not be merely as a quotation but a genuine personal
experience. If we apply the criterion of personal experience to the traditional
doctrine of Israel's election, we can come to but one conclusion, viz., that we
cannot thank God for having exalted us above all tongues without stultifying
ourselves religiously.

The reasoning by which we arrive at this conclusion is very simple.
Throughout the past it did not occur to anyone, Jew or Gentile, to doubt the
historicity of the miraculous events recorded in the Torah concerning the
Patriarchs and their descendants in Egypt. But by far the most significant of those
events was the one of God's self-revelation to Israel on Mount Sinai and the
divine announcement of at least two of the Ten Commandments. To question
the truth of these events was regarded as far less reasonable than to question what
one perceived with his senses when he was wide awake. With not even a scintilla
of doubt concerning the historic actuality of the supernatural events which took
place entirely for the sake of Israel, how could anyone in his right mind regard
Israel as other than the chosen of God? No other people were privileged to have
deserved in the least that God should make the slightest change in the normal
course of events for its sake. Never did God appoint any one from among them
as a prophet to make known his message to them. For him to reveal himself to
them was absolutely inconceivable. So long as our fathers held to these beliefs,
how could they possible regard themselves, who were the descendants of those
to whom all these self-manifestations of God took place, as other than the most
privileged of all peoples? It should not at all surprise us that the belief in Israel's
election was formerly as pervasive as an atmosphere, pervading everything that
had to do with the religion of the Jew. What the Jew really thanked for when he
pronounced the benediction over the fact that he belonged to a God-chosen
people, a people superior to all other nations, was that God had performed all
those miracles for his forefathers and had revealed himself to them and given
them a Torah. Insofar as the Jew believed in the literal truth of all these events,
they constituted for him actual experience. He lived them over again in his imagination every time he came across any reference to them. For that reason Jews

had a perfect right to regard themselves as being more closely related to God than any other people.

Those conditions no longer obtain with the majority of modern-minded men and women. They cannot possibly consider the miraculous events as recorded in the Torah and in the rest of the Bible as historic. The archaeological discoveries, to be sure, have confirmed the historic character of the manner and customs which form the background of the ancient saga, but they never will confirm the actual saga themselves. We shall never have the means of knowing whether the Patriarchs were historic persons who actually figured in events such as are described in the Torah. No evidence of their having received such divine communications as indicat[ions] that they were the beloved of God and singled out for divine favor can ever be forthcoming. The likelihood, therefore, that the patriarchal stories will ever be regarded as historic is out of the question. How, then, can the modern-minded Jew accept literally the argument developed by the Deuteronomist with regard to God's selection of Israel, when he says, "The Lord did not set his love upon you, nor choose you because you were more in number than any other people, for ye were fewest of all peoples but because the Lord loved you and because he would keep the oath which he swore unto your fathers" (Deut. 7:7–8)? This does not at all preclude our reading these texts in the Torah as part of our religious regimen, since one of the main functions of that regimen is to keep alive the remembrance of the past. The past of the Jewish people is not one that is crowded with stirring military or political events. It is one that is interesting mainly because of the notion-making and character-shaping beliefs and sagas. We cannot afford to dispense with the remembrance of our ancient thought life, however much we may have outgrown it. But when it comes to affirming what we ourselves believe with regard to God's relation to us, we dare not content ourselves with quoting what our ancestors believed. We must express forthrightly what we ourselves believe. With the main foundation for this belief in God's selection of Israel undermined by our present knowledge of the past, it is nothing less than sacrilege to address God with an untruth.

So important is it to make the past inner experiences of our people part of our own consciousness that we often have to resort to the process of interpretation in order that we may understand those experiences in terms of their original setting, historical and psychological. The process of interpretation is intended to acquaint us with as much as possible of the content of life to which belong the values and ideals of our forebears, in order that those values and ideals shall be rendered so vivid as to be properly understood and appreciated by us. But when we reinterpret those values and ideals, we go one step further and seek to equate them with our own actually experienced wants or with such needs as we deem it necessary to cultivate. Thus it is highly essential that we interpret the doctrine of the chosen people, for the very reason that it played so central a part in the consciousness of our forebears. But that doctrine does not lend itself to reinterpretation in that it cannot be equated with any value to which we might aspire today. What stands in the way of its reinterpretation will appear in the sequel.

In interpreting the doctrine of the Chosen People, we are chiefly interested in discovering what it was in the past that motivated that doctrine. We may well assume that something more than delusion was the source of the belief held by our ancestors that they were God's chosen. They unquestionably wanted to voice their sense of superiority to the other nations. But when we analyze that urge, we should try to understand what really led them to regard themselves as superior. Their criterion of value may prove abiding, though we reject their egotism. If we delve into the inner meaning of the entire scriptural context to which the assumption of Israel's election belongs, we find that as far as the Torah is concerned, the main point in the reiteration of Israel's election is that the God whom Israel worshiped was so much superior to the gods of the other nations that Israel might well consider itself fortunate in being his people, in having the opportunity to worship him and obey his laws. Being the only true God alongside the gods of the other nations, who were nothing, his law alone is worthy of respect and obedience. From the realization of the superiority of their God and of their law they concluded that only a people with such a God and such a law is a real people. By virtue of all these facts, the Jews regarded themselves as singularly fortunate, as God's own in a sense that no other people was.

More on Israel's Election

Friday, May 2, 1941

Thus by the process of interpretation we are able to distinguish between fact and fancy in the ancient texts which emphasize Israel's superiority to the other nations. That part of Jewish consciousness which depends upon the remembrance of the past calls for periodic quotation of those ancient texts so that we may not forget the fact element which they contain. The fact is that the Jewish people during the first millennium of its existence somehow did achieve a unique conception of God, a conception which displaced all the others held by the peoples of the Occident and the Near East. It is moreover an indisputable fact that the Jews as a people evolved a more rational and humane code of conduct than did all other peoples in ancient times. So long as that fact operated, we may without resorting to the traditional saga, claim for Israel the right to have called itself the chosen of God.

The preceding analysis of the sense of superiority implied in the doctrine of the chosen people applies mainly to the first millennium of Jewish history. The analysis of the doctrine of election as held by our ancestors during the Christian centuries reveals that the affirmation of superiority became part of the Jewish people's struggle for existence. With the destruction of the State and the forced dispersion of the Jews among the other nations, that struggle became embittered. No less intense than the physical war waged against the Jews was the war of nerves. It consisted then as now of unrelenting defamation. By the time the Christian church was firmly established and its doctrine became fairly crystallized, that defamation acquired a definite pattern which was calculated to make it extremely effective. The pattern consisted in basing the defamation on the very conception of God which the Jews had evolved and on the very scriptures which the Jews themselves regarded as the word of God. The very doctrine of election was used as a weapon against them. Christianity, both authoritative and sectarian, went far beyond Judaism in the utilization of the doctrine of election. That doctrine became its very raison d'être. It set itself the task of realigning mankind into the chosen and the damned. The criterion was faith in Jesus as the Son of God and identical with God. The objective was the establishment of the Church that was to supersede all human governments. In this process the Jewish people was singled out as the people which, having at one time been the elect of God, repudiated him and thereby became a people accursed and damned.

In the face of this ruthless attack on its reputation, what else was there for the Jewish people to do but so elaborate its traditional claims to superiority as to counter effectively the claims to superiority advanced by the Church? With the interest of modern mankind during the pre-modern Christian centuries focused on the question of salvation and of eligibility for it, all of its thinking was cast in the mold of the doctrine of divine election. All of creation was regarded as having come into being for the sake of those who were worthy of being God's chosen. The company of the elect by reason of their chosen kinship with God wielded a power not vouchsafed to ordinary mortals. Not only did they vanquish death but, even in this life, they exercised, especially in their collective capacity as the divine ecclesia, an influence over the very course of nature. Thus did the doctrine of election to whomever applied, or by whomever used, connote two specific ideas: one that of centrism, the other that of mystical or demonic power.

Both of these ideas entered into the conception of the Church. The Church regarded itself as the Israel of the New Covenant and as the heir of the Israel of the old covenant. As such it took over the Israelocentric conception of history and of creation. The whole of creation was pictured as a cosmic drama in which the denouement was enacted by Christ through the medium of the Church. Paul greets "those who are faithful in Jesus Christ" with the words, "He chose us in him ere the world was founded, to be consecrated and unblemished in his sight . . . so richly has God lavished upon us his grace . . . showing us how it was the purpose of his design so to order it in the fulness of the ages that all things in heaven and earth alike should be gathered up in Christ" (Ephesians 1:3–10). The church, moreover, viewed itself as a fellowship with divine gifts, to use the technical phrase of Christian theology. The well-known phrase of Athanasius, "For he (Christ) became man that we might become divine," implies that sacramental presence of God in the Church. The Eastern Church especially, where we would expect the nearest approach to the Jewish conception of Israel as it was then shaping itself, is said to have thought of itself "as a mysterious hierurgical saving institution" (Hastings, [*Encyclopaedia of Religion and Ethics*], III:6220). Due to the part played by the mysteries in the early development of Christianity, the mystical power of the church was translated into the complicated regiment of the sacraments. Though the Jewish conception of the ecclesia of Israel did not attain in practice that theurgic character, in theory it might well have done so had the institution of sacrifices been permitted.

Whether in direct response to the challenge of the church, or as a spontaneous reaction to claims which began to be voiced by various religious sects during the first centuries of the Christian era, the Jews likewise advanced the claim of centrism and mystic and demonic power for their own people, which henceforth is designated not only *umah*, or nation, but *kneset*, or ecclesia, the exact analogue of church. Throughout rabbinic writings the Israelocentric conception of the cosmos and of human history is the theme of numerous aggadic homilies. To select but one of the numerous typical passages which illustrate just in what sense the idea of Israel was taken by the rabbis:

> The straw, the stubble and the chaff were disputing with one another. Each one said, "For my sake was the field sown." Said the wheat, "Wait until you get to the threshing floor; then we shall know for whose sake the field was sown." When they arrived at the threshing floor and the owner went out to winnow the grain, he scattered the chaff in the wind, he took the straw and threw it on the ground, and the stubble he burned. But the wheat he took and piled up into a heap, and whoever passed by fondled it with admiration. Likewise do all the nations content among themselves, each claiming, "The world was created for my sake." But Israel retorts, "Wait until the day of reckoning comes. Then we shall know for whom the world was created." (*Gen. R.* 83:5 and *Cant. R.* on 7:3)[3]

Likewise was the claim of mystic power made for Israel. According to R. Eliezer ben R. Jose, the Galilean God said to the angel of death, "Although I have given the power over every one of my creatures, you can have no power over this nation" (Israel) (*Cant. R.* on 8:6). Time and again we come across statements which express the apotheosis of Israel. Israel is a people transfigured and deathless, occupying a rank equal to that of angels or holy princes (Cf. *Cant. R.* on 1:2a). This implies that the ecclesia of Israel possesses a supernatural or demonic status.

---

3. Kaplan is referring here to the rabbinic commentary on the Torah called the Midrash, particularly *Midrash Rabbah*, on Genesis and the Song of Songs. Both of these are available in translation. The Midrash formed the primary content of Kaplan's classes in the Rabbinical School at JTS.

What is the pragmatic purpose of both of these claims—centrism and demonism? The answer is contained in some of the foregoing passages which voice those claims. These claims are intended to furnish the basis for the assumption that only those identified either with the Church, for the Christian, or with the Ecclesia of Israel, for the Jew, are eligible to salvation, which for pre-modern man had one outstanding significance—that of being able to vanquish death and enjoy immortal bliss in the hereafter. To be the elect of God, therefore, meant to be of that society of human beings for whom alone the world was created and who had the exclusive opportunity of the blessed life in the hereafter. The Church claimed these prerogatives by virtue of its constituting the body of which the head was Christ. The Ecclesia of Israel based its claim to these prerogatives by virtue of its possession of the Torah. (The exception in favor of the *hasidei umot ha-olam* [Heb., the righteous of the nations] only proves the rule.)

It should by this time be clear how little there is in common between the idea of chosen people as promulgated in the Judeo-Christian tradition and the idea of a master race which is arrogantly proclaimed by the Germans. The former is the expression of a claim to exclusive possession of the way of life by which mankind can be saved; the latter is an expression of the will to power. The only excuse for putting them in the same category is that the group which lays claim to being the sole possessor of the key to salvation more often than not exploits that claim for the purpose of achieving power over other groups. Yet it is unfair to hold the doctrine of divine election responsible for the promulgation of the pseudo-scientific doctrine of Nordic race supremacy. The very statement in Deut. VII:7 deprecates the identification of divine election with natural selection.

By a strong concatenation of circumstances, the doctrine of election of Israel crops up in the most unexpected quarters and in the guise of that very chauvinism which is a form of the will to power, a form which the weakest of peoples often indulge in as a mental compensation for their very weakness. I refer to the fact that Jews who have lost all interest in the inner spiritual life of their people, whose attachment to that people is due mainly to the refusal of non-Jewish society to accept them completely, very often try to convince themselves that they belong to an inherently superior race, superior especially in being intellectually gifted. Even if true, that fact is merely one of natural or artificial selection to which Jews have been subjected by the process of discrimination. Jews have had to wage a keener struggle for existence than other peoples. Those who survive would naturally possess certain qualities that make for survival, both group and individual. But this superiority is bound to disappear the moment the process of natural selection would relent, and has nothing whatever in common with the doctrine of Israel as the chosen people.

This kind of Jewish chauvinism, which some Jews express through the medium of the doctrine of Israel's election, is a misconceived effort at reinterpreting that doctrine; the process of reinterpretation sets in when a traditional doctrine or value has become irrelevant on account of the change in the context of life and world outlook. To maintain the community with the past, some particular aspect in that doctrine or value is sought out which may happen to be not only relevant to the current context of experience but which may also continue to be desirable by reason of its intrinsic worth. Chauvinism is an aspect of the doctrine of election, an aspect which, when singled out, may be relevant to current experience; but it cannot be regarded by those who realize its menace as by any means desirable. That is sufficient reason for condemning such reinterpretation as invalid, to say nothing of the fact that in transforming a religious value into one of natural selection, the value is multiplied.

The question, however, remains: Why should it not be possible, on the basis of the interpretations of the doctrine yielded us by the analysis of it, to give it a valid reinterpretation, and thus retain it as part of the developing Jewish consciousness? The answer is that no matter what aspect of that doctrine we shall choose to preserve, whether it be the true conception of God, the humane character of the ancient code, [or] the possession of the key to salvation, we cannot possibly eliminate from the doctrine itself the element of comparison with other peoples and the claim to superiority of some kind over them. For that there can be neither factual nor moral justification at the present time.

The Dangers of the Doctrine of Election

FRIDAY, MAY 9, 1941

Far from being a factor for Jewish survival, the doctrine of Israel's election is ideologically henceforth bound to be the greatest hindrance to it. For this and for no other reason do I deem it necessary to have the affirmation of it expunged from our prayers of thanksgiving. In its traditional form, that doctrine belongs to the same universe of discourse as the one in which God was conceived as a magnified human being sitting on a great throne in the heavens, surrounded by hosts of angels and demons who are at his beck and call, ready to carry out his will on earth. It belongs to the universe of discourse in which the supernatural miracles believed to have taken place in the past were a guarantee of supernatural miracles which will take place in the future, and one in which the divine sound of the Shofar on Sinai was an assurance of the shofar of the messiah at the end of days. It belongs to the same universe of discourse as the one in which all human suffering, even the fact of death, was attributed to sin, in which animal sacrifice was accepted as an indispensable means of atoning for sin, and in which a whole people could be conceived as subjected to unceasing torment of body and mind for centuries because of failure to atone for some anonymous ancestral sin. It is possible for those who have become habituated to a Copernican-Newtonian-Einsteinian physical cosmos, to a Lockian, Rousseaunian, Kantian, Jeffersonian, and Lincolnian political and social cosmos to get back to that pre-modern universe of discourse only as one revisits the scene of one's childhood, perhaps out of a certain nostalgia, but certainly not with a view to making it one's home.

If the Jewish people is to have a future, it must reconstruct its entire ideology so that it may feel itself perfectly at home in the universe of discourse in which those who are most advanced intellectually, morally, and spiritually at present dwell. In this modern universe of discourse, religion is not based on the tradition of miraculous events and theophanies supposed to have taken place in ancient times. To the modern man, religion is based on the fundamental fact that all normal human beings are endowed with a capacity for salvation, provided that individually and collectively they coordinate their conduct and their institutions with the functioning of God as the power within and without them that makes for salvation. That conception of religion points to a better world in which we Jews, without giving up our historical uniqueness and continuity as a people, want to have a share. In that better world the orchestration of human life is not to serve merely as an accompaniment to any one nation or ecclesia playing solo. A far nobler motive for Jewish survival than the assertion of claims to spiritual superiority is the need for a people always to strive to outdo itself, always to keep on growing in moral and spiritual capacity. There can be no better evidence of such growth than the surrender of notions and beliefs which may have served a useful function in a people's childhood or youth, but which are out of place in a people which has attained maturity in the modern world.

Not Chosenness but Vocation

SUNDAY, MAY 11, 1941

Jewish survival depends entirely upon our achieving a moral realism, [which] on the one hand will wean us away from futile compensatory mechanisms of imagined superiority and, on the other hand, will enable us to find the basis for intrinsic worth of Jewish life in the daily round of contemporary living. It is a mistake to imagine that once we abandon the doctrine of Israel's election, there is no alternative except that of treating Jewish life as a purely secular affair, whether we are assimilationists and would prefer to see it liquidated, or we are Jewish nationalists and would like to see it enter the world arena of modern nations contending for a place in the sun. There is a third alternative which Reconstructionism submits for consideration. It is an alternative which would have the Jews realize that the only kind of Jewish survival which would constitute a creative adjustment to the world in which we now live is one in which the two elements of their tradition would continue to function, viz., Jewish nationhood and Jewish religion, but on terms radically different from those in the past. The essence of Jewish nationhood can no longer be identified with political unity or with religious uniformity. The political unity must be confined to Jews living in their homeland; the uniformity must be cultural rather than religious. Likewise, the essence of Jewish religion can no longer be regarded as dependent upon the historicity of the supernatural events which are recorded in the Torah and as its logical conclusion of the election of Israel. Instead, it will have to be based on what the objective study has shown to be the function of a religion in the life of a people. That function is so to inspire and direct the life of a people that it will help its individual men and women to make the most of their lives, or to achieve salvation.

With this alternative in mind, it becomes clear that the place previously occupied in the Jewish consciousness by the doctrine of election would have to be taken by the doctrine of vocation. The theological use of both terms "election" and "vocation" is one met with in Christianity, especially in Protestant teaching. Christianity was not contented with applying the doctrine of election to the church as a whole; it applied it also to the individual human being. It thereby indicated that the individual was subjected to some predestined divine decree which determined whether or not he was eligible to salvation. Jewish religion knows of no such invidious distinction among individuals. It is more inclined to give to its concept a collective significance. I submit, therefore, that it ought to do the same to the Christian doctrine of vocation. It ought to extend the present theological significance of vocation to include nations as well as individuals. No nation is chosen or elected or superior to any other, but every nation should discover its vocation or calling and utilize that vocation as a source of religious experience and as a medium of salvation to its individual men and women.

I shall avail myself of a definition of the theological concept of vocation as formulated by Robert Louis Calhoun[4] in his book *God and the Common Life* to indicate what its application would signify for the collective life of the Jewish people. An individual, according to him, may experience the presence of God in his life and have a sense of a divine calling, if he is engaged in doing needful work, if that work calls into play his best powers and makes for the[ir] development, and finally if it enables him to contribute his share to the world's work and the common life. If the Jews throughout the world would reckon in their various collective efforts with these three principles of vocation, their religion would experience a revival which would be tantamount to divine revelation. For the Jews as a people to be engaged in needful work at the present time means for them to accept the threefold task of (1) salvaging the millions of our people who are menaced with extinction, (2) reclaiming and rebuilding our ancient homeland for the homeless millions of Jews and reconstituting them into a creative commonwealth, and (3) organizing Jewish communal life in the Diaspora on a religion-cultural basis. If this vocation is to be accepted by Jews in the spirit of

---

4. The Rev. Robert L. Calhoun (1897–1983) was the Sterling Professor of Historical Theology at Yale University and a leading figure in Protestant scholarship and ecumenism.

religion, then it must be able to enlist the highest abilities of our gifted men and women. It must provide work for their talents and of those talents such fields for self-expression and development that their possessors would not have to feel that they are stunting their powers by employing them for the expression of Jewish values. Finally, the very method and spirit in which the Jews as a people would carry on the urgently needful work described in the foregoing should be of such a character as to make them sharers in the efforts to solve the fundamental problem involved in the art of living together as individuals and as groups. This certainly is a vocation to which we Jews might well consecrate ourselves and one which by giving meaning and direction to our lives would give content and a sense of reality to our religion. We shall then no longer need to have our morale bolstered up by such a spiritual anachronism as extolling God for not having made us like the other nations, etc. Instead, we shall find our calling as a people so absorbing, so satisfying, and so spiritually thrilling that we shall have every reason in the world to thank God for having manifested his love unto us by sanctifying us by his commandments, by bringing us nigh unto his service, and by rendering us worthy to be identified with his great and holy name.

Opposition to the Haggadah at JTS

Monday, May 12, 1941

I was unaware at the time I made my entry on April 29 that all the members of the faculty of the Seminary were being corralled to sign their names to a letter in which they declare that they find themselves compelled to dissociate themselves from my theology and from the *New Haggadah*.

Kaplan Challenged by Louis Ginzberg at the Rabbinical Assembly

May 13, 1941

After dinner we all convened in the auditorium of [Isaac] Klein's synagogue. Klein, as chairman of the evening session, introduced Prof. L. Ginzberg. Klein's remarks were those of a high-school adolescent trying to be humorous. Then the great man arose and everybody rose in his honor. . . . Again he repeated almost word for word what he had said a few months ago when he took part in the conference called by the Committee on Law, and what he said about four or five years ago in answer to a paper I had read at one of the conventions of the Rabbinical Assembly. Only a Saadia and a Maimonides had a right to philosophize about Judaism because they came to it with a full knowledge of it, he went on to say, but not a Philo, who came to Judaism merely with a knowledge of philosophy. So people who come nowadays from sociology and reduce the mitzvot, which Judaism considers as divine commands, to folkways (he kept on saying "fokesvays") are destroying Judaism. Then came the climax. "Such people have no right to remove the doctrine of the election of Israel from Judaism. Anyone who denies that doctrine reads himself out of Judaism."

I did not feel inclined to reply to him right there and then; I would have created a disturbance. After all, the platform was his and he had a right to go on. After having delivered the foregoing tirade, on which he spent at least 25 minutes, he proceeded to give the talk on the subject announced. He repeated for the most part what he had said at the dinner given in his honor a few weeks ago. When he was through, it was 10:20. [Max] Kadushin, who had been scheduled to read a paper in Hebrew on the "Doctrine of Election in Rabbinic Literature," must have been on tenterhooks waiting for Ginzberg to get through. I was not going to interrupt the program at that point. Kadushin dealt with his subject from a historical point of view. Toward the end of his paper he brought his argument to a head by saying that the Sages had no abstract concept corresponding with the term "election," but that the idea of election functioned for them only in conjunction with a context which contained references to God's having brought them near to his service and having given them commandments.

When Kadushin was through, I asked for the floor. Klein called me to the platform. I got quite an ovation, which contrasted strongly with the small applause which had greeted Ginzberg's statement about the doctrine of Israel's election. In calm fashion I pointed out that Ginzberg transgressed his own principle of not making generalizations without basis in fact when he read me out of Judaism because I did not include in the Haggadah reference to the doctrine of election. As I said this, he called out, "I mean historical Judaism." I replied at once, "But historical Judaism is a developing Judaism." However, I added that insofar as facts were concerned, the facts mentioned by Kadushin confirmed my position in the matter rather than his.

The majority of those present were very happy over what I said and the way I said it. . . .

The sum total of the convention is that the men are more in the dark than ever as to what Conservative Judaism stands for. When one of the men complained that such was the case after 41 years of the RA's existence, Simon Greenberg said that Judaism has been in existence over 3,000 years and we still don't know what it is. To what may we ascribe this kind of sophistry, to a perverted mind or to a perverted will?

What to Do When Rabbinical Students Don't Finish

Friday, May 16, 1941

On Wednesday afternoon I attended a meeting of the Seminary faculty which was devoted mainly to the question of what to do with members of the graduating class who had failed to complete the necessary requirements of some of the courses. . . . Although every member of the faculty argued against graduating them, Finkelstein used all kinds of specious arguments in favor of graduating them. One of his tricks in the argument was to divert the discussion to the question of what measures to adopt in the future against similar recurrences. L. Ginzberg, not wishing to find himself on the losing side, discovered that F. was right, and that ended the discussion.

As the meeting was about to adjourn, F. made reference to the correspondence in relation to the *New Haggadah* and stated that the matter would be further discussed at a meeting specially devoted to the issues raised in the correspondence.

What Is at Stake in the Controversy over the Chosen People

MAY 16, 1941

What, then, is really at stake in this controversy [over eliminating the concept of the chosen people from the liturgy]? First, the religious and ethical growth of the Jewish people. If those who happen to possess the power of the press or of an institution should succeed in strangling the sincere effort of any group of men and women to reformulate Jewish belief so as to bring it into conformity with what they conscientiously regard as the highest ethical and religious truth, the Jewish people would be condemned to spiritual stagnation. A second matter at stake is religious freedom in Jewish life. It is not the purpose of the Reconstructionist movement to legislate for the whole of Jewry. It merely wishes to formulate a philosophy and a program for those who find the existing programs and philosophies of Judaism unsatisfactory. If there are Jews who do not want their religious worship vitiated by sentiments that offend their reason or their moral sense, should they be restrained from obeying the dictates of their conscience? Is it a crime to exact of oneself absolute sincerity when addressing God? Does the future of Judaism depend upon that regimentation of beliefs and conviction which we condemn when practiced by other peoples? There was a time when no unity could be conceived without absolute uniformity. Totalitarianism is seeking to bring back that time into our own era. But we Jews who are the most tragic victims of totalitarianism should be the first to respect the principle of democracy and live up to the principle of the worth of individuality, which we proclaim in season and out of season.

Thinking Once Again of Resigning from JTS

MONDAY, MAY 19, 1941

I have done it! My position in the Seminary has become quite untenable. It is depriving me not only of peace of mind, without which I cannot do any creative thinking, but of the freedom to develop the philosophy and program of Reconstructionism. I have therefore taken a decisive step which I hope will lead to my emancipation. Last Saturday afternoon I went to see Stephen Wise and, after telling him about Finky's and Ginzberg's maneuverings to scotch the Reconstructionist movement, I asked him whether there was still a niche for me in his institution, the JIR [Jewish Institute of Religion]. He could not of course give me a definite answer, but he expressed satisfaction that I had applied to him when I did, because the amalgamation with the Hebrew Union College was liable to be consummated any day, and then it would have been too late perhaps to consider my application. (He did not use the terms "apply" and "application." These are my own terms.)

Last night I gave the principal address at the second annual meeting of the Reconstructionist Foundation, which took place at the synagogue of the SAJ. My subject was "The Doctrine of the Chosen People." I was pleasantly surprised at the large attendance—over 400—which the meeting drew. We had planned to have the meetings take place in the social hall, which seats only about 120 people, but we soon found that it could not possibly accommodate the number likely to come.

Woman Dies after Shaking Kaplan's Hand

SATURDAY, MAY 24, 1941

When the Sunday night meeting was over, a number of people felicitated me on my address. Among them was Mrs. Blume Lubetkin, the wife of Louis Lubetkin.[5] Immediately after she shook my hand, she sank to the floor. Three physicians who happened to be among the crowd, which by this time had virtually cleared out of the auditorium, were called back, but they could do nothing for her because she was dead.

The funeral took place in that same auditorium Tuesday morning.

Life has become so unreal these days that death seems to have lost its terrors.

Kaplan Defends His Haggadah at a Seminary Faculty Meeting

FRIDAY, JUNE 6, 1941

After the Seminary faculty at its meeting yesterday afternoon was through with its regular business, it took up the discussion of the matter of its correspondence with me [about the *New Haggadah*]. F. opened the discussion with some general remarks. He contrasted the wide variety of belief and practice within Judaism with the uniformity and authoritative character of whatever came forth from the Catholic Church. If the Seminary is to be the hub of American

---

5. Louis Lubetkin (1880–1964) was a business executive, community leader, and founding member of the SAJ.

Jewry (referring to a remark I had made at the recent convention of the Rabbinical Assembly), it must be in a position to present a united front (this expression is mine) and not create confusion in the minds of its graduates. (He didn't put it quite as emphatically, but in his mealy-mouthed way this is what he wanted to express.) Then he called upon Prof. [Louis] Ginzberg.

Ginzberg directed himself in his remarks specifically to me. He said in substance the following:

The Seminary was established mainly to foster knowledge of the past development of Judaism. It could not, however, avoid the task of affording guidance to its students in problems which had to do with the future. In all such matters it assumed considerable latitude in theory but not in practice. The Karaites[6] were fought bitterly by the Rabbamites[7] because they departed from the established practice. In contrast, there were always heretics who, because they conformed to the established code, were not molested. Conformity with the spirit of the Seminary implied subscribing to historical Judaism.[8] Historical Judaism does not permit any changes except from the standpoint of the law as it came down from the past. It is averse to any interpretation or modification of the law which comes from philosophical premises. We cannot permit majorities in congregations to decide what is permitted and what is not. The fact that certain manufacturers[9] approve of changes does not render them legitimate. That was the misfortune with the Reform movement. How, then, does anyone venture to lay hands on the liturgy? It has been sanctified by the ages. It is like a cathedral. If the windows of a cathedral need repair, only a skilled artist should undertake to repair them. He (Ginzberg) knows something about the liturgy. He should have been consulted and not young boys who are totally ignorant of such matters.

It looks as though this last statement contains the basic reason for this entire fuss. I understand that Ginzberg's refusal to support [Louis] Epstein's efforts to ease the Jewish law with regard to the *agunah* is due to the fact that Epstein had not consulted Ginzberg before he published his proposed measures. In a way he cannot be blamed for wanting to make us [aware] of all that learning which he has accumulated, but it is entirely his own fault that he is not consulted. He has never given the slightest indication of reckoning with the fact that we are living in a different world from the one in which what he calls Historical Judaism arose. Being

---

6. Karaite Judaism was a movement in the eighth century CE that rejected all authority outside the Hebrew scriptures. It was centered in present-day Iraq.

7. That is, the Rabbinites, traditional Jews who opposed the Karaites.

8. Historical Judaism was a nineteenth-century movement in Central Europe that originated in protests inaugurated against Reform Jews. It is an early name for Conservative Judaism, which emphasizes continuity with the past, although it is open to change.

9. "Certain manufacturers" may be a reference to the fact that a number of clothing manufacturers were strong supporters of Kaplan at the SAJ. Joseph Levy of Crawford Clothes was the most important.

fundamentally a skeptic, he has no confidence in the deliberate human effort to improve life. Unfortunately, the mess that some of the modern world improvers have made of life plays into the hands of Conservative skeptics like him.

After he was through, F. called on Prof. Marx, who merely reiterated in very general terms what Ginzberg had said. My turn came next.

I told the story of how I came to deal with the problems of the Jewish future in my teaching in the Seminary and the TI. The Seminary had omitted the teaching of the Pentateuch from its curriculum because it hoped in this way to evade the problems arising out of the documentary theory. Being faced with the task of teaching the men the interpretation of the Pentateuch, which I deemed central to Judaism, I had to evolve the functional approach which was compatible with the documentary theory. (With their permission, I quoted what [Israel] Friedlaender told me Schechter had said to him when he was being interviewed with regard to joining the Seminary faculty.[10] This remark is quoted in one of the earlier volumes of this journal.)[11]

From that point on I gave a brief résumé of my experiences with Adler and Ginzberg, who had indicated on different occasions their disapproval of what I was teaching and writing. But I had to shoulder the responsibility of grappling with problems of Jewish life which they could very well evade. Ginzberg was entirely wrong in believing that I catered to the wishes of "certain manufacturers." I was chiefly concerned in winning for Judaism the thinking men and women.

I seldom spoke with such calm and poise at a faculty meeting. As a rule, I always feel tense and uncomfortable when I am with them, even when the subject discussed does not pertain to me personally. This time, however, I felt as though I had the better of them and that they were on the defensive, and yet I said nothing that indicated an awareness of the ridiculous position in which they were maneuvering themselves with every remark that they made.

As illustrations of how glad I was to discuss with them these problems I mentioned two: one, the doctrine of Israel's election, and [the] other the assumption that liturgy must be uniform.

[Hillel] Bavli, who may be a good Hebrew versifier but who is all muddled up when it comes to analytic thinking, had to put his word in.[12] It did not

---

10. The Torah (Pentateuch) was not taught at the Seminary under Schechter. Friedlaender was prohibited from teaching it because he accepted the fundamentals of biblical criticism.

11. The remark Kaplan refers to is not in M. M. Kaplan, *Communings of the Spirit: The Journals of Mordecai M. Kaplan*, vol. 1, *1913–1934*, ed. Mel Scult (Detroit: Wayne State University Press and the Reconstructionist Press, 2001). Truth be told, I am not sure where it is in the early diary. The first volume of *Communings of the Spirit* contains only about 25 percent of the total material for the years covered by that volume.

12. Bavli spoke Hebrew as though he were reading poetry. As one of his students, I know he was very much appreciated at the Teachers Institute. The classes at the Teachers Institute and at the evening division, the Seminary College, were conducted in Hebrew.

take him long to expose his chauvinistic nationalism, which I at once punctured by saying that it was further removed from the traditional conception of Jewish nationhood than was my conception of nationalism.

I omitted in the above summary of my answer to Ginzberg the following: He had referred to the Seminary as representing Historical Judaism. In reply I pointed out that with the advent of Schechter, there took place a greater departure from what the Seminary originally stood for than the departure implied in my conception of Judaism, from what Ginzberg said the Seminary now stood for. I then told how shocked we students were at the time when Schechter made his first appearance at the old Seminary on a bright sunny Sabbath carrying a huge umbrella and books and papers. That action came under the category of violation of the Sabbath, which, according to Orthodox Judaism to which the Seminary under Morais had been dedicated, was punishable by stoning.

I also pointed out that I took issue with Ginzberg as to what we are to understand by Historical Judaism. His was a static conception. I preferred to view it dynamically as still in the process of development.

F. from his side and I from mine succeeded in keeping the discussion from becoming a free-for-all fight. F. deprecated some of the strong words used by Ginzberg, and I made them understand that I invited this kind of discussion.

After the meeting G. said to me that he had never intended to read me out of Judaism. What he said at the recent convention of the Rabbinical Assembly of Philadelphia had reference to Historical Judaism. Anyone who denies the doctrine of Israel's election reads himself out of Historical Judaism. Since Historical Judaism means for him traditional Judaism, his statement is entirely tautological.

Celebrations

MONDAY, JUNE 16, 1941

Wednesday (June 11) of last week was an extraordinarily happy day for me. In the morning I attended the graduation exercises at the U. campus, which Naomi [Kaplan's daughter] got her degree. There were virtually a replica of Columbia graduation exercises of the week before which I had also attended because Ira then got his Ph. degree [i.e., his PhD]. Both of these events together with the occasion of my 60th birthday were celebrated at a family gathering at our home on Wednesday night. Judith and Ira got up the enclosed "Ballad for American Jews," a take-off on the present popular "Ballad for Americans."

A Guide for Jewish Usage

MONDAY, JUNE 16, 1941

Some time ago the *Recon.* Edit. Board decided to hold a series of sessions during the period of June 10–20 for the purpose of discussing the formulation of a

"Guide for Jewish Usage."[13] We met last week on Tuesday, Thursday, and Friday. Our fourth session took place this morning. . . .

As was to be expected, we have had to make clear to ourselves some of the fundamental principles of Reconstructionism. The specific purpose of the sessions has so far been carried out to the extent that we have discussed quite in detail the observance of the Sabbath.

Two problems emerged from the discussions: (1) How to reconcile the two purposes of Reconstructionism, that of stressing the totality and unity of Jewish life with that of formulating specific ideas and patterns of conduct which, while they may satisfy those who are dissatisfied with the traditional ideas and patterns, are certain to arouse opposition and to cause division. This is a problem of strategy; (2) How to reconcile the two purposes of Reconstructionism in dealing with tradition, that of maintaining the continuity of Jewish life and thought and that of incorporating new truth and new ethical lines of action. This calls for the setting up of norms of interpretation.

An interesting classification of folkways was that suggested by Milton Steinberg (who was prevented on account of illness from attending two out of the four sessions but who otherwise has been an active participant). He said that folkways may be (1) irrational in form and in content, (2) rational in content and irrational in form, and (3) rational in form and rational in content. This suggestion came in the course of the discussion on whether or not to permit smoking on the Sabbath.

The one disturbing factor at these sessions is the presence of [Ben Zion] Bokser. He has been, as Rabbi [Charles I.] Hoffman put it, more of an

---

13. The *Guide* has an important but complicated history. The earliest efforts were issued in a series of articles titled "Toward a Guide for Ritual Usage" in the *Reconstructionist* in the issues for November 14, 1941, December 12, 1941, and January 9, 1942. In Kaplan's *Future of the American Jew* (New York: Macmillan, 1948) there is a chapter titled "Toward a Guide for Ritual Usage" that deals with ritual in a general way but does not outline specific recommendations. The most complete guide is *A Guide to Jewish Ritual* (New York: Reconstructionist Press, 1962). Ira Eisenstein wrote the introduction. It is not clear who actually wrote this pamphlet, though of course Kaplan would have had final approval. For the most recent efforts to offer a guide to religious practice, see David Teutsch, *A Guide to Jewish Practice* (Wyncote, PA: Reconstructionist Press, 1989). Teutsch's most recent work—*A Guide to Jewish Practice: Shabbat and Holidays*, vol. 1 (Wyncote PA: Reconstructionist College Press, 2011)—supersedes and will eventually incorporate all the previous guides. The format of this most recent book is extremely provocative, with a central text on ritual and ethical issues together with reactions by selected rabbis and laypersons within the Jewish community. Teutsch's previous contributions to the Guide series were published in 2000 (*Kashrut*), 2005 (*Bioethics and Tzedakah*), 2006 (*Ethics of Speech*), 2007 (*Organizational Ethics and Economic Justice*), 2009 (*Community, Gemilut Hesed, and Tikun Olam*), and 2010 (*Family and Sexual Ethics and Everyday Spirituality*). Rabbi Richard Hirsh, former executive director of the Reconstructionist Rabbinical Association, has edited a booklet titled *Welcoming Children*. For more information, see www.rrc.edu/ethics-center/publications/a-guide-jewish-practice-welcoming-children.

obstructionist than a Reconstructionist. The position he has been defending at the sessions has been that we should retain the statement concerning Israel's superiority over the other nations, because it may be reinterpreted to mean that in the particular area of life occupied by Israel, Israel has achieved a degree of excellence unequaled by other people in that same area. Despite the utter nonsense of that interpretation, he kept on defending it with a sophistry that tried the patience of the rest of us. By the same token, he would object to the elimination of the prayer for the restoration of the Temple and the animal sacrifices. They could be made to mean, according to him, something entirely acceptable to us. All in all, he has been a nuisance ever since he has been with us. If we have permitted him to go along with us, it has been because we have ascribed to him a certain nuisance value. We have been afraid of our becoming ingrown and lacking in the stimulus of challenge, and we have believed that his presence would guard us against such danger. But his general bearing toward Reconstructionism has been that of the Rasha[14] in the Haggadah who keeps on saying "to you" and excluding himself from the generality of our consensus in matters both practical and theoretical. There is also the possibility of his acting as a conscious or unconscious stooge of Finky's. For that reason, nothing would please us better than if he were to ease himself out of our company.

Germany Declares War on Russia

TUESDAY, JUNE 24, 1941

Two days ago Germany declared war on Russia, and the experts are already reported to be discussing whether it will take her four weeks or three months to complete the job of conquering Russia and how she would be able to hold and consolidate her conquests. Possibly mankind is living over again what the population in Europe experienced when the Huns ravaged it. But never in the entire past were there such rapid and such large-scale reshuffling of facts, adherence, and policies. All the ideologies which have been developed in democratic countries to counter the communal-pact which was in force till the day before yesterday will have to be scrapped. Willy-nilly human beings will have to learn, if they can, to make subtle distinctions, such as those between fascist totalitarianism and communist totalitarianism, between democracy and fascism, on the one hand, and democracy and communism on the other, etc., ad infinitum. In the meantime Hitler, who has the predominance in weight of metal and the highly mechanized organization of peace and war industries, is sweeping everything before him.

If most of us go on working and striving as if there will still be a world worth living in, it is because the will to live gets the better of our calculations and our fears. With conditions so unpredictable, despite the fact that in each case so

---

14. Rasha is the evil son in the Passover liturgy who takes himself out of the community.

far it has always been the greatest evil which has managed to be the unforeseen, it is natural to hope that some unforeseen good will emerge. That is the way I feel about Russia's being forced to fight Germany. By the same token that she proved Napoleon's undoing, she will in all likelihood prove Hitler's nemesis.

In the meantime, new horrors are undoubtedly being visited upon the Jews who are in the direct path of the brutal German armies. If we were to do what we should, we ought to indicate in some way that we share with those Jews the hellish agonies through which they are passing. We ought to deny ourselves the comforts of life and fast and pray and determine to go on living and fighting for those ideals which alone give any sense to the Jewish tragedy. But it would be nothing less quixotic even to suggest such measures. Hence we go on living like dumb brutes until our time comes to be taken to the house of slaughter.

Kaplan Under Sustained Attack at the Seminary

JUNE 24, 1941

It seems incongruous, after realizing what a new tornado has struck the world in the recent break between Germany and Russia, to be recording the trivialities of one's own life. Yet we go on eating and drinking and leisuring and sleeping, so why not proceed with noting down the things that matter in one's own life?

The war of nerves which Finky with the aid of Ginzy [Louis Ginzberg] has been carrying on against me since I have come back from Palestine is also spreading over a wider front. First it was the Friedlaender classes,[15] then the Teachers Institute, then the *Reconstructionist* campaign, then the Haggadah, and now it is the courses I'm giving in Homiletics.

Today was the second of the third-degree torture sessions held for my "benefit" by the Seminary Faculty. It was a continuation of the one that was held a few weeks ago. After the routine business of the Faculty meeting was over, F. [Finkelstein] began gropingly by suggesting that some method be found for going on with the discussions. Ginzberg, ignoring the suggestion, addressed himself directly to me. He wanted me to answer the following two points: (1) In the first place, he understood me to say that I considered it my duty to teach the students at the Seminary practically all the subjects of the curriculum—Talmud, Bible, History, and whatnot. How is it possible for one person to master all those subjects? Even he wouldn't think of teaching a subject like Bible. (2) Secondly, reverting to the Haggadah and the implied freedom to make changes in doctrine and practice, he wanted to know what was to prevent me from going still further and introducing a Sunday-Sabbath or, with [Joseph] Klausner, declaring Jesus to have been a Jewish prophet. As a matter of fact, one student this year actually preached a sermon on a New Testament text. This was a deliberate perversion of

---

15. Adult education classes at the JTS named after Israel Friedlaender.

the truth. [Abraham] Winokur, who took as his text *al tadun et haverkha . . .* [Heb., "Do not judge your neighbor (until you have stood in his place)"],[16] stated in his introductory remarks that in contrast with the New Testament teaching that we should not judge, the Rabbis gave sounder advice in that they said *al tadun et haverkha* [Heb.]. We have, for example, the age old belief in the establishment of *malkhut bet david* [Heb., the Kingdom of David]. How did I take it upon myself to elide it from the Grace after Meals? Again he repeated the statement about a certain person who wanted to know from him whether I advocated the abolition of circumcision because I omitted the reference to it. Of course G. [Ginzberg] told him I still believe in it, but that did not alter the impression that the Seminary tolerated one of its Faculty members to publish a kind of Haggadah which broke with tradition. There must be a distinction between breaking with tradition and continuing a tradition. He wanted to know where I drew the line and what common ground there could be between me and the rest of the Faculty. Once more he alluded to the distinction I drew between Kashrut in the home and Kashrut outside the home.

In my reply I stated the following: I denied what G. has ascribed to me, giving the impression that I voiced the opinion of the faculty. As for my saying that I deemed it my duty to teach or interpret all the subjects of the curriculum, of course that was too absurd to require refutation. I may be wrong in my views, but I still have some common sense. What I did say was that I have to bear the responsibility of guiding the men in what they are to preach and therefore have to deal with the future. In order, however, to have that future be in line of continuity with the past, I find myself compelled to do with the other subjects of the curriculum what the one who teaches philosophy has to do with the extant sciences. That does not mean that the philosopher presumes to be a master of all the sciences. Some, of course, would deny philosophy any legitimate place in the organization of thought; but most thinkers do accord it a place, due to the fact that the mind demands a unification of the sciences.

Concretely speaking, it is necessary for me to get the students to realize that there are preachable values to the Bible apart from the particular questions dealt with in the scientific study of the Bible. It takes them a long time to acquire that kind of approach. This is what I meant by saying that I had occasion to touch upon their other studies.

As for the second point raised by G., I pointed out that throughout all the years I have been associated with the Seminary I have openly taken issue with the position of the Historical school, which does not permit itself to legitimize any change until after it has been adopted by catholic Israel. The only way to meet the future is to introduce whatever changes are likely to produce a more intensive Jewish life. This does not mean that I am averse to having specific norms

---

16. This statement is from the *Ethics of the Fathers* 2:5.

which would indicate how far we may go on changing without imperiling Jewish life and continuity.

However, as to the difference between breaking with tradition and continuing it, I definitely took issue with Ginzberg. He stresses the point that the practice is everything and that any deliberate departure from the standard ritual or liturgy is a break with tradition. I contend that the break takes place the moment we stop believing what the traditionalist believed. As soon as we find ourselves incapable of subscribing to the supernatural origin of the Torah, the restoration of the sacrificial cult, the advent of a personal messiah, we have broken with tradition.

Translating the changed belief into changed practice is not altogether unknown within the Seminary circles. The United Synagogue has published a special Machzor for the Conservative Jews. The only difference, to be sure, is that in place of *she-sham na-ase lefanekha* [Heb., "There we will offer before (the Lord)"], it read *she-sham asu* [Heb., "There we offered . . ."].[17] Though this change is not followed through consistently, it is sufficient to indicate that the principle of deliberate change has begun to penetrate even the Seminary.

G. had mentioned that there ought to be some set of principles which should govern us when dealing with such problems. I agreed that it would be a fine thing for those who have the ability to formulate such principles to shoulder the responsibility for doing so. But unfortunately, after more than half a century of existence, Historical Judaism has not even made a beginning in that direction.

[Saul] Lieberman, who has been added only recently to the Faculty, found it necessary to have his say, and to question me how I came to publish the Haggadah without consulting Ginzberg, Marx, and Finkelstein. Am I not aware that I am hurting the reputation and influence of the Seminary with the masses?

The impudence of this recent arrival, taking me to task for jeopardizing the interests of the Seminary, was only equalled by [Hillel] Bavli's outburst against me, charging me with secularizing Judaism in addition to destroying the ancient forms which constitute its pageantry. Yet I held myself in check and tried to reply calmly to their insults.

But Finky, realizing that I was getting the better of the argument, started a new line of attack. He let the cat out of the bag when he said that "the main cause of all the rancor" was the nature of the sermons delivered every Sabbath in the Seminary synagogue by the students.[18] He described them as consisting of "half-truths and half-heresies." His own daughter Hadassah had sworn off

---

17. These passages refer to the traditional language of the liturgy, which states "We look forward to the restoration of sacrifices," which was changed in Conservative prayer books to "We offered . . ." (i.e., offerings were made in the past and sacrifices will not be renewed).

18. Students prepared trial sermons in Kaplan's homiletics class and then delivered them in the Seminary synagogue each Sabbath.

attending the services because she could not bear to listen to those sermons. He could not see of what good such sermons were. They could not be preached before any congregation to which the students applied for positions. They emphasized what Jews cannot and should not believe instead of what Jews should believe. This diatribe of Finky's was followed up by Ginzberg's, who mentioned the sermon which dealt with the belief in the world-to-come as having been particularly offensive. "Why should Jews be told," said G., "that they don't have to believe in personal immortality? Why preach such ideas altogether?"

Even this outbreak of Finky's didn't cause me to lose my temper. I merely said I should like to have the Faculty read the sermons and see whether they bear out the charges made by F. He quickly took up my suggestion and appointed Gordis, Greenberg, and Arzt[19] as a committee to study the sermons delivered by the men this year.

This ordeal lasted from about 11:00 to 1:00.

Immediately after lunch I phoned Stephen S. Wise [president of the JIR] to ask him whether he had any news for me.[20] He asked me whether I was speaking from the Seminary, because he didn't want to be overheard by what he described as the "Seminary Gestapo." He just got through, he said, reading a review in a European periodical of Finky's *The Pharisees*,[21] in which F. got a lambasting. As for news, he promised to call me up on Thursday afternoon after he came back from the convention of the CCAR [Central Conference of American Rabbis].

Kaplan Under Attack

WEDNESDAY, JUNE 25, 1941

This campaign that F. is waging against me is not only a war of nerves but it is also an ideological war. Unfortunately, however, human nature is so constituted that the ego is always implicated in ideologies. It would be intolerant of me to blame F. for the distaste he has toward Reconstructionism, although here again I find it impossible to clear him of the guilt of intellectual dishonesty in that he insists on the new dualism that has emerged in the sphere of religion. Formerly, the new dualism was between faith and reason, revelation and philosophy. Now it is between what you believe and what you say you believe. He and

---

19. Robert Gordis was a member of the faculty. Simon Greenberg and Max Arzt were members of the Seminary administration. Kaplan related to me that he had hoped Gordis would be more supportive at this moment.

20. On the long-term relationship between Kaplan and Wise, see Mel Scult, *Judaism Faces the Twentieth Century: A Biography of Mordecai M. Kaplan* (Detroit: Wayne State University Press, 1993), 268–79.

21. Louis Finkelstein, *The Pharisees: The Sociological Background of Their Faith*, 2 vols. (Philadelphia: Jewish Publication Society of America, 1938; repr. 1962).

Ginzberg et al. have long ceased to believe in a personal God, in a supernatural Torah, in the historicity of the miracles, in the resurrection of the dead, in personal immortality, and in a personal Messiah. Yet they assume that the way to teach and preach religion today is as though the Jews still continued believing in these dogmas. They resent bitterly my attempt to work out a Jewish ideology that frankly recognizes the denial of those dogmas and that seeks to reinterpret them from a functional point of view, thereby identifying them with some of the universally accepted spiritual beliefs of our day. This resentment is perhaps in part due to an understandable resistance bred of long habituation in traditional patterns of life and thought. But it is also due, no doubt, to a feeling that with all their gains either in scholarly prestige or in administrative power, they do not affect that actual thinking of most of the men who are trained in the Seminary. This is what I mean by the element of the ego being mixed up with ideology. Theirs is the dog in the manger policy. Because they have nothing to do with the current problems of Jewish life, they resent my attempting to do so. Week in and week out they hear the students trying to articulate the ideas they learn in my class. I can imagine how being reminded constantly of their own failure irritates and provokes Finky and Ginzy. Throughout this last year the students who preached would tell me about their being assailed by F. for having made some statements that displeased him. Every time a student showed a tendency to make use of some phrase or concept typical of Reconstructionism, I would plead with him to avoid using it because it would be like waving a red flag before a bull. This explains the malignity of F.'s campaign against me.

There is not the least question in my mind that he would welcome my resignation. On the other hand, I cannot see how I can continue teaching at the Seminary. With Finky's increasingly watchful opposition and with his determination to combat all I represent, there is really nothing left for me to do in that institution. If F. and company succeed in purging the Seminary of me or in crippling the Reconstructionist movement, that would mean an additional nail in the coffin of Judaism.

The Atlantic Charter

THURSDAY, AUGUST 14, 1941

I have just heard Atlee's statement from London giving the result of the conference held at sea between Pres. Roosevelt and Prime Minister Churchill.[22] The peace aims which he read off sounded millennial. Perhaps mankind will really get the fabled honey out of the carcass of the Aryan beast. But it certainly is a great moment in the history of the world. Despite the gloom which envelops

---

22. This meeting defined the aims of the Allies, although the United States was not yet officially in the war.

human life at the present time, it is a privilege to have been present at an event that presages so definitely a better future, and out of which there has emerged a purpose worth living and fighting for. For this privilege I thank God.

Basic Principles of Reconstructionism

SUNDAY, AUGUST 24, 1941

About two weeks ago I discussed with Ira the question of whether Reconstructionism should be the philosophy of a school of thought or the program of a party in Jewish life alongside the existing parties or denominations. We agreed that for the sake of clarity and effectiveness, it is advisable to steer the movement in the direction of a party rather than a school. This led to my suggestion that we formulate once again the Guiding Principles of Reconstructionism. The following is the outcome of our discussions:

1. The Jewish people must preserve its historic sense of national solidarity, but it must reconstruct that solidarity to fit its need of being integrated into the life of other nations. To accomplish this, the Jewish people must do the following:
   a. Accept the state of dispersion among other nations as due to persist into the discernible future.
   b. Reinterpret its nationhood so as to render it capable of being hyphenated with the nationhood of other peoples.
   c. Continue the upbuilding of Palestine as its primary national task.
   d. Deal with all problems of defense and relief in a spirit of mutual responsibility.
2. Religion is the element in Jewish life which alone can give spiritual significance to Jewish nationhood and point the way to individual salvation. In order that it may function effectively, religion must be constantly reinterpreted in the light of ever increasing knowledge of the truth, and enriched by the creation of new content and forms.
3. Judaism must make for preoccupation with the ethical aspect of all social relationship, especially the economic and the family, with a view to raising the ethical standards of Jewish and general life.
4. The form of Jewish organization in America should be the Federation of Jewish Communities, composed of democratically organized local communities of the various cities throughout the land serving the physical, recreational, cultural, and spiritual needs of their constituents. All activities of the Jewish community must be directed toward the twofold purpose of (a) providing for the needs of the Jews, and (b) perpetuating and enriching the distinctive life of the Jewish people. Affiliation with one's local Jewish community must constitute an earnest [dedication to] Jewish loyalty.

5. Jewish education must constitute a basic activity in the lives of Jews from their early childhood on. It should foster a knowledge and appreciation of the Jewish past, a sense of common destiny among all Jews, and a desire to participate to the fullest degree in the present life of the Jewish people.

6. The arts constitute an indispensable means of Jewish self-expression and must be encouraged. The esthetic aspect of Judaism should include music, poetry, prose, drama, painting, dance, sculpture, and architecture.

Predicate Theology

THURSDAY, AUGUST 28, 1941

The fog of vagueness and confusion which envelops most of the affirmative concerning God and self would lift if we realized that the fundamental fallacy in our thinking about those two concepts is that we tend to treat them as subjects instead of as predicates. If instead of saying "God is one, omniscient, activity minus potentiality, omnipotent, etc.," the medievalist thinkers had said "oneness is God," "omniscience is God," etc., their efforts to render existence intelligible would take on meaning. Their way of stating their ideas seems on the whole . . . irrelevant, because it is apparent that in their pretentious structures of reasoning they only arrive at conclusions which they implied in their very premises. They are the master violators of *petito principia*.[23] If we come to these concepts with a fresh and open mind—which is something not even Descartes succeeded in doing but which we will ultimately have to learn to do—we cannot help noting that we have no direct knowledge either of self or of God. Since, however, we use these terms, it can only be because we attach them to areas of immediate experience. But before we can answer that question, we must have specific knowledge of the areas of immediate experience which evoke those concepts. Such knowledge, if organized, would give rise to the history of the God idea and of the idea of personality. Such a history, however, was impossible so long as men labored under the assumption that the God they know and believed in was the only true God, while the gods that other men knew or believed in were either not gods or nonentities altogether. Its rise was further prevented by the medieval approach which departed from naive religion in deliberately making the idea of God the subject of all its judgments. By doing so, it necessarily took pains to conceive God in accordance with what it regarded as absolute truth. It was therefore forced to treat all other notions as false. Naive religion claimed that the manifestations of divine power which its adherents experienced were without parallel, as did Jewish religion, Christianity, and Islam. Such claim justifies the denial or disparagement of other gods as absolutely false. That was because naive religion

---

23. *Petito principia* is begging the question, that is, assuming the initial point, and is a type of logical fallacy in which a statement refers to its own assertion to prove the assertion.

identified certain specific beings as God, either YHWH, Christ, or Allah. Likewise, Akhenaton, who identified the sun as the only god, could well pronounce the other deities illusory. But the philosophic conception of God differs radically from the naive conception in that it does not identify God with any one being. Whereas in all naive religion God is predicate, philosophy has tried to make God the subject. God is omnipotent, omniscient. The Shema reads, "YHWH is our God." The Israelites on Carmel cried out, "YHWH is God." YHWH represented a definite area of experience for the Jews as Christ for the Christians. Each called his particular area of experience "God." But the philosopher or theologian treats the God concept as subject. In doing so, he covertly identifies God with an area of experience. The moment he attaches a predicate to it, he merely brings out like the magician what he already has up his sleeve. It is this sleight of hand of the medieval thinker which has become boring, now that we have become too mature to enjoy it.

Transcendence and Immanence

AUGUST 28, 1941

The emphasis upon transcendence, which characterizes both naive and philosophic conceptions of God, is motivated by the intuition that the life goals are never achieved, that they are always in advance of the actual, however far the actual may be ahead of the past. The point that Niebuhr continually dwells on (one that I believe he took over from Barth) is that the ideals of ethics and religion can never be achieved in history. This, according to him, is the basis of the sense of sin. We no sooner achieve in solving one problem than two arise in its place. This fact simply means that there are no limits to human growth or to the abundance of human life. Salvation is not static; hence the power that makes for salvation is transcendent. This principle applies in a smaller scale to humanity as a whole and in toto to the self or personality of the individual, since both humanity and personality are the two life goals which with the life goal—God—constitute in their dynamic attainment the criteria of salvation.

Needs and Ethics and Fulfillment

OCTOBER 13, 1941

In human beings, with memory and imagination and abstraction enabling them to contemplate modification in the functioning of their own innate needs and native capacities as well as in their given natural and social environment, the will to live expresses itself through acquired needs. But many, if not most, of the acquired needs are of the wrong kind, in that they either interfere with the normal functioning of the innate needs, etc., or artificially augment their functioning to such a degree as to lead to the disintegration of personality and of society. The problem of human character and conduct is how to harmonize the inborn with the acquired needs. This is essentially the problem of soterics.[24]

WEDNESDAY, OCTOBER 15, 1941

The goals of self-preservation and the perpetuation of the species belong to the final values; the former develop the value of "selfhood," [and] the other into that of "humanity." In traditional religion the use of self-preservation has given rise to the belief in bodily resurrection and personal immortality. In a modern soteric system the urge to self-preservation would involve, in addition to living a healthy, dignified, and creative life, also self-identification with a group which is expected to live on indefinitely and with humanity as a whole, whose eternity is a goal of the individual's life. Moreover, to the extent that the individual achieves both these goals, he identifies himself with the reality of godhood or the Power that makes for maximum life.

In the sub-human creatures both self-preservation and perpetuation of the species are striven for un-self-consciously, on the level of functional needs. By very reason of that fact, they are very much more precarious, and even when secured, they fail to give rise to the entire cluster of acquired needs that constitute self-consciousness and civilization. Like all needs, the cluster of acquired needs introduces a corresponding cluster of frustrations and conflicts, but that only means that self-consciousness has introduced more life, for life is inherently "a series of needs, frustrations, and the activities directed toward overcoming them."

A need is a physical or mental state of disequilibrium. It leads to activity called drive in order that the equilibrium be restored. The object which, when attained, restores the equilibrium is value. The drive expresses itself as greater sensitivity and modifiability of conduct and quicker learning. Both modifiability and learning refer to the substitution of one means for another in the attainment of objectives. Repetition of what is learned forms habit. Once the habit is established, it becomes a need and furnishes drives on its own account.

Functional needs may be divided into viscerogenci and psychologenci (H. A. Murray and others, *Explorations in Personality*, 76). Viscerogenic needs are those which arise from the bodily tissues. Psychogenic [needs] are those which arise from the mental life and behavior.

---

24. Soterics is the name that Kaplan gave to his ideology. It comes from the Greek root *soter*, which means "to save." He intended his ideology to be scientific, like physics, so he called it soterics. The term was used in the 1930s and 1940s.

More on Human Needs and Salvation

THURSDAY, OCTOBER 16, 1941

The two outstanding facts about human drives (of which there are infinitely more than sub-human) are (1) they continually meet with *frustration*—they are blocked by external factors—and (2) they are continually in mutual *conflict*—they are blocked by one another.

The purpose of all social and political ordering is to minimize the occasions of frustrations and conflict. The purpose of all educational disciplines like religion, ethics, etc., is to develop in individuals and groups not only the art of minimizing occasions of frustration and conflict but also the arts of tolerating frustration or otherwise reacting adequately to them (see *The Dynamics of Human Behavior*, P. Symonds, Ch. I) ("frustration tolerance") and resolving conflicts. All social and political ordering and educational disciplines operate with formal values. But educational disciplines go a step further. They introduce final values in dealing with frustration and conflicts.

The life story told in *The Good Fight* is an illustration of expertness in "frustration tolerance." While the author does not employ the conventional religious terminology to explain what conception of life or what final values stimulated him to fight down shame, envy, and self-pity, he very definitely indicates that it was the conviction of life's inherent worthwhileness which impelled him to keep up the struggle against his handicaps. As he says, he does not care who the author of the book of life is, but he finds the contents of the book intrinsically fascinating. To conceive of life as a continuous story that not only makes sense but that outdoes any human classic, is to assume that it has an author who gives it its meaning. This is fundamentally to believe in God.

The operation of formal values in resolving conflicts can best be understood in the light of what we know concerning what happens when there is a conflict between needs or drives. Percival M. Symonds[25] in *Dynamics of Behavior*, Ch. II, classifies the methods of meeting conflict in the following way: (1) One method is to fight one's way through so as to achieve both ends. In the majority of genuine conflicts this results in failure. It is like trying to be in two places at the same time. (2) A second method is to run away from the conflict (phantasy, withdrawal). (3) A third method, and one which is the most common, is to repress one arm of the conflict and allow the other to have free expression. "Usually this method of handling conflict is satisfactory, if the outer frustrations are not too great. If, however, the outer frustrations become too intense, an individual may not be able to manage his repressed tendencies. They may press for some form of outward expression and the conflict itself then becomes intense and hard

---

25. Percival Symonds (1893–1960) was a psychologist who wrote about methods of projective testing.

to manage." (I quote this in full because of the remarkable way in which it explains the conduct of the assimilated Jew who comes up against anti-Semitism.) (4) A fourth method is some sort of compromise. This is the neurotic method. An attempt is made to satisfy both demands without satisfying either. It is meaningless behavior in that it is not appropriate to the situation. This is due to the fact that it is a conflict of a conscious with a sub-conscious drive. (5) Finally there is the integrated solution. In this case both drives in the conflict are fully in view in consciousness. "The individual must be in a position to weigh their relative values, to see to what extent through modification of them or through substitute gratification, values in each may be to a degree realized. . . . The integrated solution cannot be achieved until the unconscious arm of the conflict is brought up to clear view in awareness so that it can be dealt with on the basis of reality."

In the light of the foregoing, it is apparent that the first four methods of meeting conflicts are, or result in, formal disvalues, and that only the fifth method is or results in formal values like justice, loyalty, decency, etc.

The formal values . . . are part of a culture or social heritage or the generalization of successful integrations of past conflicts. These generalizations are intended to serve in the resolution of subsequent conflicts.

There are numerous situations in life when the formal needs or drives are themselves in conflict. The attempt to resolve such conflict independently of the functional drives or needs that are involved is responsible for most of the ethical casuistry which usually ends up in sophistry.

The weakness of the Humanist interpretation of the "final needs or drives" is nowhere so clearly expressed as in the Humanist statement of those needs or drives contained in M. C. Otto's *Things and Ideals*, Ch. XII.[26] I shall first quote what he has to say concerning the "Hunger for Cosmic Support" and then summarize the interpretation he gives to it.

"There is a rock fact of human nature," he says (p. 283)

> against which the waives of rhetoric and logic dash in vain; a rock fact which after all the proofs and disproofs have fallen back into the sea of words from which they came, stands forth the clearer for the spray dashed over it. What is this stubborn fact? It is the fact that human beings refuse to be psychically alone in the universe; the fact that they demand that somehow there shall be a Power at the heart of things which shall not let them suffer ultimate defeat, let appearances be what they may.

He comes to this conclusion after having shown that despite the repeated refutations of the conception of God by the succession of discoveries and

---

26. M. C. Otto, *Things and Ideals* (New York: Henry Holt, 1924).

the widening of man's horizons, that conception is reborn in some new avatar time and time again. But instead of drawing the logical conclusion from that fact, he is led off on a tangent by falling into the well-worn groove of thinking to the effect that the hunger for cosmic support is purely a matter of feeling. He indulges in an eloquent passage on the indispensability of the emotions. "The logically best society," he goes on to say,

> may turn up its nose at the tang and piquancy of emotion; may attempt to act upon exclusively intellectual quarter out of its reach, where no weeds of fallacy nor wild flowers of fancy shall be permitted to grow, where syllogistic calm and order shall reign unchallenged. Life will overflow any such endeavor and be the richer for it. But to recognize the inevitability and worth of feeling is not to admit that everything that is longed for is there to be had. And the fact that man naturally objects to being quite alone in the universe and thus craves fellowship with a great Guarantor of his interests and his personal continuance, is no proof that anything corresponding to the object of his longing exists. It may rather testify to the vestigial remains of an elemental hunger brought down from the dim past, and transfigured by all manner of accretions through institutions and customs.

In the first place, his accounting for the hunger for cosmic support as a feeling that enriches life is entirely gratuitous. He might as well dilate on the enrichment of life through the hunger for nourishment. He fails to realize that life is hunger and that, in the case of human life, that hunger includes the hunger for cosmic support. Secondly, to argue that this hunger for cosmic support is "vestigial remains of an elemental hunger brought down from the dim past and transfigured by all manner of accretions etc." is to fly in the face of the facts which fill the preceding part of the chapter, to the effect that, despite the destruction of all those accretions, the elemental hunger turns out to be what is still appears, a hunger for cosmic support. To introduce at this point Gilbert Murray's conjecture that this yearning may in origin be "the groping of a lonely-souled gregarious animal to find its herd or its herd leader in the great spaces between the stars," is to display a hunger for authoritative support for a weak argument. As a matter of fact, one might even grant that "in origin" man's hunger for cosmic support expresses itself as a "groping to find the herd or herd-leader," and yet maintain that, with the ripening of intelligence, man comes to realize that it is cosmic support as such that he really yearns for. The development of self-consciousness from consciousness is also represented by the development from "groping after the herd and herd leader" to "yearning after cosmic support." In all instances of development from consciousness to self-consciousness, we take for granted that the revelations of the self-consciousness are a closer approximation to reality than those of mere consciousness. Why not take the same for granted in the case of the advance from the "groping" after the herd to the "yearning" for cosmic support, that the latter is more likely to approximate the truth?

But the Humanist interpretation is at its weakest when it assumes that the recognition that the yearning for cosmic support is only the groping for the support of the herd would lead to improvement in human life and conduct. And strange to say, he quotes a passage from Dewey which does not altogether jibe with the argument in hand. "God (*sic!*) only knows," says Dewey, "how many of the sufferings of life are due to the belief that the natural scene and operation of our life are lacking in ideal import, and to the consequent tendency to flee to the lacking ideal factors to some other world inhabited exclusively by ideals." Dewey is talking here of the Platonic dichotomy between real and ideal. What has that to do with the yearning for cosmic support?

To accept the "stern condition of being psychically alone in all the reach of space and time" is, according to Otto, "the challenge of these supreme times." "The hope of a new world is alive today," he goes on to say, "in millions of hearts the world around. May we not take courage from past achievement?" But we may well ask, "Does not that past achievement owe something at least to man's past habit of trying to satisfy his hunger for cosmic support, a hunger which Otto himself has shown to be irrepressible?"

Kaplan Contra Adler

OCTOBER 16, 1941

With the same mail that brought me the above-mentioned letter came another reminder of how well nigh impossible it is to live up to one's ideals. I refer to the copy of the *Congress Weekly* (Oct. 3, [19]41),[27] containing the Theodore Lewis review of Cyrus Adler's *I Have Considered the Days*.[28] It is a frank and honest description of that book, which should never have been published. Besides being inherently infantile in form and content, it reveals the inner rottenness of American Jewish life. That a man of such limited understanding and imagination should have been entrusted with ranking leadership is a stigma on the

---

27. The *Congress Weekly* was a publication of the American Jewish Congress.

28. *I Have Considered the Days* was Cyrus Adler's memoir. Adler, in addition to being president of the Seminary, was also president of Dropsie College at the same time. He was quite active in Jewish life and involved in a whole host of organizations. On Adler, see Cyrus Adler, *Cyrus Adler: Selected Letters*, 2 vols., ed. Ira Robinson (Philadelphia: Jewish Publication Society of America, 1985). Kaplan's negative attitude toward Adler in evidence here may be due in part to Adler's lack of knowledge of Jewish sources. Kaplan and perhaps others thought that Adler was a tool of the wealthy German Jews, including Jacob Schiff, who supported the Seminary. Most of the faculty did not support Adler when he became acting president on the death of Solomon Schechter. Most perhaps thought that Louis Ginzberg or Israel Friedlaender should have succeeded Schechter, not Adler.

collective life of American Jewry. The *Reconstructionist* magazine should have been the first to debunk that man, in the interests of an effective Jewish leadership for which it is supposed to be contending. Yet when Theodore Lewis, who is a member of the Editorial Board, asked whether we would publish his review of the book, I said no. If I had allowed that review to appear in the *Reconstructionist*, I would have been called an ingrate and a traitor and whatnot, and would probably have had to resign from the Seminary.

Although I owe it to Adler that I have been allowed to teach in the Seminary, he is also responsible for the ill will which most of my colleagues and members of the Seminary Board bear toward me. It is he who has gotten them to think of me as a radical and a secular nationalist. The fact is that when I credit Adler with having made it possible for me to remain at the Seminary, I am aware that it was not some profound recognition on his part of the value of what I had to give to the students that prompted him to let me alone, but rather that he was so ununderstanding and uninterested in the basic problems of Jewish life and religion that he didn't realize what I was trying to accomplish. Fundamentally, what decided him to let me alone was the cliche about academic freedom, which he honored too much to start proceedings against me. Now that he is gone, Ginzy would like to see me out.

11

October 17, 1941–December 30, 1941

On the Soul

FRIDAY, OCTOBER 17, 1941

The religious attitude toward life places as much emphasis upon the belief in the human soul as it does upon the belief in God. Therefore, in challenging the religious attitude, men challenge the belief in the human soul by the same token that they challenge the belief in God. It is not surprising that that should be the case, since, as the analysis of the belief in the human soul will show, the affirmation that man possesses a soul is the correlative of the belief that the cosmos is divine or possesses godhood. (Examples of challenge to belief in the human soul are given by M. C. Otto in *Things and Ideals*, 1924).[1]

To meet the challenge to the belief in human soul, it is necessary in the first place to note the various formulations of that belief since it was first held. To begin with, that belief was based upon the inference from dreams that every one had a ghost-like double, shade, or phantom. . . . Plotinus contributed largely to the dualism which marked the religious thinking of Western mankind for centuries. Descartes stated that the soul dwelt in the pineal gland. Since animals did not possess a soul, they were mere mechanisms. Modern psychology began by denying the existence of the soul and has ended up in denying the reality of consciousness. The saying goes that it first lost its soul, then its mind, and finally its consciousness. Laplace[2] claimed that he searched the heavens with his telescope and did not find God. He claimed there was no need for the hypothesis of God's existence to understand the universe. The psychologist studies the behavior of

---

1. M. C. Otto, *Things and Ideals* (New York: Henry Holt, 1924). Max Otto (1876–1968) was a philosopher and a Unitarian humanist who tended in his thought toward the nontheistic. He was a dean at the University of Wisconsin.

2. Marquis de Laplace, the title of Pierre Simon (1749–1847), was a French mathematician and astronomer.

the human body and, not finding any evidence of mind, soul, or consciousness, likewise denies their existence.

What is wrong with the conclusions of the psychologist is analogous to what is wrong with Laplace's statement about God. Both fail to realize that when a belief both persists and undergoes metamorphoses, there must be some vital human experience which men attempt to register by means of that belief, some reality which they attempt to represent as best they can in accordance with their intellectual equipment. When that equipment is so enlarged as to render the representations of a preceding age obsolete, it is necessary to find a more fitting representation for that persistent belief, but not to treat it as meaningless. Spencer in his *First Principles* has pointed out that there must be a grain of truth in the most fantastic belief.

In the perennial belief in the human soul, it seems to me men have sought to register the experience that *there is more to the human being than meets the eye* and to express the hope that *every human being will learn so to live as to bring that more to the surface.* This experience and hope are implied in every one of the ancient conceptions of the soul from the most primitive to the most philosophic, from the belief in the ghost-double to the belief in some static immortal essence.

We thus have in man's belief in the human soul the intuitive awareness that there is so much that is latent and potential in the human being, that no statement about him, no description of his powers or achievements, no definition of his being, can fully exhaust all that there is to him and in him. Thanks to this inexhaustible fund of potentiality which man possesses, he is not a fixed quantity or quality; he is incalculable and unpredictable, but above all he is creative. One of the answers to the question, Have you a soul? quoted by Otto coincides most strikingly with this conception of soul. That answer reads as follows: "Yes, indeed, I have a soul. . . . I know that it is something big and overpowering and that at other times it seems almost to leave me. I feel it most when I rise above life's sordidness and meanness and follow my better impulses. How to define it I don't know, but it is the best part of me."

The soul is human nature plus, in the same way as God is all nature plus, for God represents the inexhaustible fund of potentiality that exists in nature, that aspect of latency by virtue of which it is creative and not merely mechanical. Any organism in which the whole is more than the sum of its parts illustrates the meaning of the plus. This parallelism between God and the soul is recognized in traditional religion, as is evident from the conception of man as created in the image of God, and from the Psalmist's outcry, "Thou hast made him little less than divine." As some will put it, "Thou! Drop God out of one end of the sentence and man falls out of the other." Belief in the soul is an affirmation of the infinite worth of man as the belief in God is affirmation of the infinite worth of the cosmos. The Jewish mystic who speaks of the soul as "a portion of the God above" and the poet who pictures man as "a bit of God himself" sense the truth of the mutuality between the two concepts. Perhaps the relation of the apex of the pyramid to the rest of the pyramid might be used to symbolize that mutuality. Neither the human plus (soul) nor the cosmic plus (God) can be exhaustively described in any affirmative definitions. Definition in their case must consist mostly in negating inadequate description.

It follows from the foregoing that we must never reckon with anything human, whether in our own life or in the lives of others, in terms only of the visible, the immediate, and the actual, but we must also take into account the invisible, the imponderable, the potential.

Kaplan's Experience That Led to His Ideas on the Soul

SATURDAY NIGHT, OCTOBER 18, 1941

I came upon the theme of the soul in the course of my thinking about soterics. It occurred to me that it would be an appropriate subject for this morning's sermon, since we were to read the story of the creation. But my problem was how to popularize whatever ideas I had on the subject. It would not do to discuss it in such technical terms as implied in the concept "final values." Yesterday morning I had little more than the students' answers given by Otto. I was really wondering whether I should go with Lena, as we had planned, to look over a farm in Stony Ridge which is for sale. But I trusted to luck that I will hit upon the necessary catalytic idea that would help me crystallize my thoughts on the subject. As I sat in the automobile during the two and a half hour trip to the farm, I seemed to make no headway. But somehow I did not get panicky. On the way back, about four o'clock, as I was sitting back all relaxed, the idea that the belief in the soul registers the intuition that there is more to man than what meets the eye came like a flash. From that moment every other thought I had about the soul fell into its place. Last night I wrote up the preceding two pages and this morning I preached the sermon. The fact that the attendance was rather small didn't annoy me as much as the general haphazard fashion in which things are run at the SAJ. Despite that, I managed to get my sermon across and those who were present seemed to enjoy it very much. This afternoon at the Oneg Shabbat in honor of the Hattan Torah and Hattan Bereshit,[3] Ira pronounced it one of the best ever given at the SAJ services.

In the talk this afternoon I carried out the idea of the soul in things and applied it to the need of our realizing that there was a soul to the Torah.

---

3. The *Hattan Torah* (Bridegroom of the Torah) and *Hattan Bereshit* (Bridegroom of the Creation) are honors given to individuals on Simchat Torah when the reading of Deuteronomy is ended (*Hattan Torah*) and the reading is begun anew with Genesis (*Hattan Bereshit*). In many Reconstructionist congregations one of these honors is given to a woman as *Kalat Bereshit*.

Kaplan Surveys the Religious Beliefs of His Students

MONDAY, OCTOBER 20, 1941

When I met my new class in the TI a few weeks ago for the first time, I gave them a written test to find out what their attitude was toward Judaism. I asked them to answer the following questions: (1) State on what grounds you consider yourself Orthodox, Conservative, Reform, rationalists, or anything else in Judaism. (2) To what extent do you observe the Sabbath, Kashrut, recital of prayers? (3) Do you regard the stories of creation of the world and of man, of the Patriarchs, of the ten plagues in Egypt, of the revelation on Mt. Sinai, of the standing still of the sun for Joshua as fact or fiction? If you consider those stories important to Jewish life, state your reason why. (4) What do you expect from the course in religion?

After reading the answers, I found that the students might be divided into three groups: (1) 11 Orthodox; (2) 8 Conservatives; (3) 6 rationalists; the only thing they have in common is their nationalism and the observance of Sabbath and kashrut. The Orthodox take the position that the supernatural origin of Judaism is the only guarantee of its truth. From that standpoint nothing in the Bible is incredible or subject to the canons of reason. The Conservatives are befuddled. The rationalists insist that Judaism must be compatible with modern science. The average age of the students is 19–20. Their academic status is two years out of high school or Soph/Junior. On the whole, the test shows that young people who get an intensive Jewish education are left intellectually and spiritually maladjusted, and unable to cope with the problem of living in two civilizations. So long as no provision is made to overcome this maladjustment, there can be no future to Judaism, and the Jews are bound to be the victims of hatred from without and conflict from within.

On Adler and Finkelstein

OCTOBER 29, 1941

Neither was I much encouraged by the Seminary celebration last night. Years ago I recorded in the journal my complaint against Cyrus Adler that he does nothing to bring the Seminary closer to the people. Finkelstein is now doing that with a vengeance, because the Seminary has now become almost entirely dependent on popular support. By the way he does it is disgusting. He plays up the tendency of the Jews to curry the favor of the Gentiles. To that end he organized the Conference on Science, Philosophy, and Religion[4] in which Judaism did not have a voice last year, and this year just got something of a squeak. At the

---

4. The Conference on Science, Philosophy, and Religion was founded by Louis Finkelstein and included many prominent intellectual leaders, both Jewish and Christian. Periodic meetings lasted until 1968. Conference papers were published in a series of volumes.

celebration last night, which was called "Inaugural Assembly," the main address was given by Dr. John A. Mackey, the dean of the Princeton Theological Seminary. It was a good sermon with a good Christian climax. All the other Christian theological seminaries were represented. It was in fact a resplendent Christian representation. Judaism was represented by our own Ginzy.⁵ The talk he made was "ginzy." It was unprepared, casual, and pointless. For the first ten minutes, he marshaled two old stories which always call forth a ha-ha from his "hasidism" and some hackneyed wisecracks of his about rabbis who are real rabbis and rabbis who are preachers and orators, and all such nonsense. This was followed by a catalogue of the different places where Jews had academies, beginning with Babylon and ending with Vilna, to prove that they had amount[ed] to nothing so long as they had no academies. But strange as it may seem, time and again in the course of his half-hour of persiflage [frivolous discussion] he interlarded it with snide remarks about Reconstructionism, even going so far as to say that what we need is to reconstruct the Jew, but we do not need to reconstruct Judaism. Another pointed remark of his was that we cannot sum up Judaism in a slogan. To drive that remark home, he even thought it fit to criticize Hillel for trying to answer the would-be proselyte while the latter was standing on one foot. On the whole, that performance of Ginzy's was in bad taste, and the entire affair—which incidentally was poorly attended from the standpoint of the audience—did not raise my hopes concerning the future of Judaism.

On Studying Talmud and Saul Lieberman's Inaugural Lecture

OCTOBER 20, 1941

Before writing down the preceding item, I was debating with myself whether I should resume the study of Talmud, something I have been wanting to do for the longest time, or use the hours which I happen to have free to note down the contents of that item. I asked myself what would I get from the study of a passage in the Talmud. Certainly nothing to exalt or edify me; nor would it be in any degree informative. All it might do would be to revive in me the remembrance of some forgotten text. The recollection of it would afford me momentary satisfaction, and that is all.

I came a little while ago from the Seminary, where this evening Saul Lieberman, the newly appointed professor of Palestinian literature, read a chapter of his forthcoming book on Palestinian piety of the second to fourth centuries. It was a brilliant lecture and displayed wise reading in ancient and modern languages, keen power of analysis, and synthesis. The lecture dealt with instances

---

5. Ginzy was Kaplan's nickname for Louis Ginzberg. In the 1950s rabbinical students at the JTS called Kaplan Kappy, although I am not sure he was aware of this.

of magic, astrology, and incantations which the rabbis managed to reinterpret and cast into the mold of Jewish teaching. It not only gave a highly interesting picture of inner Jewish life during those early centuries but it demonstrated to what extent the method of the rabbis was to accept prevailing ideas and practices and give them a Jewish significance instead of trying to suppress them. When one knows Talmud that way, one should spend time on it. But just to read it with the aid of the traditional commentaries is like trying to read the Bible that way. It is a most unrewarding task.

Kaplan Thinks Other JTS Faculty Are Also Somewhat Heretical

WEDNESDAY, OCTOBER 22, 1941

When I think of the radical views expressed by every one of the four speakers—the four new professors at the Seminary—I am flabbergasted. That people holding such views were not ashamed to sign the letter of protest against the *New Haggadah* is too ridiculous for words. [Saul] Lieberman stated that the rabbis did not suppress the heathen magic and incantations which the people were in the habit of resorting to, but that they reinterpreted them in the light of Jewish teaching. H. L. Ginsberg said that we cannot be certain whether Moses was a monotheist or not, and that the Israelites were influenced for the good in their general and religious life by the Canaanites; [Robert] Gordis' thesis was that, [because] the entire wisdom literature belongs to the proto-Sadducean[6] trend in Judaism and [because] all of its ideas, social, political, and economic, are determined by the class attitude of the writers, who belonged to the wealthy ruling element in Jewry, [this] cannot but have a devastating effect on the traditional spirit of reverence with which that literature has historically been regarded in Judaism. Even [Alexander] Sperber's paper cut the ground from under the sacredness of the Masoretic text, which Jewish tradition has jealously defended. I dare say that I have something of a share in the freedom with which those gentlemen permit themselves to air such highly heterodox views, in that I have openly challenged the traditional assumptions instead of doing so *sub-rosa*. Yet these same men gang themselves up against me to please Finkelstein and [Louis] Ginzberg.

Kaplan vs. Ginzberg—The Last Word

WEDNESDAY, OCTOBER 22, 1941

I have just come back from the Seminary, where I scored one of those rare triumphs which enable me to withstand the hostility of my colleagues. I was scheduled to act as chairman of the evening to introduce Hillel Bavli, who was

---

6. The Sadducees were a priestly party in the late Second Temple period who traced their descent from Tzaddok, a biblical priest.

to read a paper on "The Universal Aspects of Hebrew Poetry." Smarting under Louis Ginzberg's[7] attack on Reconstructionism last Sunday, I made up my mind to get even with him in my introductory remarks this evening. For a moment I hesitated whether I should venture on what might be criticized as controversial territory. I was even afraid that Finkelstein might try to stop me and create a scandal. And when I saw Ginzberg and his wife in the audience, I almost got cold feet. But I would have been very unhappy had I yielded to these fears. And now that I came out of the ordeal with flying colors, I am indeed happy. Even Arzt, now Finkelstein's henchman, remarked, "It is a good thing to carry on the controversy on so high a level."

This is what I said: One of the things in Rabbinic Judaism I am profoundly grateful for is that R. Judah the Prince found it necessary, when compiling the Mishnah, to record not only the majority of opinion but also the minority opinion. At one of the sessions this week, the majority opinion was expressed in criticism of Reconstruction in Jewish life, to the effect that we should reconstruct the Jew not Judaism. From the same authoritative source came the suggestions (1) that Judaism cannot be compressed within any slogan and (2) we should not resort to make generalizations. In registering the minority opinion in favor of Reconstructionism, my purpose is not to enter into any controversy, but to introduce a point which will lead up to the theme of tonight, "The Universal Aspect of Hebrew Poetry."

In declaring that no slogan can do justice to Judaism, the speaker found fault with Hillel, who tried to convey the essence of Judaism in a brief principle even though Hillel had guarded himself against criticism by adding, "The rest is commentary; go and learn." Moreover I'd rather be wrong with Hillel than right with Shammai.[8] Besides, the statement "We should reconstruct the Jew but not Judaism" is itself a slogan and a very expressive one—though when we analyze it we find it quite untenable, for what makes a Jew if not Judaism? When therefore you reconstruct him, you cannot help reconstructing Judaism. But we need not press that point. Reconstruction in Jewish life means not so much reconstructing Judaism as reconstructing our idea of Judaism.

That purpose, I believe, is well served by the conception of Judaism as an evolving religious civilization. That it is religious, there can be no two opinions among us. That it is evolving, even to a breathtaking degree, was amply demonstrated in the four brilliant lectures which were delivered from this platform the last two nights. But we deem it important also to emphasize that it is a civilization, consisting of a cluster of elements such as land, language, poetry.

---

7. Kaplan and Ginzberg had been in conflict since the 1920s. See Mel Scult, *Judaism Faces the Twentieth Century: A Biography of Mordecai Kaplan* (Detroit: Wayne State University Press, 1993), esp. 209–13.

8. Hillel and Shammai were ancient rabbis who usually disagreed. Ordinarily the law takes the opinion of Hillel as the accepted rule.

How important it is to stress that conception of Judaism, because clear to me again is the other day when I learned that in one of the congregation schools on the West Side (82 St. Cong.), where weekday teaching of Hebrew was recently introduced, the rabbi (Schactel) told the teachers that when they would have occasion to explain the school to the parents of the children, they should be careful not to speak of it as a Hebrew school but as a religious school. No civilization can exist without poetry, and no poetry without a civilization, etc. Hence, Bavli. His paper was excellent.

A New Year of Teaching Begins

MONDAY, OCTOBER 27, 1941, 7:30 A.M.

I feel this morning like a schoolboy resuming his school attendance after a long vacation, all ready and eager to go back to school, with his books in his briefcase, face shining, shoes polished, and clothes all trim. Although the classes have long been in session and I have found my work with them this year delightful, mainly because of the ease with which I have at last learned to lecture in Hebrew, this is my first day at the Seminary. I am extremely eager to begin my course in Soterics to see how it will work out.

Like a flash of light, the thought came to me while I had a few moments with Ira last Saturday afternoon that the second chapter in "Soterics,"[9] which is to deal with the will to maximum life, should make the point that the essence of the will to maximum life, as distinguished from the will to life, is that the former is an urge for the potential. The awareness of the potential is perhaps, of all suggested human differential, the most characteristic.

Sermons — How Should They Be Constructed?

OCTOBER 27, 1941, 3:00 P.M.

At the end of the first lecture this morning at the Seminary which dealt with Soterics, I was applauded to the echo. I was wondering what called forth that applause, which Ribner explained to me that the students wanted to express their acclaim of the stand I was taking vis-à-vis the members of the Faculty who are forever criticizing me and the Reconstructionist movement. Later I learned that Louis Ginzberg again took a fling at me after last Wednesday night, making the point that like Philo and unlike Maimonides, I come as a non-Jew to Judaism.

In addition, the older students are all worked up on account of my departure from the method I had employed with the men who gave their sermons

---

9. Kaplan was working on a manuscript which he never finished. Part of it was apparently translated into Hebrew and appeared in 1954 as *Ha-emunah ve-hamusar* [Faith and Ethics] (Jerusalem: Reuben Mass, 1954). In my opinion, this work is Kaplan's best book.

in class preparatory to giving them in the Seminary synagogue. After Finkelstein's assertion that the main cause for the Faculty's protest against me was the type of sermons the students were teaching, I made up my mind to have the students preach along Levinthalian[10] lines—employing some generally admitted truth around a number of rabbinic quotations. Consequently, the first two sermons this year, one by Barish and the other by [Solomon] Bernards, which were given in class today, dealt with Palestine and with the importance of hospitality in the conventional manner in which one hears sermons preached in Conservative congregations. [Moshe] Davis, [Max] Vorspan, Jack Cohen, and a few others have been pestering me ever since they got wind of this new method and are raising quite a howl. They feel that they are being muzzled and deprived of an opportunity to do any genuine individual thinking about contemporary Jewish and spiritual problems.

For the first time in all the years that I have been teaching at the Seminary, I permitted myself today to open the academic year with prayer. I asked the students to recite with me the prayer *Ve-ha-arev nah* [Heb., "May the words of the Lord be sweet in our mouths . . ."].[11]

Looking for Jewish Heroes—A. D. Gordon

WEDNESDAY, OCTOBER 29, 1941

We Jews are sacrificing important contemporary values for the sake of maintaining a sense of continuity with the past. As I was trying to put down a number of names of men whose biographies I should like to see figure in the Friday night readings the Reconstructionist group is working on, I was struck by the paucity of outstanding characters which the past contributed in comparison with the large number of great Jewish contemporaries. Whether this is the case because there really were but few outstanding men in the last twenty centuries of our history, or because the habit of noting and recording the values of personality was not in vogue is a moot question. For example, the few I can think of just now are Hillel, Akiba, Rashi, Maimonides. Their lives have universal significance and are a source of inspiration to a Jewish future. On the other hand, the last two or

---

10. Referring to Israel Levinthal. Kaplan tried to convince Levinthal, a "Conservadox" Jew, that one could be observant and Reconstructionist at the same time.

11. This is the first evidence of Kaplan opening his classes with a prayer. The prayer here is in the morning daily service and begins with the blessing praising God, "who gave us the mitzvah to study words of Torah." In the diary Kaplan refers here to the line after this initial blessing. We do not know how much of the paragraph he had the students recite. At the end of the paragraph in question there is a reference to Israel being the "Chosen people" in having received the gift of the Torah. We do not know if Kaplan ended with these final words. Considering Kaplan's rejection of the chosen people concept, it is more likely that he ended with the blessing with praise for God, who "teaches Torah to his people Israel."

three generations are replete with names of great Jewish characters whose lives deserve to be better shown and to become Jewish sancta.

What made me think of all this was the article by Hans Kohn on A. D. Gordon[12] in the *Menorah Journal* [19]32, which I read yesterday, probably for the first time. I had known the usual facts about Gordon, but what I read in that article was a revelation to me. The central thought of his philosophy—that this would be a better world if the individual worker were interested not merely in improving his personal lot, but in transforming himself into an agent for the improvement of human life as a whole—is a new and refreshing approach to the apparently insoluble problems of social conflict. This I had not known. A. D. Gordon, however, did not merely theorize. He lived his philosophy. His was not the sterile saintliness of the sanctified egoists who figure in history. His example is an inspiration to high thinking and simple living. I know of no one in the entire roster of our ancient great men—outside the prophets—that can compare with him.

The idea that the will to life abundant is basically the will to actualize the maximum possible number of potentialities is most fecund. The fact that man is acutely aware of his limitations and that he refuses to accept them is part of that same will to salvation. Hence the tendency at first to identify salvation with personal immortality. As man learns to manipulate the physical processes of nature, the division of labor, the arts of exchange, new vistas of life open up before him. To occupy and exploit them seems to mean to him salvation, and his interest is transferred from personal immortality to the improvement of this world.

Two Types of Sermons

OCTOBER 29, 1941

A committee of three students—Bennet, [Hayyim] Kieval, and [Max] Vorspan—appointed to see me about the course in homiletics conferred with me tonight. As a result of the discuss[ion], we decided that I should leave it to the student-preacher to express his preference either for the midrash type of sermon or for the analytic type.[13] In case a student took the midrash type of sermon, I would spend the hour following on the one in which he gave the sermon demonstrating what might be done with that topic if it were treated from the analytic

---

12. Aaron David Gordon (1856–1922) was an early Zionist ideologue of Labor Zionism. As a spiritual leader, he emphasized the religion of labor. Kaplan found Gordon's emphasis on individual fulfillment appealing and opened his 1954 Hebrew work *Ha-emunah Ve-hamusar* with an epigraph from A. D. Gordon. This little known work is one of Kaplan's best, but we do not have the English original. Unfortunately, Gordon is little known among American Jews but highly valued in Israel for his emphasis on moral perfectionism.

13. Kaplan apparently distinguished between a midrashic sermon, in which one emphasized the way scriptural verses could be interpreted, and an analytic type of sermon, which centered around a general concept.

point of view. Those who will undertake to preach an analytic type of sermon are willing to face the consequences in case they have a run-in with Finkelstein or any other member of the faculty.

One World

NOVEMBER 8, 1941

Since human relationships are at the center of the problem of salvation, and since salvation is to mean for us the conquest of fear and the maximum actualization of potentialities, the question arises, How large an area of human relationships is necessary for the achievement of salvation? Hitherto it was some people, church, or nation that constituted an adequate area. Bitter experience has proved up to the hilt the tragic fallacy of such assumptions. The reduction of the planet to a single neighborhood has rendered all of mankind as the area within which the human relationships of every human being must be normalized, if we are to be emancipated from the besetting anxieties that stand in the way of salvation.

. . . But the will to salvation cannot be content with the mere overcoming of fears. The very ability which man displays in overcoming the more intense and complex fears reveals to him unsuspected potentialities of a creative character, which, when realized, give rise to goods inherently worthwhile. This is the creative aspect of salvation, which led the ancients to picture life in the hereafter not merely as secure existence but as bliss or as basking in the glory of God.

Salvation and Growth

NOVEMBER 10, 1941

There is no such thing, therefore, as a static attainment of salvation. To be equal to the implications of his surplus energy in terms of creative potentialities and ever widening scope of life, man has come to regard growth itself as an indispensable factor for salvation. He has acquired the conscious need of finding something new all the time to learn and to master, new perceptions, new comprehension, new insights, ever increasing relationships among the different parts of reality and experience, increasing capacity in doing things, increasing sensitivity in appreciating values and differences between values. The entire range of formal interests which are synonymous with a life of reason comes within the process of growth, which man has learned to regard as indispensable, if he is to achieve salvation in a progressively richer existence, which he must learn to make his own or lose his soul.

Everyday Life and Salvation

NOVEMBER 10, 1941

"The earth belongs to the Lord and all [that the] earth holds, the world and its inhabitants" [Psalms 24:1]. The psalmist probably meant to express by this verse nothing more than the general idea that God possesses all that there is. But what did he want the reader to infer from this fact? That God can wreak his will upon the world and its inhabitants? Hardly that. In view of what follows, which describes the kind of man who is worthy of ascending God's hill, it would seem that the psalmist wants the reader to realize that everything which exists, including men and their ways, constitute God's kingdom or field of action. From the standpoint of salvation, this implication of the psalmist's statement is the one to be stressed in the conception of God as the power that makes for salvation. The tragedy of religion has been man's tendency to abstract God from the everyday realities of life other than those which, in his primitive thinking, he regarded as harboring dangers beyond his control. Realities like plagues, enemies, death by which he was ever surrounded, were regarded by him as occasions for calling on God. But the ordinary pursuits and pleasures, the affairs of mine and thine, of social intercourse and banter, the world of small kindnesses and petty strifes and jealousies, he treated as something that constituted a kind of limbo which was not to be invaded by God. God was only in temples and churches, visiting the world on Sabbath and holy days when men and women were dressed in all their fineries and everybody was on his good behavior.

On the principle that no interest is conducive to salvation, unless suffused by something of every other interest, the conception of God is empty of all content and meaning, unless it is so closely identified with the functional interests as to include "everyone and everything—all interests, all commerce, all government, all art, all amusements, all staid pursuits of the old and all the ardor of the young, all sport, all laughter, all that makes for gladness." It is only as we succeed in identifying the business of daily living, striving, and pleasuring as God's kingdom that we can hope to expel from our lives the element of fear that robs us of all joy in what we have, makes us envious of what others have, and destroys all likelihood of our making the most of our opportunities.

Moreover, we must remember that not only the world but also its inhabitants are the Lord's. No! Life can have no meaning to any one of us apart from his family, his employers, his community, his country, and in the final analysis, mankind. These are all to be viewed as members of God's kingdom, and our relation to God or membership in that kingdom can be expressed in no other way than through the medium of our responsibilities to our fellowmen who inhabit it. "If I forget them, I forget God, God expressing himself to me through men in general as through my family and my employers in particular."

Growth Is the Essence

NOVEMBER 21, 1941

Life abundant is essentially growth. Man differs from the rest of creation in not being entirely limited by the data of his existence. He can not only further and modify the growth of plants and animals by means of special cultivation, grafting, and breeding. He can also further and modify his own growth as a human being by means of environmental changes and educational processes to such an extent as to overcome in progressive measure the limitations implied in the data of his existence. Overcoming consists either in transforming or transcending limitations, of which the fact of death is the most challenging. Self-identification of individual with group and of group with humanity is indispensable both to the transformation and transcendence of limitations.

To maintain the process of continuous growth, man has to be forever engaged in reconstructing himself and his environment. Whereas other creatures begin and end with the same fund of transmitted interests and capacities, man envisages indefinite increase of that fund. Progress in knowledge of human nature is to be counted on for achieving effective methods of education and self-improvement. This applies also to reconstruction of social heritage. On the other hand, the reconstruction of environment, which until modern times proceeded slowly, has been given by technology a momentum which promises far-reaching improvements in the outward conditions of living.

Stages of Salvation

DECEMBER 2, 1941

The following is a summary of the different stages of human behavior as reflected in man's striving for salvation:

Spiritual Values	Means of Salvation	Nature of Salvation
Spirits and gods	Theurgic (conscious) + soteric (unconscious)	Security against disease, privation, enemies
Emergence of group god	Theurgic & soteric (both conscious)	Security for individual and group
Emergence of universal god	Divinely revealed law	Security + group expansion
Universal God as redeemer	Self-identification with God	Individual redemption from sin and death (otherworldliness)
God as immanent and transcendent	Knowledge of the right translated into habits	Ethical personality
Power that makes for salvation	Knowledge of rational and functional values translated into individual habits and attitudes and into social institutions and ideals	Growth, individual and collective

Pearl Harbor

SUNDAY, DECEMBER 7, 1941

When I was through teaching at the Institute this evening at 5:00, one of the students told me he had just heard over the radio that Japan had bombarded Manila and had declared war against our country. God knows what is in store for us. Now is the time to be prepared for the worst and to hope for the best.

Kaplan Comes Out Against American Jewish Isolationists

MONDAY, DECEMBER 8, 1941

It now turns out that it was Hawaii (Pearl Harbor) that was attacked yesterday and not Manila. The latter city was raided this morning.

After lecturing the first hour at the Seminary this morning on Soterics, I was approached by a student with the request that, instead of taking up the Midrash during the second hour, I say something about the article by Judge Jerome Frank which appeared in this week's issue of the *Saturday Evening Post*, and by another student that I say something about the war between Japan and the Allies. Although I knew very well that the requests were prompted mainly by the desire to know what to say to those whom they would have occasion to address at the coming Friday night services, I acceded to their wishes. Fortunately, I had given some thought to the article by Jerome Frank. In fact, I used its contents as a jumping-off base for my talk last week at Pottsville, and I was even contemplating writing a reply to it. Although I did not have my notes before me, I recollected enough of what I had planned to say that I was able to give the men a rather lengthy statement on the subject. As I warmed up to the theme, I found myself formulating an idea which served as a natural transition to the discussion of our entry into the war. The idea was the following: Frank, as an assimilationist Jew, takes the position (in his article titled "The Red-White-and-Blue Herring") that Jews, in coming here, must sever all connections with their fellow-Jews as a group, either here or abroad, in order to be 100 percent loyal to America. This assumption is in keeping with the general pattern of thinking American isolationists, one of whom Frank confesses himself to be. He merely applies the same principle of selfishness that makes him indifferent to and irresponsible for his fellow-Jews as members of a group also to international relations. This policy of American isolationists, which has prevented America from interfering with the international banditry that strong nations were perpetrating upon weak nations, is one of the contributing factors to our present world tragedy. This policy is that of Cain who could not see why he should be expected to be his brother's keeper. By the same token that a man like Frank acts selfishly toward his fellow-Jews, he acts as an American and would have all Americans act toward other nations.

I concluded my closing session a few minutes before the regular time so that the students should not miss listening in on the radio at 12:30, at which time the President was expected to address Congress and to call upon them to declare war against Japan. The students went to the students' lounge and I went to Greenberg and Charry's room to hear the address, which was very brief and to the point.

The Reconstructionist *Board Supports Indicted Communist*

WEDNESDAY, DECEMBER 10, 1941

Last night we had the first of the evening meetings of the *Reconstructionist* Editorial Board, which we had been wanting to hold for the longest time but which we had to put off from week to week because it interfered with one or another's schedule. Those present were Ira [Eisenstein], Eugene Kohn, Milton Steinberg, Abe Duker, The. N. Lewis, Bernard Heller, Sam Dinin, Israel S. Chipkin, Mrs. Grossman, and I.

I had asked a young man, Eli Jaffe (27) of Oklahoma and now of Brooklyn, to come and present his case to the group. He has been sentenced to ten years' state prison and $5,000 fine for being a communist. That being a communist rendered one guilty of a criminal act was argued by the county attorney on the ground of the communist literature found in his possession. He was one of four who were sentenced on these grounds. They are at present out on bail and are being enabled principally by the International Labor Defense, a communist organization, to appeal to the higher courts. The entire matter had been called to my attention by Mrs. Guggenheimer, a former friend of Mrs. Lindheim. She had introduced this Jaffe, a young Jewish journalist, and I had him come before our group in the hope that he might interest them in the so-called "Oklahoma Witch Hunt." Duker and Dinin, who are somewhat familiar with the tortuous workings of the communists, identified the International Labor Defense as being communist. We therefore made it clear to Jaffe that we could work only through the Civil Liberties League, whom we shall ask in what way we could be of help in this matter.

After that I discussed the editorials which have to be written up for the coming issue of the *Reconstructionist*. The outbreak of the war with Japan demanded that we have something to say about it in next week's issue.

Establishing a Reconstructionist Fellowship — Moving Beyond a "School of Thought"

DECEMBER 10, 1941

The main subject of the evening's discussion was the idea of organizing a Reconstructionist Order, or as it later developed, a Reconstructionist Fellowship, to be known as The Religious Fellowship of Jewish Reconstructionists. After realizing that we could not expect to make much headway with our movement if we were content to remain a kind of esoteric school of thought, and that we would waste our energy in polemics if we were to set up as a rival to any of the existing denominations, I came to the conclusion that the organizational framework most suited to our purpose was that of a lay religious order or fellowship. The suggestion met with approval from most of those present. Chipkin was virtually the only doubting Thomas.

As I envisage the Fellowship, it would develop along the following lines: To begin with, we would have to formulate the specific regimen of principles and duties to which a member of such a Fellowship would have to dedicate himself. They would have to be principles and duties relating to his personal life and conduct. We would have to find at least a "minyan"[14] [of] persons from among our own group to constitute themselves the first chapter. This chapter would then contact individuals who, with the assistance of one or two of their close friends, could organize "minyanim," or chapters, from among their acquaintances. The procedure of Ahad Ha-Am's "Bne Moshe"[15] might be followed in our case, except that it could not afford to confine itself as that fellowship did to a few very select people. It would have to be more inclusive and democratic, seeking to elicit devotion to Judaism in lay people willing to lead Jewish lives and to bring up their children as Jews, instead of assuming a highly developed interest as already present.

Give Up the Material, Maintain the Spiritual — FDR and the Declaration of War Against Germany and Italy

FRIDAY, DECEMBER 12, 1941

Yesterday Germany and Italy declared war against our country, and our country is at last united on the only course that will save the world from the desperadoes who have gotten a stranglehold on it. No one expects that we should interrupt our normal pursuits or stop meeting our normal needs, because we are at war. It is otherwise with activities of a cultural and spiritual character. Many of our people who have felt some obligation to engage in such activities are only too glad to find an excuse for placing a moratorium on them at this time. They are even ready to regard the blackout of Jewish interests as a patriotic duty. Fortunately, President Roosevelt in his address last Tuesday night — for which our Reconstructionist group suspended its discussions to listen to — said something which is a charter for carrying on our Jewish life. "And I am sure," he said, "that

---

14. A minyan is a quorum of ten persons needed to have a public service. Only men are counted in traditional settings; liberal sects include women.

15. B'nai Moshe was the organization of Ahad Ha-Am's followers. For more on Kaplan and Ahad Ha-Am, see Mel Scult, *The Radical American Judaism of Mordecai Kaplan* (Bloomington: Indiana University Press, 2013), 46–51. Also see Steven Zipperstein, "On Reading Ahad Ha-Am as Mordecai Kaplan Read Him," *Jewish Social Studies* 12.2 (2006): 30–39. This issue of *Jewish Social Studies* contains all the papers delivered at the 2004 conference on Kaplan at Stanford University.

the people in every part of the nation are prepared in their individual living to win the war. . . . I am sure that they will cheerfully give up those material things that they are asked to give up. And I am sure that they will retain all those great spiritual things without which we cannot win through."

I used the foregoing as my opening text in my talk last Wednesday night and last night. Last night I presented Reconstructionism to a small group of people at the home of Mr. Doniger, who lives in the same apartment house that we do. One would imagine that when people accept an invitation to meet me and to hear me discuss Reconstructionism, they are at least vitally concerned in the conservation of Jewish life, and that the discussion would turn upon the question of how it may best be achieved. Instead of which they would like me to prove to them why we should remain Jews. And when I succeed in diverting them from that question to the question "How?" they take a critically negative attitude. When I give them the general purposes to which we must dedicate ourselves, they complain that those purposes are too general. When I detail a list of specific activities, they find fault with this or that detail. I nearly lost my temper but managed to hold myself back. What I did say was that we are not coming to them with a supernatural revelation. We merely propose certain general purposes and ask those who are interested in remaining Jews to make the reconstruction of Jewish life and thought their problem and responsibility. If they do not care enough about Judaism to realize that, it is as much their problem as ours; nothing that we say or do is of any avail.

Remembering His Own Student Days

DECEMBER 12, 1941

I have just come from Rodeph Sholom Temple of West 83 St., where I spoke on "What Jews Need Most Today" before a group of about 175 people of Louis I. Newman's congregation. This was the first time he tried out a kind of "Oneg Shabbat" gathering for the purpose of infusing in his people something of the Sabbath spirit which is probably lacking in their homes.

That Temple was among the first to introduce Friday night services. I recall the days when I was a student at the old Seminary, which was housed in a brownstone private house at 736 Lexington Ave. For about two years (1896–98) I lived in the dormitory, which consisted of the top floor. On Friday nights we used to attend services in what was then the Rodeph Sholom Temple on cor. Lexington Ave. and 63 St. It was originally a church, and it had all the beauty and comfort of a church. Rev. Dr. Rudolph Grossman was the rabbi. He was a little, pale-faced man who pronounced his r's like w's. He was therefore known as Wudolph Gwossman. Before coming to the Temple, he had been Kohler's assistant at Temple Beth El, where he used to officiate without a hat. But when he came to Rodeph Sholom, he had to don a kind of episcopal hat because a member had left money in his will for the congregation and had stipulated that the rabbi must worship with covered head. That ruling is kept up to this day. Grossman was a very fluent and interesting preacher. At least so it seemed to us students at the time. Charles Kauvar, of Denver, for the last 40 years used to write out on Saturday night [when he was a student at JTS] the summary of the sermons he heard Grossman deliver Friday nights. He could have wanted no better course in homiletics.

On Arthur Hertzberg

MONDAY, DECEMBER 15, 1941

The Seminary students whose attitude in class is generally challenging to the point of being ill-mannered are those who regard themselves as the defenders of the faith. They generally come from the Yeshivah or from some similar Talmudical academy where they have absorbed considerable knowledge of Talmud text but little of anything else. There is so much about them that is reminiscent of Jesuitry that I never feel comfortable when they try to engage me in debate. It is never a discussion for the sake of learning, but to put me in the wrong. There are two men particularly who get on my nerves. They are [Arthur] Hertzberg[16] and Sam Cohen. They possess a considerable degree of general knowledge and mental ability, but unfortunately because of their cock-sureness and impudence, they will utilize their knowledge and ability more in the interests of power for themselves than of good for our poor leaderless people.

This morning I had occasion to explain the midrash in *Mekilta*[17] on *ve-ra-iytah et ha-dam* [Heb., "When I see the blood I will Passover you, so that no plague will destroy you when I strike the land of Egypt" (Exodus 12:13)], which is interpreted as meaning *ro-eh ani dam akeydato shel Yitzhak* [Heb.] (*Mekilta parsha zayin*, Lauterbach, vol. 1, page 57, "I see the blood of the sacrifice of Isaac").

I pointed out that it implied an idea which figures prominently in Christology, namely, that redemption requires a blood sacrifice. I then went on to

---

16. Arthur Hertzberg (1921–2006), ordained JTS, was a Jewish American scholar, activist, and Zionist leader. He served as president of the American Jewish Congress for many years. Hertzberg was an important public intellectual in the mid-twentieth century.

17. *Mekhilta*, the Rabbinic Midrash on Exodus. See Jacob Z. Lauterbach, ed., *Mekilta de Rabbi Ishmael* (Philadelphia: Jewish Publication Society, 1949). Lauterbach's book is part of a series of ancient and medieval Jewish sources titled "The Schiff Classics" after Jacob Schiff, who underwrote the program. The series is meant to be a Jewish alternative to the Harvard Loeb Classics project of Greek and Roman writers. The Schiff Classics were small, inexpensive volumes with facsimile pages of the original on one page and the English translation on the facing page. Solomon Schechter was a key person at the beginning of the series. Kaplan's translation of Moses Hayyim Luzzatto's *Mesillat Yesharim: Path of the Righteous* appeared in this series. Kaplan was informed that he was to do the translation the day that Schechter passed away in 1915. Kaplan took many years to finish the translation, which was not published until 1936. Although he was critical of the translation, Ira Stone used it in the publication of his commentary on *Mesillat Yesharim*, which was published in 2010.

remark that there are many such parallels between Jewish and Christian religion. As one such parallel, I mentioned the principle of vicarious atonement, according to which the premature death of a righteous man may be due to sin of his contemporaries, for which it is an expiation. Hertzberg maintained that no such teaching can be found in Jewish religion. In all such situations I find myself helpless because I cannot quote chapter and verse. I merely said that the next time we meet, I will indicate a number of passages substantiating my contention.

When I came home, I found a whole section in Moore's *Judaism*[18] devoted to the idea of vicarious atonement. There is some mention of it in the *Jewish Encyclopedia*. In the *Encyclopedia of Religion and Ethics*, which has an article on Atonement, there is not the slightest allusion to that doctrine. This is what I was afraid of. Our Jewish theologians are too stupid or too dishonest to admit that such a doctrine was advanced by the ancient Sages. I would therefore not be able to convince a stubborn mule like Hertzberg if I didn't have Moore's text to substantiate what I said.

A *Slip of the Tongue*

Tuesday, December 23, 1941

Last week at the SAJ was quite a notable one. The Sabbath was the sixth day of Hanukkah and the first day of Rosh Hodesh [New Moon]. In addition, there was to be a short service on the occasion of our country's entry into the war. The choral group, consisting of about 25 women of the SAJ and about 5 men whom Judith had been training, were scheduled to sing two songs in honor of Hanukkah and I was to give the sermon. I somehow could not relax while I was speaking; the needed words did not come in time and I felt tense almost all through the course of the sermon. This feeling started almost in the first sentence when, by a slip of the tongue, I said "the persecution of the war" instead of "the prosecution of the war." We had a good attendance. I did not speak long and everything else came off smoothly, so that the people were pleased.

Students at the Teachers Institute Are Not Exempt from the Draft

December 23, 1941

Yesterday Abraham Barras, a student of the Teachers Institute in his third year, came to tell me that at the insistent urging of his parents, he is withdrawing from the Institute [at JTS] and joining the Teachers Institute of the Yeshiva

---

18. George Foot Moore, *Judaism in the First Centuries of the Christian Era*, 2 vols. (Cambridge, MA: Harvard University Press, 1954). This authoritative work on the early rabbinic period was written by a non-Jewish scholar.

because the latter institution makes it possible for its students to be exempted from the draft. The Yeshiva recognizes them as theological students and therefore brackets them with those who are training for the ministry.

Some time ago the question of the status of students of the Seminary outside the Rabbinical School came up at a Seminary faculty meeting, and the sentiment was almost unanimous that such students be not regarded as theological students, even where there had been a bona fide declaration long before the war of intention to prepare for entering the rabbinical school. In the meantime, the Teachers Institute is bound to lose its men students. In addition to the numerous handicaps under which it is laboring, such as the negative attitude on the part of the Seminary authorities led by Finkelstein, the more intensive training and dormitory facilities plus college education afforded by the Yeshivah, the difficulty of getting jobs for the graduates in the weekday schools which are mostly Orthodox, this one of having to compete with a draft-exempting institution like the Yeshiva is likely to ruin our Teachers Institute.

Kaplan Comments on His Amazingly Mixed Reading Diet

DECEMBER 23, 1941

My mind is all in a whirl. After the strain of the last weekend I feel too tired to attend to routine tasks. Whenever I feel that way, I take to the most promiscuous [sic] kind of reading of both serious and light stuff. Right now I have on my desk the following, which I have been reading from alternately virtually all day (with the exception of one hour when I had Meyer Fishman of the Jewish Welfare Board come to see me to discuss the organization of Jewish community): *Sources of Religious Insight* by Royce, *The Crisis of Our Age* by Sorokin, Augustine's *Confessions*, the most recent issue of the CCAR *Yearbook* (1914), an abridged version of *Byron in Italy* by Peter Quenell, Byron's *Poems*.

The outcome of this odd diet is a kind of mental indigestion. I cannot get Sorokin's reactionary scoldings and Royce's pious abstractions to mix with the picaresque accounts of Byron's amorous adventures or with his sentiments in *Don Juan*. What becomes of all my theories with regard to making the most out of life? Would Byron have enriched English poetry as he did if he had lived a staid and normal life? Was his complete flouting of conventions a prerequisite to his creativity? "No theory, however comprehensive, no type, however detailed and well established, will quite cover any single human being," says Quenell. In trying to analyze Byron's numerous philanderings, Quenell points out that they are to be explained in terms of psychological rather than physical causes. "Were the sexual impulse always governed by sexual motives," he says, "human relationships would present a somewhat easier study." He finds psychological, glandular, social, and literary causes necessary to be taken into account, if we want to understand fully the behavior of a Byron. From Byron's own idea of his life, we gather that he could not have been a very happy man. He did not expect to live long. When he was thirty, he was determined, he told his friend Moore, that "he would make what he could of the remainder of his youth. He would work its mine to the last vein . . . and then good night." He could feel that he had enjoyed and lived. The need of achieving self-possession or integration, which Royce regards as common to all mankind and therefore as the initial source of religious insight, was furthest from the mind of Byron. He was inwardly the most disintegrated type of person outside a lunatic asylum. Yet it may well be that, but for such inner disintegration, he might never have written a single line of his beautiful poetry.

There is one thing, however, that does emerge from these considerations, and that is that great art not only often goes along with individual degeneracy but may also accompany social corruption and cruelty. Wagner's music is an illustration of how both individual and social deterioration may dwell together with great music and drama. Perhaps in this instance Sorokin's eternal croakings about sensate culture have some warrant. It may not be fashionable to apply any standards of a moral or social character to artistic expression. Yet the failure to do so may not have done Western civilization too much good.

The first time I read Royce's *Sources of Religious Insight* was in 1914.[19] Like most of his writings which I have read, this one too raised greater expectations than it fulfills. He has a wholesome sense of reality, but it is neutralized by his idealistic absolutism. I was amazed when I picked up the book again yesterday to discover how much likeness there is between my notion of soterics and his recognition of the centrality of salvation in the understanding of religion. So far, he is the third writer I have come across who appreciates the place of the striving after the salvation in human life. The other two are George Foote Moore and Irwin Edman. Of the three, Edman has the most comprehensive conception of the meaning of salvation. The other two can think of it only either as the source or objective of religion only. That prevents them from comprehending its far-reaching implications for the understanding of an aspect of human life.

The first three chapters in Royce's *Sources* have a bearing on the final interests. Self-possession, human brotherhood, and cosmic rationality, as interpreted in those chapters, correspond, respectively, to the three categories of values: self, humanity, and God. What he argues is that the need[s] for self-possession, human brotherhood, and cosmic rationality are sources of religious insight—they reveal God. He falls into the common error of treating salvation as achievable through

19. Josiah Royce (1855–1916) was a prominent professor of philosophy at Harvard. His conception of loyalty was especially interesting to Kaplan. Royce was one of the big three philosophers at Harvard in the first decade of the twentieth century (the other two were William James and George Santayana). The Ethical Culture Society offered Kaplan a scholarship to study philosophy at Harvard, but he turned it down. On Kaplan and Felix Adler, founder of the Ethical Culture Society, see Scult, *Radical American Judaism*, 66–87.

the attainment only of the final values. If those three needs are for him more than final values, but also include the formal and functional values without which they have no meaning, he does not make that fact in the least explicit.

Among the formal values the one which it seems to me has the greatest potency in bringing under control both the desires of the flesh and of the mind, is that of faithfulness to any relationship, natural or contractual, which carries with it certain expectations. That, rather than love, is what binds the human world together. To violate the plighted word is "to strike at the very center of life, at the spirit of the universe."

Fundamental Values

DECEMBER 26, 1941

Another way of naming the final values is *self-possession, human brother-hood, godhood*. To have one's faith in them reenforced, to keep on growing in the achievement of what they imply, is the goal of human activity, the end for which the formal interests seek to regulate our functional interests.

On Courage and the Will to Live

SATURDAY NIGHT, DECEMBER 27, 1941

One of the facts I point out in connection with the will to live is that it is infectious. The same is true of the will to salvation. We cannot have our attention called to a fine example of endurance or heroism without being stimulated to bear up under the hardships that weigh us down or to fight on bravely against overwhelming odds. The example of Roosevelt and Churchill facing all kinds of enemies and carrying on with undaunted courage is a challenge to me personally in my desperate struggle to lay the foundation for a Jewish future in America. Yet I become discouraged most of the time. I long for rest; I yearn to be relieved of my duties. I am quite sure that if I did not have the responsibility of helping Mother and Sophie,[20] I would have asked to be retired both by the Seminary and the SAJ. Does my attitude disprove the truth of what I said before about the infectious character of endurance and courage?

The answer is that it is one thing to fight against overwhelming odds and another to fight in a losing cause. Both Roosevelt and Churchill are heading a cause which is daily gaining in strength, however great the enemy's forces and advantage of initiative may be. They have sufficient reason for being confident of the final outcome. In my case, unfortunately, the cause for which I am fighting is daily becoming weaker. There is not a single manifestation of Jewish life or

---

20. Sophie Kaplan Israeli, Kaplan's older sister. Sophie married a classmate of Kaplan's from JTS. For more on Sophie Israeli, see Scult, *Judaism Faces the Twentieth Century*, 23, 26, 31. For a photo of Sophie Kaplan Israeli, see my Facebook page.

interest anywhere on the American scene to give me the least assurance of a halt in the process of Jewish disintegration. Wherever I look, whether it be within the circle of Jewish activities or without, there is nothing but chaos, indolence, preoccupation with trivialities, perverted thinking due to vested interests, and stubborn and willful blindness to realities. How little we can expect from our professional Jewish leaders—I refer especially to the rabbinate—who are presumably engaged in salvaging Jewish life, may be inferred from this one fact among a thousand others, namely, that of the eighteen Jewish chaplains in the army five have had to be brought up for charges of one kind or another. The rabbinical training schools do not pay the least attention to the personal character of the men they train, and certainly do not imbue them with the need of placing the cause of Judaism above their professional success. A goodly number in the rabbinate work hard and are conscientious in the performance of their duties, but for some reason or other the problem of Jewish life as a whole is the last thing they would ever think of getting their congregants interested in. Take, for example, the *Reconstructionist* magazine. Its reading material is remarkably adopted for study and discussion of various phases of Jewish life. If the rabbis who are in sympathy with the Reconstructionist outlook would really be concerned in training a number of men and women to think constructively about Judaism, they could want no better medium. If they would avail themselves of the *Reconstructionist* as such a medium, it would have a circulation of at least 10,000. The fact that after seven years of existence we have not been able to raise its circulation above 2,000 or 2,200 is an index of the futility of our efforts.

Royce on Loyalty—Valuable for the Concept of Salvation

DECEMBER 27, 1941

The trouble with Royce's *Sources of Religious Insight*, as with all attempts to make the problem of salvation subordinate to that of religion instead of vice versa, is that both salvation and religion are seen in the wrong perspective. His book would have been much more instructive if he had come to grips directly with the question that constitutes salvation and how is it to be attained. The most significant portion of the book is undoubtedly the one which discusses loyalty. Instead of trying to answer the question "Why is loyalty necessary as a means to salvation?" he tries to answer the question "How does loyalty reveal God?" Yet there is undoubtedly much in the way he deals with the matter of loyalty that might throw a great deal of light on loyalty as a means to salvation.

Loyalty is only another term for faithfulness. By itself it is merely a formal interest. It calls for a functional interest to supply it with content and final interest to give it meaning. The functional interest necessarily pertains to the concrete needs which human beings experience in the physical, social, and mental aspects of their lives. The final interests, in which all loyalties are rooted, are phases of human brotherhood. The synthesis of these two groups of interests figures as a cause to which the attitude of loyalty is directed.

What Royce says about loyalty to loyalty translated into the final interest of human brotherhood means that the scope of brotherhood must be coextensive with all of humanity and with all group interests in human life that do not call for the elimination of other group interests in order to survive.

In applying the principle of loyalty as a means of salvation to any concrete situation, such as loyalty to Jewish life, the questions to be answered are: (1) Is the loyalty related to a genuine functional need of the human beings involved in the cause, and (2) Is the loyalty to the cause so interpreted as not to be prejudicial to loyalty as a universal principle of human life?

Law of Justice and Law of Love

Sunday, December 28, 1941

It seems to me that soterics promises to give us a truer comprehension of the relation of the law of justice to the law of love than anything that has thus so far been said on the subject. All we have to do is merely to recognize that the law of justice belongs to the formal interests, whereas the law of love belongs to the final interests. The particular area to which it belongs is the goal of human brotherhood. In the light of this relation of the law of love to the law of justice, all the finely spun of our arguments about the one superseding the other or rendering the other unnecessary or supplementing each other is entirely beside the point.

In the field of formal interests the most important consideration is that urged constantly by Reinhold Niebuhr, viz.:

> It is necessary to insist that the moral achievement of individual good will is not a substitute for the mechanisms of social control. It may perfect and purify, but it cannot create basic justice. Basic justice in any society depends upon the right organization of men's labor, the equalization of their social power, regulation of their common interests and adequate restraint upon the inevitable conflict of competing interests. The health of a social organism depends upon the adequacy of its social structure as much as does the health of a body upon the biochemical processes. No degree of good will alone can cure a deficiency in glandular secretions; and no moral idealism can overcome a basic mechanical defect in the social structure. (*An Interpretation of Christian Ethics*, pp. 181–82)

The foregoing implies that it is misrepresenting the formal need for justice to say that all it asks for is that each one experiences a due sense of what is fair in his dealings with his fellows. The fact is that in the very will to salvation or to make the most of human life is the inherent demand as much for the very mechanisms and agencies of social control as for the element of good will as each individual. Insofar as man is a political animal, he yearns for institutions and laws which regulate the life of society as for the spirit of justice which is in each individual human being. [There is] no better proof of this inherent yearning than the fact that man has always valued those institutions and laws so highly and regarded them as so indispensable to his existence as to ascribe them to some superhuman source.

More on Niebuhr

DECEMBER 29, 1941

The will to salvation cannot achieve its objective merely by taking thought. No mere deliberate desire to exercise will can strengthen one's will. "What men are able to win depends not upon the strength of their willing, but upon the strength which enters their will and over which their will has little control," says R. Niebuhr (217). The problem of salvation is, accordingly, so to cooperate with our social environment as to have it provide us with the strength which is stronger than our own individual vacillating wills.

"Whether a man stands or yields in the hour of crisis is of course determined by commitments made before the crisis arises" (*ibid.*). If this is true, we should not permit ourselves to remain footloose, but enter into covenants and relationships which will in time of crisis give us the strength to do what we would not do if we were thrown entirely upon the inherent strength of our own individual wills. Those moral and religious anarchists, who dread making commitments because they maintain that pledges are made only to be broken, fail to reckon with the overpowering strength of the biological impulses. Granted even that pledges are broken, but they are not broken without causing a trauma. The healing of that trauma only adds to the appreciation of the need for keeping the pledges. In the sense of sin and repentance, the individual keenly realizes his dependence upon society for the integrity and salvation of his personality and is thus sensitized to the significance of human brotherhood.

The moral or religious anarchist who claims to possess such will power as to be independent of any strength from without cannot place a high value upon human brotherhood. This describes the attitude of a Nietzsche. He was himself no flouter of high ideals. "No complete moral nihilism is of course possible. Some recognition of the principle of law and order is inevitable even in the most consistent vitalism. In Nietzsche this is done in minimal terms by the insistence that the will to power of his superman will create aristocratic societies of higher worth than the rationalized societies in which the morality of 'herd animals' has gained ascendancy" (R. Niebuhr, *The Nature and Destiny of Man*, p. 34). What objective ground is there for regarding the individual as more normal than the herd? He had a morality and religion of his own. They were based on the assumption that a human being, to be distinctively human, ought to depend upon his own inner strength. But by the same token, he renounced the ideal of human brotherhood.

This, incidentally, makes clear why the Fascist and Nazi utilization of Nietzsche as one of their patron saints is based on a falsification of his philosophy. Any totalitarian system is at the very opposite pole of Nietzsche's anarchism. Mussolini justified Fascism on the ground that men were "tired of liberty" and the youth of today "desire order, hierarchy and discipline." Unfortunately there is sufficient truth in Mussolini's assertion to render Fascism plausible and alluring. The truth is that men look for strength from without to fortify their will to salvation, to protect them against themselves as well as against outward enemies. It is this fact which democracy has overlooked, and in overlooking it has had to yield to totalitarian systems of life.

On Schechter's Higher Criticism

TUESDAY, DECEMBER 30, 1941

Schechter's designation of Higher Criticism as "Higher anti-Semitism"[21] has not done the cause of Jewish biblical scholarship any good. It has proved to be a stumbling block in the way of honest research and frank discussion of the problems raised by a scientific and historical approach to the Bible. It belongs to the same class of cheap and dangerous wit as William Jennings Bryan's famous crack at the theory of evolution: "I am more interested in the Rock of Ages than in the age of rocks."

Exactly the same kind of argument was advanced by Bryan against evolution as is advanced by the fundamentalists against the scientific approach to the Bible. He too maintained "that evolution was not a theory but a hypothesis; that since the evolutionists could not agree among themselves on the origin of species, since important changes had been made since Darwin first promulgated his findings, evolution was, therefore, an incoherent mass of conjecture and guesswork with neither a scientific nor factual base."

On Clarence Darrow and Lord Byron

DECEMBER 30, 1941

If Soterics is ever to deserve the name of a normative science, it should be able to bring within its perspective the entire range of creatures that call

---

21. "Higher anti-Semitism" was originally used in an address delivered in honor of Kaufman Kohler. The address, titled "Higher Criticism—Higher Anti-Semitism," was published in Solomon Schechter, *Seminary Addresses and Other Papers*, intro. Louis Finkelstein (New York: Burning Bush Press, 1959), 35–41.

themselves human and evaluate each of them by some comparative standard. Take two such entirely dissimilar characters like Clarence Darrow[22] and Byron[23] (both of whose abridged biographies I have read in *Omnibook* of Dec. 1941). Darrow was a normal human being who lived a long and useful life. He was a true warrior knight if ever there was one. He was a zealous defender of the weak against the strong, of the persecuted against the persecutor. The more helpless the persecuted, the more powerful the persecutor, the greater Darrow's zeal. He was a lover of the truth and an ardent hater of ignorance and superstition. That he belongs to those "whom the forgotten never forget" (an expression Rabbi Goldenson used in his prayer at the funeral of Sol H. Stroock) is attested by the following:

> At all hours of the day and night people filed past to say their farewells: workingmen from the stock yards and steel mills in their overalls; scrub women in their Mother Hubbards; colored men with their lunch baskets under their arms; colored women with groups of wide-eyed little children who had been brought to see the white man who fought for their race; the cold and frightened one who had gone to him to warm their hands at his fire; the weak and confused and indeterminate ones who had been strengthened by his boldness and resolution; the harassed, the unhappy, the mentally ill, whose plight he had tried to make intelligible; teachers whose freedom he had broadened by his struggles; students whose minds had been stimulated by his iconoclasm; lawyers to whose trade he had given another dimension; clergymen to whom he had revealed Christianity at work; those who came from no specific class or section; the indescribable ones who had spilled out their grief to him and whose worries had been lightened by his sympathy; the misfits whom he had defended and for whom he had pleaded in a harsh and cruel world; the labor leaders and union members whose organizations he had preserved under fire; the liberals for whose middle of the road navigation he had fought increasingly for half a century; the radical for whose freedom of thought and speech he had endured the spleen of reaction; the long line of men accused of crime for whom he had earned another chance; those who had killed and who lived now only because this dead man had lived; the middle class folk for whom he had been a rallying point, a debunker, an intellectual spark.

22. Clarence Darrow (1857–1938) was a famous controversial lawyer, civil libertarian, and agnostic. He defended John Thomas Scopes in the "Scopes Monkey Trial" of 1925. An account of this trial was made into the movie *Inherit the Wind*, starring Spencer Tracy and Fredrick March. Darrow also defended Leopold and Loeb in the murder of Bobby Franks in 1924.

23. George Gordon, Lord Byron (1788–1924) was a famous Romantic poet.

"The masks of battle are all over his face," wrote H. L. Mencken. "He has been through more wars than a whole regiment of Pershings. And most of them have been struggles to the death, without codes or quarter."

Men of the Darrow type are unfortunately too few to make a dent on the kind of a world we live in. To realize what kind of a world it is, one has but to note the vast array of evil forces with which Darrow tried to grapple. To take as an example only one aspect of it, the religious with which I have firsthand familiarity, the biographer has this interesting fact to record: In his old age Darrow went around the country with three representatives of religion—a Jew, a Catholic, and a Protestant—debating the subject of religion. He was the protagonist of Agnosticism. I dare say that from the standpoint of religion at its best, there was more and higher religion in his agnosticism than in the kind of religion which was represented by its official defenders. He was eager to bring about a mutual understanding among the representatives of the different religions, by having them become acquainted with one another's religion. "Yet," says his biographer, "of the four men on the platform in each of the cities, the only one who was received with suspicion, fear and dislike was the agnostic among them. Eighty per cent of the audiences hated Darrow's point of view reports Whitehead" (his lecture manager). This figure tells the whole story of what anyone must put up with who challenges the imbecilities and hypocrisies which beset the cause of sincere and intelligent religion. Certainly no smaller is the percentage of the evil forces which dominate the rest of human life.

Let us take a look now at Byron. I am not in the least interested in passing judgment on his wallowing in sensuality. His poetic gifts apart, he strikes me as a human bull much sought after by lady cows. That all such people can afford to play dalliance at love without having to do a stitch of honest work indicates how far parasitism is still an accepted part of social life. There is nothing in his personal life that can serve as a stimulus nor in his thinking that can serve as a guide to the striving for salvation. Yet I suppose there must be something in the very frustration of his personal life that can throw light on the problem of soterics as a whole. Just what it is I cannot at this moment say. . . .

From the subjective standpoint, it can be conjectured with a great deal of certainty that Byron was a far less happy man than Darrow, and that despite the great fame and influence of his poetry. This can be seen from what Shelley said about him when the two were together in Italy: "He is heartily and deeply discontented with himself; and contemplating in the distorted mirror of his own thoughts the nature and the habits of men, what can he behold but objects of contempt and despair?" Byron was evidently quite a misanthrope. Darrow it seems, must have been quite a lover of mankind. The mere fact that his experience with the McNamara case did not embitter him against the workers' organizations is sufficient testimony to his love for his fellow men.

In the light of soterical analysis of the final interests, a misanthrope is one who cannot set up humanity or the brotherhood of mankind as a goal to live for. By the same token that he hates mankind, he hates himself, and therefore must also lack any personality-goal to live for. As for God or a rational cosmos, that is out of the question. This means that, subjectively, a person like Byron achieves nothing but perdition in this life. On the other hand, Darrow must have felt, despite occasional lapses into states of mental depression, that he was living for purposes that made his life worthwhile to himself and to others. Subjectively he surely achieved salvation.

More on Niebuhr

DECEMBER 30, 1941

Whatever else soterics may accomplish, it certainly can furnish the key to many an enigmatic philosophy of religion, whether traditional or mystic, as well as a criterion by which to judge the completeness or significance of any modern philosophy of life. This time I shall make use of the soterical analysis to render R. Niebuhr's opening chapter of his *The Nature and Destiny of Man* not only more understandable, but more successful in proving its point.

The chapter is called "Man as a Problem to Himself." After pointing out the paradoxes inherent in man's conception of himself and of his place in the universe, Niebuhr finds that they are due to the fact that man views himself in twofold fashion: as a child of nature and as spirit transcending nature. The rationalist recognizes such transcendence in man's rational capacity. But the degree of his transcendence is much greater than that connoted in "reason," for man has the further ability to stand outside himself, even outside reason, as when he submits to inquiry the affirmations of reason.

In terms of the soterical analysis into four factors or causes of salvation, the foregoing means that man functions not only in the functional interests (nature or world) and the rational or formal interests (reason), but also in the final or purposive interests. The values Personality, Humanity, God represent man's self-transcendence or ability to make himself the object of his consciousness.

Soterical View of Human Nature—Classical and Christian Also

DECEMBER 30, 1941

II. *The Classical View of Man.* Both according to Plato and to Aristotle, man is a body-mind dualism. For Aristotle the "mind" in that dualism is passive in contrast to "active *nous*" (mind). In Stoicism the relation of mind or reason to nature is not always consistent; at times it is the antithesis of nature (as in impulse) and at times it is regarded as synonymous with nature or God (pantheism).

The Greek dramatists represent the principle of order, whose protagonist is Zeus, as being defied by the vitalities, whose protagonist is Dionysus.

Translated into soterical terms, the classical view of man compares him to a battlefield wherever the functional and the rational interests contend with each other. According to Aristotle, the immortal principle is other than the reason which is hyphenated with or involved in the body. The "active mind" belongs to the category of final values. According to Plato, the formal values themselves are the external ideals. The Greek dramatists with a sense for life's realities appreciate the creative element in the functional interests, but also their tendency to disrupt measure, law, reason.

III. *The Christian View of Man.* "The Christian faith in God," says N., "as creator of the world transcends the canons and autonomies of rationality, particularly the autonomy between mind and matter, between consciousness and extension." I confess that without the soterical analysis, this statement of N. would be to me completely meaningless. This, however, is what it means to me in terms of that analysis: The faith in God as creator of the world introduces a new category into our understanding of man, viz., the category of purpose. To realize the connection between the conception of God as creator and the category of purpose, it is necessary to realize that for ancient man the discovery of what he regarded as purpose was so overwhelming that he personified the purpose and ascribed to it not only the factor of initiative but also the factor of creativity. In fact, even we moderns are wont to identify initiative with creativity.

The final values, of which godhood is the most representative, cannot be identified with either the functional or the formal. Insofar as it is in those final values rather than in the functional or rational that we discover the uniqueness of man, there can be no inherent contradiction between the two latter. This conclusion is in accord with the biblical conception of the unity of body and soul—the soul corresponding to the rational principle in the Greek conception of man.

What N. speaks of as "the homelessness of the human spirit" refers to the fact that man stands outside both the necessity of nature and the laws of rationality in that he can contemplate them, view them from without. This constitutes his freedom, which alone gives meaning to his life. But what else is this freedom and its concomitant transcendence of nature and rationality if not the domain of purposive values? It is from that standpoint that he must see himself to understand himself as man. "To understand himself truly," says N., "means to begin with a faith that he is understood from beyond himself, that he is known and loved of God and must find himself in terms of obedience to the divine will." This means that man cannot understand himself truly unless he reckons with those values of purpose which man must follow, obey, in order to achieve salvation. Following those values constitutes obeying God's will.

But the same Christian faith that sees man's essence in his relation to God sees man's inherent failure in the fact that man "refuses to admit his creatureliness." In the soterical analysis the purposive values are personality, humanity, God. They are interdependent, but not coordinate. God is creator, personality is creature, humanity is mediator between creator and creature. Whenever the individual forgets his role as creature, and humanity (or its representative, the clan, tribe, or nation) its role as intermediary, they set themselves up as God. That is the cardinal sin.

Time Line of Kaplan's Life

June 11, 1881	Mordecai M. Kaplan is born in Sventzian, Lithuania. Kaplan learns the English date of his birth only when he goes to the New York Public Library and looks up the Hebrew date.
1888	Kaplan spends a year in Paris with his mother and sister. His father came to New York first.
1889	Kaplan comes to America.
1893	Kaplan enrolls at the Jewish Theological Seminary (JTS) of New York.
1895	Kaplan enrolls at City College of New York.
1900	Kaplan graduates from City College.
1900	Kaplan registers at Columbia University in the Master's program.
1902	Kaplan is ordained as a rabbi at the JTS.
1902	Solomon Schechter becomes head of the newly reorganized JTS.
1903	Kaplan becomes minister of the Orthodox congregation Kehilath Jeshurun.
1905	Kaplan receives his Master's degree from Columbia University and writes his thesis on Henry Sidgwick.
1908	Kaplan marries Lena Rubin, a member of Kehilath Jeshurun.
1908	Kaplan leaves Kehilath Jeshurun.
1908	Kaplan receives rabbinic ordination (*smicha*) from Rabbi Isaac Jacob Reines while on his honeymoon in Europe.
1909	Kaplan becomes principal of the newly formed Teachers Institute at the JTS.
1909	Birth of Judith, Kaplan's first child.
1910	Kaplan begins to teach Homiletics at the JTS rabbinical school.
1912	Birth of Hadassah, Kaplan's second child.

1913	Beginning of Kaplan's major diary.
1914	Birth of Naomi, Kaplan's third child.
1915	Solomon Schechter dies.
1915	Birth of Selma, Kaplan's fourth child, named after Solomon Schechter.
1917	Kaplan's father, Rabbi Israel Kaplan, dies.
1917	Kaplan becomes rabbi of the newly formed Jewish Center, "the shul with a pool and a school."
1922	Kaplan leaves the Jewish Center and organizes the Society for the Advancement of Judaism (SAJ). He is called the Leader but later changes his title to rabbi.
1922	Bat mitzvah of Judith Kaplan, the first bat mitzvah in the United States.
1923	Kaplan attends the Zionist Congress in Karlsbad, Germany.
1925	SAJ purchases a building on West 86th Street in New York City. Kaplan is distressed because he realizes that the SAJ will be a congregation and not the beginning of a new movement.
1927	Kaplan leaves the JTS for a position at the Jewish Institute of Religion but returns after three months.
1929	Kaplan receives an honorary doctorate from the JTS.
1930	Ira Eisenstein, Kaplan's most devoted disciple, becomes executive director at the SAJ.
1931	Kaplan establishes the Seminary College of Jewish Studies, the evening division of the Teachers Institute.
1934	Publication of *Judaism as a Civilization*.
1934	Judith Kaplan and Ira Eisenstein are married.
1935	*The Reconstructionist* begins publication.
1935	Kaplan becomes a grandfather for the first time. Jeremy Musher, "eight pounds of potentiality," as Kaplan notes in his diary, is born to Sidney and Hadassah Kaplan Musher.
1936	Publication of *Judaism in Transition*, which deals with Marx and Maimonides.

1936	Publication of *Mesillat Yesharim: The Path of the Upright*, with introduction and a new translation by Kaplan.
1937	Kaplan lives in Jerusalem, teaching education at The Hebrew University in the fall. Kaplan meets and has dialogues with Martin Buber, although he feels that Buber never initiates conversation.
1937	Publication of *The Meaning of God in Modern Jewish Religion*.
1939	Kaplan leaves Jerusalem and comes home during the summer. Cyrus Adler refuses to let Kaplan teach in Jerusalem every other summer. "He froze to the occasion," Kaplan notes.
1941	Publication of *The New Haggadah*.
1945	Publication of *The Sabbath Prayer Book*.
1945	Kaplan is excommunicated by the ultra-Orthodox Agudat Rabbanim of the United States and Canada at Hotel McAlpin, across from Macy's.
1945	Kaplan retires as dean of the Teachers Institute.
1945	With Kaplan's assistance, Abraham Joshua Heschel joins the faculty at the JTS.
1948	Kaplan attends the opening of the University of Judaism in Los Angeles, which he helped to establish.
1948	Publication of the *Future of the American Jew*.
1951	Publication of *The Faith of America: Prayers, Readings, and Songs for the Celebration of American Holidays*.
1951	Kaplan turns seventy.
1952	Publication of *Mordecai M. Kaplan, An Evaluation*, edited by Ira Eisenstein and Eugene Kohn.
1954	Publication of *Ha-emunah ve-hamusar* (Faith and Ethics).
1955	Publication of *A New Zionism*.
1955	Establishment of the Federation of Congregations and Havurot. These congregations were Reconstructionist and Kaplan supporters.
1956	Publication of *Questions Jews Ask*.
1958	Publication of *Judaism Without Supernaturalism*.

1958   Death of Lena Rubin Kaplan, Kaplan's wife.

1959   Kaplan marries Rivka Rieger, noted Israeli artist and all-around great person.

1960   Publication of *A Greater Judaism in the Making: A Study of the Modern Evolution of Judaism.*

1963   Kaplan retires from the JTS.

1964   Publication of *The Purpose and Meaning of Jewish Existence: A People in the Image of God.*

1966   Publication of *Not So Random Thoughts: Witty and Profound Observations on Society, Religion, and Jewish Life.*

1968   Opening of the Reconstructionist Rabbinical College. Kaplan travels to Philadelphia to teach at the college.

1970   Publication of *The Religion of Ethical Nationhood: Judaism's Contribution to World Peace.*

1973   Publication of *If Not Now, When? Toward a Reconstruction of the Jewish People: Conversations Between Mordecai M. Kaplan and Arthur A. Cohen.*

1975   Kaplan makes aliyah (immigrates) to Israel.

1978   Last entries in Kaplan's diary, twenty-seven volumes in all. The original is housed at the JTS. The digitized diary is available at www.Kaplancenter.org.

1979   Kaplan returns from Israel and moves into the Hebrew Home for the Aged in Riverdale, New York.

November 8,   Kaplan dies.
1983

Glossary

The asterisk indicates that more information can be found in Mel Scult, *Judaism Faces the Twentieth Century: A Biography of Mordecai M. Kaplan* (Detroit: Wayne State University Press, 1993).

Abbreviations

CCNY, City College of New York
HUC, Hebrew Union College
JIR, Jewish Institute of Religion
JTS, Jewish Theological Seminary
SAJ, Society for the Advancement of Judaism
TI, Teachers Institute
ZOA, Zionist Organization of America

*Cyrus Adler (1863–1940), PhD, Johns Hopkins University; national community leader; president of Dropsie College, 1908–1940; president of JTS, 1915–1940; president of the American Jewish Committee, 1929–1940; editor of the *American Jewish Year Book*. Adler was instrumental in establishing the Jewish Publication Society (1888) and the American Jewish Historical Society (1892). His autobiography is *I Have Considered the Days* (Philadelphia: Jewish Publication Society, 1941). There is no definitive scholarly biography of Adler. The best one can do is read the collection of his letters: *Cyrus Adler: Selected Letters*, ed. Ira Robinson (Philadelphia: Jewish Publication Society, 1985; digitized 2006).

*Felix Adler (1851–1933), PhD; philosopher, rationalist, and religious leader; founder of the Ethical Culture Movement who also established the Ethical Culture Society; professor of political and social ethics at Columbia University. Kaplan studied with Adler and was deeply influenced by his concern for the ethical. On Kaplan and Adler, see Mel Scult, *The Radical American Judaism of Mordecai M. Kaplan* (Bloomington: Indiana University Press, 2013), 66–87.

Morris Adler (1906–1966), ordained JTS; rabbi in Detroit; World War II chaplain.

Jacob Agus (1911–1986), graduate of Yeshiva University; PhD, Harvard University; U.S. rabbi, scholar, philosopher; rabbi at Beth El Synagogue in Baltimore; professor of religion at Temple University; member of the faculty of the Reconstructionist Rabbinical College. Although there were many differences between them, Agus and Kaplan had a long and fruitful relationship. See Scult, *Radical American Judaism*, 246. Agus wrote Kaplan after many years that it was because of Kaplan's recommendation that Agus went to Harvard and studied philosophy with Harry A. Wolfson, the preeminent scholar of the time. Agus was a congregational rabbi and a prolific author. His finest work is *The Evolution of Jewish Thought from Biblical Times to the Opening of the Modern Era* (New York: Abelard-Schuman, 1959). Also see Zach Mann, "The American Judaism of Jacob Agus," PhD diss., Jewish Theological Seminary, 2012.

Ahad Ha-Am (Asher Ginzberg) (1856–1927), essayist and philosopher of cultural Zionism; major figure in the development of Zionism. Ahad Ha-Am opposed Herzl on many issues. Kaplan was his most important disciple.

Joseph Albo (c. 1380–1444), Jewish philosopher and rabbi who lived in Spain during the fifteenth century; known chiefly as the author of *Sefer Ha-Ikkarim* (Book of Principles), the classic work on the fundamentals of Judaism.

William F. Albright (1891–1971), American archaeologist, biblical scholar (one of the most important on the American scene in the early twentieth century), and philologist.

Gordon Allport (1897–1967), prominent American scholar on psychology; founding figure in personality theory. Kaplan was well acquainted with Allport's work. On the way that midcentury social scientists fit into Kaplan's thought, see Mel Scult, "Kaplan and Personality," in *Reappraisals and New Studies of the Modern Jewish Experience: Essays in Honor of Robert Seltzer*, ed. Brian Smollett and Christian Wiese (Leiden: Brill, 2014), 162–80.

Max Arzt (1897–1975), ordained JTS; author; administrator at JTS, 1939–1962; vice-chancellor of JTS; president of the Rabbinical Assembly.

Salo W. Baron (1895–1989), PhD; ordained JTS (Vienna); historian, author, and editor; faculty member at Columbia University.

Alexander Basel (1882–1941), graduate of Columbia University; ordained JTS; author and a chaplain for the Bronx County Jail.

Hillel Bavli (1893–1961), Hebrew poet and literary critic; faculty member at TI. Bavli spoke Hebrew as though he were reading poetry.

*****Samson Benderly** (1876–1944), U.S. educator (important especially to American Jewish education) who was born in Palestine; director of the Bureau of Jewish Education of the New York Kehillah. Benderly is the only person in the 1920s and 1930s whom Kaplan considered a close personal friend. They frequently met for lunch when the TI was in the East Village and Benderly worked nearby. Benderly's students, all later leaders in Jewish education, were called the Benderly Boys, although there was one woman, Rebecca Aronson, who eventually married Barnett Brickner, a leading Reform rabbi. On Benderly in general, see Jonathan Krasner, *The Benderly Boys and American Jewish Education* (Waltham, MA: Brandeis University Press, 2011).

Joseph Bentwich (1902–1982), educator and mathematician; teacher at Hebrew Reali School in Haifa (Bentwich settled in Palestine in 1924); inspector of schools for the Mandate Government; biographer of Solomon Schechter.

Norman de Mattos Bentwich (1883–1971), British lawyer and legal academic; Legal Secretary and first attorney general of Mandatory Palestine (1918–1929); president of the Jewish Historical Society; biographer of Solomon Schechter and Judah Magnes. Bentwich was the eldest son of Herbert Bentwich. His papers, stored at the National Zionist Archives in Jerusalem, contain a wealth of Schechter materials.

Samuel Hugo Bergman (1883–1975), German and Israeli Jewish philosopher, scholar of Jewish philosophy, and author; professor at the Hebrew University; first director of the National and University Library; member of Brit Shalom, a group advocating a binational Jewish-Arab state; close associate of Martin Buber. Bergman was born in Prague and was a classmate of Kafka's there. He was a Zionist who emigrated to Eretz Yisrael in 1920.

Henri Bergson (1859–1941), French philosopher. Bergson was widely read in the first half of the twentieth century and was influential on Kaplan's thinking. Concept of élan vital comes from Bergson. Kaplan read Bergson's work throughout his life, especially his *Creative Evolution*.

Rabbi Solomon Bernards (1914–2004), ordained JTS; director of interreligious cooperation at the Anti-Defamation League for twenty-two years. Bernards was a dedicated Kaplan supporter.

Hayim Nahman Bialik (1873–1934), greatest Hebrew poet of modern times, essayist, story writer, translator, and editor; profound influence on modern Jewish culture.

Frederick Simon Bodenheimer (1897–1959), zoologist and entomologist; professor at Hebrew University. Bodenheimer's survey of the Sinai in 1927 revealed the origin of the biblical phenomenon of the falling of the manna. Bodenheimer was born in Cologne, Germany.

Ben Zion Bokser (1907–1984), leading Conservative rabbi and author; founder of the Center for the Study of Ethics at Queens College; active member of the Rabbinical Assembly; disciple of Abraham Isaac Kook.

Barnett Brickner (1892–1958), leading Reform rabbi, Zionist, and author. Brickner was involved in numerous national Jewish educational activities. He is the father of Balfour Brickner, also a leading Reform rabbi. Barnett was the husband of Rebecca Aronson Brickner (1894–1981), a leading figure in Jewish education. She studied with Kaplan and Samson Benderly and was the only female member of the Benderly Boys.

Ruth Brin (1921–2009), graduate of Vassar College; master's degree, University of Minnesota; honorary doctorate, Reconstructionist Rabbinical College; poet, liturgical pioneer, and author. Brin's most important book is *Harvest: Collected Poems and Prayers* (Duluth, MN: Holy Cow! Press, 1999).

Selig Brodetsky (1888–1954), Russian-born English mathematician; member of the World Zionist Executive Committee; second president of the Hebrew University.

Martin Buber (1878–1965), Austrian-born Jewish philosopher best known for his philosophy of dialogue. Emigrated to Jerusalem, for a position at the Hebrew University, in 1938. Kaplan met Buber a number of times when he was in Jerusalem in the 1930s. Kaplan was also involved with Buber when the latter visited the United States in 1951. Kaplan thought that Buber's most important contribution was to make the biblical text available to German Jews in a language they would appreciate.

Alexander Burnstein (1900–1980), ordained JTS; active in interfaith concerns.

Paul Chertoff (1880–1966), rabbi and talmudist; faculty member at TI. Chertoff was a supporter of Kaplan.

Israel Chipkin (1891–1955), community educator at the Bureau of Jewish Education; director of the Friedlaender classes and registrar at TI. Chipkin was a strong supporter of Kaplan.

Armand Cohen (1909–2007), ordained JTS; rabbi at the Park Synagogue in Cleveland.

Boaz Cohen (1899–1968), ordained JTS; PhD, Columbia University; rabbinic scholar; faculty member at JTS, teaching Jewish law; author on comparative law.

Hermann Cohen (1842–1918), German Jewish philosopher who is often held to be the most important Jewish philosopher of the nineteenth century; one of the founders of the Marburg School of Neo-Kantianism. Although Kaplan was critical of Cohen's philosophy, he valued Cohen highly. Kaplan's primary work on Cohen is *The Purpose and Meaning of Jewish Existence: A People in the Image of God* (Philadelphia: Jewish Publication Society, 1964). The core of the book is an epitome of Cohen's major work, *Religion der Vernuft*, presented in an aphoristic style and commented on by Kaplan.

Jack Cohen (1919–2012), ordained JTS; educational director and rabbi at SAJ; director of Hillel at the Hebrew University; faculty member at Hebrew University; founder of Congregation Mevakshei Derech in Jerusalem; author of several books, including *Judaism in a Post Halakhic Age* and *Guide for an Age of Confusion: Studies in the Thinking of Avraham I. Kook and Mordecai M. Kaplan*. Cohen made aliyah in 1961. He was a lifelong Kaplan disciple.

Rabbi Jehudah Cohen (1907–1966), Reform rabbi and social worker; regional director of Hillel in Ann Arbor, Michigan.

*Joseph H. Cohen (1877–1961), businessman and philanthropist; key figure in the founding of the Jewish Center; board member of Beth Israel Hospital for many years. Cohen's business firm manufactured men's clothing, with stores throughout the Northeast. Born in Russia, Cohen came to the United States at the age of 4. He had a rather complicated relationship with Kaplan, being both a supporter and later a critic.

Morris Raphael Cohen (1880–1947), writer, philosopher, and legal scholar; well-known professor at CCNY. Kaplan and Cohen knew each other as teenagers and attended CCNY at the same time. Kaplan studied the classical curriculum and Cohen the science curriculum.

Samuel Cohen (1886–1945), ordained JTS; executive director of the United Synagogue of America.

*Israel Davidson (1870–1939), scholar of medieval Hebrew literature who was born in Lithuania; faculty member at JTS; editor of the four-volume *Thesaurus of Medieval Hebrew Poetry*, his magnum opus.

Moshe Davis (1916–1996), ordained JTS; PhD, Hebrew University; Conservative leader and scholar of American Jewish history; registrar of TI in the early 1940s; founder of the Institute for Contemporary Jewry at Hebrew University. Davis was a strong supporter of Kaplan and helped to reconcile Kaplan and Louis Finkelstein. He was proud of this accomplishment and mentioned it every time I met him in Jerusalem.

David de Sola Pool (1885–1970), rabbi at Sheareth Israel, the Spanish Portuguese Synagogue, where he served for sixty-three years.

*Samuel Dinin (1902–1972), PhD, Columbia University; community leader and editor; executive director of the SAJ; faculty member at JTS and TI.

*Max Drob (1887–1959), ordained JTS; founder of United Synagogue; president of the Rabbinical Assembly.

Abraham Duker (1907–1987), PhD; scholar, author, and librarian; faculty member at Brooklyn College. Duker compiled the index for Kaplan's *Judaism as a Civilization.*

*Alexander Dushkin (1890–1976), PhD, Columbia University; educator and rabbi; community educator in New York City and Jerusalem; founder of the College of Jewish Studies in Chicago; organized the Department of Education at Hebrew University; editor of *Jewish Education* from 1929 to 1935 and from 1939 to 1949. Dushkin was born in Poland and immigrated to the United States in 1901. He became an important disciple of Kaplan and was responsible for bringing him to Hebrew University to teach in 1937 and 1938.

Irwin Edman (1896–1954), author; professor of philosophy at Columbia University noted for the charm and grace of his writing. Edman was a supporter of John Dewey. Kaplan valued his work.

Azriel Eisenberg (1903–1985), leader in Jewish education; author; dean of Gratz College.

*Ira Eisenstein (1906–2001), ordained JTS; leader of the Reconstructionist movement; leader of the SAJ; president of the Reconstructionist Foundation; founder of the Reconstructionist Rabbinical College. Eisenstein is Kaplan's most important disciple and his son-in-law (he married Kaplan's daughter Judith).

*Judah David Eisenstein (1854–1956), Hebraist, author, encyclopedist, and translator; grandfather of Ira and Myron Eisenstein.

*Judith Kaplan Eisenstein (1909–1996), PhD; author and expert on Jewish music; eldest of Kaplan's four daughters and his favorite philosophical companion. The other daughters all reported to me that at the dinner table Kaplan talked only to Judith. Kaplan noted that when she was away, he missed discussing his latest ideas with her. She was 14 at the time. Her diary reveals her as a precocious young woman.

Ismar Elbogen (1874–1943), Jewish German rabbi, scholar, and historian; expert in Jewish liturgy.

Hyman Enelow (1876–1934), noted Reform rabbi, scholar, and author; raised money for Israel Davidson's *Thesaurus of Medieval Hebrew Poetry.*

Louis Epstein (1887–1949), ordained JTS; authority on Jewish law and marriage; president of the Rabbinical Assembly. Epstein opposed Kaplan on many issues.

Yitzhak Epstein (1862–1943), Hebrew writer and linguist; pioneer in modern Hebrew education in Eretz Yisrael and in the Diaspora.

*Louis Finkelstein (1895–1991), Conservative rabbi, talmudist, and author; president of JTS, 1940–1972 (Finkelstein became president of the seminary when

Cyrus Adler died). Finkelstein respected Kaplan, but they differed on a host of issues and had a difficult time with each other from the start. Kaplan once reported
in the diary that he was inflicted with "Finkitus." If looks could kill, they would
both be dead; see the photo in Scult, *Judaism Faces the Twentieth Century*, 231.

Rabbi Henry Fischer (1903–?), ordained JTS; rabbi in Arverne, New York,
where Kaplan and members of his congregation, the Jewish Center, regularly
summered.

Abraham H. Fraenkl (1891–1965), mathematician; dean of mathematics and
rector at Hebrew University. Fraenkl, a Zionist, was born in Germany.

Solomon Freehof (1892–1990), prominent Reform Rabbi, author, expert in Jewish law, and authority on responsa.

*Israel Friedlaender (1876–1920), Semitics scholar and community leader; professor of biblical literature at the JTS, starting in 1903. Adult education classes at
JTS are named after him. Friedlaender was born in Russia and was killed in the
Ukraine in 1920 while on a relief mission. His philosophy has much in common
with Kaplan's. Kaplan greatly respected him.

Emanuel Gamoran (1895–1962), PhD; noted community educator and author;
president of the National Council for Jewish Education; editor of *The Jewish
Teacher*.

Joel S. Geffen (1903–1988), ordained JTS; Associate Director of Field Activities
at the JTS beginning in 1944, becoming the department's director a few years
later. Geffen is the father of noted Judaica scholar Rela Geffen.

Harold Louis Ginsberg (1903–1990), biblical scholar and author; professor of
Bible at JTS; expert on ancient Canaanite myths. Ginzberg was born in Montreal
and studied in London.

Adele Ginzberg (1886–1980), influential figure in the Conservative movement;
wife of Louis Ginzberg. Before Louis Ginzberg married Adele, he was involved
for a short time with Henrietta Szold, the founder of Hadassah. On this relationship and its connection to Adele Ginzberg, see Henrietta Szold, *Lost Love:, The
Untold Story of Henrietta Szold—Unpublished Diary and Letters*, ed. and trans.
Baila Round Shargel (Philadelphia: Jewish Publication Society, 1997).

*Louis Ginzberg (1873–1953), Talmud and Midrash scholar and author;
faculty member of JTS; one of the founders of the Conservative movement.
Ginzberg was a primary faculty critic of Kaplan, and the two men had a complex
relationship.

Nahum N. Glatzer (1903–1990), German Jewish scholar, writer, and anthol-
ogist; professor of Judaic Studies at Brandeis University and also head of the

department. Glatzer introduced the work of Franz Rosenzweig to the United States.

*Solomon Goldman (1893–1953), Conservative rabbi and Zionist leader. Goldman was a key disciple of Kaplan.

David Goldstein (1902–1990), ordained JTS; rabbi at Har Zion synagogue in Philadelphia; prominent thinker in the Conservative movement.

Israel Goldstein (1896–1986), ordained JTS; Jewish historian, author, and Zionist leader; one of the founders of Brandeis University; member of the New York Board of Rabbis; officer of the ZOA.

Jacob Golub (1895–1959), ordained JTS; LL.B. and PhD; community education administrator and author; educational director of the ZOA.

*Robert Gordis (1908–1992), ordained JTS (1932); leading Conservative rabbi; noted Bible scholar who published extensively on the Bible and other topics; rabbi in Rockaway Park, 1931–1968; founder of the first Conservative day school; president of the Rabbinical Assembly; professor at JTS (1940–1992); teacher at Columbia University and the Union Theological Seminary. Gordis was primarily responsible for the Rabbinical Assembly siddur published by JTS in 1946. He had a complex relationship with Kaplan.

Albert I. Gordon (1903–1958), ordained JTS; author; executive director of the United Synagogue; faculty member at Boston University.

*Simon Greenberg (1901–1993), ordained JTS; PhD, Dropsie College; Conservative leader; executive director of the United Synagogue of America; president of the Rabbinical Assembly. Simon Greenberg is the father of biblical scholar Moshe Greenberg and of scholar and educator Daniel Greenberg. Simon Greenberg admired Kaplan but was critical of him.

Julius Greenstone (1873–1955), ordained JTS; religious educator; administrator and principal of Gratz College. Greenstone was a longtime friend of Kaplan.

Jacob Grossman (1886–1970s?), BA, Columbia University; ordained JTS, 1911; rabbi in New York City and in Flushing, New York; one of the founders of Camp Tabor. Grossman frequented the Kaplan household to discuss sermon material.

Julius (Yizhak) Guttman (1880–1950), philosopher and historian of Jewish philosophy.

Herman Hailperin (1899–1973), ordained JTS; PhD, University of Pittsburgh; author; expert on medieval Jewish scholarship.

Abraham Halkin (1904–1990), scholar, author (publishing in the area of medieval Jewish studies), and teacher; teacher of Hebrew language, culture, and history at CCNY and at JTS. Abraham Halkin is the father of author Hillel Halkin and the brother of Shimon Halkin. He spoke beautiful Hebrew.

Shimon Halkin (1898–1987), Hebrew poet, novelist, and critic; professor of modern Hebrew literature at the Hebrew University. Shimon Halkin is the brother of Abraham Halkin and uncle of Hillel Halkin. He was born in Russia but was raised in the United States. He settled in Palestine in 1932.

Harry Halpern (1899–1981), ordained JTS; noted preacher; president of the Rabbinical Assembly.

James Heller (1892–1971), Reform rabbi and Zionist leader; faculty member at the University of Cincinnati; president of the Central Conference of American Rabbis.

Joseph Hertz (1872–1946), ordained JTS (the first graduate, in fact); served as rabbi in Johannesburg; Chief Rabbi of the British Empire, beginning in 1913 until his death; author of a widely used Torah commentary.

Arthur Hertzberg (1921–2006), ordained JTS; Jewish American scholar, activist, and Zionist leader; president of the American Jewish Congress for many years. Hertzberg was an important public intellectual in the mid-twentieth century.

Theodor Herzl (1860–1904), Austrian Jew; founder of modern political Zionism; founder of the World Zionist Organization; promoter of immigration to Palestine in an effort to establish a Jewish state.

Rabbi Isaac Herzog (1888–1959), doctorate in literature, London University; rabbinical scholar, linguist, and mathematician; rabbi in Dublin and Belfast, Ireland; chief rabbi of Eretz Yisrael from 1936 to 1959. Herzog was born in Lomza, Poland, and raised in England. The charm of his personality, which combined ascetic unworldliness with conversational wit and diplomatic talents, made a great impression.

Michael Higger (1898–1952), PhD, Columbia University; ordained JTS; Talmud scholar and author.

*****Charles I. Hoffman** (1864–1945), ordained JTS; journalist and Conservative leader; editor of the *Jewish Exponent*; friend of Solomon Schechter. Hoffman lived with the Schechters when he was a student at JTS.

Leo Honor (1894–1956), PhD; community educator in New York City and then Chicago; leader in Jewish education; author; member of the Bureau of Jewish Education, New York; faculty member at the College of Jewish Studies, Chicago. Honor was trained by Samson Benderly and Kaplan. He was a member of the group known as the Benderly Boys, all of whom became important in Jewish education.

Jacob Hoschander (1874–1933), biblical scholar and Assyriologist; faculty member at JTS.

Henry Hurwitz (1886–1961), educator, editor, essayist, and community worker; organizer of the Harvard Menorah Society (1906); founder of the Intercollegiate Menorah Association (1913); founder (in 1915) and editor of the *Menorah Journal*. Hurwitz was born in Lithuania and immigrated to the United States at the age of 5. Hurwitz was a friend and admirer of Kaplan.

Moses Hyamson (1862–1949), rabbi and scholar; chairman of the Beth Din of the British Empire; faculty member at JTS, teaching Talmud and Codes.

Elias Inselbuch (1866–1936), Orthodox leader; one of the founders of Mizrachi; member of the Executive Committee of the Union of Orthodox Rabbis. Inselbuch migrated to the United States in 1903 and then to Palestine in 1932.

*****Phineas Israeli** (1880–1948), ordained JTS, 1902; rabbi in Des Moines, Iowa (also in Brooklyn and Massachusetts). Israeli was Kaplan's brother-in-law; he was married to Kaplan's sister Sophie.

Sophie Kaplan Israeli (1879?–1950?), Kaplan's older sister. She was well educated and helped teach Hebrew to Kaplan. See photo of her on my Facebook page.

Vladimir (Ze'ev) Jabotinsky (1880–1940), writer, orator, Zionist leader, and militant revisionist; founder of Betar; spiritual father of the Irgun.

Selma Kaplan Jaffe-Goldman (1915–2008), television production and syndication worker. Selma is Kaplan's fourth and therefore youngest daughter. She was named after Solomon Schechter. She married Saul Jaffe (1913–1977), an attorney and radio and TV producer; she later married Joseph L. Goldman (1904–1991), a physician and chief of the Department of Otolaryngology at Mt. Sinai Hospital.

Leo Jung (1892–1987), Orthodox leader and rabbi at the Jewish Center; author. Jung succeeded Kaplan as rabbi at the center.

*****Max Kadushin** (1895–1980), ordained JTS; scholar of rabbinic Judaism, author, and educator; faculty member at JTS. Kadushin was an important disciple of Kaplan but was critical of him in later life.

Lena Rubin Kaplan (1884–1958), participant in the founding of Hadassah and active member of the SAJ. Lena was Kaplan's wife, marrying him in 1908. She was the youngest of ten children.

Maurice Karpf (1889–1964), PhD, Columbia University; Jewish social work administrator and author; director of the Training School for Jewish Social Work.

Ezekiel Kaufman (1889–1963), PhD, University of Berne; sociological thinker, biblical scholar, and author; teacher at the Reali School in Haifa and at Hebrew University. Kaufman was born in Podolia, Ukraine, and received a traditional education. He immigrated to Israel in the early 1930s. Kaufman challenged theories of biblical criticism and wrote a sociology of Jewish history that Kaplan valued. He also wrote a multivolume history of the religion of Israel. Kaufman's theories about the development of biblical religion dominated the JTS at midcentury.

*****Charles E. H. Kauvar** (1879–1971), ordained JTS; author; president of the United Synagogue of America. Kauvar was a cousin of Kaplan and inspired Kaplan to seek out and attend JTS.

Israel Kazis (1911–2001), Conservative rabbi and World War II chaplain; rabbi at Mishkan Tefila, Boston; founder of the Solomon Schechter Day School in Newton, Massachusetts.

Hayyim Kievel (d. 1991), ordained JTS; rabbi at Temple Israel of Albany. The Hayyim and Esther Kieval Institute of Jewish-Christian Studies at Siena College is named for him.

Joseph Klausner (1874–1958), historian and professor of Hebrew Literature and literary critic; faculty member at Hebrew University; chief redactor of *The Hebrew Encyclopedia*; editor of the journal *Ha-Shiloah*; author of *Jesus of Nazareth: His Life, Times, and Teaching*. Klausner was an ardent Zionist polemicist, supportive of Revisionist and religious and ideologies, and a candidate for president in the first Israeli presidential election.

Isaac Klein (1905–1979), ordained JTS; prominent Conservative rabbi and halachic authority; president of the Rabbinical Assembly; author of *A Guide for Jewish Religious Practice*, the standard legal guide for observant Conservative Jews.

Israel Jacob Kligler (1889–1944), bacteriologist; director of the Department of Hygiene of Hebrew University.

*****Eugene Kohn** (1887–1977), rabbi in Baltimore; Reconstructionist; edited Reconstructionist prayer books with Kaplan and Rabbi Ira Eisenstein. Eugene Kohn is the brother of Jacob Kohn, also a JTS graduate. He was a close disciple of Kaplan; Kaplan, Ira Eisenstein, and Kohn were called the Father, the Son-in-Law, and the Holy Ghost Writer, a trinity coined by Eisenstein (or at least related by him).

Samuel Calmen Kohs (1890–1984), PhD, Stanford University; social worker and psychologist.

Rabbi Abraham Isaac Kook (1865–1935), religious Zionist and Kabbalist; first chief rabbi of Palestine under the British Mandate. Kook was born in Eastern

Europe and attended Volozhin Yeshiva. He immigrated to Israel in 1905. Kook's religious ideology has many affinities with Kaplan's. On Kaplan and Kook, see Jack Cohen, *Guides for an Age of Confusion: Studies in the Thinking of Abraham Y. Kook and Mordecai Kaplan* (New York: Fordham University Press, 1999).

Louis Kraft (1891–1975), community worker and author; executive director of the Jewish Welfare Board.

Harold Laski (1893–1950), British political theorist, economist, author, and lecturer.

Irving Lehman (1876–1945), legal philosopher; judge for the State Supreme Court of New York; board member of the Union of American Hebrew Congregations (UAHC); judge for the Rosenwald contest (see Chapter 4). Lehman appreciated Kaplan's submission to the Rosenwald contest but thought that it had significant weaknesses.

Gershon Levi (1909–1990), graduate of JTS; president of the Rabbinical Assembly; author.

Morris Levine (1881–1935), rabbi; much respected faculty member at JTS. Levine was primarily responsible for bringing Hebrew to TI (the original language of instruction at TI was English, but Samson Benderly succeeded so well with the Talmud Torahs in New York City that the language was switched to Hebrew c. 1915).

Israel Levinthal (1888–1982), ordained JTS; D.H.L.; Conservative leader, well-known rabbi, and author; rabbi at the Brooklyn Jewish Center, which was modeled after Kaplan's Jewish Center in Manhattan; member of the National Executive Committee of the ZOA. Levinthal was traditional in his thought and observance. His father was Rabbi Bernard Levinthal, a well-known Orthodox rabbi who opposed his son going to JTS.

Louis Levitsky (1897–1975), ordained JTS; president of the Rabbinical Assembly; author.

Felix Alexander Levy (1884–1963), Reform rabbi. Although born in New York City, Levy served a Chicago Reform congregation. He influenced the Reform Columbus Platform of 1937.

Joseph Levy (?–1944), businessman and president of Crawford Clothes; one of the founders of the SAJ and a consistently generous supporter of it.

Saul Lieberman (1898–1983), rabbi and Talmud scholar; influential faculty member at JTS. For an informative work, see Marc Shapiro, *Saul Lieberman and the Orthodox* (Scranton, PA: University of Scranton Press, 2006). On the Finkelstein era, when Lieberman was so central to JTS administration, see

Michael B. Greenbaum, *Louis Finkelstein and the Conservative Movement: Conflict and Growth* (Binghamton, NY: Global, 2001). See also Neil Gillman, *Conservative Judaism: The New Century* (West Orange, NJ: Behrman House, 1993).

Abraham Liebovitz (1878–1964), manufacturer and community fundraiser; one of the founders of SAJ; officer of the Jewish Reconstructionist Foundation.

Harry Liebovitz (1882–?), clothing manufacturer; president of the Jewish Education Association; board member of the SAJ.

Irma Levy Lindheim (1886–1978), educator and author; wealthy Zionist fundraiser; president of Hadassah and of the Women's Zionist Organization. Lindheim studied at Columbia and the JIR. She settled in Israel in 1933. See volume 1 of *Communings of the Spirit* for Kaplan's conversations with her.

*****Judah L. Magnes** (1877–1948), PhD, Heidelberg University, 1902; American Reform rabbi and Zionist leader; president of the New York Kehillah; chancellor (1924–1935) and then first president of Hebrew University. Magnes was born in San Francisco. He was a pacifist and believed in a binational Jewish state. Kaplan and Magnes knew each other well. See the fine collection of his letters and speeches, Judah L. Magnes, *Dissenter in Zion: From the Writings of Judah L. Magnes*, ed. Arthur A. Goren (Cambridge, MA: Harvard University Press, 1982).

*****Moses Sebulun Margolies** (1851–1936), Orthodox rabbi and community leader; rabbi at Kehilath Jeshurun in 1905 along with Kaplan. Kaplan respected him, although they had their differences. Ramaz School is named after him. Kehilath Jeshurun is still one of the primary Orthodox congregations in Manhattan.

Max Margolis (1866–1932), PhD, Columbia University; Semitic philologist and Septuagint scholar; author with Alexander Marx of the early standard history of the Jewish people, *A History of the Jewish People* (Philadelphia: Jewish Publication Society, 1945); faculty member at Hebrew Union College and Dropsie College.

*****Louis Marshall** (1856–1929), lawyer and community leader; one of the founders of the American Jewish Committee; member of the Board of JTS; important spokesman for Jewish rights; key figure of the German Jewish elite.

*****Alexander Marx** (1878–1953), historian, librarian, and author; faculty member at JTS and largely responsible for making the school's collection one of the largest Jewish libraries in the world.

Sidney Matz (1899–1946), MA, Harvard University; business executive; one of the founders of the American Economic Committee for Palestine.

*****Sabato Morais** (1823–1897), Sephardic rabbi in Philadelphia; one of the founders and first president of JTS; friend of Italian nationalist thinker Giuseppe

Mazzini. See Arthur Kiron, "Golden Ages, Promised Lands: The Victorian Rabbinic Humanism of Sabato Morais," PhD diss., Columbia University, 1999.

Julian Morgenstern (1881–1976), rabbi, biblical and Semitic language scholar, and author; appointed president of HUC in 1922.

Louis J. Moss (1884–1948), lawyer and community leader; officer of the ZOA; president of the United Synagogue of America.

Hadassah Kaplan Musher (1912–2013), educator; active in the SAJ; one of the organizers of the Reconstructionist Women's Organization. Hadassah was Kaplan's second eldest daughter, and she married Sidney Musher. She was a strong supporter of Kaplan's projects.

Sidney Musher (1905–1990), inventor, pharmaceuticals executive, and philanthropist, particularly philanthropy concerning Israel; chairman of the PEF–Israel Endowment Fund for many years (PEF was the Palestine Endowment Fund, the name used before the State of Israel was established). Musher was the husband of Hadassah Kaplan Musher.

Adolf Judah Nadich (1912–2007), ordained JTS; radio lecturer, author, and scholar; rabbi at Park Avenue Synagogue in New York City; active in the Bureau of Jewish Education.

Moshe Nathanson (1899–1981), cantor at the SAJ for forty-eight years. Nathanson was born in Jerusalem and emigrated to the United States in 1922. He studied law and music. As a composer, he is most known for music widely used for the Grace After Meals and the well-known Hebrew song "Hava Nagila," which some say he wrote at age 12.

Abraham Neuman (1890–1970), ordained JTS; president of Dropsie College, 1940–1966; editor of the *Jewish Quarterly Review*; author of the two-volume work *The Jews in Spain*.

Emanuel Neuman (1893–1980), New York University law graduate; Zionist leader and fundraiser; president of Keren HaYesod; founder of the Herzl Foundation.

Louis I. Newman (1893–1972), ordained JIR; PhD, Columbia University; Reform rabbi, Zionist, and civic leader who supported the Irgun.

Reinhold Niebuhr (1892–1971), prominent American Protestant theologian; commentator on public affairs; author of the serenity prayer ("God, grant me the serenity to accept the things I cannot change, The courage to change the things I can, And the wisdom to know the difference"); intellectual opponent of John Dewey. Niebuhr started out on the left and ended up an advocate of neo-Orthodox theology. Niebuhr is noted for saying, "Man's capacity for justice makes democracy possible; but man's inclination to injustice makes democracy necessary."

Max Nordau (1849–1923), philosopher, writer, orator, and physician; co-founder of the World Zionist Organization.

Herbert Parzen (1897–1985), ordained JTS; author; state director of the United Synagogue of America; chaplain for the New York City Department of Correction. Parzen lost a rabbinical post because he took a shower.

Joseph Proskauer (1877–1971), lawyer and New York State Supreme Court judge; civic and community leader in New York City, and philanthropist; president of the Federation of Jewish Philanthropies.

***Bernard Revel** (1885–1940), educator, scholar, and author; reorganizer of the Rabbi Isaac Elhanan Theological Seminary; founder of Yeshiva College, which later became Yeshiva University. Revel was Kaplan's neighbor at one point.

Albert Rosenblatt (1872–1944), clothing manufacturer and SAJ member.

***Henry Rosenthal** (1906–1977), ordained JTS; philosopher and author; faculty member of Hunter College. Rosenthal was a favorite student of Kaplan's.

***Julius Rosenwald** (1862–1932), merchant (Sears Roebuck) and philanthropist. Rosenwald established the Rosenwald Fund, which ran an essay contest that Kaplan won. Kaplan used the money to support the publication of his book *Judaism as a Civilization*, which had been submitted to the contest (essays were invited on the state of American Jewry and proposals for improvement).

Franz Rosenzweig (1886–1929), German Jewish philosopher and educator; author of *The Star of Redemption* (1921). Rosenzweig worked with Martin Buber on a German translation of the Bible, which Buber finished alone after Rosenzweig's death.

Abraham Rothstein (1857–1939), cotton merchant and labor arbitrator. Rothstein was active in the Jewish Center.

Max Routtenberg (1909–1987), Conservative rabbi who served in Reading, Pennsylvania, and in Rockville Center, New York; author; president of the Rabbinical Assembly; officer of the JTS.

***Herman H. Rubenovitz** (1883–1966), graduate of JTS, 1908; rabbi and Zionist; rabbi at Temple Mishkan Tefila, Boston, 1910–1946. Rubenovitz was a disciple of Kaplan and one of his strongest supporters.

Bertrand Russell (1872–1970), third Earl Russell; well-known British philosopher, logician and mathematician, historian, social critic, and political activist. In 1940 Russell's appointment at CCNY was revoked before his arrival because of public protests and a legal judgment in which Russell was found morally unfit to teach at the college.

Jessie Ethel Sampter (1883–1938), influential Zionist educator and Zionist pioneer; author and poet. Sampter was born in New York City on March 22, 1883, and died at Kibbutz Givat Brenner on November 11, 1938. Sampter immigrated to Eretz Yisrael in 1919 and did social work among the Yemenite Jews. Her books include *A Course in Zionism* (1915), *Modern Palestine* (1933), and the poetry collection *Brand Plucked from the Fire* (1937). She was a friend of Kaplan's and an admirer of his work.

Maurice Samuel (1895–1972), Romanian British and American novelist, translator, and lecturer.

Zevi Scharfstein (1884–1972), Hebrew editor, educator, and textbook writer; active in the Bureau of Jewish Education; faculty member at TI.

*****Solomon Schechter** (1847–1915), well-known rabbinic scholar who discovered the large cache of medieval Jewish documents in Cairo called the Geniza; primary force in creating Conservative Judaism in America; first president of the reorganized JTS, 1902–1915. Schechter liked Kaplan but was critical of him.

*****Jacob Schiff** (1847–1920), financier and noted community leader; involved with virtually every major institution in the Jewish community. Schiff had a reputation for inspecting the bed sheets at the hospitals he supported.

Zalman Schocken (1877–1959), Zionist, businessman, collector, bibliophile and publisher, and philanthropist; patron of the Hebrew writer Samuel Joseph Agnon; rector of Hebrew University. See the well-written biography by Anthony David, *The Patron: A Life of Salman Schocken, 1977–1959* (New York: Henry Holt, 2003).

Gershom Scholem (1897–1982), preeminent scholar of Jewish mysticism; professor at Hebrew University. Scholem had a significant friendship with Walter Benjamin. Scholem's most important work is *Major Trends in Jewish Mysticism* (New York: Schocken Books, 1941). Kaplan knew this work well, and when A. J. Heschel came to the Seminary in 1945, Kaplan expected him to teach from it, but he did not. For interesting perspectives on Scholem, see Gershom Scholem, *A Life in Letters, 1914–1982*, ed. and trans. Anthony David Skinner (Cambridge, MA: Harvard University Press, 2002).

Albert Schoolman (1894–1980), MA, Columbia University; Teachers Diploma, JTS; president of the National Council for Jewish Education; founder of the Central Jewish Institute. Schoolman was one of Kaplan's disciples and a friend. The two men spent many summers together at Camp Cejwin.

Abraham Schwadron (Sharon) (1878–1957), folklorist, collector, and Hebrew writer, translator, and composer of music. Schwadron was a Zionist who insisted on total commitment to Eretz Yisrael. He immigrated to Palestine in 1927.

Alice Seligsberg (1873–1940), BA, Barnard College; Zionist leader, social worker, and author; national president of Hadassah. See *Communings of the Spirit*, 1: 220, for an interesting theological discussion Kaplan had with Seligsberg.

Bernard Semel (1878–1959), businessman, community leader, and Zionist in New York City.

David Werner Senator (1896–1953), social scientist, welfare worker, and Zionist; supporter and leading member of Brit Shalom; administrator of Hebrew University; member of the Executive Committee of the Jewish Agency. Senator was born in Germany and settled in Palestine in 1924.

Abba Hillel Silver (1893–1963), internationally known Reform rabbi, Zionist, author, and social activist. Silver's most important book is *Where Judaism Differed.*

Morris Silverman (1894–1972), eminent Conservative rabbi; writer; editor of a number of prayer books that became the basis for the Conservative prayer book issued by the Rabbinical Assembly. Silverman was a sometime supporter of Kaplan.

Akiba Ernst Simon (1899–1988), Jewish educator and religious philosopher; professor of education at Hebrew University; founder, along with Martin Buber and Judah Magnes, of Brit Shalom, an early peace group that advocated a binational state. Simon emigrated from Germany to Israel. Akiba Simon is the father of Uri Simon, noted Israeli biblical scholar.

Nahum Sokolow (1860–1936), Zionist leader and Hebrew journalist; General Secretary of the World Zionist Organization; key negotiator of the Balfour Declaration.

Alexander Sperber (1897–1970), PhD, University of Bonn; Semitics scholar; faculty member at JTS. Sperber was born in Cernowitz.

*\ **Shalom Spiegel** (1899–1984), PhD, University of Vienna; scholar of Hebrew literature; faculty member at JTS; lecturer at the SAJ. Spiegel was much admired by Kaplan, especially for his spoken elegant Hebrew.

Joshua Starr (1907–1949), ordained JTS; Jewish historian, community worker, and linguist.

*\ **Milton Steinberg** (1903–1950), ordained JTS; outstanding Conservative rabbi schooled in Jewish philosophy; Zionist instructor at CCNY and at JTS; author of, among other works, the novel *As a Driven Leaf.* Steinberg was a disciple and supporter of Kaplan and a favorite, although he was critical of him in his later years.

Lewis L. Strauss (1896–1974), banker, naval officer, community leader, and officer of the American Jewish Committee.

Solomon Strook (1973–1941), lawyer and national, civic, and community leader; president of the Federation of Jewish Philanthropies; supporter of the JTS and of the American Jewish Committee.

*****Henrietta Szold** (1860–1945), national Zionist leader and author; founder of Hadassah; editorial secretary of the Jewish Publication Society. Szold aided the resettlement to Palestine of Jewish refugee children. Kaplan met Szold in 1903 when she came to study at JTS. She and Kaplan sat in Schechter's classes together. She greatly admired Kaplan and in 1910 said, "He grows every day." Szold was an intellect of the highest order.

Saul Tchernikhowski (1875–1943), physician and Hebrew poet who revolted against the moral emphasis in Hebrew poetry and wrote poems of nature.

*****Chaim Tchernowitz** (pseud. Rav Za'ir, which means "young rabbi") (1871–1949), PhD; Talmud scholar, Hebrew author, and Zionist; faculty member at JIR; editor of *Bizaron.* Tchernowitz wrote a fine series of portraits of early Hebrew writers in *Masekhet Zichronotai.* He lived in Odessa along with the major figures in Jewish thought; at the turn of the twentieth century Ahad Ha-Am, Hayim Nahman Bialik, Mendele Moche Sefarim, and Vladimir Jabotinsky all lived in Odessa and knew each other.

Harry Torczyner (Tur Sinai) (1886–1973), Bible scholar, author, and linguist. Torczyner was instrumental in the revival of the Hebrew language.

*****Israel Unterberg** (1863–1934), wealthy clothing manufacturer; member of Kaplan's congregation (the SAJ). Unterberg was a strong supporter of Kaplan and donated money for the TI building at the JTS (the Unterberg Memorial Building).

Menahem Ussishkin (1863–1941), Zionist leader; member of Hovevei Zion (Lovers of Zion); president of the Jewish National Fund.

Max Vorspan (1916–2002), ordained JTS; author; official of the University of Judaism in Los Angeles.

*****Felix Warburg** (1871–1937), banker and noted philanthropist and prominent civic, cultural, and community leader; a partner of Jacob Schiff in Kuhn Loeb and Company; supporter of many agencies and causes throughout the Jewish community. Warburg was born in Germany and immigrated to the United States. He married Frieda Schiff, the daughter of philanthropist Jacob Schiff.

Naomi Kaplan Wenner (1914–1997), psychiatrist who retired in 1982 to take up sculpture full-time. She created a fine "head" of Kaplan, which is now in my possession. Naomi is Kaplan's third daughter. She married Seymour Wenner (1913–1993), an administrative law judge at several U.S. government agencies.

Henry Nelson Wieman (1884–1975), author, philosopher, Protestant thinker, and theologian of religious theocentric naturalism; author of *Religious Experience and Scientific Method* (1926) and *The Wrestle of Religion with Truth* (1927). Wieman's thinking was close to Kaplan's and has been chronicled in a number of essays by Professor Emanuel S. Goldsmith, for example, "Religious Naturalism in Defense of Democracy," in *Religious Experience and Ecological Responsibility*, ed. Donald A. Crosby and Charley Hardwick (New York: Peter Lang, 1996), 317–35.

Joseph Willen (1897–1985), social welfare activist, businessman, and fundraiser; executive officer of the Federation of Jewish Philanthropies; active in the American Jewish Committee.

Isaac Mayer Wise (1819–1900), rabbi, editor, and author; founder and president of Hebrew Union College from 1875 until his death. Wise immigrated to New York in 1846.

*Stephen Wise (1872–1949), outstanding liberal rabbi and Zionist; founder of the Free Synagogue and the JIR. Wise admired Kaplan and hoped he would be associated with the JIR. In 1927, when Kaplan left JTS for JIR and then returned to JTS, Wise wrote Judge Mack that "maybe we have misjudged him."

Louis Wolsey (1877–1953), ordained HUC; national and community leader; president of the Central Conference of American Rabbis.

Hayyim Yassky (1896–1948), physician and medical administrator. Yassky emigrated to Palestine in 1919 and joined the Hadassah organization in 1921. He was killed on April 13, 1948, when the Arabs massacred a truck convoy to Mt. Scopus.

David Yellin (1864–1941), educator and one of the leaders of the Yishuv in pre-independence Palestine.

Index

References in italics refer to illustrations

Aaron (brother of Moses), as peacemaker, 63
Aaronson, Rabbi, 304, 305
the absolute, and Power for salvation, 262
Abulafia, Abraham ben Samuel, 218
Abuya, Elisha ben, 220
acosmism, 264
Adler, Alfred, 31
Adler, Cyrus, 6, 14, 397; anger at lecturers, 42–43; attack on Kaplan, 47; contact with students, 292; death of, 226; educational failures of, 70–71; and Finkelstein, 187, 247; funeral of, 6, 226, 229–330; *I Have Considered the Days*, 359; illness of, 173; and JTS finances, 27–28; at JTS social gatherings, 91; Kaplan and, 47, 226–29, 343, 359n28, 360, 364; and Kaplan's sabbatical, 93, 96, 151; and Kaplan's salary, 173, 174; on loyalty oath, 20; nine live of, 230; presidency of Dropsie College, 359n28; presidency of JTS, 359n28; at Rabbinical Assembly, 44–45; and Teachers' Institute, 216; wealthy supporters of, 359n28
Adler, Felix, 43–44, 397; Ethical Culture Society of, 107, 285; Kaplan and, 107n33, 381n19; rejection of Judaism, 285n24; universalism of, 107n33
Adler, Morris, 25, 397; at Shaarey Zedek Synagogue, 244
Adler, Mortimer J., 314
adult study, Jewish, 324–25; at Jewish Theological Seminary, 12, 68, 247, 249, 291–92. *See also* Friedlaender Classes (JTS)
Agudah (ultra-Orthodox Jews), 51

agunah problem (separated women), 72–73; Epstein and, 191, 313, 342; Ginzberg and, 342
Agus, Jacob B. (Jacob Agushewitz), 397–98; on Judaism as civilization, 62–63; and Orthodoxy, 62n32, 63; Reconstructionism of, 205; Yeshibah education of, 63
Ahad Ha-Am (Asher Ginsberg), 6–7, 135, 319n42, 398; Bne Moshe organization of, 376; Kaplan and, 9, 376n15; on Palestine, 209; writing style of, 163
Akhenaton, idea of God, 354
Akiba, Rabbi: Finkelstein's work on, 56–57; as hero, 369
Albania, refugees from, 152
Albany (New York), Jewish community of, 23
Albo, Joseph, 398; on chosen people, 327; concept of God, 121–22; on reward and punishment, 123; *Sefer ha-Ikkarim*, 121n7, 126–27
Albright, William F., 243, 398; and Gordis, 242
Alexandria (Egypt), Jews of, 272
alienage, Jewish, 237, 238
aliyah: American Jewish life and, 88; Second, 158
Aliyot (blessings), 206
Allport, Gordon, 131, 277, 279, 398
American Jewish Committee, 219, 220; and Pan-American Jewish Congress, 318; and Reconstructionism, 301
Amos 3:2, chosen people concept in, 238–39
anarchy, religious, 385
Anderson, Maxwell: *Key Largo*, 211